PEARSON CUSTOM LIBRARY

3rd Custom Edition for Royal Roads University & Faculty of Management

PEARSON

V092

ISBN 10: 1-269-83448-7
ISBN 13: 978-1-269-83448-3

PEARSON

Table of Contents

VALUES, ATTITUDES, AND WORK BEHAVIOUR

From Chapter 4 of *Organizational Behaviour*, Ninth Edition. Gary Johns and Alan M. Saks. Copyright © 2014 by Pearson Education Canada. All rights reserved.

VALUES, ATTITUDES, AND WORK BEHAVIOUR

LEARNING OBJECTIVES

After reading this chapter, you should be able to:

1 Define *values* and discuss the implications of cross-cultural variation in values for organizational behaviour.

2 Define *attitudes* and explain how people develop attitudes.

3 Explain the concept of *job satisfaction* and discuss some of its key contributors, including discrepancy, fairness, disposition, mood, and emotion.

4 Explain the relationship between job satisfaction and absenteeism, turnover, performance, organizational citizenship behaviour, and customer satisfaction.

5 Differentiate *affective*, *continuance*, and *normative commitment* and explain how organizations can foster *organizational commitment*.

L'ORÉAL CANADA

Montreal's L'Oréal Canada is a subsidiary of the French L'Oréal Group, a prominent producer of cosmetics and personal care products. Their lines include L'Oréal Paris, Giorgio Armani, Ralph Lauren, Redken, Garnier, Biotherm, and The Body Shop. Journalist Donna Nebenzahl describes three generations of L'Oréal employees.

It's not a new phenomenon, three generations in a single workplace, but the latest generation on the scene is causing a flurry of concern. That message came loud and clear to Marjolaine Rompré, director of learning development at L'Oréal Canada, a company that hires a large number of the Gen Y population, the most recent generation in the workplace.

By the late 1990s, the company realized that a work population that is one-third boomer (1947–1966), one-third Generation X (1967–1979), and one-third Generation Y (1980–1995) was going to have to figure out how to cope with the winds of change blown in by this younger generation. So it was up to Rompré, a young boomer (born in 1961), to do something to alleviate the stress. Earlier generations, when they started at work, would go into meetings and observe and hardly speak, not wanting to ruffle feathers. Not so for the Gen Y population. "This new generation is so candid about participating and a lot freer," she said. "When we saw that, we realized we could

be faced with an interesting problem. We called it Generation Shock."

So they decided to create a program for L'Oréal workers that would "valorize generational differences," which became the title, because they felt that Gen Y already received a lot of attention and the goal was to ensure that every group understood the other. In the end, she says, "the Ys told us they were so happy to learn why the baby boomers were so conservative and why Gen X didn't want to share information with them." They have brought in 500 employees so far, in an effort to reveal the values of each generation—and the common truth that each generation is more rebellious than the one before and always wants to change the world.

For instance, when they talk about security, the groups learn that for the post-war generation, the smallest, oldest group now known as Traditionalists, security meant their savings. "They bought with cash and they had money in the bank," she said. For baby boomers, "their security was in the pension plan, because that was really created with their generation. You just had job security and pension plan." For the X generation, who came into a saturated market and had to fight for their jobs, security meant having a strong resume. On the other hand, Rompré says, "for Gen Y, *security* is not a word in their

L'Oréal employees Jean Cardinal, Rosalie Nolin, and Dominic Savaria span the baby boom–Gen X–Gen Y gap.

vocabulary because they have such a safety net; their parents are there for them. They don't have the same outlook."

There's a certain self importance in this group, she says, mixed with extreme loyalty toward their colleagues, with whom many form lasting friendships. "There's a greater sense of community than among the Gen X. Baby boomers are about the team, while Gen X were very career-oriented, all about themselves." This, of course, is a response to Gen X's entrée into a very competitive and tight workplace, compared with Gen Y, who see work as a continuum from university. "For them, it's just another way of learning. They're really focused on their development," Rompré said. "They want to continue to grow and learn." At the same time, she points out, "they have an amazing sense of community and friendship. Families are smaller, with fewer siblings, so friends are important when growing up. Plus, mom and daddy are working." So when they get into the workplace, their colleagues become their friends and their social life takes place partly at work.

On the other hand, the previous generations were a lot more career and results focused. It was clear that when you started in a company, you would start at the bottom and work hard in order to earn your place. Not so for Gen Y. "This generation is the most schooled generation ever, and they want to have responsibility very early on," she said. They really want to be autonomous, yet they also want validation. They want to be independent, but like to work in teams. They want rapid success within the company, yet have a very strong desire to maintain work–life balance. They practise extensive freedom of speech and are very candid, but they lack political savvy. They want to be everywhere at the same time, but have real difficulty managing priorities. They have great tolerance about religion, race, and nationality, but are very quick to pass judgment on the competency of their bosses. "They won't respect you because you're their boss. They'll respect you because you're competent and approachable," Rompré said.

At L'Oréal, the course has been a huge success, generating so much buzz that the company had to add to the half-day sessions. Another sidenote within the company, where there are actually a number of Gen Ys who are now managing boomers and Gen Xs: Most of the Ys are children of baby boomers so there is an interesting relationship between the two groups. "The Xs had to fight much more, waiting for boomers to get out, but the baby boomers aren't threatened by Gen Y," she said. "In fact, they love to share and to show them the ropes."[1]

The L'Oréal Canada story illustrates how generational differences in values and work attitudes affect workplace behaviour. In this chapter we will discuss such values and attitudes. Our discussion of values will be particularly oriented toward cross-cultural variations in values and their implications for organizational behaviour. Our discussion of attitudes will explain attitude formation. Two critical attitudes are job satisfaction and organizational commitment. We will consider the causes and consequences of both.

LO **1**

Define *values* and discuss the implications of cross-cultural variation in values for organizational behaviour.

Values. A broad tendency to prefer certain states of affairs over others.

WHAT ARE VALUES?

We might define **values** as "a broad tendency to prefer certain states of affairs over others."[2] The *preference* aspect of this definition means that values have to do with what we consider good and bad. Values are motivational, since they signal the attractive aspects of our environment that we seek and the unattractive aspects that we try to avoid or change. They also signal how we believe we *should* and *should not* behave.[3] The words *broad tendency* mean that values are very general and that they do not predict behaviour in specific situations very well. Knowing that a person generally embraces the values that support capitalism does not tell us much about how he or she will respond to a homeless person on the street this afternoon.

People tend to hold values structured around such factors as achievement, power, autonomy, conformity, tradition, and social welfare.[4] Not everyone holds the same values. Managers might value high productivity (an achievement value), while union officials might be more concerned with enlightened supervision and full employment (social values). We learn values through reinforcement processes. Most are socially reinforced by parents, teachers, and representatives of religions.

To solidify your understanding of values and their impact on organizational behaviour, let's examine some generational differences in values and see how work values differ across cultures.

Generational Differences in Values

Like L'Oréal Canada, many contemporary organizations are attempting to understand the implications of having four rather distinctive generations in the workplace who are often required to work with one another. As shown in Exhibit 1, these generations comprise what are often called the Traditionalists, the baby boomers, Generation X, and the Millennials (or Generation Y). These generations are of course demarcated by being of different ages, but they are also distinguished by having grown up under rather different socialization experiences. For example, many Traditionalists grew up in the shadow of two wars, baby boomers faced a vibrant economy (not to mention the sexual revolution and the advent of rock 'n' roll!), and Gen X and Y experienced more dual-career families and more divorce when growing up. It has been argued that these contrasting experiences, in turn, have led to notable value differences between the generations. For example, "latchkey kids" and those who know divorce might come to value the advice of authority figures less and the advice of friends more, compared to earlier generations. Such value differences might then underlie the differential workplace assets and preferences for leadership style highlighted in Exhibit 1.

The popular press contains many stereotypes concerning the generations, some of which are apparent in the exhibit.[5] Thus, the Traditionalists are portrayed as being respectful of authority and having a high work ethic; boomers are viewed as optimistic workaholics; Gen X is seen as cynical, confident, and pragmatic; and Gen Y is said to be confident, social, demanding of feedback, and somewhat unfocused. In general, the latter two generations are seen as more accepting of diversity and striving for good work–life balance, and their comfort with technology is notable.

Are these stereotypes accurate? It has to be said that the study of inter-generational values and of related attitudes and behaviour is in its infancy. And it is inherently hard to tease

Generation	Percentage of Workforce	Assets in the Workplace	Leadership Style Preferences
Traditionalists Born 1922–1945	8%	Hard working, stable, loyal, thorough, detail-oriented, focused, emotional maturity	Fair, consistent, clear, direct, respectful
Baby Boomers Born 1946–1964	44%	Team perspective, delicated, experienced, knowledgeable, service-oriented	Treat as equals, warm and caring, mission-defined, democratic approach
Generation X Born 1965–1980	34%	Independent, adaptable, creative, techno-literate, willing to challenge the status quo	Direct, competent, genuine, informal, flexible, results-oriented, supportive of learning opportunities
Millennials Born 1981–2000	14% and increasing rapidly	Optimistic, able to multitask, tenacious, technologically savvy, driven to learn and grow, team-oriented, socially responsible	Motivational, collaborative, positive, educational, organized, achievement-oriented, able to coach

EXHIBIT 1

Four generations in today's workplace.
Source: Society for Human Resource Management (2009). The multigenerational workforce: Opportunity for competitive success. *SHRM Research Quarterly*, First Quarter, 1–9. Compiled from AARP (2007). *Leading a multigenerational workforce.* Washington, DC: AARP; Sabatini Fraone, J., Hartmann, D., & McNally, K. (2008). *The multigenerational workforce: Management implications and strategies for collaboration.* Boston: Boston College Center for Work & Family; Zemke, R., Raines, C., & Filipezak, B. (2000). *Generations at work.* New York: American Management Association.

out generational effects from those that simply reflect age or work experience. Most recent research points to more similarities than differences in values across generations.[6] However, there is some indication that Gen X and Y are more inclined to value money, status, and rapid career growth than are boomers.[7] This may reflect valuing what one does not yet have, but it could also reflect the positive self-esteem movement to which later generations have been exposed. Indeed, there is evidence that the self-esteem of university students has increased over the years, along with narcissism.[8] There is also evidence that Gen Ys and Xs, compared to boomers, see work as less central, value leisure more, and are more inclined toward work–life balance.[9] Research conducted by the Center for Creative Leadership concluded that all work generations share the same values but express them differently. For instance, most people value respect, but for older employees this means being deferred to, while for Gen X and Y this means being listened to.[10]

Any generational differences in work values or in the way values are expressed is important because there is much evidence that good "fit" between a person's values and those of the organization (person–organization fit) leads to positive work attitudes and behaviours, including reduced chances of quitting.[11] This means that organizations may have to tailor job designs, leadership styles, and benefits to the generational mix of their workforces.

Go to MyManagementLab to see an annotated version of this figure.

Cultural Differences in Values

It is by now a cliché to observe that business has become global in its scope—Korean cars dot North American roads, your Dell helpdesk service provider resides in India, and entire lines of "Italian" cookware are made in China. All this activity obscures just how difficult it can be to forge business links across cultures. For example, research shows that anywhere from 16 to 40 percent of managers who receive foreign assignments terminate them early because they perform poorly or do not adjust to the culture.[12] Similarly, a lengthy history of failed business negotiations is attributable to a lack of understanding of cross-cultural differences. At the root of many of these problems is a lack of appreciation of basic differences in work-related values across cultures.

WORK CENTRALITY Work itself is valued differently across cultures. One large-scale survey of over 8000 individuals in several nations found marked cross-national differences in the extent to which people perceived work as a central life interest.[13] Japan topped the list, with very high work centrality. Belgians and Americans exhibited average work centrality, and the British scored low. One question in the survey asked respondents whether they would continue working if they won a large amount of money in a lottery. Those with more central interest in work were more likely to report that they would continue working despite the new-found wealth.

Customer-friendly service is a high work priority in Japan. Tokyo Disneyland is considered the safest, cleanest, and most orderly Disney park in the world.

The survey also found that people for whom work was a central life interest tended to work more hours. A reflection of this can be seen in Exhibit 2, which shows great variation in vacation time across cultures. This illustrates how cross-cultural differences in work centrality can lead to adjustment problems for foreign employees and managers. Imagine the unprepared British executive who is posted to Japan only to find that Japanese managers commonly work late and then socialize with co-workers or customers long into the night. In Japan, this is all part of the job, often to the chagrin of the lonely spouse. On the other hand, consider the Japanese executive posted to Britain who finds out that an evening at the pub is *not* viewed as an extension of the day at the office and is therefore not a time to continue talking business.

HOFSTEDE'S STUDY Dutch social scientist Geert Hofstede questioned over 116 000 IBM employees located in 40 countries about their work-related values. In subsequent work he added another 36 countries and regions to his database.[14] When Hofstede analyzed the results, he discovered four basic dimensions along which work-related values differed across cultures: power distance, uncertainty avoidance, masculinity/femininity, and individualism/

EXHIBIT 2
Vacation time across cultures.
Source: World Tourism Organization (WTO) as cited in Travel Industry Association of America (2002). World Tourism Overview. Retrieved July 18, 2003, from http://www.tia.org/ivis/worldtourism.asp#vacation. Reprinted by permission. © UNWTO, 9284403309.

Explore

Go to MyManagementLab to see an annotated version of this figure.

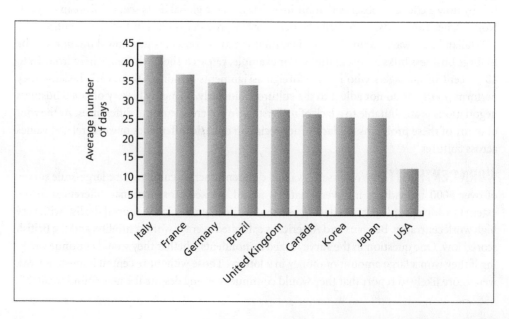

collectivism. Subsequent work with Canadian Michael Bond that catered more to Eastern cultures resulted in a fifth dimension, the long-term/short-term orientation.[15] More recently, the dimensions were verified and supplemented by the GLOBE project, headed by Professor Robert House.[16]

- *Power distance.* **Power distance** refers to the extent to which society members accept an unequal distribution of power, including those who hold more power and those who hold less. In small power distance cultures, inequality is minimized, superiors are accessible, and power differences are downplayed. In large power distance societies, inequality is accepted as natural, superiors are inaccessible, and power differences are highlighted. Small power distance societies include Denmark, New Zealand, Israel, and Austria. Large power distance societies include the Philippines, Russia, and Mexico. Out of 76 countries and regions, Canada and the United States rank 15 and 16, respectively, falling on the low power distance side of the average, which would be 38.

  Power distance. The extent to which an unequal distribution of power is accepted by society members.

- *Uncertainty avoidance.* **Uncertainty avoidance** refers to the extent to which people are uncomfortable with uncertain and ambiguous situations. Strong uncertainty avoidance cultures stress rules and regulations, hard work, conformity, and security. Cultures with weak uncertainty avoidance are less concerned with rules, conformity, and security, and hard work is not seen as a virtue. However, risk taking is valued. Strong uncertainty avoidance cultures include Japan, Greece, and Portugal. Weak uncertainty avoidance cultures include Singapore, Denmark, and Sweden. On uncertainty avoidance, the United States and Canada are well below average (i.e., exhibiting weak uncertainty avoidance), ranking 13 and 15, respectively, out of 76.

  Uncertainty avoidance. The extent to which people are uncomfortable with uncertain and ambiguous situations.

- *Masculinity/femininity.* More masculine cultures clearly differentiate gender roles, support the dominance of men, and stress economic performance. More feminine cultures accept fluid gender roles, stress sexual equality, and stress quality of life. In Hofstede's research, Slovakia and Japan are the most masculine societies, followed by Austria, Venezuela, and Mexico. The Scandinavian countries are the most feminine. Canada ranks about mid-pack, and the United States is fairly masculine, falling about halfway between Canada and Japan. The GLOBE research identified two aspects to this dimension—how assertive people are and how much they value gender equality.

- *Individualism/collectivism.* More **individualistic** societies tend to stress independence, individual initiative, and privacy. More **collective** cultures favour interdependence and loyalty to one's family or clan. The United States, Australia, Great Britain, and Canada are among the most individualistic societies. Venezuela, Columbia, and Pakistan are among the most collective, with Japan falling about mid-pack. The GLOBE research uncovered two aspects to this dimension—how much the collective distribution of resources is stressed and how much one's group or organization elicits loyalty.

  Individualism vs. collectivism. Individualistic societies stress independence, individual initiative, and privacy. Collective cultures favour interdependence and loyalty to family or clan.

- *Long-term/short-term orientation.* Cultures with a long-term orientation tend to stress persistence, perseverance, thrift, and close attention to status differences. Cultures with a short-term orientation stress personal steadiness and stability, face-saving, and social niceties. China, Hong Kong, Taiwan, Japan, and South Korea tend to be characterized by a long-term orientation. The United States, Canada, Great Britain, Zimbabwe, and Nigeria characterized by a more short-term orientation. Hofstede and Bond argue that the long-term orientation, in part, explains prolific East Asian entrepreneurship.

Exhibit 3 compares the United States, Canada, Mexico, Japan, and West Africa on Hofstede's value dimensions. Note that the profiles for Canada and the United States are very similar, but they differ considerably from that of Mexico.

Hofstede has produced a number of interesting "cultural maps" that show how countries and regions cluster together on pairs of cultural dimensions. The map in Exhibit 4 shows

EXHIBIT 3

Cross-cultural value comparisons.

Note: Time orientation data for Mexico unavailable.

Source: Graph by Gary Johns and Alan Saks. Based on data from Hofstede, G. (2005). Cultures and organizations: Software of the mind.

Go to MyManagementLab to see an annotated version of this figure.

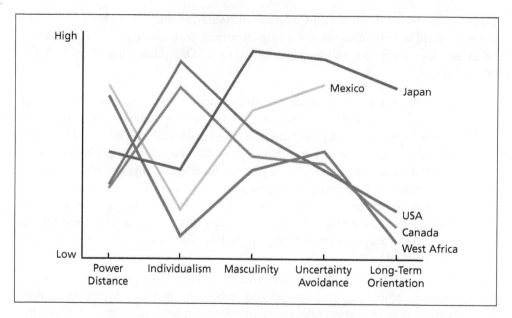

the relationship between power distance and degree of individualism. As you can see, these two values tend to be related. Cultures that are more individualistic tend to downplay power differences, while those that are more collectivistic tend to accentuate power differences.[17]

Implications of Cultural Variation

EXPORTING OB THEORIES

An important message from the cross-cultural study of values is that organizational behaviour theories, research, and practices from North America might not translate well to other societies, even the one located just south of Texas.[18] The basic questions (How should I lead? How should we make this decision?) remain the same. It is just the *answers* that differ. For example, North American managers tend to encourage participation in work decisions by employees. This corresponds to the fairly low degree of power distance valued here. Trying to translate this leadership style to cultures that value high power distance might prove unwise. In these cultures, people might be more comfortable deferring to the boss's decision. Similarly, in individualistic North America, calling attention to one's accomplishments is expected and often rewarded in organizations. In more collective Asian or South American cultures, individual success might be devalued, and it might make sense to reward groups rather than individuals. Finally, in extremely masculine cultures, integrating women into management positions might require special sensitivity.

IMPORTING OB THEORIES

Not all theories and practices that concern organizational behaviour are designed in North America or even in the West. The most obvious examples are "Japanese management" techniques, such as quality circles, total quality management, and just-in-time production. Although there are success stories of importing these techniques from Japan to North America, there are also examples of difficulties and failure. Many of the problems stem from basic value differences between Japan and North America. For example, the quest for continuous improvement and the heavy reliance on employee suggestions for improvement has had a mixed reaction.[19] In Japan, cultural values have traditionally dictated a fairly high degree of employment security. Thus, working at a fast pace and providing suggestions for improvement will not put one out of a job. North American workers are uncertain about this.

Many of the Japanese-inspired means of organizing work are team-oriented. Since Japan has fairly collective cultural values, submerging one's own interests in those of the team is natural. Although employers have successfully used teams in North America, our more individualistic culture dictates that careful selection of team members is necessary.

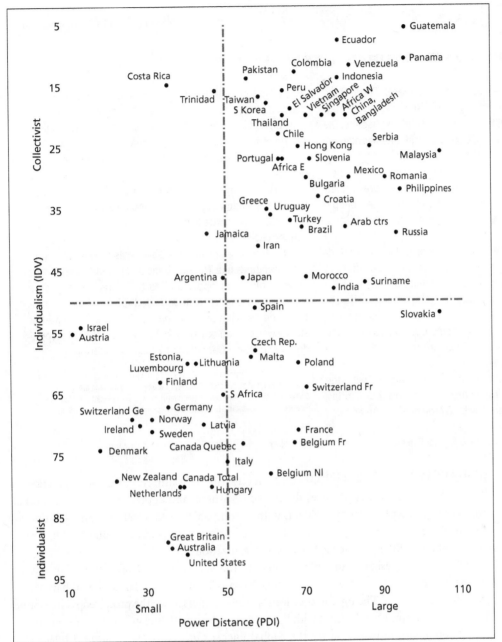

EXHIBIT 4
Power distance and individualism values for various countries and regions.
Source: Adapted from Hofstede, G., Hofstede, G.J., & Minkov, M. (2010). *Cultures and organizations: Software of the mind* (3rd ed.). New York: McGraw-Hill, p. 103.

Understanding cultural value differences can enable organizations to successfully import management practices by tailoring the practice to the home culture's concerns.

APPRECIATING GLOBAL CUSTOMERS An appreciation of cross-cultural differences in values is essential to understanding the needs and tastes of customers or clients around the world. Once relegated to the status of a marketing problem, it is now clear that such understanding fundamentally has to do with organizational behaviour. Errors occur with regularity. For instance, the initial French response to the Disneyland Paris theme park was less enthusiastic than Disney management had expected, probably due in part to Disney's failure to truly appreciate French tastes in food, lifestyle, and entertainment. South Korea's Samsung recalled a calendar featuring models displaying its products that was destined for overseas customers. Some North Americans were offended by Miss July's see-through blouse.

Appreciating the values of global customers is also important when the customers enter your own culture. Many firms have profited from an understanding of the increasing ethnic diversity in the United States, Canada, and Australia.

GLOBAL FOCUS

CANADIANS HAVE CULTURAL INTELLIGENCE

First there was IQ—intelligence quotient. Then there was EQ—emotional intelligence. Now there's a new kind of intelligence that is increasingly indispensable in today's global village. CQ—cultural intelligence—is a must-have skill, not just for foreign diplomats but also for business people, public sector workers, military personnel, and just about everyone in multicultural societies. And Canadians score more highly in it than people in the United States, United Kingdom, and France, according to a recent study.

CQ is a heightened awareness of cultures—including one's own—that makes a person more sensitive to people from diverse origins. It implies having a broad knowledge of customs and beliefs among different nationalities, ethnic groups, and faiths. It also reflects a person's motivation to overcome cultural barriers and confidence in one's ability to communicate with people from different cultures.

Four out of ten Canadians strongly agreed with the statement: "I enjoy interacting with people from different cultures," compared with 37 percent of Americans,

24 percent of Britons, and 30 percent of French respondents. Sixteen percent of Canadians strongly agreed that: "I have a good knowledge of the cultural values and religious beliefs of some other cultures," compared with 13 percent of Americans, 9 percent of Britons, and 5 percent of French respondents. Fifteen percent of Canadians strongly agreed that: "I adjust my behaviour when I meet people from a culture that is unfamiliar to me," compared with 13 percent of Americans, 10 percent of British residents, and 12 percent of people in France.

Canadians' relatively high CQ reflects the fact that multicultural cities like Toronto, Vancouver, and Montreal give citizens plenty of opportunities to interact with people from diverse origins, said Jack Jedwab, executive director of the Association for Canadian Studies. The internet survey was carried out among 3000 international respondents and 2345 Canadians by Léger Marketing.

Source: Excerpted from Scott, M. (2012, January 5). Canadians are leaders in cultural intelligence. *The Gazette* (Montreal), p. A4. © Copyright The Montreal Gazette. For more about the scientific underpinnings of CI see www.culturalq.com.

DEVELOPING GLOBAL EMPLOYEES Success in translating management practices to other cultures, importing practices developed elsewhere, and appreciating global customers are not things that happen by accident. Rather, companies need to select, train, and develop employees to have a much better appreciation of differences in cultural values and the implications of these differences for behaviour in organizations.

To get their designers to better appreciate the values of the North American market, Japanese and Korean car makers, including Nissan, Toyota, Hyundai, and Kia, have design studios in California. The top ranks of Detroit's automakers, once the protected realm of midwesterners, are now liberally filled with Europeans or those with European or Asian experience.

Before continuing, please see the Global Focus: *Canadians Have Cultural Intelligence*. As you proceed through the text, you will encounter further discussion about the impact of cultural values on organizational behaviour. Now, let's examine attitudes and see how they are related to values.

LO **2**

Define *attitudes* and explain how people develop attitudes.

Attitude. A fairly stable evaluative tendency to respond consistently to some specific object, situation, person, or category of people.

WHAT ARE ATTITUDES?

An **attitude** is a fairly stable evaluative tendency to respond consistently to some specific object, situation, person, or category of people. First, notice that attitudes involve *evaluations* directed toward *specific* targets. If I inquire about your attitude toward your boss, you will probably tell me something about how well you *like* him or her. This illustrates the evaluative aspect of attitudes. Attitudes are also much more specific than values, which dictate only broad preferences. For example, you could value working quite highly but still dislike your specific job.

Our definition indicates that attitudes are *tendencies to respond* to the target of the attitude. Thus, attitudes often influence our behaviour toward some object, situation, person, or group.

Attitude ⟶ Behaviour

Of course, not everyone who likes the boss goes around praising him or her in public for fear of being seen as too political. Similarly, people who dislike the boss do not always engage in public criticism for fear of retaliation. These examples indicate that attitudes are not always consistent with behaviour, and that attitudes provide useful information over and above the actions that we can observe. Behaviour is most likely to correspond to attitudes when people have direct experience with the target of the attitude and when the attitude is held confidently.[20]

Where do attitudes come from? Put simply, attitudes are a function of what we think and what we feel. That is, attitudes are the product of a related belief and value.[21] Given this point of view, we can now expand the attitude model presented above to include the thinking and feeling aspects of attitudes represented by beliefs and values.

$$\text{BELIEF} + \text{VALUE} \Rightarrow \text{Attitude} \longrightarrow \text{Behaviour}$$

Thus, we can imagine the following sequence of ideas in the case of a person experiencing work–family conflict:

"My job is interfering with my family life." (Belief)

"I dislike anything that hurts my family." (Value)

"I dislike my job." (Attitude)

"I'll search for another job." (Behaviour)

This simple example shows how attitudes (in this case, job satisfaction) develop from basic beliefs and values, and how they affect organizational behaviour (in this case, turnover from the organization). The specific attitudes we are now going to cover, job satisfaction and organizational commitment, have a strong impact on people's positive contributions to their work.[22]

WHAT IS JOB SATISFACTION?

Job satisfaction refers to a collection of attitudes that people have about their jobs. We can differentiate two aspects of satisfaction. The first of these is facet satisfaction, the tendency for an employee to be more or less satisfied with various facets of the job. The notion of facet satisfaction is obvious when we hear someone say, "I love my work but hate my boss" or "This place pays lousy, but the people I work with are great." Both these statements represent different attitudes toward separate facets of the speaker's job. The most relevant attitudes toward jobs are contained in a rather small group of facets: the work itself, compensation, career opportunities, recognition, benefits, working conditions, supervision, co-workers, and organizational policy.[23]

In addition to facet satisfaction, we can also conceive of overall satisfaction, an overall or summary indicator of a person's attitude toward his or her job that cuts across the various facets.[24] The statement "On the whole, I really like my job, although a couple of aspects could stand some improvement" is indicative of the nature of overall satisfaction. Overall satisfaction is an average or total of the attitudes individuals hold toward various facets of the job. Thus, two employees might express the same level of overall satisfaction for different reasons.

A popular measure of job satisfaction is the *Job Descriptive Index* (JDI).[25] This questionnaire is designed to evaluate five facets of satisfaction: people, pay, supervision, promotions, and the work itself. Employees are asked to respond "yes," "no," or "?" (cannot decide) in describing whether a particular word or phrase is descriptive of these facets. For example, for the pay facet, they are asked whether they are "well paid." A scoring system is available to provide an index of satisfaction for each facet. In addition, there is a scale that provides an overall measure of satisfaction.

Another carefully constructed measure of satisfaction, using a somewhat different set of facets, is the *Minnesota Satisfaction Questionnaire* (MSQ).[26] On this measure, respondents indicate how happy they are with various aspects of their job on a scale ranging from "very satisfied" to "very dissatisfied." Sample items from the short form of the MSQ include

- the competence of my supervisor in making decisions;
- the way my job provides for steady employment; and
- my pay and the amount of work I do.

JOIE DE VIVRE HOSPITALITY: EMPLOYEE MOTIVATION Go to MyManagementLab to watch a video about employee motivation.

PTC: EMPLOYEE ENGAGEMENT Go to MyManagementLab to watch a video about employee engagement.

Explain the concept of *job satisfaction* and discuss some of its key contributors, including discrepancy, fairness, disposition, mood, and emotion.

Job satisfaction. A collection of attitudes that workers have about their jobs.

Scoring the responses to these items provides an index of overall satisfaction as well as satisfaction on the facets on which the MSQ is based.

Firms such as Best Buy, Marriott, Scotiabank, The Keg, and Microsoft make extensive use of employee attitude surveys.

WHAT DETERMINES JOB SATISFACTION?

When employees on a variety of jobs complete the JDI or the MSQ, we often find differences in the average scores across jobs. Of course, we could almost expect such differences. The various jobs might differ objectively in the facets that contribute to satisfaction. Thus, you would not be astonished to learn that a corporate vice-president was more satisfied with her job than a janitor in the same company. Of greater interest is the fact that we frequently find decided differences in job satisfaction expressed by individuals performing the same job in a given organization. For example, two nurses who work side by side might indicate radically different satisfaction in response to the MSQ item "The chance to do things for other people." How does this happen?

Discrepancy

You will recall that attitudes, such as job satisfaction, are the product of associated beliefs and values. These two factors cause differences in job satisfaction even when jobs are identical. First, people might differ in their beliefs about the job in question. That is, they might differ in their *perceptions* concerning the actual nature of the job. For example, one of the nurses might perceive that most of her working time is devoted to direct patient care, while the other might perceive that most of her time is spent on administrative functions. To the extent that they both value patient care, the former nurse should be more satisfied with this aspect of the job than the latter nurse. Second, even if individuals perceive their jobs as equivalent, they might differ in what they *want* from the jobs. Such desires are preferences that are dictated, in part, by the workers' value systems. Thus, if the two nurses perceive their opportunities to engage in direct patient care as high, the one who values this activity more will be more satisfied with the patient care aspect of work. The **discrepancy theory** of job satisfaction asserts that satisfaction is a function of the discrepancy between the job outcomes people want and the outcomes that they perceive they obtain.[27] For instance, there is strong evidence that satisfaction with one's pay is high when there is a small gap between the pay received and the perception of how much pay *should* be received.[28] For example, at L'Oréal generational differences in values could have an impact on job satisfaction levels.

Discrepancy theory. A theory that job satisfaction stems from the discrepancy between the job outcomes wanted and the outcomes that are perceived to be obtained.

Fairness

In addition to the discrepancy between the outcomes people receive and those they desire, another factor that determines job satisfaction is fairness. Issues of fairness affect both what people want from their jobs and how they react to the inevitable discrepancies of organizational life. As you will see, there are three basic kinds of fairness. Distributive fairness has to do with the outcomes we receive, procedural fairness concerns the process that led to those outcomes, and interactional fairness concerns how these matters were communicated to us.[29]

DISTRIBUTIVE FAIRNESS **Distributive fairness** (often called *distributive justice*) occurs when people receive the outcomes they think they deserve from their jobs; that is, it involves the ultimate *distribution* of work rewards and resources. Above, we indicated that what people want from their jobs is a partial function of their value systems. In fact, however, there are

Distributive fairness. Fairness that occurs when people receive the outcomes they think they deserve from their jobs

practical limitations to this notion. You might value money and the luxurious lifestyle that it can buy very highly, but this does not suggest that you expect to receive a salary of $200 000 a year. In the case of many job facets, individuals want "what's fair." And how do we develop our conception of what is fair? **Equity theory** states that the inputs that people perceive themselves as investing in a job and the outcomes that the job provides are compared against the inputs and outcomes of some other relevant person or group.[30] Equity will be perceived when the following distribution ratios exist:

$$\frac{\text{My outcomes}}{\text{My inputs}} = \frac{\text{Other's outcomes}}{\text{Other's inputs}}$$

In these ratios, **inputs** consist of anything that individuals consider relevant to their exchange with the organization, anything that they give up, offer, or trade to their organization. These might include factors such as education, training, seniority, hard work, and high-quality work. **Outcomes** are those factors that the organization distributes to employees in return for their inputs. The most relevant outcomes are represented by the job facets we discussed earlier—pay, career opportunities, supervision, the nature of the work, and so on. The "other" in the ratio above might be a co-worker performing the same job, a number of co-workers, or even one's conception of all the individuals in one's occupation.[31] For example, the CEO of Microsoft probably compares his outcome/input ratio with those that he assumes exist for the CEOs of Google and Intel. You probably compare your outcome/input ratio in your organizational behaviour class with that of one or more fellow students.

Equity theory has important implications for job satisfaction. First, inequity itself is a dissatisfying state, especially when we are on the "short end of the stick." For example, suppose you see the hours spent studying as your main input to your organizational behaviour class and the final grade as an important outcome. Imagine that a friend in the class is your comparison person. Under these conditions, the following situations appear equitable and should not provoke dissatisfaction on your part:

You	Friend		You	Friend
C grade	A grade	Or	A grade	C grade
50 hours	100 hours		60 hours	30 hours

In each of these cases, a fair relationship seems to exist between study time and grades distributed. Now consider the following relationships:

You	Friend		You	Friend
C grade	A grade	Or	A grade	C grade
100 hours	50 hours		30 hours	60 hours

In each of these situations, an unfair connection appears to exist between study time and grades received, and you should perceive inequity. However, the situation on the left, in which you put in more work for a lower grade, should be most likely to prompt dissatisfaction. This is a "short end of the stick" situation. For example, the employee who frequently remains on the job after regular hours (input) and receives no special praise or extra pay (outcome) might perceive inequity and feel dissatisfied. Equity considerations also have an indirect effect on job satisfaction by influencing what people want from their jobs. If you study for 100 hours while the rest of the class averages 50 hours, you will expect a higher grade than the class average.

Consider a practical example of equity in action. During a business recession, the Canadian-based luxury hotel company Four Seasons did not lay off employees and thus threaten customer service like many of its competitors. Rather, executives accepted a pay freeze and workers were asked to vote on a temporary move to a four-day work week rather than five.

Equity theory. A theory that job satisfaction stems from a comparison of the inputs one invests in a job and the outcomes one receives in comparison with the inputs and outcomes of another person or group.

Inputs. Anything that people give up, offer, or trade to their organization in exchange for outcomes.

Outcomes. Factors that an organization distributes to employees in exchange for their inputs.

The offer was accepted enthusiastically because it was seen as fair given extensive industry layoffs and the sacrifices made by company executives.[32]

The equity concept suggests that outcomes should be tied to individual contributions or inputs. This corresponds well with the individualistic North American culture. In more collective cultures, *equality* of outcomes might produce more feelings of distributive fairness. In more feminine cultures, allocating outcomes according to *need* (rather than performance) might provide for distributive fairness.

PROCEDURAL FAIRNESS

Procedural fairness (often called *procedural justice*) occurs when individuals see the process used to determine outcomes as reasonable; that is, rather than involving the actual distribution of resources or rewards, it is concerned with how these outcomes are decided and allocated. An example will illustrate the difference between distributive and procedural fairness. Out of the blue, Greg's boss tells him that she has completed his performance evaluation and that he will receive a healthy pay raise starting next month. Greg has been working very hard, and he is pleased with the pay raise (distributive fairness). However, he is vaguely unhappy about the fact that all this occurred without his participation. Where he used to work, the employee and the boss would complete independent performance evaluation forms and then sit down and discuss any differences. This provided good feedback for the employee. Greg wonders how his peers who got less generous raises are reacting to the boss's style.

Procedural fairness is particularly relevant to outcomes such as performance evaluations, pay raises, promotions, layoffs, and work assignments. In allocating such outcomes, the following factors contribute to perceptions of procedural fairness.[33] The allocator

- follows consistent procedures over time and across people;
- uses accurate information and appears unbiased;
- allows two-way communication during the allocation process; and
- welcomes appeals of the procedure or allocation.

Procedural fairness is especially likely to provoke dissatisfaction when people also see distributive fairness as being low.[34] One view notes that dissatisfaction will be "maximized when people believe that they *would* have obtained better outcomes if the decision maker had used other procedures that *should* have been implemented."[35] (Students who receive lower grades than their friends will recognize the wisdom of this observation!) Thus, Greg, mentioned above, will probably not react too badly to the lack of consultation while his peers who did not receive large raises might strongly resent the process that the boss used.

INTERACTIONAL FAIRNESS

Interactional fairness (often called *interactional justice*) occurs when people feel that they have received respectful and informative communication about some outcome.[36] In other words, it extends beyond the actual procedures used to the interpersonal treatment received when learning about the outcome. Respectful communication is sincere and polite and treats the individual with dignity; informative communication is candid, timely, and thorough. Interactional fairness is important because it is possible for absolutely fair outcomes or procedures to be perceived as unfair when they are inadequately or uncaringly explained.

Sometimes, lower-level managers have little control over procedures that are used to allocate resources. However, they almost always have the opportunity to explain these procedures in a thorough, truthful, and caring manner. Frequently, people who experience procedural unfairness are dissatisfied with the "system." On the other hand, people who experience interactional unfairness are more likely to be dissatisfied with the boss.

Both procedural and interactional fairness can to some extent offset the negative effects of distributive unfairness. In one interesting study, nurses who received a pay cut due to hospital policy changes exhibited less insomnia when their supervisors were trained in the principles of interactional fairness compared to nurses with untrained supervisors.[37]

Procedural fairness. Fairness that occurs when the process used to determine work outcomes is seen as reasonable.

Interactional fairness. Fairness that occurs when people feel they have received respectful and informative communication about an outcome.

GLOBAL FOCUS

IS THE IMPORTANCE OF FAIRNESS UNIVERSAL ACROSS CULTURES?

Most research concerning fairness at work has been done in North America. In general, this research shows that fairness is an important determinant of job satisfaction, commitment to the organization, and trust in the organization and managers. But are these findings universal across cultures, or is fairness a particular preoccupation of North Americans?

Andrew Li and Russell Cropanzano compared the research on fairness at work that has been done in North America with that conducted in East Asia (mainland China, Japan, Hong Kong, South Korea, Taiwan, and Singapore). On one hand, we might guess that individualistic, low-power–distance North Americans would be more sensitive to incidents of unfairness. On the other hand, most such incidents are interpersonal (e.g., a boss gives a biased performance evaluation), and the more collective, social features of East Asian cultures might point to greater fairness sensitivity.

Li and Cropanzano found that distributive and procedural fairness predicted satisfaction, commitment, and trust in both regions. However, the associations were somewhat weaker in East Asia, suggesting a greater tolerance for unfairness there. The authors suggested that a need for interpersonal harmony, prevalent in the more collective East Asian cultures, might have led to this result.

The authors concluded that fairness seems important for people with a range of cultural backgrounds. However, they also noted that managers should be extra alert for feelings of unfairness among East Asians because they might not signal it in their attitudes and behaviour, hoping to maintain social harmony.

Source: Li, A., & Cropanzano, R. (2009). Do East Asians respond more/less strongly to organizational justice than North Americans? *Journal of Management Studies, 46,* 787–805.

Before continuing, see the Global Focus: *Is the Importance of Fairness Universal across Cultures?*

Disposition

Could your personality contribute to your feelings of job satisfaction? This is the essential question guiding research on the relationship between disposition and job satisfaction. Underlying the dispositional view is the idea that some people are *predisposed* by virtue of their personalities to be more or less satisfied despite changes in discrepancy or fairness. Some of the research that suggests that disposition contributes to job satisfaction is fascinating:[38]

- Identical twins raised apart from early childhood tend to have similar levels of job satisfaction.

- Job satisfaction tends to be fairly stable over time, even when changes in employer occur.

- Disposition measured early in adolescence is correlated with one's job satisfaction as a mature adult.

Taken together, these findings suggest that some personality characteristics originating in genetics or early learning contribute to adult job satisfaction. In fact, recent research has linked dopamine and serotonin genes to satisfaction.[39]

Research on disposition and job satisfaction has centred around the Big Five personality traits. People who are extraverted and conscientious tend to be more satisfied with their jobs, while those high in neuroticism are less satisfied.[40] Also, people who are high in self-esteem and internal locus of control are more satisfied.[41] Thus, in general, people who are more optimistic and proactive report higher job satisfaction. Mood and emotion may contribute to this connection, so we will now examine these topics.

EAST HAVEN FIRE DEPARTMENT: EMOTIONS AND MOODS Go to MyManagementLab to watch a video about emotions and moods.

Emotions. Intense, often short-lived feelings caused by a particular event.

Moods. Less intense, longer-lived, and more diffuse feelings.

Emotional contagion. Tendency for moods and emotions to spread between people or throughout a group.

Emotional regulation. Requirement for people to conform to certain "display rules" in their job behaviour in spite of their true mood or emotions.

Mood and Emotion

The picture we have painted so far of the determinants of job satisfaction has been mostly one of calculation and rationality: people calculate discrepancies, compare job inputs to outcomes, and so on. But what about the intense feelings that are sometimes seen in work settings—the joy of a closed business deal or the despair that leads to workplace homicides? Or what about that vague feeling of a lack of accomplishment that blunts the pleasure of a dream job? We are speaking here about the role of affect as a determinant of job satisfaction. Affect is simply a broad label for feelings. These feelings include **emotions**, which are intense, often short-lived, and caused by a particular event such as a bad performance appraisal. Common emotions include joy, pride, anger, fear, and sadness. Affect also refers to **moods**, which are less intense, longer-lived, and more diffuse feelings.

How do emotions and moods affect job satisfaction? Affective events theory, proposed by Howard Weiss and Russell Cropanzano, addresses this question.[42] Basically, the theory reminds us that jobs actually consist of a series of events and happenings that have the potential to provoke emotions or to influence moods, depending on how we appraise these events and happenings. Thus, seeing a co-worker being berated by a manager might provoke emotional disgust and lower one's job satisfaction, especially if it is a frequent occurrence. This illustrates that perceived unfairness, as discussed earlier, can affect job satisfaction via emotion.[43] Also, a person's disposition can interact with job events to influence satisfaction. For instance, those who are neurotic and pessimistic may react to a minor series of job setbacks with a negative mood that depresses their job satisfaction.

An interesting way in which mood and emotion can influence job satisfaction is through **emotional contagion**. This is the tendency for moods and emotions to spread between people or throughout a group. Thus, people's moods and emotions tend to converge with interaction. Generally, teams experiencing more positive affect tend to be more cooperative, helpful, and successful, all of which are conditions that contribute to job satisfaction.[44] Emotional contagion can also occur in dealing with customers such that pleasant service encounters contribute to the service provider's satisfaction as well as to that of the customer.

Another interesting way in which mood and emotion can influence job satisfaction is through the need for **emotional regulation**. This is the requirement for people to conform to certain "display rules" in their job behaviour, in spite of their true mood or emotions. Often, this is referred to informally as "emotional labour." In one version, employees are expected to be perky and upbeat whether they feel that way or not, thus exaggerating positive emotions. In the other version, employees are supposed to remain calm and civil even when hassled or insulted, thus suppressing negative emotions. One study found that call centre employees averaged 10 incidents of customer aggression a day.[45] All jobs have their implicit display rules, such as not acting angry in front of the boss. However, service roles such as waiter, bank teller, and flight attendant are especially laden with display rules, some of which may be made explicit in training and via cues from managers.

What are the consequences of the requirement for emotional regulation? There is solid evidence that the frequent need to suppress negative emotions and fake emotions that you do not really feel take a toll on job satisfaction and increase stress.[46] Flight attendants can humour only so many drunk or angry air passengers before the experience wears thin! On the other hand, the jury is still out on the requirement to express positive emotions, especially when you really are feeling positive. Some research suggests that this display rule boosts job satisfaction.[47] If so, positive contagion from happy customers may be responsible. Of course, disposition may again enter the picture, as extraverts may be energized by requirements for positive display.

Do organizations pay a premium for emotional labour? The answer is sometimes. Theresa Glomb, John Kammeyer-Mueller, and Maria Rotundo studied the emotional labour and cognitive demands (thinking, decision making) required in various occupations (see Exhibit 5).[48]

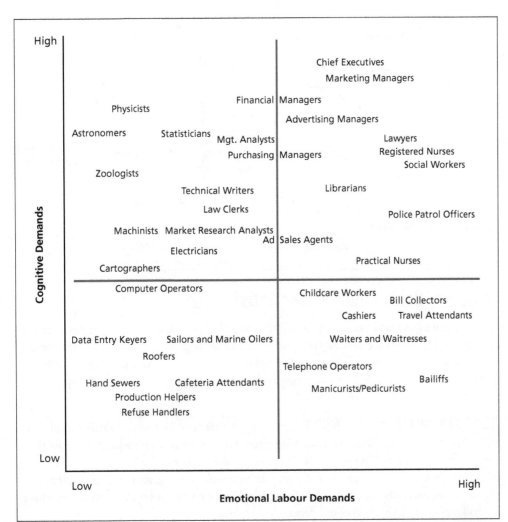

EXHIBIT 5
Occupations plotted by emotional labour and cognitive demands.
Source: Adapted from Glomb, T.M., Kammeyer-Mueller, J.D., & Rotundo, M. (2004). Emotional labor demands and compensating wage differentials. *Journal of Applied Psychology*, 89, 700–714.

Go to MyManagementLab to see an annotated version of this figure.

They found that those in occupations with high cognitive demands (the upper portion of the exhibit) tend to be paid more when the jobs are also high in emotional labour. Thus, lawyers tend to earn more than zoologists. On the other hand, occupations with low cognitive demands entail a wage penalty when emotional labour is higher. Thus, the "people jobs" in the lower right quadrant of the exhibit tend to be less well paid than the jobs in the lower left quadrant. As we will see shortly, pay is an important determinant of job satisfaction.

Consideration of mood and emotion helps explain a curious but commonplace phenomenon: how people with similar beliefs and values doing the same job for the same compensation can still exhibit very different satisfaction levels. This difference is probably a result of emotional events and subtle differences in mood that add up over time.

Exhibit 6 summarizes what research has to say about the determinants of job satisfaction. To recapitulate, satisfaction is a function of certain dispositional factors, the discrepancy between the job outcomes a person wants and the outcomes received, and mood and emotion. More specifically, people experience greater satisfaction when they meet or exceed the job outcomes they want, perceive the job outcomes they receive as equitable compared with those others receive, and believe that fair procedures determine job outcomes. The outcomes that people want from a job are a function of their personal value systems, moderated by equity considerations. The outcomes that people perceive themselves as receiving from the job represent their beliefs about the nature of that job.

EXHIBIT 6
How discrepancy, fairness, disposition, mood, and emotion affect job satisfaction.

Explore

Go to MyManagementLab to see an annotated version of this figure.

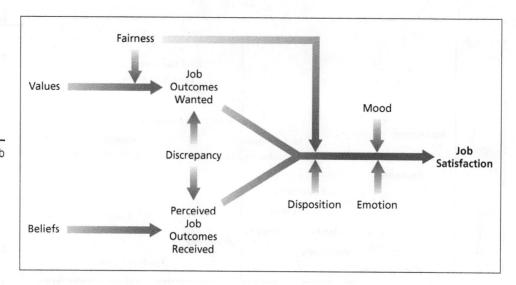

Some Key Contributors to Job Satisfaction

From what we have said thus far, you might expect that job satisfaction is a highly personal experience. While this is essentially true, we can make some general statements about the facets that seem to contribute the most to feelings of job satisfaction for most North American workers. These include mentally challenging work, adequate compensation, career opportunities, and friendly or helpful colleagues.[49]

MENTALLY CHALLENGING WORK This is work that tests employees' skills and abilities and allows them to set their own working pace. Employees usually perceive such work as personally involving and important. It also provides the worker with clear feedback regarding performance. Of course, some types of work can be too challenging, and this can result in feelings of failure and reduced satisfaction. In addition, some employees seem to prefer repetitive, unchallenging work that makes few demands on them.

ADEQUATE COMPENSATION It should not surprise you that pay and satisfaction are positively related. However, not everyone is equally desirous of money, and some people are certainly willing to accept less responsibility or fewer working hours for lower pay. In most companies, one finds a group of employees who are especially anxious to earn extra money through overtime and another group that actively avoids overtime work.

CAREER OPPORTUNITIES The availability of career opportunities contributes to job satisfaction. Opportunity for promotion is an important contributor to job satisfaction because promotions contain a number of valued signals about a person's self-worth. Some of these signals may be material (such as an accompanying raise), while others are of a social nature (recognition within the organization and increased prestige in the community). Of course, there are cultural and individual differences in what people see as constituting a fair promotion system. Some employees might prefer a strict seniority system, while others might wish for a system based strictly on job performance. Many of today's flatter organizations no longer offer the promotion opportunities of the past. Well-run firms have offset this by designing lateral moves that provide for challenging work. Also, career development helps prepare employees to assume challenging assignments.

PEOPLE It should not surprise you that friendly, considerate, good-natured superiors and co-workers contribute to job satisfaction, especially via positive moods and emotions. There is, however, another aspect to interpersonal relationships on the job that contributes to job satisfaction. Specifically, we tend to be satisfied in the presence of people who help us attain job outcomes that we value. Such outcomes might include doing our work better or more easily, obtaining a raise or promotion, or even staying alive. For example, a company of soldiers in battle might be less concerned with how friendly their commanding officer is than with how competently he is able to act to keep them from being overrun by the enemy. Similarly, an aggressive young executive might like a considerate boss but prefer even more a boss who can clarify her work objectives and reward her for attaining them. The friendliness aspect of interpersonal relationships seems most important in lower-level jobs with clear duties and in various dead-end jobs. If pay is tied to performance or as jobs become more complex or promotion opportunities increase, the ability of others to help us do our work well contributes more to job satisfaction.

Context can certainly affect what contributes most to job satisfaction. Exhibit 7 shows the results of a survey conducted by the Society for Human Resource Management in 2011. As you can see, job security and the organization's financial stability were high on the list.

In the high-tech and creative domains, organizational success depends on attracting and retaining the very best talent and creating an atmosphere free from distractions and inconveniences so that the creative juices can flow. The stress of project deadlines is commonplace. Because of these factors, firms such as Google, Microsoft, Pixar, and Research In Motion (RIM) go to extraordinary lengths to foster employee job satisfaction. Perks range from the provision of "fun" campus-like environments to free meals to the availability of services such as transportation, dry cleaning, and car washes. To see how Capital One enhances job satisfaction, check out You Be the Manager.

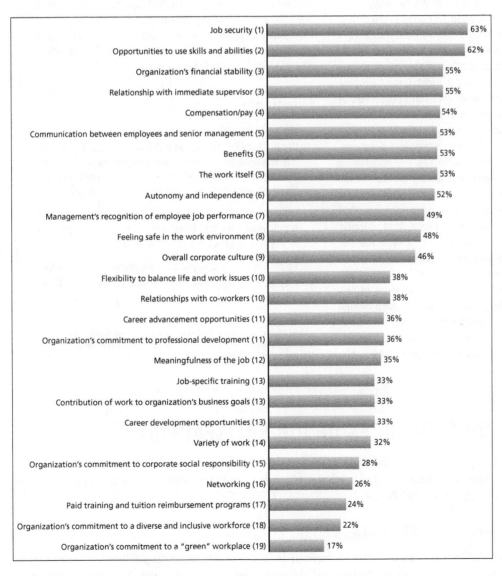

EXHIBIT 7
"Very important" aspects of employee job satisfaction.
Note: Percentages reflect respondents who answered "very important" on a scale where 1 = "very unimportant" and 4 = "very important." *Source:* Society for Human Resource Management. (2011). *2011 Employee job satisfaction and engagement.* Alexandria, VA: SHRM, p.7. © Society for Human Resource Management. Used by permission.

YOU BE THE MANAGER

The Future of Work @ Capital One

The nature of the work to which people are drawn reflects the values that individuals espouse. Over the past century, work has moved from primarily blue collar, assembly-line jobs toward white collar, knowledge-based jobs. With the transition, employee values have also changed. Knowledge workers, who make up approximately one-third of the workforce in North America, seek a work environment that supports not only teamwork and collaboration but also privacy and flexibility. When the work environment cannot support these needs, employees can become dissatisfied because inability to concentrate and accomplish tasks can create frustration and anxiety, as can the challenges of trying to balance worklife with personal life. When employees are not able to work when they want, how they want, and with whom they want, satisfaction can decline, resulting in absenteeism, turnover, and lower productivity.

At Capital One, one of the top 15 banks in the United States, caring for their knowledge workers has always been a top priority. Considered one of the best places to work by *Fortune* magazine, Capital One's key values include "Excellence" and "Do the Right Thing." Employees are encouraged to achieve corporate objectives by thinking independently and taking ownership of their ideas. The "test and learn" culture is played out through teamwork, collaboration, and innovative work practices. At the core of Capital One's culture is the importance of making data-driven decisions, which has positioned the IT function, and technology itself, in a strategic role.

To satisfy their knowledge workers, Capital One has invested in creating workspaces that support employee values. In the late 1990s, they embarked on a program with the aim of creating state-of-the-art facilities that encourage teamwork and collaboration. Drawing on theories of building and furniture utilization, Capital One implemented a standardized design of offices, cubicles, and conference rooms. But Capital One soon discovered a significant underutilization of office resources. They found that, on a daily basis,

40 percent of cubicles were left vacant, while another 30 percent were unoccupied for certain hours of the day. It appeared that employees were not using their workspace as originally intended. Capital One took this problem seriously. Even though the company had been recognized for its state-of-the-art facilities, changing workplace values were signalling that standard office designs were a thing of the past.

Questions

1. Although Capital One had implemented a state-of-the-art facility, employees did not appear to be taking advantage of the office resources in the way management intended. How could the work environment be affecting employees' job satisfaction?

2. How could the office space be redesigned to meet employees' needs? What role could technology play in the redesign of the office space?

To find out how Capital One increased job satisfaction by redesigning their office space, see The Manager's Notebook at the end of the chapter.

Source: Adapted from Khana, S., & New, J.R. (2008). Revolutionizing the workplace: A case study of the future of work program at Capital One. *Human Resource Management, 47*, 795–808.

LO 4

Explain the relationship between job satisfaction and absenteeism, turnover, performance, organizational citizenship behaviour, and customer satisfaction.

CONSEQUENCES OF JOB SATISFACTION

Dell, Sears, and L'Oréal Canada are firms that have maintained a competitive advantage by paying particular attention to employee satisfaction. Why is this so? Let's look at some consequences of job satisfaction.

Absence from Work

Absenteeism is an expensive behaviour in North America, costing billions of dollars each year. Such costs are attributable to "sick pay," lost productivity, and chronic overstaffing to compensate for absentees. Many more days are lost to absenteeism than to strikes and other industrial disputes. Research shows that less-satisfied employees are more likely to be absent and that satisfaction with the content of the work is the best predictor of absenteeism.[50] However, the absence–satisfaction connection is not very strong. Several factors constrain the ability of many people to convert their like or dislike of work into corresponding attendance patterns:

- Some absence is simply unavoidable because of illness, weather conditions, or child care problems. Thus, some very happy employees will occasionally be absent owing to circumstances beyond their control.

- Some organizations have attendance control policies that influence absence more than satisfaction does. In a company that does not pay workers for missed days (typical of many workplaces with hourly pay), absence may be more related to economic needs than to dissatisfaction. The unhappy worker who absolutely needs money will probably show up for work. By the same token, dissatisfied and satisfied workers might be equally responsive to threats of dismissal for absenteeism.

- In many jobs it may be unclear to employees how much absenteeism is reasonable or sensible. With a lack of company guidelines, workers may look to the behaviour of their peers for a norm to guide their behaviour. This norm and its corresponding "absence culture" might have a stronger effect than the individual employee's satisfaction with his or her job.[51]

Turnover

Turnover refers to resignation from an organization, and it can be incredibly expensive. For example, it costs several thousand dollars to replace a nurse or a bank teller who resigns. As we move up the organizational hierarchy, or into technologically complex jobs, such costs escalate dramatically. For example, it costs millions of dollars to hire and train a single military fighter pilot. Estimates of turnover costs usually include the price of hiring, training, and developing to proficiency a replacement employee. Such figures probably underestimate the true costs of turnover, however, because they do not include intangible costs, such as work group disruption or the loss of employees who informally acquire special skills and knowledge over time on a job. All this would not be so bad if turnover were concentrated among poorer performers. Unfortunately, this is not always the case. In one study, 23 percent of scientists and engineers who left an organization were among the top 10 percent of performers.[52]

What is the relationship between job satisfaction and turnover? Research indicates a moderately strong connection, with less-satisfied workers being more likely to quit.[53] However, the relationship between the attitude (job satisfaction) and the behaviour in question (turnover) is far from perfect. Exhibit 8 presents a model of turnover that can help explain this.[54] In the model, circles represent attitudes, ovals represent elements of the turnover process, and squares denote situational factors. The model shows that job satisfaction as well as commitment to the organization and various "shocks" (both discussed below) can contribute to intentions to leave. Research shows that such intentions are very good predictors of turnover.[55] As shown, such intentions sometimes prompt turnover directly, even impulsively. On the other hand, reduced satisfaction or commitment can also stimulate a more deliberate evaluation of the utility of quitting and a careful job search and evaluation of job alternatives. The following are some reasons why satisfied people sometimes quit their jobs or dissatisfied people stay:

- Certain "shocks," such as a marital breakup, the birth of a child, or an unsolicited job offer in an attractive location, might stimulate turnover despite satisfaction with the current job.

- An employee's dissatisfaction with his or her specific job might be offset by a strong commitment to the overall values and mission of the organization.

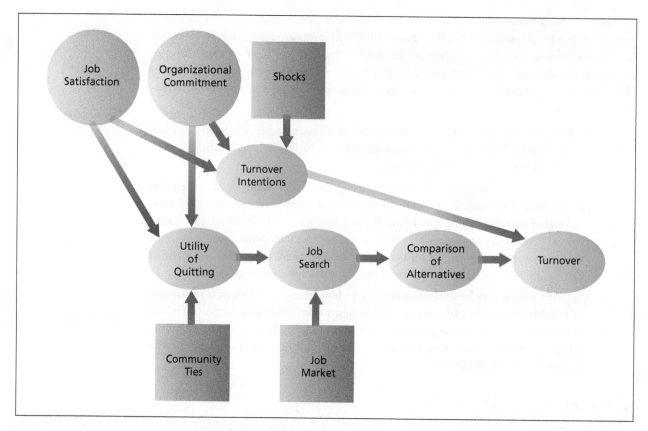

EXHIBIT 8
A model of employee turnover.

Go to MyManagementLab to see an annotated version of this figure.

- An employee might be so embedded in the community (due to involvement with churches, schools, or sports) that he or she is willing to endure a dissatisfying job rather than move.

- A weak job market might result in limited employment alternatives. Dissatisfaction is most likely to result in turnover when jobs are plentiful.[56]

Despite these exceptions, a decrease in job satisfaction often precedes turnover, and those who quit experience a boost in satisfaction on their new job. However, some of this boost might be due to a "honeymoon effect," in which the bad facets of the old job are gone, the good facets of the new job are apparent, and the bad facets of the new job are not yet known. Over time, as these bad facets are recognized, a "hangover effect" can occur, in which overall satisfaction with the new job decreases.[57] This pattern is shown in Exhibit 9, which traces job satisfaction at five points in time as a person moves between jobs A and B.

Performance

It seems sensible that job satisfaction contributes to less absenteeism and turnover, but does it also lead to improved job performance? After all, employees might be so "satisfied" that no work is accomplished! In fact, research has confirmed what folk wisdom and business magazines have advocated for many years—job satisfaction is associated with enhanced performance.[58] However, the connection between satisfaction and performance is complicated, because many factors influence motivation and performance besides job satisfaction. Thus, research has led to some qualifications to the idea that "a happy worker is a productive worker."

All satisfaction facets are not equal in terms of stimulating performance. The most important facet has to do with the content of the work itself.[59] Thus, interesting, challenging jobs are most likely to stimulate high performance. One consequence of this is the fact that the connection between job satisfaction and performance is stronger for complex, high-tech jobs

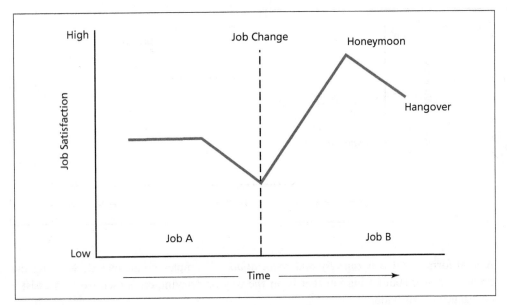

EXHIBIT 9
The honeymoon–hangover effect.
Source: Drawing by the authors, based on Boswell, W.R., Boudreau, J.W., & Tichy, J. (2005). The relationship between employee job change and job satisfaction: The honeymoon–hangover effect. *Journal of Applied Psychology, 90,* 882–892.

Go to MyManagementLab to see an annotated version of this figure.

in science, engineering, and computers and less strong for more routine labour jobs. In part, this is because people doing complex jobs have more control over their level of performance.

Another issue in the connection between job satisfaction and performance has to do with which of these is the cause and which the effect. Although job satisfaction contributes to performance, performance could also contribute to job satisfaction.[60] When good performance is *followed by rewards*, employees are more likely to be satisfied. However, many organizations do not reward good performance sufficiently. Thus, contemporary research indicates that satisfaction is more likely to affect performance, rather than the reverse.[61]

In addition to boosting formal job performance, satisfaction can also contribute to employees' informal, everyday behaviour and actions that help their organizations and their co-workers. Let's turn now to a discussion of this.

Organizational Citizenship Behaviour

Organizational citizenship behaviour (OCB) is voluntary, informal behaviour that contributes to organizational effectiveness.[62] In many cases, the formal performance evaluation system does not detect and reward it. Job satisfaction contributes greatly to the occurrence of OCB, more than it does to regular task performance, in fact.[63]

An example of OCB should clarify the concept. You are struggling to master a particularly difficult piece of software. A colleague at the next desk, busy on her own rush job, comes over and offers assistance. Irritated with the software, you are not even very grateful at first, but within 10 minutes you have solved the problem with her help. Notice the defining characteristics of this example of OCB:

- The behaviour is voluntary. It is not included in her job description.
- The behaviour is spontaneous. Someone did not order or suggest it.
- The behaviour contributes to organizational effectiveness. It extends beyond simply doing you a personal favour.
- The behaviour is unlikely to be explicitly picked up and rewarded by the performance evaluation system, especially since it is not part of the job description.

What forms might OCB take? As the software example indicates, one prominent form is *helping* behaviour, offering assistance to others. Another might be *conscientiousness* to the details of work, including getting in on the snowiest day of the year and not wasting organizational resources. A third involves being a *good sport* when the inevitable frustrations of organizational life crop up—not everyone can have the best office or the best parking spot.

Organizational citizenship behaviour (OCB). Voluntary, informal behaviour that contributes to organizational effectiveness.

EXHIBIT 10
Progression of withdrawal

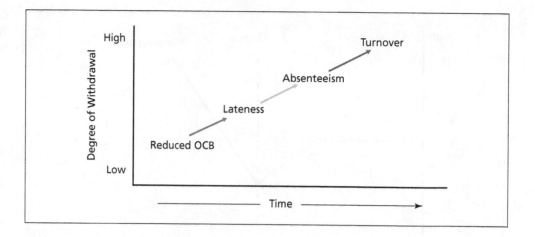

A final form of OCB is *courtesy and cooperation*.[64] Examples might include warning the photocopy unit about a big job that is on the way or delaying one's own work to assist a colleague on a rush job.

Just how does job satisfaction contribute to OCB? Fairness is the key. Although distributive fairness (especially in terms of pay) is important, procedural and interactional fairness from a supportive manager seem especially critical.[65] If the manager strays from the prescriptions for procedural fairness we gave earlier, OCB can suffer. If one feels unfairly treated, it might be difficult to lower formal performance for fear of dire consequences. It might be much easier to withdraw the less visible, informal activities that make up OCB. On the other hand, fair treatment and its resulting satisfaction might be reciprocated with OCB, a truly personalized input. OCB is also influenced by employees' mood at work. People in a pleasant, relaxed, optimistic mood are more likely to provide special assistance to others.[66]

OCB contributes to organizational productivity and efficiency and to reduced turnover.[67] Because of this, some firms do try to formally recognize OCBs. Xilinx, the highly innovative leader in programmable logic components, fosters and publicizes nominations of people who go "above and beyond duty" to help peers, selecting some for special recognition and a token cash award.[68]

Research shows that there is sometimes a progression of withdrawal in response to job dissatisfaction (and to reduced commitment, discussed below).[69] That is, people withdraw their attention or work effort in an attempt to compensate for dissatisfaction, beginning with more subtle behaviours and progressing to more extreme, until some equilibrium is struck. As shown in Exhibit 10, reduction of OCB is often the first withdrawal response, as these are voluntary behaviours. This may be followed, in turn, by coming to work late, then absenteeism, and ultimately turnover. Managers should be alert to increases in the lower forms of withdrawal, because they may signal bigger problems in the future.

Customer Satisfaction and Profit

So far, we have established that job satisfaction can reduce employee absenteeism and turnover and increase employee performance and citizenship behaviour. But is it possible that employee satisfaction could actually affect *customer* satisfaction? That is, do happy employees translate into happy customers? And do happy employees actually contribute to the bottom line of the organization by increasing organizational profits? After all, we have warned that the translation of positive attitudes into positive employee behaviours is less than perfect and that such attitudes therefore might not affect the bottom line.

A growing body of evidence has established that employee job satisfaction is indeed translated into customer or client satisfaction and organizational profitability.[70] Thus, organizations with higher average levels of employee satisfaction are more effective. The same

When one worker voluntarily helps out another, it is an example of organizational citizenship, which positively affects organizational effectiveness.

applies to units within larger organizations. Hence, local bank branches or insurance claims offices with more satisfied employees should tend to have more satisfied clients and generate more profits for the larger firm. Thus, it makes good sense to use employee satisfaction as one criterion in judging the effectiveness of local unit managers.

How does employee satisfaction translate into customer satisfaction? Reduced absenteeism and turnover contribute to the seamless delivery of service, as do the OCBs that stimulate good teamwork. Also, the mood mechanism, mentioned earlier, should not be discounted, as good mood among employees can be contagious for customers.

The Ford Motor Company and Sears have been particularly attentive to the links among employee satisfaction, customer satisfaction, and profit. In an 800-store study, Sears found a clear positive relationship between employee satisfaction and store profitability. In addition, improvements in employee satisfaction were mirrored in customer satisfaction, resulting in an estimated $200 million in added annual revenue.[71]

Let's turn now to another important work attitude—organizational commitment.

WHAT IS ORGANIZATIONAL COMMITMENT?

Organizational commitment is an attitude that reflects the strength of the linkage between an employee and an organization. This linkage has implications for whether someone tends to remain in an organization. Researchers John Meyer and Natalie Allen have identified three very different types of organizational commitment:[72]

- **Affective commitment** is commitment based on a person's identification and involvement with an organization. People with high affective commitment stay with an organization because they *want* to.

- **Continuance commitment** is commitment based on the costs that would be incurred in leaving an organization. People with high continuance commitment stay with an organization because they *have* to.

- **Normative commitment** is commitment based on ideology or a feeling of obligation to an organization. People with high normative commitment stay with an organization because they think that they *should* do so.

LO 5

Differentiate *affective*, *continuance*, and *normative commitment* and explain how organizations can foster *organizational commitment*.

Organizational commitment. An attitude that reflects the strength of the linkage between an employee and an organization.

Affective commitment. Commitment based on identification and involvement with an organization.

Continuance commitment. Commitment based on the costs that would be incurred in leaving an organization.

Normative commitment. Commitment based on ideology or a feeling of obligation to an organization.

25

Employees can be committed not only to their organization but also to various constituencies within and outside the organization. Thus, each type of commitment could also apply to one's work team, union, or profession.[73]

Key Contributors to Organizational Commitment

The causes of the three forms of commitment tend to differ. By far the best predictor of affective commitment is interesting, satisfying work of the type found in enriched jobs.[74] One mistake that organizations sometimes make is starting employees out in unchallenging jobs so they do not make any serious errors. This can have a negative impact on affective commitment. Role clarity and having one's expectations met after being hired also contribute to affective commitment.[75]

Continuance commitment occurs when people feel that leaving the organization will result in personal sacrifice, or they perceive that good alternative employment is lacking. Building up "side bets" in pension funds, obtaining rapid promotion, or being well integrated into the community where the firm is located can lock employees into organizations even though they would rather go elsewhere. Not surprisingly, continuance commitment increases with the time a person is employed by an organization.

Normative commitment ("I *should* stay here") can be fostered by benefits that build a sense of obligation to the organization. These might include tuition reimbursements or special training that enhances one's skills. Strong identification with an organization's product or service ("I should stay here because the Sierra Club is doing important work") can also foster normative commitment. Finally, certain socialization practices that emphasize loyalty to the organization can stimulate normative commitment. For example, sports coaches often haze players who miss practice to stress the importance of loyalty to the team.

Consequences of Organizational Commitment

There is good evidence that all forms of commitment reduce turnover intentions and actual turnover.[76] Organizations plagued with turnover problems among key employees should look carefully at tactics that foster commitment. This is especially called for when turnover gets so bad that it threatens customer service. Many service organizations (e.g., restaurants and hotels), however, have traditionally accepted high turnover rates.

Organizations should take care, though, in their targeting of the kind of commitment to boost. Affective commitment is positively related to performance because it focuses attention on goals and thus enhances motivation.[77] However, continuance commitment is *negatively* related to performance, something you might have observed in dealing with burned-out bureaucrats.[78] An especially bad combination for both the employee and the organization is high continuance commitment coupled with low affective commitment—people locked into organizations that they detest. This happens very frequently during recessions.

Is there a downside to organizational commitment? Very high levels of commitment can cause conflicts between family life and worklife. Also, very high levels of commitment have often been implicated in unethical and illegal behaviour, including a General Electric price-fixing conspiracy. Finally, high levels of commitment to a particular *form* or *style* of organization can cause a lack of innovation and lead to resistance when a change in the culture is necessary.[79]

Changes in the Workplace and Employee Commitment

Organizations are experiencing unprecedented change as a result of shifts in workforce demographics, technological innovations, and global competition.[80] In an era of layoffs, downsizing, outsourcing, restructuring, and reengineering, there is evidence that employees are losing commitment to their organizations.[81] People often view their careers as a series of jobs with a variety of potential employers, or they even see themselves as freelancers rather than having a series of jobs in one organization.

John Meyer, Natalie Allen, and Laryssa Topolnytsky have studied commitment in a changing world of work, and they note that the impact of changes in the workplace on employee commitment can be seen in three main areas:[82]

- *Changes in the nature of employees' commitment to the organization.* Depending on the nature of workplace changes and how they are managed, employees' levels of affective, continuance, and normative commitment can increase or decrease. Thus, the commitment profiles of employees following a change will be different from what they were prior to the change, and maintaining high levels of affective commitment will be particularly challenging. Changes that are made in the organization's best interest but that are detrimental to employees' well-being are most likely to damage affective commitment.

- *Changes in the focus of employees' commitment.* Employees generally have multiple commitments. In particular, employee commitment can be directed to others within the organization, such as subunits or divisions, teams, the "new" organization, as well as entities outside the organization, such as one's occupation, career, or union. Therefore, changes in the workplace might alter the focus of employees' commitments both within and outside of the organization. As organizations increase in size following mergers and acquisitions, for example, employees are likely to shift their commitment to smaller organizational units, such as their particular division, branch, or team. As well, changes that threaten employees' future in the organization might result in a shift in commitment to entities outside the organization, such as one's profession, occupation, or personal career.

- *The multiplicity of employer–employee relationships within organizations.* As organizations attempt to cope and adapt to rapid change, they need to be flexible enough to shrink or expand their workforce. At the same time, they need a workforce that is flexible enough to get any job done. This creates a potential conflict as employees who do not have guaranteed job security may be unwilling to be as flexible as the organization would like or to have a strong affective commitment toward the organization. A potential solution to this problem is for organizations to have different relationships with employee groups. For example, an organization might have a group of core employees who perform the key operations required for organizational success. It would be important for this group of employees to have a high level of affective organizational commitment. Other employee groups would consist of those with contractual arrangements or individuals hired on a temporary basis who do not perform the core tasks and whose commitment to the organization is not as important.

In summary, changes in the workplace are having an impact on the nature of employee commitment and employee–employer relationships. It is therefore important that organizations understand how changes in the workplace can change the profile and focus of employees' commitment and the impact this can have on employee behaviour and organizational success.

THE MANAGER'S NOTEBOOK

Capital One

1. Capital One's original workspace design was based on a "one size fits all" approach. Using conventional theories of building and furniture utilization, they standardized the size of offices and cubicles and assigned office space based on hierarchy. Conference rooms were established as iconic representations of the corporate culture, taking up ample space in prime areas of the building. Although employees were provided with the tools to do their work, such as high-powered desktop computers and feature-rich phones, the design was based on the assumption that employees would either be in their cubicles working or in conference rooms for meetings. Capital One did not consider that their knowledge workers sought a diversity of workspace solutions that allowed them to work anywhere (within or outside the building), whenever and however they wanted. In lieu of working the way they were expected, they sought out workspaces that supported their need to collaborate, work independently, and work away from the office when required. Upon realizing the underutilization of resources, Capital One established a new program, called "The Future of Work." With the intent to increase job satisfaction, and ultimately business productivity, Capital One focused the program on the employee. With their employees they aimed to discover what their knowledge workers needed to be most productive and most happy. Capital One realized that, with the many generations of workers in their company and with the diversity of cultures, employee needs varied considerably throughout the workday and the workweek. Their Future of Work program sought to provide a rich variety of work environments that allowed employees the flexibility they craved.

2. Capital One's Future of Work program was primarily concerned with the satisfaction of employees.

Although reducing facility costs and boosting productivity were also considered important, Capital One believed that things start with the employee. The Future of Work program therefore redirected the facility savings into technology programs in order to "untether" employees from their desks. Mobility tools such as laptops, mobile phones, BlackBerries, and voice-over-Internet Protocol (VOIP) telephone solutions were made available to ensure that employees could work from anywhere, whenever they chose, as long as WiFi or hard-wired internet connections were available. Workers were classified by the type of work they did and their mobility preferences. Each type of worker was then assigned a certain amount of office space and a set of mobility tools to support their work habits. For example, executives and directors were provided with both office space and BlackBerries or laptops, since they are often in the office during the day but also continue working when they leave. Teleworkers and mobile workers, on the other hand, were provided with plenty of mobility tools, but with shared rather than dedicated office space, in consideration of the fact that they were in the office less. In addition to the technology, the workspace itself was redesigned to include a variety of spaces, ranging from small enclaves to large project rooms, along with lounges and café-style settings, supported by power and data connections. Did all this work? Employees reported a 41 percent increase in overall workplace satisfaction, while facilities costs per employee dropped by almost half. Although overall productivity increases are difficult to measure, employees did report a greater facility in getting their work done, on their own and with their teams.

MyManagementLab   Visit MyManagementLab at **www.mymanagementlab .com** for access to online tutorials, interactive exercises, videos, and much more.

LEARNING OBJECTIVES CHECKLIST

1 *Values* are broad preferences for particular states of affairs. Values tend to differ across generations and across cultures. Critical cross-cultural dimensions of values include power distance, uncertainty avoidance, masculinity/femininity, individualism/collectivism, and time orientation. Differences in values across cultures set constraints on the export and import of organizational behaviour theories and management practices. They also have implications for satisfying global customers and developing globally aware employees.

2 *Attitudes* are a function of what we think about the world (our beliefs) and how we feel about the world (our values). Attitudes are important because they influence how we behave, although we have discussed several factors that reduce the correspondence between our attitudes and behaviours.

3 *Job satisfaction* is an especially important attitude for organizations. Satisfaction is a function of the discrepancy between what individuals want from their jobs and what they perceive that they obtain, taking into account fairness. Dispositional factors, moods, and emotions also influence job satisfaction. Factors such as challenging work, adequate compensation, career opportunities, and friendly, helpful co-workers contribute to job satisfaction.

4 Job satisfaction is important because it promotes several positive outcomes for organizations. Satisfied employees tend to be less likely to be absent or leave their jobs. While links between satisfaction and performance are not always strong, satisfaction with the work itself has been linked to better performance. Satisfaction linked to perceptions of fairness can also lead to citizenship behaviours on the part of employees. Satisfied workers may also enhance customer satisfaction.

5 *Organizational commitment* is an attitude that reflects the strength of the linkage between an employee and an organization. *Affective commitment* is based on a person's identification with an organization. *Continuance commitment* is based on the costs of leaving an organization. *Normative commitment* is based on ideology or feelings of obligation. Changes in the workplace can change the nature and focus of employee commitment as well as employer–employee relationships. To foster commitment, organizations need to be sensitive to the expectations of employees and consider the impact of policy decisions beyond economic issues.

DISCUSSION QUESTIONS

1. What are some of the conditions under which a person's attitudes might not predict his or her work behaviour?

2. What is the difference between procedural and interactional fairness? Give an example of each.

3. Explain how these people might have to regulate their emotions when doing their jobs: hair salon owner, bill collector, police officer, teacher. How will this regulation of emotion affect job satisfaction?

4. Using the model of the turnover process in Exhibit 8, explain why a very dissatisfied employee might not quit his or her job.

5. Explain why employees who are very satisfied with their jobs might not be better performers than those who are less satisfied.

6. Use equity theory to explain why a dentist who earns $100 000 a year might be more dissatisfied with her job than a factory worker who earns $40 000.

7. Mexico has a fairly high power distance culture, while the United States and Canada have lower power distance cultures. Discuss how effective management techniques might vary between Mexico and its neighbours to the north.

8. Describe some job aspects that might contribute to job satisfaction for a person in a more collective culture. Do the same for a person in a more individualistic culture.

9. Give an example of an employee who is experiencing distributive fairness but not procedural fairness. Give an example of an employee who is experiencing procedural fairness but not distributive fairness.

INTEGRATIVE DISCUSSION QUESTIONS

1. What role do perceptions play in the determination of job satisfaction? Refer to the components of perception and describe how perception plays a role in the determination of job satisfaction according to discrepancy theory, equity theory, and dispositions. How can perceptions be changed to increase job satisfaction?

2. Does personality influence values and job attitudes? Discuss how the Big Five personality dimensions—locus of control, self-monitoring, self-esteem, and positive and negative affectivity—might influence occupational choice, job satisfaction, and organizational commitment (affective, continuance, and normative). If personality influences job satisfaction and organizational commitment, how can organizations foster high levels of these attitudes?

ON-THE-JOB CHALLENGE QUESTION

Mr. Winston

In 2006, Arthur Winston died at age 100. He had worked for 76 years for the Los Angeles Metropolitan Transportation Authority cleaning trains and buses. Although this is remarkable enough, it is even more remarkable that he missed only one day of work in his last 72 years, the day of his wife's funeral in 1988. At the time of his retirement on the eve of becoming 100, he headed a crew of 11 workers. Although he had aspired to become a mechanic when younger, the racial biases of the 1930s and 1940s prevented this career advancement. In 1996, Mr. Winston received a congressional citation from the U.S. president as "Employee of the Century." Mr. Winston's incredible record was the object of extensive media coverage, both at home and abroad.

Use the material in the chapter to speculate on various reasons for Mr. Winston's awesome attendance record. What accounts for the great media interest in Mr. Winston?

Sources: (2006, April 14). MTA employee who retired at 100 has died in his sleep. http://cbs2.com/local/Arthur.Winston.MTA.2.515610.html; Marquez, M. (2006, March 22). Los Angeles man retires at 100. abcnews.go.com/US/WNT/story?id=1756219.

EXPERIENTIAL EXERCISE

Attitudes Toward Absenteeism from Work

In this exercise we will examine your attitudes toward absenteeism from work. Although you learned in the chapter that absence can stem from job dissatisfaction, the scenarios below show that a number of other factors can also come into play.

1. Working alone, please indicate the extent to which you think that the employee's absence in each of the following scenarios is legitimate or illegitimate by using one of the six answer categories that appear below. A legitimate absence might be considered acceptable, while an illegitimate absence might be considered unacceptable. This is a measure of your personal attitudes; there are no right or wrong answers. Add up your scores and divide by 7 to obtain an average. Lower scores represent less favourable attitudes toward absenteeism.

2. Working in groups of 3 to 5 people, discuss the ratings that each of you gave to each scenario. What are the major reasons that contributed to each of your ratings? Compare your average scores.

3. As a group, decide which scenario is *most* legitimate, and explain why. Then decide which scenario is *least* legitimate, and explain why. Compare with the norms provided below.

4. As managers, how would you react to the least legitimate situation? What would you do?

6	5	4	3	2	1
Extremely legitimate	Moderately legitimate	Slightly legitimate	Slightly illegitimate	Moderately illegitimate	Extremely illegitimate

1. Susan is a highly productive employee, but she is absent more often than her co-workers. She has decided to be absent from work to engage in some recreational activities because she believes that her absence would not affect her overall productivity. _____

2. John is an active member of his community social club. Occasionally, the club organizes community activities with the aim of improving the quality of community life. A few days before a planned community activity, much of the work has not been done and the club members are concerned that the activities will be unsuccessful. John has therefore decided to be absent from work to help the club organize its forthcoming activities. _____

3. Peter is a member of a project team that was charged with the responsibility of converting the company's information systems. The work entailed long hours, but the team was able to finish the project on time. Now that the project is completed, the long working hours have taken a toll and Peter feels quite stressed, so he has decided to stay away from work to recuperate. _____

4. Jane works in a low-paying job for which she is over-qualified. She has been searching for a more suitable job through advertisements in the newspapers. She has been called for a job interview and has decided to call in sick to attend the interview. _____

5. Frank has a few months before his retirement and has lost the enthusiasm he used to have for his work. He believes he has contributed to making the company the success it is today. He recently joined a retired persons association where he feels his services are needed more. The association is organizing a safety awareness pro-gram for senior citizens, so he has decided to stay away from work to help. _____

6. Joan's co-workers normally use up all their sick leave. She is moving into a new house, and since she has not used up all her permitted sick leave, she has decided to call in sick so that she can finish packing for the move. _____

7. Anne does not feel challenged by her job and believes that she is not making any meaningful contribution to her organization. Her mother is going to the doctor for a routine medical checkup and because Anne believes the company will not miss her, she decided to stay away from work to accompany her mother. _____

Source: Scenarios developed by Helena M. Addae. Used with permission.

Scoring and Interpretation

As noted, lower scores represent less favourable attitudes toward absenteeism. Helena Addae, who developed the scenarios, administered them to over 1500 employees in nine countries. The average rating across the 7 scenarios was 3.09. Respectively, the average ratings for each scenario were: S1 = 2.39; S2 = 2.88; S3 = 3.96; S4 = 3.52; S5 = 3.12; S6 = 3.03; S7 = 2.70. Higher numbers indicate more legitimacy.

CASE INCIDENT

How Much Do You Get Paid?

Joan had been working as a reporter for a large television network for seven years. She was an experienced and hardworking reporter who had won many awards over the years for her outstanding work. The work was exciting and challenging, and at $75 000 a year plus benefits she felt well paid and satisfied. Then she found out that two recent graduates from one of the best schools of journalism in the United States had just been hired by her network at a starting salary of $80 000. Further, two other reporters who worked with Joan and had similar track records had just received job offers from American networks and were being offered $150 000 plus $10 000 for every award won for their reporting.

1. According to equity theory, how will these incidents influence Joan's job satisfaction and behaviour?

2. What should Joan do in response to her situation? What should her organization do?

CASE STUDY

Gen Y in the Workforce

"RU BRD?"[1]

The text message from Ashok stood out in bold block letters on the small screen of Josh Lewis's iPhone. Am I ever, Josh thought, stuffing the device back into his pocket and emphatically rolling his chair away from his PC and the backlit spreadsheets and formulas that had made his eyes bloodshot and his mood sour. He stood up, stretched, and took a minute to consider his plight: For the past three days, he'd been crunching U.S. and international

1 Are you bored?

film sales, attendance, and merchandising figures nonstop for his boss, Sarah Bennett, the marketing chief of the movie division of Rising Entertainment. Bennett and her team were in the midst of prepping the promotions, advertising, and branding plan for the next *Fire Force Five* film; her presentation to the company's CEO, its head of distribution, and other unit leaders was planned for Friday.

Two more days—many more hours, many more stats to go over before I sleep, the 23-year-old marketing associate estimated. He plunked himself back down in his chair.

A recent graduate of the University of Southern California, Josh had had visions of making films that offered strong social commentary—like Al Gore's *An Inconvenient Truth* or Morgan Spurlock's *Super Size Me*—and distributing them on open platforms so that his message could reach the greatest number of people. With some championing from his uncle—a well-regarded TV producer who knew people who knew people—Josh joined Rising Entertainment, one of the top three multimedia production and distribution houses in the world. The company boasted large film, television, home video, music, and licensed merchandise units, with a catalogue of thousands of properties. Josh expected that the studio, with its location in the heart of Los Angeles and satellite offices in six countries, would offer plenty of excitement and opportunity—ever-present TV and film shoots on the lots, hobnobbing with industry power brokers, the inevitable offers from competing studios, and, of course, the terrific LA nightlife. But now, with 10 months on job, and most of that time relegated to mundane ancillary projects that informed the bigger initiatives his boss was spearheading, Josh was feeling numb. Who would have thought that life in a big movie studio could be so routine? He thought to himself.

Suddenly there was that familiar vibration from his iPhone and another text message from Ashok: "WRUD? TAB?"[2] A break sounded great. He replied immediately—"BRT"[3]—and set off for their favourite meeting spot. As he was heading out, it occurred to Josh that he should let Sarah know where he was. He fired off another quick text message.

---

2 What are you doing? Take a break?

3 Be right there

Sounding Bored

By the time Josh got to the high-backed purple booth in the corner of the commissary, Ashok and Jessica were already there. Ashok Devi worked in Rising Entertainment's TV division as a promotions associate. Jessica Sadler had started out in the film division but, for now at least, was working as an assistant in the company's legal group—ostensibly to help out a team in transition but really to figure out if law school was in her future. The three had been at USC together, studying a broad mix of business, communications, and film, but they had become particularly good friends since joining the company around the same time, braving orientation together, and now commiserating with one another about the flaws in their respective work groups—in which each was among the youngest on staff.

"Aw, what's wrong, Josh?" Jessica said, noticing Josh's serious expression as he shuffled over to the table. "Did your mom call HR again?" Ashok, who was sitting next to Jessica, just grinned and shook his head.

Josh shot them both a look. "Whatever. I've been buried all week with ridiculous busy-work. Sarah's all amped about this distribution and marketing plan for the Triple-F series. But I'm just not feeling it," he vented.

"Have you tried explaining that to Sarah?" Jessica asked.

Josh had. A few weeks earlier, during a small team meeting in which Sarah was outlining her marketing premise for *Fire Force Five: Resignation*—the details of which centered primarily on TV ads and an aggressive print campaign—Josh had causally joked about how 1990s the whole plan was. It was as though DVRs, film-related websites and blogs, virtual worlds, and YouTube didn't exist, he thought. As though the question of how to capitalize on the free-content movement was still something plaguing the guys in the record business and not anyone else.

No one watches network TV anymore—or network TV ads, Josh had pointed out during the meeting. Instead of relying chiefly on traditional marketing channels, he said, why not try new media? Make the movie theme song available for download for Guitar Hero. Or, even better, make one or more of the *Fire Force Five* movies available online and embed teasers for the latest sequel within them.

Sarah had immediately balked, noting the creaky Rising Entertainment website, which boasted very little traffic and even less functionality. A "successful" online campaign for the third Triple-F movie in 2005 had nearly taken down the studio's entire network—including critical sales force connections.

"So how about striking deals with, like, Hulu or There or Gaia? They're well suited to handle the traffic—much better than we are," Josh replied. These days it was just so much easier to download music, movies, and TV shows how and when you wanted them. To have, as Jessica joked, old *90210* and new *90210* existing peacefully on your laptop. "We'd be leveraging one of Rising Entertainment's biggest strengths, its library, in a way that gets the company out in front of the movement to free content."

"All great points," Sarah had responded. "But our budget is soft right now—everything is soft right now. I'm not sure we have the time and resources to throw at these channels." Josh opened his mouth to respond, but the marketing chief cut off the discussion there and went on to her other notes.

That was the end of that, Josh explained to his friends. "I guess I just expected that I would get to act on more of my ideas," he complained, as they finished crunching through a large order of lime-cilantro chips and salsa. "And that the higher-ups here would have figured out by now that the model's changing." By the time Ashok, Jessica, and Josh had gotten down to salty crumbs, the three were in firm agreement: Sarah just didn't get it.

The View from Above

Should all the bullet points be flame balls? Sarah Bennett wondered, only half joking with herself. She was in the midst of building her PowerPoint slides for Friday's meeting with CEO Sam Smith stone and, as always, fighting the urge to add crazy animation and special effects to her presentation. After 10 years at Rising Entertainment, the 37-year-old marketing chief still saw herself as a budding creative rather than an established suit. But she understood her role in the hierarchy: manage the people and the details.

Still, it was a far cry from where she started. A native of Long Island, Sarah had gotten her MBA from New York University's Stern School of Business and held an undergraduate degree in film studies from NYU's prestigious Tisch School. She moved to Los Angeles and worked her way up in Rising Entertainment, from an entry-level copywriter, to

marketing associate, to head of the 22-person film-marketing unit. Sarah had a lot riding on the latest *Fire Force Five* release. A big opening weekend would go a long way toward helping her lobby for one of the positions she was really interested in: EVP in either international business development or family films.

The *Fire Force Five* series was one of the company's strongest and best-known properties: The three Triple-F movies released over the past 10 years had generated more than $2.4 billion in box-office receipts and almost as much in merchandise sales. The buzz was building for the upcoming fourth release. Already, Sarah had leveraged the decade-long relationships she'd cultivated with reporters at *Entertainment Weekly*, *Variety*, and other magazines to place behind-the-scenes and making-of feature articles—each of which stoked the chatter and anticipation among Triple-F fans. She'd overseen the production of a high-impact trailer that would be reviewed in Friday's meeting, and she'd also been coordinating with Rising Entertainment's publicity department to get most of the *Fire Force* quintet booked on the usual morning and late-night talk shows.

Now, Sarah was staring anxiously at the envelope icon in the bottom-right corner of her screen: Where were the numbers she'd asked Josh to generate? Sarah just couldn't afford to stay at the office tonight; every minute she was late to pick up four-month-old Rosie from day care was costing her (financially and psychically), and she had already logged plenty of overtime this week. Sarah was ready to alert her husband that he'd have to handle the pickup, when the Outlook message popped up: "You have new unopened items." It was close to 5:30 PM when Josh's report arrived, and the last couple of case studies looked pretty sketchy, as if he'd thrown them together quickly. But there wasn't enough time to send them back for revision, Sarah decided. She'd work on them further in the morning.

Sarah quickly dropped the numbers into her slide deck and was about to log off when she spotted the bright pink "coaching" sticky note slapped on the side of her monitor. A few months ago she and the other frontline managers at Rising Entertainment had gone through a special HR-facilitated training session about integrating the newer, younger hires into the company. "Invest the time," the managers were told. But what many of them heard was "Sugarcoat."

Sarah quickly dashed off an e-mail to Josh. "Great job! You're the best." Who was she kidding? He'd done a half-assed job, and he knew it. Like so many of the young people hired by the studio recently, Sarah thought, Josh was far more concerned with *getting* praise than with *earning* praise. How else to explain that "look at me" move in the team meeting a few weeks back? Not that Josh's ideas were bad, Sarah recalled. They just weren't very well informed; he hadn't bothered to think about things like, well, money and infrastructure and talent. If I had tried something like that when I was an associate, I would have been back at square one in a heartbeat, she thought.

No one had even bothered to show her the ropes until she'd been on board awhile, Sarah recalled. But, following HR's directives, she promised herself she'd take time to explain to Josh exactly how his analysis had been received, how it fit into the overall presentation, and how she'd structured the pitch—after the meeting. The clock was ticking.

Bypassing the Boss

Sam Smithstone was already late for a dinner meeting with a couple of potential clients at the Ivy. The freeway would be murder. So he didn't take too kindly to Josh Lewis's overly solicitous greeting in the hallway late on Thursday and his attempts to conduct a drive-by pitch. "Stop by my office at 8:15 a.m. tomorrow," he told the marketing associate. "Or walk with me, if you want. But keep up."

The break-time discussion with his friends the day before had emboldened Josh. As soon as he'd returned to his cubicle, he sent Jessica and Ashok an urgent e-mail: "Who would know details of our current distribution and intellectual property agreements for the Triple-F films?" Jessica shared the name of a veteran IP lawyer in her department. Ashok had no contacts to share but responded nonetheless with a morale-boosting "XLNT!"[4] Rather than devote even more time to Sarah's assignment, Josh opted to turn in a "good enough" version near day's end. Then he had raced off to legal to find Jessica's colleague. He'd spent most of Thursday morning and afternoon fleshing out his plan.

Now, walking alongside the studio head, Josh took a moment to establish his pedigree, telling the executive where he went to school and why he chose Rising Entertainment. As Josh chatted up the CEO with ease, Sam was instantly reminded of his daughter—who was around the same age, now living back at home, and would similarly corral him to talk gadgets, politics, and pop culture.

"I'm glad you're enjoying it here—so what did you want to run by me?" Sam said, trying to get Josh to cut to the chase before they reached the lobby.

Josh carefully but quickly laid out his ideas for putting the Triple-F series online as a marketing ploy for the new instalment and employing nontraditional distribution and promotion channels. Even before Josh was done, Sam stopped and smiled. "That's some fresh thinking—I like it," he said. "Can you talk through these ideas during tomorrow's meeting? Maybe provide some P&L projections or a point-by-point comparison of your plan against the plans we've used to market and distribute Triple-F in the past?"

"I can," Josh replied, neglecting to tell the senior leader that he hadn't actually been invited to the meeting and wasn't even sure where it was being held. "I will. Thanks, Mr. Smithstone." Sam was only seconds out the door when Josh grabbed for his phone and typed an urgent message to Ashok and Jessica: "AYT?[5] SOS!"

"Oops!" Sarah literally bumped into her boss as they were both getting coffee in the commissary early on Friday morning. She had been so fixated on the slight stain on her blouse—spit-up? orange juice?—that she hadn't even seen Sam Smithstone approaching, Styrofoam cup in hand. Good thing there's a cover on that, Sarah thought.

"Great work cultivating the new guys, Sarah. I'm looking forward to hearing more from Josh," the CEO said in passing. "I love his approach, and even better, I love the wiki he sent around last night explaining his idea. See you in a bit."

Sarah stared after Sam. What? Wikis? She was amazed on every level, starting with the fact that the CEO even knew who Josh was. I wasn't even sure he knew who *I* was, she thought. Her astonishment slowly abated—replaced with a burning desire to talk things over with her young marketing colleague, particularly before the Triple-F meeting in a few hours.

Sarah pulled out her BlackBerry and punched out a message: "Josh, in my office please, in 10."

Source: Case prepared by Tamara J. Erikson.

---

4 Excellent!

5 Are you there?

QUESTIONS

1. What are the sources of generational conflict between Josh Lewis and Sarah Bennett? How do their values differ?

2. What are the sources of job dissatisfaction for Josh? What are the sources of job dissatisfaction for Sarah? In both cases, consider discrepancy between wanted and received job outcomes and issues of fairness.

3. Was Josh correct to bypass Sarah and intervene directly with studio head Sam Smithstone?

4. In this series of events, could Josh have acted more effectively? Could Sarah have acted more effectively? In each case, explain your reasoning.

5. What should Sarah do right now? Should she punish Josh, or commend his diligence, or invite him to the meeting, or commandeer his ideas, or something else?

6. What should Sarah do in the longer term?

REFERENCES

1. Excerpted from Nebenzahl, D. (2009, February 28). Managing the generation gap. *The Gazette* (Montreal), G1–G2. Reprinted by the express permission of Montreal Gazette Group Inc., a Can-West Partnership.

2. Hofstede, G. (1980). *Culture's consequences: International differences in work-related values.* Beverly Hills, CA: Sage, 19; see also Rokeach, M. (1973). *The nature of human values.* New York: Free Press.

3. Meglino, B. M., & Ravlin, E. C. (1998). Individual values in organizations: Concepts, controversies, and research. *Journal of Management, 24,* 351–389.

4. Schwartz, S. H. (1992). Universals in the content and structure of values: Theoretical advances and empirical tests in 20 countries. *Advances in Experimental Social Psychology, 25,* 1–65.

5. See for example Hammill, G. (2005, Winter/Spring). Mixing and managing four generations of employees. *FDU Magazine*(online), http://view.fdu.edu/default.aspx?id=1144.

6. Cennamo, L., & Gardner, D. (2008). Generational differences in work values, outcomes and person–organisation fit. *Journal of Managerial Psychology, 23,* 891–906; Hess, N., & Jepsen, D. M. (2009). Career stage and generational differences in psychological contracts. *Career Development International, 14,* 261–283; Wong, M., Gardiner, E., Lang, W., & Coulon, L. (2008). General differences in personality and motivation: Do they exist and what are the implications for the workplace? *Journal of Managerial Psychology, 23,* 878–890; Deal, J. J. (2007). *Retiring the generation gap: How employees young and old can find common ground.* San Francisco: Jossey-Bass.

7. Westerman, J. W., & Yamamura, J. H. (2007). Generational preferences for work environment fit: Effects on employee outcomes. *Career Development International, 12,* 150–161; Cennamo & Gardner, 2008; Wong et al., 2008.

8. Twenge, J. M. (2010). A review of the empirical evidence on generational differences in work attitudes. *Journal of Business and Psychology, 25,* 201–210.

9. Twenge, 2010; Twenge, J. M., Campbell, S. M., Hoffman, B. J., & Lance, C. E. (2010). Generational differences in work values: Leisure and extrinsic values increasing, social and intrinsic values decreasing. *Journal of Management, 36,* 1117–1142.

10. Deal, 2007.

11. Meglino & Ravlin, 1998; Kristof, A. L. (1996). Person-organization fit: An integrative review of its conceptualizations, measurement, and implications. *Personnel Psychology, 49,* 1–49.

12. Black, J. S., & Mendenhall, M. (1990). Cross-cultural training effectiveness: A review and theoretical framework for future research. *Academy of Management Review, 15,* 113–136.

13. MOW International Research Team. (1987). *The meaning of working.* London: Academic Press.

14. Hofstede, G., Hofstede, G. J., Minkov, M. (2010). *Cultures and organizations: Software of the mind* (3rd ed.). New York: McGraw-Hill.

15. Hofstede, G. (1991). *Cultures and organizations: Software of the mind.* London: McGraw-Hill; Hofstede, G., & Bond, M. H. (1988). The Confucius connection: From cultural roots to economic growth. *Organizational Dynamics, 16*(4), 4–21.

16. House, R. J., Hanges, P. J., Javidan, M., Dorfman, P. W., & Gupta, V. (Eds.) (2004). *Culture, leadership, and organizations: The GLOBE study of 62 societies.* Thousand Oaks, CA: Sage.

17. For a meta-analysis of the correlates of Hofstede's cultural dimensions see Taras, V., Kirkman, B. L., & Steel, P. (2010). Examining the impact of *Culture's Consequences*: A three-decade, multilevel, meta-analytic review of Hofstede's cultural value dimensions. *Journal of Applied Psychology, 95,* 405–439.

18. Hofstede, G. (1984). The cultural relativity of the quality of life concept. *Academy of Management Review, 9,* 389–398; Hofstede, G. (1993, February). Cultural constraints in management theories. *Academy of Management Executive,* 81–94.

19. Young, S. M. (1992). A framework for successful adoption and performance of Japanese manufacturing practices in the United States. *Academy of Management Review, 17,* 677–700; Basadur, M. (1992, May). Managing creativity: A Japanese model. *Academy of Management Executive,* 29–42.

20. Glasman, L. R., & Albarracín, D. (2006). Forming attitudes that predict future behavior: A meta-analysis of the attitude-behavior relation. *Psychological Bulletin, 132,* 778–821.

21. The following syllogistic construction of attitudes can be found in Jones, E. E., & Gerard, H. B. (1967). *Foundations of social psychology.* New York: Wiley.

22. Harrison, D. A., Newman, D. A., & Roth, P. L. (2006). How important are job attitudes? Meta-analytic comparisons of integrative behavioral outcomes and time sequences. *Academy of Management Journal, 49,* 305–325.

23. Locke, E. A. (1976). The nature and causes of job satisfaction. In M. D. Dunnette (Ed.), *Handbook of industrial and organizational psychology.* Chicago: Rand McNally. See also Rice, R. W., Gentile, D. A., & McFarlin, D. B. (1991). Facet importance and job satisfaction. *Journal of Applied Psychology, 76,* 31–39.

24. Smith, P. C. (1992). In pursuit of happiness: Why study general job satisfaction? In C. J. Cranny, P. C. Smith, & E. F. Stone (Eds.), *Job satisfaction.* New York: Lexington.

25. Smith, P. C., Kendall, L. M., & Hulin, C. L. (1969). *The measurement of satisfaction in work and retirement.* Chicago: Rand McNally; Bowling Green State University (2009). *The job descriptive index.* Bowling Green, OH: Department of Psychology, Bowling Green State University.

26. Weiss, D. J., Dawis, R. V., England, G. W., & Lofquist, L. H. (1967). *Manual for the Minnesota satisfaction questionnaire: Minnesota studies in vocational rehabilitation.* Minneapolis: Vocational Psychology Research, University of Minnesota.

27. Locke, E. A. (1969). What is job satisfaction? *Organizational Behavior and Human Performance, 4,* 309–336; Rice, R. W., McFarlin, D. B., & Bennett, D. E. (1989). Standards of comparison and job satisfaction. *Journal of Applied Psychology, 74,* 591–598.

28. Williams, M. L., McDaniel, M. A., & Nguyen, N. T. (2006). A meta-analysis of the antecedents and consequences of pay level satisfaction. *Journal of Applied Psychology, 91,* 392–413.

29. For a good overview of fairness research, see Greenberg, J., & Colquitt, J. A. (2005). *Handbook of organizational justice.* Mahwah, NJ: Lawrence Erlbaum Associates. For empirical reviews of the literature, see Colquitt, J. A., Conlon, D. E., Wesson, M. J., Porter, C. O. L. H., & Ng, K. Y. (2001). Justice at the millennium: A meta-analytic review of 25 years of organizational justice research. *Journal of Applied Psychology, 86,* 425–445; Cohen-Charash, Y., & Spector, P. E. (2001). The role of justice in organizations: A meta-analysis. *Organizational Behavior and Human Decision Processes, 86,* 278–321.

30. Adams, J. S. (1963). Toward an understanding of inequity. *Journal of Abnormal and Social Psychology, 67,* 422–436.

31. See Kulik, C. T., & Ambrose, M. L. (1992). Personal and situational determinants of referent choice. *Academy of Management Review, 17*, 212–237.

32. Sharp, I. (2009, April 15). A few bumps in the road. *Globe and Mail*, B3.

33. Greenberg, J. (1987). A taxonomy of organizational justice theories. *Academy of Management Review, 12*, 9–22.

34. Brockner, J., & Wisenfeld, B. M. (1996). An integrative framework for explaining reactions to decisions: Interactive effects of outcomes and procedures. *Psychological Bulletin, 120*, 189–208; Brockner, J., & Wiesenfeld, B. (2005). How, when, and why does outcome favorability interact with procedural fairness? In Greenberg & Colquitt, 2005.

35. Cropanzano, R., & Folger, R. (1989). Referent cognitions and task decision autonomy: Beyond equity theory. *Journal of Applied Psychology, 74*, 293. See also Folger, R. (1987). Reformulating the preconditions of resentment: A referent cognitions model. In J. C. Masters & W. P. Smith (Eds.), *Social comparison, justice, and relative deprivation: Theoretical, empirical, and policy perspectives*. Hillsdale, NJ: Erlbaum.

36. Colquitt, J. A., Greenberg, J., & Zapata-Phelan, C. P. (2005). What is organizational justice? A historical overview. In Greenberg & Colquitt, 2005; Bies, R. J. (2005). Are procedural justice and interactional justice conceptually distinct? In Greenberg & Colquitt, 2005.

37. Greenberg, J. (2006). Losing sleep over organizational injustice: Attenuating insomniac reactions to underpayment inequity with supervisory training in interactional justice. *Journal of Applied Psychology, 91*, 58–69.

38. Judge, T. A. (1992). The dispositional perspective in human resources research. *Research in Personnel and Human Resources Management, 10*, 31–72. See also Staw, B. M., & Cohen-Charash, Y. (2005). The dispositional approach to job satisfaction: More than a mirage, but not yet an oasis. *Journal of Organizational Behavior, 26*, 59–78; Bowling, N. A., Beehr, T. A., Wagner, S. H., & Libkuman, T. M. (2005). Adaptation-level theory, opponent process theory, and dispositions: An integrated approach to the stability of job satisfaction. *Journal of Applied Psychology, 90*, 1044–1053.

39. Song, Z., Li, W., & Arvey, R. D. (2011). Associations between dopamine and serotonin genes and job satisfaction: Preliminary evidence from the Add Health Study. *Journal of Applied Psychology, 96*, 1223–1233.

40. Judge, T. A., Heller, D., & Mount, M. K. (2002). Five-factor model of personality and job satisfaction: A meta-analysis. *Journal of Applied Psychology, 87*, 530–541.

41. Judge, T. A., Bono, J. E., & Locke, E. A. (2000). Personality and job satisfaction: The mediating role of job characteristics. *Journal of Applied Psychology, 85*, 237–249.

42. Weiss, H. M., & Cropanzano, R. (1996). Affective events theory: A theoretical discussion of the structure, causes and consequences of affective experiences at work. *Research in Organizational Behavior, 18*, 1–74.

43. Barsky, A., Kaplan, S. A., & Beal, D. J. (2011). Just feelings? The role of affect in the formation of organizational fairness judgments. *Journal of Management, 37*, 248–279.

44. Barsade, S. G. (2002). The ripple effect: Emotional contagion and its influence on group behavior. *Administrative Science Quarterly, 47*, 644–675; see also Vijayalakshmi, V., & Bhattacharyya, S. (2012). Emotional contagion and its relevance to individual behavior and organizational processes: A position paper. *Journal of Business and Psychology*, 1–12.

45. Grandey, A. A., Dickter, D. N., & Sin, H. P. (2004). The customer is *not* always right: Customer aggression and emotion regulation of service employees. *Journal of Organizational Behavior, 25*, 397–418.

46. Hülsheger, U. R., & Schewe, A. F. (2011). On the costs and benefits of emotional labor: A meta-analysis of three decades of research. *Journal of Occupational Health Psychology, 16*, 361–389.

47. Côté, S., & Morgan, L. M. (2002). A longitudinal analysis of the association between emotion regulation, job satisfaction, and intentions to quit. *Journal of Organizational Behavior, 23*, 947–962.

48. Glomb, T. M., Kammeyer-Mueller, J. D., & Rotundo, M. (2004). Emotional labor demands and compensating wage differentials. *Journal of Applied Psychology, 89*, 700–714.

49. This material draws upon Locke, 1976.

50. Hackett, R. D. (1989). Work attitudes and employee absenteeism: A synthesis of the literature. *Journal of Occupational Psychology, 62*, 235–248; Hackett, R. D., & Guion, R. M. (1985). A reevaluation of the absenteeism-job satisfaction relationship. *Organizational Behavior and Human Decision Processes, 35*, 340–381.

51. Johns, G. (2008). Absenteeism and presenteeism: Not at work or not working well. In C. L. Cooper & J. Barling (Eds.), *The Sage handbook of organizational behavior* (Vol. 1). London: Sage; Nicholson, N., & Johns, G. (1985). The absence culture and the psychological contract—Who's in control of absence? *Academy of Management Review, 10*, 397–407.

52. Farris, G. F. (1971). A predictive study of turnover. *Personnel Psychology, 24*, 311–328. However, the more general relationship between performance and voluntary turnover is negative, as shown by Bycio, P., Hackett, R. D., & Alvares, K. M. (1990). Job performance and turnover: A review and meta-analysis. *Applied Psychology: An International Review, 39*, 47–76; Williams, C. R., & Livingstone, L. P. (1994). Another look at the relationship between performance and voluntary turnover. *Academy of Management Journal, 37*, 269–298.

53. Hom, P. W., & Griffeth, R. W. (1995). *Employee turnover*. Cincinnati, OH: South-Western.

54. This model is based on Hom & Griffeth, 1995; Lee, T. W., & Mitchell, T. R. (1994). An alternative approach: The unfolding model of voluntary employee turnover. *Academy of Management Review, 19*, 51–89; Mitchell, T. R., Holtom, B. C., Lee, T. W., Sablynski, C. J., & Erez, M. (2001). Why people stay: Using job embeddedness to predict voluntary turnover. *Academy of Management Journal, 44*, 1102–1121.

55. Hom & Griffeth, 1995.

56. Carsten, J. M., & Spector, P. E. (1987). Unemployment, job satisfaction, and employee turnover: A meta-analytic test of the Muchinsky model. *Journal of Applied Psychology, 72*, 374–381.

57. Boswell, W. R., Boudreau, J. W., & Tichy, J. (2005). The relationship between employee job change and job satisfaction: The honeymoon-hangover effect. *Journal of Applied Psychology, 90*, 882–892; see also Boswell, W. R., Shipp, A. J., Payne, S. C., & Culbertson, S. S. (2009). Changes in newcomer satisfaction over time: Examining the pattern of honeymoons and hangovers. *Journal of Applied Psychology, 94*, 844–858.

58. Judge, T. A., Thoresen, C. J., Bono, J. E., & Patton, G. K. (2001). The job satisfaction-job performance relationship: A qualitative and quantitative review. *Psychological Bulletin, 127*, 376–407.

59. Iaffaldano, M. T., & Muchinsky, P. M. (1985). Job satisfaction and job performance: A meta-analysis. *Psychological Bulletin, 97*, 251–273.

60. Lawler, E. E., III (1973). *Motivation in organizations*. Monterey, CA: Brooks/Cole.

61. Riketta, M. (2008). The causal relationship between job attitudes and performance: A meta-analysis of panel studies. *Journal of Applied Psychology, 93*, 472–481.

62. Organ, D. W. (1988). *Organizational citizenship behavior: The good soldier syndrome*. Lexington, MA: Lexington; Podsakoff, P. M., MacKenzie, S. B.,

Paine, J. B., & Bachrach, D. G. (2000). Organizational citizenship behaviors: A critical review of the theoretical and empirical literature and suggestions for future research. *Journal of Management, 26*, 513–563.

63. Lepine, J. A., Erez, A., & Johnson, D.E. (2002). The nature and dimensionality of organizational citizenship behavior: A critical review and meta-analysis. *Journal of Applied Psychology, 87*, 52–65; Organ, D. W., & Ryan, K. (1995). A meta-analytic review of attitudinal and dispositional predictors of organizational citizenship behavior. *Personnel Psychology, 48*, 775–802; Hoffman, B. J., Blair, C. A., Meriac, J. P., & Woehr, D. J. (2007). Expanding the criterion domain? A quantitative review of the OCB literature. *Journal of Applied Psychology, 92*, 555–566.

64. Organ, 1988.

65. Lepine et al., 2002; Fassina, N. E., Jones, D. A., & Uggerslev, K. L. (2008). Meta-analytic tests of relationships between organizational justice and citizenship behavior: Testing agent-system and shared-variance models. *Journal of Organizational Behavior, 29*, 805–828.

66. George, J. M. (1991). State or trait: Effects of positive mood on prosocial behaviors at work. *Journal of Applied Psychology, 76*, 299–307.

67. Podsakoff, N. P., Whiting, S. W., Podsakoff, P. M., & Blume, B. D. (2009). Individual- and organizational-level consequences of organizational citizenship behaviors: A meta-analysis. *Journal of Applied Psychology, 94*, 122–141.

68. Leavy, B. (2005). Innovation at Xilinx: A senior operating manager's view. *Strategy & Leadership, 33*(4), 33–37.

69. Berry, C.M., Lelchook, A.M., & Clark, M.A. (2011). A meta-analysis of the interrelationships between employee lateness, absenteeism, and turnover: Implications for models of withdrawal behavior. *Journal of Organizational Behavior, 33*(5), 678–699; Harrison et al., 2006.

70. Harter, J.K, Schmidt, F.L., & Hayes, T.L. (2002). Business-unit level relationship between employee satisfaction, employee engagement, and business outcomes: A meta-analysis. *Journal of Applied Psychology, 87*, 268–279.

71. Laabs, J. (1999, March). The HR side of Sears' comeback. *Workforce*, 24–29.

72. Meyer, J.P., & Allen, N.J. (1997). *Commitment in the workplace*. Thousand Oaks, CA: Sage; for a recent critique and revised conception of commitment see Klein, H.J., Molloy, J.C., & Brinsfield, C.T. (2012). Reconceptualizing workplace commitment to redress a stretched construct: Revisiting assumptions and removing confounds. *Academy of Management Review, 37*, 130–151.

73. Meyer, J.P., Allen, N.J., & Topolnytsky, L. (1998). Commitment in a changing world of work. *Canadian Psychology, 39*, 83–93; see also Meyer, J.P., Jackson, T.A., & Maltin, E.R. (2008). Commitment in the workplace: Past, present, and future. In J. Barling & C.L. Cooper (Eds.), *The Sage handbook of organizational behavior* (Vol. 1). London: Sage.

74. Meyer, J.P, Stanley, D.J., Herscovitch, L., & Topolnytsky, L. (2002). Affective, continuance, and normative commitment to the organization: A meta-analysis of antecedents, correlates, and consequences. *Journal of Vocational Behavior, 61*, 20–52.

75. Meyer et al., 2002.

76. Meyer et al., 2002; for a careful study, see Jaros, S.J., Jermier, J.M., Koehler, J.W., & Sincich, T. (1993). Effects of continuance, affective, and moral commitment on the withdrawal process: An evaluation of eight structural equation models. *Academy of Management Journal, 36*, 951–995.

77. Meyer, J.P., Becker, T.E., & Vandenberghe, C. (2004). Employee commitment and motivation: A conceptual analysis and integrative model. *Journal of Applied Psychology, 89*, 991–1007.

78. Meyer, J.P., Paunonen, S.V., Gellatly, I.R., Goffin, R.D., & Jackson, D.N. (1989). Organizational commitment and job performance: It's the nature of the commitment that counts. *Journal of Applied Psychology, 74*, 152–156.

79. Randall, D.M. (1987). Commitment and the organization: The organization man revisited. *Academy of Management Review, 12*, 460–471.

80. Meyer, Allen, & Topolnytsky, 1998.

81. Cascio, W.F. (1993, February). Downsizing: What do we know? What have we learned? *Academy of Management Executive*, 95–104.

82. Meyer, Allen, & Topolnytsky, 1998; see also Meyer et al., 2008.

PHOTO CREDITS

Credits are listed in order of appearance.

PERCEPTION, ATTRIBUTION, AND DIVERSITY

PERCEPTION, ATTRIBUTION, AND DIVERSITY

LEARNING OBJECTIVES

After reading this chapter, you should be able to:

1 Define *perception* and discuss some of the general factors that influence perception.

2 Explain *social identity theory* and *Bruner's model* of the perceptual process.

3 Describe the main biases in person perception.

4 Describe how people form *attributions* about the causes of behaviour.

5 Discuss various biases in attribution.

6 Discuss the concepts of *workforce diversity* and valuing diversity.

7 Discuss how racial, ethnic, religious, gender, and age *stereotypes* affect organizational behaviour and what organizations can do to manage diversity.

8 Define *trust* perceptions and *perceived organizational support*, and describe *organizational support theory*.

9 Discuss person perception and perceptual biases in human resources.

KPMG

KPMG is a leading accounting and professional services firm that provides audit, tax, and financial advisory services to businesses across Canada. KPMG is one of Canada's oldest accounting firms with offices in 33 locations across the country and more than 675 partners and 5000 employees.

Several years ago, Michael Bach, a manager in the professional services IT consulting practice at KPMG in Toronto, approached the human resources director about creating a full-time position responsible for diversity and promoting diversity at the company. He was told to write a business case. So he did.

His business case was about bringing the company's diversity practices under one umbrella and making them a companywide priority. A month later, he presented it to the board of directors and got a new job, a team, and a budget of just over $500 000. "I was told to go rock the boat," said Bach, who is now KPMG's national director of diversity, equity, and inclusion and reports directly to the chief HR officer and CEO.

In four years, Bach launched initiatives and programs to recruit and retain employees from diverse backgrounds

as well as a mandatory online-training program for employees on diversity issues. KPMG now has diversity councils at many of its 33 offices in Canada. The company also has a number of social clubs, including an international club, where members meet regularly to offer support to employees who are new to the country. Bach has also introduced networks and clubs such as Women's Interchange Network, Parents of Children with Special Needs, religious groups, and pride@kpmg, a network for LGBT employees.

Bach also created an open recruiting process for skilled immigrants and introduced diversity training for all new hires and cultural competence training for managers. "There was a lot of education, making sure that people got that being educated and working outside of Canada is not a bad thing," said Bach. A targeted recruitment strategy to increase the number of women and visible minority employees by 10 percent over five years was also implemented.

Other initiatives Bach has spearheaded include reaching out to immigrant communities through career fairs to identify professional candidates and participating in the

Michael Bach of KPMG has initiated many diversity programs at KPMG, and the firm is now recognized as one of Canada's Best Diversity Employers and one of the Best Employers for New Canadians.

Internationally Educated Professionals conference. But Bach is most proud of the fact that KPMG helps immigrants with foreign accounting accreditation attain their Canadian designation, be it a Certified Accountant (CA) or Certified Public Accountant (CPA) designation.

When KPMG looked at women's advancement into its equity partnership they saw that they had only moved about 3 percent and were only at about 10 percent to begin with. "Quite frankly, they were at a glacier pace," said Bach. So they set targets for women to become partners at the firm and became the first accounting firm in Canada to do so.

Multipurpose reflection rooms have also been created in most KPMG offices. They are a dedicated space for quiet observation, prayers, meditation, or breast-feeding. The idea came from a Muslim employee who wondered aloud if there was some quiet place at work where he could pray for a few minutes. "I realized it was a reasonable request, and we need a place for not only prayers, but others things, too," said Bach.

The biggest roadblock was lack of understanding and awareness, said Bach. "There was some skepticism as people thought they would lose out in some way when we talked about being more diverse. The message that we had was: It's not about losing anything, but offering everyone equal opportunities and that can benefit the company."

Today, almost 15 percent of the firm's workforce in the Toronto area is foreign-trained and nearly 40 percent were born outside Canada. The number of women partners has now reached 18 percent and the proportion of women and visible minorities in new partner classes at KPMG has gone from 40 percent in 2009 to 51 percent in 2010.

For his work, Bach received the *Canadian HR Reporter* Individual Achievement award as part of the Toronto Region Immigrant Employment Council's (TRIEC's) fourth annual Immigrant Success (IS) Awards, which recognize innovation and leadership in integrating skilled immigrants into the workplace. Catalyst Canada also recognized Bach in 2011 for his work to improve diversity within KPMG.

In 2012, KPMG was chosen as one of Canada's Best Diversity Employers and one of the Best Employers for New Canadians for the fifth year in a row, in addition to being selected as one of Canada's Top 100 Employers.[1]

Why has KPMG made workplace diversity a top priority? What effect do diversity programs have on employee attitudes and behaviour? And why do organizations often harbour false assumptions and myths about women, visible minority employees, and immigrants? These are the kinds of questions that we will attempt to answer in this chapter. First, we will define *perception* and examine how various aspects of the perceiver, the object or person being perceived, and the situation influence perception. Following this we will present a theory and model of the perceptual process and we will consider some of the perceptual tendencies that we employ in forming impressions of people and attributing causes to their behaviour. We will then examine the role of perception in achieving a diverse workforce and how to manage diversity, perceptions of trust, perceived organizational support, and person perception in human resources. In general, you will learn that perception and attribution influence who gets into organizations, how they are treated as members, and how they interpret this treatment.

WHAT IS PERCEPTION?

LO 1

Define *perception* and discuss some of the general factors that influence perception.

Perception. The process of interpreting the messages of our senses to provide order and meaning to the environment.

Perception is the process of interpreting the messages of our senses to provide order and meaning to the environment. Perception helps sort out and organize the complex and varied input received by our senses of sight, smell, touch, taste, and hearing. The key word in this definition is *interpreting*. People frequently base their actions on the interpretation of reality that their perceptual system provides, rather than on reality itself. If you perceive your pay to be very low, you might seek employment in another firm. The reality—that you are the best-paid person in your department—will not matter if you are unaware of the fact. However, to go a step further, you might be aware that you are the best-paid person and *still* perceive your pay as low in comparison with that of the CEO of your organization or your ostentatious next-door neighbour.

Some of the most important perceptions that influence organizational behaviour are the perceptions that organizational members have of each other. Because of this, we will concentrate on person perception in this chapter.

COMPONENTS OF PERCEPTION

Perception has three components—a perceiver, a target that is being perceived, and some situational context in which the perception is occurring. Each of these components influences the perceiver's impression or interpretation of the target (Exhibit 1).

"I'm only firing you to impress the people that I'm not firing."

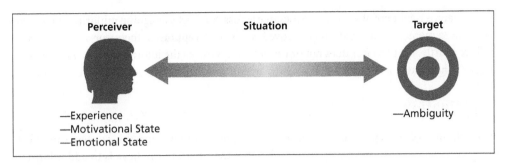

EXHIBIT 1
Factors that influence perception.

Go to MyManagementLab to see an annotated version of this figure.

The Perceiver

The perceiver's experience, needs, and emotions can affect his or her perceptions of a target.

One of the most important characteristics of the perceiver that influences his or her impressions of a target is experience. Past experiences lead the perceiver to develop expectations, and these expectations affect current perceptions. An interesting example of the influence of experience on perception is shown in Exhibit 2. It illustrates the perceptions of 268 managerial personnel in a Fortune 500 company concerning the influence of race and gender on promotion opportunities. As you can see, Caucasian men were much less likely to perceive race or gender barriers to promotion than were Caucasian women, non-Caucasian men, and non-Caucasian women.[2] Remember, these people were ostensibly viewing the same "objective" promotion system.

Frequently, our needs unconsciously influence our perceptions by causing us to perceive what we wish to perceive. Research has demonstrated that perceivers who have been deprived of food will tend to "see" more edible things in ambiguous pictures than will well-fed observers. Similarly, lonely university students might misperceive the most innocent actions of members of the opposite sex as indicating interest in them.

Emotions, such as anger, happiness, or fear, can influence our perceptions. We have all had the experience of misperceiving the innocent comment of a friend or acquaintance when we were angry. For example, a worker who is upset about not getting a promotion might perceive the consolation provided by a co-worker as gloating condescension. On the other hand, consider the worker who does get a promotion. She is so happy that she fails to notice how upset her co-worker is because he was not the one promoted.

In some cases, our perceptual system serves to defend us against unpleasant emotions. This phenomenon is known as **perceptual defence**. We have all experienced cases in which we "see what we want to see" or "hear what we want to hear." In many of these instances, our perceptual system is working to ensure that we do not see or hear things that are threatening.

Perceptual defence. The tendency for the perceptual system to defend the perceiver against unpleasant emotions.

Go to MyManagementLab to see an annotated version of this figure.

EXHIBIT 2
Ratings of the perceived importance of race and gender for promotion opportunity in executive jobs.
Note: Table values are the percentages saying that race or gender was important or very important. N = number of cases.
Source: Reprinted with permission of the publisher from *Cultural diversity in organizations: Theory, research, & practice.* © 1993 by T. Cox Jr. Berrett-Koehler Publishers, Inc., San Francisco, CA. All rights reserved. www.bkconnection. com.

The Target

Perception involves interpretation and the addition of meaning to the target, and ambiguous targets are especially susceptible to interpretation and addition. Perceivers have a need to resolve such ambiguities. You might be tempted to believe that providing more information about the target will improve perceptual accuracy. Unfortunately, this is not always the case. Writing

	Caucasian Men (N = 123)	Caucasian Women (N = 76)	Non-Caucasian Men (N = 52)	Non-Caucasian Women (N = 17)
Race	26	62	75	76
Gender	31	87	71	82

clearer memos might not always get the message across. Similarly, assigning minority workers to a prejudiced manager will not always improve his or her perceptions of their true abilities. As we shall see shortly, the perceiver does not or cannot always use all the information provided by the target. In these cases, a reduction in ambiguity might not be accompanied by greater accuracy.

The Situation

Every instance of perception occurs in some situational context, and this context can affect what one perceives. The most important effect that the situation can have is to add information about the target. Imagine a casual critical comment about your performance from your boss the week before she is to decide whether or not you will be promoted. You will likely perceive this comment very differently from how you would if you were not up for promotion. Also, a worker might perceive a racial joke overheard on the job very differently before and after racial strife has occurred in the plant. In both of these examples, the perceiver and the target are the same, but the perception of the target changes with the situation.

LO 2

Explain *social identity theory* and *Bruner's model* of the perceptual process.

Social identity theory. A theory that states that people form perceptions of themselves based on their personal characteristics and memberships in social categories.

SOCIAL IDENTITY THEORY

In the previous section, we described how characteristics of the perceiver, the target, and the situation influence the perceiver's interpretation of the target. In this section, we discuss social identity theory to help us understand how this happens. Let's begin with a simple question: "Who are you?" Chances are when you answer this question you say things like "student," "Canadian," "accountant," and so on. In other words, you respond in terms of various social categories to which you believe you belong. This is what social identity theory is all about.

According to **social identity theory**, people form perceptions of themselves based on their personal characteristics and memberships in social categories. As a result, our sense of self is composed of a personal identity and a social identity. Our *personal identity* is based on our unique personal characteristics, such as our interests, abilities, and traits. *Social identity* is based on our perception that we belong to various social groups, such as our gender, nationality, religion, occupation, and so on. Personal and social identities help us answer the question "Who am I?"

But why and how do we do this? As individuals, we categorize ourselves and others to make sense of and understand the social environment. The choice of specific categories depends on what is most salient and appropriate to the situation. For example, we might define people in a meeting according to their job title. Once a category is chosen, we tend to see members of that category as embodying the most typical attributes of that category, or what are called "prototypes." Similarly, once we locate ourselves in a social category we tend to perceive ourselves as embodying the prototypical characteristics of the category. In this way, we develop a sense of who and what we are, as well as our values, beliefs, and ways of thinking, acting, and feeling.[3]

In addition to forming self-perceptions based on our social memberships, we also form perceptions of others based on their memberships in social categories. This is because social identities are relational and comparative. In other words, we define members of a category relative to members of other categories. For example, the category of professor is meaningful in relation to the category of student. As the comparison category changes, so will certain aspects of the focal social identity. So when the authors of this text are in the classroom, they are perceived as professors by their students and as having whatever attributes the students attribute to professors. However, one of the authors of this text lives next door to a university student who perceives him not as a professor, but as a "baby boomer." Notice how her social categorization differs from those of the students in the classroom. As a result, her perception of the author will also differ because the attributes and characteristics associated with the generation category of a "baby boomer" differ from those of the occupational category of "professor."

Social identity theory helps us understand how the components of the perceptual system operate in the formation of perceptions. We perceive people in terms of the attributes and characteristics that we associate with their social category relative to other categories. Thus, your perception of others is a function of how you categorize yourself (e.g., student) and your target (e.g., professor). If the situation changes, so might the categorization and the relation between the perceiver and the target. For example, in a hospital, medical students might be perceived as doctors by nurses and patients, but in the classroom they are perceived as medical students by their professors.[4]

Because people tend to perceive members of their own social categories in more positive and favourable ways than those who are different and belong to other categories, social identity theory is useful for understanding stereotyping and discrimination, topics we discuss later in this chapter. Now let's turn to a more detailed understanding and model of the perceptual process.

A MODEL OF THE PERCEPTUAL PROCESS

In the previous section, we described how we form perceptions of ourselves and others based on social categories. But exactly how does the perceiver go about putting together the information contained in the target and the situation to form a picture of the target? Respected psychologist Jerome Bruner has developed a model of the perceptual process that can provide a useful framework for this discussion.[5] According to Bruner, when the perceiver encounters an unfamiliar target, the perceiver is very open to the informational cues contained in the target and the situation surrounding it. In this unfamiliar state, the perceiver really needs information on which to base perceptions of the target and will actively seek out cues to resolve this ambiguity. Gradually, the perceiver encounters some familiar cues (note the role of the perceiver's experience here) that enable her or him to make a crude categorization of the target, which follows from social identity theory. At this point, the cue search becomes less open and more selective. The perceiver begins to search out cues that confirm the categorization of the target. As this categorization becomes stronger, the perceiver actively ignores or even distorts cues that violate initial perceptions (see the left side of Exhibit 3). This does not mean that an early categorization cannot be changed. It does mean, however, that it will take a good many contradictory cues before one re-categorizes the target, and that these cues will have to overcome the expectations that have been developed.

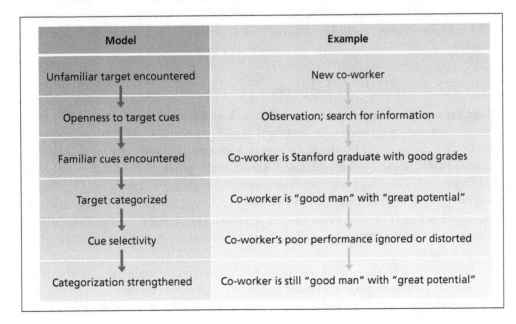

Model	Example
Unfamiliar target encountered	New co-worker
Openness to target cues	Observation; search for information
Familiar cues encountered	Co-worker is Stanford graduate with good grades
Target categorized	Co-worker is "good man" with "great potential"
Cue selectivity	Co-worker's poor performance ignored or distorted
Categorization strengthened	Co-worker is still "good man" with "great potential"

EXHIBIT 3
Bruner's model of the perceptual process and an example.

 Explore

Go to MyManagementLab to see an annotated version of this figure.

Let's clarify your understanding of Bruner's perceptual model with an example, shown on the right side of Exhibit 3. Imagine that a woman who works as an engineer for a large aircraft company is trying to size up a newly hired co-worker. Since he is an unfamiliar target, she will be especially open to any cues that might provide information about him. In the course of her cue search, she discovers that he has a master's degree in aeronautical engineering from Stanford University and that he graduated with top grades. These are familiar cues because she knows that Stanford is a top school in the field, and she has worked with many excellent Stanford graduates. She then proceeds to categorize her new co-worker as a "good man" with "great potential." With these perceptions, she takes a special interest in observing his performance, which is good for several months. This increases the strength of her initial categorization. Gradually, however, the engineer's performance deteriorates for some reason, and his work becomes less and less satisfactory. This is clear to everyone except the other engineer, who continues to see him as adequate and excuses his most obvious errors as stemming from external factors beyond his control.

Bruner's model demonstrates three important characteristics of the perceptual process. First, perception is *selective*. Perceivers do not use all the available cues, and those they do use are thus given special emphasis. This means that our perception is efficient, and this efficiency can both aid and hinder our perceptual accuracy. Second, Bruner's model illustrates that our perceptual system works to paint a constant picture of the target. Perceptual *constancy* refers to the tendency for the target to be perceived in the same way over time or across situations. We have all had the experience of "getting off on the wrong foot" with a teacher or a boss and finding it difficult to change his or her constant perception of us. Third, the perceptual system also creates a consistent picture of the target. Perceptual *consistency* refers to the tendency to select, ignore, and distort cues in such a manner that they fit together to form a homogeneous picture of the target. We strive for consistency in our perception of people. We do not tend to see the same person as both good and bad or dependable and untrustworthy. Often, we distort cues that are discrepant with our general image of a person to make the cues consistent with this image. In the next section, we consider some specific perceptual biases that contribute to selectivity, constancy, and consistency in our perception of people.

LO 3

Describe the main biases in person perception.

BASIC BIASES IN PERSON PERCEPTION

For accuracy's sake, it would be convenient if we could encounter others under laboratory conditions, in a vacuum or a test tube, as it were. Because the real world lacks such ideal conditions, the impressions that we form of others are susceptible to a number of perceptual biases.

Primacy and Recency Effects

Primacy effect. The tendency for a perceiver to rely on early cues or first impressions.

Given the examples of person perception that we have discussed thus far, you might gather that we form our impressions of others fairly quickly. One reason for this fast impression formation is our tendency to rely on the cues that we encounter early in a relationship. This reliance on early cues or first impressions is known as the **primacy effect**. Primacy often has a lasting impact. Thus, the worker who can favourably impress his or her boss in the first few days on the job is in an advantageous position due to primacy. Similarly, the labour negotiator who comes across as "tough" on the first day of contract talks might find this image difficult to shake as the talks continue. Primacy is a form of selectivity, and its lasting effects illustrate the operation of constancy.

Recency effect. The tendency for a perceiver to rely on recent cues or last impressions.

Sometimes, a **recency effect** occurs, in which people give undue weight to the cues they encountered most recently. In other words, last impressions count most. Landing a big contract today might be perceived as excusing a whole year's bad sales performance.

Reliance on Central Traits

Even though perceivers tend to rely on early information when developing their perceptions, these early cues do not receive equal weight. People tend to organize their perceptions around **central traits**, personal characteristics of the target that are of special interest to them. In developing her perceptions of her new co-worker, the experienced engineer seemed to organize her impressions around the trait of intellectual capacity. The centrality of traits depends on the perceiver's interests and the situation. Thus, not all engineers would organize their perceptions of the new worker around his intellectual abilities, and the established engineer might not use this trait as a central factor in forming impressions of the people she meets at a party.

Central traits often have a very powerful influence on our perceptions of others. Physical appearance is a common central trait in work settings that is related to a variety of job-related outcomes. Research shows an overwhelming tendency for those who are "attractive" to also be perceived as "good," especially when it comes to judgments about their social competence, qualifications, and potential job success.[6]

In general, research shows that conventionally attractive people are more likely to fare better than unattractive people in terms of a variety of job-related outcomes, including employment potential, getting hired, being chosen as a business partner, receiving good performance evaluations, or being promoted.[7] Physical height, which is one of the most obvious aspects of appearance, has also been found to be related to job performance, promotions, and career success.[8] Taller and more attractive people are also more likely to be paid more. However, as discussed in the Research Focus: *Weight-Based Bias in the Workplace*, individuals who are overweight tend to be evaluated negatively on a number of workplace outcomes. This bias is particularly troublesome given that the rate of obesity among adults in North America has been increasing over the last 20 years.

Central traits. Personal characteristics of a target person that are of particular interest to a perceiver.

Implicit Personality Theories

Each of us has a "theory" about which personality characteristics go together. These are called **implicit personality theories**. Perhaps you expect hardworking people to also be honest. Perhaps you feel that people of average intelligence tend to be most friendly. To the extent that such implicit theories are inaccurate, they provide a basis for misunderstanding.[9] The employee who assumes that her very formal boss is also insensitive might be reluctant to discuss a work-related problem with him that could be solved fairly easily.

Implicit personality theories. Personal theories that people have about which personality characteristics go together.

Projection

In the absence of information to the contrary, and sometimes in spite of it, people often assume that others are like themselves. This tendency to attribute one's own thoughts and feelings to others is called **projection**. In some cases, projection is an efficient and sensible perceptual strategy. After all, people with similar backgrounds or interests often *do* think and feel similarly. Thus, it is not unreasonable for a capitalistic business person to assume that other business people favour the free enterprise system and disapprove of government intervention in this system. However, projection can also lead to perceptual difficulties. The chairperson who feels that an issue has been resolved and perceives committee members to feel the same way might be very surprised when a vote is taken. The honest warehouse manager who perceives others as honest might find inventory disappearing. In the case of threatening or undesirable characteristics, projection can serve as a form of perceptual defence. The dishonest worker might say, "Sure I steal from the company, but so does everyone else." Such perceptions can be used to justify the perceiver's thievery.

Projection. The tendency for perceivers to attribute their own thoughts and feelings to others.

Stereotyping

One way to form a consistent impression of other people is simply to assume that they have certain characteristics by virtue of some category that they fall into as suggested by social identity theory. This perceptual tendency is known as **stereotyping**, or the tendency to generalize about people in a social category and ignore variations among them. Categories on which people might base a stereotype include race, age, gender, ethnic background, religion, social class, and occupation.[10] There are three specific aspects to stereotyping.[11]

- We distinguish some category of people (university professors).

- We assume that the individuals in this category have certain traits (absent-minded, disorganized, ivory-tower mentality).

- We perceive that everyone in this category possesses these traits ("All my professors this year will be absent-minded, disorganized, and have an ivory-tower mentality").

People can evoke stereotypes with incredibly little information. In a "first impressions" study, the mere fact that a woman preferred to be addressed as "Ms." led to her being perceived as more masculine, more achievement-oriented, and less likeable than those who preferred the traditional titles "Miss" or "Mrs."[12]

Not all stereotypes are unfavourable. You probably hold favourable stereotypes of the social categories of which you are a member, such as student. However, these stereotypes

Stereotyping. The tendency to generalize about people in a certain social category and ignore variations among them.

RESEARCH FOCUS

WEIGHT-BASED BIAS IN THE WORKPLACE

Researchers have been investigating how body weight affects workplace outcomes such as hiring decisions and performance appraisals for nearly 30 years. Many studies have found evidence of a bias against overweight individuals in the workplace and have concluded that overweight individuals are systematically denigrated in comparison to their non-overweight co-workers. In fact, the evidence for discrimination against overweight individuals can be found at virtually every stage of the employment process, including hiring, placement, compensation, promotion, discipline, and termination.

Research on negative attitudes toward overweight people in the workplace has found that overweight individuals are perceived by their co-workers and supervisors as lacking self-discipline and self-control, being lazy and not trying as hard as others at work, possessing poor work habits, and having less conscientiousness, competency, skills, and ability than individuals of "average" weight. Overweight individuals are also viewed as being more likely to be absent from work and less likely to get along with and be accepted by their co-workers and subordinates.

In an effort to better understand the extent of the bias against overweight individuals in the workplace, Cort Rudolph and colleagues examined the results of previous research on body weight and workplace outcomes. Based on the results of 25 studies that have investigated weight-based bias in the workplace, the authors found that there is a significant negative relationship between body weight across all relevant evaluative workplace outcomes, including hiring decisions, promotion, and performance evaluation.

They also found that the negative effect of weight bias on hiring outcomes was significantly stronger than the effect on performance outcomes. Why might this be? The authors suggest that it is because the effects of bias are stronger when decision makers lack performance-relevant information about a target, such as when making hiring decisions. On the other hand, when decision makers have performance-relevant information about a target, such as when making performance evaluations or promotion decisions, the effects of bias are much lower. Without relevant information about a target, a decision maker is more likely to resort to body weight stereotypes and to make biased decisions.

Source: Reprinted from *Journal of Vocational Behaviour*, *74*, Rudolph, C.W., Wells, C.L., Weller, M.D., & Baltes, B.B. A meta-analysis of empirical studies of weight-based bias in the workplace, 1–10, Copyright © 2009, with permission from Elsevier.

are often less well developed and less rigid than others you hold. Stereotypes help us develop impressions of ambiguous targets, and we are usually pretty familiar with the people in our own groups. In addition, this contact helps us appreciate individual differences among group members, and such differences work against the development of stereotypes.

Language can be easily twisted to turn neutral or even favourable information into a basis for unfavourable stereotypes. For example, if British people do tend to be reserved, it is fairly easy to interpret this reserve as snobbishness. Similarly, if women who achieve executive positions have had to be assertive, it is easy to interpret this assertiveness as pushiness.

Knowing a person's occupation or field of study, we often make assumptions about his or her behaviour and personality. Accountants might be stereotyped as compulsive, precise, and one-dimensional, while engineers might be perceived as cold and calculating. Reflect on your own stereotypes of psychology or business students.

Not all stereotypes are inaccurate. You probably hold fairly correct stereotypes about the educational level of the typical university professor and the on-the-job demeanour of the typical telephone operator. These accurate stereotypes ease the task of developing perceptions of others. However, it is probably safe to say that most stereotypes are inaccurate, especially when we use them to develop perceptions of specific individuals. This follows from the fact that stereotypes are most likely to develop when we do not have good information about a particular group.

This raises an interesting question: If many stereotypes are inaccurate, why do they persist?[13] After all, reliance on inaccurate information to develop our perceptions would seem to be punishing in the long run. In reality, a couple of factors work to *reinforce* inaccurate stereotypes. For one thing, even incorrect stereotypes help us process information about others quickly and efficiently. Sometimes, it is easier for the perceiver to rely on an inaccurate stereotype than it is to discover the true nature of the target. The male manager who is required to recommend one of his 20 employees for a promotion might find it easier to automatically rule out promoting a woman than to carefully evaluate all his employees, regardless of gender. Second, inaccurate stereotypes are often reinforced by selective perception and the selective application of language that was discussed above. The Hispanic worker who stereotypes all non-Hispanic managers as unfair might be on the lookout for behaviours to confirm these stereotypes and fail to notice examples of fair and friendly treatment. If such treatment *is* noticed, it might be perceived as patronizing rather than helpful.

ATTRIBUTION: PERCEIVING CAUSES AND MOTIVES

Thus far, we have considered the components of perception, social identity theory, and Bruner's model of the perceptual process, and we have discussed some specific perceptual tendencies that operate as we form impressions of others. We will now consider a further aspect of impression formation—how we perceive people's motives. **Attribution** is the process by which we assign causes or motives to explain people's behaviour. The attribution process is important because many rewards and punishments in organizations are based on judgments about what really caused a target person to behave in a certain way.

In making attributions about behaviour, an important goal is to determine whether the behaviour is caused by dispositional or situational factors. **Dispositional attributions** suggest that some personality or intellectual characteristic unique to the person is responsible for the behaviour and that the behaviour thus reflects the "true person." If we explain a behaviour as a function of intelligence, greed, friendliness, or laziness, we are making dispositional attributions.

Situational attributions suggest that the external situation or environment in which the target person exists was responsible for the behaviour and that the person might have had little control over the behaviour. If we explain behaviour as a function of bad weather, good luck, proper tools, or poor advice, we are making situational attributions.

 LO **4**

Describe how people form *attributions* about the causes of behaviour.

Attribution. The process by which causes or motives are assigned to explain people's behaviour.

Dispositional attributions. Explanations for behaviour based on an actor's personality or intellect.

Situational attributions. Explanations for behaviour based on an actor's external situation or environment.

Obviously, it would be nice to be able to read minds to understand people's motives. Since we cannot do this, we are forced to rely on external cues and make inferences from these cues. Research indicates that as we gain experience with the behaviour of a target person, three implicit questions guide our decisions as to whether we should attribute the behaviour to dispositional or situational causes.[14]

- Does the person engage in the behaviour regularly and consistently? (Consistency cues)
- Do most people engage in the behaviour, or is it unique to this person? (Consensus cues)
- Does the person engage in the behaviour in many situations, or is it distinctive to one situation? (Distinctiveness cues)

Let's examine consistency, consensus, and distinctiveness cues in more detail.

Consistency Cues

Consistency cues.
Attribution cues that reflect how consistently a person engages in a behaviour over time.

Consistency cues reflect how consistently a person engages in a behaviour over time. For example, unless we see clear evidence of external constraints that force a behaviour to occur, we tend to perceive behaviour that a person performs regularly as indicative of his or her true motives. In other words, high consistency leads to dispositional attributions. Thus, one might assume that the professor who has generous office hours and is always there for consultation really cares about his or her students. Similarly, we are likely to make dispositional attributions about workers who are consistently good or poor performers, perhaps perceiving the former as "dedicated" and the latter as "lazy." When behaviour occurs inconsistently, we begin to consider situational attributions. For example, if a person's performance cycles between mediocre and excellent, we might look to variations in workload to explain the cycles.

Consensus Cues

Consensus cues.
Attribution cues that reflect how a person's behaviour compares with that of others.

Consensus cues reflect how a person's behaviour compares with that of others. In general, acts that deviate from social expectations provide us with more information about the actor's motives than conforming behaviours do. Thus, unusual, low-consensus behaviour leads to more dispositional attributions than typical, high-consensus behaviour. The person who acts differently from the majority is seen as revealing more of his or her true motives. The informational effects of low-consensus behaviour are magnified when the actor is expected to suffer negative consequences because of the deviance. Consider the job applicant who makes favourable statements about the role of big business in society while being interviewed for a job at General Electric. Such statements are so predictable in this situation that the interviewer can place little confidence in what they really indicate about the candidate's true feelings and motives. On the other hand, imagine an applicant who makes critical comments about big business in the same situation. Such comments are hardly expected and could clearly lead to rejection. In this case, the interviewer would be more confident about the applicant's true disposition regarding big business.

Distinctiveness Cues

Distinctiveness cues.
Attribution cues that reflect the extent to which a person engages in some behaviour across a variety of situations.

Distinctiveness cues reflect the extent to which a person engages in some behaviour across a variety of situations. When a behaviour occurs across a variety of situations, it lacks distinctiveness, and the observer is prone to provide a dispositional attribution about its cause. We reason that the behaviour reflects a person's true motives if it "stands up" in a variety of environments. Thus, the professor who has generous office hours, stays after class to talk to students, and attends student functions is seen as truly student-oriented. The worker whose performance was good in his first job as well as several subsequent jobs is perceived as having real ability. When a behaviour is highly distinctive, in that it occurs in only one situation, we are likely to assume that some aspect of the situation caused the behaviour. If the only student-oriented behaviour that we observe is generous office hours, we assume that they are dictated by department policy. If a worker performed well on only one job, back in 1995, we suspect that his uncle owned the company!

Attribution in Action

Frequently, observers of real-life behaviour have information at hand about consistency, consensus, and distinctiveness. Let's take an example that shows how the observer puts such information together in forming attributions. At the same time, the example will serve to review the previous discussion. Imagine that Roshani, Mika, and Sam are employees who work in separate firms. Each is absent from work today, and a manager must develop an attribution about the cause to decide which action is warranted.

- *Roshani*—Roshani is absent a lot, her co-workers are seldom absent, and she was absent a lot in her previous job.
- *Mika*—Mika is absent a lot, her co-workers are also absent a lot, but she was almost never absent in her previous job.
- *Sam*—Sam is seldom absent, her co-workers are seldom absent, and she was seldom absent in her previous job.

Just what kind of attributions are managers likely to make regarding the absences of Roshani, Mika, and Sam? Roshani's absence is highly consistent, it is a low-consensus behaviour, and it is not distinctive, since she was absent in her previous job. As shown in Exhibit 4, this combination of cues is very likely to prompt a dispositional attribution, perhaps that Roshani is lazy or irresponsible. Mika is also absent consistently, but it is high-consensus behaviour in that her peers also exhibit absence. In addition, the behaviour is highly distinctive—she is absent only on this job. As indicated, this combination of cues will usually result in a situational attribution, perhaps that working conditions are terrible, or that the boss is nasty. Finally, Sam's absence is inconsistent. In addition, it is similar to that of co-workers and not distinctive, in that she was inconsistently absent on her previous job as well. As shown, this combination of cues suggests that some temporary, short-term situational factor is causing her absence. It is possible that a sick child occasionally requires her to stay home.

Biases in Attribution

As the preceding section indicates, observers often operate in a rational, logical manner in forming attributions about behaviour. The various cue combinations and the resulting attributions have a sensible appearance. This does not mean that such attributions are always correct, but they do represent good bets about why some behaviour occurred. Having made this observation, it would be naïve to assume that attributions are always free from bias or error. Earlier, we discussed a number of very basic perceptual biases, and it stands to reason that the complex task of attribution would also be open to bias. Let's consider three biases in attribution: the fundamental attribution error, actor–observer effect, and self-serving bias.[15]

LO **5**

Discuss various biases in attribution.

	Consistency	Consensus	Distinctiveness	Likely Attribution
Roshani	High	Low	Low	Disposition
Mika	High	High	High	Situation
Sam	Low	High	Low	Temporary Situation

EXHIBIT 4
Cue combinations and resulting attributions.

 Explore

Go to MyManagementLab to see an annotated version of this figure.

FUNDAMENTAL ATTRIBUTION ERROR

FUNDAMENTAL ATTRIBUTION ERROR Suppose you make a mistake in attributing a cause to someone else's behaviour. Would you be likely to err on the side of a dispositional cause or a situational cause? Substantial evidence indicates that when we make judgments about the behaviour of people other than ourselves, we tend to overemphasize dispositional explanations at the expense of situational explanations. This is called the **fundamental attribution error.**[16]

Why does the fundamental attribution error occur? For one thing, we often discount the strong effects that social roles can have on behaviour. We might see bankers as truly conservative people because we ignore the fact that their occupational role and their employer dictate that they act conservatively. Second, many people whom we observe are seen in rather constrained, constant situations (at work or at school) that reduce our appreciation of how their behaviour may vary in other situations. Thus, we fail to realize that the observed behaviour is distinctive to a particular situation. That conservative banker might actually be a weekend skydiver!

The fundamental attribution error can lead to problems for managers of poorly performing employees. It suggests that dispositional explanations for the poor performance will sometimes be made even when situational factors are the true cause. Laziness or low aptitude might be cited, while poor training or a bad sales territory is ignored. However, this is less likely when the manager has had actual experience in performing the employee's job and is thus aware of situational roadblocks to good performance.[17]

ACTOR–OBSERVER EFFECT

ACTOR–OBSERVER EFFECT It is not surprising that actors and observers often view the causes for the actor's behaviour very differently. This difference in attributional perspectives is called the **actor–observer effect.**[18] Specifically, while the observer might be busy committing the fundamental attribution error, the actor might be emphasizing the role of the situation in explaining his or her own behaviour. Thus, as actors, we are often particularly sensitive to those environmental events that led us to be late or absent. As observers of the same behaviour in others, we are more likely to invoke dispositional causes.

We see some of the most striking examples of this effect in cases of illegal behaviour, such as price fixing and the bribery of government officials. The perpetrators and those close to them often cite stiff competition or management pressure as causes of their ethical lapses. Observers see the perpetrators as immoral or unintelligent.[19]

Why are actors prone to attribute much of their own behaviour to situational causes? First, they might be more aware than observers of the constraints and advantages that the environment offered. At the same time, they are aware of their private thoughts, feelings, and intentions regarding the behaviour, all of which might be unknown to the observer. Thus, I might know that I sincerely wanted to get to the meeting on time, that I left home extra early, and that the accident that delayed me was truly unusual. My boss might be unaware of all of this information and figure that I am just unreliable.

Research on the actor–observer effect has recently found that the effect is not as pervasive as once believed. For example, it appears to be more likely under particular conditions such as when explaining negative events. The opposite effect seems to occur for positive events (i.e., the actor makes a dispositional attribution while the observer makes a situational attribution).[20]

SELF-SERVING BIAS

SELF-SERVING BIAS It has probably already occurred to you that certain forms of attributions have the capacity to make us feel good or bad about ourselves. In fact, people have a tendency to take credit and responsibility for successful outcomes of their behaviour and to deny credit and responsibility for failures.[21] This tendency is called **self-serving bias,** and it is interesting because it suggests that people will explain the very same behaviour differently on the basis of events that happened *after* the behaviour occurred. If the vice-president of marketing champions a product that turns out to be a sales success, she might attribute this to her retailing savvy. If the very same marketing process leads to failure, she might attribute this to the poor performance of the marketing research firm that she used. Notice that the self-serving

Fundamental attribution error. The tendency to overemphasize dispositional explanations for behaviour at the expense of situational explanations.

Actor–observer effect. The propensity for actors and observers to view the causes of the actor's behaviour differently.

Self-serving bias. The tendency to take credit for successful outcomes and to deny responsibility for failures.

bias can overcome the tendency for actors to attribute their behaviour to situational factors. In this example, the vice-president invokes a dispositional explanation ("I'm an intelligent, competent person") when the behaviour is successful.

Self-serving bias can reflect intentional self-promotion or excuse making. However, again, it is possible that it reflects unique information on the part of the actor. Especially when behaviour has negative consequences, the actor might scan the environment and find situational causes for the failure.[22] To be sure, when a student does very well on an exam, she is very likely to make a dispositional attribution. However, upon receiving a failing grade, the same student is much more likely to find situational causes to explain her grade!

PERSON PERCEPTION AND WORKFORCE DIVERSITY

The realities of workforce diversity have become an important factor for many organizations in recent years. **Workforce diversity** refers to differences among employees or potential recruits in characteristics such as gender, race, age, religion, cultural background, physical ability, or sexual orientation. The interest in diversity stems from at least two broad facts. First, the workforce is becoming more diverse. Second, there is growing recognition that many organizations have not successfully managed workforce diversity.

The Changing Workplace

The composition of the Canadian labour force is changing.[23] Fifty years ago, it was mainly Caucasian and male. Now, changing immigration patterns, the aging of baby boomers, and the increasing movement of women into paid employment result in a lot more variety. Immigrants to Canada from all parts of the world are making the Canadian population and labour force increasingly multicultural and multiethnic. The diversity of Canada's population is expected to continue to grow during the next 20 years. According to Statistics Canada, the number of visible minorities in Canada is expected to double by 2017 and visible minorities will form more than half the population in greater Toronto and Vancouver. If current trends continue, one in every five persons in Canada will be non-white when Canada celebrates its 150th birthday in 2017.[24] According to projections, between 25 and 28 percent of the Canadian population will be foreign-born by 2031, and in less than a decade 48 percent of Canada's working-age population will be between the ages of 45 and 64.[25]

The labour pool is changing, and at the same time many organizations are seeking to recruit more representatively from this pool so that they employ people who reflect their customer base—an effort to better mirror their markets. This is especially true in the growing service sector, where contact between organizational members and customers is very direct. As discussed in the chapter-opening vignette, KPMG has been very active in developing programs to hire, develop, and promote visible minorities, women, and immigrants, as have many other companies, including the YMCA in Toronto, Shell Canada Ltd., Federal Express Canada Ltd., and the Royal Bank of Canada (RBC).[26]

The changing employment pool is not the only factor that has prompted interest in diversity issues. Globalization, mergers, and strategic alliances mean that many employees are required to interact with people from substantially different national or corporate cultures. Compounding all this is an increased emphasis on teamwork as a means of job design and quality enhancement.

Valuing Diversity

In the past, organizations were thought to be doing the right thing if they merely tolerated diversity—that is, if they engaged in fair hiring and employment practices with respect to women and minorities. Firms were considered to be doing especially well if they assisted these

LO **6**

Discuss the concepts of *workforce diversity* and valuing diversity.

Workforce diversity. Differences among recruits and employees in characteristics such as gender, race, age, religion, cultural background, physical ability, or sexual orientation.

 Watch

VERIZON: DIVERSITY Go to MyManagementLab to watch a video about diversity.

 Simulate

GLOBAL CULTURE AND DIVERSITY Go to MyManagementLab to complete a simulation about global culture and diversity.

EXHIBIT 5
Competitive advantages to valuing and managing a diverse workforce.
Source: Cox, T.H., & Blake, S. (1991, August). Managing cultural diversity: Implications for organizational competitiveness. *Academy of Management Executive, 47,* 45–56.

1. Cost Argument	As organizations become more diverse, the cost of a poor job in integrating workers will increase. Those who handle this well will thus create cost advantages over those who don't.
2. Resource-Acquisition Argument	Companies develop reputations on favourability as prospective employers for women and ethnic minorities. Those with the best reputations for managing diversity will win the competition for the best personnel. As the labour pool shrinks and changes composition, this edge will become increasingly important.
3. Marketing Argument	For multinational organizations, the insight and cultural sensitivity that members with roots in other countries bring to the marketing effort should improve these efforts in important ways. The same rationale applies to marketing to subpopulations within domestic operations.
4. Creativity Argument	Diversity of perspectives and less emphasis on conformity to norms of the past (which characterize the modern approach to management of diversity) should improve the level of creativity.
5. Problem-Solving Argument	Heterogeneity in decision and problem solving groups potentially produces better decisions through a wider range of perspectives and more thorough critical analysis of issues.
6. System Flexibility Argument	An implication of the multicultural model for managing diversity is that the system will become less determinant, less standardized, and therefore more fluid. The increased fluidity should create greater flexibility to react to environmental changes (i.e., reactions should be faster and at less cost).

people to "fit in" with the mainstream corporate culture by "fixing" what was different about them.[27] For example, women managers were sometimes given assertiveness training to enable them to be as hard-nosed and aggressive as their male counterparts!

Recently, some have argued that organizations should *value* diversity, not just tolerate it or try to blend everyone into a narrow mainstream. To be sure, a critical motive is the basic fairness of valuing diversity. However, there is increasing awareness that diversity and its proper management can yield strategic and competitive advantages. These advantages include the potential for improved problem solving and creativity when diverse perspectives are brought to bear on an organizational problem such as product or service quality. They also include improved recruiting and marketing when the firm's human resources profile matches that of the labour pool and customer base (see Exhibit 5). The results of a recent study indicate that more organizations are adopting diversity as part of their corporate strategy to improve their competitiveness in global markets. Furthermore, a diversity climate (the extent to which an organization promotes equal employment opportunity and inclusion) has been found to be associated with business-unit performance. Another study found that organizations with more gender-diverse management teams have superior financial performance.[28]

However, if there is a single concept that serves as a barrier to valuing diversity, it is the stereotype. Let's now examine several workplace stereotypes and their consequences.

Discuss how racial, ethnic, religious, gender, and age *stereotypes* affect organizational behaviour and what organizations can do to manage diversity.

Stereotypes and Workforce Diversity

As described earlier, a stereotype is the tendency to generalize about people in a certain social category and ignore variations among them. Common workplace stereotypes are based on gender, age, race, religion, and ethnicity. In the following section, we describe how stereotypes can have negative effects on how individuals are treated in organizations. It is also worth noting that in some situations in which a negative stereotype is salient, just the perception that one might be judged on the basis of a stereotype can have a negative effect on their behaviour and performance, something that is known as stereotype threat.

Stereotype threat occurs when members of a social group (e.g., visible minorities or women) feel they might be judged or treated according to a stereotype and that their behaviour and/or performance will confirm the stereotype. Thus, the existence of a stereotype threat can undermine a person's performance. Research has found evidence for stereotype threat effects for ethnicity/race stereotypes and gender-based stereotypes. The activation of a salient negative stereotype threat in a testing situation (e.g., asking test takers to report demographics prior to taking a test) has been found to result in lower cognitive ability and math test performance scores of minorities and women compared to non-threatening situations.[29] Let's now consider the nature of these stereotypes and their consequences in the workplace.

Stereotype threat. Members of a social group feel they might be judged or treated according to a stereotype and that their behaviour and/or performance will confirm the stereotype.

RACIAL, ETHNIC, AND RELIGIOUS STEREOTYPES

Racial, ethnic, and religious stereotypes are pervasive, persistent, frequently negative, and often self-contradictory. Most of us hold at least some stereotypical views of other races, religions, or cultures. Over the years, such stereotypes exhibit remarkable stability unless some major event, such as a war, intervenes to change them. Then, former allies can acquire negative attributes in short order.

Personal experience is unnecessary for such stereotype formation. In one study, people were asked to describe the traits of a number of ethnic groups, including several fictional ones. Although they had never met a Danerian, a Pirenian, or a Wallonian, this did not inhibit them from assigning traits, and those they assigned were usually unfavourable![30] Such stereotypes often contain contradictory elements. A common reaction is to describe a particular group as being too lazy, while at the same time criticizing it for taking one's job opportunities away.

There is a remarkable shortage of serious research into racial, ethnic, and religious matters in organizations.[31] However, what evidence there is shows that just getting in the door can be a problem. For example, whites have been found to advance further in the hiring process than blacks even when the applicants are the same age and physical size, have identical education and work experience, and share similar personalities.[32] A study on religious discrimination found that female job applicants who appeared to be Muslim experienced more negative interpersonal behaviour and discrimination (e.g., rudeness or hostility) than non-Muslim female applicants.[33] Discrimination in hiring has also been found to occur when job applicants have an ethnic-sounding name. To learn more, see the Ethical Focus: *What's in a Name? You're Hired…or Not!*

Even after visible minorities get in the door, career advancement based on racial or ethnic stereotypes are common. A study on the career satisfaction and advancement of visible minorities in Canada found that visible minorities perceive more barriers in their career advancement, including a lack of fairness in the process, and report less career satisfaction than white colleagues. In addition, 47 percent of visible minority managers and professionals reported feeling they were held to a higher standard of performance and 69 percent of visible minority respondents reported that in their career, "who you know" is more important than "what you know."[34] In the United States, almost one-quarter of workers from diverse backgrounds reported being discriminated against or treated unfairly at work. The most common example was not receiving credit for their work.[35]

Attributions can play an important role in determining how job performance is interpreted. For example, one study found that good performance on the part of African-American managers was seen to be due to help from others (a situational attribution), while good performance by Caucasian managers was seen to be due to their effort and abilities (a dispositional attribution).[36]

Racial and ethnic stereotypes are also important in the context of the increasing globalization of business. In one study, researchers asked American business students to describe Japanese and American managers along a number of dimensions. The students viewed Japanese managers as having more productive employees and being better overall managers. However, the students preferred to work for an American manager.[37] One can wonder how such students will respond to international assignments. Of course, all groups have stereotypes of each other. Japanese stereotypes of Americans probably contribute to Americans not being promoted above a certain level in Japanese firms.

ETHICAL FOCUS

WHAT'S IN A NAME? YOU'RE HIRED . . . OR NOT!

Have you ever thought about how your name might influence your chances of being invited for a job interview or receiving a job offer? Chances are you probably have not thought about this.

However, there is evidence that name discrimination is a problem when it comes to screening resumes and that having an ethnic-sounding name might put a job applicant at a disadvantage. Furthermore, this might explain in part why the unemployment rate of recent immigrants to Canada is almost twice as high as similarly aged non-immigrants even though Canada's immigration policy focuses on skilled immigrants with high levels of education and experience.

To find out if the name of a job applicant influences recruiter decisions, a study was conducted by Metropolis British Columbia and authors Philip Oreopoulos and Diane Dechief of the University of Toronto. The study involved sending out over 7000 resumes by email in response to job postings across multiple occupations in Toronto, Montreal, and Vancouver. The jobs required at least a bachelor's degree, fluency in English, and four to six years of work experience. All of the resumes indicated that the applicant had Canadian work experience, Canadian education, and solid credentials. However, they differed in terms of the name of the applicant. Some of the resumes had common Anglophone sounding names such as John Smith, while others had popular Greek, Indian, or Chinese names.

The main outcome variable of the study was whether or not a resume generates a callback from an employer indicating interest in meeting or further discussing the applicant's credentials. A callback is the most important step for obtaining a job offer.

The results indicated that resumes with English-sounding names were 35 percent more likely to receive a callback for a job interview than resumes with Indian or Chinese names across the three cities. Resumes with English-sounding names also received more callbacks than resumes with Greek-sounding names. These results remained even when taking into account many other factors on the resumes such as a degree from a top-ranking university, active social extracurricular activities, or job experience from a large, multinational firm.

These results indicate the existence of employer discrimination against job applicants with ethnic-sounding names. According to the authors of the study, subconscious or implicit discrimination may be one reason why recruiters are less likely to call back applicants with ethnic-sounding names. An applicant's name or country of origin may trigger stereotypes that cause employers to focus on the stereotype and overemphasize potential concerns such as social and language skills and to ignore other important factors on the resume such as education and experience.

These results provide one explanation for a common complaint from immigrants to Canada that they never hear back from prospective employers, even when they apply for jobs that precisely match their expertise. What's more, the results also indicate that even Canadian-raised and educated job applicants might be discriminated against if they have an ethnic-sounding name.

Sources: Oreopoulos, P., & Dechief, D. (2011). *Why do some employers prefer to interview Matthew, but not Samir? New evidence from Toronto, Montreal, and Vancouver.* Metropolis British Columbia Centre of Excellence for Research on Immigration and Diversity, Working Paper Series, No.11-13; Dobson, S. (2011, November 21). "Matthew, you're hired. Good luck next time, Samir." *Canadian HR Reporter, 24*(20), 1, 20; Immen, W. (2011, November 18). How an ethnic-sounding name may affect the job hunt; Hiring managers tend to bypass resumes with foreign-sounding names even if education, experience meet the grade, study finds. *The Globe and Mail*, B21.

Finally, recent evidence suggests that organizations are simply reflections of the environments of which they are a part. Thus, if prejudice, negative stereotyping, ethnocentrism, and discrimination exist within the environment that an organization inhabits, it is very likely that these problems will surface within the organization itself.[38]

GENDER STEREOTYPES One of the most problematic stereotypes for organizations is the gender stereotype. Considering their numbers in the workforce, women are severely underrepresented in managerial and administrative jobs. Although women now occupy a significant and growing proportion of entry- and mid-level management positions, this is not the case for top-level positions, where they remain significantly underrepresented. According to a study of 500 of Canada's top companies by Catalyst Canada, women hold only 14.4 percent of corporate officer positions, including presidents, executive vice-presidents, and chief operating officers. As a result, it's predicted that women's overall representation in corporate Canada will not reach 25 percent until 2025.[39]

There is evidence that gender stereotypes are partially responsible for discouraging women from business careers and blocking their ascent to managerial positions. This under-representation of women managers and administrators happens because stereotypes of women do not correspond especially well with stereotypes of business people or managers.

What is the nature of gender stereotypes? A series of studies have had managers describe men in general, women in general, and typical "successful middle managers." These studies have determined that successful middle managers are perceived as having traits and atti-tudes that are similar to those generally ascribed to men. That is, successful managers are seen as more similar to men in qualities such as leadership ability, competitiveness, self-confidence, ambitiousness, and objectivity.[40] Thus, stereotypes of successful middle manag-ers do not correspond to stereotypes of women. The trend over time in the results of these studies contains some bad news and some good news. The bad news is that *male* managers today hold the same dysfunctional stereotypes about women and management that they held in the early 1970s when researchers conducted the first of these studies. At that time, women managers held the same stereotypes as the men. The good news is that the recent research shows a shift by the women—they now see successful middle managers as possessing atti-tudes and characteristics that describe *both* men and women in general. However, although good managers are described today as possessing fewer masculine characteristics than in past decades, the recent research indicates that both men and women of varying age, educa-tion, and work experience still describe a good manager as possessing predominantly mascu-line characteristics. In other words, the stereotype of a leader is culturally masculine. People perceive leaders as similar to men but not very similar to women.[41]

Granting that gender stereotypes exist, do they lead to biased human resources deci-sions? The answer would appear to be yes. In a typical study, researchers asked male bank supervisors to make hypothetical decisions about workers who were described equivalently except for gender.[42] Women were discriminated against for promotion to a branch manager's position. They were also discriminated against when they requested to attend a professional development conference. In addition, female supervisors were less likely than their male counterparts to receive support for their request that a problem employee be fired. In one case, bias worked to *favour* women. The bank supervisors were more likely to approve a request for a leave of absence to care for one's children when it came from a female. This finding is similar to others that show that gender stereotypes tend to favour women when they are being considered for "women's" jobs (such as secretary) or for "women's" tasks (such as supervising other women), but not for traditional male jobs.[43] One recent study found that when women are successful in traditional male jobs, they are less liked, and being disliked had a negative effect on their evaluations and recommendations for rewards, including salary and special job opportunities.[44]

In general, research suggests that the above findings are fairly typical. Women suffer from a stereotype that is detrimental to their hiring, development, promotion, and salaries. Female managers are also more likely than male managers to have to make off-the-job sacri-fices and compromises in family life to maintain their careers.[45] However, there is growing evidence that the detrimental effects of such stereotypes are reduced or removed when deci-sion makers have good information about the qualifications and performance of particular women and an accurate picture of the job that they are applying for or seeking promotion into.[46] In particular, several studies reveal convincingly that women do not generally suffer from gender stereotypes in *performance evaluations* that their supervisors provide.[47] This is not altogether surprising. As we noted earlier, stereotypes help us process information in ambiguous situations. To the extent that we have good information on which to base our perceptions of people, reliance on stereotypes is less necessary. Day-to-day performance is often fairly easy to observe, and gender stereotypes do not intrude on evaluations. Along these lines, a recent review of research on gender differences in job performance ratings found that females scored slightly higher than males; however, males received higher ratings of promotion potential.[48]

1. L.V. Lomes Limited
2. Admiral Insurance
3. DEL Property Management Inc.
4. Nycomed, a Takeda Company
5. Royal Lepage Performance Realty
6. SaskCentral (Credit Union Central of Saskatchewan)
7. Ariad Communications
8. T4G Limited
9. Lutherwood
10. Achievers (Formerly I Love Rewards)

Fortunately, as shown in Exhibit 6, many Canadian organizations have made efforts to ensure that women are represented in senior positions and have been recognized for their endeavours. For example, at Shell Canada Ltd. of Calgary there are more women than men on the list of potential senior managers.[49] Women have made the most significant progress moving into senior management and executive positions in the financial services industry. On the other hand, industries that tend to be stereotypically male, such as paper and forest products, steel production, motor vehicles and parts, oil and gas, and general manufacturing and construction, continue to have the lowest representation of women in senior positions.[50]

AGE STEREOTYPES Another kind of stereotype that presents problems for organizations is the age stereotype. Knowing that a person falls into a certain age range or belongs to a particular age generation, we have a tendency to make certain assumptions about the person's physical, psychological, and intellectual capabilities.

What is the nature of work-related age stereotypes? Older workers are seen as having less *capacity for performance.* They tend to be viewed as less productive, creative, logical, and capable of performing under pressure than younger workers. In addition, older workers are seen as having less *potential for development.* Compared with younger workers, they are considered more rigid and dogmatic and less adaptable to new corporate cultures. Not all stereotypes of older workers are negative, however. They tend to be perceived as more honest, dependable, and trustworthy (in short, more *stable*). In general, these stereotypes are held by both younger and older individuals.[51]

It is worth noting that these stereotypes are essentially inaccurate. For example, age seldom limits the capacity for development until post-employment years.[52] Furthermore, the most comprehensive study on age and job performance found that age is not related to task performance or creativity but it is related to other forms of job performance. For example, older workers were found to exhibit more citizenship behaviours and greater safety-related behaviour, and fewer counterproductive work behaviours. Older workers were also found to exhibit less workplace aggression, on-the-job substance use, tardiness, and absenteeism. Thus, by all accounts older workers perform as well or better than younger workers across numerous dimensions of job performance.[53]

However, the relevant question remains: Do age stereotypes affect human resources decisions? It would appear that such stereotypes can affect decisions regarding hiring, promotion, and skills development. In one study, researchers had university students make hypothetical recommendations regarding younger and older male workers. An older man was less likely to be hired for a finance job that required rapid, high-risk decisions. An older man was considered less promotable for a marketing position that required creative solutions to difficult problems. Finally, an older worker was less likely to be permitted to attend

A public awareness campaign to combat age stereotypes and discrimination sponsored by Canada's Association for the Fifty-Plus and the Ontario Human Rights Commission featured this poster with the tag line "Nobody has a shelf life."

a conference on advanced production systems.[54] These decisions reflect the stereotypes of the older worker depicted above, and they are doubtless indicative of the tendency for older employees to be laid off during corporate restructuring.

Unfortunately, the reality for older workers is consistent with the research. According to the Ontario Human Rights Commission, discrimination on the basis of age is experienced by people as young as 40 to 45, who are often passed over for merit pay and promotions or pressured to take early retirement. In a blatant example of such discrimination, a job fair held in Toronto several years ago stated that the target audience was 18- to 54-year-olds. Many older workers were offended, and a complaint was made to the Ontario Human Rights Commission.[55] Again, however, we should recognize that age stereotypes may have less impact on human resources decisions when managers have good information about the capacities of the particular employee in question.

Walmart Canada is a repeat winner of the Best Employer Awards for 50-plus Canadians for its efforts in attracting and hiring older workers.

To combat age stereotypes and discrimination, Canada's Association for the Fifty-Plus (CARP) has worked with the Ontario Human Rights Commission on a public awareness campaign that included a poster featuring photographs of older people with the tag line "Nobody has a shelf life. Stop age discrimination now."[56] Some organizations have implemented programs and practices to promote the hiring and retention of older workers. A good example is Walmart Canada, which has been recognized for its efforts in attracting and hiring older workers. The company is a repeat winner of the Best Employer Awards for 50-plus Canadians.[57]

Managing Workforce Diversity

◄◉─Simulate

HUMAN RESOURCES AND DIVERSITY Go to MyManagementLab to complete a simulation about human resources and diversity.

Given the prevalence of the stereotypes noted above, valuing diversity is not something that occurs automatically. Rather, diversity needs to be *managed* to have a positive impact on work behaviour and an organization. What can organizations do to achieve and manage a diverse workforce? Before continuing, try to answer this question by taking another look at the chapter-opening vignette on KPMG to see what they do to manage a diverse workforce.

Exhibit 7 lists some of the common activities that are often included in diversity programs. Some additional examples are listed below.[58]

EXHIBIT 7
Common activities included in diversity programs.
Source: Jayne, M.E.A., & Dipboye, R.L. (2004, Winter). Leveraging diversity to improve business performance: Research findings and recommendations for organizations. *Human Resource Management, 43(4),* 409–424. © 2004 John Wiley & Sons, Inc. Used by permission.

Strategic Initiative	Sample Interventions
Recruiting	• Employee referral programs • Diverse recruiting teams • Internship programs and sponsored scholarships • Job posting and advertising initiatives targeting specific groups • Minority conference and job fair attendance • Recruiting efforts targeting universities and community colleges with diverse student bodies
Retention	• Corporate-sponsored employee resource or affinity groups • Employee benefits (e.g., adoption, domestic partner, elder care, flexible health, and dependent spending accounts) • Work–life programs and incentives (e.g., on-site child care, flexible work schedules, and on-site lactation facilities)
Development	• Leadership development training programs • Mentoring programs
External Partnership	• Minority supplier programs • Community service outreach
Communication	• Award programs providing public recognition of managers and employees for diversity achievement • Newsletters, internal websites on diversity • Senior leadership addresses, town hall meetings, business updates
Training	• Awareness training on the organization's diversity initiative • Issue-based/prevention training (e.g., sexual harassment and men and women as colleagues) • Team-building and group-process training
Staffing and Infrastructure	• Dedicated diversity staff • Executive and local diversity councils

- Select enough minority members to get them beyond token status. When this happens, the majority starts to look at individual accomplishments rather than group membership because they can see variation in the behaviours of the minority. In recent years, an increasing number of Canadian organizations have become more interested in diversity recruiting and, as indicted in the chapter-opening vignette, KPMG actively recruits immigrants and has set targets for promoting women.[59]

- Encourage teamwork that brings minority and majority members together.

- Ensure that those making career decisions about employees have accurate information about them rather than having to rely on hearsay and second-hand opinion.

- Train people to be aware of stereotypes and to value diversity. As indicated in the chapter-opening vignette, KPMG made diversity training mandatory for all employees and new hires.

A good example of a company that manages workforce diversity is Boeing Canada, which has been recognized as one of Canada's Best Diversity Employers. The company actively promotes diversity, which helps to create a positive and respectful workplace and contributes to the overall success of the organization. In addition to employing deaf people and providing them with BlackBerrys to communicate with co-workers and their supervisors, the company also employs the following diversity strategies:[60]

- Diversity days that feature a lunch from a particular culture accompanied by presentations that include dancers and singers to help employees learn about the diverse backgrounds of their co-workers.

- Diversity training that includes formal educational classes on respecting and honouring co-worker's origins, leanings, and affiliations.

- Language training for recent immigrants and others who want to improve their English, as well as training in American Sign Language (ASL).

- Monthly awareness campaigns that profile events in the calendar such as Ramadan.

- Aboriginal recruitment in partnership with the Centre for Aboriginal Human Resource Development in Winnipeg.

- A women's committee to assist female employees with personal and professional development.

- Partnering with the Society for Manitobans with Disabilities (SMD) to provide employment opportunities to disabled job seekers.

- Job shadowing in cooperation with Red River College's deaf students program in Winnipeg so that students can see and communicate with deaf employees at work.

- A volunteer employment equity and diversity team that meets biweekly to identify and discuss diversity initiatives and plan awareness programs.

Although diversity training programs are one of the most common approaches for managing diversity, there is little hard research on the success of these programs. However, there is some anecdotal evidence that these programs can actually cause disruption and bad feelings when all they do is get people to open up and voice their stereotypes and then send them back to work.[61] Awareness training should be accompanied by skills training that is relevant to the particular needs of the organization. This might include training in resolving intercultural conflict, team building, handling a charge of sexual harassment, or learning a second language. Basic awareness and skills training are not the only components of managing diversity. Organizations must use a number of other tactics. What is perhaps most important is that organizations integrate diversity into all of its policies and practices rather than treat diversity as a stand-alone practice. Organizations that have been successful in managing diversity have an inclusive culture that values individual differences.[62]

Here are some additional diversity practices:

- The implications of generational differences in values and work attitudes.
- Recognizing diversity in employee needs and motives.
- Using alternative working schedules to offer employees flexibility.
- Using employee surveys to foster better communication.

YOU BE THE MANAGER

American Express Canada's Skilled Immigrant Strategy

American Express in Canada operates as AMEX Canada Inc. and AMEX Bank of Canada. AMEX Canada Inc. and AMEX Band of Canada employ over 3000 Canadians in 13 cities coast to coast.

AMEX Canada has had a diverse workforce for many years. However, with the expected growth in the coming years, the company realized that it needed to do more to attract, retain, and develop skilled immigrants.

Nancy Steele, Director of AMEX technologies (AET), was puzzled that the company's policy of hiring skilled immigrant workers seemed to be failing. "Quite often, you would on-board them, then find they weren't successful and have to remove them and have them leave the organization" she said.

As a solution, Steele initiated a skilled immigrant strategy. "The broader strategy was to look at talent in general across the organization," she said. "As we're going to grow, take on new people and invest a lot in Canada, we looked at what we're going to do to keep up the pace of growth and diversity a little bit."

In looking at ways to hire new employees, she realized there needed to be more work done to hire immigrants. "There were a lot of gaps in the process of how we hire and recruit, where we hire and recruit, and the type of talent we're getting," she said. "There were many opportunities we didn't see."

Furthermore, managers sometimes struggled to understand other cultures and help staff to succeed.

To retain skilled immigrants, Steele implemented initiatives to encourage these employees to grow within the company. "We looked at strategies to improve the process to help individuals not only get better jobs or jobs that are more suited to their skills, but develop them when they're on-site and help them progress in their career," she said.

What should AMEX Canada do to improve the hiring and retention of skilled immigrants? You be the manager.

Fernanda Silva (left) is a Brazillian immigrant who was hired by AMEX technologies as a quality assurance analyst through a skilled immigrant hiring program that was initiated by company director, Nancy Steele.

Questions

1. What should AMEX Canada do to attract and hire skilled immigrants?

2. What strategies are needed to develop and retain skilled immigrants?

To find out what AMEX Canada did, consult The Manager's Notebook at the end of the chapter.

Sources: Based on Silliker, A. (2011, March 28). Firms honoured for work with skilled immigrants. *Canadian HR Reporter, 24*(6), 1, 20; Dalby, P. (2011, March 9). New hiring approach improves success rate for immigrants. *Toronto Star*, www.thestar.com/printarticle/950769; Anonymous (2011, October 6). Nancy Steele spearheads skilled immigrant strategy at American Express Canada. *TRIEC*, www.triec.ca/2011/nancy-steele-spearheads-skilled-immigrant-strategy; www.americanexpress.com/ca.

Finally, one area of diversity that is of particular concern to governments and organizations is the hiring and integration of skilled immigrants, something that KPMG has been doing very well. To find out how another organization is doing this, read *You Be the Manager: American Express Canada's Skilled Immigrant Strategy.*

PERCEPTIONS OF TRUST

 LO **8**

Do you trust your boss and organization? What about your co-workers? These are questions that more and more people are asking themselves today, and research has found that employee trust toward management is on the decline.[63] One survey found that 47 percent of those who responded agreed that a lack of trust is a problem in their organization. In another survey, 40 percent indicated that they do not believe what management says.[64] A decline in trust can be a serious problem because trust perceptions influence organizational processes and outcomes, such as sales levels, net profits, and employee turnover.[65]

Trust has been defined as a willingness to be vulnerable and to take risks with respect to the actions of another party.[66] More specifically, "trust is a psychological state comprising the intention to accept vulnerability based upon positive expectations of the intentions or behaviour of another."[67] Trust perceptions toward management are based on three distinct perceptions: ability, benevolence, and integrity.[68] *Ability* refers to employee perceptions regarding management's competence and skills. *Benevolence* refers to the extent that employees perceive management as caring and concerned for their interests and willing to do good for them. *Integrity* refers to employee perceptions that management adheres to and behaves according to a set of values and principles that the employee finds acceptable. The combination of these three factors influences trust perceptions.

Not surprisingly, higher perceptions of management ability, benevolence, and integrity are associated with greater perceptions of trust. There is also some evidence that perceptions of fairness are associated with trust perceptions. Employees who perceived their supervisor as more fair report higher levels of trust.[69] Furthermore, perceptions of trust in management are positively related to job satisfaction, organizational commitment, job performance, and organizational citizenship behaviour, and negatively related to turnover intentions.[70]

Trust is also considered to be the most critical factor when judging best workplaces in Canada. According to the Great Place to Work Institute Canada, trust is the foundation for quality jobs and performance excellence. When the institute evaluates organizations for the best workplaces, they use a "Trust Index" to assess employees' perspective on what it is like to work in their organization. As shown in Exhibit 8, the trust model consists of five dimensions. To create a great workplace, managers need to build trust, which is achieved by practising credibility, respect, and fairness, and by encouraging pride and camaraderie among employees.[71]

Finally, it should also be noted that trust among co-workers is also important. A study of firefighters found that higher levels of trust toward one's co-workers was related to fewer physical symptoms (e.g., trouble sleeping) and less withdrawal (e.g., thoughts of being absent).[72]

PERCEIVED ORGANIZATIONAL SUPPORT

Whether or not you trust your boss and organization probably has a lot to do with how much they support you or, rather, your perceptions of support. **Perceived organizational support** (POS) refers to employees' general belief that their organization values their contribution and cares about their well-being. When employees have positive perceptions of organizational support, they believe their organization will provide assistance when they need it to perform their job effectively and to deal with stressful situations.[73]

Sidebar notes:

Define *trust* perceptions and *perceived organizational support,* and describe *organizational support theory.*

Trust. A psychological state in which one has a willingness to be vulnerable and to take risks with respect to the actions of another party.

Perceived organizational support (POS). Employees' general belief that their organization values their contribution and cares about their well-being.

EXHIBIT 8
Trust model.
Source: © 2005 Great Place to Work® Institute, Inc. All Rights Reserved.

Explore

Go to MyManagementLab to see an annotated version of this figure.

Organizational support theory. A theory that states that employees who have strong perceptions of organizational support feel an obligation to care about the organization's welfare and to help the organization achieve its objectives.

According to **organizational support theory**, employees who have strong perceptions of organizational support feel an obligation to care about the organization's welfare and to help the organization achieve its objectives. They feel a greater sense of purpose and meaning, and a strong sense of belonging to the organization. As a result, employees incorporate their membership and role within the organization into their social identity. In addition, when POS is strong, employees feel obligated to reciprocate the organization's care and support. As a result, POS has a number of positive consequences.

Research has found that employees who have greater POS have higher job performance and are more satisfied with their jobs, more committed to the organization, and less likely to be absent from work and to quit. They are also more likely to have a positive mood at work and to be more involved in their job, and they are less likely to experience strain symptoms such as fatigue, burnout, anxiety, and headaches.[74]

As shown in Exhibit 9, there are a number of factors that contribute to employees' POS. First, because supervisors function as representatives of the organization through their actions and decisions, they represent the organization to employees. As a result, favourable treatment and support from supervisors, or *perceived supervisor support*, contributes strongly to POS. Interestingly, supervisors with more positive perceptions of POS are themselves perceived by employees as being more supportive. In addition, fair organizational procedures as well as favourable rewards and job conditions are also strongly related to POS.[75]

What can organizations do to improve employee perceptions of organizational support? One study found that supportive human resources practices that demonstrate an investment

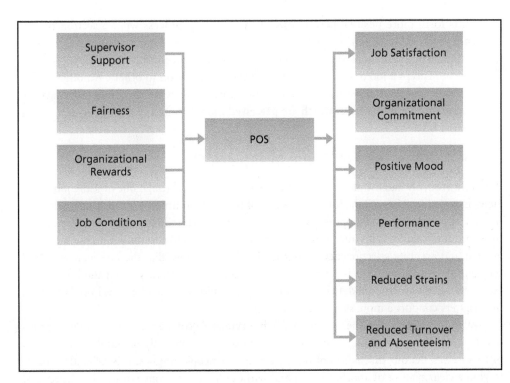

EXHIBIT 9
Predictors and consequences of perceived organizational support.
Source: Based on Rhoades, L., & Eisenberger, R. (2002). Perceived organizational support: A review of the literature. *Journal of Applied Psychology,* *87,* 698–714.

Go to MyManagementLab to see an annotated version of this figure.

in employees and recognition of employee contributions are most likely to lead to the development of greater POS. Such practices signal to employees that the organization values and cares about them. Some examples of supportive human resources practices include participation in decision making, opportunities for growth and development, and a fair reward and recognition system.[76] Of course, equality and diversity programs such as those at KPMG also help to increase POS.

PERSON PERCEPTION IN HUMAN RESOURCES

LO 9

Discuss person perception and perceptual biases in human resources.

Perceptions play an important role in human resources and can influence who gets hired and how employees are evaluated once they are hired. Job applicants also form perceptions during the recruitment and selection process, and their perceptions influence their attraction to an organization and whether or not they decide to accept a job offer.

In this section, we consider the role of perceptions in three important areas of human resources: recruitment and selection, the employment interview, and the performance appraisal.

Perceptions of Recruitment and Selection

When you meet recruiters and complete employment tests, chances are you form perceptions of the organization. In fact, research indicates that how job applicants are treated during the recruitment and selection process influences their perceptions toward the organization and their likelihood of accepting a job offer. According to **signalling theory**, job applicants have incomplete information about jobs and organizations so they interpret their recruitment experiences as cues or signals about unknown characteristics of an organization and what it would be like to work there. For example, questions that are invasive and discriminatory might send a signal that the organization discriminates and does not value diversity; poor treatment during the hiring process might signal a lack of professionalism and respect of employees. These perceptions are important because they influence a job applicant's likelihood of remaining in the selection process and accepting a job offer.[77]

Signalling theory. Job applicants interpret their recruitment experiences as cues or signals about unknown characteristics of an organization and what it will be like to work in an organization.

Applicants also form perceptions toward organizations based on the selection tests used for hiring. This research has its basis in *organizational justice theory.* Essentially, job

65

applicants form more positive perceptions of the selection process when selection procedures are perceived to be fair. Furthermore, applicants who have more positive perceptions of selection fairness are more likely to view the organization favourably and to have stronger intentions to accept a job offer and recommend the organization to others. Among various selection procedures, employment interviews and work samples are perceived more favourably than cognitive ability tests, which are perceived more favourably than personality tests and honesty tests.[78]

Perceptions in the Employment Interview

You have probably had the pleasure (or displeasure!) of sitting through one or more job interviews in your life. After all, the interview is one of the most common organizational selection devices, applied with equal opportunity to applicants for everything from the janitorial staff to the executive suite. With our futures on the line, we would like to think that the interview is a fair and accurate selection device, but is it? Research shows that the interview is a valid selection device, although it is far from perfectly accurate, especially when the interviewer conducts it in an unstructured, free-form format. The validity of the interview improves when interviewers conduct a more structured interview.[79]

What factors threaten the validity of the interview? To consider the most obvious problem first, applicants are usually motivated to present an especially favourable impression of themselves. As our discussion of the perception of people implies, it is difficult enough to gain a clear picture of another individual without having to cope with active deception! A couple of the perceptual tendencies that we already discussed in this chapter can also operate in the interview. For one thing, there is evidence that interviewers compare applicants to a stereotype of the ideal applicant.[80] In and of itself, this is not a bad thing. However, this ideal stereotype must be accurate, and this requires a clear understanding of the nature of the job in question and the kind of person who can do well in this job. This is a tall order, especially for the interviewer who is hiring applicants for a wide variety of jobs. Second, interviewers have a tendency to exhibit primacy reactions.[81] Minimally, this means that information the interviewer acquired early in the interview will have an undue impact on the final decision. However, it also means that information the interviewer obtained *before* the interview (for instance, by scanning the application form or resume) can have an exaggerated influence on the interview outcome.

The interview is a difficult setting in which to form accurate impressions about a candidate. Interview validity increases when interviews are more structured.

A couple of perceptual tendencies that we have not discussed are also at work in interviews. First, interviewers have a tendency to give less importance to positive information about the applicant.[82] This tendency means that negative information has undue impact on the decision.[83] It might occur because interviewers get more feedback about unsuccessful hiring than successful hiring ("Why did you send me that idiot?"). It might also happen because positive information is not perceived as telling the interviewer much, since the candidate is motivated to put up a good front. In addition, **contrast effects** sometimes occur in the interview.[84] This means that the applicants who have been interviewed earlier affect the interviewer's perception of a current applicant, leading to an exaggeration of differences between applicants. For example, if the interviewer has seen two excellent candidates and then encounters an average candidate, she might rate this person lower than if he had been preceded by two average applicants (see Exhibit 10). This is an example of the impact of the situation on perception.

Contrast effects. Previously interviewed job applicants affect an interviewer's perception of a current applicant, leading to an exaggeration of differences between applicants.

It is clear that the interview constitutes a fairly difficult setting in which to form accurate impressions about others. It is of short duration, a lot of information is generated, and the applicant is motivated to present a favourable image. Thus, interviewers often adopt "perceptual crutches" that hinder accurate perception. At KPMG, employees involved in the recruitment process receive bias-free interview training.[85]

Earlier, we noted that the validity of the interview improves when it is structured. But what exactly is a structured interview? According to a study by Derek Chapman of the

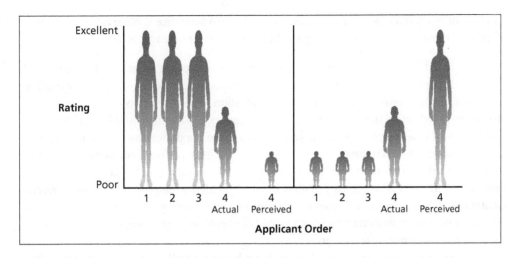

EXHIBIT 10
Two examples of contrast effects.

✖ Explore

Go to MyManagementLab to see an annotated version of this figure.

University of Calgary and David Zweig of the University of Toronto, interview structure involves four dimensions: *evaluation standardization* (the extent to which the interviewer uses standardized and numeric scoring procedures); *question sophistication* (the extent to which the interviewer uses job-related behavioural questions and situational questions); *question consistency* (the extent to which the interviewer asks the same questions in the same order of every candidate); and *rapport building* (the extent to which the interviewer does *not* ask personal questions that are unrelated to the job). They also found that interviews were more likely to be structured when the interviewer had formal interview training and focused on selection rather than recruitment during the interview.[86] Structured interviews probably reduce information overload and ensure that applicants can be more easily compared, since they have all responded to an identical sequence of questions.[87]

Perceptions and the Performance Appraisal

Once a person is hired, however imperfectly, further perceptual tasks confront organization members. Specifically, the organization will want some index of the person's job performance for decisions regarding pay raises, promotions, transfers, and training needs.

OBJECTIVE AND SUBJECTIVE MEASURES It is possible to find objective measures of performance for certain aspects of some jobs. These are measures that do not involve a substantial degree of human judgment. The number of publications that a professor has in top journals is a good example. In general, though, as we move up the organizational hierarchy, it becomes more difficult to find objective indicators of performance. Thus, it is often hard to find quantifiable evidence of a manager's success or failure. When objective indicators of performance do exist, they are often contaminated by situational factors. For example, it might be very difficult to compare the dollar sales of a snowmobile salesperson whose territory covers British Columbia with one whose territory is Nova Scotia. Also, while dollar sales might be a good indicator of current sales performance, it says little about a person's capacity for promotion to district sales manager.

Because of the difficulties that objective performance indicators present, organizations must often rely on subjective measures of effectiveness, usually provided by managers. However, the manager is confronted by a number of perceptual roadblocks. He or she might not be in a position to observe many instances of effective and ineffective performance. This is especially likely when the employee's job activities cannot be monitored directly. For example, a police sergeant cannot ride around in six squad cars at the same time, and a telephone company supervisor cannot visit customers' homes or climb telephone poles with all of his or her installers. Such situations mean that the target (the employee's performance) is frequently ambiguous, and we have seen that the perceptual system resolves ambiguities in an efficient but often inaccurate manner. Even when performance is observable, employees often alter their behaviour so that they look good when their manager is around.

RATER ERRORS Subjective performance appraisal is susceptible to some of the perceptual biases we discussed earlier—primacy, recency, and stereotypes. In addition, a number of other perceptual tendencies occur in performance evaluation. They are often called rater errors. One interrelated set of these tendencies includes leniency, harshness, and central tendency (Exhibit 11). **Leniency** refers to the tendency to perceive the performance of one's ratees as especially good, while **harshness** is the tendency to see their performance as especially ineffective. Lenient raters tend to give "good" ratings, and harsh raters tend to give "bad" ratings. Professors with reputations as easy graders or tough graders exemplify these types of raters. **Central tendency** involves assigning most ratees to a middle-range performance category—the extremes of the rating categories are not used. The professor who assigns 80 percent of her students *C*s is committing this error.

Each of these three rating tendencies is probably partially a function of the rater's personal experiences. For example, the manager who has had an especially good group of employees might respond with special harshness when management transfers him to supervise a group of slightly less able workers. It is worth noting that not all instances of leniency, harshness, and central tendency necessarily represent perceptual errors. In some cases, raters intentionally commit these errors, even though they have accurate perceptions of workers' performance. For example, a manager might use leniency or central tendency in performance reviews so that his employees do not react negatively to his evaluation.

Another perceptual error that is frequently committed by performance raters is called the **halo effect**.[88] The halo effect occurs when the observer allows the rating of an individual on one trait or characteristic to colour the ratings on other traits or characteristics. For example, in a teacher evaluation system, a student might perceive his instructor as a nice person, and this might favourably influence his perception of the instructor's knowledge of the material and speed in returning exams and papers. Similarly, a manager might rate an employee as frequently late for work, and this might in turn lead her to devalue the employee's productivity and quality of work. As these examples illustrate, halo can work either for or against the ratee. In both cases, the rater fails to perceive differences *within* ratees. The halo effect tends to be organized around central traits that the rater considers important. The student feels that being nice is an especially important quality, while the manager places special emphasis on promptness. Ratings on these characteristics then affect the rater's perceptions of other characteristics.

The **similar-to-me effect** is an additional rater error that may, in part, reflect perceptual bias. The rater tends to give more favourable evaluations to people who are similar to the rater in terms of background or attitudes. For example, the manager with an MBA degree

---

Leniency. The tendency to perceive the job performance of ratees as especially good.

Harshness. The tendency to perceive the job performance of ratees as especially ineffective.

Central tendency. The tendency to assign most ratees to middle-range job performance categories.

Halo effect. The rating of an individual on one trait or characteristic tends to colour ratings on other traits or characteristics.

Similar-to-me effect. A rater gives more favourable evaluations to people who are similar to the rater in terms of background or attitudes.

EXHIBIT 11
Leniency, harshness, and central tendency rater errors.

✱⊣Explore

Go to MyManagementLab to see an annotated version of this figure.

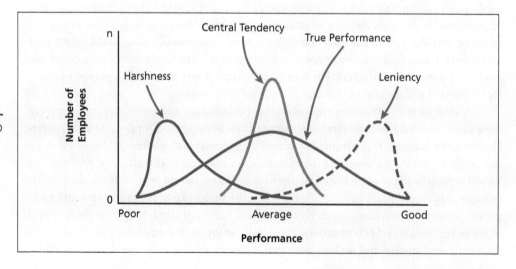

who comes from an upper-middle-class family might perceive a similar employee as a good performer even though the person is only average. Similarly, a rater might overestimate the performance of an individual who holds similar religious and political views. Such reactions probably stem from a tendency to view our own performance, attitudes, and background as "good." We then tend to generalize this evaluation to others who are, to some degree, similar to us. Raters with diverse employees should be especially wary of this error.

Given all these problems, it should be clear that it is difficult to obtain good subjective evaluations of employee performance. Because of this, human resources specialists have explored various techniques for reducing perceptual errors and biases. There has been a tendency to attempt to reduce rater errors by using rating scales with more specific behavioural labels. The assumption here is that giving specific examples of effective and ineffective performance will facilitate the rater's perceptual processes and recall.

Exhibit 12 shows a **behaviourally anchored rating scale (BARS)** that gives very specific behavioural examples (from top to bottom) of good, average, and poor customer service. It was developed for the J.C. Penney Company. With such an aid, the rater may be less susceptible to perceptual errors when completing the rating task, although the evidence for this is mixed.[89]

Another approach for reducing perceptual errors and biases and improving the accuracy of performance appraisals is rater training. One of the best known approaches is

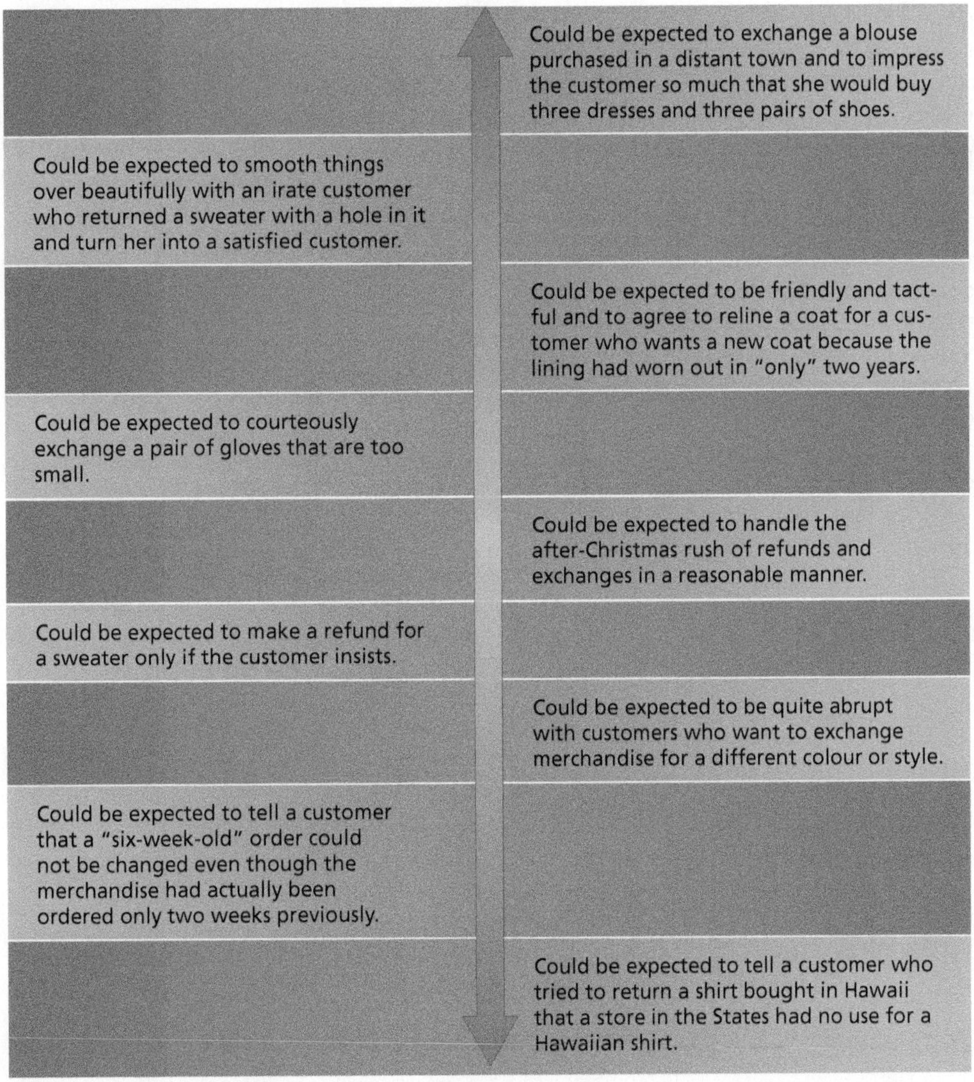

Behaviourally anchored rating scale (BARS). A rating scale with specific behavioural examples of good, average, and poor performance.

EXHIBIT 12
Behaviourally anchored rating scale (BARS) for rating customer service.
Source: Campbell, J.P., Dunnette, M.D., Lawler, E.E., III, & Weick, K.E., Jr. (1970). *Managerial behavior, performance, and effectiveness.* New York: McGraw-Hill. © The McGraw-Hill Companies, Inc. Used by permission.

✳─[Explore

Go to MyManagementLab to see an annotated version of this figure.

Could be expected to exchange a blouse purchased in a distant town and to impress the customer so much that she would buy three dresses and three pairs of shoes.

Could be expected to smooth things over beautifully with an irate customer who returned a sweater with a hole in it and turn her into a satisfied customer.

Could be expected to be friendly and tactful and to agree to reline a coat for a customer who wants a new coat because the lining had worn out in "only" two years.

Could be expected to courteously exchange a pair of gloves that are too small.

Could be expected to handle the after-Christmas rush of refunds and exchanges in a reasonable manner.

Could be expected to make a refund for a sweater only if the customer insists.

Could be expected to be quite abrupt with customers who want to exchange merchandise for a different colour or style.

Could be expected to tell a customer that a "six-week-old" order could not be changed even though the merchandise had actually been ordered only two weeks previously.

Could be expected to tell a customer who tried to return a shirt bought in Hawaii that a store in the States had no use for a Hawaiian shirt.

Frame-of-reference (FOR) training. A training method to improve rating accuracy that involves providing raters with a common frame of reference to use when rating individuals.

called **frame-of-reference (FOR) training**. FOR training involves providing raters with a common frame of reference to use when rating individuals. Raters learn about each performance dimension and are provided with examples of good, average, and poor performance. They then practise making performance ratings and receive feedback on their accuracy. As a result, raters learn what behaviours reflect different levels of performance on each performance dimension and to use the same frame of reference when rating all individuals. Research on FOR training has shown that it is a very effective method for improving rating accuracy.[90]

THE MANAGER'S NOTEBOOK

American Express Canada's Skilled Immigrant Strategy

AMEX Canada's skilled immigrant strategy was implemented in 2009 and earned Nancy Steele the *Canadian HR Reporter* Individual Achievement Award in 2011 at the Immigrant Success Awards presented by the Toronto Region Immigrant Employment Council (TRIEC). This is a good example of how a strategy for managing diversity includes skilled immigrants and that this requires special initiatives for hiring, developing, and retaining them. In 2012, AMEX Canada was named one of Canada's Best Diversity Employers.

1. To recruit skilled immigrants, Nancy Steele worked with TRIEC and organized a mass recruitment day. TRIEC, which pre-screens applicants, brought in 200 immigrants and 10 managers and went through the interview process with the recruits. There have been two sessions like this to date, with more scheduled. So far 11 skilled immigrants have been hired through the program, or 10 percent of hires in the AET division. They have filled key positions such as quality assurance analysts, business analysts, project managers, and programming.

2. To develop and retain skilled immigrants, a number of initiatives were implemented. Language training is available for those skilled immigrants whose language skills many not be "quite as robust" as what is needed, said Steele. English language training enhances integration and promotion. Managers undergo cross-cultural training to learn how to understand the challenges immigrants might be facing and evaluate any potential gaps in their training or performance, so they can coach them appropriately, said Steele. The success of the program is demonstrated in improved retention rates. "What makes me most proud is the feedback I get directly from our new skilled immigrant hires. They thank me for the opportunity to work here and grow their career with the company," says Steele.

Sources: Based on Silliker, A. (2011, March 28). Firms honoured for work with skilled immigrants. *Canadian HR Reporter, 24*(6), 1, 20; Dalby, P. (2011, March 9). New hiring approach improves success rate for immigrants. *Toronto Star,* www.thestar.com/printarticle/950769; Anonymous (2011, October 6). Nancy Steele spearheads skilled immigrant strategy at American Express Canada. *TRIEC,* www.triec.ca/2011/nancy-steele-spearheads-skilled-immigrant-strategy; www.americanexpress.com/ca.

MyManagementLab   Visit MyManagementLab at **www.mymanagementlab** **.com** for access to online tutorials, interactive exercises, videos, and much more.

LEARNING OBJECTIVES CHECKLIST

1 *Perception* involves interpreting the input from our senses to provide meaning to our environment. Any instance of perception involves a perceiver, a target, and a situational context. The experience, needs, and emotions of the perceiver affect perception, as does the ambiguity of the target.

2 According to *social identity theory*, people form perceptions of themselves and others based on their characteristics and memberships in social categories. Bruner's model of the perceptual process suggests that we are very receptive to cues provided by the target and the situation when we encounter an unfamiliar target. However, as we discover familiar cues, we quickly categorize the target and process other cues in a selective manner to maintain a consistent and constant picture of the target.

3 The main biases in person perception include *primacy*, *recency*, *implicit personality theory*, *reliance on central traits*, *projection*, and *stereotyping*. Stereotypes of gender, age, race, ethnicity, and religion are especially problematic for organizations.

4 *Attribution* is the process of assigning causes or motives to people's behaviour. The observer is often interested in determining whether the behaviour is due to *dispositional* (internal) or *situational* (external) causes. Behaviour is likely to be attributed to the disposition of the actor when the behaviour (1) is performed consistently, (2) differs from that exhibited by other people, and (3) occurs in a variety of situations or environments. An opposite set of cues will prompt a situational attribution.

5 The tendency of observers to overemphasize dispositional attributions is known as the *fundamental attribution error*. In contrast, actors are more likely to explain their own behaviour in situational terms, and this actor–observer difference in attributions is known as the *actor–observer effect*. Our tendency to take credit for success and to deny responsibility for failure is known as the *self-serving bias*.

6 The changing nature of the workplace and increasing diversity have highlighted the importance of valuing and managing employee diversity, which can yield strategic, competitive, and performance advantages for the organization.

7 Racial, ethnic, religious, gender, and age stereotypes can result in discriminatory human resources decisions and are a major barrier to valuing diversity. Organizations can use a number of tactics, including training, to manage diversity. However, to be most effective, diversity should be integrated into all organization policies and practices and part of an inclusive culture that values individual differences.

8 Perceptions of *trust* involve a willingness to be vulnerable and to take risks with respect to the actions of another party. Trust perceptions toward management are based on perceptions of ability, benevolence, and integrity. *Perceived organizational support* (POS) refers to perceptions about how much an organization values an individual's contribution and cares about one's well-being. According to *organizational support theory*, employees who have strong perceptions of organizational support feel an obligation to care about the organization's welfare and to help the organization achieve its objectives.

9 According to *signalling theory*, job applicants have incomplete information about jobs and organizations so they interpret their recruitment and selection experiences as cues or signals about unknown characteristics of an organization. Job applicants form more positive perceptions of the selection process when the selection procedures are perceived to be fair. Judging the suitability of job applicants in an interview and appraising job performance are especially difficult perceptual tasks, in part because the target is motivated to convey a good impression. In addition, interviewers and performance raters exhibit a number of perceptual tendencies that are reflected in inaccurate judgments, including *leniency*, *harshness*, *central tendency*, and *contrast*, *halo*, and *similar-to-me effects*. Structured interviews can improve the accuracy of perceptions in the employment interview, and *behaviourally anchored rating scales (BARS)* and *frame-of-reference (FOR)* training can improve the accuracy of performance appraisals.

DISCUSSION QUESTIONS

1. Discuss how differences in the experiences of students and professors might affect their perceptions of students' written work and class comments.

2. Using implicit personality theory, explain how physical attractiveness influences job-related outcomes in employment interviews and performance appraisals.

3. Discuss the occupational stereotypes that you hold about computer programmers, the clergy, truck drivers, bartenders, and bankers. How do you think these stereotypes have developed? Has an occupational stereotype ever caused you to commit a socially embarrassing error when meeting someone for the first time?

4. Use Bruner's perceptual model (Exhibit 3) and social identity theory to explain why performance appraisals and interviewers' judgments are frequently inaccurate.

5. Discuss how perceptions of organizational support can influence employees' attitudes and behaviour. What can organizations do to develop positive perceptions of organizational support?

6. Suppose an employee does a particularly poor job on an assigned project. Discuss the attribution process that this person's manager will use to form judgments about this poor performance. Be sure to discuss how the manager will use consistency, consensus, and distinctiveness cues.

7. A study of small business failures found that owners generally cited factors such as economic depression or strong competition as causes.

However, creditors of these failed businesses were much more likely to cite ineffective management. What attribution bias is indicated by these findings? Why do you think the difference in attribution occurs?

8. Discuss the factors that make it difficult for employment interviewers to form accurate perceptions of interviewees. Explain why a gender or racial stereotype might be more likely to affect a hiring decision than a performance appraisal decision. How can interviews and performance appraisals be designed to improve the accuracy of perceptions?

9. What are the implications of social identity theory for diversity in organizations? Describe some of the things that an organization can do to remove the barriers to workplace diversity. List some of the advantages gained by organizations that effectively manage a diverse workforce.

10. Explain stereotype threat effects and provide some examples of how they might occur in organizations and the consequences. What can organizations do to prevent stereotype threat effects?

11. Review the Ethical Focus feature, *What's in a Name? You're Hired . . . or Not!*, and use Bruner's model of the perceptual process to explain why job applicants with ethnic-sounding names are less likely to receive callbacks. What perceptual biases might explain the lower callbacks received for resumes with ethnic-sounding names? What should organizations do to avoid name discrimination? What should job applicants do?

INTEGRATIVE DISCUSSION QUESTIONS

1. Describe how the principles of operant learning theory and social cognitive theory can be used to manage workplace diversity and reduce the effects of workplace stereotypes. How can the organizational learning practices be used for managing diversity?

2. Consider how the four basic types of managerial activities (i.e., routine communication,

traditional management, networking, and human resource management) can influence employees' perceptions of trust and perceived organizational support (POS). How should managers perform each of these activities to improve employees' perceptions of trust and POS?

ON-THE-JOB CHALLENGE QUESTION 1

Australia's Jobs Bonus Initiative

In 2012, the Australian government launched a new initiative that will pay employers to hire older workers. Employers will receive $1000 for every worker aged 50 or older that they hire and retain for at least three months. The government has committed $10 million over four years to the Jobs Bonus initiative in response to a report which highlights the value of older workers.

According to Mark Butler, the Minister for Ageing, "We still need to deal with a cultural issue in the Australian business community that sometimes looks past the value of older workers. We know that older workers have lower absenteeism, they have higher retention rates, and they bring with them extraordinary wisdom and experience. We just need to push through this barrier that some Australian employers still have."

However, according to Susan Eng, vice-president of advocacy at CARP, a Toronto-based advocacy group for people over 50, this may not be the right course of action. "I understand the motivation but I'm not particularly thrilled with the method. It suggests that an older worker is somehow flawed and you, therefore, have to pay somebody to hire them," she said. "If you're trying to resolve and overcome age discrimination in hiring, why reinforce this stereotype by offering a sweetener?"

What do you think about the Australian government's Jobs Bonus initiative? Do perceptions have anything to do with this initiative? Do you think this will help or hurt older workers and the perception and stereotype of them? Is this something that Canadian governments should consider doing? What are the implications for employees and organizations?

Source: Silliker, A. (2012, May 21). Australia offers $1000 for hiring of older workers. *Canadian HR Reporter, 25*(10), 1, 10.

ON-THE-JOB CHALLENGE QUESTION 2

Citizens Medical Centre's New Hiring Policy

Citizens Medical Centre, a hospital in Victoria, Texas, recently instituted a new hiring policy that bans job applicants from employment for being overweight. The new policy states that the hospital will not hire anyone with a body mass index (BMI which is a formula used to determine fat) of 35 or higher. This is the equivalent of someone who is five feet five inches tall and weighs 210 pounds or someone who is 5 feet 10 inches tall and weighs 245 pounds.

According to the policy, an employee's physique "should fit with a representational image or specific mental projection of the job of a health-care professional." David Brown, the hospital's CEO, stated, "The majority of our patients are over 65 and they have expectations that cannot be ignored in terms of personal appearance." He further stated that, "We have the ability as an employer to characterize our process and to have a policy that says what's best for our business and our patients."

As part of the hiring process, job applicants are screened by a physician who assesses their fitness for work, which includes their body mass index. Existing workers who become obese during employment are not terminated; however, job applicants have been turned away as a result of the policy.

Although the laws in Texas do not prohibit weight discrimination in hiring, they do prohibit discrimination based on race, age, or religion.

However, according to Peggy Howell, public relations director for the National Association to Advance Fat Acceptance, "This is discrimination plain and simple. So the field of medicine is no longer an option for people of larger body size? What a waste of talent." She said that a hospital should know that lots of medical conditions lead to obesity or weight gain.

According to CEO David Brown, excessive weight has "all kinds of encumbrances" for the hospital and its health plan, and there's evidence that extremely obese employees are absent from work more often.

What do you think about Citizens Medical Centre's new hiring policy? Do perceptions, attributions, and stereotypes have anything to do with the hiring policy? What do you think is the reason for such a policy and do you believe it is in the best interests of the hospital and its patients? Is this something that other organizations should consider doing? What are the implications?

Sources: Silliker, A. (2012, May 21). U.S. hospital balks a hiring obese workers. *Canadian HR Reporter, 25*(10), 1, 3; Ramshaw, E. (March 26, 2012). Victoria hospital won't hire very obese workers. *The Texas Tribune*, www.texastribune.org; (2012, April 5). Hospital in weight row after hiring policy BANS obese job applicants. *Daily Mail Reporter*, www.dailymail.co.uk/news/article-2125385.

EXPERIENTIAL EXERCISE

Beliefs about Older Workers

Answer the 27 questions listed here. The questions are an attempt to assess the attitudes people have about older workers. The statements cover many different points of view; you may find yourself agreeing strongly with some of the statements, disagreeing just as strongly with others, and perhaps feeling uncertain about others. After you have answered all 27 questions, follow the instructions below to obtain your score.

Read each statement carefully. Using the numbers from 1 to 5 on the rating scale, mark your personal opinion about each statement in the blank space next to each statement. Remember, give your personal opinion according to how much you agree or disagree with each item. In all cases, older refers to people who are 50 years of age or older.

——1———	—2—	———3———	——4——	——5—
Strongly agree	Agree	Neither agree nor disagree	Disagree	Strongly disagree

____ 1. Older employees have fewer accidents on the job.

____ 2. Most companies are unfair to older employees.

____ 3. Older employees are harder to train for jobs.

____ 4. Older employees are absent more often than younger employees.

____ 5. Younger employees have more serious accidents than older workers.

____ 6. If two workers had similar skills, I'd pick the older worker to work with me.

____ 7. Occupational diseases are more likely to occur among younger employees.

____ 8. Older employees usually turn out work of higher quality.

____ 9. Older employees are grouchier on the job.

____ 10. Younger workers are more cooperative on the job.

____ 11. Older workers are more dependable.

____ 12. Most older workers cannot keep up with the speed of modern industry.

____ 13. Older employees are most loyal to the company.

____ 14. Older workers resist change and are too set in their ways.

____ 15. Younger workers are more interested than older workers in challenging jobs.

____ 16. Older workers can learn new skills as easily as other employees.

____ 17. Older employees are better employees.

____ 18. Older employees do not want jobs with increased responsibilities.

____ 19. Older workers are not interested in learning new skills.

____ 20. Older employees should "step aside" (take a less demanding job) to give younger employees advancement opportunities.

____ 21. The majority of older employees would quit work if they could afford it.

____ 22. Older workers are usually outgoing and friendly at work.

____ 23. Older workers prefer less challenging jobs than those they held when they were younger.

____ 24. It is a better investment to train younger workers rather than older workers.

____ 25. Older employees in our department work just as hard as anyone else.

____ 26. Given a choice, I would not work with an older worker on a daily basis.

____ 27. A person's performance declines significantly with age.

Scoring and Interpretation

The scale you have just completed measures your attitudes toward older workers. To score your beliefs about older workers, subtract your responses to each of the following items from 6: 1, 2, 5, 6, 7, 8, 11, 13, 16, 17, 22, and 25. For example, if you put 2 for item 1, give yourself a 4 (6 minus 2). Then simply add up your resulting responses to all 27 items. Your score

should fall somewhere between 27 and 135. Low scores indicate an overall negative belief about older workers, while high scores indicate positive beliefs. The higher your score, the more favourable your attitudes are toward older workers.

Research on older workers has generally found that a negative stereotype of older workers exists in organizations. The danger of this is that it can lead to negative attitudes and discriminatory behaviour toward older workers.

A study of 179 employees from three organizations obtained scores that ranged from 54 to 118. The average score was 90, which indicated somewhat positive beliefs about older workers. As reported in other studies, older workers had more positive beliefs about older workers than younger workers. However, younger workers who had more interactions with older workers were found to have more positive beliefs about older workers.

To facilitate class discussion and your understanding of age stereotypes, form a small group with several other members of the class and consider the following questions. (Note that the instructor can also do this as a class exercise. Students should write their score, age, and interactions with older workers on a piece of paper and hand it in to the instructor, who can then determine the relationship between age, interactions with older workers, and beliefs about older workers.)

1. Students should first compare their scores to each other's and to the average score indicated above (90). Do group members have positive or negative beliefs about older workers? Do some group members have more positive or negative beliefs than others in the group?

2. Each member of the group should indicate his or her age. Determine the average age of the group and categorize those members above the average as being "older" and those below the average as being "younger." Then calculate the average score of the two age groups. Is there a difference in beliefs about older workers between older and younger group members?

3. Each group member should indicate how often they interact with older workers (daily, several times a week, once a week, or monthly). Based on group members' responses, create two categories that correspond to high and low interactions with older workers. Calculate the average score of these two groups. Is there a difference in beliefs about older workers between those who have more and those you have less interaction with older workers?

4. Why do some students have positive or negative beliefs about older workers? What are the implications of these beliefs at work and outside of work?

5. What can you do to develop more positive beliefs about older workers? What are the implications of doing so?

Source: Hassell, B.L., & Perrewe, P.L. (1995). An examination of beliefs about older workers: Do stereotypes still exist? *Journal of Organizational Behavior, 16,* 457–468.

CASE INCIDENT

The New CEO

In March 2009, the Canadian National Institute for the Blind (CNIB) announced the appointment of John M. Rafferty as the organization's new president and CEO. CNIB is a nationwide charity that provides services and support to Canadians who are blind or visually impaired. Rafferty left a lucrative private-sector job to join CNIB. According to Al Jameson, chair of CNIB's national board of directors, Rafferty is an exceptional business leader whose skills and experience make him an excellent fit for CNIB. In fact, Rafferty has 13 years of national and international experience as a senior executive who has served in numerous leadership positions.

However, Rafferty's appointment upset many people in the community and prompted criticism of CNIB. Some even referred to his hiring as despicable and a step backward. Unlike all his predecessors and every top executive in the 91-year history of

CNIB, Rafferty can see. He is CNIB's first "sighted" president and CEO. His hiring resulted in a complicated debate about identity and employment equity within Canada's diverse blind and visually impaired community.

According to John Rae, vice-president of the Alliance for Equality of Blind Canadians (AEBC), the hiring of a sighted person as CEO is yet another example of CNIB "turning its back on the people it was set up to serve." By selecting Rafferty, CNIB has implied that blind Canadians qualified to lead a major organization do not exist. How can CNIB lobby corporations to hire the blind when it will not do so itself?

Sources: Dale, D. (2009, May 3). Debate stirs over hiring of sighted CNIB head: Board defends choice as critics ask how it can lobby firms to hire blind when it will not do so itself. *Toronto Star,* A1; Meet the President: John M. Rafferty. www.cnib.ca/en/about/who/president/default.aspx.

1. Discuss the role of perceptions in people's reactions to the hiring of John Rafferty. Use Bruner's model of the perceptual process and social identity theory to explain people's perceptions and reactions.

2. Do you think CNIB should have hired John Rafferty as the organization's new president and

CEO, or should they have hired an individual who is blind or visually impaired? Explain your answer.

3. Does this incident have anything to do with equity and diversity? Explain your answer.

CASE STUDY

CTV Newsnet

On January 15, 2000, Henry Kowalski, senior vice-president, news, had to move quickly to save the reputation of CTV (Canadian Television) Newsnet. Because of a technical error, a tape of its anchorperson, Avery Haines, making degrading remarks about various minorities, had been aired during a newscast. He had no doubt whatsoever about the integrity of Haines and that the apparent slurs were part of a private self-deprecating joke made, she believed, off-air. Still, none of these facts made his dilemma easier. It was up to him to address the situation, without delay.

CTV's Position in the Canadian Broadcasting Industry

CTV Inc. was one of Canada's pre-eminent communications companies, with conventional television operations across Canada. Its broadcasting signals reached 99 percent of English-speaking Canadians and offered a wide range of quality news, sports, information, and entertainment programming. CTV Inc. had been in preliminary discussions with BCE (Bell Canada Enterprises), which announced a formal offer to purchase in March 2000.

During the previous four years, the company saw significant growth from its roots in family-run regional broadcasting, such as CFTO in Toronto. In February 1999, CTV Inc. was hoping to complete strategic negotiations that would expand the scale of its online operations. It was planning to launch an interactive site in the fall of 2000. At the CTV Inc. annual general meeting, Ivan Fecan, the chief executive officer, announced: "We expect to move into entertainment content production in a meaningful way, in fiscal 2000." While Fecan was clearly excited and optimistic about the direction

the company was taking, he also, however, drew attention to the extra interest costs that would be incurred by acquisitions.

CTV's main competitor was Global Television, and at the beginning of the year both companies were claiming to have won the 1999 fall ratings war, each interpreting differently the statistics compiled by Nielsen Research. Each of the competing broadcasters would have liked to be able to demonstrate definitively its edge in viewer numbers over the other, knowing the weight that advertisers would give to such ratings.

CTV's Goals and Corporate Philosophy

Fiscal 1999 was the first year of operation for the newly formed CTV Inc., although the brand known as CTV Network had been very well-known to Canadian audiences and advertisers for the past two decades. The consolidation of CTV and its owned affiliates, along with recent restructuring and innovations, had resulted in the creation of a truly integrated Canadian broadcasting and communications company.

Scope of operations included 25 television stations in Ontario, Saskatchewan, Alberta, British Columbia, Nova Scotia, and New Brunswick. Of these stations, 18 were affiliates of CTV, six were CBC affiliate television stations and one, CIVT, Vancouver, was an independent television station. CTV also owned ASN, a satellite-to-cable program undertaking and had ownership interests in four speciality cable television services: The Comedy Network; Outdoor Life Network; a headline news channel, CTV Newsnet; and CTV Sportsnet.

CTV Inc. had a 12 percent interest in History Television Inc. and held a licence for an additional speciality service, TalkTV, which was scheduled to launch in September 2000. CTV Inc. also had a controlling interest in Sports Specials/Pay-Per-View for digital and DTH.

On March 5, 1999, CTV acquired a 68.46 percent interest in NetStar Communications Inc. The acquisition of NetStar was held in trust pending regulatory approvals. NetStar owned the Sports Network Inc. (TSN); Le Reseau des Sports (RDS) Inc.; Dome Productions Inc. (one of the largest mobile production facilities in Canada); and, through its 80 percent owned subsidiary, operated the Discovery Channel. NetStar also had a 24.95 percent interest in Viewer's Choice Canada Inc. CTV Inc. also had a 50 percent interest in Landscape Entertainment Corp., a production venture that would produce worldwide content for film, television, and the Internet.

At fiscal year-end 1999, CTV Inc.'s. balance sheet showed total assets of $1.1 billion compared with $760 million at end of the previous year. Revenues for the first quarter of 2000 showed a slight decline over the same period the previous year, due mostly to softness in conventional television, which was down four percent compared with the previous year. Consequently, speciality channels such as CTV Newsnet and the Comedy Network were making significant revenue contributions and it was in this area that CTV Inc. would continue to focus.

Ivan Fecan further remarked that "CTV Inc. is still in the process of becoming the powerful, integrated broadcasting and communications organization it can and will be. We are leveraging the strengths of every part of the company to create a strong whole." He emphasized the company goal of helping clients to "extend their brands along the entire value chain, from the internet to local retail," and the need to maintain strong personal relationships and community roots across Canada.

CTV Inc. was clearly moving forward and enthusiastic about further expansion in the future, but it was also determined to continue to demonstrate that social commitment was still a priority. Fecan commended the involvement of individual employees in various fundraising and charitable activities. He also pointed to the contribution of CTV's programming, especially the Signature Series, which "had a significant impact on national awareness of injustice and sexual harassment of children," and stated the intention do many more projects like that.

The 24-hour news channel, CTV Newsnet, had always observed the company philosophy in its reporting, giving generous broadcast time to social issues, local, national, and global. In January 2000, Canadian farmers were voicing their desperation about the crisis in Canadian agriculture, and the impossibility of family-owned farms remaining viable without increased government support. On January 16, a massive benefit concert was planned in Toronto solely to create awareness among urban dwellers on the problems faced by Canadian farmers.

One organizer, Liberal MP (Broadview-Greenwood) Dennis Mills, was quoted in *The Toronto Star* (January 13) as saying: "if we can get people to make legislators who live in cities—and 80 percent of Canada's parliamentarians do—more accountable in dealing with farming and agricultural issues, we'll have succeeded."

Canada's public station, CBC (Canadian Broadcasting Corporation), was planning to air a farm crisis program from 10:00 am Sunday, January 16 until 2:00 AM Monday, January 17. On the morning of Saturday, January 15, CTV Newsnet, in keeping with its social awareness and community interest policies, was about to air the first of a series of its reports on the situation.

Henry Kowalski

Kowalski was a 25-year veteran of television news and had been with the CTV family since 1984. In the first six years of his career, he worked as head of assignment, specials producer, Toronto bureau chief, and Vancouver bureau chief. In 1992, he was promoted to chief news editor, where he retooled the newscast and added several innovative features and segments.

His responsibilities included CTV's flagship *CTV News* with Lloyd Robertson and Sandie Rinaldo, all local newscasts on CTV's owned and operated stations across Canada, *Canada AM*, and the highly acclaimed *W5*. Under his leadership, *CTV News* became Canada's most-watched newscast, consistently ranking in the Nielsen top twenty.

In January 1997, Kowalski was promoted to senior vice-president and general manager, CTV News. He was responsible for guiding a team towards the successful launch of CTV Newsnet in October 1997 and for the remake of CFTO News, where he increased the audience and cemented it in first place in the competitive Toronto/Hamilton market.

CTV Newsnet's mandate was to become a significant force in Canadian journalism. In the highly competitive and over-serviced Canadian television market, Kowalski knew that a significant effort would be required to build a new service that would take a leadership position. He was no stranger to this type of challenge.

A New Anchorperson

Early in December 1999, Kowalski signed 33-year-old Haines on a probationary contract to anchor the station's 24-hour cable news channel. Haines had been with the Toronto radio station CFRB for 11 years, having been hired straight from college by Bill Carroll, its news director.

Haines was eager to make the move from radio to television, and Kowalski was impressed with her qualifications; not only had she won several awards in newscasting, but she was well liked and respected by her peers and superiors and was already a popular radio personality with an enthusiastic following. He felt that she would be a good fit in the fast-paced and demanding milieu of television news and had the ability, ambition, and charisma that CTV Newsnet was looking to acquire. He had enjoyed the interview and found Haines relaxed, animated, composed, and personable. In all, he was very confident that Haines would quickly adapt and grow into this challenging position.

An Excellent Fit

Nearly two months had passed, and Kowalski was very pleased with Haines's progress. She had adjusted adeptly to the new medium, and her charisma translated well from voice to visual; she had impressive screen presence. Besides the implicit public approval, Haines seemed already to have gained the support and even affection of all her co-workers. She appeared inherently interested in everyone and everything and exuded a natural enthusiasm and charm.

It was not only personality, however, that distinguished the new employee but also her work ethic. Haines gave full commitment to her job; always willing to accept criticism and advice, to apply herself completely to every task, she was also creative and innovative where appropriate. Kowalski felt he had made a good decision and had acquired an employee who would be a great asset to CTV Newsnet.

Flubbed Lines

On Saturday, January 15, Haines was in the studio taping an introduction to a report on aid for Canadian farmers. For some reason, whether through lack of concentration, or simply because of a slip of the tongue, Haines stammered her way through the opening lines and completely garbled the message. Fortunately this was not a live broadcast, but as a relative newcomer in a very responsible position, Haines felt vulnerable and awkward.

Partly to cover her own embarrassment, but also to ease the tension for the other people in the studio, Haines started to make fun of her own ineptness. "I kind of like the stuttering thing," she laughed, "It's like equal opportunity, right? We've got a stuttering newscaster. We've got the black; we've got the Asian; we've got the woman. I could be a lesbian-folk-dancing-black-woman-stutterer." Someone joined in the banter, adding a few other possibilities, and Haines, responded in kind: "In a wheelchair…with a gimping rubber leg. Yeah, really. I'd have a successful career, let me tell you." Everyone in the studio knew the statements were very politically incorrect, but the repartee was harmless among those who understood its self-deprecating context and so typical of the gallows humour among journalists. No one was in the least offended, since Haines herself was a woman of African-Asian heritage. They knew she was poking fun at herself.

Meanwhile, everyone had relaxed, the technicians were ready to roll with a new tape, the original with the flubbed lines having been set aside. Haines went flawlessly through her farm-and-aid report, and the segment was ready to be aired later in the day.

A Technical Error

It had been a busy Saturday for the technical crew, but despite the re-take, everything was ready to go for the latest broadcast. The control room technician hit play and Haines, composed and pleasant, was on screen—stumbling through her intro to the farm-aid report. "Oh—! Oh—! Wrong tape! Wrong tape!" The cries went up in the studio control room. But things got worse. They realized that not only was the audience seeing Haines, CTV's Newsnet anchor, talking gibberish, they were watching and listening to the appallingly inappropriate exchange that had followed the flawed intro. The tape was rolling and the technical crews were so stunned that before they could react, the short tape had been played in its entirety.

Public Reaction

The phone lines at CTV's Agincourt studios were flashing instantly with messages from horrified and angry viewers, viewers who had come to trust the integrity and professionalism of CTV. Haines was doing another taped interview when her line-up editor rushed in to tell her about the awful error. Everyone scrambled, as they knew that Haines's comments would be aired by every competitive media source in the Greater Toronto area and could potentially spread beyond. It was essential to apologize on air as soon as possible. Haines was shaken and devastated, more for those she must have horribly offended than for her own sake. She was deeply disturbed that the public would inevitably, and quite understandably, assume that her remarks represented her real views. She also knew that her position on CTV Newsnet was in jeopardy.

Henry Kowalski's Dilemma

Even before Haines's apologies were aired, Kowalski was in the CTV Newsnet studio, quickly trying to get a take on public reaction and to establish just how this major breach of process could have happened. Regardless of the details or of who was to blame, he was ultimately responsible for managing the brand created by CTV News and now he was faced with the unthinkable—damage control in the wake of a serious error.

Avery Haines had already demonstrated her talent and potential and clearly was a victim in the fiasco. Nevertheless, Kowalski had to consider the effects of the incident not so much on individuals as on the growing reputation of CTV Newsnet and its ultimate backlash on the parent company, CTV Inc. They could lose major advertisers if the right actions weren't taken. Clearly, this was not going to be a good weekend.

Source: Professors Carol Tattersall and Christina A. Cavanagh prepared this case solely to provide material for class discussion. The authors do not intend to illustrate either effective or ineffective handling of a managerial situation. The authors may have disguised certain names and other identifying information to protect confidentiality.

QUESTIONS

1. What are people's perceptions of Avery Haines? Be sure to refer to the perceptions of Henry Kowalski, her co-workers, and CTV Newsnet viewers.

2. Why do viewers have different perceptions of Avery Haines than her co-workers? Use Bruner's model of the perceptual process to explain people's perceptions of Avery Haines.

3. Use attribution theory to explain how co-workers and viewers responded to Haines's inappropriate comments. Why did her co-workers and the public react so differently?

4. Do you think the public's reaction to Haines's comments was reasonable? Discuss the possibility that the public response may be due to biases in person perception and attribution.

5. Haines was deeply disturbed that the public would assume that the bigotry inherent in her remarks represented her real views. Use the material in the chapter on perceptions and attributions to explain why the public believed that her remarks represented her real views. What does this case tell us about perceptions and attributions?

6. What do you think Avery Haines should do? What should Henry Kowalski do? Should Avery Haines be fired? Explain your answers.

REFERENCES

1. Klie, S. (2010, April 19). IS Awards honour diversity. *Canadian HR Reporter, 23*(8), 1, 18; Bach, M. (2011, October 24). A little recognition goes a long way. *Canadian HR Reporter, 24*(18), 23; Dobson, S. (2011, November 7). Catalyst honours champions of women in business. *Canadian HR Reporter, 24*(19), 1, 17; Aulakh, R. (2010, March 25). He created a job out of diversity. *Toronto Star,* www.thestar.com; One of Canada's Best Diversity Employers for 2012, www.eluta.ca/diversity-at-kpmg; One of Canada's Top 100 Employers and Greater Toronto's Top Employers for 2012, www.eluta.ca/top-employer-kpmg; www.kpmg.com/ca/en (Catalytst Canada Honors KPMG's very own Michael Bach; Who we are; KPMG named one of Canada's Best Diversity Employers).

2. Cox, T., Jr. (1993). *Cultural diversity in organizations: Theory, research, & practice.* San Francisco: Berrett-Koehler.

3. Ashforth, B. E. (2001). *Role transitions in organizational life: An identity-based persepctive.* Mahwah, NJ: Lawrence Erlbaum Associates, Inc.; Ashforth, B. E., & Mael, F. (1989). Social identity theory and the organization. *Academy of Management Review, 14,* 20–39.

4. Ashforth, 2001; Ashforth & Mael, 1989.

5. Bruner, J. S. (1957). On perceptual readiness. *Psychological Review, 64,* 123–152.

6. Eagly, A. H., Ashmore, R. D., Makhijani, M. G., & Longo, L. C. (1991). What is beautiful is good, but...: A meta-analytic review of research on the physical attractiveness stereotype. *Psychological Bulletin, 110,* 109–128; Hosoda, M., Stone-Romero, E. F., & Coats, G. (2003). The effects of physical attractiveness on job-related outcomes: A meta-analysis of experimental studies. *Personnel Psychology, 56,* 431–462.

7. Stone, E. F., Stone, D. L., & Dipboye, R. L. (1992). Stigmas in organizations: Race, handicaps, and physical unattractiveness. In K. Kelley (Ed.), *Issues, theory and research in industrial/organizational psychology.* New York: Elsevier; Hosoda, Stone-Romero, & Coats, 2003.

8. Judge, T. A., & Cable, D. M. (2004). The effect of physical height on workplace success and income: Preliminary test of a theoretical model. *Journal of Applied Psychology, 89,* 428–441.

9. See Krzystofiak, F., Cardy, R., & Newman, J. E. (1988). Implicit personality and performance appraisal: The influence of trait inferences on evaluations of behavior. *Journal of Applied Psychology, 73,* 515–521.

10. Fiske, S. T. (1993). Social cognition and social perception. *Annual Review of Psychology, 44,* 155–194.

11. Secord, P. F., Backman, C. W., & Slavitt, D. R. (1976). *Understanding social life: An introduction to social psychology.* New York: McGraw-Hill. For elaboration, see Wilder, D. A. (1986). Social categorization: Implications for creation and reduction of intergroup bias. *Advances in Experimental Social Psychology, 19,* 291–349.

12. Dion, K. L., & Schuller, R. A. (1991). The Ms. stereotype: Its generality and its relation to managerial and marital status stereotypes. *Canadian Journal of Behavioural Science, 23,* 25–40.

13. For a more complete treatment see Falkenberg, L. (1990). Improving the accuracy of stereotypes within the workplace. *Journal of Management, 16,* 107–118.

14. Kelley, H. H. (1972). Attribution in social interaction. In E. E. Jones, D. E. Kanhouse, H. H. Kelley, R. E. Nisbett, S. Valins, & B. Weiner (Eds.), *Attribution: Perceiving the causes of behavior.* Morristown, NJ: General Learning Press. For an integrative attribution model, see Medcof, J. W. (1990). PEAT: An integrative model of attribution processes. *Advances in Experimental Social Psychology, 23,* 111–209.

15. This discussion of attribution biases draws upon Fiske, S. T., & Taylor, S. E. (1984). *Social cognition.* Reading, MA: Addison-Wesley.

16. Jones, E. E. (1979). The rocky road from acts to dispositions. *American Psychologist, 34,* 107–117; Ross, L. (1977). The intuitive psychologist and his shortcomings: Distortions in the attribution process. *Advances in Experimental Social Psychology, 10,* 173–220.

17. Mitchell, T. R., & Kalb, L. S. (1982). Effects of job experience on supervisor attributions for a subordinate's poor performance. *Journal of Applied Psychology, 67,* 181–188.

18. Watson, D. (1982). The actor and the observer: How are their perceptions of causality divergent? *Psychological Bulletin, 92,* 682–700.

19. Sonnenfeld, J. (1981). Executive apologies for price fixing: Role biased perceptions of causality. *Academy of Management Journal, 24,* 192–198; Waters, J. A. (1978, Spring). Catch 20.5. Corporate morality as an organizational phenomenon. *Organizational Dynamics,* 2–19.

20. Malle, B. F. (2006). The actor-observer asymmetry in attribution: A (surprising) meta-analysis. *Psychological Bullentin, 132,* 895–919.

21. Greenwald, A. G. (1980). The totalitarian ego: Fabrication and revision of personal history. *American Psychologist, 35,* 603–618; Tetlock, P. E. (1985). Accountability: The neglected social context of judgment and choice. *Research in Organizational Behavior, 7,* 297–332.

22. Pyszczynski, T., & Greenberg, J. (1987). Toward an integration of cognitive and motivational perspectives on social inference: A biased hypothesis-testing model. *Advances in Experimental Social Psychology, 20,* 197–340.

23. This section relies on Jackson, S. E., & Alvarez, E. B. (1992). Working through diversity as a strategic imperative. In S. E. Jackson (Ed.), *Diversity in the workplace: Human resources initiatives.* New York: Guilford Press; Mahoney, J. (2005, March 23). Visible majority by 2017. *Globe and Mail,* A1, A7.

24. Mahoney, 2005, March 23.

25. Mingail, H. (2004, September 29). Wise ways for retraining older workers. *Globe and Mail,* C8; Dobson, S. (2010, April 5). HR by the numbers. *Canadian HR Reporter, 23*(7), 4.

26. Crawford, T. (2006, April 1). A better mix. *Toronto Star,* L1, L2; Galt, V. (2005, March 2). Diversity efforts paying off: Shell CFO. *Globe and Mail,* B1, B20; Vu, U. (2004, November 8). FedEx holds managers accountable for diversity. *Canadian HR Reporter, 17*(19), 3; Shaw, A. (2006, May 22). Hiring immigrants makes good business sense. *Canadian HR Reporter, 19*(10), 21; Keung, N. (2006, March 18). Wanted: Minorities. *Toronto Star,* B1, B3.

27. Cox, 1993; Cox, T., Jr. (1991, May). The multicultural organization. *Academy of Management Executive, 5,* 34–47.

28. Crone, G. (1999, February 18). Companies embracing workplace diversity. *Financial Post,* C11; Galt, V. (2004, January 27). Firms excel with women in senior ranks: Study. *Globe and Mail,* B5; McKay, P. F., Avery D. R., & Morris, M. A. (2009). A tale of two climates: Diversity climate from subordinates' and managers' perspectives and their role in store unit sales performance. *Personnel Psychology, 62,* 767–791.

29. Nguyen, H.-H. D., & Ryan, A. M. (2008). Does stereotype threat affect test performance of minorities and women? A meta-analysis of experimental evidence. *Journal of Applied Psychology, 93,* 1314–1334.

30. Hartley, E. L. (1946). *Problems in prejudice.* New York: King's Crown Press.

31. Alderfer, C. P., & Thomas, D. A. (1988). The significance of race and ethnicity for organizational behavior.

In C. L. Cooper & I. Robertson (Eds.), *International review of industrial and organizational psychology*. New York: Wiley; Cox, T., Jr., & Nkomo, S. M. (1990). Invisible men and women: A status report on race as a variable in organization behavior research. *Journal of Organizational Behavior, 11*, 419–431.

32. Sharpe, R. (1993, September 14). Losing ground. *Wall Street Journal*, A1, 12, 13.

33. King, E. B., & Ahmad, A. S. (2010). An experimental field study of interpersonal discrimination toward Muslim job applicants. *Personnel Psychology, 63*, 881–906.

34. Immen, W. (2007, June 29). Minorities still see barriers in way to the top. *Globe and Mail*, C1.

35. (2007, June 29). Discrimination reported as a continuing issue in U.S. *Globe and Mail*, C1.

36. Greenhaus, J. H., & Parasuraman, S. (1993). Job performance attributions and career advancement prospects: An examination of gender and race effects. *Organizational Behavior and Human Decision Processes, 55*, 273–297.

37. Powell, G. N. (1992). The good manager: Business students' stereotypes of Japanese managers versus stereotypes of American managers. *Group & Organizational Management, 17*, 44–56.

38. Brief, A. P., Umphress, E. E., Dietz, J., Burrows, J. W., Butz, R. M., Scholten, L. (2005). Community matters: Realistic group conflict theory and the impact of diversity. *Academy of Management Journal, 48*, 830–844.

39. Galt, V. (2005, May 4). Glass ceiling still tough to crack. *Globe and Mail*, C1, C2; Flavelle, D. (2005, April 28). Women advance up ranks slowly. *Toronto Star*, D1, D12; Perry, A. (2009, March 6). Women climbing corporate ranks: Study. *Toronto Star*, B3.

40. Brenner, O. C., Tomkiewicz, J., & Schein, V. E. (1989). The relationship between sex role stereotypes and requisite management characteristics revisited. *Academy of Management Journal, 32*, 662–669; Heilman, M. E., Block, C. J., Martell, R. F., & Simon, M. C. (1989). Has anything changed? Current characterizations of men, women, and managers. *Journal of Applied Psychology, 74*, 935–942; Schein, V. E. (1975). Relationships between sex role stereotypes and requisite management characteristics among female managers. *Journal of Applied Psychology, 60*, 340–344.

41. Brenner et al., 1989; Powell, G. N., Butterfield, D. A., & Parent, J. D. (2002). Gender and managerial stereotypes: Have the times changed? *Journal of Management, 28*(2), 177–193; Koenig, A. M., Eagly, A. H., Mitchell, A. A., & Ristikari, T. (2011). Are leader stereotypes masculine? A meta-analysis

of three research paradigms. *Psychological Bulletin, 137*, 616–642.

42. Rosen, B., & Jerdee, T. H. (1974). Influence of sex role stereotypes on personnel decisions. *Journal of Applied Psychology, 59*, 9–14.

43. Cohen, S. L., & Bunker, K. A. (1975). Subtle effects of sex role stereotypes on recruiters' hiring decisions. *Journal of Applied Psychology, 60*, 566–572. See also Rose, G. L., & Andiappan, P. (1978). Sex effects on managerial hiring decisions. *Academy of Management Journal, 21*, 104–112.

44. Heilman, M. E., Wallen, A. S., Fuchs, D., & Tamkins, M. M. (2004). Penalties for success: Reactions to women who succeed at male gender-typed tasks. *Journal of Applied Psychology, 89*, 416–427.

45. Parasuraman, S., & Greenhaus, J. H. (1993). Personal portrait: The lifestyle of the woman manager. In E. A. Fagenson (Ed.), *Women in management: Trends, issues, and challenges in managerial diversity*. Newbury Park, CA: Sage; Cleveland, J. N., Vescio, T. K., & Barnes-Farrell, J. L. (2005). Gender discrimination in organizations. In R. L. Dipboye & A. Colella (Eds.), *Discrimination at work: The psychological and organizational bases*. Mahwah, NJ: Lawrence Erlbaum Associates.

46. Tosi, H. L., & Einbender, S. W. (1985). The effects of the type and amount of information in sex discrimination research: A meta-analysis. *Academy of Management Journal, 28*, 712–723.

47. For a review, see Latham, G. P., Skarlicki, D., Irvine, D., & Siegel, J. P. (1993). The increasing importance of performance appraisals to employee effectiveness in organizational settings in North America. In C. L. Cooper & I. Robertson (Eds.), *International review of industrial and organizational psychology*. New York: Wiley. For a representative study, see Pulakos, E. D., White, L. A., Oppler, S. A., & Borman, W. C. (1989). Examination of race and sex effects on performance ratings. *Journal of Applied Psychology, 74*, 770–780; Cleveland, Vescio, & Barnes-Farrell, 2005.

48. Roth, P. L., Purvis, K. L., & Bobko, P. (2012). A meta-analysis of gender group differences for measures of job performance in field studies. *Journal of Management, 38*, 719–739.

49. Galt, 2005, March 2.

50. Galt, 2005, May 4.

51. Rosen, B., & Jerdee, T. H. (1976). The nature of job-related age stereotypes. *Journal of Applied Psychology, 61*, 180–183. See also Gibson, K. J., Zerbe, W. J., & Franken, R. E. (1992). Job search strategies for older job hunters: Addressing employers' perceptions.

Canadian Journal of Counselling, 26, 166–176.

52. Gibson et al., 1992.

53. Ng, T. W. H., & Feldman, D. C. (2008). The relationship of age to ten dimensions of job performance. *Journal of Applied Psychology, 93*, 392–423; McEvoy, G. M., & Cascio, W. F. (1989). Cumulative evidence of the relationship between employee age and job performance. *Journal of Applied Psychology, 74*, 11–17. For a broader review on age, see Rhodes, S. R. (1983). Age related differences in work attitudes and behavior. *Psychological Bulletin, 93*, 328–367.

54. Rosen, B., & Jerdee, T. H. (1976). The influence of age stereotypes on managerial decisions. *Journal of Applied Psychology, 61*, 428–432. Also see Dietrick, E. J., & Dobbins, G. J. (1991). The influence of subordinate age on managerial actions: An attributional analysis. *Journal of Organizational Behavior, 12*, 367–377.

55. Galt, V. (2002, October 16). What am I, chopped liver? *Globe and Mail*, C1, C6.

56. Galt, 2002, October 16.

57. Dobson, S. (2011, March 14). 50-plus awards celebrate older workers. *Canadian HR Reporter, 24*(5), 1, 6.

58. Falkenberg, 1990; Fiske, S. T., Beroff, D. N., Borgida, E., Deaux, K., & Heilman, M. E. (1991). Use of sex stereotyping research in Price Waterhouse v. Hopkins. *American Psychologist, 46*, 1049–1060.

59. Dobson, S. (2010, May 3). HR by the numbers. *Canadian HR Reporter, 23*(9), 4.

60. Shaw, A. (2008, May 5). Boeing puts diversity to work—silently. *Canadian HR Reporter, 21*(9), 18; Caballero, R., & Yerema, R. (2009, February 19). Employer Review: Boeing Canada Operations Limited: Chosen as one of Canada's Best Diversity Employers for 2009. www.eluta.ca/diversity-at-boeing-canada; Chosen as one of Canada's Best Diversity Employers for 2012. www.eluta.ca/diversity-at-boeing-canada.

61. Caudron, S. (1993, April). Training can damage diversity efforts. *Personnel Journal*, 51–62.

62. Scott, K. A., Heathcote, J. M., & Gruman, J. A. (2011). The diverse organization: Finding gold at the end of the rainbow. *Human Resource Management, 50*, 735–755.

63. Mayer, R. C., & Davis, J. H. (1999). The effect of the performance appraisal system on trust for management: A field quasi-experiment. *Journal of Applied Psychology, 84*, 123–136.

64. Lee, C. (1997, January). Trust. *Training, 34*(1), 28–37.

65. Mayer & Davis, 1999; Davis, J. H., Mayer, R. C., & Schoorman, F. D. (1995, October). The trusted general manager

and firm performance: Empirical evidence of a strategic advantage. Paper presented at the 15th annual meeting of the Strategic Management Society, Mexico City, Mexico. Cited in Mayer & Davis, 1999.

66. Davis, Mayer, & Schoorman, 1995; Mayer, R. C., Davis, J. H., & Schoorman, F. D. (1995). An integrative model of organizational trust. *Academy of Management Review, 20,* 709–734; Rousseau, D. M., Sitkin, S. B., Burt, R. S., & Camerer, C. (1998). Not so different after all: A cross-discipline view of trust. *Academy of Management Review, 23,* 393–404.

67. Mayer, Davis, & Schoorman, 1995.

68. Mayer & Davis, 1999; Mayer, Davis, & Schoorman, 1995.

69. Colquitt, J. A., & Rodell, J. B. (2011). Justice, trust, and trustworthiness: A longitudinal analysis integrating three theoretical perspectives. *Academy of Management Journal, 54,* 1183–1206.

70. Dirks, K. T., & Ferrin, D. L. (2002). Trust in leadership: Meta-analytic findings and implications for research and practice. *Journal of Applied Psychology, 87,* 611–628.

71. Neto, J. T. (2009, April 6). About this survey. *A special national report for the Great Place to Work Institute Canada. Globe and Mail,* GPTW2.

72. Colquitt, J. A., Lepine, J. A., Zapata, C. P., & Wild, R. E. (2011). Trust in typical and high-reliability contexts: Building and reacting to trust among firefighters. *Academy of Management Journal, 54,* 999–1015.

73. Rhoades, L., & Eisenberger, R. (2002). Perceived organizational support: A review of the literature. *Journal of Applied Psychology, 87,* 698–714.

74. Rhoades & Eisenberger, 2002.

75. Shanock, L. R., & Eisenberger, R. (2006). When supervisors feel supported: Relationships with subordinates' perceived supervisor support, perceived organizational support, and performance. *Journal of Applied Psychology, 91,* 689–695.

76. Allen, D. G., Shore, L. M., & Griffeth, R. W. (2003). The role of perceived organizational support and supportive human resource practices in the turnover process. *Journal of Management, 29(1),* 99–118.

77. Rynes, S. L., Bretz, R., & Gerhart, B. (1991). The importance of recruitment in job choice: A different way of looking. *Personnel Psychology, 44,* 487–521.

78. Hausknecht, J. P., Day, D. V., & Thomas, S. C. (2004). Applicant reactions to selection procedures: An updated model and meta-analysis. *Personnel Psychology, 57,* 639–683.

79. Campion, M. A., Palmer, D. K., and Campion, J. E. (1997). A review of structure in the selection interview. *Personnel Psychology, 50,* 655–702; McDaniel, M. A., Whetzel, D. L., Schmidt, F. L., & Maurer, S. D. (1994). The validity of employment interviews: A comprehensive review and meta-analysis. *Journal of Applied Psychology, 79,* 599–616; Wiesner, W. H., & Cronshaw, S. F. (1988). A meta-analytic investigation of the impact of interview format and degree of structure on the validity of the employment interview. *Journal of Occupational Psychology, 61,* 275–290.

80. Hakel, M.D. (1982). Employment interviewing. In K. M. Rowland & G. R. Ferris (Eds.), *Personnel management.* Boston: Allyn and Bacon.

81. Hakel, 1982; Dipboye, R. L. (1989). Threats to the incremental validity of interviewer judgments. In R. W. Eder & G. R. Ferris (Eds.), *The employment interview: Theory, research, and practice.* Newbury Park, CA: Sage.

82. Hollmann, T. D. (1972). Employment interviewers' errors in processing positive and negative information. *Journal of Applied Psychology, 56,* 130–134.

83. Rowe, P. M. (1989). Unfavorable information in interview decisions. In R. W. Eder & G. R. Ferris (Eds.), *The employment interview: Theory, research, and practice.* Newbury Park, CA: Sage.

84. Maurer, T. J., & Alexander, R. A. (1991). Contrast effects in behavioral measurement: An investigation of alternative process explanations. *Journal of Applied Psychology, 76,* 3–10; Maurer, T. J., Palmer, J. K., & Ashe, D. K. (1993). Diaries, checklists, evaluations, and contrast effects in measurement of behavior. *Journal of Applied Psychology, 78,* 226–231; Schmitt, N. (1976). Social and situational determinants of interview decisions: Implications for the employment interview. *Personnel Psychology, 29,* 70–101.

85. One of Canada's Best Diversity Employers for 2012, www.eluta.ca/diversity-at-kpmg.

86. Chapman, D. S., & Zweig, D. I. (2005). Developing a nomological network for interview structure: Antecedents and consequences of the structured selection interview. *Personnel Psychology, 58,* 673–702.

87. For other reasons and a review of the interview literature, see Harris, M. M. (1989). Reconsidering the employment interview: A review of recent literature and suggestions for future research. *Personnel Psychology, 42,* 691–726.

88. Balzer, W. K., & Sulsky, L. M. (1992). Halo and performance appraisal research: A critical examination. *Journal of Applied Psychology, 77,* 975–985; Cooper, W. H. (1981). Ubiquitous halo. *Psychological Bulletin, 90,* 218–244; Murphy, K. R., Jako, R. A., & Anhalt, R. L. (1993). Nature and consequences of halo error: A critical analysis. *Journal of Applied Psychology, 78,* 218–225.

89. Kingstrom, P. D., & Bass, A. R. (1981). A critical analysis of studies comparing behaviorally anchored rating scales (BARS) and other rating formats. *Personnel Psychology, 34,* 263–289; Landy, F. J., & Farr, J. L. (1983). *The measurement of work performance.* New York: Academic Press.

90. Roch, S. G., Woehr, D. J., Mishra, V., & Kieszczynska, U. (2012). Rater training revisited: An updated meta-analytic review of frame-of-reference training. *Journal of Occupational and Organizational Psychology, 85,* 370–395.

PHOTO CREDITS

PERSONALITY AND LEARNING

From Chapter 2 of *Organizational Behaviour*, Ninth Edition. Gary Johns and Alan M. Saks. Copyright © 2014 by Pearson Education Canada. All rights reserved.

PERSONALITY AND LEARNING

LEARNING OBJECTIVES

After reading this chapter, you should be able to:

1. Define *personality* and discuss its general role in influencing organizational behaviour.

2. Describe the *dispositional*, *situational*, and *interactionist* approaches to organizational behaviour and *trait activation theory*.

3. Discuss the Five-Factor Model of personality.

4. Describe and discuss the consequences of *locus of control, self-monitoring*, and *self-esteem*.

5. Discuss *positive* and *negative affectivity, proactive personality, general self-efficacy*, and *core self-evaluations* and their consequences.

6. Define *learning* and describe what is learned in organizations.

7. Explain *operant learning theory* and differentiate between *positive* and *negative reinforcements*.

8. Explain when to use immediate versus delayed reinforcement and when to use continuous versus partial reinforcement.

9. Distinguish between *extinction* and *punishment* and explain how to use punishment effectively.

10. Explain *social cognitive theory* and discuss *observational learning, self-efficacy beliefs*, and *self-regulation*.

11. Describe the following organizational learning practices: *organizational behaviour modification, employee recognition programs, training and development programs*, and *career development*.

ECONOMICAL INSURANCE

Economical Insurance is a property and casualty insurance company that was founded in 1871. Its first insurance policy was written on a barn in Berlin, Ontario. Today, Economical has nearly 2500 employees and it is one of the largest property and casualty insurance companies in Canada. From its head office in Waterloo, Ontario, and an additional 17 branches and member companies across Canada, Economical offers a wide range of personal, commercial, farm, and surety products.

A few years ago, the company's medical plan costs had been increasing at an annual rate of 8 to 12 percent. So in the summer of 2008, members of the human resources department began to think seriously about a wellness strategy. Economical needed a program that would meet the following goals: build employee awareness of individual health; enhance employee engagement; reward employees for a broad range of wellness behaviours; enhance organiza-

tional health; have the flexibility to evolve as needs change; and produce measureable results in group benefits experience, absenteeism, and other key areas in three to five years.

In the first year of the program, the company focused on enhancing the awareness of individual employees and overall organizational health, as this would set the baseline for future strategies and initiatives. A wellness campaign was designed, including biometric clinics and wellness assessments, and a new personal wellness account was introduced.

The biometric screening clinics involved voluntary, confidential 15-minute appointments with a registered nurse to look for six heart disease risk factors. Employees were provided with wallet cards documenting their measures so they could monitor changes, speak with their physicians, and enter the information into their wellness assessments.

The confidential wellness assessment was housed on the benefit carrier's website and contained 32 questions

assessing 10 health risks (such as health habits, readiness to change, culture, and productivity). Each employee received an individualized report summarizing their results, along with tips to improve areas needing attention. Employees who completed the assessment within the promoted time frame were provided with $300 in wellness credits deposited into a personal wellness account through their flexible benefit plan. The credits can be used for things such as fitness/sports equipment, lessons, and weight management programs. More than one-half (54 percent) of employees participated.

In the second year of the program, Economical added a team wellness challenge to the program to create action and behaviour changes. This required employees to take action by focusing on particular risk areas. Teams worked toward common health goals and logged activities using an online journal.

The main challenge included a minimum amount of physical activity. For each minute of exercise, participants got a point. In addition, teams received bonus points for participation in focus areas (e.g., eating five fruits and veggies a day, drinking water, and taking time for oneself). Individual scores were combined to make team scores and the team with the most points won.

Employees who did the team challenge were rewarded with $150 for their personal wellness accounts while those who completed a wellness assessment received a further $150. The change in the incentive strategy from the first year to the second year is a purposeful, multi-year approach that progressively requires employees to adjust behaviours.

To create a year-round focus on physical activity, Economical also launched a four-week spring walking challenge (Stride into Summer) that involved more than 70 percent of employees walking more than 112 000 kilometres. Senior executives acted as role models by sharing their personal wellness-related stories.

Reviewing the results against the objectives indicates that employees are learning more about their individual health. Ninety-two percent of biometric screening participants said it helped them learn more about cardiovascular health and 71 percent said they will be making changes to their lifestyle. Testimonials from employees who have begun to change their lifestyles and see real health gains also indicate that the program has been effective.

Employees will now be challenged to sustain the changes they have made in their behaviour. Economical expects that within another two years, the program should see measureable improvements in the group benefits experience and absenteeism. It is also hoped that the program will enhance employee engagement and productivity, and help contain rising health-care costs.[1]

Learning is a critical requirement for effective organizational behaviour, and as you probably have heard, for organizations to remain competitive in today's rapidly changing and competitive environment, employee learning must be continuous and lifelong. As you can tell from the opening vignette, employees at Economical are learning about their health and changing their behaviour to live healthier lifestyles. But how do people learn and how can organizations change employees' behaviour? What learning principles and theories are involved? In this chapter we will focus on the learning process and see how learning in organizations takes place. While learning is necessary for people to change their behaviours, studies in organizational behaviour have shown that behaviour is also a function of people's personalities. Therefore, we begin this chapter by considering personality and organizational behaviour.

Kirmac Collision Services focuses on personality when recruiting and hiring employees.

LO ①

Define *personality* and discuss its general role in influencing organizational behaviour.

Personality. The relatively stable set of psychological characteristics that influences the way an individual interacts with his or her environment.

WHAT IS PERSONALITY?

The notion of personality permeates thought and discussion in our culture. We are bombarded with information about "personalities" in the print and broadcast media. We are sometimes promised exciting introductions to people with "nice" personalities. We occasionally meet people who seem to have "no personality."

Personality is so important that some companies focus on personality when hiring employees. For example, Kirmac Collision Services, an automotive collision repair company based in Coquitlam, British Columbia, has taken a new approach to recruiting and hiring employees that focuses less on industry-specific experience and skills and more on personality.[2] But what exactly *is* personality?

Personality is the relatively stable set of psychological characteristics that influences the way an individual interacts with his or her environment and how he or she feels, thinks, and behaves. An individual's personality summarizes his or her personal style of dealing with the world. You have certainly noticed differences in personal style among your parents, friends, professors, bosses, and employees. They are reflected in the distinctive way that they react to people, situations, and problems.

Where does personality come from? Personality consists of a number of dimensions and traits that are determined in a complex way by genetic predisposition and by one's long-term learning history. Although personality is relatively stable, it is certainly susceptible to change through adult learning experiences. And while we often use labels such as "high self-esteem" to describe people, we should always remember that people have a *variety* of personality characteristics. Excessive typing of people does not help us to appreciate their unique potential to contribute to an organization.

PERSONALITY AND ORGANIZATIONAL BEHAVIOUR

Personality has a rather long and rocky history in organizational behaviour. Initially, it was believed that personality was an important factor in many areas of organizational behaviour, including motivation, attitudes, performance, and leadership. In fact, after the Second World War, the use of personality tests for the selection of military personnel became widespread, and, in the 1950s and 1960s it became popular in business organizations.

This approach to organizational behaviour is known as the **dispositional approach** because it focuses on individual dispositions and personality. According to the dispositional approach, individuals possess stable traits or characteristics that influence their attitudes and behaviours. In other words, individuals are predisposed to behave in certain ways. However, decades of research produced mixed and inconsistent findings that failed to support the usefulness of personality as a predictor of organizational behaviour and job performance. As a result, there was a dramatic decrease in personality research and a decline in the use of personality tests for selection.

Researchers began to shift their attention to factors in the work environment that might predict and explain organizational behaviour. This approach became known as the **situational approach**. According to the situational approach, characteristics of the organizational setting, such as rewards and punishment, influence people's feelings, attitudes, and behaviour. For example, many studies have shown that job satisfaction and other work-related attitudes are largely determined by situational factors such as the characteristics of work tasks.[3]

Over the years, proponents of both approaches have argued about the importance of dispositions versus the situation in what is known as the "person–situation debate." Although researchers argued over which approach was the right one, it is now believed that both approaches are important for predicting and understanding organizational behaviour. This led to a third approach to organizational behaviour, known as the "interactionist approach," or "interactionism." According to the **interactionist approach**, organizational behaviour is a function of both dispositions and the situation. In other words, to predict and understand organizational behaviour, one must know something about an individual's personality and the setting in which he or she works. This approach is now the most widely accepted perspective within organizational behaviour.[4]

To give you an example of the interactionist perspective, consider the role of personality in different situations. To keep it simple, we will describe situations as being either "weak" or "strong." In weak situations it is not always clear how a person should behave, while in strong situations there are clear expectations for appropriate behaviour. As a result, personality has the most impact in weak situations. This is because in these situations (e.g., a newly formed volunteer community organization) there are loosely defined roles, few rules, and weak reward and punishment contingencies. However, in strong situations, which have more defined roles, rules, and contingencies (e.g., routine military operations), personality tends to have less impact.[5] Thus, as you can see, the extent to which personality influences people's attitudes and behaviour depends on the situation. Later in the text you will learn that the extent to which people perceive stressors as stressful and the way they react to stress is also influenced by their personality. This is another example of the interactionist approach to organizational behaviour.

One of the most important implications of the interactionist perspective is that some personality characteristics are useful in certain organizational situations. According to

Simulate

INDIVIDUAL BEHAVIOUR Go to MyManagementLab to complete a simulation about individual behaviour.

LO 2

Describe the *dispositional, situational,* and *interactionist* approaches to organizational behaviour and *trait activation theory.*

Dispositional approach. Individuals possess stable traits or characteristics that influence their attitudes and behaviours.

Situational approach. Characteristics of the organizational setting influence people's attitudes and behaviour.

Interactionist approach. Individuals' attitudes and behaviour are a function of both dispositions and the situation.

Trait activation theory.
Traits lead to certain behaviours only when the situation makes the need for the trait salient.

trait activation theory, traits lead to certain behaviours only when the situation makes the need for that trait salient. In other words, personality characteristics influence people's behaviour when the situation calls for a particular personality characteristic.[6] Thus, there is no one best personality and managers need to appreciate the advantages of employee diversity. A key concept here is *fit*: putting the right person in the right job, group, or organization and exposing different employees to different management styles.

In recent years, there has been a resurgence of interest in personality research in organizational behaviour. One of the main problems with the early research on personality was the use of inadequate measures of personality characteristics. However, advances in measurement and trends in organizations have prompted renewed interest. For example, increased emphasis on service jobs with customer contact, concern about ethics and integrity, and contemporary interest in teamwork and cooperation all point to the potential contribution of personality.[7]

Another reason for the renewed interest in personality has been the development of a framework of personality characteristics known as the Five-Factor Model, or the "Big Five," which provides a framework for classifying personality characteristics into five general dimensions. This framework makes it much easier to understand and study the role of personality in organizational behaviour.[8]

In what follows, we first discuss the five general personality dimensions of the Five-Factor Model. Then we cover three well-known personality characteristics with special relevance to organizational behaviour. We then discuss recent developments in personality research. Later in the text, we will explore the impact of personality characteristics on job satisfaction, motivation, leadership, ethics, organizational politics, and stress.

LO 3

Discuss the Five-Factor Model of personality.

The Five-Factor Model of Personality

People are unique, people are complex, and there are literally hundreds of adjectives that we can use to reflect this unique complexity. Yet, over the years, psychologists have discovered that there are about five basic but general dimensions that describe personality. These Big Five dimensions are known as the Five-Factor Model (FFM) of personality and are summarized in Exhibit 1 along with some illustrative traits.[9] The dimensions are:

Go to MyManagementLab to see an annotated version of this figure.

- **Extraversion.** This is the extent to which a person is outgoing versus shy. Persons who score high on extraversion tend to be sociable, outgoing, energetic, joyful, and assertive. High extraverts enjoy social situations, while those low on this dimension (introverts) avoid them. Extraversion is especially important for jobs that require a lot of interpersonal interaction, such as sales and management, where being sociable, assertive, energetic, and ambitious is important for success.

- **Emotional stability/Neuroticism.** This is degree to which a person has appropriate emotional control. People with high emotional stability (low neuroticism) are self-confident and have high self-esteem. Those with lower emotional stability (high neuroticism) tend toward self-doubt and depression. They tend to be anxious, hostile, impulsive, depressed, insecure, and more prone to stress. As a result, for almost any job the performance of persons with low emotional stability is likely to suffer. Persons

EXHIBIT 1
The Five-Factor Model of personality.

Extraversion	Emotional Stability	Agreeableness	Conscientiousness	Openness to Experience
Sociable, Talkative vs. Withdrawn, Shy	Stable, Confident vs. Depressed, Anxious	Tolerant, Cooperative vs. Cold, Rude	Dependable, Responsible vs. Careless, Impulsive	Curious, Original vs. Dull, Unimaginative

who score high on emotional stability are likely to have more effective interactions with co-workers and customers because they tend to be more calm and secure.

- **Agreeableness.** This is the extent to which a person is friendly and approachable. More agreeable people are warm, considerate, altruistic, friendly, sympathetic, cooperative, and eager to help others. Less agreeable people tend to be cold and aloof. They tend to be more argumentative, inflexible, uncooperative, uncaring, intolerant, and disagreeable. Agreeableness is most likely to contribute to job performance in jobs that require interaction and involve helping, cooperating, and nurturing others, as well as in jobs that involve teamwork and cooperation.

- **Conscientiousness.** This is the degree to which a person is responsible and achievement-oriented. More conscientious people are dependable and positively motivated. They are orderly, self-disciplined, hard-working, and achievement-striving, while less conscientious people are irresponsible, lazy, and impulsive. Persons who are high on conscientiousness are likely to perform well on most jobs given their tendency toward hard work and achievement.

- **Openness to experience.** This is the extent to which a person thinks flexibly and is receptive to new ideas. More open people tend toward creativity and innovation. Less open people favour the status quo. People who are high on openness to experience are likely to do well in jobs that involve learning and creativity given that they tend to be intellectual, curious, and imaginative, and to have broad interests.

The Big Five dimensions are relatively independent. That is, you could be higher or lower in any combination of dimensions. Also, they tend to hold up well cross-culturally. Thus, people in different cultures use these same dimensions when describing the personalities of friends and acquaints. There is also evidence that the Big Five traits have a genetic basis.[10]

RESEARCH EVIDENCE Research has linked the Big Five personality dimensions to organizational behaviour. First, there is evidence that each of the Big Five dimensions is related to job performance and organizational citizenship behaviours (voluntary behaviour that contributes to organizational effectiveness such as helping co-workers).[11] Generally, traits like those in the top half of Exhibit 1 lead to better job performance and more citizenship behaviours. Further, the Big Five dimensions that best predict job performance depend on the occupation. For example, high extraversion is important for managers and salespeople. However, high conscientiousness predicts performance in all jobs across occupations and is also the strongest predictor of all the Big Five dimensions of overall job performance.[12]

Second, research has also found that the Big Five are related to other work behaviours. For example, one study showed that conscientiousness is related to retention and attendance at work and is also an important antidote for counterproductive behaviours such as theft, absenteeism, and disciplinary problems.[13] Extraversion has also been found to be related to absenteeism; extraverts tend to be absent more often than introverts.[14]

The Big Five are also related to work motivation and job satisfaction. In a study that investigated the relationship between the Big Five and different indicators of work motivation, the Big Five were found to be significantly related to motivation. Among the five dimensions, neuroticism and conscientiousness were the strongest predictors of motivation, with the former being negatively related and the latter being positively related.[15] In another study, the Big Five were shown to be significantly related to job satisfaction. The strongest predictor was neuroticism (i.e., emotional stability) followed by conscientiousness, extraversion, and, to a lesser extent, agreeableness. Openness to experience was not related to job satisfaction. Higher neuroticism was associated with lower job satisfaction, while higher extraversion, conscientiousness, and agreeableness were associated with higher job satisfaction. Similar results have been found for life satisfaction. In addition, individuals with higher conscientiousness, extraversion, agreeableness, and emotional stability perform better on a team in terms of their performance of important team-relevant behaviours such as cooperation, concern, and courtesy to team members.[16]

The Big Five are also related to job search and career success. Extraversion, conscientiousness, openness to experience, and agreeableness have been found to relate positively to the intensity of a job seeker's job search, while neuroticism was negatively related. As well, conscientiousness was found to be positively related to the probability of obtaining employment.[17] In addition, high conscientiousness and extraversion and low neuroticism have been found to be associated with a higher income and occupational status. Perhaps most interesting is the fact that these personality traits were related to career success even when the influence of general mental ability was taken into account. Furthermore, both childhood and adult measures of personality predicted career success during adulthood over a period of 50 years. These results suggest that the effects of personality on career success are relatively enduring.[18]

The above findings all indicate that one's personality can influence one's attitudes and behaviours. But can the personality of a CEO influence the performance of an organization? To find out, see the Research Focus: *CEO Personality and Firm Performance.*

As noted earlier, the Big Five personality dimensions are basic and general. However, years of research have also identified a number of more specific personality characteristics that influence organizational behaviour, including locus of control, self-monitoring, and self-esteem. Let's now consider each of these.

Locus of Control

Consider the following comparison. Laurie and Stan are both management trainees in large banks. However, they have rather different expectations regarding their futures. Laurie has just enrolled in an evening Master of Business Administration (MBA) program in a nearby university. Although some of her MBA courses are not immediately applicable to her job, Laurie feels that she must be prepared for greater responsibility as she moves up in the bank hierarchy. Laurie is convinced that she will achieve promotions because she studies hard, works hard, and does her job properly. She feels that an individual makes her own way in the world and that she can control her own destiny. She is certain that she can someday be the president of the bank if she really wants to be. Her personal motto is "I can do it."

Stan, on the other hand, sees no use in pursuing additional education beyond his bachelor's degree. According to him, such activities just do not pay off. People who get promoted are just plain lucky or have special connections, and further academic preparation or hard work has nothing to do with it. Stan feels that it is impossible to predict his own future, but he knows that the world is pretty unfair.

Laurie and Stan differ on a personality dimension called **locus of control**. This variable refers to individuals' beliefs about the *location* of the factors that control their behaviour. At one end of the continuum are high internals (like Laurie), who believe that the opportunity to control their own behaviour resides within themselves. At the other end of the continuum are high externals (like Stan), who believe that external forces determine their behaviour. Not surprisingly, compared with internals, externals see the world as an unpredictable, chancy place in which luck, fate, or powerful people control their destinies (see Exhibit 2).[19]

Internals tend to see stronger links between the effort they put into their jobs and the performance level that they achieve. In addition, they perceive to a greater degree than externals that the organization will notice high performance and reward it.[20] Since internals believe that their work behaviour will influence the rewards they achieve, they are more likely to be aware of and to take advantage of information that will enable them to perform effectively.[21]

LO **4**

Describe and discuss the consequences of *locus of control*, *self-monitoring*, and *self-esteem*.

 Explore

Go to MyManagementLab to see an annotated version of this figure.

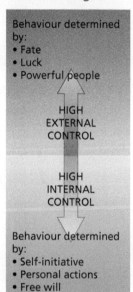

Behaviour determined by:
• Fate
• Luck
• Powerful people

HIGH EXTERNAL CONTROL

HIGH INTERNAL CONTROL

Behaviour determined by:
• Self-initiative
• Personal actions
• Free will

EXHIBIT 2
The internal/external locus of control continuum.

Locus of control.
A set of beliefs about whether one's behaviour is controlled mainly by internal or external forces.

RESEARCH FOCUS

CEO PERSONALITY AND FIRM PERFORMANCE

As organizations struggle to remain competitive in today's increasingly global environment, a key success factor is the ability to adapt quickly to environmental changes or what is known as *strategic flexibility*. Strategic flexibility has been shown to drive firm performance.

The CEO of an organization plays a key role in driving strategic change and can have a profound effect on an organization's strategic direction and performance. But can the CEO's personality influence strategic flexibility and firm performance?

To find out, Sucheta Nadkarni and Pol Herrmann conducted a study of CEOs of 195 small and medium-sized enterprises (SMEs) from the Indian business process outsourcing industry. Offshore business process outsourcing is the transfer of the operational ownership of one or more of a firm's processes to an external provider from another country that then manages the processes according to predetermined metrics. India is the leader in business process outsourcing services, an industry where strategic flexibility is central to success and survival.

The researchers predicted that a CEO's personality can influence firm performance by either enhancing or inhibiting strategic flexibility. This is because the CEO's personality will influence how he/she searches for and interprets information that is central to developing strategic flexibility.

Nadkarni and Herrmann focused on the five dimensions of the Five-Factor Model and predicted that each dimension will be positively or negatively related to strategic flexibility. The CEOs completed a personality and demographic survey, and at least two top managers that report directly to the CEO completed a strategic flexibility survey. Financial performance records were obtained from each firm.

The results indicated that emotional stability, extraversion, and openness to experience were positively related to strategic flexibility while conscientiousness was negatively related. Medium levels of agreeableness were related to the most strategic flexibility. In addition, strategic flexibility was positively related to firm performance.

These results indicate that CEO extraversion, emotional stability, and openness to experience enhanced firm performance by fostering strategic flexibility, whereas CEO conscientiousness undermined firm performance by inhibiting flexibility. Medium levels of agreeableness maximized strategic flexibility and firm performance.

This study highlights the importance of CEO personality in fostering strategic flexibility and firm performance.

Source: Based on Nadkarni, S., & Herrmann, P. (2010). CEO personality, strategic flexibility, and firm performance: The case of the Indian business process outsourcing industry. *Academy of Management Journal, 53,* 1050–1073.

Research shows that locus of control influences organizational behaviour in a variety of occupational settings. Evidently, because they perceive themselves as being able to control what happens to them, people who are high on internal control are more satisfied with their jobs, more committed to their organizations, earn more money, and achieve higher organizational positions.[22] In addition, they seem to perceive less stress, to cope with stress better and experience less burnout, and to engage in more careful career planning. They are also less likely to be absent from work and to be more satisfied with their lives.[23]

Self-Monitoring

We are sure that you have known people who tend to "wear their heart on their sleeve." These are people who act the way they feel and say what they think in spite of their social surroundings. We are also sure that you have known people who are a lot more sensitive to their social surroundings, a lot more likely to fit what they say and do to the nature of those surroundings regardless of how they think or feel. What we have here is a contrast in **self-monitoring**, which is the extent to which people observe and regulate how they appear and behave in social settings and relationships.[24] The people who "wear their heart on their sleeve" are low self-monitors. They are not so concerned with scoping out and fitting in with those around them. Their opposites are high self-monitors, who take great care to observe the thoughts, actions, and feelings of those around them and control the images that they project. In this sense, high

Self-monitoring. The extent to which people observe and regulate how they appear and behave in social settings and relationships.

self-monitors behave somewhat like actors. In particular, high self-monitors tend to show concern for socially appropriate emotions and behaviours, to tune in to social and interpersonal cues, and to regulate their behaviour and self-presentation according to these cues.

How does self-monitoring affect organizational behaviour?[25] For one thing, high self-monitors tend to gravitate toward jobs that require, by their nature, a degree of role-playing and the exercise of their self-presentation skills. Sales, law, public relations, and politics are examples. In such jobs, the ability to adapt to one's clients and contacts is critical; so are communication skills and persuasive abilities, characteristics that high self-monitors frequently exhibit. High self-monitors perform particularly well in occupations that call for flexibility and adaptiveness in dealings with diverse constituencies. As well, a number of studies show that managers are inclined to be higher self-monitors than non-managers in the same organization. Self-monitoring is also significantly related to a number of work-related outcomes. High self-monitors tend to be more involved in their jobs, to perform at a higher level, and to be more likely to emerge as leaders. However, high self-monitors are also likely to experience more role stress and show less commitment to their organization.[26]

Promotion in the management ranks is often a function of subjective performance appraisals, and the ability to read and conform to the boss's expectations can be critical for advancement. Thus, the ability to regulate and adapt one's behaviour in social situations and to manage the impressions others form of them might be a career advantage for high self-monitors. In fact, in a study that tracked the careers of a sample of MBA graduates, high self-monitors were more likely to change employers and locations and to receive more promotions than low self-monitors.[27]

Are high self-monitors always at an organizational advantage? Not likely. They are unlikely to feel comfortable in ambiguous social settings in which it is hard to determine exactly what behaviours are socially appropriate. Dealing with unfamiliar cultures (national or corporate) might provoke stress. Also, some roles require people to go against the grain or really stand up for what they truly believe in. Thus, high self-monitoring types would seem to be weak innovators and would have difficulty resisting social pressure.

Self-Esteem

Self-esteem. The degree to which a person has a positive self-evaluation.

How well do you like yourself? This is the essence of the personality characteristic called self-esteem. More formally, **self-esteem** is the degree to which a person has a positive self-evaluation. People with high self-esteem have favourable self-images. People with low self-esteem have unfavourable self-images. They also tend to be uncertain about the correctness of their opinions, attitudes, and behaviours. In general, people tend to be highly motivated to protect themselves from threats to their self-esteem.

Behavioural plasticity theory. People with low self-esteem tend to be more susceptible to external and social influences than those who have high self-esteem.

One of the most interesting differences between people with high and low self-esteem has to do with the *plasticity* of their thoughts, attitudes, and behaviour, or what is known as "behavioural plasticity." According to **behavioural plasticity theory**, people with low self-esteem tend to be more susceptible to external and social influences than those who have high self-esteem—that is, they are more pliable. Thus, events and people in the organizational environment have more impact on the beliefs and actions of employees with low self-esteem. This occurs because, being unsure of their own views and behaviour, they are more likely to look to others for information and confirmation. In addition, people who have low self-esteem seek social approval from others, approval that they might gain from adopting others' views, and they do not react well to ambiguous and stressful situations. This is another example of the interactionist approach, in that the effect of the work environment on people's beliefs and actions is partly a function of their self-esteem.[28]

Employees with low self-esteem also tend to react badly to negative feedback—it lowers their subsequent performance.[29] This means that managers should be especially cautious when using negative reinforcement and punishment, as discussed later in this chapter, with employees with low self-esteem. If external causes are thought to be responsible for a performance problem, this should be made very clear. Also, managers should direct criticism at the performance difficulty and not at the person. As we will explain shortly, modelling the correct behaviour should be especially effective with employees with low self-esteem, who are quite willing to imitate credible models and who also respond well to mentoring. Finally, organizations should try to avoid assigning those with low self-esteem to jobs (such as life insurance sales) that inherently provide a lot of negative feedback.

Organizations will generally benefit from a workforce with high self-esteem. Such people tend to make more fulfilling career decisions, they exhibit higher job satisfaction and job performance, and they are generally more resilient to the strains of everyday worklife.[30] What can organizations do to bolster self-esteem? Opportunity for participation in decision making, autonomy, and interesting work have been fairly consistently found to be positively related to self-esteem.[31] Also, organizations should avoid creating a culture with excessive and petty work rules that signal to employees that they are incompetent or untrustworthy.[32]

NEW DEVELOPMENTS IN PERSONALITY AND ORGANIZATIONAL BEHAVIOUR

LO 5

Discuss *positive* and *negative affectivity*, *proactive personality*, *general self-efficacy*, and *core self-evaluations* and their consequences.

In recent years, there have been a number of exciting developments in personality research in organizational behaviour. In this section, we describe five recent personality variables that have been found to be important for organizational behaviour: positive and negative affectivity, proactive personality, general self-efficacy, and core self-evaluations.

Positive and Negative Affectivity

Have you ever known somebody who is always happy, cheerful, and in a good mood? Or perhaps you know someone who is always unhappy and in a bad mood. Chances are you have noticed these differences in people. Some people are happy most of the time, while others are almost always unhappy. These differences reflect two affective dispositions known as positive affectivity (PA) and negative affectivity (NA). Research has found that they are enduring personality characteristics and that there might be a genetic and biological bases to them.

People who are high on **positive affectivity** experience positive emotions and moods like joy and excitement and view the world in a positive light, including themselves and other people. They tend to be cheerful, enthusiastic, lively, sociable, and energetic. People who are high on **negative affectivity** experience negative emotions and moods like fear and anxiety and view the world in a negative light. They have an overall negative view of themselves and the world around them, and they tend to be distressed, depressed, and unhappy.[33] It is important to understand that PA and NA are not opposite ends of a continuum but are relatively independent dimensions.[34]

Unlike the other personality traits discussed in this chapter, positive and negative affectivity are emotional dispositions that predict people's general emotional tendencies. Thus, they can influence people's emotions and mood states at work and influence job attitudes and work behaviours. Research has found that people who are high on PA have higher job satisfaction, job performance, and engage in more organizational citizenship behaviours. High PA employees have also been found to be more creative at work. Individuals who are high on NA report lower job satisfaction and have poorer job performance. High NA employees tend to experience more stressful work conditions and report higher levels of workplace stress and strain. NA has also been found to be associated with counterproductive work behaviours (e.g., harassment and physical aggression), withdrawal behaviours (e.g., absenteeism and turnover), and occupational injury. Finally, there is some evidence that PA is a key factor that links happiness to success in life and at work.[35]

Positive affectivity. Propensity to view the world, including oneself and other people, in a positive light.

Negative affectivity. Propensity to view the world, including oneself and other people, in a negative light.

Proactive Personality

How effective are you at taking initiative and changing your circumstances? Taking initiative to improve one's current circumstances or creating new ones is known as **proactive behaviour**. It involves challenging the status quo rather than passively adapting to present conditions. Some people are actually better at this than others because they have a stable disposition toward proactive behaviour, known as a "proactive personality." Individuals who have a **proactive personality** are relatively unconstrained by situational forces and act to change and influence their environment. Proactive personality is a stable personal disposition that reflects a tendency to take personal initiative across a range of activities and situations and to effect positive change in one's environment.[36]

Proactive individuals search for and identify opportunities, show initiative, take action, and persevere until they bring about meaningful change. People who do not have a proactive personality are more likely to be passive and to react and adapt to their environment. As a result, they tend to endure and to be shaped by the environment instead of trying to change it.[37]

Proactive personality has been found to be related to a number of work outcomes, including job satisfaction, job performance, organizational citizenship behaviours, tolerance for stress in demanding jobs, leadership effectiveness, participation in organizational initiatives, work team performance, and entrepreneurship. One study found that proactive personality is associated with higher performance evaluations because individuals with a proactive personality develop strong supportive networks and perform initiative-taking behaviours such as implementing solutions to organization or departmental problems or spearheading new programs. Individuals with a proactive personality have also been found to have high-quality relationships with their supervisors. There is also evidence that persons with a proactive personality are more successful in searching for employment and career success. They are more likely to find a job, to receive higher salaries and more frequent promotions, and to have more satisfying careers.[38]

General Self-Efficacy

General self-efficacy (GSE) is a general trait that refers to an individual's belief in his or her ability to perform successfully in a variety of challenging situations.[39] GSE is considered to be a *motivational* trait rather than an *affective* trait because it reflects an individual's belief that he or she can succeed at a variety of tasks rather than how an individual feels about him or herself. An individual's GSE is believed to develop over the lifespan as repeated successes and failures are experienced across a variety of tasks and situations. Thus, if you have experienced many successes in your life, you probably have high GSE, whereas somebody who has experienced many failures probably has low GSE. Individuals who are high on GSE are better able to adapt to novel, uncertain, and adverse situations. In addition, employees with higher GSE have higher job satisfaction and job performance.[40]

Core Self-Evaluations

Unlike the other personality characteristics described in this chapter, which are specific in themselves, **core self-evaluations** refers to a broad personality concept that consists of more specific traits. The idea behind the theory of core self-evaluations is that individuals hold evaluations about themselves and their self-worth or worthiness, competence, and capability.[41] In a review of the personality literature, Timothy Judge, Edwin Locke, and Cathy Durham identified four traits that make up a person's core self-evaluation. The four traits have already been described in this chapter; they include self-esteem, general self-efficacy, locus of control, and neuroticism (emotional stability).

Research on core self-evaluations has found that these traits are among the best dispositional predictors of job satisfaction and job performance. People with more positive core self-evaluations have higher job satisfaction, organizational commitment, and job performance. Furthermore, research has shown that core self-evaluations measured in childhood and in early adulthood are related to job satisfaction in middle adulthood. This suggests that core self-evaluations are related to job satisfaction over time. Core self-evaluations have also been found to be positively related to life and career satisfaction, and individuals with higher CSE perceive fewer stressors and experience less stress and conflict at work. One of the reasons for the relationship between core self-evaluations and work outcomes is that individuals with a positive self-regard are more likely to perceive and pay attention to the positive aspects of their environments. They experience their job as more intrinsically satisfying and have higher perceptions of fairness and support.[42]

WHAT IS LEARNING?

LO 6

Define *learning* and describe what is learned in organizations.

So far in this chapter we have described how people's personalities can influence their work attitudes and behaviours. However, recall our earlier discussion that the organizational setting can also can have a strong effect on an individual's attitudes and behaviour. As you will learn in this section, the environment can change people's behaviour and even shape personalities. As described at the start of the chapter, employees at Economical changed their lifestyle behaviours. But how does this happen? How and why do people change their behaviour? To try and answer this question, let's examine the concept of learning.

Learning occurs when practice or experience leads to a relatively permanent change in behaviour potential. The words *practice* or *experience* rule out viewing behavioural changes caused by factors like drug intake or biological maturation as learning. One does not learn to be relaxed after taking a tranquilizer, and a boy does not suddenly learn to be a bass singer at the age of 14. The practice or experience that prompts learning stems from an environment that gives feedback concerning the consequences of behaviour. But what do employees learn in organizations?

Learning. A relatively permanent change in behaviour potential that occurs due to practice or experience.

What Do Employees Learn?

Learning in organizations can be understood in terms of taxonomies that indicate what employees learn, how they learn, and different types of learning experiences. The "what" aspect of learning can be described as learning content, of which there are four primary categories: practical skills, intrapersonal skills, interpersonal skills, and cultural awareness.[43]

Practical skills include job-specific skills, knowledge, and technical competence. Employees frequently learn new skills and technologies to continually improve performance and to keep organizations competitive. Constant improvement has become a major goal in many organizations today, and learning can give an organization a competitive advantage.[44] *Intrapersonal skills* are skills such as problem solving, critical thinking, learning about alternative work processes, and risk taking. *Interpersonal skills* include interactive skills such as communicating, teamwork, and conflict resolution. Teams are becoming the major building blocks of organizations, and effective communication is important for organizational success.

Finally, *cultural awareness* involves learning the social norms of organizations and understanding company goals, business operations, and company expectations and priorities. All employees need to learn the cultural norms and expectations of their organizations to function as effective organizational members.

Now that we have considered what people learn in organizations, let's turn to two theories that describe how people in organizations like Economical learn.

LO **7**

Explain *operant learning theory* and differentiate between *positive* and *negative reinforcements*.

Operant learning. Learning by which the subject learns to operate on the environment to achieve certain consequences.

Operant Learning Theory

In the 1930s, psychologist B.F. Skinner investigated the behaviour of rats confined in a box containing a lever that delivered food pellets when pulled. Initially, the rats ignored the lever, but at some point they would accidentally pull it and a pellet would appear. Over time, the rats gradually acquired the lever-pulling response as a means of obtaining food. In other words, they *learned* to pull the lever. The kind of learning Skinner studied is called **operant learning** because the subject learns to operate on the environment to achieve certain consequences. The rats learned to operate the lever to achieve food. Notice that operantly learned behaviour is controlled by the consequences that follow it. These consequences usually depend on the behaviour, and this connection is what is learned. For example, salespeople learn effective sales techniques to achieve commissions and avoid criticism from their managers. The consequences of commissions and criticism depend on which sales behaviours salespeople exhibit.

Operant learning can be used to increase the probability of desired behaviours and to reduce or eliminate the probability of undesirable behaviours. Let's now consider how this is done.

INCREASING THE PROBABILITY OF BEHAVIOUR

Reinforcement. The process by which stimuli strengthen behaviours.

One of the most important consequences that influences behaviour is reinforcement. **Reinforcement** is the process by which stimuli strengthen behaviours. Thus, a *reinforcer* is a stimulus that follows some behaviour and increases or maintains the probability of that behaviour. The sales commissions and criticism mentioned earlier are reinforcers for salespeople. In each case, reinforcement serves to strengthen behaviours, such as proper sales techniques, that fulfill organizational goals. In general, organizations are interested in maintaining or increasing the probability of behaviours such as correct performance, prompt attendance, and accurate decision making. As described at the beginning of the chapter, Economical is interested in maintaining and increasing the probability of various employee wellness behaviours, such as physical activity and healthy eating. As we shall see, positive reinforcers work by their application to a situation, while negative reinforcers work by their removal from a situation.

Positive Reinforcement

Positive reinforcement. The application or addition of a stimulus that increases or maintains the probability of some behaviour.

Positive reinforcement increases or maintains the probability of some behaviour by the *application* or *addition* of a stimulus to the situation in question. Such a stimulus is a positive reinforcer. In the basic Skinnerian learning situation described earlier, we can assume that reinforcement occurred because the probability of the lever operation increased over time. We can further assume that the food pellets were positive reinforcers because they were introduced after the lever was pulled.

Consider the experienced securities analyst who tends to read a particular set of financial newspapers regularly. If we had been able to observe the development of this reading habit, we might have found that it occurred as the result of a series of successful business decisions. That is, the analyst learns to scan those papers because his or her reading is positively reinforced by subsequent successful decisions. In this example, something is added to the situation (favourable decisions) that increases the probability of certain behaviour (selective reading). Also, the appearance of the reinforcer is dependent or contingent on the occurrence of that behaviour.

In general, positive reinforcers tend to be pleasant things, such as food, praise, money, or business success. However, the intrinsic character of stimuli does not determine whether they are positive reinforcers, and pleasant stimuli are not positive reinforcers when considered in the abstract. Whether or not something is a positive reinforcer depends only on whether it increases or maintains the occurrence of some behaviour by its application. Thus, it is improbable that the holiday turkey that employers give to all the employees of a manufacturing plant positively reinforces anything. The only behaviour that the receipt of the turkey is contingent on is being employed by the company during the third week of December. It is unlikely that the turkey increases the probability that employees will remain for another year or work harder.

Negative Reinforcement

Negative reinforcement increases or maintains the probability of some behaviour by the *removal* of a stimulus from the situation in question. Also, negative reinforcement occurs when a response *prevents* some event or stimulus from occurring. In each case, the removed or prevented stimulus is a *negative reinforcer*. Negative reinforcers are usually aversive or unpleasant stimuli, and it stands to reason that we will learn to repeat behaviours that remove or prevent these stimuli.

Let's repeat this point, because it frequently confuses students of organizational behaviour: Negative reinforcers *increase* the probability of behaviour. Suppose we rig a cage with an electrified floor so that it provides a mild shock to its inhabitant. In addition, we install a lever that will turn off the electricity. On the first few trials, a rat put in the cage will become very upset when shocked. Sooner or later, however, it will accidentally operate the lever and turn off the current. Gradually, the rat will learn to operate the lever as soon as it feels the shock. The shock serves as a negative reinforcer for the lever pulling, increasing the probability of the behaviour by its removal.

Managers who continually nag their employees unless the employees work hard are attempting to use negative reinforcement. The only way employees can stop the aversive nagging is to work hard and be diligent. The nagging maintains the probability of productive responses by its removal. In this situation, employees often get pretty good at anticipating the onset of nagging by the look on their boss's face. This look serves as a signal that they can avoid the nagging altogether if they work harder.

Negative reinforcers generally tend to be unpleasant things, such as shock, nagging, or threat of fines. Again, however, negative reinforcers are defined only by what they do and how they work, not by their unpleasantness. Above, we indicated that nagging could serve as a negative reinforcer to increase the probability of productive responses. However, nagging could also serve as a positive reinforcer to increase the probability of unproductive responses if an employee has a need for attention and nagging is the only attention the manager provides. In the first case, nagging is a negative reinforcer—it is terminated following productive responses. In the second case, nagging is a positive reinforcer—it is applied following unproductive responses. In both cases, the responses increase in probability.

Organizational Errors Involving Reinforcement

Experience indicates that managers sometimes make errors in trying to use reinforcement. The most common errors are confusing rewards with reinforcers, neglecting diversity in preferences for reinforcers, and neglecting important sources of reinforcement.

CONFUSING REWARDS WITH REINFORCERS

Organizations and individual managers frequently "reward" workers with things such as pay, promotions, fringe benefits, paid vacations, overtime work, and the opportunity to perform challenging tasks. Such rewards can fail to serve as reinforcers, however, because organizations do not make them contingent on specific behaviours that are of interest to the organization, such as attendance, innovation, or productivity. For example, many organizations assign overtime work on the basis of seniority, rather than performance or good attendance, even when the union contract does not require it. Although the opportunity to earn extra money might have strong potential as a reinforcer, it is seldom made contingent on some desired behaviour. Notice how the incentives and points awarded as part of Economical's wellness program were all contingent on specific behaviours.

Negative reinforcement. The removal of a stimulus that in turn increases or maintains the probability of some behaviour.

NEGLECTING DIVERSITY IN PREFERENCES FOR REINFORCERS Organizations often fail to appreciate individual differences in preferences for reinforcers. In this case, even if managers administer rewards after a desired behaviour, they may fail to have a reinforcing effect. Intuitively, it seems questionable to reinforce a workaholic's extra effort with time off from work, yet such a strategy is fairly common. A more appropriate reinforcer might be the assignment of some challenging task, such as work on a very demanding key project. Some labour contracts include clauses that dictate that supervisors assign overtime to the workers who have the greatest seniority. Not surprisingly, high-seniority workers are often the best paid and the least in need of the extra pay available through overtime. Even if it is administered so that the best-performing high-seniority workers get the overtime, such a strategy might not prove reinforcing—the usual time off might be preferred over extra money.

Managers should carefully explore the possible range of stimuli under their control (such as task assignment and time off from work) for their applicability as reinforcers for particular employees. For example, there is some evidence that employee preferences vary as a function of generational differences with younger workers in their 20s and 30s preferring cash rewards and older workers preferring more experiential rewards, like a vacation.[45] Furthermore, organizations should attempt to administer their formal rewards (such as pay and promotions) to capitalize on their reinforcing effects for various individuals.

NEGLECTING IMPORTANT SOURCES OF REINFORCEMENT There are many reinforcers of organizational behaviour that are not especially obvious. While concentrating on potential reinforcers of a formal nature, such as pay or promotions, organizations and their managers often neglect those that are administered by co-workers or are intrinsic to the jobs being performed. Many managers cannot understand why a worker would persist in potentially dangerous horseplay despite threats of a pay penalty or dismissal. Frequently, such activity is positively reinforced by the attention provided by the joker's co-workers. In fact, on a particularly boring job, such threats might act as positive reinforcers for horseplay by relieving the boredom, especially if the threats are never carried out. Two important sources of reinforcement that managers often ignore are performance feedback and social recognition.

Performance feedback. Providing quantitative or qualitative information on past performance for the purpose of changing or maintaining performance in specific ways.

- *Performance feedback.* **Performance feedback** involves providing quantitative or qualitative information on past performance for the purpose of changing or maintaining performance in specific ways. This reinforcement is available for jobs that provide feedback concerning the adequacy of performance. For example, in some jobs, feedback contingent on performance is readily available. Doctors can observe the success of their treatment by observing the progress of their patients' health, and mechanics can take the cars they repair for a test drive. In other jobs, organizations must build some special feedback mechanism into the job. Performance feedback is most effective when it is (a) conveyed in a positive manner, (b) delivered immediately after the performance is observed, (c) represented visually, such as in graph or chart form, and (d) specific to the behaviour that is being targeted for feedback.[46]

Social recognition. Informal acknowledgement, attention, praise, approval, or genuine appreciation for work well done from one individual or group to another.

- *Social recognition.* **Social recognition** involves informal acknowledgement, attention, praise, approval, or genuine appreciation for work well done from one individual or group to another. Research has shown that when social recognition is made contingent on employee behaviour it can be an effective means for performance improvement.[47]

In summary, managers should understand that positive feedback and a "pat on the back" for a job well done are positive reinforcers that are easy to administer and likely to reinforce desirable behaviours.

I THINK YOUR CONSTRUCTIVE FEEDBACK SKILLS COULD USE A LITTLE POLISHING.

REINFORCEMENT STRATEGIES

LO 8

Explain when to use immediate versus delayed reinforcement and when to use continuous versus partial reinforcement.

What is the best way to administer reinforcers? Should we apply a reinforcer immediately after the behaviour of interest occurs, or should we wait for some period of time? Should we reinforce every correct behaviour, or should we reinforce only a portion of correct responses?

To obtain the *fast acquisition* of some response, continuous and immediate reinforcement should be used—that is, the reinforcer should be applied every time the behaviour of interest occurs, and it should be applied without delay after each occurrence. Many conditions exist in which the fast acquisition of responses is desirable. These include correcting the behaviour of "problem" employees, training employees for emergency operations, and dealing with unsafe work behaviours. Consider the otherwise excellent performer who tends to be late for work. Under pressure to demote or fire this good worker, the boss might sensibly attempt to positively reinforce instances of prompt attendance with compliments and encouragement. To modify the employee's behaviour as quickly as possible, the supervisor might station herself near the office door each morning to supply these reinforcers regularly and immediately.

You might wonder when one would not want to use a continuous, immediate reinforcement strategy to mould organizational behaviour. Put simply, behaviour that individuals learn under such conditions tends not to persist when reinforced less frequently or stopped. Intuitively, this should not be surprising. For example, under normal conditions, operating the power switch on your iPod is continuously and immediately reinforced by music. If the system develops a short circuit and fails to produce music, your switch-operating behaviour will cease very quickly. In the example in the preceding paragraph, the need for fast learning justified the use of continuous, immediate reinforcement. Under more typical circumstances, we would hope that prompt attendance could occur without such close attention.

Behaviour tends to be *persistent* when it is learned under conditions of partial and delayed reinforcement. That is, it will tend to persist under reduced or terminated reinforcement when not every instance of the behaviour is reinforced during learning or when some time period elapses between its enactment and reinforcement. In most cases, the supervisor who wishes to reinforce prompt attendance knows that he or she will not be able to stand by the shop door every morning to compliment the crew's timely entry. Given this constraint, the supervisor should compliment prompt attendance occasionally, perhaps later in the day. This should increase the persistence of promptness and reduce the employees' reliance on the boss's monitoring.

Let's recap. Continuous, immediate reinforcement facilitates fast learning, and delayed, partial reinforcement facilitates persistent learning (see Exhibit 3). Notice that it is impossible to maximize both speed and persistence with a single reinforcement strategy. Also, many responses in our everyday lives cannot be continuously and immediately reinforced, so in

EXHIBIT 3 Summary of reinforcement strategies and their effects.

Explore

Go to MyManagementLab to see an annotated version of this figure.

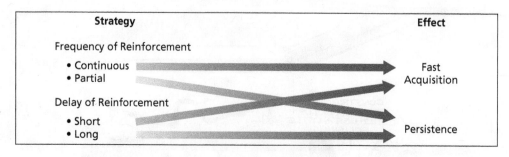

many cases it pays to sacrifice some speed in learning to prepare the learner for this fact of life. All this suggests that managers have to tailor reinforcement strategies to the needs of the situation. Often, managers must alter the strategies over time to achieve effective learning and maintenance of behaviour. For example, the manager training a new employee should probably use a reinforcement strategy that is fairly continuous and immediate (whatever the reinforcer). Looking over the employee's shoulder to obtain the fast acquisition of behaviour is appropriate. Gradually, however, the supervisor should probably reduce the frequency of reinforcement and perhaps build some delay into its presentation to reduce the employee's dependency on his or her attention.

LO 9

Distinguish between *extinction* and *punishment* and explain how to use punishment effectively.

REDUCING THE PROBABILITY OF BEHAVIOUR

Thus far in our discussion of learning, we have been interested in *increasing* the probability of various work behaviours, such as attendance or good performance. Both positive and negative reinforcement can accomplish this goal. However, in many cases, we encounter learned behaviours that we wish to *stop* from occurring. Such behaviours are detrimental to the operation of the organization and could be detrimental to the health or safety of an individual employee.

There are two strategies that can reduce the probability of learned behaviour: extinction and punishment.

Extinction

Extinction. The gradual dissipation of behaviour following the termination of reinforcement.

Extinction simply involves terminating the reinforcement that is maintaining some unwanted behaviour. If the behaviour is not reinforced, it will gradually dissipate or be extinguished.

Consider the case of a bright, young marketing expert who was headed for the "fast track" in his organization. Although his boss, the vice-president of marketing, was considering him for promotion, the young expert had developed a very disruptive habit—the tendency to play comedian during department meetings. The vice-president observed that this wisecracking was reinforced by the appreciative laughs of two other department members. He proceeded to enlist their aid to extinguish the joking. After the vice-president explained the problem to them, they agreed to ignore the disruptive one-liners and puns. At the same time, the vice-president took special pains to positively reinforce constructive comments by the young marketer. Very quickly, joking was extinguished, and the young man's future with the company improved.[48]

This example illustrates that extinction works best when coupled with the reinforcement of some desired substitute behaviour. Remember that behaviours that have been learned under delayed or partial reinforcement schedules are more difficult to extinguish than those learned under continuous, immediate reinforcement. Ironically, it would be harder to extinguish the joke-telling behaviour of a committee member who was only partially successful at getting a laugh than of one who was always successful at getting a laugh.

Punishment

Punishment. The application of an aversive stimulus following some behaviour designed to decrease the probability of that behaviour.

Punishment involves following an unwanted behaviour with some unpleasant, aversive stimulus. In theory, when the actor learns that the behaviour leads to unwanted consequences, this should reduce the probability of the response. Notice the difference between punishment and

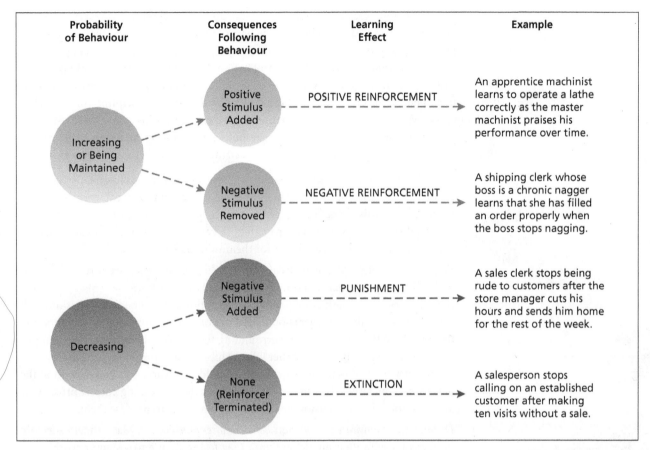

Probability of Behaviour	Consequences Following Behaviour	Learning Effect	Example
Increasing or Being Maintained	Positive Stimulus Added	POSITIVE REINFORCEMENT	An apprentice machinist learns to operate a lathe correctly as the master machinist praises his performance over time.
	Negative Stimulus Removed	NEGATIVE REINFORCEMENT	A shipping clerk whose boss is a chronic nagger learns that she has filled an order properly when the boss stops nagging.
Decreasing	Negative Stimulus Added	PUNISHMENT	A sales clerk stops being rude to customers after the store manager cuts his hours and sends him home for the rest of the week.
	None (Reinforcer Terminated)	EXTINCTION	A salesperson stops calling on an established customer after making ten visits without a sale.

EXHIBIT 4 Summary of learning effects.

 Explore

Go to MyManagementLab to see an annotated version of this figure.

negative reinforcement. In negative reinforcement a nasty stimulus is *removed* following some behaviour, increasing the probability of that behaviour. With punishment, a nasty stimulus is *applied* after some behaviour, *decreasing* the probability of that behaviour. If a boss criticizes her assistant after seeing her use the office phone for personal calls, we expect to see less of this activity in the future. Exhibit 4 compares punishment with reinforcement and extinction.

Using Punishment Effectively

In theory, punishment should be useful in eliminating unwanted behaviour. After all, it seems unreasonable to repeat actions that cause us trouble. Unfortunately, punishment has some unique characteristics that often limit its effectiveness in stopping unwanted activity. First, while punishment provides a clear signal as to which activities are inappropriate, it does not by itself demonstrate which activities should *replace* the punished response. Reconsider the executive who chastises her assistant for making personal calls at the office. If the assistant makes personal calls only when she has caught up on her work, she might legitimately wonder what she is supposed to be doing during her occasional free time. If the boss fails to provide substitute activities, the message contained in the punishment may be lost.

Both positive and negative reinforcers specify which behaviours are appropriate. Punishment indicates only what is not appropriate. Since no reinforced substitute behaviour is provided, punishment only temporarily suppresses the unwanted response. When surveillance is removed, the response will tend to recur. Constant monitoring is very time consuming, and individuals become amazingly adept at learning when they can get away with the forbidden activity. The assistant will soon learn when she can make personal calls without detection. The moral here is clear: *Provide an acceptable alternative for the punished response.*

A second difficulty with punishment is that it has a tendency to provoke a strong emotional reaction on the part of the punished individual.[49] This is especially likely when the punishment is delivered in anger or perceived to be unfair. Managers who try overly hard to be patient with employees and then finally blow up risk overemotional reactions. So do those who tolerate unwanted behaviour on the part of their employees and then impulsively decide to make an example of one individual by punishing him or her. Managers should be sure that their own emotions are under control before punishing, and they should generally avoid punishment in front of observers.[50] Because of the emotional problems involved in the use of punishment, some organizations have downplayed its use in discipline systems. They give employees who have committed infractions *paid* time off to think about their problems.

In addition to providing correct alternative responses and limiting the emotions involved in punishment, there are several other principles that can increase the effectiveness of punishment.

- *Make sure the chosen punishment is truly aversive.* Organizations frequently "punish" chronically absent employees by making them take several days off work. Managers sometimes "punish" ineffective performers by requiring them to work overtime, which allows them to earn extra pay. In both cases, the presumed punishment may actually act as a positive reinforcer for the unwanted behaviour.

- *Punish immediately.* Managers frequently overlook early instances of rule violations or ineffective performance, hoping that things will "work out."[51] This only allows these behaviours to gain strength through repetition. If immediate punishment is difficult to apply, the manager should delay action until a more appropriate time and then reinstate the circumstances surrounding the problem behaviour. For example, the bank manager who observes her teller exhibiting inappropriate behaviour might ask this person to remain after work. She should then carry out punishment at the teller's window rather than in her office, perhaps demonstrating correct procedures and then role-playing a customer to allow the employee to practise them.

- *Do not reward unwanted behaviours before or after punishment.* Many supervisors join in horseplay with their employees until they feel it is time to get some work done. Then, unexpectedly, they do an about-face and punish those who are still "goofing around." Sometimes, managers feel guilty about punishing their employees for some rule infraction and then quickly attempt to make up with displays of good-natured sympathy or affection. For example, the boss who criticizes her assistant for personal calls might show up an hour later with a gift. Such actions present employees with extremely confusing signals about how they should behave, since the manager could be unwittingly reinforcing the very response that he or she wants to terminate.

- *Do not inadvertently punish desirable behaviour.* This happens commonly in organizations. The manager who does not use all his capital budget for a given fiscal year might have the department's budget for the next year reduced, punishing the prudence of his employees. Government employees who "blow the whistle" on wasteful or inefficient practices might find themselves demoted.[52] University professors who are considered excellent teachers might be assigned to onerous, time-consuming duty on a curriculum committee, cutting into their class preparation time.

In summary, punishment can be an effective means of stopping undesirable behaviour. However, managers must apply it very carefully and deliberately to achieve this effectiveness. In general, reinforcing correct behaviours and extinguishing unwanted responses are safer strategies for managers than the frequent use of punishment.

LO 10

Explain *social cognitive theory* and discuss *observational learning, self-efficacy beliefs,* and *self-regulation.*

SOCIAL COGNITIVE THEORY

It has perhaps occurred to you that learning and behaviour sometimes takes place in organizations without the conscious control of positive and negative reinforcers by managers. People often learn and behave through their own volition and self-influence. Thus, human behaviour is not simply due to environmental influences. Rather, people have the cognitive capacity to regulate and control their own thoughts, feelings, motivation, and actions. Unlike operant learning theory, **social cognitive theory (SCT)** emphasizes the role of *cognitive processes* in regulating people's behaviour.

According to SCT, people learn by observing the behaviour of others. Individuals also manage their own behaviour by thinking about the consequences of their actions (forethought), setting performance goals, monitoring their performance and comparing it to their goals, and rewarding themselves for goal accomplishment. People also develop beliefs about their abilities through their interaction with the environment, and these beliefs influence their thoughts and behaviour.[53]

Social cognitive theory suggests that human behaviour can best be explained through a system of *triadic reciprocal causation*, in which personal factors and environmental factors work together and interact to influence people's behaviour. In addition, people's behaviour can also influence personal factors and the environment. Thus, SCT complements operant learning in explaining how people learn and organizational behaviour.[54]

According to Albert Bandura, who is responsible for the development of social cognitive theory, SCT involves three key components: observational learning, self-efficacy beliefs, and self-regulation.[55]

Social cognitive theory (SCT). Emphasizes the role of cognitive processes in learning and in the regulation of people's behaviour.

Observational Learning

Besides directly experiencing consequences, people also learn by observing the behaviour of others. For instance, after experiencing just a couple of executive committee meetings, a newly promoted vice-president might look like an "old pro," bringing appropriate materials to the meeting, asking questions in an approved style, and so on. How can we account for such learning?

Observational learning is the process of observing and imitating the behaviour of others. With observational learning, learning occurs by observing or imagining the behaviour of others (models), rather than through direct personal experience.[56] Generally, observational learning involves examining the behaviour of others, seeing what consequences they experience, and thinking about what might happen if we act the same way. If we expect favourable consequences, we might imitate the behaviour. Thus, the new vice-president doubtless modelled his behaviour on that of the more experienced peers on the executive committee. But has reinforcement occurred here? It is *self-reinforcement* that occurs in the observational learning process. For one thing, it is reinforcing to acquire an understanding of others who are viewed positively. In addition, we are able to imagine that the reinforcers that the model experiences will come our way when we imitate his or her behaviour. Surely, this is why we imitate the behaviour of sports heroes and entertainers, a fact that advertisers capitalize on when they choose them to endorse products.

Observational learning. The process of observing and imitating the behaviour of others.

What kinds of models are likely to provoke the greatest degree of imitation? In general, attractive, credible, competent, high-status people stand a good chance of being imitated. In addition, it is important that the model's behaviour provoke consequences that are seen as positive and successful by the observer. You might recall that in the chapter-opening vignette senior executives at Economical acted as role models by sharing their personal wellness-related stories.

Finally, it helps if the model's behaviour is vivid and memorable—bores do not make good models.[57] In business schools, it is not unusual to find students who have developed philosophies or approaches that are modelled on credible, successful, high-profile business leaders. Popular examples include Microsoft's Bill Gates and former General Electric CEO Jack Welch, both of whom have been the object of extensive coverage in the business and popular press.

The extent of observational learning as a means of learning in organizations suggests that managers should pay more attention to the process. For one thing, managers who operate on a principle of "do as I say, not as I do" will find that what they do is more likely to be imitated, including undesirable behaviours such as expense account abuse. Also, in the

RESEARCH FOCUS

THE TRICKLE-DOWN EFFECTS OF ABUSIVE MANAGEMENT

There is strong evidence that abusive supervisors (e.g., telling a subordinate that his or her thoughts or feelings are stupid or putting the subordinate down in front of others) result in negative employee attitudes, behaviours, and psychological health. But why are supervisors abusive and does their abusive behaviour make their employees more likely to be abusive?

To find out, Mary Bardes Mawritz and colleagues tested a model of the trickle-down effects of abusive manager behaviour that suggests that abusive behaviour in organizations can flow downward from higher levels of management to lower level employees. The model predicts that employees will be negatively impacted by abusive manager behaviour through their direct supervisor's abusive behaviour.

The model and predictions are based on social cognitive theory and observational learning such that abusive behaviour at higher levels in an organization is role modelled by those at lower levels (i.e., supervisors and employees). In other words, supervisors role model the abusive behaviour of their managers and engage in similar abusive behaviour with their own employees. Employees then model their supervisor's abusive behaviour which leads to workgroup interpersonal deviance (i.e., employees' abusive behaviours directed at other organizational members).

The researchers also predicted that the effect of abusive supervisor behaviour on workgroup interpersonal deviance will be especially strong when the workgroup climate is hostile (a climate that is characterized by consistent acrimonious, antagonistic, and suspicious feelings within the work group). In a hostile climate, workgroup members feel envious, less trusting, and aggressive toward others.

Employees in different organizations completed a survey and asked four of their co-workers and their immediate supervisor to also complete the survey. As expected, abusive manager behaviour was positively related to abusive supervisor behaviour, and abusive supervisor behaviour was positively related to workgroup interpersonal deviance. In other words, supervisors who have managers who are abusive toward them are abusive toward their employees, who in turn treat each other in an abusive manner.

The results also indicated that employees were more likely to model their supervisor's abusive behaviour when the climate of their workgroup was hostile. When the workgroup climate was non-hostile it actually reversed the negative effects of abusive supervisor behaviour on workgroup interpersonal deviance. Thus, employees in a non-hostile work climate did not model their supervisor's abusive behaviour.

These results indicate that employees observe and imitate their supervisor's negative and abusive behaviours. Thus, managers and supervisors should act as positive role models because their behaviours, both positive and negative, will trickle down and be observed and imitated by their employees.

Source: Based on Bardes Mawritz, M., Mayer, D.M., Hoobler, J.M., Wayne, S.J., & Marinova, S.V. (2012). A trickle-down model of abusive supervision. *Personnel Psychology, 65*, 325–357.

absence of credible management models, workers might imitate dysfunctional peer behaviour if peers meet the criteria for strong models. For example, one study found that the antisocial behaviour of a work group was a significant predictor of an individual's antisocial workplace behaviour. Thus, individual's antisocial workplace behaviour can be shaped, in part, through the process of observation.[58] Furthermore, as described in the Research Focus: *The Trickle-Down Effects of Abusive Management*, abusive behaviour on the part of managers and supervisors can lead to abusive behaviour among employees. On a more positive note, well-designed performance appraisal and reward systems permit organizations to publicize the kind of organizational behaviour that should be learned and imitated.

Self-Efficacy Beliefs

Self-efficacy beliefs.
Beliefs people have about their ability to successfully perform a specific task.

While observational learning may have helped the vice-president learn how to behave in an executive committee meeting, you may have wondered what made him so confident. Was he not full of self-doubt and worried that he would fail? This belief is known as self-efficacy. **Self-efficacy beliefs** refer to beliefs people have about their ability to successfully perform

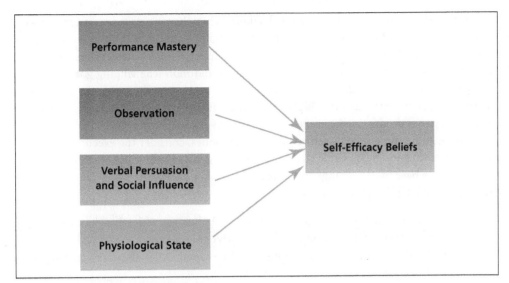

EXHIBIT 5
**Determinants of
self-efficacy beliefs.**

Go to MyManagementLab
to see an annotated
version of this figure.

a specific task. At this point, it is important to note the difference between task-specific self-efficacy and some of the general personality traits discussed earlier in the chapter. In particular, unlike self-esteem and general self-efficacy, which are general personality traits, self-efficacy is a task-specific cognitive appraisal of one's ability to perform a specific task. Thus, it is not a generalized personality trait. Furthermore, people can have different self-efficacy beliefs for different tasks. For example, the vice-president might have strong self-efficacy for conducting an executive committee meeting, but low self-efficacy for doing well in a course on organizational behaviour![59]

Because self-efficacy is a cognitive belief rather than a stable personality trait, it can be changed and modified in response to different sources of information. As shown in Exhibit 5, self-efficacy beliefs are influenced by one's experiences and success performing the task in question (performance mastery), observation of others performing the task, verbal persuasion and social influence, and one's physiological or emotional state. Thus, the self-efficacy of the vice-president could have been strengthened by observing the behaviour of others during meetings, by encouragement from peers that he would do a great job, and perhaps by his own sense of comfort and relaxation rather than feelings of anxiety and stress while attending meetings. Finally, his mastery displayed during the meeting is also likely to further strengthen his self-efficacy beliefs.

Self-efficacy beliefs are important because they influence the activities people choose to perform, the amount of effort and persistence they devote to a task, affective and stress reactions, and job performance.[60] In the case of the vice-president, his strong sense of self-efficacy beliefs obviously contributed to his ability to perform like an "old pro" at the meeting.

Self-Regulation

In much of this chapter we have been concerned with how organizations and individual managers can use learning principles to manage the behaviour of organizational members. However, according to social cognitive theory, employees can use learning principles to manage their *own* behaviour, making external control less necessary. This process is called **self-regulation**.[61]

How does self-regulation occur? You will recall that observational learning involved factors such as observation of models, imagination, imitation, and self-reinforcement. Individuals can use these and similar techniques in an intentional way to control their own behaviour. The basic process involves observing one's own behaviour (i.e., self-observation), comparing the behaviour with a standard (i.e., self-evaluation), and rewarding oneself if the behaviour meets the standard (i.e., self-reinforcement). A key part of the process is people's

Self-regulation.
The use of learning
principles to regulate one's
own behaviour.

pursuit of self-set goals that guide their behaviour. When there exists a discrepancy between one's goals and performance, individuals are motivated to modify their behaviour in the pursuit of goal attainment, a process known as *discrepancy reduction*. When individuals attain their goals, they are likely to set even higher and more challenging goals, a process known as *discrepancy production*. In this way, people continually engage in a process of setting goals in the pursuit of ever higher levels of performance. Thus, discrepancy reduction and discrepancy production lie at the heart of the self-regulatory process.[62]

To illustrate some specific self-regulation techniques, consider the executive who finds that she is taking too much work home to do in the evenings and over weekends. While her peers seem to have most evenings and weekends free, her own family is ready to disown her due to lack of attention! What can she do?[63]

- *Collect self-observation data.* This involves collecting objective data about one's own behaviour. For example, the executive might keep a log of phone calls and other interruptions for a few days if she suspects that these contribute to her inefficiency.

- *Observe models.* The executive might examine the time-management skills of her peers to find someone successful to imitate.

- *Set goals.* The executive might set specific short-term goals to reduce telephone interruptions and unscheduled personal visits, enlisting the aid of her assistant, and using self-observation data to monitor her progress. Longer-term goals might involve four free nights a week and no more than four hours of work on weekends.

- *Rehearse.* The executive might anticipate that she will have to educate her co-workers about her reduced availability. So as not to offend them, she might practise explaining the reason for her revised accessibility.

- *Reinforce oneself.* The executive might promise herself a weekend at the beach with her family the first time she gets her take-home workload down to her target level.

Research has found that self-regulation can improve learning and result in a change in behaviour. For example, one study showed how a self-regulation program was used to improve work attendance among unionized maintenance employees. Those who had used over half their sick leave were invited by the human resources department to participate in an eight-week program with the following features:

- Discussion of general reasons for use of sick leave. High on the list were transportation problems, family difficulties, and problems with supervisors and co-workers.

- Self-assessment of personal reasons for absence and development of personal coping strategies.

- Goal setting to engage in behaviours that should improve attendance (short-term goals) and to improve attendance by a specific amount (long-term goal).

- Self-observation using charts and diaries. Employees recorded their own attendance, reasons for missing work, and steps they took to get to work.

- Identification of specific reinforcers and punishers to be self-administered for reaching or not reaching goals.

Compared with a group of employees who did not attend the program, the employees who were exposed to the program achieved a significant improvement in attendance, and they also felt more confident (i.e., higher self-efficacy) that they would be able to come to work when confronted with various obstacles to attendance.[64] In another study, training in self-regulation was found to significantly improve the sales performance of a sample of insurance salespeople.[65] Self-regulation programs have been successful in changing a variety of work behaviours and are an effective method of training and learning.[66]

ORGANIZATIONAL LEARNING PRACTICES

LO

Describe the following organizational learning practices: *organizational behaviour modification, employee recognition programs, training and development programs,* and *career development.*

We began our discussion of learning by defining learning and describing learning content, and then we focused on theories of how people learn. In this final section, we review a number of organizational learning practices (including an application of operant learning called organizational behaviour modification), employee recognition programs, training and development programs, and career development.

Organizational Behaviour Modification

Most reinforcement occurs naturally, rather than as the result of a conscious attempt to manage behaviour. However, if you recall the wellness program at Economical described at the beginning of the chapter, you will notice that reinforcers (i.e., points and money) were used for specific health-related behaviours such as exercise and healthy eating. In other words, the reinforcers were made contingent on specific behaviours. This is an example of organizational behaviour modification.

Organizational behaviour modification (O.B. Mod) involves the systematic use of learning principles to influence organizational behaviour. For example, consider how one company used organizational behaviour modification through the reinforcement of safe working behaviour in a food-manufacturing plant. At first glance, accidents appeared to be chance events or wholly under the control of factors such as equipment failures. However, the researchers felt that accidents could be reduced if specific safe working practices could be identified and reinforced. These practices were identified with the help of past accident reports and advice from supervisors. Systematic observation of working behaviour indicated that employees followed safe practices only about 74 percent of the time. A brief slide show was prepared to illustrate safe versus unsafe job behaviours. Then, two reinforcers of safe practices were introduced into the workplace. The first consisted of a feedback chart that was conspicuously posted in the workplace to indicate the percentage of safe behaviours observers noted. This chart included the percentages achieved in observational sessions before the slide show, as well as those achieved every three days after the slide show. A second source of reinforcement was supervisors, who were encouraged to praise instances of safe performance that they observed. These interventions were successful in raising the percentage of safe working practices to around 97 percent almost immediately. The plant moved from last to first place in the company standings and received a safety plaque from the company "in recognition of successfully working 280 000 hours without a disabling injury" over a period of 10 months. (See Exhibit 6.)[67]

Organizational behaviour modification (O.B. Mod). The systematic use of learning principles to influence organizational behaviour.

Go to MyManagementLab to see an annotated version of this figure.

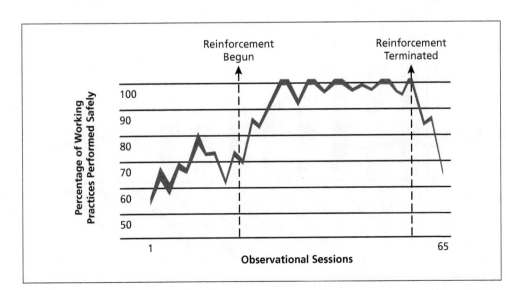

EXHIBIT 6 Percentage of safe working practices achieved with and without reinforcement.
Source: Adapted from Komaki, J., et al. (1978, August). A behavioral approach to occupational safety: Pinpointing and reinforcing safe performance in a food manufacturing plant. *Journal of Applied Psychology, 63* (4), 439. Copyright © 1978 by American Psychological Association. Adapted by permission.

In general, research supports the effectiveness of organizational behaviour modification programs. In addition to improvements in safety, O.B. Mod has also been found to have a positive effect on improving work attendance and task performance. The effects on task performance, however, tend to be stronger in manufacturing than in service organizations. As well, money, feedback, and social recognition have all been found to be effective forms of positive reinforcement. Although money has been found to have stronger effects on performance than social recognition and performance feedback, the use of all three together has the strongest effect on task performance. Research has also found that the effect of money on performance is greater when it is provided systematically through O.B. Mod compared to a routine pay-for-performance program.[68]

Employee Recognition Programs

Employee recognition programs. Formal organizational programs that publicly recognize and reward employees for specific behaviours.

A popular example of an organizational learning practice that uses positive reinforcement is employee recognition programs. **Employee recognition programs** are formal organizational programs that publicly recognize and reward employees for specific behaviours. Exhibit 7 shows some of the most popular types of employee recognition programs.

Many companies in Canada have some form of employee recognition program, and employees in the best companies to work for in Canada believe that they receive adequate recognition beyond compensation for their contributions and accomplishments. To be effective, however, a formal employee recognition program must specify (a) how a person will be recognized, (b) the type of behaviour being encouraged, (c) the manner of the public acknowledgement, and (d) a token or icon of the event for the recipient. A key part of an employee recognition program is public acknowledgement. Thus, a financial reward for good performance would not qualify as an employee recognition program if it was not accompanied by some form of public praise and recognition.[69]

Peer recognition programs. Formal programs in which employees can publicly acknowledge, recognize, and reward their co-workers for exceptional work and performance.

An increasing number of organizations have begun to implement a new kind of recognition program called peer recognition. **Peer recognition programs** are formal programs in which employees can publicly acknowledge, recognize, and reward their co-workers for exceptional work and performance. For example, at Ceridian Canada Ltd. employees can nominate co-workers for monthly prizes, quarterly cash awards, and the chance to win the annual President's Club Award, which includes a paid vacation to a holiday destination. Ceridian recognizes 28 "star" employees each quarter and gives each a $100 gift certificate. At year end, 15 are selected to go on an overseas trip with spouses and senior executives. IT/NET Ottawa Inc. has

EXHIBIT 7 Types of recognition programs.
Source: Trends in Employee Recognition/WorldatWork. (2008, August 11). Service awards most popular. *Canadian HR Reporter, 21* (14), 4.

Explore

Go to MyManagementLab to see an annotated version of this figure.

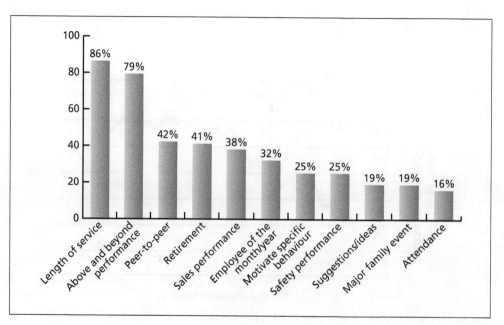

a peer-to-peer recognition program called "My Thanks," in which employees are encouraged to acknowledge co-workers' exceptional work by sending them a cash-valued gift certificate. The value of the certificate is determined by who is awarding it and it can be done any time and as often as employees choose to recognize a co-worker.[70] Before continuing, consider You Be the Manager: *Calgary International Airport's YYC Miles Recognition Program.*

Employee recognition programs have been found to result in a number of individual and organizational outcomes, including job satisfaction, performance and productivity, and lower turnover.[71] One study compared a public recognition program for improving work attendance with several other interventions. Employees with perfect attendance for an entire month had their names posted with a gold star for that month. At the end of each quarter, employees with no more than two absences received a personal card notifying and congratulating them. In addition, at the end of the year there was a plant-wide meeting to recognize good attendance, and small engraved mementos were awarded to employees who had perfect attendance during the entire year. The results indicated that employees had favourable perceptions of the program and that the program resulted in a decrease in absenteeism.[72] A survey of 26 000 employees in 31 organizations in the United States found that companies that invest the most in recognition programs have more than triple the profits of those that invest the least.[73]

Training and Development Programs

Training and development is one of the most common types of formal learning in organizations. Training refers to planned organizational activities that are designed to facilitate knowledge and skill acquisition to change behaviour and improve performance on one's current job; development focuses on future job responsibilities.[74] Employees learn a variety of skills by attending formal training and development programs. In addition to teaching employees technical skills required to perform their jobs, training and development programs also teach employees non-technical skills such as how to work in teams, how to provide excellent customer service, and ways to understand and appreciate cultural diversity.

Effective training and development programs include many of the principles of learning described earlier in the chapter, such as positive reinforcement, feedback, observational

Training and development. Training is planned organizational activities that are designed to facilitate knowledge and skill acquisition to change behaviour and improve performance on one's current job; development focuses on future job responsibilities.

YOU BE THE MANAGER

Calgary International Airport's YYC Miles Recognition Program

The Calgary Airport Authority is a not-for-profit corporation that is responsible for the management, maintenance, operation, and development of Calgary International Airport and Springbank Airport.

Several years ago, a volunteer employee committee developed a recognition program in response to a low score to a question on an employee engagement survey. The low score was for the statement, "I feel my contributions are recognized and valued."

According to Cynthia Tremblay, Senior Director of Human Resources at the Calgary Airport Authority, "We did some employee focus groups (asking), 'What can we do to help address this issue?' and a recognition program was the idea that came out of that. It is very much employee-driven," she says.

The program, called the YYC Miles recognition program—based on the Calgary airport locator code—allows employees to recognize their co-workers for going above and beyond their role, such as helping a confused passenger find his/her way around the airport.

When the program was launched, the employee committee made a promotional video based on the TV show *The Office* and showed it to all employees at a company retreat. To make sure they are continually promoting the program, the committee writes regular articles about it for the company newsletter and mentions it in meetings.

What do you think of the Calgary Airport's YYC Miles recognition program? You be the manager.

Employees at the Calgary International Airport can recognize their co-workers for going above and beyond their role.

Questions

1. How would you design the YYC Miles peer recognition program if you were using the principles of operant learning theory?

2. How should peer recognition programs be designed to be most effective?

To find learn more about the YYC miles recognition program, see The Manager's Notebook.

Sources: Based on Silliker, A. (2011, October 10). Calgary airport's recognition program—YYC Miles—takes flight. *Canadian HR Reporter, 24* (17), 19; information on Calgary International Airport (www.calgaryairport.com).

Behaviour modelling training (BMT). One of the most widely used and effective methods of training, involving five steps based on the observational learning component of social cognitive theory.

learning, strengthening employees' self-efficacy beliefs, and self-regulation. One of the most widely used and effective methods of training is **behaviour modelling training** (BMT), which is based on the observational learning component of social cognitive theory and involves the following steps:[75]

- Describe to trainees a set of well-defined behaviours (skills) to be learned.
- Provide a model or models displaying the effective use of those behaviours.
- Provide opportunities for trainees to practise using those behaviours.
- Provide feedback and social reinforcement to trainees following practice.
- Take steps to maximize the transfer of those behaviours to the job.

Many organizations have used behavioural modelling training to develop supervisory, communications, sales, and customer service skills. A review of BMT research concluded that it has a positive effect on learning, skills, and job behaviour. The effects on behaviour were greatest when trainees were instructed to set goals and when rewards and sanctions were used in the trainees' work environment.[76] Training has been found to increase trainees' self-efficacy in addition to having a positive effect on learning and job behaviour.[77]

Career Development

Career development is an ongoing process in which individuals progress through a series of stages that consist of a unique set of issues, themes, and tasks. This usually involves a career planning and career management component. Career planning involves the assessment of an individual's interests, skills, and abilities in order to develop goals and career plans. Career management involves taking the necessary steps to achieve an individual's goals and career plans. This often involves special assignments and activities that are designed to assist employees in their career development.[78]

Given the increasing emphasis on and importance of continuous and lifelong learning, many organizations now have career development programs. For example, Dun & Bradstreet Canada, a business information services company, has a career development program for all of its employees. Employees have a file called a Leadership Action Plan that lists their strengths and career aspirations as well as a plan on how they will achieve their goals. The file is reviewed by a supervisor four times a year. In addition, an intranet site is available to help employees perform career assessments and access information about job opportunities within the company.[79]

When TD Bank Financial Group surveyed its employees, it found that skills development and career development were very important factors for them. As a result, the company decided to invest more in employee career management and created a website to help employees with all aspects of managing their careers. The Career Advisor site is a comprehensive tool that enables employees to determine how best to develop themselves and overcome career challenges. Employees have access to a combination of interactive diagnostic instruments, personal reports, advice, tools, and action planning exercises.[80]

Career development. An ongoing process in which individuals progress through a series of stages that consist of a unique set of issues, themes, and tasks.

THE MANAGER'S NOTEBOOK

Calgary International Airport's YYC Miles Recognition Program

1. According to operant learning theory, rewards should be contingent on specific behaviours that are of interest to the organization, such as attendance, innovation, or productivity. This is especially important in a peer recognition program because employees are responsible for choosing co-workers for recognition, and such choices should not simply be based on who is most liked or who has the most friends in the company. The program also has to consider individual preferences for reinforcers. Rewards will not have a reinforcing effect if they are not desired by employees. Therefore, it is important that a variety of rewards be available to suit individual preferences. With respect to the YYC Miles program, each employee is given 1000 points per month to recognize co-workers. When an employee sees a co-worker go above and beyond his role, she fills out a form online saying why she's recognizing him and how many points he is receiving—which is completely at the discretion of the employee. One point is equivalent to one cent and points can be accumulated for a wide range of gifts from the YYC Miles online catalogue, starting at 1250 points for a movie ticket all the way up to 450 000 points for an LCD TV.

2. Peer recognition programs should be designed in the same manner as formal employee recognition programs. To be effective, they should specify (a) how a person will be recognized, (b) the type of behaviour being encouraged, (c) the manner of the public acknowledgement, and (d) a token or icon of the event for the recipient. Because the employee's peers are responsible for deciding who will be recognized, careful attention should be given to how this is done to ensure that the process is fair and that the expected behaviour has been demonstrated. With respect to the YYC Miles program, the committee monitors the program to make sure people are nominating each other for appropriate things. When filling out a recognition form, employees need to specify which of five pillars of excellence the co-worker displayed—dedicated people, responsible investing, great partnerships, operational efficiency, or Western hospitality.

LEARNING OBJECTIVES CHECKLIST

1 *Personality* is the relatively stable set of psychological characteristics that influences the way we interact with our environment. It has more impact on behaviour in weak situations than in strong situations.

2 According to the *dispositional approach*, stable individual characteristics influence people's attitudes and behaviours. The *situational approach* argues that characteristics in the work environment influence people's attitudes and behaviour. The *interactionist approach* posits that organizational behaviour is a function of both dispositions and the situation. According to *trait activation theory*, traits lead to certain behaviours only when the situation makes the need for that trait salient.

3 The Five-Factor Model consists of five basic dimensions of personality: *extraversion, emotional stability/neuroticism, agreeableness, conscientiousness*, and *openness to experience*. Research has found that the Big Five are related to job performance, motivation, job satisfaction, and career outcomes.

4 *Locus of control* refers to individuals' beliefs about the location of the factors that control their behaviour. High internals believe that the opportunity to control their own behaviour resides within themselves, while high externals believe that external forces determine their behaviour. People who have an internal locus of control are more satisfied with their jobs, earn more money, and achieve higher organizational positions. *Self-monitoring* is the extent to which people observe and regulate how they appear and behave in social settings and relationships. High self-monitors have good communication skills and persuasive abilities and are more likely to change employers and locations and to receive more promotions than individuals who are low self-monitors. *Self-esteem* is the degree

to which a person has a positive self-evaluation. People with high self-esteem tend to make more fulfilling career decisions, to exhibit higher job satisfaction and job performance, and to be generally more resilient to the strains of everyday worklife.

5 People who are high on *positive affectivity* experience positive emotions and moods and tend to view the world in a positive light, including themselves and other people. People who are high on *negative affectivity* experience negative emotions and moods and tend to view the world in a negative light. *Proactive personality* is a stable personal disposition that reflects a tendency to take personal initiative across a range of activities and situations and to effect positive change in one's environment. *General self-efficacy* (GSE) is a general trait that refers to an individual's belief in his or her ability to perform successfully in a variety of challenging situations. *Core self-evaluations* refer to a broad personality concept that consists of more specific traits.

6 *Learning* occurs when practice or experience leads to a relatively permanent change in behaviour potential. The content of learning in organizations consists of practical, intrapersonal and interpersonal skills, and cultural awareness.

7 *Operant learning* occurs as a function of the consequences of behaviour. If some behaviour is occurring regularly or increasing in probability, you can assume that it is being reinforced. If the reinforcer is added to the situation following the behaviour, it is a *positive reinforcer*. If the reinforcer is removed from the situation following the behaviour, it is a *negative reinforcer*.

8 Behaviour is learned quickly when it is reinforced immediately and continuously. Behaviour tends

9 If some behaviour decreases in probability, you can assume that it is being either extinguished or punished. If the behaviour is followed by no observable consequence, it is being extinguished; that is, some reinforcer that was maintaining the behaviour has been terminated. If the behaviour is followed by the application of some unpleasant consequence, it is being punished.

10 According to social cognitive theory, people have the cognitive capacity to regulate and control their own thoughts, feelings, motivation, and actions. The main components of social cognitive theory are observational learning, self-efficacy beliefs, and self-regulation. *Observational learning* is the process of imitating others. Models are most likely to be imitated when they are high in status, attractive, competent, credible, successful, and vivid. *Self-efficacy beliefs* refer to the belief that one can successfully perform a specific task and is influenced by performance mastery, observation of others performing the task, verbal persuasion and social influence, and physiological arousal. *Self-regulation* occurs when people use learning principles to manage their own behaviour, thus reducing the need for external control. Aspects of self-regulation include collecting self-observation data, observing models, goal setting, rehearsing, and using self-reinforcement.

11 Organizational learning practices include organizational behaviour modification, employee recognition programs, training and development programs, and career development. *Organizational behaviour modification* is the systematic use of learning principles to influence organizational behaviour. Companies have successfully used it to improve employees' attendance, task performance, and workplace safety. *Employee recognition programs* are formal organizational programs that publicly recognize and reward employees for specific behaviours. *Training programs* involve planned organizational activities that are designed to facilitate knowledge and skill acquisition and to change behaviour and improve performance on one's current job, while *development* focuses on future job responsibilities. *Career development* is an ongoing process in which individuals progress through a series of stages that consist of a unique set of issues, themes, and tasks. It involves a career planning and career management component.

DISCUSSION QUESTIONS

1. Consider the relevance of the dispositional, situational, and interactionist approaches to your own behaviour. Describe examples of your behaviour in a school or work situation that demonstrate each perspective of organizational behaviour.

2. Suppose that you are the manager of two employees, one who has an internal locus of control and another who has an external locus of control. Describe the leadership tactics that you would use with each employee. Contrast the management styles that you would employ for employees with high versus low self-esteem.

3. Consider some examples of behaviour that you repeat fairly regularly (such as studying or going to work every morning). What are the positive and negative reinforcers that maintain this behaviour?

4. We pointed out that managers frequently resort to punishing ineffective behaviour. What are some of the practical demands of the typical manager's job that lead to this state of affairs?

5. Discuss a situation that you have observed in which the use of punishment was ineffective in terminating some unwanted behaviour. Why was punishment ineffective in this case? What would have made it more effective?

6. Describe a situation in which you think an employer could use organizational behaviour modification and an employee recognition program to improve or correct employee behaviour. Can you anticipate any dangers in using these approaches?

7. A supervisor in a textile factory observes that one of her employees is violating a safety rule

that could result in severe injury. What combination of reinforcement, punishment, and extinction could she use to correct this behaviour? What does social cognitive theory suggest that she do to correct the behaviour?

8. Describe a job in which you think an employee recognition program might be an effective means for changing and improving employee behaviour. Explain how you would design the program and how you would use principles from operant learning theory and social cognitive theory.

9. Do you think that organizations should base their hiring decisions on applicants' personality? What are the advantages and disadvantages of doing this? If an organization were to do this, what personality characteristics do you think they should focus on when assessing and choosing applicants?

10. Refer to the Research Focus: *CEO Personality and Firm Performance* and consider the relationship between the Big Five personality characteristics and strategic flexibility. Why do you think conscientiousness was the only trait negatively related to strategic flexibility given that it has been found to be the best predictor of job performance among the Big Five? Why are openness to experience, extraversion, and emotional stability positively related, and why is medium agreeableness better for strategic flexibility than high or low agreeableness?

11. Employee of the month (EOM) programs are one of the most popular forms of recognition in organizations. However, there is some evidence that such programs are not effective and can even have detrimental effects such as sabotage and unhealthy competition. Based on the material presented in this chapter, why do you think that the typical EOM program is not effective, and how should EOM programs be designed to make them more effective?

INTEGRATIVE DISCUSSION QUESTIONS

1. Use what you know about Mintzberg's managerial roles and consider how personality might be a factor in how effectively a manager performs each role. Discuss the relationships among the Big Five personality dimensions, locus of control, self-monitoring, self-esteem, proactive personality, and general self-efficacy with each of the managerial roles.

2. Discuss how each of the organizational learning practices described in the chapter can be used by organizations to deal effectively with contemporary management concerns.

ON-THE-JOB CHALLENGE QUESTION

Playing Hooky

In the summer of 2012, a *Toronto Star* investigation reported that construction and maintenance workers who were supposed to be working at Toronto public schools were spending their mornings at Tim Hortons, drinking in bars, and even kissing in cars. One worker was spotted delivering pamphlets to houses and offering to perform odd jobs for pay on school board time. The workers submitted time sheets and were paid their wages as if they had put in a full day's work.

In some cases, workers have signed in to work at a school and then announced they had to go get "parts" and were later discovered by Toronto District School Board officials drinking in a bar. In another case, a male worker was found in a board vehicle with a female "fooling around," according to a board source. In the case of the pamphlets, board sources say a worker was using board time to distribute flyers advertising his services for odd jobs, apparently using board equipment.

How can we explain these behaviours? Based on what you know about learning theory, explain why workers engaged in these inappropriate behaviours during work hours and why they were not doing what they were supposed to be doing. What do you think needs to be done to stop these behaviours and increase the probability that workers will do what they are supposed to be doing?

Source: Based on Donovan, K., & Welsh, M. (2012, June 22). School workers playing hooky. *Toronto Star*, A1, A4.

EXPERIENTIAL EXERCISE

Proactive Personality Scale

Do you have a proactive personality? To find out, answer the 17 questions below as frankly and honestly as possible using the following response scale:

1–Disagree very much

2–Disagree moderately

3–Disagree slightly

4–Neither agree or disagree

5–Agree slightly

6–Agree moderately

7–Agree very much

____ 1. I am constantly on the lookout for new ways to improve my life.

____ 2. I feel driven to make a difference in my community, and maybe the world.

____ 3. I tend to let others take the initiative to start new projects.

____ 4. Wherever I have been, I have been a powerful force for constructive change.

____ 5. I enjoy facing and overcoming obstacles to my ideas.

____ 6. Nothing is more exciting than seeing my ideas turn into reality.

____ 7. If I see something I don't like, I fix it.

____ 8. No matter what the odds, if I believe in something I will make it happen.

____ 9. I love being a champion for my ideas, even against others' opposition.

____ 10. I excel at identifying opportunities.

____ 11. I am always looking for better ways to do things.

____ 12. If I believe in an idea, no obstacle will prevent me from making it happen.

____ 13. I love to challenge the status quo.

____ 14. When I have a problem, I tackle it head-on.

____ 15. I am great at turning problems into opportunities.

____ 16. I can spot a good opportunity long before others can.

____ 17. If I see someone in trouble, I help out in any way I can.

Source: Bateman, T.S., & Crant, J.M. (1993). The proactive component of organizational behavior: A measure and correlates. *Journal of Organizational Behavior, 14*, 103–118. © 1993 John Wiley & Sons Limited. Reprinted with permission.

Scoring and Interpretation

You have just completed the Proactive Personality Scale developed by Thomas Bateman and J. Michael Crant.

To obtain your score, first subtract your response to question 3 from 8. For example, if you gave a response of 7 to question 3, give yourself a 1 (8 minus 7). Then add up your scores to all 17 items. Your total should be somewhere between 17 and 119. The higher you scored, the more proactive your personality is—you feel that you can change things in your environment.

The average score of 134 first-year MBA students with full-time work experience was 90.7. Thus, these people tended to see themselves as very proactive. In this research, people with a proactive personality tended to report more extracurricular and service activities and major personal achievements that involve making constructive changes to the world around them.

General Self-Efficacy

Want to learn about your general self-efficacy? Answer the eight questions below as frankly and honestly as possible using the following response scale:

1–Strongly disagree

2–Disagree

3–Neither agree nor disagree

4–Agree

5–Strongly agree

6–Agree moderately

____ 1. I will be able to achieve most of the goals that I have set for myself.

____ 2. When facing difficult tasks, I am certain that I will accomplish them.

____ 3. In general, I think that I can obtain outcomes that are important to me.

____ 4. I believe I can succeed at most any endeavour to which I set my mind.

____ 5. I will be able to successfully overcome many challenges.

____ 6. I am confident that I can perform effectively on many different tasks.

____ 7. Compared to other people, I can do most tasks very well.

____ 8. Even when things are tough, I can perform quite well.

Source: Chen, G., Gully, S.M., & Eden, D. (2001). Validation of a new general self-efficacy scale. *Organizational Research Methods, 4*, 62–83.

Scoring and Interpretation

You have just completed the New General Self-Efficacy Scale developed by Gilad Chen, Stanley M. Gully, and Dov Eden. To obtain your general self-efficacy (GSE) score, add up your scores to all 8 items and divide by 8. Your score should be somewhere between 1 and 5. The higher your score, the greater your general self-efficacy.

GSE enables individuals to effectively adapt to novel and adverse environments and can help to explain motivation and performance in a variety of work contexts. The average score of 323 undergraduate students enrolled in several upper-level psychology courses was 3.87.

The Core Self-Evaluations Scale (CSES)

To find out about your core self-evaluations, answer the 12 questions below as frankly and honestly as possible using the following response scale:

1–Strongly disagree

2–Disagree

3–Neither agree nor disagree

4–Agree

5–Strongly agree

____ 1. I am confident I get the success I deserve in life.

____ 2. Sometimes I feel depressed.

____ 3. When I try, I generally succeed.

____ 4. Sometimes when I fail I feel worthless.

____ 5. I complete tasks successfully.

____ 6. Sometimes, I do not feel in control of my work.

____ 7. Overall, I am satisfied with myself.

____ 8. I am filled with doubts about my competence.

____ 9. I determine what will happen in my life.

____ 10. I do not feel in control of my success in my career.

____ 11. I am capable of coping with most of my problems.

____ 12. There are times when things look pretty bleak and hopeless to me.

Source: Judge, T.A., Erez, A., Bono, J.E., & Thoresen, C.J. (2003). The core self-evaluations scale: Development of a measure. *Personnel Psychology, 56,* 303–313.

Scoring and Interpretation

You have just completed the Core Self-Evaluations Scale (CSES) developed by Timothy Judge, Amir Erez, Joyce Bono, and Carl Thoresen. To obtain your score, first subtract your response to questions 2, 4, 6, 8, 10, and 12 from 6. For example, if you gave a response of 1 to question 2, give yourself a 5 (6 minus 1). Then add up your scores to all 12 items and divide by 12. Your score should be somewhere between 1 and 5. The higher your score, the higher your core self-evaluations.

Core self-evaluations (CSE) are a broad personality concept that reflect evaluations people hold about themselves and their self-worth. Core self-evaluations consist of self-esteem, general self-efficacy, locus of control, and neuroticism. The average score of undergraduate students in two studies was 3.83 and 3.78. Scores on the CSES have been found to be positively related to job satisfaction, job performance, and life satisfaction.

Questions

To facilitate class discussion and your understanding of proactive personality, GSE, and CSE, form a small group with several other members of the class and consider the following questions:

1. Each group member should present their proactive personality, GSE, and CSE scores. Next, consider the extent to which each member has been involved in extracurricular and service activities and in personal accomplishments that involved making changes to their circumstances and how they have adapted to novel and difficult situations. Each member should also consider how satisfied they are with a current or previous job and how satisfied they are with their life (1 = not satisfied at all to 5 = very satisfied). Have students with higher proactive personality scores been more involved in extracurricular and service activities? What about personal accomplishments and constructive change? Have students with higher GSE scores been more effective in adapting to novel and difficult situations? And are students with higher CSE scores more satisfied with their current or a previous job and are they more satisfied with their life? (Alternatively, members of the class may write their proactive personality, GSE, and CSE scores, extracurricular and service activities, personal accomplishments, experiences adapting to novel and difficult situations, and job and life satisfaction on a piece of paper and hand it in to the instructor. The instructor can then write the responses on the board for class discussion.)

2. When are a proactive personality, GSE, and CSE most likely to be beneficial? When are they least likely to be beneficial?

3. Do you think organizations should hire people based on whether they have a proactive personality and on their GSE and CSE scores? What are the implications of this?

4. Based on your proactive personality, GSE, and CSE scores, what have you learned about yourself and your behaviour in different situations?

5. How can your knowledge of your proactive personality, GSE, and CSE scores help you at school and at work? What can you do to become more proactive? What can you do to strengthen your GSE and CSE?

CASE INCIDENT

Courier Cats

To stay competitive, many organizations regularly upgrade their computer technology. This was the case for Courier Cats, a small but profitable courier firm. To improve the delivery and tracking of parcels, the company decided to invest in new software. It was expected that the new software would not only allow the company to expand its business but also improve the quality of service. Because the new software was much more complex and sophisticated than what the company had been using, employees had to attend a one-day training program to learn how to use the new system. However, six months after the system was implemented, many employees were still using the old system. Some employees refused to use the new software, while others did not think they would ever be able to learn how to use it.

1. Why do you think that the employees did not use the new software?

2. Can personality explain why some employees refused to use the new software? What personality characteristics are most relevant for explaining why some employees refused to use the new software while others had no trouble learning and using it?

3. What are some of the implications that stem from operant learning theory and social cognitive theory for increasing the probability that the employees will use the new software? What do you recommend for improving the use of the new software?

CASE STUDY

Howe 2 Ski Stores

The Howe 2 Ski Stores are a chain of three ski and windsurfing shops located in the suburbs of a large western coastal city. Maria Howe, a ski enthusiast and business major, opened the first store 10 years ago after her university graduation with financial backing from her family and several friends. From its inception, the Howe 2 store was intended to provide state-of-the-art equipment and clothing for skiers at all ski levels, from beginner to champion. It was to be staffed by employees who were themselves advanced skiers and could provide expert advice on the choice of clothing and equipment, and it was intended to have a quick response time that would permit the last-minute purchase of equipment and clothing to a ski trip.

Howe originally drew from a pool of skiing friends and fellow students to staff the stores and still prefers to hire part-time employees with skiing expertise who might leave in a year over more stable, full-time employees with less expertise and interest in the sport. Whether administrative staff, cashiers, clerks, or moulders (employees who fit bindings to skis), employees were encouraged to keep up to date on the latest skiing equipment and trends, attend ski vendor shows, try out demo equipment, and give feedback on the store's inventory to help provide the highest quality equipment and advice for the customer. Suggestion boxes were placed in the store, and Howe herself regularly collected, read, and acted upon the suggestions made by the clerks and customers. She developed special advertising campaigns to build an image for the nearby slopes to increase the market. As the business grew, Howe even added a line of rental equipment to lower the costs and encourage people to try the sport.

Although profits grew irregularly due to weather effects and the faddish nature of the sport, Howe's efforts paid off in the long term, and within four years business had grown sufficiently to permit the opening of a second Howe 2 Ski Store in another suburb about 16 kilometres from the location of the first store. To even out sales across the year, about six years ago Howe took a chance on the growing windsurfing market and the coastal location and added a line of equipment for this sport. This expanded market has enabled her to smooth out the number of sales occurring throughout the year.

Three years ago, Howe was able to open a third store, located within a 25-kilometre radius of the other two locations. Although managers have been hired to run each of the stores and the total number of employees has grown to 65, Howe's basic strategy has remained the same—high quality, state-of-the-art products, a knowledgeable staff, and quick response time. Profits from the stores have continued to grow, although at a slower rate. Competition from other ski stores has also increased noticeably within the last two years.

The threat of increased competition has been exacerbated by signs that employee productivity has begun to slide. Last year, there were eight occasions where expensive ski orders were not delivered in time for the customer's ski vacation. Although Howe used a variety of manoeuvres to retain the customers' patronage (e.g., paying for the customer to rent equipment of equivalent quality, arranging express delivery of the equipment to the customer as soon as it was received at the store, and lowering the price of the equipment), the costs of these late orders were high. She realized that word of mouth about these kinds of incidents could significantly damage the store's reputation. Furthermore, at least 15 percent of all ski orders were delivered more than two days late, even though customers did not miss a trip or vacation as a result.

In an attempt to respond to these difficulties, Howe instituted a merit performance system for the moulders (employees who fit the binding to skis). Although productivity seemed to increase for a while, waves of discontent popped up all over the stores. The moulders felt that their merit ratings were inaccurate because the store managers could not observe them working much of the time. Further, they argued that their performance levels would have been much higher had not other employees interrupted them with questions about appropriate bindings or failed to clearly identify the appropriate equipment on the sales orders. Other employees also complained because they were not given the opportunity for merit pay. The buyers, who visit ski shows, examine catalogues, and talk with sales representatives to decide on the inventory, argued that their work was essential for high sales figures and quality equipment. Sales clerks claimed that their in-depth familiarity with an extensive inventory and their sales skills were essential to increasing sales. They also noted their important role in negotiating a delivery date that the moulders could meet. Similar arguments were made by the people in the credit office who arranged for short-term financing if necessary and the cashiers who verified costs and checked credit card approvals. Even the stockers noted that the store would be in a bad way if they did not locate the correct equipment in a warehouse full of inventory and deliver it in a timely manner to the moulders.

Howe had to concede that the employees were correct on many of these points, so she suspended the merit plan at the end of the ski season and promised to re-evaluate its fairness. Even more convincing were several indications that productivity problems were not limited to moulder employees. Complaints about customer service increased 20 percent during the year. Several customers noted that they were allowed to stand, merchandise in hand, waiting for a clerk to help them, while clerks engaged in deep conversations among themselves. Although Howe mentioned this to employees in the stores when she visited and asked the store managers to discuss it in staff meetings, the complaints continued. A record number of "as is" skis were sold at the end of the season sale because they were damaged in the warehouse or the store or by the moulders. The closing inventory revealed that 20 percent of the rental equipment had been lost or seriously damaged without resulting charges to the renters because records were poorly maintained. Regular checks of the suggestion boxes in the store revealed fewer and fewer comments. Although less extreme, similar problems occurred in windsurfing season. Employees just didn't seem to notice these problems or, worse, didn't seem to care.

Howe was very bothered by all these factors and felt they could not be attributed to the growth of the business alone. She knew it would be impossible to maintain her competitive position with these events occurring.

Source: From NKOMO/MCAFEE/QUARRIE. Applications in Human Resource Management, 1E. © 2007 Nelson Education Ltd. Reproduced by permission. www.cengage.com/permissions

QUESTIONS

1. What are the main problems occurring in the Howe 2 Ski Stores? To what extent are the problems due to personality and characteristics of the work environment?

2. What behaviours need to be maintained or increased, and what behaviours should be reduced or eliminated?

3. What do you think of Maria Howe's attempt to respond to the difficulties in the stores? Use operant learning theory and social cognitive theory to explain the effects of her merit performance system. Why wasn't it more effective?

4. What do you think Maria Howe should do to respond to the difficulties in the stores? Refer to operant learning theory and social cognitive theory in answering this question.

5. What organizational learning practices might be effective for changing employee behaviours? Consider the potential of organizational behaviour modification, employee recognition programs, and training and development programs. Explain how you would implement each of these and their potential effectiveness.

6. What advice would you give Maria Howe on how to address the problems in her stores? Should she pay more attention to the personalities of the people she hires and/or should she make changes to the work environment? What employees and what behaviours should she focus on? Explain your answer.

REFERENCES

1. Hubbard, J. (2011, January 31). From awareness to action: Employee wellness. *Canadian HR Reporter, 24*(2), 32; Smith, B. (2011, April 18). TEIG shares wellness program success. *Benefits Canada*, www.benefitscanada.com; Freifeld, L. (2011, January/February). TEIG locks in on leadership. *Training, 48*(1), 34-39.

2. Dobson, S. (2012, February 13). Revving up interest. *Canadian HR Reporter, 25*(3), 13, 18.

3. George, J. M. (1992). The role of personality in organizational life: Issues and evidence. *Journal of Management, 18*, 185–213; Mount, M. K., & Barrick, M. R. (1995). The big five personality dimensions: Implications for research and practice in human resources management. In K. M. Rowland & G. Ferris (Eds.), *Research in personnel and human resources management* (Vol. 13, 153–200). Greenwich, CT: JAI Press.

4. George, 1992; Weiss, H. M., & Adler, S. (1984). Personality and organizational behavior. In B. M. Staw & L. L. Cummings (Eds.), *Research in organizational behavior* (Vol. 6, 1–50). Greenwich, CT: JAI Press.

5. Adler, S., & Weiss, H. M. (1988). Recent developments in the study of personality and organizational behavior. In C. L. Cooper & I. Robertson (Eds.), *International review of industrial and organizational psychology*. New York: Wiley.

6. Tett, R. P., & Burnett, D. D. (2003). A personality trait-based interactionist model of job performance. *Journal of Applied Psychology, 88*, 500–517.

7. Moses, S. (1991, November). Personality tests come back in I/O. *APA Monitor*, 9.

8. Mount & Barrick, 1995.

9. Digman, J. M. (1990). Personality structure: Emergence of the five-factor model. *Annual Review of Psychology, 41*, 417–440; Hogan, R. T. (1991). Personality and personality measurement. In M. D. Dunette & L. M. Hough (Eds.), *Handbook of industrial and organizational psychology* (2nd ed., Vol. 2). Palo Alto, CA: Consulting Psychologists Press; Barrick, M. R., & Mount, M. K. (1991). The big five personality dimensions and job performance: A meta-analysis. *Personnel Psychology, 44*, 1–26; Barrick, M. R., Mount, M. K., & Judge, T. A. (2001). Personality and performance at the beginning of the new millennium: What do we know and where do we go next? *International Journal of Selection and Assessment, 9*, 9–30; Barrick, M. R., Mount, M. K., & Gupta, R. (2003). Meta-analysis of the relationship between the five-factor model of personality and Holland's occupational types. *Personnel Psychology, 56*, 45–74; Ng, T. W. H., Eby, L. T., Sorensen, K. L., & Feldman, D. C. (2005). Predictors of objective and subjective career success: A meta-analysis. *Personnel Psychology, 58*, 367–408.

10. Judge, T. A., Higgins, C. A., Thorensen, C. J., & Barrick, M. R. (1999). The Big Five personality traits, general mental ability, and career success across the life span. *Personnel Psychology, 52*, 621–652.

11. Chiaburu, D. S., Oh, I., Berry, C. M., Li, N., & Gardner, R. G. (2011). The five-factor model of personality traits and organizational citizenship behaviors: A meta-analysis. *Journal of Applied Psychology, 96*, 1140–1166; Hough, L. M., Eaton, N. K., Dunnette, M. D., Kamp, J. D., & McCloy, R. A. (1990). Criterion-related validities of personality constructs and the effect of response distortion on those validities. *Journal of Applied Psychology, 75*, 581–595; Tett, R. P., Jackson, D. N., & Rothstein, M. (1991). Personality measures as predictors of job performance: A meta-analytic review. *Personnel Psychology, 44*, 703–742.

12. Barrick & Mount, 1991; Ones, D. S., Dilchert, S., Viswesvaran, C., & Judge, T. A. (2007). In support of personality assessment in organizational settings. *Personnel Psychology, 60*, 995–1027; Barrick, M. R., Mount, M. K., & Judge, T. A. (2001).

13. Ones, D. S., Viswesvaran, C., & Schmidt, F. L. (1993). Comprehensive meta-analysis of integrity test validities: Findings and implications for personnel selection and theories of job performance. *Journal of Applied Psychology, 78*, 679–703.

14. Judge, Higgins, Thorensen, & Barrick, 1999.

15. Judge, T. A., & Ilies, R. (2002). Relationship of personality to performance motivation: A meta-analytic review. *Journal of Applied Psychology, 87*, 797–807.

16. Judge, T. A., Heller, D., & Mount, M. K. (2002). Five-factor model of personality and job satisfaction: A meta-analysis. *Journal of Applied Psychology, 87*, 530–541; Morgeson, F. P., Reider, M. H., & Campion, M. A. (2005). Selecting individuals in team settings: The importance of social skills, personality characteristics, and team work knowledge. *Personnel Psychology, 58*, 583–611.

17. Kanfer, R., Wanberg, C. R., & Kantrowitz, T. M. (2001). Job search and employment: A personality-motivational analysis and meta-analytic review. *Journal of Applied Psychology, 86*, 837–855.

18. Judge, Higgins, Thorensen, & Barrick, 1999.

19. Rotter, J. B. (1966). Generalized expectancies for internal versus external controls of reinforcement. *Psychological Monographs, 80* (Whole no. 609).

20. Szilagyi, A. D., & Sims, H. P., Jr. (1975). Locus of control and expectancies across multiple organizational levels. *Journal of Applied Psychology, 60*, 638–640.

21. Szilagyi, A. D., Sims, H. P., Jr., & Keller, R. T. (1976). Role dynamics, locus of control, and employee attitudes and behavior. *Academy of Management Journal, 19*, 259–276.

22. Andrisani, P. J., & Nestel, G. (1976). Internal-external control as contributor to and outcome of work experience. *Journal of Applied Psychology, 61*, 156–165.

23. Wang, Q., Bowling, N. A., & Eschleman, K. J. (2010). A meta-analytic examination of work and general locus of control. *Journal of Applied Psychology, 95*, 761–768. For evidence on stress and locus of control, see Anderson, C. R. (1977). Locus of control, coping behaviors, and performance in a stress setting: A longitudinal study. *Journal of Applied Psychology, 62*, 446–451. For evidence on career planning, see Thornton, G. C., III. (1978). Differential effects of career planning on internals and externals. *Personnel Psychology, 31*, 471–476.

24. Snyder, M. (1987). *Public appearances/private realities: The psychology of self-monitoring*. New York: W. H. Freeman; Gangestad, S. W., & Snyder, M. (2000). Self-monitoring: Appraisal and reappraisal. *Psychological Bulletin, 126*(4), 530–555.

25. Snyder, 1987; Gangestad & Snyder, 2000.

26. Day, D. V., Schleicher, D. J., Unckless, A. L., & Hiller, N. J. (2002). Self-monitoring personality at work: A meta-analytic investigation of construct validity. *Journal of Applied Psychology, 87*, 390–401.

27. Kilduff, M., & Day, D. V. (1994). Do chameleons get ahead? The effects of self-monitoring and managerial careers. *Academy of Management Journal, 37*(4), 1047–1060.

28. Brockner, J. (1988). *Self-esteem at work: Research, theory, and practice*. Lexington, MA: Lexington.

29. Brockner, 1988.

30. Brockner, 1988.

31. Pierce, J. L., Gardner, D. G., Cummings, L. L., & Dunham, R. B. (1989). Organization-based self-esteem: Construct definition, measurement,

and validation. *Academy of Management Journal, 32,* 622–648; Tharenou, P. (1979). Employee self-esteem: A review of the literature. *Journal of Vocational Behavior, 15,* 1–29.

32. Pierce, J. L., Gardner, D. G., Dunham, R. B., & Cummings, L. L. (1993). Moderation by organization-based self-esteem of role condition–employee response relationships. *Academy of Management Journal, 36,* 271–288.

33. George, J. M. (1996). Trait and state affect. In K. R. Murphy (Ed.), *Individual differences and behavior in organizations.* San Francisco, CA: Jossey-Bass.

34. Johnson, R. E., Tolentino, A. L., Rodopman, O. B., & Cho, E. (2010). We (sometimes) know not how we feel: Predicting job performance with an implicit measure of trait affectivity. *Personnel Psychology, 63,* 197–219.

35. Johnson et al., 2010; George, 1996; Thoresen, C. J., Kaplan, S.A., Barsky, A. P., Warren, C. R., & de Chermont, K. (2003). The affective underpinnings of job perceptions and attitudes: A meta-analytic review and integration. *Psychological Bulletin, 129,* 914–945; Lyubomirsky, S., King, L., & Diener, E. (2005). The benefits of frequent positive affect: Does happiness lead to success? *Psychological Bulletin, 131,* 803–855; Kaplan, S., Bradley, J. C., Luchman, J. N., & Haynes, D. (2009). On the role of positive and negative affectivity in job performance: A meta-analytic investigation. *Journal of Applied Psychology, 94,* 162–176.

36. Crant, M. J. (2000). Proactive behaviour in organizations. *Journal of Management, 26,* 435–462; Seibert, S. E., Kraimer, M. L., & Crant, J. M. (2001). What do proactive people do? A longitudinal model linking proactive personality and career success. *Personnel Psychology, 54,* 845–874.

37. Bateman, T. S., & Crant, J. M. (1993). The proactive component of organizational behavior: A measure and correlates. *Journal of Organizational Behavior, 14,* 103–118.

38. Li, N., Liang, J., & Crant, J. M. (2010). The role of proactive personality in job satisfaction and organizational citizenship behavior: A relational perspective. *Journal of Applied Psychology, 95,* 395–404; Seibert, Kraimer, & Crant, 2001; Thompson, J. A. (2005). Proactive personality and job performance: A social capital perspective. *Journal of Applied Psychology, 90,* 1011–1017; Brown, D. J., Cober, R. T., Kane, K., Levy, P. E., & Shalhoop, J. (2006). Proactive personality and the successful job search: A field investigation with college graduates. *Journal of Applied Psychology, 91,* 717–726.

39. Chen, G., Gully, S. M., & Eden, D. (2001). Validation of a new general self-efficacy scale. *Organizational Research Methods, 4,* 62–83.

40. Chen, Gully, & Eden, 2001.

41. Judge, T. A., Erez, A., Bono, J. E., & Thoresen, C. J. (2003). The core self-evaluation scale: Development of a measure. *Personnel Psychology, 56,* 303–331.

42. Chang, C., Ferris, D. L., Johnson, R. E., Rosen, C. C., & Tan, J. A. (2012). Core self-evaluations: A review and evaluation of the literature. *Journal of Management, 38,* 81–128; Judge, T. A., & Bono, J. E. (2001). Relationship of core self-evaluations traits—self-esteem, generalized self-efficacy, locus of control, and emotional stability—with job satisfaction and job performance: A meta-analysis. *Journal of Applied Psychology, 86,* 80–92; Judge, T. A., Bono, J. E., & Locke, E. A. (2000). Personality and job satisfaction: The mediating role of job characteristics. *Journal of Applied Psychology, 85,* 237–249; Judge, Erez, Bono, & Thoresen, 2003; Judge, T. A., Locke, E. A., & Durham, C. C. (1997). The dispositional causes of job satisfaction: A core evaluations approach. In B. M. Staw & L. L. Cummings (Eds.), *Research in organizational behavior* (Vol. 19, 151–188). Greenwich, CT: JAI Press; Judge, T. A., Bono, J. E., Erez, A., & Locke, E. A. (2005). Core self-evaluations and job and life satisfaction: The role of self-concordance and goal attainment. *Journal of Applied Psychology, 90,* 257–268; Kammeyer-Mueller, J. D., Judge, T. A., & Scott, B. A. (2009). The role of core self-evaluations in the coping process. *Journal of Applied Psychology, 94,* 177–195; Judge, T. A. (2009). Core self-evaluations and work success. *Current Directions in Psychological Science, 18,* 58–62; Johnson, R. E., Rosen, C. C., & Levy, P. E. (2008). Getting to the core of core self-evaluation: A review and recommendations. *Journal of Organizational Behavior, 29,* 391–413.

43. Day, N. (1998, June). Informal learning gets results. *Workforce,* 31–35.

44. Pfeffer, J. (1994). *Competitive advantage through people: Unleashing the power of the work force.* Boston, MA: Harvard Business School Press.

45. Immen, W. (2012, June 20). Companies boosting incentive programs. *Globe and Mail,* B17.

46. Peterson, S. J., & Luthans, F. (2006). The impact of financial and nonfinancial incentives on business-unit outcomes over time. *Journal of Applied Psychology, 91,* 156–165.

47. Peterson & Luthans, 2006.

48. Luthans, F., & Kreitner, R. (1975). *Organizational behavior modification.* Glenview, IL: Scott, Foresman.

49. However, more research is necessary to establish the extent of this in organizations. See Arvey, R. D., & Ivancevich, J. M. (1980). Punishment in organizations: A review, propositions, and research suggestions. *Academy of Management Review, 5,* 123–132.

50. Punishment in front of others can be effective under restricted conditions. See Trevino, L. K. (1992). The social effects of punishment in organizations: A justice perspective. *Academy of Management Review, 17,* 647–676.

51. Orsgan, D. W., & Hamner, W. C. (1982). *Organizational behavior: An applied psychological approach* (Revised ed.). Plano, TX: Business Publications.

52. See Parmerlee, M. A., Near, J. P., & Jensen, T. C. (1982). Correlates of whistle-blowers' perceptions of organizational retaliation. *Administrative Science Quarterly, 27,* 17–34.

53. Bandura, A. (1991). Social cognitive theory of self-regulation. *Organizational Behavior and Human Decision Processes, 50,* 248–287.

54. Bandura, A. (1989). Human agency in social cognitive theory. *American Psychologists, 44,* 1175–1184. For a presentation of operant learning theory, see Honig, W. K., & Staddon, J. E. R. (Eds.). (1977). *Handbook of operant behavior.* Englewood Cliffs, NJ: Prentice-Hall. For a presentation of social learning theory, see Bandura, A. (1986). *Social foundations of thought and action.* Englewood Cliffs, NJ: Prentice-Hall.

55. Bandura, 1986.

56. Luthans, F., & Kreitner, R. (1985). *Organizational behavior modification and beyond: An operant and social learning approach.* Glenview, IL: Scott, Foresman; Manz, C. C., & Sims, H. P., Jr. (1981). Vicarious learning: The influence of modeling on organizational behavior. *Academy of Management Review, 6,* 105–113.

57. Bandura, 1986; Goldstein, A. P., & Sorcher, M. (1974). *Changing supervisor behavior.* New York: Pergamon.

58. Robinson, S. L., & O'Leary-Kelly, A. M. (1998). Monkey see, monkey do: The influence of work groups on the anti-social behavior of employees. *Academy of Management Journal, 41,* 658–672; Goulet, L. R. (1997). Modelling aggression in the workplace: The role of role models. *Academy of Management Executive, 11,* 84–85.

59. Bandura, A. (1997). *Self-efficacy: The exercise of control.* New York, NY: W. H. Freeman.

60. Bandura, 1997; Stajkovic, A. D., & Luthans, F. (1998). Self-efficacy and work-related performance: A meta-analysis. *Psychological Bulletin, 124,* 240–261.

61. Bandura, 1991; Manz, C. C., & Sims, H. P., Jr. (1980). Self-management as a substitute for leadership: A social learning theory perspective. *Academy of Management Review, 5*, 361–367; Hackman, J. R. (1986). The psychology of self-management in organizations. In M. S. Pollack & R. Perloff (Eds.), *Psychology and work*. Washington, DC: American Psychological Association.

62. Bandura, 1986, 1989, 1991; Kanfer, F. H. (1980). Self-management methods. In F. H. Kanfer & A. P. Goldstein (Eds.), *Helping people change: A textbook of methods* (2nd ed.). New York: Pergamon.

63. Luthans & Kreitner, 1985; Manz & Sims, 1980.

64. Frayne, C., & Latham, G. (1987). Application of social learning theory to employee self-management of attendance. *Journal of Applied Psychology, 72*, 387–392.

65. Frayne, C. A., & Geringer, J. M. (2000). Self-management training for improving job performance: A field experiment involving salespeople. *Journal of Applied Psychology, 85*, 361–372.

66. Gist, M. E., Stevens, C. K., & Bavetta, A. G. (1991). Effects of self-efficacy and post-training intervention on the acquisition and maintenance of complex interpersonal skills. *Personnel Psychology, 44*, 837–861; Stevens, C. K., Bavetta, A. G., & Gist, M. E. (1993). Gender differences in the acquisition

of salary negotiation skills: The role of goals, self-efficacy, and perceived control. *Journal of Applied Psychology, 78*, 723–735.

67. Komaki, J., Barwick, K. D., & Scott, L. R. (1978). A behavioral approach to occupational safety: Pinpointing and reinforcing safe performance in a food manufacturing plant. *Journal of Applied Psychology, 63*, 434–445. For a similar study, see Haynes, R. S., Pine, R. C., & Fitch, H. G. (1982). Reducing accident rates with organizational behavior modification. *Academy of Management Journal, 25*, 407–416.

68. Stajkovic, A. D., & Lutans, F. (1997). A meta-analysis of the effects of organizational behavior modification on task performance, 1975–95. *Academy of Management Journal, 40*, 1122–1149; Stajkovic, A. D., & Luthans, F. (2003). Behavioral management and task performance in organizations: Conceptual background, meta-analysis, and test of alternative models. *Personnel Psychology, 56*, 155–194; Stajkovic, A. D., & Luthans, F. (2001). Differential effects of incentive motivators on work performance. *Academy of Management Journal, 44*, 580–590.

69. Markham, S. E., Scott, K. D., & McKee, G. H. (2002). Recognizing good attendance: A longitudinal, quasi-experimental field study. *Personnel Psychology, 55*, 639–660.

70. Anonymous. (2008, April 28). The power of peer recognition. A special

report for the Great Place to Work® Institute Canada. *Globe and Mail*, GPTW5; Marron, K. (2006, February 15). High praise from colleagues counts. *Globe and Mail*, C1, C6.

71. Markham, Scott, & McKee, 2002; Well-structured employee reward/recognition programs yield positive results. (1999, November). *HRFocus, 1*, 14, 15.

72. Markham, Scott, & McKee, 2002.

73. Klie, S. (2006, August 14). Recognition equals profits. *Canadian HR Reporter, 19*(14), 18.

74. Saks, A. M., & Haccoun, R. R. (2010). *Managing performance through training and development* (5th ed.). Toronto: Nelson.

75. Taylor, P. J., Russ-Eft, D. F., & Chan, D. W. L. (2005). A meta-analytic review of behavior modeling training. *Journal of Applied Psychology, 90*, 692–709.

76. Taylor, Russ-Eft, & Chan, 2005.

77. Saks, A. M. (1997). Transfer of training and self-efficacy: What is the dilemma? *Applied Psychology: An International Review, 46*, 365–370.

78. DeSimone, R. L., Werner, J. M., & Harris, D. M. (2002). *Human resource development*. Orlando, FL: Harcourt College.

79. Harding, K. (2003, February 5). Firms offer a hand up the ladder. *Globe and Mail*, C3.

80. Brown, D. (2005, June 20). TD gives employees tool to chart career paths. *Canadian HR Reporter, 18*(12), 11, 13.

PHOTO CREDITS

THEORIES OF WORK MOTIVATION

THEORIES OF WORK MOTIVATION

LEARNING OBJECTIVES

After reading this chapter, you should be able to:

1 Define *motivation*, discuss its basic properties, and distinguish it from *performance*.

2 Compare and contrast *intrinsic* and *extrinsic motivation* and describe *self-determination theory, autonomous motivation*, and *controlled motivation*.

3 Explain and discuss the different factors that predict *performance* and define *general cognitive ability* and *emotional intelligence*.

4 Explain and discuss *need theories* of motivation.

5 Explain and discuss *expectancy theory*.

6 Explain and discuss *equity theory*.

7 Explain and discuss *goal setting theory, goal orientation*, and *proximal* and *distal goals*.

8 Discuss the cross-cultural limitations of theories of motivation.

9 Summarize the relationships among the various theories of motivation, performance, and job satisfaction.

GREAT LITTLE BOX COMPANY LTD.

Great Little Box Company Ltd. (GLBC) is a leading designer and manufacturer of custom and stock corrugated boxes, point-of-purchase displays, folding cartons, labels, and protective packaging. It began operations in 1982 in Burnaby, British Columbia, with just three employees. Today, the company has grown to more than 200 full- and part-time employees. It has locations in Kelowna, Victoria, and Everett, Washington, in addition to its head office in Vancouver.

The company has had remarkable success since it began, with annual sales today of $35 million. Much of its success is attributed to the hard work and dedication of its employees, who receive ongoing skills training and career and personal development, as well as above-average compensation and benefits. To ensure that salaries are competitive, the company participates in salary surveys and reviews individual salaries every 12 months.

Incentive compensation is linked to the company's overall business goals and to objectives that are part of employees' goals. At the beginning of each year, employees meet with their immediate supervisor to set individual performance goals. Performance reviews are held every three months, and employees meet with their supervisor to review how well they met their goals and to establish goals for the next quarter. Performance feedback is also obtained from co-workers and managers who are familiar with each employee's work.

Exceptional performance is recognized with special dinners, cash awards, and preferred parking spots. A suggestion program rewards employees for cost-saving ideas. Employees whose suggestions are implemented receive a share of the financial savings to the company. Employees can also receive a $10 reward any day of the week for catching a mistake, improving a work process, or providing better ideas for manufacturing in what is known as the $10'ers program. Incentives have also been established for each department and are paid out weekly, monthly, and quarterly.

GLBC also has a profit-sharing plan and encourages employees to save for their retirement through matching RSP contributions. Employees are kept up to date on the company's profits through monthly meetings that include frank discussions about all financial matters relating to the business. The company opens its books to employees and provides details on the company's financial status. The meetings ensure that employees know how the company is doing and what can be done to improve things. The meetings are also a forum for employee input and for recog-

Motivated employees are the key to the success of the Great Little Box Company, which has been named one of Canada's Top 100 Employers and one of British Columbia's Top Employers.

nizing and rewarding employees for their efforts. Every month, 15 percent of the previous month's profits are shared equally among all employees regardless of an employee's position, seniority, and wage.

Employees also share the benefits of the company's success when it reaches its annual profitability goal. The annual profitability goal is known as the Big Outrageous Xtravaganza goal (or BOX goal), and when it is reached, the company treats all of its employees to an all-expenses-paid vacation to a sunny destination. Over the past 13 years, GLBC employees have enjoyed vacations to places such as Cabo San Lucas, Puerto Vallarta, and Las Vegas.

GLBC has consistently been recognized as one of Canada's Best Managed Companies and a great employer. In 2012 it was chosen as one of Canada's Top 100 Employers, one of the *Financial Post*'s Ten Best Companies to Work For, and one of British Columbia's Top Employers. According to GLBC president and CEO Robert Meggy, "It is clear that happy and motivated employees are the key to success and longevity."[1]

Would you be motivated if you worked for Great Little Box Company? What kind of person would respond well to the company's motivational techniques? What underlying philosophy of motivation is GLBC using and what effect does it have on employees' motivation and performance? These are some of the questions that this chapter will explore.

First we will define motivation and distinguish it from performance. After that we will describe several popular theories of work motivation and contrast them. Then we will explore whether these theories translate across cultures. Finally we will present a model that links motivation, performance, and job satisfaction.

WHY STUDY MOTIVATION?

Motivation is one of the most traditional topics in organizational behaviour, and it has interested managers, researchers, teachers, and sports coaches for years. However, a good case can be made that motivation has become even more important in contemporary organizations. Much of this is a result of the need for increased productivity to be globally competitive. It is also a result of the rapid changes that contemporary organizations are undergoing. Stable systems of rules, regulations, and procedures that once guided behaviour are being replaced by requirements for flexibility and attention to customers that necessitate higher levels of initiative. This initiative depends on motivation. According to GLBC president and CEO Robert Meggy, "Everything we do has to be by people who are well-motivated. I see it in the bottom line for us."[2]

What would a good motivation theory look like? In fact, as we shall see, there is no single all-purpose motivation theory. Rather, we will consider several theories that serve somewhat different purposes. In combination, though, a good set of theories should recognize human diversity and consider that the same conditions will not motivate everyone. Also, a good set of theories should be able to explain how it is that some people seem to be self-motivated, while others seem to require external motivation. Finally, a good set of theories should recognize the social aspect of human beings—people's motivation is often affected by how they see others being treated. Before getting to our theories, let's first define motivation more precisely.

Sidebar

Define *motivation*, discuss its basic properties, and distinguish it from *performance*.

Motivation. The extent to which persistent effort is directed toward a goal.

 Watch

JOIE DE VIVRE HOSPITALITY: EMPLOYEE MOTIVATION Go to MyManagementLab to watch a video about employee motivation.

WHAT IS MOTIVATION?

The term *motivation* is not easy to define. However, from an organization's perspective, when we speak of a person as being motivated, we usually mean that the person works "hard," "keeps at" his or her work, and directs his or her behaviour toward appropriate outcomes.

Basic Characteristics of Motivation

We can formally define **motivation** as the extent to which persistent effort is directed toward a goal.[3]

EFFORT The first aspect of motivation is the strength of the person's work-related behaviour, or the amount of *effort* the person exhibits on the job. Clearly, this involves different kinds of activities on different kinds of jobs. A loading-dock worker might exhibit greater effort by carrying heavier crates, while a researcher might reveal greater effort by searching out an article in some obscure foreign technical journal. Both are exerting effort in a manner appropriate to their jobs.

PERSISTENCE The second characteristic of motivation is the *persistence* that individuals exhibit in applying effort to their work tasks. The organization would not be likely to think of the loading-dock worker who stacks the heaviest crates for two hours and then goofs off for six hours as especially highly motivated. Similarly, the researcher who makes an important discovery early in her career and then rests on her laurels for five years would not be considered especially highly motivated. In each case, workers have not been persistent in the application of their effort.

DIRECTION Effort and persistence refer mainly to the quantity of work an individual produces. Of equal importance is the quality of a person's work. Thus, the third characteristic of motivation is the *direction* of the person's work-related behaviour. In other words, do workers channel persistent effort in a direction that benefits the organization? Employers expect motivated stockbrokers to advise their clients of good investment opportunities and motivated software designers to design software, not play computer games. These correct decisions increase the probability that persistent effort is actually translated into accepted organizational outcomes. Thus, motivation means working smart as well as working hard.

GOALS Ultimately, all motivated behaviour has some goal or objective toward which it is directed. We have presented the preceding discussion from an organizational perspective—that is, we assume that motivated people act to enhance organizational objectives. In this case, employee goals might include high productivity, good attendance, or creative decisions. Of course, employees can also be motivated by goals that are contrary to the objectives of the organization, including absenteeism, sabotage, and embezzlement. In these cases, they are channelling their persistent efforts in directions that are dysfunctional for the organization.

Extrinsic and Intrinsic Motivation and Self-Determination Theory

Some hold the view that people are motivated by factors in the external environment (such as supervision or pay), while others believe that people can, in some sense, be self-motivated without the application of these external factors. You might have experienced this distinction. As a worker, you might recall tasks that you enthusiastically performed simply for the sake of doing them and others that you performed only to keep your job or placate your boss.

Experts in organizational behaviour distinguish between intrinsic and extrinsic motivation. At the outset, we should emphasize that there is only weak consensus concerning the exact definitions of these concepts and even weaker agreement about whether we should label specific motivators as intrinsic or extrinsic.[4] However, the following definitions and examples seem to capture the distinction fairly well.

Intrinsic motivation stems from the direct relationship between the worker and the task and is usually self-applied. Feelings of achievement, accomplishment, challenge, and competence derived from performing one's job are examples of intrinsic motivators, as is sheer interest in the job itself. Off the job, avid participation in sports and hobbies is often intrinsically motivated.

Extrinsic motivation stems from the work environment external to the task and is usually applied by someone other than the person being motivated. Pay, fringe benefits, company policies, and various forms of supervision are examples of extrinsic motivators. At GLBC, profit sharing and cash awards for exceptional performance are examples of extrinsic motivators.

Obviously, employers cannot package all conceivable motivators as neatly as these definitions suggest. For example, a promotion or a compliment might be applied by the boss but might also be a clear signal of achievement and competence. Thus, some motivators have both extrinsic and intrinsic qualities.

The relationship between intrinsic and extrinsic motivators has been the subject of a great deal of debate.[5] Some research studies have reached the conclusion that the availability of extrinsic motivators can reduce the intrinsic motivation stemming from the task itself.[6] The notion is that when extrinsic rewards depend on performance, then the motivating potential of intrinsic rewards decreases. Proponents of this view have suggested that making extrinsic rewards contingent on performance makes individuals feel less competent and less in control of their own behaviour. That is, they come to believe that their performance is controlled by the environment and that they perform well only because of the money.[7] As a result, their intrinsic motivation suffers.

However, a review of research in this area reached the conclusion that the negative effect of extrinsic rewards on intrinsic motivation occurs only under very limited conditions, and

Intrinsic motivation. Motivation that stems from the direct relationship between the worker and the task; it is usually self-applied.

Extrinsic motivation. Motivation that stems from the work environment external to the task; it is usually applied by others.

they are easily avoidable.[8] As well, in organizational settings in which individuals see extrinsic rewards as symbols of success and as signals of what to do to achieve future rewards, they increase their task performance.[9] Thus, it is safe to assume that both kinds of rewards are important and compatible in enhancing work motivation.

Despite the fact that the distinction between intrinsic and extrinsic motivation can be fuzzy, many theories of motivation make the distinction. For example, intrinsic and extrinsic factors are used in **self-determination theory** (SDT) to explain what motivates people and whether motivation is autonomous or controlled. When people are motivated by intrinsic factors, they are in control of their motivation or what is known as **autonomous motivation**. When motivation is autonomous, individuals are engaged in a task because they choose to be and their actions are internally regulated. This is often the case when people perform a task because they find it interesting or fun to do.

When people are motivated to obtain a desired consequence or extrinsic reward, their motivation is controlled externally or what is known as **controlled motivation**. When motivation is controlled, individuals feel they have no choice and they have to engage in a task. Thus, their behaviour is externally regulated. This is the case when people do something to obtain a desired consequence, avoid punishment, or because the boss is watching them.

The distinction between autonomous and controlled motivation is important because autonomous motivation has been shown to facilitate effective performance, especially on complex tasks. Autonomous motivation is also associated with other work outcomes such as positive work attitudes and psychological well-being.[10] Later in the chapter you will see how other theories of motivation treat intrinsic and extrinsic motivation. Let's now consider the relationship between motivation and performance.

Motivation and Performance

At this point, you may well be saying, "Wait a minute, I know many people who are 'highly motivated' but just don't seem to perform well. They work long and hard, but they just don't measure up." This is certainly a sensible observation, and it points to the important distinction between motivation and performance. **Performance** can be defined as the extent to which an organizational member contributes to achieving the objectives of the organization.

Some of the factors that contribute to individual performance in organizations are shown in Exhibit 1.[11] While motivation clearly contributes to performance, the relationship is not one-to-one because a number of other factors also influence performance. For example, personality traits such as the Big Five and core self-evaluations also predict job performance. You might also be wondering about the role of intelligence—doesn't it influence performance? The answer, of course, is yes—intelligence, or what is also known as mental ability, does predict performance. Two forms of intelligence that are particularly important for performance are general cognitive ability and emotional intelligence. Let's consider each before we discuss motivation.

GENERAL COGNITIVE ABILITY The term *cognitive ability* is often used to refer to what most people call intelligence or mental ability. Although there are many different types of specific cognitive abilities, in organizational behaviour we are often concerned with what is known as *general cognitive ability*. **General cognitive ability** is a term used to refer to a

Self-determination theory. A theory of motivation that considers whether people's motivation is autonomous or controlled.

Autonomous motivation. When people are self-motivated by intrinsic factors.

Controlled motivation. When people are motivated to obtain a desired consequence or extrinsic reward.

LO 3

Explain and discuss the different factors that predict *performance* and define *general cognitive ability* and *emotional intelligence*.

Performance. The extent to which an organizational member contributes to achieving the objectives of the organization.

General cognitive ability. A person's basic information-processing capacities and cognitive resources.

EXHIBIT 1
Factors contributing to individual job performance.

Explore

Go to MyManagementLab to see an annotated version of this figure.

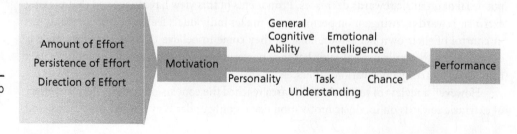

person's basic information-processing capacities and cognitive resources. It reflects an individual's overall capacity and efficiency for processing information, and it includes a number of cognitive abilities, such as verbal, numerical, spatial, and reasoning abilities, that are required to perform mental tasks. Cognitive ability is usually measured by a number of specific aptitude tests that measure these abilities.[12]

Research has found that general cognitive ability predicts learning, training, and career success as well as job performance in all kinds of jobs and occupations, including those that involve both manual and mental tasks. This should not come as a surprise because many cognitive skills are required to perform most kinds of jobs. General cognitive ability is an even better predictor of performance for more complex and higher-level jobs that require the use of more cognitive skills and involve more information processing.[13] Thus, both general cognitive ability and motivation are necessary for performance.

Given that cognitive ability is a strong predictor of performance, you might also wonder about the role of education in job performance. As you probably know, education is an important indicator of one's intelligence and it is important for obtaining employment. But how important is education for job performance? To find out, see the Research Focus: *Does Education Predict Job Performance?*

EMOTIONAL INTELLIGENCE Although the importance of general cognitive ability for job performance has been known for many years, researchers have only recently begun to study emotional intelligence. **Emotional intelligence** (EI) has to do with an individual's ability to understand and manage his or her own and others' feelings and emotions. It involves the ability to perceive and express emotion, assimilate emotion in thought, understand and reason about

Emotional intelligence.
The ability to understand and manage one's own and other's feelings and emotions.

RESEARCH FOCUS

DOES EDUCATION PREDICT JOB PERFORMANCE?

Most organizations use education as an indicator of a job applicant's skill levels and ability and use education as a prerequisite in hiring decisions. There is substantial evidence that individuals' educational attainments are associated with positive career outcomes, including salary level, number of promotions, development opportunities, and job mobility. But does educational level predict job performance?

To find out, Thomas W.H. Ng and Daniel C. Feldman examined the results of 293 studies on education and job performance. They looked at three kinds of job performance. Core task performance refers to the basic required duties of a particular job. Citizenship performance refers to those extra behaviours engaged in by employees, over and above their core task requirements, that actively promote and strengthen an organization's effectiveness (e.g., creativity). Counterproductive performance refers to voluntary behaviours that harm the well-being of the organization (e.g., theft, absenteeism). Education level refers to the academic credentials or degrees an individual has obtained.

The authors predicted that education would be positively related to core task performance and citizenship performance and negatively related to counterproductive performance as a result of the acquisition of

task-relevant knowledge and work values that promote organizational effectiveness.

The results indicated that education was related to all three types of performance. More highly educated workers have higher core task performance, display greater creativity, and demonstrate more citizenship behaviours than less educated workers. Highly educated workers also engage in less counterproductive behaviours (i.e., workplace aggression, substance use, and absenteeism). The authors also found that the relationships between education and performance were stronger for men than for women and stronger for Caucasian employees than for racial minorities. In addition, the relationship between education and core task performance was stronger for more complex jobs.

Overall, the results of this study confirm the long-held belief that education predicts job performance and provides some validity for the use of education level as a factor in the hiring process and for the benefits of an educated workforce.

Source: Excerpted from Ng, T.W.H., & Feldman, D.C. (2009). How broadly does education contribute to job performance? *Personnel Psychology, 62,* 89–134. Reprinted with permission of Wiley-Blackwell Publishing.

emotions, and manage emotions in oneself and others. Individuals high in EI are able to identify and understand the meanings of emotions and to manage and regulate their emotions as a basis for problem solving, reasoning, thinking, and action.[14]

Peter Salovey and John Mayer, who are credited with first coining the term *emotional intelligence*, have developed an EI model that consists of four interrelated sets of skills, or branches. The four skills represent sequential steps that form a hierarchy. The perception of emotion is at the bottom of the hierarchy, followed by (in ascending order) using emotions to facilitate thinking, understanding emotions, and managing and regulating emotions. The four-branch model of EI is shown in Exhibit 2 and described below.[15]

1. *Perceiving emotions accurately in oneself and others:* This involves the ability to perceive emotions and to accurately identify one's own emotions and the emotions of others. An example of this is the ability to accurately identify emotions in people's faces and in non-verbal behaviour. People differ in the extent to which they can accurately identify emotions in others, particularly from facial expressions.[16] This step is the most basic level of EI and is necessary to be able to perform the other steps in the model.

2. *Using emotions to facilitate thinking:* This refers to the ability to use and assimilate emotions and emotional experiences to guide and facilitate one's thinking and reasoning. This means that one is able to use emotions in functional ways, such as making decisions and other cognitive processes (e.g., creativity, integrative thinking, and inductive reasoning). This stage also involves being able to shift one's emotions and generate new emotions that can help one to see things in different ways and from different perspectives. This is an important skill because emotions and moods affect what and how people think when making decisions.[17]

3. *Understanding emotions, emotional language, and the signals conveyed by emotions:* This stage involves being able to understand emotional information, the determinants and consequences of emotions, and how emotions evolve and change over time. At this stage, people understand how different situations and events generate emotions as well as how they and others are influenced by various emotions.[18] Individuals who are good at this know not to ask somebody who is in a bad mood for a favour, but rather to wait until the person is in a better mood or to just ask somebody else!

4. *Managing emotions so as to attain specific goals:* This involves the ability to manage one's own and others' feelings and emotions as well as emotional relationships. This is the highest level of EI because it requires one to have mastered the previous stages. At this stage, an individual is able to regulate, adjust, and change his or her own emotions as well as others' emotions to suit the situation. Examples of this include being able to stay calm when feeling angry or upset; being able to excite and enthuse others; or being able to lower another person's anger. To be effective at managing emotions one must be able to perceive emotions, integrate and assimilate emotions, and be knowledgeable of and understand emotions.

Research on EI has found that it predicts performance in a number of areas, including job performance and academic performance.[19] One study found that college students' EI measured at the start of the academic year predicted their grade point averages at the end of the year. A review of research on emotional intelligence and job performance found that EI is not only positively related to job performance, but that it predicts job performance above and beyond cognitive ability and the Big Five personality variables.[20] There is also some evidence that EI is most strongly related to job performance in jobs that require high levels of emotional labour, such as police officers and customer service representatives.[21] According to the results of one study, the importance of emotional intelligence for job performance depends on one's cognitive ability. Emotional intelligence was found to be most important for the job performance of employees with lower levels of cognitive ability and of less importance for the job performance of employees with high levels of cognitive ability.[22]

Explore

Go to MyManagementLab to see an annotated version of this figure.

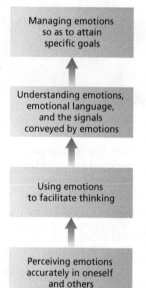

EXHIBIT 2
Four-branch model of emotional intelligence.
Source: Based on Mayer, J.D., Caruso, D.R., & Salovey, P. (2000). Emotional Intelligence meets traditional standards for an intelligence. *Intelligence, 27*, 267–298; Salovey, P., & Mayer, J.D. (1990). Emotional Intelligence. *Imagination, Cognition & Personality, 9*, 185–211. Used by permission of Baywood Publishing.

The Motivation–Performance Relationship

As shown in Exhibit 1, it is certainly possible for performance to be low even when a person is highly motivated. In addition to personality, general cognitive ability, and emotional intelligence, poor performance could also be due to a poor understanding of the task or luck and chance factors that can damage the performance of the most highly motivated individuals. Of course, an opposite effect is also possible. An individual with rather marginal motivation might have high general cognitive ability or emotional intelligence or might understand the task so well that some compensation occurs—what little effort the individual makes is expended very efficiently in terms of goal accomplishment. Also, a person with weak motivation might perform well because of some luck or chance factor that boosts performance. Thus, it is no wonder that workers sometimes complain that they receive lower performance ratings than colleagues who "don't work as hard."

In this chapter, we will concentrate on the motivational components of performance rather than on the other determinants in Exhibit 1. However, the message here should be clear: We cannot consider motivation in isolation. High motivation will not result in high performance if employees have low general cognitive ability and emotional intelligence, do not understand their jobs, or encounter unavoidable obstacles over which they have no control. Motivational interventions, such as linking pay to performance, simply *will not work* if employees are deficient in important skills and abilities.[23] Let's now turn to theories of motivation to better understand what motivates people and the process of motivation.

NEED THEORIES OF WORK MOTIVATION

The first three theories of motivation that we will consider are **need theories**. These theories attempt to specify the kinds of needs people have and the conditions under which they will be motivated to satisfy these needs in a way that contributes to performance. Needs are physiological and psychological wants or desires that individuals can satisfy by acquiring certain incentives or achieving particular goals. It is the behaviour stimulated by this acquisition process that reveals the motivational character of needs:

$$\text{NEEDS} \longrightarrow \text{BEHAVIOUR} \longrightarrow \text{INCENTIVES AND GOALS}$$

Notice that need theories are concerned with *what* motivates workers (needs and their associated incentives or goals). They can be contrasted with *process theories*, which are concerned with exactly *how* various factors motivate people. Need and process theories are complementary rather than contradictory. Thus, a need theory might contend that money can be an important motivator (what), and a process theory might explain the actual mechanics by which money motivates (how).[24] In this section, we will examine three prominent need theories of motivation.

Maslow's Hierarchy of Needs

Abraham Maslow was a psychologist who developed and refined a general theory of human motivation.[25] According to Maslow, humans have five sets of needs that are arranged in a hierarchy, beginning with the most basic and compelling needs (see the left side of Exhibit 3). These needs include

1. *Physiological needs.* These include the needs that must be satisfied for the person to survive, such as food, water, oxygen, and shelter. Organizational factors that might satisfy these needs include the minimum pay necessary for survival and working conditions that promote existence.

2. *Safety needs.* These include needs for security, stability, freedom from anxiety, and a structured and ordered environment. Organizational conditions that might meet these needs

Watch

MOTIVATION Go to MyManagementLab to watch a video about motivation.

LO 4

Explain and discuss *need theories* of motivation.

Need theories. Motivation theories that specify the kinds of needs people have and the conditions under which they will be motivated to satisfy these needs in a way that contributes to performance.

EXHIBIT 3
Relationship between Maslow's and Alderfer's need theories.

Explore

Go to MyManagementLab to see an annotated version of this figure.

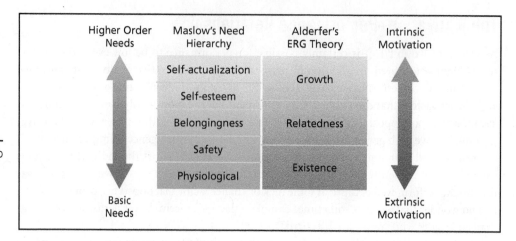

include safe working conditions, fair and sensible rules and regulations, job security, a comfortable work environment, pension and insurance plans, and pay above the minimum needed for survival.

3. *Belongingness needs.* These include needs for social interaction, affection, love, companionship, and friendship. Organizational factors that might meet these needs include the opportunity to interact with others on the job, friendly and supportive supervision, opportunity for teamwork, and opportunity to develop new social relationships.

4. *Esteem needs.* These include needs for feelings of adequacy, competence, independence, strength, and confidence, and the appreciation and recognition of these characteristics by others. Organizational factors that might satisfy these needs include the opportunity to master tasks leading to feelings of achievement and responsibility. Also, awards, promotions, prestigious job titles, professional recognition, and the like might satisfy these needs when they are felt to be truly deserved.

5. *Self-actualization needs.* These needs are the most difficult to define. They involve the desire to develop one's true potential as an individual to the fullest extent and to express one's skills, talents, and emotions in a manner that is most personally fulfilling. Maslow suggests that self-actualizing people have clear perceptions of reality, accept themselves and others, and are independent, creative, and appreciative of the world around them. Organizational conditions that might provide self-actualization include absorbing jobs with the potential for creativity and growth as well as a relaxation of structure to permit self-development and personal progression.

Given the fact that individuals may have these needs, in what sense do they form the basis of a theory of motivation? That is, what exactly is the motivational premise of **Maslow's hierarchy of needs**? Put simply, the lowest-level unsatisfied need category has the greatest motivating potential. Thus, none of the needs is a "best" motivator; motivation depends on the person's position in the need hierarchy. According to Maslow, individuals are motivated to satisfy their physiological needs before they reveal an interest in safety needs, and safety must be satisfied before social needs become motivational, and so on. When a need is unsatisfied, it exerts a powerful effect on the individual's thinking and behaviour, and this is the sense in which needs are motivational. However, when needs at a particular level of the hierarchy are satisfied, the individual turns his or her attention to the next higher level. Notice the clear implication here that a *satisfied need is no longer an effective motivator.* Once one has adequate physiological resources and feels safe and secure, one does not seek more of the factors that met these needs but looks elsewhere for gratification. According to Maslow, the single exception to this rule involves self-actualization needs. He felt that these were "growth" needs that become stronger as they are gratified.

Maslow's hierarchy of needs. A five-level hierarchical need theory of motivation that specifies that the lowest-level unsatisfied need has the greatest motivating potential.

Alderfer's ERG Theory

Clayton Alderfer developed another need-based theory, called **ERG theory**.[26] It streamlines Maslow's need classifications and makes some different assumptions about the relationship between needs and motivation. The name ERG stems from Alderfer's compression of Maslow's five-category need system into three categories—existence, relatedness, and growth needs.

ERG theory. A three-level hierarchical need theory of motivation (existence, relatedness, growth) that allows for movement up and down the hierarchy.

1. *Existence needs.* These are needs that are satisfied by some material substance or condition. As such, they correspond closely to Maslow's physiological needs and to those safety needs that are satisfied by material conditions rather than interpersonal relations. These include the need for food, shelter, pay, and safe working conditions.

2. *Relatedness needs.* These are needs that are satisfied by open communication and the exchange of thoughts and feelings with other organizational members. They correspond fairly closely to Maslow's belongingness needs and to those esteem needs that involve feedback from others. However, Alderfer stresses that relatedness needs are satisfied by open, accurate, honest interaction rather than by uncritical pleasantness.

3. *Growth needs.* These are needs that are fulfilled by strong personal involvement in the work setting. They involve the full utilization of one's skills and abilities and the creative development of new skills and abilities. Growth needs correspond to Maslow's need for self-actualization and the aspects of his esteem needs that concern achievement and responsibility.

As you can see in Exhibit 3, Alderfer's need classification system does not represent a radical departure from that of Maslow. In addition, Alderfer agrees with Maslow that as lower-level needs are satisfied, the desire to have higher-level needs satisfied will increase. Thus, as existence needs are fulfilled, relatedness needs gain motivational power. Alderfer explains this by arguing that as more "concrete" needs are satisfied, energy can be directed toward satisfying less concrete needs. Finally, Alderfer agrees with Maslow that the least concrete needs—growth needs—become *more* compelling and *more* desired as they are fulfilled.

It is, of course, the differences between ERG theory and the need hierarchy that represent Alderfer's contribution to the understanding of motivation. First, unlike the need hierarchy, ERG theory does not assume that a lower-level need *must* be gratified before a less concrete need becomes operative. Thus, ERG theory does not propose a rigid hierarchy of needs. Some individuals, owing to background and experience, might seek relatedness or growth even though their existence needs are ungratified. Hence, ERG theory seems to account for a wide variety of individual differences in motive structure. Second, ERG theory assumes that if the higher-level needs are ungratified, individuals will increase their desire for the gratification of lower-level needs. Notice that this represents a *radical* departure from Maslow. According to Maslow, if esteem needs are strong but ungratified, a person will not revert to an interest in belongingness needs because these have necessarily already been gratified. (Remember, he argues that satisfied needs are not motivational.) According to Alderfer, however, the frustration of higher-order needs will lead workers to regress to a more concrete need category. For example, the software designer who is unable to establish rewarding social relationships with superiors or co-workers might increase his interest in fulfilling existence needs, perhaps by seeking a pay increase. Thus, according to Alderfer, an apparently satisfied need can act as a motivator by substituting for an unsatisfied need.

Given the preceding description of ERG theory, we can identify its two major motivational premises as follows:

1. The more lower-level needs are gratified, the more higher-level need satisfaction is desired.

2. The less higher-level needs are gratified, the more lower-level need satisfaction is desired.

McClelland's Theory of Needs

Psychologist David McClelland has spent several decades studying the human need structure and its implications for motivation. According to **McClelland's theory of needs**, needs reflect relatively stable personality characteristics that one acquires through early life experiences and exposure to selected aspects of one's society. Unlike Maslow and Alderfer, McClelland has not been interested in specifying a hierarchical relationship among needs. Rather, he has been more concerned with the specific behavioural consequences of needs. In other words, under what conditions are certain needs likely to result in particular patterns of motivation? The three needs that McClelland studied most have special relevance for organizational behaviour—needs for achievement, affiliation, and power.[27]

Individuals who are high in **need for achievement** (*n* Ach) have a strong desire to perform challenging tasks well. More specifically, they exhibit the following characteristics:

- *A preference for situations in which personal responsibility can be taken for outcomes.* Those high in *n* Ach do not prefer situations in which outcomes are determined by chance because success in such situations does not provide an experience of achievement.

- *A tendency to set moderately difficult goals that provide for calculated risks.* Success with easy goals will provide little sense of achievement, while extremely difficult goals might never be reached. The calculation of successful risks is stimulating to the high–*n* Ach person.

- *A desire for performance feedback.* Such feedback permits individuals with high *n* Ach to modify their goal attainment strategies to ensure success and signals them when success has been reached.[28]

People who are high in *n* Ach are concerned with bettering their own performance or that of others. They are often concerned with innovation and long-term goal involvement. However, these things are not done to please others or to damage the interests of others. Rather, they are done because they are *intrinsically* satisfying. Thus, *n* Ach would appear to be an example of a growth or self-actualization need.

People who are high in **need for affiliation** (*n* Aff) have a strong desire to establish and maintain friendly, compatible interpersonal relationships. In other words, they like to like others, and they want others to like them! More specifically, they have an ability to learn social networking quickly and a tendency to communicate frequently with others, either face to face, by telephone, or in writing. Also, they prefer to avoid conflict and competition with others, and they sometimes exhibit strong conformity to the wishes of their friends. The *n* Aff motive is obviously an example of a belongingness or relatedness need.

People who are high in **need for power** (*n* Pow) strongly desire to have influence over others. In other words, they wish to make a significant impact or impression on them. People who are high in *n* Pow seek out social settings in which they can be influential. When in small groups, they act in a "high-profile," attention-getting manner. There is some tendency for those who are high in *n* Pow to advocate risky positions. Also, some people who are high in *n* Pow show a strong concern for personal prestige. The need for power is a complex need because power can be used in a variety of ways, some of which serve the power seeker and some of which serve other people or the organization. However, *n* Pow seems to correspond most closely to Maslow's self-esteem need.

McClelland predicts that people will be motivated to seek out and perform well in jobs that match their needs. Thus, people with high *n* Ach should be strongly motivated by sales jobs or entrepreneurial positions, such as running a small business. Such jobs offer the feedback, personal responsibility, and opportunity to set goals, as noted above. People who are high in *n* Aff will be motivated by jobs such as social work or customer relations because these jobs have as a primary task establishing good relations with others.

Finally, high *n* Pow will result in high motivation in jobs that enable one to have a strong impact on others—jobs such as journalism and management. In fact, McClelland has found that the most effective managers have a low need for affiliation, a high need for power, and the ability to direct power toward organizational goals.[29]

Research Support for Need Theories

Maslow's need hierarchy suggests two main hypotheses. First, specific needs should cluster into the five main need categories that Maslow proposes. Second, as the needs in a given category are satisfied, they should become less important, while the needs in the adjacent higher-need category should become more important. This second hypothesis captures the progressive, hierarchical aspect of the theory. In general, research support for both these hypotheses is weak or negative. This is probably a function of the rigidity of the theory, which suggests that most people experience the same needs in the same hierarchical order. However, there is fair support for a simpler, two-level need hierarchy comprising the needs toward the top and the bottom of Maslow's hierarchy.[30]

This latter finding provides some indirect encouragement for the compressed need hierarchy found in Alderfer's ERG theory. Several tests indicate fairly good support for many of the predictions generated by the theory, including expected changes in need strength. Particularly interesting is the confirmation that the frustration of relatedness needs increases the strength of existence needs.[31] The simplicity and flexibility of ERG theory seem to capture the human need structure better than the greater complexity and rigidity of Maslow's theory.

McClelland's need theory has generated a wealth of predictions about many aspects of human motivation. Researchers have tested more and more of these predictions in organizational settings, and the results are generally supportive of the idea that particular needs are motivational when the work setting permits the satisfaction of these needs.[32]

Managerial Implications of Need Theories

The need theories have some important things to say about managerial attempts to motivate employees.

APPRECIATE DIVERSITY The lack of support for the fairly rigid need hierarchy suggests that managers must be adept at evaluating the needs of individual employees and offering incentives or goals that correspond to their needs. Unfounded stereotypes about the needs of the "typical" employee and naïve assumptions about the universality of need satisfaction are bound to reduce the effectiveness of chosen motivational strategies. The best salesperson might not make the best sales manager! The needs of a young recent college graduate probably differ from those of an older employee preparing for retirement. Thus, it is important to survey employees to find out what their needs are and then offer programs that meet their needs. For example, GLBC conducts an annual employee satisfaction survey to find out what employees want most and what they think of their salary.[33]

APPRECIATE INTRINSIC MOTIVATION The need theories also serve the valuable function of alerting managers to the existence of higher-order needs (whatever specific label we apply to them). The recognition of these needs in many employees is important for two key reasons. One of the basic conditions for organizational survival is the expression of some creative and innovative behaviour on the part of members. Such behaviour seems most likely to occur during the pursuit of higher-order need fulfillment, and ignorance of this factor can cause the demotivation of the people who have the most to offer the organization. Second, observation and research evidence support Alderfer's idea that the frustration of higher-order needs prompts demands for greater satisfaction of lower-order needs. This can lead to a vicious motivational cycle—that is, because the factors that gratify lower-level needs are fairly easy to administer (e.g., pay and fringe benefits), management has grown to rely on them to motivate employees. In turn, some employees, deprived of higher-order need gratification, come to expect more and more of these extrinsic factors in exchange for their services. Thus, a cycle of deprivation, regression, and temporary gratification continues, at great cost to the organization.[34]

How can organizations benefit from the intrinsic motivation that is inherent in strong higher-order needs? First, such needs will fail to develop for most employees unless lower-level needs are reasonably well gratified.[35] Thus, very poor pay, job insecurity, and unsafe working conditions will preoccupy most workers at the expense of higher-order outcomes. Second, if basic needs are met, jobs can be "enriched" to be more stimulating and challenging and to provide feelings of responsibility and achievement. Finally, organizations could pay more attention to designing career paths that enable interested workers to progress through a series of jobs that continue to challenge their higher-order needs. Individual managers could also assign tasks to employees with this goal in mind.

PROCESS THEORIES OF WORK MOTIVATION

Process theories.
Motivation theories that specify the details of how motivation occurs.

In contrast to need theories of motivation, which concentrate on *what* motivates people, **process theories** concentrate on *how* motivation occurs. In this section, we will examine three important process theories—expectancy theory, equity theory, and goal setting theory.

LO **5**

Explain and discuss *expectancy theory.*

Expectancy Theory

Expectancy theory.
A process theory that states that motivation is determined by the outcomes that people expect to occur as a result of their actions on the job.

The basic idea underlying **expectancy theory** is the belief that motivation is determined by the outcomes that people expect to occur as a result of their actions on the job. Psychologist Victor Vroom is usually credited with developing the first complete version of expectancy theory and applying it to the work setting.[36] The basic components of Vroom's theory are shown in Exhibit 4 and are described in more detail below.

Outcomes. Consequences that follow work behaviour.

- **Outcomes** are the consequences that may follow certain work behaviours. First-level outcomes are of particular interest to the organization, such as high productivity versus average productivity, illustrated in Exhibit 4, or good attendance versus poor attendance. Expectancy theory is concerned with specifying how an employee might attempt to choose one first-level outcome instead of another. Second-level outcomes are consequences that follow the attainment of a particular first-level outcome. Contrasted with first-level outcomes, second-level outcomes are most personally relevant to the individual worker and might involve amount of pay, sense of accomplishment, acceptance by peers, fatigue, and so on.

Instrumentality. The probability that a particular first-level outcome will be followed by a particular second-level outcome.

- **Instrumentality** is the probability that a particular first-level outcome (such as high productivity) will be followed by a particular second-level outcome (such as pay) (this is also known as the *performance → outcome* link). For example, a bank teller might figure that the odds are 50/50 (instrumentality = .5) that a good performance rating will result in a pay raise.

Valence. The expected value of work outcomes; the extent to which they are attractive or unattractive.

- **Valence** is the expected value of outcomes, the extent to which they are attractive or unattractive to the individual. Thus, good pay, peer acceptance, the chance of being fired, or any other second-level outcome might be more or less attractive to particular workers. According to Vroom, the valence of first-level outcomes is the sum of products of the associated second-level outcomes and their instrumentalities—that is,

$$\text{the valence of a particualr frist-level outcome} = \sum \text{instrumentalities} \times \text{second-level valences}$$

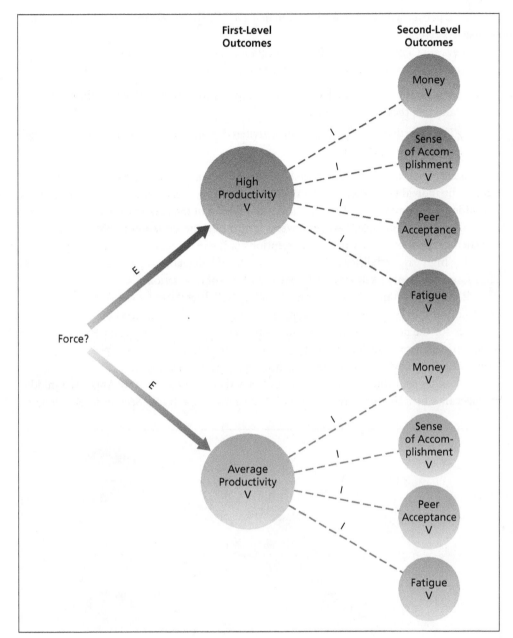

EXHIBIT 4
A hypothetical
expectancy model
(E = Expectancy, I =
Instrumentality, V =
Valence).

❋-⎸Explore

Go to MyManagementLab
to see an annotated
version of this figure.

In other words, the valence of a first-level outcome depends on the extent to which it leads to favourable second-level outcomes.

- **Expectancy** is the probability that the worker can actually achieve a particular first-level outcome (this is also known as the *effort ⟶ performance* link). For example, a machinist might be absolutely certain (expectancy = 1.0) that she can perform at an average level (producing 15 units a day), but less certain (expectancy = .6) that she can perform at a high level (producing 20 units a day).

- **Force** is the end product of the other components of the theory. It represents the relative degree of effort that will be directed toward various first-level outcomes.

According to Vroom, the force directed toward a first-level outcome is a product of the valence of that outcome and the expectancy that it can be achieved. Thus,

$$force = first\text{-}level\ valence \times expectancy$$

We can expect an individual's effort to be directed toward the first-level outcome that has the largest force product. Notice that no matter the valence of a particular first-level

Expectancy. The probability that a particular first-level outcome can be achieved.

Force. The effort directed toward a first-level outcome.

outcome a person will not be motivated to achieve it if the expectancy of accomplishment approaches zero.

Believe it or not, the mechanics of expectancy theory can be distilled into a couple of simple sentences! In fact, these sentences nicely capture the premises of the theory:

- People will be motivated to perform in those work activities that they find attractive and that they feel they can accomplish.

- The attractiveness of various work activities depends on the extent to which they lead to favourable personal consequences.

It is extremely important to understand that expectancy theory is based on the perceptions of the individual worker. Thus, expectancies, valences, instrumentalities, and relevant second-level outcomes depend on the perceptual system of the person whose motivation we are analyzing. For example, two employees performing the same job might attach different valences to money, differ in their perceptions of the instrumentality of performance for obtaining high pay, and differ in their expectations of being able to perform at a high level. Therefore, they would likely exhibit different patterns of motivation.

Although expectancy theory does not concern itself directly with the distinction between extrinsic and intrinsic motivators, it can handle any form of second-level outcome that has relevance for the person in question. Thus, some people might find second-level outcomes of an intrinsic nature, such as feeling good about performing a task well, positively valent. Others might find extrinsic outcomes, such as high pay, positively valent.

To firm up your understanding of expectancy theory, consider Tony Angelas, a middle manager in a firm that operates a chain of retail stores (Exhibit 5). Second-level outcomes

EXHIBIT 5
Expectancy model for Tony Angelas (E = Expectancy, I = Instrumentality, V = Valence).

Explore

Go to MyManagementLab to see an annotated version of this figure.

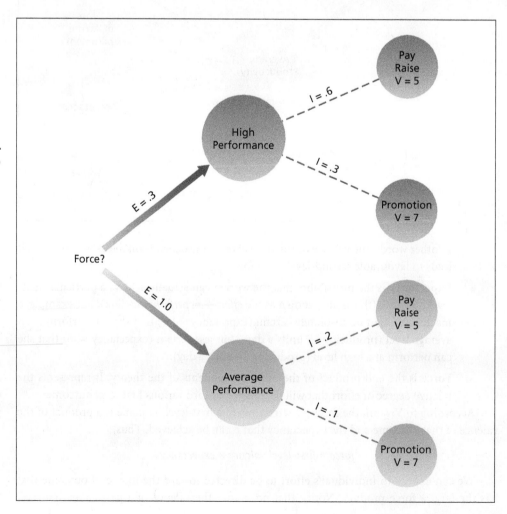

that are relevant to him include the opportunity to obtain a raise and the chance to receive a promotion. The promotion is more highly valent to Tony than the raise (7 versus 5 on a scale of 10) because the promotion means more money *and* increased prestige. Tony figures that if he can perform at a very high level in the next few months, the odds are 6 in 10 that he will receive a raise. Thus, the instrumentality of high performance for obtaining a raise is .6. Promotions are harder to come by, and Tony figures the odds at .3 if he performs well. The instrumentality of average performance for achieving these favourable second-level outcomes is a good bit lower (.2 for the raise and only .1 for the promotion). Recall that the valence of a first-level outcome is the sum of the products of second-level outcomes and their instrumentalities. Thus, the valence of high performance for Tony is $(5 \times .6) + (7 \times .3) = 5.1$. Similarly, the valence of average performance is $(5 \times .2) + (7 \times .1) = 1.7$. We can conclude that high performance is more valent for Tony than average performance.

Does this mean that Tony will necessarily try to perform at a high level in the next few months? To determine this, we must take into account his expectancy that he can actually achieve the competing first-level outcomes. As shown in Exhibit 5, Tony is absolutely certain that he can perform at an average level (expectancy = 1.0) but much less certain (.3) that he can sustain high performance. Force is a product of these expectancies and the valence of their respective first-level outcomes. Thus, the force associated with high performance is .3 $\times$ 5.1 = 1.53, while that associated with average performance is 1.0 $\times$ 1.7 = 1.70. As a result, although high performance is attractive to Tony, he will probably perform at an average level.

With all this complicated figuring, you might be thinking, "Look, would Tony really do all this calculation to decide his motivational strategy? Do people actually think this way?" The answer to these questions is probably no. Rather, the argument is that people *implicitly* take expectancy, valence, and instrumentality into account as they go about their daily business of being motivated. If you reflect for a moment on your behaviour at work or school, you will realize that you have certain expectancies about what you can accomplish, the chances that these accomplishments will lead to certain other outcomes, and the value of these outcomes for you.

Research Support for Expectancy Theory

Tests have provided moderately favourable support for expectancy theory.[37] In particular, there is especially good evidence that the valence of first-level outcomes depends on the extent to which they lead to favourable second-level consequences. We must recognize, however, that the sheer complexity of expectancy theory makes it difficult to test. We have already suggested that people are not used to *thinking* in expectancy terminology. Thus, some research studies show that individuals have a difficult time discriminating between instrumentalities and second-level valences. Despite this and other technical problems, experts in motivation generally accept expectancy theory.

Managerial Implications of Expectancy Theory

The motivational practices suggested by expectancy theory involve "juggling the numbers" that individuals attach to expectancies, instrumentalities, and valences.

BOOST EXPECTANCIES One of the most basic things managers can do is ensure that their employees *expect* to be able to achieve first-level outcomes that are of interest to the organization. No matter how positively valent high productivity or good attendance might be, the force equation suggests that workers will not pursue these goals if expectancy is low. Low expectancies can take many forms, but a few examples will suffice to make the point.

- Employees might feel that poor equipment, poor tools, or lazy co-workers impede their work progress.

- Employees might not understand what the organization considers to be good performance or see how they can achieve it.

- If performance is evaluated by a subjective supervisory rating, employees might see the process as capricious and arbitrary, not understanding how to obtain a good rating.

Although the specific solutions to these problems vary, expectancies can usually be enhanced by providing proper equipment and training, demonstrating correct work procedures, carefully explaining how performance is evaluated, and listening to employee performance problems. The point of all this is to clarify the path to beneficial first-level outcomes.

CLARIFY REWARD CONTINGENCIES Managers should also attempt to ensure that the paths between first- and second-level outcomes are clear. Employees should be convinced that first-level outcomes desired by the organization are clearly *instrumental* in obtaining positive second-level outcomes and avoiding negative outcomes. If a manager has a policy of recommending good performers for promotion, she should spell out this policy. Similarly, if managers desire regular attendance, they should clarify the consequences of good and poor attendance. To ensure that instrumentalities are strongly established, they should be clearly stated and then acted on by the manager. Managers should also attempt to provide stimulating, challenging tasks for workers who appear to be interested in such work. On such tasks, the instrumentality of good performance for feelings of achievement, accomplishment, and competence is almost necessarily high. The ready availability of intrinsic motivation reduces the need for the manager to constantly monitor and clarify instrumentalities.[38]

APPRECIATE DIVERSE NEEDS Obviously, it might be difficult for managers to change the valences that employees attach to second-level outcomes. Individual preferences for high pay, promotion, interesting work, and so on are the product of a long history of development and are unlikely to change rapidly. However, managers would do well to analyze the diverse preferences of particular employees and attempt to design individualized "motivational packages" to meet their needs. Recall that at GLBC exceptional performance is recognized by a variety of rewards such as cash, special dinners, and preferred parking spots. Of course, all concerned must perceive such rewards to be fair. Let's examine another process theory that is concerned specifically with the motivational consequences of fairness.

Equity Theory

LO 6

Explain and discuss *equity theory.*

Equity theory. A process theory that states that motivation stems from a comparison of the inputs one invests in a job and the outcomes one receives in comparison with the inputs and outcomes of another person or group.

Equity theory can be used in explaining job satisfaction. The theory asserts that workers compare the inputs that they invest in their jobs and the outcomes that they receive against the inputs and outcomes of some other relevant person or group. When these ratios are equal, the worker should feel that a fair and equitable exchange exists with the employing organization. Such fair exchange contributes to job satisfaction. When the ratios are unequal, workers perceive inequity, and they should experience job dissatisfaction, at least if the exchange puts the worker at a disadvantage vis-à-vis others.

But in what sense is equity theory a theory of motivation? Put simply, *individuals are motivated to maintain an equitable exchange relationship.* Inequity is unpleasant and tension-producing, and people will devote considerable energy to reducing inequity and achieving equity. What tactics can do this? Psychologist J. Stacey Adams has suggested the following possibilities:[39]

- Perceptually distort one's own inputs or outcomes.
- Perceptually distort the inputs or outcomes of the comparison person or group.
- Choose another comparison person or group.
- Alter one's inputs or alter one's outcomes.
- Leave the exchange relationship.

Notice that the first three tactics for reducing inequity are essentially psychological, while the last two involve overt behaviour.

To clarify the motivational implications of equity theory, consider Terry, a middle manager in a consumer products company. He has five years' work experience and an MBA degree and considers himself a good performer. His salary is $75 000 a year. Terry finds out that Maxine, a co-worker with whom he identifies closely, makes the same salary he does. However, she has only a Bachelor's degree and one year of experience, and he sees her performance as average rather than good. Thus, from Terry's perspective, the following outcome/input ratios exist:

$$\frac{\text{TERRY \$75 000}}{\text{Good performance MBA, 5 years}} \neq \frac{\text{MAXINE \$75 000}}{\text{Average performance Bachelor's, 1 year}}$$

In Terry's view, he is underpaid and should be experiencing inequity. What might he do to resolve this inequity? Psychologically, he might distort the outcomes that he is receiving, rationalizing that he is due for a certain promotion that will bring his pay into line with his inputs. Behaviourally, he might try to increase his outcomes (by seeking an immediate raise) or reduce his inputs. Input reduction could include a decrease in work effort or perhaps excessive absenteeism. Finally, Terry might resign from the organization to take what he perceives to be a more equitable job somewhere else.

Let's reverse the coin and assume that Maxine views the exchange relationship identically to Terry—same inputs, same outcomes. Notice that she too should be experiencing inequity, this time from relative overpayment. It does not take a genius to understand that Maxine would be unlikely to seek equity by marching into the boss's office and demanding a pay cut. However, she might well attempt to increase her inputs by working harder or enrolling in an MBA program. Alternatively, she might distort her view of Terry's performance to make it seem closer to her own. As this example implies, equity theory is somewhat vague about just when individuals will employ various inequity reduction strategies.

GENDER AND EQUITY As an addendum to the previous example, it is extremely interesting to learn that both women and men have some tendency to choose same-sex comparison persons—that is, when judging the fairness of the outcomes that they receive, men tend to compare themselves with other men, and women tend to compare themselves with other women. This might provide a partial explanation for why women are paid less than men, even for the same job. If women restrict their equity comparisons to (lesser paid) women, they are less likely to be motivated to correct what we observers see as wage inequities.[40]

Research Support for Equity Theory

Most research on equity theory has been restricted to economic outcomes and has concentrated on the alteration of inputs and outcomes as a means of reducing inequity. In general, this research is very supportive of the theory when inequity occurs because of *underpayment*.[41] For example, when workers are underpaid on an hourly basis, they tend to lower their inputs by producing less work. This brings inputs in line with (low) outcomes. Also, when workers are underpaid on a piece-rate basis (e.g., paid $1 for each market research interview conducted), they tend to produce a high volume of low-quality work. This enables them to raise their outcomes to achieve equity. Finally, there is also evidence that underpayment inequity leads to resignation. Presumably, some underpaid workers thus seek equity in another organizational setting.

The theory's predictions regarding *overpayment* inequity have received less support.[42] The theory suggests that such inequity can be reduced behaviourally by increasing inputs or by reducing one's outcomes. The weak support for these strategies suggests either that people tolerate overpayment more than underpayment, or that they use perceptual distortion to reduce overpayment inequity.

Managerial Implications of Equity Theory

The most straightforward implication of equity theory is that perceived underpayment will have a variety of negative motivational consequences for the organization, including low productivity, low quality, theft, or turnover. On the other hand, attempting to solve organizational problems through overpayment (disguised bribery) might not have the intended motivational effect. The trick here is to strike an equitable balance.

But how can such a balance be struck? Managers must understand that feelings about equity stem from a *perceptual* social comparison process in which the worker "controls the equation"—that is, employees decide what are considered relevant inputs, outcomes, and comparison persons, and management must be sensitive to these decisions. For example, offering the outcome of more interesting work might not redress inequity if better pay is considered a more relevant outcome. Similarly, basing pay only on performance might not be perceived as equitable if employees consider seniority an important job input.

Understanding the role of comparison people is especially crucial.[43] Even if the best engineer in the design department earns $2000 more than anyone else in the department, she might still have feelings of inequity if she compares her salary with that of more prosperous colleagues in *other* companies. Awareness of the comparison people chosen by workers might suggest strategies for reducing felt inequity. Perhaps the company will have to pay even more to retain its star engineer.

Notice how equity is achieved at GLBC. Salary surveys are conducted and individual salaries are reviewed every 12 months to make sure that salaries are competitive. In addition, all employees share equally in profit sharing. President and CEO Robert Meggy says, "I certainly believe in fair pay. You don't have to be the best paying but you have to be fair."[44]

LO 7

Explain and discuss *goal setting theory, goal orientation,* and *proximal* and *distal goals.*

Goal. The object or aim of an action.

Goal Setting Theory

At the beginning of the chapter, motivation was defined as persistent effort directed toward a goal. But what is a goal? A **goal** is the object or aim of an action.[45] One of the basic characteristics of all organizations is that they have goals. As indicated in the chapter-opening vignette, GLBC sets business goals and objectives for the organization as well as departments. In addition, employees meet with their immediate supervisor to set individual performance goals and to review how well they have met their goals. Thus, if employees are to achieve acceptable performance, some method of translating organizational goals into individual goals must be implemented.

Unfortunately, there is ample reason to believe that personal performance goals are vague or nonexistent for many organizational members. Employees frequently report that their role in the organization is unclear, or that they do not really know what their boss expects of them. Even in cases in which performance goals would seem to be obvious because of the nature of the task (e.g., filling packing crates to the maximum to avoid excessive freight charges), employees might be ignorant of their current performance. This suggests that the implicit performance goals simply are not making an impression.

The notion of goal setting as a motivator has been around for a long time. However, theoretical developments and some very practical research have demonstrated when and how goal setting can be effective.[46]

Goal setting theory. A process theory that states that goals are motivational when they are specific, challenging, when organizational members are committed to them, and when feedback about progress toward goal attainment is provided.

What Kinds of Goals Are Motivational?

According to **goal setting theory**, goals are most motivational when they are *specific* and *challenging* and when organizational members are *committed* to them. In addition, *feedback* about progress toward goal attainment should be provided.[47] The positive effects of goals are due to four mechanisms: they *direct* attention toward goal-relevant activities, they lead to greater *effort,* they increase and prolong *persistence,* and they lead to the discovery and use of task-relevant

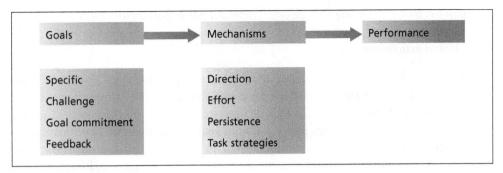

EXHIBIT 6
The mechanisms of goal setting.
Source: Locke, E.A., & Latham, G.P. (2002). Building a practically useful theory of goal setting and task motivation. *American Psychologist, 57*, 705–717.

Go to MyManagementLab to see an annotated version of this figure.

strategies for goal attainment.[48] Exhibit 6 shows the characteristics of goals that are motivational and the mechanisms that explain the effects of goals on performance.

GOAL SPECIFICITY Specific goals are goals that specify an exact level of achievement for people to accomplish in a particular time frame. For example, "I will enrol in five courses next semester and achieve a B or better in each course" is a specific goal. Similarly, "I will increase my net sales by 20 percent in the coming business quarter" is a specific goal. On the other hand, "I will do my best" is not a specific goal, since level of achievement and time frame are both vague.

GOAL CHALLENGE Obviously, specific goals that are especially easy to achieve will not motivate effective performance. But goal challenge is a much more personal matter than goal specificity, since it depends on the experience and basic skills of the organizational member. One thing is certain, however—when goals become so difficult that they are perceived as *impossible* to achieve, they will lose their potential to motivate. Thus, goal challenge is best when it is pegged to the competence of individual workers and increased as the particular task is mastered. One practical way to do this is to base initial goals on past performance. For example, an academic counsellor might encourage a D student to set a goal of achieving Cs in the coming semester and encourage a C student to set a goal of achieving Bs. Similarly, a sales manager might ask a new salesperson to try to increase his sales by 5 percent in the next quarter and ask an experienced salesperson to try to increase her sales by 10 percent.

GOAL COMMITMENT Individuals must be committed to specific, challenging goals if the goals are to have effective motivational properties. The effect of goals on performance is strongest when individuals have high goal commitment. In a sense, goals really are not goals and cannot improve performance unless an individual accepts them and is committed to working toward them. This is especially important when goals are challenging and difficult to achieve. In a following section, we will discuss some factors that affect goal commitment.

GOAL FEEDBACK Specific and challenging goals have the most beneficial effect when they are accompanied by ongoing feedback that enables the person to compare current performance with the goal. This is why a schedule of tasks to be completed often motivates goal accomplishment. Progress against the schedule provides feedback. To be most effective, feedback should be accurate, specific, credible, and timely. Recall that at GLBC performance reviews are held every three months at which time employees meet with their supervisor to review how well they met their goals and to establish goals for the next quarter. Performance feedback is also obtained from co-workers and managers who are familiar with each employee's work and informal progress reviews are also held throughout the year.

Enhancing Goal Commitment

It has probably not escaped you that the requirements for goal challenge and goal commitment seem potentially incompatible. After all, you might be quite amenable to accepting an easy goal but balk at accepting a tough one. Therefore, it is important to consider some of the factors that might affect commitment to challenging, specific goals, including participation, rewards, and management support.

PARTICIPATION It seems reasonable that organizational members should be more committed to goals that are set with their participation than to those simply handed down by their superior. Sensible as this sounds, the research evidence on the effects of participation is very mixed—sometimes participation in goal setting increases performance, and sometimes it does not.[49] If goal commitment is a potential *problem*, participation might prove beneficial.[50] When a climate of distrust between superiors and employees exists, or when participation provides information that assists in the establishment of fair, realistic goals, then it should facilitate performance. On the other hand, when employees trust their boss and when the boss has a good understanding of the capability of the employees, participation might be quite unnecessary for goal commitment.[51] Interestingly, research shows that participation can improve performance by increasing the *difficulty* of the goals that employees adopt.[52] This might occur because participation induces competition or a feeling of team spirit among members of the work unit, which leads them to exceed the goal expectations of the supervisor.

REWARDS Will the promise of extrinsic rewards (such as money) for goal accomplishment increase goal commitment? Probably, but there is plenty of evidence that goal setting has led to performance increases *without* the introduction of monetary incentives for goal accomplishment. One reason for this might be that many ambitious goals involve no more than doing the job as it was designed to be done in the first place. For example, encouraging employees to pack crates or load trucks to within 5 percent of their maximum capacity does not really involve a greater expenditure of effort or more work. It simply requires more attention to detail. Goal setting should, however, be compatible with any system to tie pay to performance that already exists for the job in question.

SUPPORTIVENESS There is considerable agreement about one factor that will *reduce* commitment to specific, challenging performance goals. When supervisors behave in a coercive manner to encourage goal accomplishment, they can badly damage employee goal commitment. For goal setting to work properly, supervisors must demonstrate a desire to assist employees in goal accomplishment and behave supportively if failure occurs, even adjusting the goal downward if it proves to be unrealistically high. Threat and punishment in response to failure will be extremely counterproductive.[53]

"Nobody came back from the Goal Setting
Workshop. They all left to find better jobs."

Goal Orientation and Proximity

A recent development in goal setting theory is research on people's preferences for different kinds of goals, or what is known as *goal orientation*. **Goal orientation** refers to an individual's goal preferences in achievement situations. It is a stable individual difference that affects performance. Some individuals have a preference for learning goals while others have a preference for performance goals (performance-prove or performance-avoid goals). Individuals with a **learning goal orientation** are most concerned about learning something new and developing their competence in an activity by acquiring new skills and mastering new situations; they focus on acquiring new knowledge and skills and developing their competence. Individuals with a **performance-prove goal orientation** are concerned about demonstrating their competence in performing a task by seeking favourable judgments about the outcome of their performance. Individuals with a **performance-avoid goal orientation** are concerned about avoiding negative judgments about the outcome of their performance.[54]

In the last several years, research has found that goal orientation is important for learning and performance. For example, a learning goal orientation has been found to be positively related to learning as well as academic, task, and job performance, while a performance-avoid orientation is negatively related to learning and lower task and job performance. A performance-prove orientation is not related to learning or performance outcomes. Thus, a learning goal orientation is most effective for learning and performance outcomes, while a performance-avoid goal orientation is detrimental for learning and performance.[55]

Goals can also be distinguished in terms of whether they are distal or proximal goals. A **distal goal** is a long-term or end goal, such as achieving a certain level of sales performance. A **proximal goal** is a short-term goal or sub-goal that is instrumental for achieving a distal goal. Proximal goals involve breaking down a distal goal into smaller, more attainable sub-goals. Proximal goals provide clear markers of progress toward a distal goal because they result in more frequent feedback. As a result, individuals can evaluate their ongoing performance and identify appropriate strategies for the attainment of a distal goal. Distal goals are too far removed to provide markers of one's progress, making it difficult for individuals to know how they are doing and to adjust their strategies.[56]

Research Support for Goal Setting Theory

Goal setting theory is considered to be one of the most valid and practical theories of employee motivation. Several decades of research have demonstrated that specific, difficult goals lead to improved performance and productivity on a wide variety of tasks and occupations, including servicing drink machines, entering data, selling, teaching, and typing text. Further, the effect of group goal setting on group performance is similar to the effect of individual goal setting. Group goals result in superior group performance, especially when groups set specific goals and when the group members participate in setting the goals.[57] Studies also reveal that the positive effects of goal setting are not short lived—they persist over a long enough time to have practical value.[58]

For example, in a now classic study conducted at Weyerhaeuser Company, a large forest products firm headquartered in Tacoma, Washington, truck drivers were assigned a specific, challenging performance goal of loading their trucks to 94 percent of legal weight capacity. Before setting this goal, management had simply asked the drivers to do their best to maximize their weight. Over the first several weeks, load capacity gradually increased to more than 90 percent and remained at this high level for seven years! In the first nine months alone, the company accountants conservatively estimated the savings at $250 000. These results were achieved without driver participation in setting the goal and without monetary incentives for goal accomplishment. Drivers evidently found the 94 percent goal motivating in and of itself; they frequently recorded their weights in informal competition with other drivers.[59]

In recent years, research has found that the effects of goal setting on performance depend on a number of factors. For example, when individuals lack the knowledge or skill to

Goal orientation. An individual's goal preferences in achievement situations.

Learning goal orientation. A preference to learn new things and develop competence in an activity by acquiring new skills and mastering new situations.

Performance-prove goal orientation. A preference to obtain favourable judgments about the outcome of one's performance.

Performance-avoid goal orientation. A preference to avoid negative judgments about the outcome of one's performance.

Distal goal. Long-term or end goal.

Proximal goal. Short-term goal or sub-goal.

Drivers at Weyerhaeuser Company were assigned a specific, challenging performance goal of loading their trucks to 94 percent of legal weight capacity.

perform a novel or complex task, a specific and challenging performance goal can decrease rather than increase performance relative to a do-your-best goal. On the other hand, when a task is straightforward, a specific, high-performance goal results in higher performance than a do-your-best goal. Thus, a high-performance goal is most effective when individuals already have the ability to perform a task. However, when individuals are learning to perform a novel or complex task, setting a specific, high-learning goal that focuses on knowledge and skill acquisition will be more effective than a specific, high-performance goal or a do-your-best goal. This is because effective performance of complex tasks requires the acquisition of knowledge and skills, and a specific learning goal focuses one's attention on learning.[60]

In addition, proximal goals have been found to be especially important for novel and complex tasks and distal goals can have a negative effect. However, when distal goals are accompanied with proximal goals they have a significant positive effect on the discovery and use of task-relevant strategies, self-efficacy, and performance.[61]

Research on goal setting theory has recently begun to consider the potential effects of subconscious goals. To learn more, see the Research Focus: *Effects of Subconscious Goals on Performance.*

Managerial Implications of Goal Setting Theory

The managerial implications of goal setting theory seem straightforward: set specific and challenging goals and provide ongoing feedback so that individuals can compare their performance with the goal. While goals can be motivational in certain circumstances, they obviously have some limitations. For example, as indicated earlier, the performance impact of specific, challenging goals is stronger for simpler jobs than for more complex jobs, such as scientific and engineering work. Thus, when a task is novel or complex and individuals need to acquire new knowledge and skills for good performance, setting a specific learning goal will be more effective than setting a high-performance goal. Setting a high-performance goal will be most effective when individuals already have the ability to perform a task effectively. In addition, proximal goals should be set in conjunction with distal goals when employees are learning a new task or performing a complex one.[62] A more elaborate application of goal setting theory is called *Management by Objectives.*

Now that you are familiar with the motivation theories, please consult You Be the Manager: *Your Tips or Your Job.*

RESEARCH FOCUS

EFFECTS OF SUBCONSCIOUS GOALS ON PERFORMANCE

When we think of goals and goal setting, we naturally assume that it is a conscious process, and in fact goal setting theory is focused entirely on conscious motivation. But there is some evidence that subconscious goals can have the same effect on behaviour and performance as conscious goals. But how can people have subconscious goals?

The answer is priming. Participants are exposed to stimuli such as a word or a picture of something relevant to the goal that one wants to prime them for. The stimulus triggers automatic goal activation that affects goal-directed cognition and behaviour without the person being aware of the process. Thus, subconscious goal motivation operates automatically, without intention, awareness, or conscious guidance.

A number of laboratory experiments have found that priming results in subconscious goals that influence behaviour and performance. But can priming result in subconscious goals in the workplace? To find out, Amanda Shantz and Gary Latham conducted an experiment in which they tested the effect of a primed goal alone and a specific, difficult, consciously set goal on the performance of call centre employees who were fundraising for a university. Employees were randomly assigned to one of four conditions: a primed goal only, a conscious goal only, a primed goal and conscious goal, and a "do-your-best" goal condition.

At the start of their three-hour shift, the employees received an information packet that contained information about the university for whom they would be soliciting donations and recent awards to faculty and the university. To prime a subconscious goal, an achievement-related photograph of a woman winning a race was shown in the backdrop of the paper that the information was printed on. The photograph was of Sonia O'Sullivan, an Irish athlete who won a silver medal in the 2000 Olympics. Participants in the conscious goal condition were given a specific high goal of $1200 to attain on their shift. The employees were told that management wanted to determine the usefulness of the information in the packet on their ability to raise money. They did not know that they were in an experiment.

To test the effects of the goal conditions, the employees in the four groups were compared on the amount of dollars they raised at the end of their shift. The results indicated that employees who were primed raised significantly more money than employees who were not primed and that employees who were assigned a conscious, difficult goal raised more money than employees who were told to do their best. Thus, both the primed and conscious goals increased performance. However, employees in the conscious goal condition raised more money than employees in the primed-subconscious goal condition.

The results of this study suggest that organizations can motivate employees to achieve higher levels of performance by priming them with a subconscious achievement-related goal through the use of an image that depicts achievement. This study also shows that motivation is not always conscious and that subconscious goals can be activated through priming.

Sources: Reprinted from *Organizational Behavior and Human Decision Processes, 109,* Shantz, A., & Latham, G. P., An exploratory field experiment of the effect of subconscious and conscious goals on employee performance, 9–17, Copyright © 2009 Elsevier Inc. All rights reserved; Stajkovic, A.D., Locke, E.A., & Blair, E.S. (2006). A first examination of the relationships between primed subconscious goals, assigned conscious goals, and task performance, *Journal of Applied Psychology, 91,* 1172–1180. Copyright © 2006 by American Psychological Association. Reprinted by permission.

DO MOTIVATION THEORIES TRANSLATE ACROSS CULTURES?

LO

Discuss the cross-cultural limitations of theories of motivation.

Are the motivation theories that we have described in this chapter culture-bound? That is, do they apply only to North America, where they were developed? The answer to this question is important for North American organizations that must understand motivational patterns in their international operations. It is also important to foreign managers, who are often exposed to North American theory and practice as part of their training and development.

It is safe to assume that most theories that revolve around human needs will come up against cultural limitations to their generality. For example, both Maslow and Alderfer suggest that people pass through a social stage (belongingness, relatedness) on their way to a

YOU BE THE MANAGER

Your Tips or Your Job

During the summer of 2012, a Marriott beach resort hotel in Ontario, The Rousseau Muskoka, issued an ultimatum to its spa employees. The ultimatum came in the form of a three-page letter to employees that made the front page of the *Toronto Star*.

In the letter, the employees were informed that spa customers will be charged a new higher gratuity fee (20 percent) on manicures, body wraps, massages, and other treatments and spa employees will receive 50 percent of the gratuity.

The gratuity was previously 18 percent with 2 percent going to the spa's administrative staff and the rest to the spa employee who performed the service. Under the new gratuity policy, the spa staff will receive 10 percent, 8.75 percent will go to the hotel, and 1.25 will go to administrative staff. If customers wish to tip more than the 20 percent gratuity, the extra portion would go to the employee.

The letter indicated that the new policy is necessary to efficiently manage costs and to remain competitive within the industry. Employees were told that if the new policy was not acceptable to them, their employment would be terminated.

Under the *Employment Standards Act*, there is nothing to stop organizations and managers from taking tips from their employees. However, at the time of the letter, New Democrat MPP Michael Prue introduced a private member's bill at Queen's Park that would outlaw owners and managers from taking a cut of worker's tips. Prue's proposal would amend the law to specify "an employer shall not take any portion of an employee's tips or other gratuities."

In the *Toronto Star* article, it was reported that sources at the hotel said most spa employees had reluctantly consented to the new policy because they

Employees at the Rousseau Muskoka were told to accept a reduction in gratuities or have their employment terminated.

need their jobs. But what about their motivation and job performance? You be the manager.

Questions

1. What do you think of the resort's new policy? Use the theories of motivation to explain the effects it might have on employees' motivation and performance.

2. Do you think the resort should proceed with its new policy? Explain your answer.

To find out what happened, see The Manager's Notebook at the end of the chapter.

Sources: Based on Ferguson, R. (June 27, 2012). Your tips or your jobs, posh hotel warns staff. *Toronto Star*, A1, A6; Ferguson, R. (June 29, 2012). Staff can keep tips—and their jobs. *Toronto Star*, A1, A14; Silliker, A. (2012). Hotel nixes plan to skim employee tips. *Canadian HR Reporter, 25*(14), 3, 6.

higher-level personal growth or self-actualization stage. However, it is well established that there are differences in the extent to which societies value a more collective or a more individualistic approach to life.[63] In individualistic societies (e.g., Canada, the United States, Great Britain, and Australia), people tend to value individual initiative, privacy, and taking care of oneself. In more collective societies (e.g., Mexico, Singapore, and Pakistan), more closely knit social bonds are observed, in which members of one's in-group (family, clan, or organization) are expected to take care of each other in exchange for strong loyalty to the in-group.[64] This suggests that there might be no superiority to self-actualization as a motive in more collective cultures. In some cases, for example, appealing to employee loyalty might prove more motivational than the opportunity for self-expression because it relates to strong belongingness needs that stem from cultural values. Also, cultures differ in the extent to which they value achievement as it

Cultures differ in how they define achievement. In collective societies where group solidarity is dominant, achievement may be more group-oriented than in individualistic societies.

is defined in North America, and conceptions of achievement might be more group-oriented in collective cultures than in individualistic North America. Similarly, the whole concept of intrinsic motivation might be more relevant to wealthy societies than to developing societies.

With respect to equity theory, we noted earlier that people should be appropriately motivated when outcomes received "match" job inputs. Thus, higher producers are likely to expect superior outcomes compared with lower producers. This is only one way to allocate rewards, however, and it is one that is most likely to be endorsed in individualistic cultures. In collective cultures, there is a tendency to favour reward allocation based on equality rather than equity.[65] In other words, everyone should receive the same outcomes despite individual differences in productivity, and group solidarity is a dominant motive. Trying to motivate employees with a "fair" reward system might backfire if your definition of fairness is equity and theirs is equality.

Because of its flexibility, expectancy theory is very effective when applied cross-culturally. The theory allows for the possibility that there may be cross-cultural differences in the expectancy that effort will result in high performance. It also allows for the fact that work outcomes (such as social acceptance versus individual recognition) may have different valences across cultures.[66]

Finally, setting specific and challenging goals should also be motivational when applied cross-culturally, and, in fact, goal setting has been found to predict, influence, and explain behaviour in numerous countries around the world.[67] However, for goal setting to be effective, careful attention will be required to adjust the goal setting process in different cultures. For example, individual goals are not likely to be accepted or motivational in collectivist cultures, where group rather than individual goals should be used. Power distance is also likely to be important in the goal setting process. In cultures where power distance is large, it would be expected that goals be assigned by superiors. However, in some small power distance cultures in which power differences are downplayed, participative goal setting would be more appropriate. One limitation to the positive effect of goal setting might occur in those (mainly Far Eastern) cultures in which saving face is important. That is, a specific and challenging goal may not be very motivating if it suggests that failure could occur and if it results in a negative reaction. This would seem to be especially bad if it were in the context of the less-than-preferred individual goal setting. Failure in the achievement of a very specific goal could lead to loss of face. As well, in the so-called being-oriented cultures where people work only as much as needed to live and avoid continuous work, there tends to be some resistance to goal setting.[68]

International management expert Nancy Adler has shown how cultural blinders often lead to motivational errors.[69] A primary theme running through this discussion is that appreciating cultural diversity is critical in maximizing motivation.

LO **9**

Summarize the relationships among the various theories of motivation, performance, and job satisfaction.

PUTTING IT ALL TOGETHER: INTEGRATING THEORIES OF WORK MOTIVATION

In this chapter, we have presented several theories of work motivation and attempted to distinguish between motivation and performance. At this point, it seems appropriate to review just how all these concepts fit together with job performance and job satisfaction. Exhibit 7 presents a model that integrates these relationships.

Each of the theories helps us to understand the motivational process. First, for individuals to obtain rewards they must achieve designated levels of performance. We know from earlier in this chapter that performance is a function of motivation as well as other factors, such as personality, general cognitive ability, emotional intelligence, understanding of the task, and chance. In terms of motivation, we are concerned with the amount, persistence, and direction of effort. Therefore, Boxes 1 through 5 in Exhibit 7 explain these relationships.

Perceptions of expectancy and instrumentality (expectancy theory) relate to all three components of motivation (*Box 1*). In other words, individuals direct their effort toward a particular first-level outcome (expectancy) and increase the amount and persistence of effort to the extent that they believe it will result in second-level outcomes (instrumentality). Goal setting theory (*Box 2*) indicates that specific and challenging goals that people are committed to, as well as feedback about progress toward goal attainment, will have a positive effect on amount, persistence, and direction of effort. Goal specificity should also strengthen both expectancy and instrumentality connections. The individual will have a clear picture of a first-level outcome to which her effort should be directed and greater certainty about the consequences of achieving this outcome.

Boxes 3 through 5 illustrate that motivation (*Box 3*) will be translated into good performance (*Box 5*) if the worker has the levels of general cognitive ability and emotional intelligence relevant to the job, and if the worker understands the task (*Box 4*). Chance can also help to translate motivation into good performance. If these conditions are not met, high motivation will not result in good performance.

 Explore

Go to MyManagementLab to see an annotated version of this figure.

EXHIBIT 7
Integrative model of motivation theories.

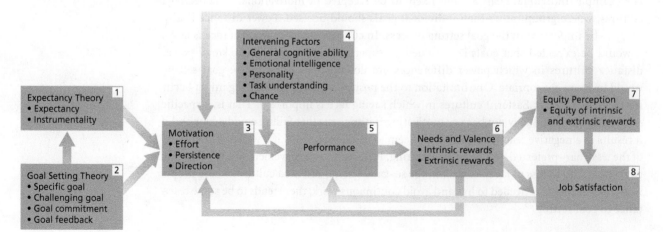

Second, a particular level of performance (*Box 5*) will be followed by certain outcomes. To the extent that performance is followed by outcomes that fulfill individual needs (need theory) and are positively valent second-level outcomes (expectancy theory), they can be considered rewards for good performance (*Box 6*). In general, the connection between performance and the occurrence of intrinsic rewards should be strong and reliable because such rewards are self-administered. For example, the nurse who assists several very sick patients back to health is almost certain to feel a sense of competence and achievement because such feelings stem directly from the job. On the other hand, the connection between performance and extrinsic rewards might be much less reliable because the occurrence of such rewards depends on the actions of management. Thus, the head nurse may or may not recommend attendance at a nursing conference (an extrinsic fringe benefit) for the nurse's good performance.

THE MANAGER'S NOTEBOOK

Your Tips or Your Job

1. According to one employee at the spa, "Everyone feels disgusted. Morale is low." The theories of motivation suggest that the new policy is also going to hurt employee motivation. The employees are probably motivated to fulfill their physiological or existence needs and are thus motivated to earn the extra money they receive from tips. The reduction in tips will lower their motivation given that they will be receiving lower tips for the same work. Their lower motivation is most clearly evident from an equity theory perspective. According to equity theory, workers compare the inputs that they invest in their jobs and the outcomes that they receive against the inputs and outcomes of some other relevant person or group. When these ratios are equal, the worker should feel that a fair and equitable exchange exists with the employing organization. When the ratios are unequal, workers perceive inequity. The employees at the resort will perceive their situation as inequitable because they will be obtaining lower outcomes (i.e., tips) for the same amount of work (i.e., inputs). Given that individuals are motivated to maintain an equitable exchange relationship, we would expect the employees to lower their inputs to bring them in line with the lower tips they will be receiving. This could include a decrease in work effort or quality, or perhaps excessive absenteeism. Employees might also try to increase their outcomes through theft. Expectancy theory also suggests that employees will lower their motivation because performing at the same level will no longer result in the same outcome. As a result, employees might be motivated to work at a lower level given that a high level of performance is not going to result in the same outcome as previously. In expectancy theory terms, the valence of the tip (second-level outcome) might be reduced thereby lowering the valence of the first-level outcome (e.g., high performance). Ultimately, what might happen is that the employees will work faster so that they can service more clients, which will result in more tips. This will probably result in poorer customer service (e.g.; less time to chat with customers), lower quality work, and a greater potential for mistakes.

2. It didn't take long for the resort to change its mind about the new policy. An angry public and media backlash forced them to scrap the new policy just two days after the story appeared on the front page of the *Toronto Star*. In a statement to the *Star*, the general manager said, "In response to feedback from staff and clientele about our company's recent decision to change our current gratuity structure at Spa Rousseau, we believe it prudent to reverse this decision and to maintain the gratuity structure as it is." He also told the *Star* that other steps will be taken to ensure the financial viability of the spa.

Sources: Based on Ferguson, R. (June 27, 2012). Your tips or your jobs, posh hotel warns staff. *Toronto Star*, A1, A6; Ferguson, R. (June 29, 2012). Staff can keep tips—and their jobs. *Toronto Star*, A1, A14.

Third, to the extent that the rewards fulfill individual needs (need theory), then they will be motivational, as depicted by the path from rewards (*Box 6*) to motivation (*Box 3*). In addition, the rewards that individuals receive are also the outcomes of the equity theory equation and will be used by individuals to form perceptions of equity (*Box 7*). Perceptions of equity also influence motivation (*Box 3*) and job satisfaction (*Box 8*). According to equity theory, individuals in a state of equity have high job satisfaction. Individuals who are in a state of inequity experience job dissatisfaction. Also, good performance leads to job satisfaction if that performance is rewarded, and job satisfaction in turn leads to good performance. In summary, each theory of motivation helps us to understand a different part of the motivational process.

MyManagementLab   Visit MyManagementLab at **www.mymanagementlab .com** for access to online tutorials, interactive exercises, videos, and much more.

LEARNING OBJECTIVES CHECKLIST

1 *Motivation* is the extent to which persistent effort is directed toward a goal. *Performance* is the extent to which an organizational member contributes to achieving the objectives of the organization.

2 *Intrinsic motivation* stems from the direct relationship between the worker and the task and is usually self-applied. *Extrinsic motivation* stems from the environment surrounding the task and is applied by others. *Self-determination theory* focuses on whether motivation is autonomous or controlled. Motivation is *autonomous* when people are motivated by intrinsic factors and they are in control of their motivation. Motivation is *controlled* when people are motivated to obtain a desired consequence or extrinsic reward.

3 *Performance* is influenced by motivation as well as personality, general cognitive ability, emotional intelligence, task understanding, and chance factors. *General cognitive ability* refers to a person's basic information-processing capacities and cognitive resources. *Emotional intelligence* refers to the ability to manage one's own and other's feelings and emotions. Motivation will be translated into good performance if an individual has the general cognitive ability and

emotional intelligence relevant to the job, and if he or she understands the task.

4 *Need theories* propose that motivation will occur when employee behaviour can be directed toward goals or incentives that satisfy personal wants or desires. The three need theories discussed are *Maslow's need hierarchy, Alderfer's ERG theory,* and *McClelland's theory of needs* for achievement, affiliation, and power. Maslow and Alderfer have concentrated on the hierarchical arrangement of needs and the distinction between intrinsic and extrinsic motivation. McClelland has focused on the conditions under which particular need patterns stimulate high motivation.

5 *Process theories* attempt to explain how motivation occurs rather than what specific factors are motivational. *Expectancy theory* argues that people will be motivated to engage in work activities that they find attractive and that they feel they can accomplish. The attractiveness of these activities depends on the extent to which they lead to favourable personal consequences.

6 *Equity theory* states that workers compare the inputs that they apply to their jobs and the outcomes that they get from their jobs with the inputs and outcomes of others. When these outcome/input ratios are unequal, inequity exists, and workers will be motivated to restore equity.

7 *Goal setting theory* states that goals are motivational when they are specific and challenging and when workers are committed to them and receive feedback about progress toward goal attainment. In some cases, companies can facilitate goal commitment through employee participation in goal setting and by financial incentives for goal attainment, but freedom from coercion and punishment seems to be the key factor in achieving goal commitment. *Goal orientation* refers to an individual's goal preferences in achievement situations. A *learning* goal orientation is a preference to learn new things and develop competence in an activity by acquiring new skills and mastering new situations. A *performance-prove goal orientation* is a preference to obtain favourable judgments about the outcome of one's performance, and a *performance-avoid goal orientation* is a preference to avoid negative judgments about the outcome of one's performance. A *distal goal* is a long-term or end goal, and a *proximal goal* is a short-term goal or sub-goal.

8 There are some cross-cultural limitations of the theories of motivation. For example, most theories that revolve around human needs will come up against cultural limitations to their generality as a result of differences in values across cultures. As for equity theory, trying to motivate employees with a "fair" reward system might backfire if the definition of fairness is other than

equity (e.g., equality). Because of its flexibility, expectancy theory is very effective when applied cross-culturally and allows for the possibility that there may be cross-cultural differences in the expectancy that effort will result in high performance. It also allows for the fact that work outcomes (such as social acceptance versus individual recognition) may have different valences across cultures. Setting specific and challenging goals should also be motivational when applied cross-culturally. However, for goal setting to be effective, careful attention will be required to adjust the goal setting process in different cultures.

9 Performance is a function of motivation as well as other factors, such as personality, general cognitive ability, emotional intelligence, understanding of the task, and chance. Perceptions of expectancy and instrumentality influence motivation, as do specific and challenging goals that people are committed to and that are accompanied with feedback. Motivation will be translated into good performance if the worker has the levels of general cognitive ability and emotional intelligence relevant to the job and if the worker understands the task. Chance can also help to translate motivation into good performance. To the extent that performance leads to rewards that fulfill individual needs and are positively valent, they will be motivational. When the rewards are perceived as equitable, they will have a positive effect on motivation and job satisfaction. Furthermore, good performance leads to job satisfaction if that performance is rewarded, and job satisfaction in turn leads to good performance.

DISCUSSION QUESTIONS

1. Many millionaires continue to work long, hard hours, sometimes even beyond the usual age of retirement. Use the ideas developed in the chapter to speculate about the reasons for this motivational pattern. Is the acquisition of wealth still a motivator for these individuals?

2. Discuss a time when you were highly motivated to perform well (at work, at school, in a sports contest) but performed poorly in spite of your high motivation. How do you know that your

motivation was really high? What factors interfered with good performance? What did you learn from this experience?

3. Use Maslow's hierarchy of needs and Alderfer's ERG theory to explain why assembly line workers and executive vice-presidents might be susceptible to different forms of motivation.

4. Colleen is high in need for achievement, Eugene is high in need for power, and Max is high in need for affiliation. They are thinking about

starting a business partnership. To maximize the motivation of each, what business should they go into, and who should assume which roles or jobs?

5. Reconsider the case of Tony Angelas, which was used to illustrate expectancy theory. Imagine that you are Tony's boss and you think that he can be motivated to perform at a high level. Suppose you cannot modify second-level outcomes or their valences, but you can affect expectancies and instrumentalities. What would you do to motivate Tony? Prove that you have succeeded by recalculating the force equations to demonstrate that Tony will now perform at a high level.

6. Debate the following statements: Of all the motivational theories we discussed in this chapter, goal setting theory is the simplest to implement. Goal setting is no more than doing what a good manager should be doing anyway.

7. What are the implications of goal orientation for motivating a group of employees? When would it be best to set a learning goal versus a performance goal? When it would be best to set a proximal versus a distal goal? Describe a situation in which it would be best to set a learning goal and a situation in which it would be best to set a performance goal. Describe a situation in which it would be best to set a proximal goal and a situation in which it would be best to set a distal goal.

8. Critique the following assertion: People are basically the same. Thus, the motivation theories discussed in the chapter apply equally around the globe.

9. Describe self-determination theory and provide an example of when your motivation was controlled and when it was autonomous. What factors contributed to your autonomous and controlled motivation and what effect did your motivation have on your performance?

10. What is the relationship between cognitive ability and emotional intelligence with job performance? When would emotional intelligence be most important for a person's job performance? When is cognitive ability especially important for job performance?

INTEGRATIVE DISCUSSION QUESTIONS

1. With respect to the cross-cultural dimensions of values (i.e., work centrality, power distance, uncertainty avoidance, masculinity/femininity, individualism/collectivism, and long-term/short-term orientation), discuss the implications of each value for exporting the work motivation theories discussed in this chapter across cultures. Based on your analysis, how useful are the theories described in this chapter for understanding and managing motivation across cultures? What are the implications?

2. Consider the basic characteristics of motivation in relation to operant learning theory and social cognitive theory. What are the implications of operant learning theory and social cognitive theory for motivation, and how do they compare to the theories of work motivation described in this chapter?

ON-THE-JOB CHALLENGE QUESTION

Employee Time Theft

Employee theft is a major problem for organizations in Canada and the United States. According to one study, employee theft costs Canadian organizations more than $120 billion a year and is the cause of 30 percent of business failures. The study also found that 79 percent of employees admit to stealing or considering it. Another study found that as many as one out of every 28 employees was apprehended for theft in 2007 in the United States. Although employee theft has usually involved things like inflated expense accounts, cooking the books, stealing merchandise, or pocketing money from cash sales, organizations are increasingly finding themselves the victims of time theft.

Time theft occurs when employees steal their employer's time by engaging in unauthorized personal activities during working hours, such as visiting social networking sites and chat lines or spending time out of the office fulfilling one's personal agenda (e.g., playing golf) rather than meeting with clients or making sales calls. Time theft also occurs when employees take longer breaks for coffee or meals, make personal phone calls at work, send or receive email not related to work, and surf the Web for personal reasons.

Why are employees motivated to steal from their organization? Use the theories of motivation discussed in the chapter to answer this question. What can organizations do to prevent employee time theft? Consider the implications of each

theory of motivation for preventing all forms of employee theft.

Sources: Sherr, I. (2009, July 11). U.S. retailers struggle with theft by employees; Outpaces shoplifting, fraud. Tech solutions yield surprises. *Gazette* (Montreal), C6; Levitt, H. (2009, May 20). Employers must beware of the time wasters: Ways to make staff accountable for time away from the office. *Edmonton Journal*, F4; Levitt, H. (2008, August 20). Hands off the cookie jar or pay the price. *Ottawa Citizen*, F3; Buckingham, R. (2008, April 1). Time theft growing in the workplace. *Telegraph-Journal* (Saint John), B1.

EXPERIENTIAL EXERCISE

What Is Your Goal Orientation?

The following scale is a measure of goal orientation. Answer each of the statements as accurately and honestly as possible using the following response scale:

1–Strongly disagree

2–Moderately disagree

3–Slightly disagree

4–Neither disagree nor agree

5–Slightly agree

6–Moderately agree

7–Strongly agree

____ 1. It's important for me to impress others by doing a good job.

____ 2. If I don't succeed at a difficult task, I plan to try harder the next time.

____ 3. I worry that I won't always be able to meet the standards set by others.

____ 4. I avoid tasks that I may not be able to complete.

____ 5. It's better to stick with what works than risk failing at a task.

____ 6. The opportunity to extend my range of abilities is important to me.

____ 7. I avoid circumstances where my performance will be compared to that of others.

____ 8. I like to meet others' expectations of me.

____ 9. The opportunity to learn new things is important to me.

____ 10. I'm not interested in impressing others with my performance.

____ 11. I am always challenging myself to learn new concepts.

____ 12. I get upset when other people do better than I do.

____ 13. Most of the time, I stay away from tasks that I know I won't be able to complete.

____ 14. I don't care what others think of my performance.

____ 15. I don't enjoy taking on tasks if I am unsure whether I will complete them successfully.

____ 16. The opportunity to do challenging work is important to me.

____ 17. Typically, I like to be sure that I can successfully perform a task before I attempt it.

____ 18. I value what others think of my performance.

____ 19. I prefer to work on tasks that force me to learn new things.

____ 20. In learning situations, I tend to set fairly challenging goals for myself.

____ 21. I don't like having my performance compared negatively to that of others.

Scoring and Interpretation

To obtain your score, first subtract your response to questions 10 and 14 from 8. For example, if you gave a response of 1 to question 10, give yourself a 7 (8 minus 1). To obtain your score on each type of goal orientation, add your scores as follows:

Learning goal orientation: Add items 2, 6, 9, 11, 16, 19, and 20.

Performance-prove goal orientation: Add items 1, 5, 8, 12, 18, and 10.

Performance-avoid goal orientation: Add items 3, 4, 7, 13, 15, 17, and 21.

Your total for each of the three goal orientations should be somewhere between 7 and 49. The higher your score, the higher your goal orientation. Rank your scores from highest to lowest to identify your primary goal orientation. To facilitate class discussion and your understanding of goal orientation, form a small group with several other members of the class and consider the following questions:

1. Each group member should present their goal orientation scores. Rank your three scores from highest to lowest. What is your primary goal orientation? What is the primary goal orientation of most members of your group?

2. Given your primary goal orientation, how might it affect your academic performance? How might it affect your performance at work?

3. Given your primary goal orientation, what type of goal should you set for yourself in the future? When should you set a learning goal versus a performance goal?

4. How can knowledge of your primary goal orientation help you in your future studies and grades? How can it help you at work and in your career?

5. Based on the results of this exercise, what have you learned about yourself? What kind of goals should you focus on at school and at work? Explain your answers.

Source: Zweig, D., and Webster, J. (2004). Validation of a multidimensional measure of goal orientation. *Canadian Journal of Behavioural Science, 36*(3), 232–243. Copyright 2004, Canadian Psychological Association. Used with permission.

CASE INCIDENT

Mayfield Department Stores

As competition in the retail market began to heat up, it became necessary to find ways to motivate the sales staff of Mayfield Department Stores to increase sales. Therefore, a motivational program was developed with the help of a consulting firm. Each month, employees in the department with the highest sales would have a chance to win a trip to Mexico. At the end of the year, the names of all employees in those departments that had the highest sales for at least one month would have their name entered into a draw and three names would be chosen to win a one-week trip to Mexico paid for by Mayfield.

1. According to need theories of motivation and goal setting theory, will this program be motivational? Explain your answer.

2. Discuss the motivational potential of the program according to expectancy theory and equity theory. Will the program motivate the sales staff and improve sales?

3. How would you change the program to make it more effective for motivating employees? Use expectancy theory, equity theory, and goal setting theory to support your plan to make the program more effective.

CASE STUDY

DATATRONIC

DATATRONIC is a company started by George Pandry and Rolin Martin, two friends who had just graduated with degrees in business administration and saw an opportunity to start their own business. With an increasing number of organizations conducting employee attitude surveys, they saw a need for data input and analyses as well as for the design of Web-based surveys. With a loan from their parents, they rented space, purchased 20 used computers, and set up shop. They hired some students they knew at the university and began advertising their services. Employees were paid minimum wage and usually worked three-hour shifts in the mornings and afternoons several days a week.

The assignment of projects to employees was fairly straightforward. Whenever a new project was accepted by DATATRONIC, Rolin would review the job and then set a deadline for completion based on the nature of the project and the customer's needs. While some employees only worked on Web-based surveys, all employees were able to input data and conduct some basic data analyses. If a project required more advanced data analysis, it was assigned to one of a handful of employees who were able to do it. It was George's responsibility to check on the progress of projects and make sure they were completed by the deadline. Once a project was completed, Rolin would review it and check for mistakes and errors. If a project was found to have errors, Rolin would send it back to the employee who worked on it, with instructions on what needed to be corrected and the new deadline. If the corrections were minor, then the employee would be asked to do them immediately and put aside what he or she was currently working on. If the corrections were more substantial, then the employee's current project would be given to another employee so that the employee could work on the project that required corrections.

Within a relatively short period of time, DATA-TRONIC was having trouble keeping up with demand. In fact, business was so good they had to hire more employees and purchase more computers. After about six months, however, they began to notice some problems. An increasing number of projects were not being completed on time, and customers were beginning to complain. In some cases, George and Rolin had to give big discounts to customers who threatened to take their business elsewhere.

In order to try to deal with the increasing missed deadlines, George decided to keep a close eye on employees during their shifts. He soon came to the conclusion that many of them were friends and spent too much time chatting and socializing while they were supposed to be working.

After discussing the problem with Rolin, it was decided that the best thing to do was to keep a closer eye on employees while they worked. So the next day, George began watching employees and even standing over them while they worked. Whenever some of the employees began to talk with each other, George rushed over to remind them that they were there to work and not to talk. Some of the employees were surprised at this sudden change and didn't understand what the problem was. George told them that too many projects were not being completed on time

and that talking would no longer be tolerated while employees are working. "You get paid for working here, not socializing and talking to your friends," George was often heard saying. "Stop talking and get back to work."

By the end of the month, however, things still had not improved. While the employees were no longer talking to each other when George was watching over them, many projects were still not being completed on time. George and Rolin decided that they should focus on those employees who were the main source of the problem. After reviewing the records of all employees, they made a list showing the number of projects each employee had completed on time as well as the number that were late. They then posted the list on a large board at the front of the room. Employees were told that from now on, George and Rolin would be keeping track of how many employees' projects were completed on time and that they would fire people who were late completing more than one project a month.

This did not sit well with the employees. Many of them complained that it was unfair to blame them for being late because some projects were much more demanding than others and the deadlines were often unreasonable. However, George and Rolin insisted that the deadlines were based on the size and difficulty of the projects.

Many of the students relied on the extra money they made from DATATRONIC to pay for their books, supplies, and the occasional dinner or night out, so being fired was a concern to them. Within a few weeks, almost all projects were being completed on time. George and Rolin concluded that their latest strategy was working, and the list of employees at the front of the room was showing a marked increase in projects completed on time for all employees.

However, by the end of the month a new problem became apparent. Many of the completed data files were full of mistakes, the data analysis was often incomplete and incorrect, and the Web-based surveys were often missing questions and contained all sorts of errors. As a result, almost 50 percent (15 jobs per month) of all jobs had to be completely redone. This turned out to be a rather costly problem. Each job took between 10 and 50 hours and cost DATATRONIC hundreds of dollars to fix. This also meant that projects were not being completed on time because they had to be redone and checked after the deadline. More and more customers began to complain and to demand a reduction in the cost of their projects.

To make matters worse, some of the best employees decided to quit. Over a period of three months, DATATRONIC lost an average of three employees a month. Every time an employee quit, they had to replace him or her, and the cost of replacement was beginning to be a problem. The cost of advertising, interviewing, and hiring a new employee was estimated to be about $5000.

While employees were at one time bringing their friends to work DATATRONIC, this was no longer enough to fill all the jobs. As a result, it became increasingly difficult to find and hire new workers. In desperation, George and Rolin decided to increase the pay to new hires to above minimum wage. This, however, did not sit well with current employees, some of whom had been with DATATRONIC since it first began. Some of DATATRONIC's experienced employees threatened to quit if they did not receive a pay increase. George and Rolin did not see how they could increase the pay of all their current employees. However, they realized that something had to be done—and fast.

They came up with a three-pronged approach. First, they decided to give those employees who were threatening to quit a pay increase equal to what new hires were receiving. Second, they decided to offer a $100 bonus at the end of every month to the employee who performed best on completion time and quality. The employee with the most projects completed with the fewest errors would receive the bonus. And third, they decided that employees who turned in projects with substantial errors would be required to correct them on their own time, without pay.

When the employees heard about these changes they became less cooperative with each other and less willing to offer help and assistance. Before the announcement, although employees engaged in less socializing during working hours, they maintained a friendly and collegial atmosphere, with workers frequently asking each other for help and providing assistance to new hires. However, with the new bonus program and the possibility of having to correct errors without pay, this was no longer the case. Employees not only stopped talking to each other, they also stopped helping each other.

This was especially hard on the new hires who often needed help and advice from the more experienced employees.

At the end of the first month under the new bonus program, George and Rolin called a meeting and told the employees that Mika Salomn had completed three projects and had made only one error. She happily accepted her bonus of $100 and was congratulated for her excellent performance. Some of the other employees clapped and congratulated her, but others seemed less enthused. Nonetheless, the number of mistakes and projects that had to be returned to workers for corrections began to decline.

George and Rolin felt that they had finally found the solution to solving the problems at DATATRONIC. However, by the end of the week, three other employees began demanding a pay increase and several others complained that they should have received the bonus because their performance was just as good as Mika's. To make matters worse, three new hires and two of DATATRONIC's most experienced employees decided to quit.

George and Rolin couldn't understand how something so good had become so bad. They wondered whether they should give all employees a pay increase equal to the new hires or perhaps they need to do something about the bonus program. They were at a loss as to what to do next and wondered if maybe they needed to hire a consultant to provide some advice and direction.

QUESTIONS

1. What factors do you think contribute to the performance of the employees at DATATRONIC? Refer to Exhibit 1 to explain your answer.
2. Consider the needs of the employees at DATATRONIC. What is most likely to motivate them? How important are intrinsic and extrinsic motivators? Is their motivation autonomous or controlled?
3. Discuss the motivational strategies being used at DATATRONIC. What are employees motivated to do? How do the theories of motivation help us understand employees' motivation and performance and the effectiveness of the motivational strategies?

4. Using the theories of motivation, what advice would you give George and Rolin on how to motivate employees at DATATRONIC? Be sure to refer to the need theories and the process theories of motivation.

5. What would you do to motivate DATATRONIC employees? Be specific in terms of how to motivate them to complete projects on time, to complete projects without errors, and to continue to work at DATATRONIC. Justify your answers using the theories of motivation.

REFERENCES

1. Brooks, Y. (2006, December). Handle with care. *BC Business* (online), bcbusinessonline.ca; Colman, R. (2007, March). Packing the perfect HR punch: Great Little Box Company president and CEO Robert Meggy, CMA, FCMA, knows that people make a business. His unique approach to employee engagement proves it. *Entrepreneur* (online), www.entrepreneur.com; Great Little Box Company: A team approach to success. *Managing for Business Success.* Industry Canada, www.ic.gc.ca; Atkinson, C. (2008, July 2). The total package: Anatomy of a great place to work, *Globe and Mail*, B6; Brent, P. (2005, October). Packaging loyalty: A Vancouver maker thrives by finding employees who fit. *National Post*, WK2; Yerema, R. (2009, January 12). Employer Review: The Great Little Box Company Ltd.: Chosen as one of Canada's Top 100 employers and BC's top employers for 2009. www.eluta.ca; Great Little Box Company, www.greatlittlebox.com/about/history; Chosen as one of Canada's Top 100 employers, *Financial Post*'s Ten Best Companies to Work For and BC's Top Employers for 2012, www.eluta.ca/top-employer-great-little-box company.

2. Great Little Box Company: A team approach to success. *Managing for Business Success.* Industry Canada, www.ic.gc.ca.

3. Campbell, J.P., Dunnette, M.D., Lawler, E.E., III, & Weick, K.E., Jr. (1970). *Managerial behavior, performance, and effectiveness.* New York: McGraw-Hill. Also see Blau, G. (1993). Operationalizing direction and level of effort and testing their relationship to job performance. *Organizational Behavior and Human Decision Processes, 55*, 152–170.

4. Dyer, L., & Parker, D.F. (1975). Classifying outcomes in work motivation research: An examination of the intrinsic-extrinsic dichotomy. *Journal of Applied Psychology, 60*, 455–458; Kanungo, R.N., & Hartwick, J. (1987). An alternative to the intrinsic-extrinsic dichotomy of work rewards. *Journal of Management, 13*, 751–766. Also see Brief, A.P., & Aldag, R.J. (1977). The intrinsic-extrinsic dichotomy: Toward conceptual clarity. *Academy of Management Review, 2*, 496–500.

5. Vallerand, R.J. (1997). Toward a hierarchical model of intrinsic and extrinsic motivation. *Advances in Experimental Social Psychology, 29*, 271–360.

6. Deci, E.L., & Ryan, R.M. (1985). *Intrinsic motivation and self-determination in human behavior.* New York: Plenum.

7. Deci & Ryan, 1985.

8. Eisenberger, R., & Cameron, J. (1996). Detrimental effects of reward: Reality or myth? *American Psychologist, 51*, 1153–1166.

9. Guzzo, R.A. (1979). Types of rewards, cognitions, and work motivation. *Academy of Management Review, 4*, 75–86; Wiersma, U.J. (1992). The effects of extrinsic rewards in intrinsic motivation: A meta-analysis. *Journal of Occupational and Organizational Psychology, 65*, 101–114.

10. Gagné, M., & Deci, E.L. (2005). Self-determination theory and work motivation. *Journal of Organizational Behavior, 26*, 331–362.

11. Based on Campbell, J.P., & Pritchard, R.D. (1976). Motivation theory in industrial and organizational psychology. In M.D. Dunnette (Ed.), *Handbook of industrial and organizational psychology.* Chicago: Rand McNally.

12. O'Reilly, C.A. III, & Chatman, J.A. (1994). Working smarter and harder: A longitudinal study of managerial success. *Administrative Science Quarterly, 39*, 603–627.

13. Lang, J.W.B., Kersting, M., Hulsheger, U.R., & Lang, J. (2010). General mental ability, narrower cognitive abilities, and job performance: The perspective of the nested-factors model of cognitive abilities. *Personnel Psychology, 63*, 595–640; Hunter, J.E. (1986). Cognitive ability, cognitive aptitudes, job knowledge, and job performance. *Journal of Vocational Behavior, 29*, 340–362; Schmidt, F.L., & Hunter, J.E. (1998). The validity and utility of selection methods in personnel psychology: Practical and theoretical implications of 85 years of research findings. *Psychological Bulletin, 124*, 262–274; Judge, T.A., Klinger, R.L., & Simon, L.S. (2010). Time is on my side: Time, general mental ability, human capital, and extrinsic career success. *Journal of Applied Psychology, 95*, 92–107.

14. Mayer, J.D., Caruso, D.R., & Salovey, P. (2000). Emotional intelligence meets traditional standards for an intelligence. *Intelligence, 27*, 267–298; Salovey, P., & Mayer, J.D. (1990). Emotional intelligence. *Imagination, Cognition and Personality, 9*,185–211.

15. Mayer, Caruso, & Salovey, 2000.

16. George, J.M. (2000). Emotions and leadership: The role of emotional intelligence. *Human Relations, 53*, 1027–1055.

17. George, 2000.

18. George, 2000.

19. Van Rooy, D.L., & Viswesvaran, C. (2004). Emotional intelligence: A meta-analytic investigation of predictive validity and nomological net. *Journal of Vocational Behavior, 65*, 71–95.

20. O'Boyle, E.H., Jr., Humphrey, R.H., Pollack, J.M., Hawver, T.H., & Story, P.A. (2011). The relation between emotional intelligence and job performance: A meta-analysis. *Journal of Organizational Behavior, 32*, 788–818.

21. Schutte, N.S., Malouff, J.M., Hall, L.E., Haggerty, D.J., Cooper, J.T., Golden, C.J., & Dornheim, L. (1998). Development and validation of a measure of emotional intelligence. *Personality and Individual Differences, 25*, 167–177; Wong, C., & Law, K.S. (2002). The effects of leader and follower emotional intelligence on performance and attitude: An exploratory study. *The Leadership Quarterly, 13*, 243–274; Daus, C.S., & Ashkanasy, N.M. (2005). The case for the ability-based model of emotional intelligence in organizational behaviour. *Journal of Organizational Behavior, 26*,453–466; Joseph, D.L., & Newman, D.A. (2010). Emotional intelligence: An integrative meta-analysis and cascading model. *Journal of Applied Psychology, 95*, 54–78.

22. Côté, S., & Miners, C.T.H. (2006). Emotional intelligence, cognitive intelligence, and job performance. *Administrative Science Quarterly, 51*, 1–28.

23. See Henkoff, R. (1993, March 22). Companies that train best. *Fortune*, 62–75.

24. The distinction between need (content) and process theories was first made by Campbell et al., 1970.

25. Maslow, A.H. (1970). *Motivation and personality* (2nd ed.). New York: Harper & Row.

26. Alderfer, C.P. (1969). An empirical test of a new theory of human needs. *Organizational Behavior and Human Performance, 4*, 142–175. Also see Alderfer, C.P. (1972). *Existence, relatedness, and growth: Human needs in organizational settings.* New York: The Free Press.

27. McClelland, D.C. (1985). *Human motivation.* Glenview, IL: Scott, Foresman.

28. McClelland, D.C., & Winter, D.G. (1969). *Motivating economic achievement.* New York: The Free Press, 50–52.

29. McClelland, D.C., & Boyatzis, R.E. (1982). Leadership motive pattern and long-term success in management. *Journal of Applied Psychology, 67*, 737–743; McClelland, D.C., & Burnham, D. (1976, March–April). Power is the great motivator. *Harvard Business Review*, 159–166. However, need for power might not be the best motive pattern for managers of technical and professional people. See Cornelius,

E.T., III, & Lane, F.B. (1984). The power motive and managerial success in a professionally oriented service industry organization. *Journal of Applied Psychology, 69,* 32–39.

30. Wahba, M.A., & Bridwell, L.G. (1976). Maslow reconsidered: A review of research on the need hierarchy theory. *Organizational Behavior and Human Performance, 15,* 212–240.

31. Schneider, B., & Alderfer, C.P. (1973). Three studies of measures of need satisfaction in organizations. *Administrative Science Quarterly, 18,* 498–505. Also see Alderfer, C.P., Kaplan, R.E., & Smith, K.K. (1974). The effect of relatedness need satisfaction on relatedness desires. *Administrative Science Quarterly, 19,* 507–532. For a disconfirming test, see Rauschenberger, J., Schmitt, N., & Hunter, J.E. (1980). A test of the need hierarchy concept by a Markov model of change in need strength. *Administrative Science Quarterly, 25,* 654–670.

32. McClelland, 1985; Spangler, W.D. (1992). Validity of questionnaire and TAT measures of need for achievement: Two meta-analyses. *Psychological Bulletin, 112,* 140–154.

33. Great Little Box Company: A team approach to success. *Managing for Business Success.* Industry Canada, www .ic.gc.ca.

34. Herzberg, F. (1966). *Work and the nature of man.* Cleveland: World Publishing.

35. Lawler, E.E., III. (1973). *Motivation in work organizations.* Monterey, CA: Brooks/Cole.

36. Vroom, V.H. (1964). *Work and motivation.* New York: Wiley.

37. Mitchell, T.R. (1974). Expectancy models of job satisfaction, occupational preference, and effort: A theoretical, methodological, and empirical appraisal. *Psychological Bulletin, 81,* 1053–1077. Also see Pinder, C.C. (1984). *Work motivation: Theory, issues, and applications.* Glenview, IL: Scott, Foresman; Kanfer, R. (1990). Motivation theory in industrial and organizational psychology. In M.D. Dunnette & L.M. Hough (Eds.), *Handbook of industrial and organizational psychology* (2nd ed., Vol. 1). Palo Alto, CA: Consulting Psychologists Press.

38. A good discussion of how managers can strengthen expectancy and instrumentality relationships is presented by Strauss, G. (1977). Managerial practices. In J.R. Hackman & J.L. Suttle (Eds.), *Improving life at work: Behavioral science approaches to organizational change.* Glenview, IL: Scott, Foresman.

39. Adams, J.S. (1965). Injustice in social exchange. *Advances in Experimental Social Psychology, 2,* 267–299.

40. Kulik, C.T., & Ambrose, M.L. (1992). Personal and situational determinants of referent choice. *Academy of Management Review, 17,* 212–237.

41. Carrell, M.R., & Dittrich, J.E. (1978). Equity theory: The recent literature, methodological considerations, and new directions. *Academy of Management Review, 3,* 202–210; Mowday, R.T. (1991). Equity theory predictions of behavior in organizations. In R.M. Steers & L.W. Porter (Eds.), *Motivation and work behavior,* 111–131. New York: McGraw-Hill.

42. Mowday, 1991; Carrell & Dittrich, 1978.

43. See Kulik & Ambrose, 1992.

44. Colman, R. (2007, March).

45. Locke, E.A., & Latham, G.P. (2002). Building a practically useful theory of goal setting and task motivation. *American Psychologist, 57,* 705–717.

46. The best-developed theoretical position is that of Locke, E.A., & Latham, G.P. (1990). *A theory of goal setting and task performance.* Englewood Cliffs, NJ: Prentice-Hall.

47. Locke & Latham, 2002.

48. Locke & Latham, 2002.

49. Locke, E.A., Latham, G.P., & Erez, M. (1988). The determinants of goal commitment. *Academy of Management Review, 13,* 23–39.

50. See Erez, M., Earley, P.C., & Hulin, C.L. (1985). The impact of participation on goal acceptance and performance: A two-step model. *Academy of Management Journal, 28,* 50–66.

51. Latham, G.P., Erez, M., & Locke, E.A. (1988). Resolving scientific disputes by the joint design of crucial experiments by the antagonists: Application to the Erez-Latham dispute regarding participation in goal setting. *Journal of Applied Psychology, 73,* 753–772.

52. Latham, G.P., Mitchell, T.R., & Dosset, D.L. (1978). The importance of participative goal setting and anticipated rewards on goal difficulty and job performance. *Journal of Applied Psychology, 63,* 163–171; Saari, L.M., & Latham, G.P. (1979). The effects of holding goal difficulty constant on assigned and participatively set goals. *Academy of Management Journal, 22,* 163–168.

53. For a discussion of this issue, see Saari & Latham, 1979.

54. Payne, S.C., Youngcourt, S.S., & Beaubien, J.M. (2007). A meta-analytic examination of the goal orientation nomological net. *Journal of Applied Psychology, 92,* 128–150; Zweig, D., & Webster, J. (2004). Validation of a multidimensional measure of goal orientation. *Canadian Journal of Behavioural Science, 36*(3), 232–243.

55. Seijts, G.H., Latham, G.P., Tasa, K., & Latham, B.W. (2004). Goal setting and goal orientation: An integration of two different yet related literatures. *Academy of Management Journal, 47,* 227–239; Button, S.B., Mathieu, J.E., & Zajac, D.M. (1996). Goal orientation in organizational research: A conceptual and empirical foundation. *Organizational Behavior and Human Decision Processes, 67,* 26–48; VandeWalle, D., Brown, S.P., Cron, W.L., & Slocum, J.W., Jr. (1999). The influence of goal orientation and self-regulation tactics on sales performance: A longitudinal field test. *Journal of Applied Psychology, 84,* 249–259; VandeWalle, D., Cron, W.L., & Slocum, J.W., Jr. (2001). The role of goal orientation following performance feedback. *Journal of Applied Psychology, 86,* 629–640; Kozlowski, S.W.J., Gully, S.M., Brown, K.G., Salas, E., Smith, E.M., & Nason, E.R. (2001). Effects of training goals and goal orientation traits on multidimensional training outcomes and performance adaptability. *Organizational Behavior and Human Decision Processes, 85,* 1–31.

56. Latham, G.P., & Seijts, G.H. (1999). The effects of proximal and distal goals on performance on a moderately complex task. *Journal of Organizational Behavior, 20,* 421–429; Seijts, G.H., & Latham, G.P. (2001). The effect of distal learning, outcome, and proximal goals on a moderately complex task. *Journal of Organizational Behavior, 22,* 291–307.

57. O'Leary-Kelly, A.M., Martocchio, J.J., & Frink, D.D. (1994). A review of the influence of group goals on group performance. *Academy of Management Journal, 37,* 1285–1301; Kleingeld, A., van Mierlo, H., & Arends, L. (2011). The effect of goal setting on group performance: A meta-analysis. *Journal of Applied Psychology, 96,* 1289–1304.

58. Locke, E.A., & Latham, G.P. (1984). *Goal setting—A motivational technique that works.* Englewood Cliffs, NJ: Prentice-Hall.

59. Latham, G.P., & Baldes, J.J. (1975). The "practical significance" of Locke's theory of goal setting. *Journal of Applied Psychology, 60,* 122–124; Latham, G.P., & Locke, E. (1979, Autumn). Goal setting—a motivational technique that works. *Organizational Dynamics, 8*(2), 68–80.

60. Payne et al., 2007; Seijts, Latham, Tasa, & Latham, 2004; Seijts, G., & Latham, G.P. (2005). Learning versus performance goals: When should each be used? *Academy of Management Executive, 19,* 124–131.

61. Latham & Seijts, 1999; Seijts & Latham, 2001.

62. Seijts, Latham, Tasa, & Latham, 2004; Seijts & Latham, 2005; Latham & Seijts, 1999; Seijts & Latham, 2001.

63. Kagitcibasi, C., & Berry, J.W. (1989). Cross-cultural psychology: Current research and trends. *Annual Review of Psychology, 40,* 493–531.

64. Hofstede, G. (1980). *Culture's consequences: International differences in work-related values.* Beverly Hills, CA: Sage.

65. For a review, see Kagitcibasi & Berry, 1989.

66. Adler, N.J. (1992). *International dimensions of organizational behaviour* (2nd ed.). Belmont, CA: Wadsworth.

67. Locke & Latham, 2002.

68. Kirkman, B.L., & Shapiro, D.L. (1997). The impact of cultural values on employee resistance to teams: Toward a model of globalized self-managing work team effectiveness. *Academy of Management Review, 22,* 730–757.

69. Adler, 1992, 159.

PHOTO CREDITS

Credits are listed in order of appearance.

Courtesy of Great Little Box Company; Randy Glasbergen; Weyerhauser; Sergej Khackimullin/Fotolia; The Canadian Press/Bebeto Matthews.

GROUPS AND TEAMWORK

From Chapter 7 of *Organizational Behaviour*, Ninth Edition. Gary Johns and Alan M. Saks. Copyright © 2014 by Pearson Education Canada. All rights reserved.

GROUPS AND TEAMWORK

IDEO

IDEO is considered to be one of the most innovative and influential global design and innovation consultancy firms in the world. IDEO has received numerous domestic and international awards for design excellence, including 38 Red Dot awards and 28 iF Hanover awards. Signature products have included the first Apple computer mouse, Nike sunglasses, and the Steelcase Node chair.

With offices in major cities in the U.S., Europe, and Asia, IDEO employs people working on projects for clients ranging from startups to premier organizations in food and beverage (Nestlé), retail (Target), philanthropy (Oxfam), telecommunications (Nokia), computing (Microsoft), medicine (Mayo Clinic), banking (Bank of America), and manufacturing (Ford Motor Company).

As a design firm, IDEO uses an approach that relies heavily on interdisciplinary project teams. For example, for a Kentucky-based project headed by The Community Builders, the largest nonprofit developer of public housing in the U.S., an IDEO team was assembled consisting of anthropologists, architects, psychologists, and industrial designers. To accomplish their mandate, team members interviewed builders, urban planners, municipal authorities, and service providers. The real insights, however, occurred when the team broke into groups to stay overnight with three families from Park DuValle, a mixed-income community in Louisville. By doing so, the team was able to uncover the latent needs of home dwellers whose income levels and life trajectories were vastly different from one another.

Since the challenges facing IDEO are complex, assembling the right teams is critical to ensuring its success. In his book *Change by Design*, CEO Tim Brown suggests that a popular saying throughout the company – "All of us are smarter than any of us" – is purportedly what drives the company's insistence on a collective ownership of ideas. Staffing a project with teammates from a multiplicity of disciplines takes patience, however. To become part of an IDEO team, an individual must possess not only depth in the skill required to make a tangible contribution, but also

a capacity for handling role ambiguity and a disposition for collaborating with others across fields. Several best practices are therefore instilled to provide the firm with guidance in designing effective teams.

First, since new teams are marshaled for every project, team members must be passionate about the project they are assigned to. Without passion, IDEO believes that the motivation needed to generate creative solutions will be absent.

Second, status differences between team members are eliminated because IDEO considers hierarchy as stifling to innovation. As such, formal position titles on business cards and segregated corner offices are rejected because they impose mental and physical barriers between teams and individuals. Another element minimizing employee status differences and facilitating virtual communication is the company's intranet, known widely as "The Tube." Considered to be the centerpiece of how IDEO interacts as a global organization, The Tube encourages teams to collaborate and share their passions and expertise through social-networking tools such as blogs, wikis, and real-time screen sharing.

An innovation project with a dedicated beginning, middle, and end is more likely to keep the team motivated and focused on moving forward. Since clients may unnecessarily delay their engagement after the presentation of a consultant's report, IDEO encourages its client to participate in all aspects of the team's research, analysis, and development process. Unlike many traditional design consulting firms, IDEO's teams help shorten the time between conception and sale, thereby reinforcing its competitive advantage.[1]

This vignette shows how critical groups or teams are in determining organizational success. In this chapter, we will define the term *group* and discuss the nature of formal groups and informal groups in organizations. After this, we will present the details of group development. Then, we will consider how groups differ from one another structurally and explore the consequences of these differences. We will also cover the problem of social loafing. Finally, we will examine how to design effective work teams.

WHAT IS A GROUP?

We use the word "group" rather casually in everyday discourse—for example, special-interest group or ethnic group. However, for behavioural scientists, a **group** consists of two or more people interacting interdependently to achieve a common goal.

Interaction is the most basic aspect of a group—it suggests who is in the group and who is not. The interaction of group members need not be face to face, and it need not be verbal. For example, employees who telecommute can be part of their work group at the office even though they live kilometres away and communicate via email. Interdependence simply means that group members rely to some degree on each other to accomplish goals. All groups have one or more goals that their members seek to achieve. These goals can range from having fun to marketing a new product to achieving world peace.

Group memberships are very important for two reasons. First, groups exert a tremendous influence on us. They are the social mechanisms by which we acquire many beliefs, values, attitudes, and behaviours. Group membership is also important because groups provide a context in which *we* are able to exert influence on *others*.

Formal work groups are groups that organizations establish to facilitate the achievement of organizational goals. They are intentionally designed to channel individual effort in an appropriate direction. The most common formal group consists of a manager and the employees who report to that manager. In a manufacturing company, one such group might consist of a production manager and the six shift supervisors who report to him or her. In turn, the shift supervisors head work groups composed of themselves and their respective subordinates. Thus, the hierarchy of most organizations is a series of formal, interlocked work groups.

Other types of formal work groups include task forces, project teams, and committees. *Task forces* and *project teams* are temporary groups that meet to achieve particular goals or to solve particular problems, such as suggesting productivity improvements. At IDEO, the design of products and services is accomplished via formal but temporary interdisciplinary project teams. *Committees* are usually permanent groups that handle recurrent assignments outside the usual work group structures. For example, a firm might have a standing committee on work–family balance.

In addition to formal groups sanctioned by management to achieve organizational goals, informal grouping occurs in all organizations. **Informal groups** are groups that emerge naturally in response to the common interests of organizational members. They are seldom sanctioned by the organization, and their membership often cuts across formal groups. Informal groups can either help or hurt an organization, depending on their norms for behaviour. We will consider this in detail later.

GROUP DEVELOPMENT

Even relatively simple groups are actually complex social devices that require a fair amount of negotiation and trial and error before individual members begin to function as a true group. While employees often know each other before new teams are formed, simple familiarity does not replace the necessity for team development.

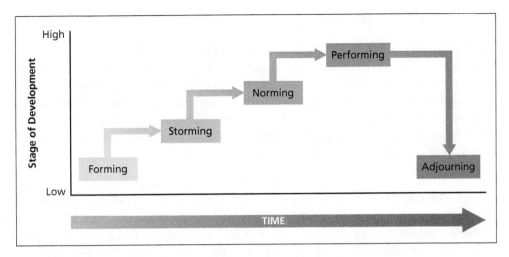

EXHIBIT 1 Stages of group development.

 Explore

Go to MyManagementLab to see an annotated version of this figure.

Typical Stages of Group Development

Leaders and trainers have observed that many groups develop through a series of stages over time.[2] Each stage presents the members with a series of challenges they must master to achieve the next stage. These stages (forming, storming, norming, performing, and adjourning) are presented in Exhibit 1.

FORMING At this early stage, group members try to orient themselves by "testing the waters." What are we doing here? What are the others like? What is our purpose? The situation is often ambiguous, and members are aware of their dependency on each other.

STORMING At this second stage, conflict often emerges. Confrontation and criticism occur as members determine whether they will go along with the way the group is developing. Sorting out roles and responsibilities is often at issue here. Problems are more likely to happen earlier, rather than later, in group development.

NORMING At this stage, members resolve the issues that provoked the storming, and they develop social consensus. Compromise is often necessary. Interdependence is recognized, norms are agreed to, and the group becomes more cohesive (we will study these processes later). Information and opinions flow freely.

PERFORMING With its social structure sorted out, the group devotes its energies toward task accomplishment. Achievement, creativity, and mutual assistance are prominent themes of this stage.

ADJOURNING Some groups, such as task forces and design project teams, have a definite lifespan and disperse after achieving their goals. Also, some groups disperse when corporate layoffs and downsizing occur. At this adjourning stage, rites and rituals that affirm the group's previous successful development are common (such as ceremonies and parties). Members often exhibit emotional support for each other.[3]

The stages model is a good tool for monitoring and troubleshooting how groups are developing. However, not all groups go through these stages of development. The process applies mainly to new groups that have never met before. Well-acquainted task forces and committees can short-circuit these stages when they have a new problem to work out.[4] Also, some organizational settings are so structured that storming and norming are unnecessary for even strangers to coalesce into a team. For example, most commercial airline cockpit crews perform effectively even though they can be made up of virtual strangers who meet just before takeoff.[5]

Punctuated Equilibrium

When groups have a specific deadline by which to complete some problem-solving task, we can often observe a very different development sequence from that described above. Connie Gersick, whose research uncovered this sequence, describes it as a **punctuated equilibrium model** of group development.[6] *Equilibrium* means stability, and the research revealed apparent stretches of group stability punctuated by a critical first meeting, a midpoint change in group activity, and a rush to task completion. In addition to many business work groups, Gersick studied student groups doing class projects, so see if this sequence of events sounds familiar to you.

PHASE 1 Phase 1 begins with the first meeting and continues until the midpoint in the group's existence. The very first meeting is critical in setting the agenda for what will happen in the remainder of this phase. Assumptions, approaches, and precedents that members develop in the first meeting end up dominating the first half of the group's life. Although it gathers information and holds meetings, the group makes little visible progress toward the goal.

MIDPOINT TRANSITION The midpoint transition occurs at almost exactly the halfway point in time toward the group's deadline. For instance, if the group has a two-month deadline, the transition will occur at about one month. The transition marks a change in the group's approach, and how the group manages the change is critical for the group to show progress. The need to move forward is apparent, and the group may seek outside advice. This transition may consolidate previously acquired information or even mark a completely new approach, but it crystallizes the group's activities for Phase 2 just as the first meeting did for Phase 1.

PHASE 2 For better or for worse, decisions and approaches adopted at the midpoint get played out in Phase 2. It concludes with a final meeting that reveals a burst of activity and a concern for how outsiders will evaluate the product.

Exhibit 2 shows how the punctuated equilibrium model works for groups that successfully or unsuccessfully manage the midpoint transition.

What advice does the punctuated equilibrium model offer for managing product development teams, advertising groups, or class project groups?[7]

- Prepare carefully for the first meeting. What is decided here will strongly determine what happens in the rest of Phase 1. If you are the coach or adviser of the group, stress *motivation and excitement* about the project.

- As long as people are working, do not look for radical progress during Phase 1.

- Manage the midpoint transition carefully. Evaluate the strengths and weaknesses of the ideas that people generated in Phase 1. Clarify any questions with whoever is

Punctuated equilibrium model. A model of group development that describes how groups with deadlines are affected by their first meetings and crucial midpoint transitions.

EXHIBIT 2
The punctuated equilibrium model of group development for two groups.

 Explore

Go to MyManagementLab to see an annotated version of this figure.

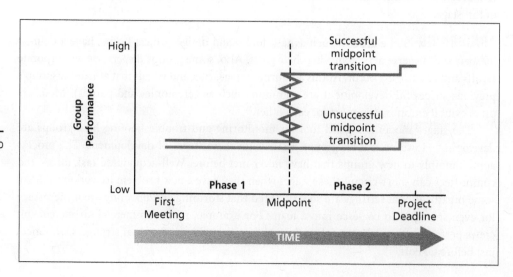

commissioning your work. Recognize that a fundamental change in approach must occur here for progress to occur. Essential issues are not likely to "work themselves out" during Phase 2. At this point, a group coach should focus on the *strategy* to be used in Phase 2.

- Be sure that adequate resources are available to actually execute the Phase 2 plan.
- Resist deadline changes. These could damage the midpoint transition.

As noted, the concept of punctuated equilibrium applies to groups with deadlines. Such groups might also exhibit some of the stages of development noted earlier, with a new cycle of storming and norming following the midpoint transition.

GROUP STRUCTURE AND ITS CONSEQUENCES

Group structure refers to the characteristics of the stable social organization of a group—the way a group is "put together." The most basic structural characteristics along which groups vary are size and member diversity. Other structural characteristics are the expectations that members have about each other's behaviour (norms), agreements about "who does what" in the group (roles), the rewards and prestige allocated to various group members (status), and how attractive the group is to its members (cohesiveness).

Group Size

Of one thing we can be certain—the smallest possible group consists of two people, such as a manager and a particular employee. It is possible to engage in much theoretical nitpicking about just what constitutes an upper limit on group size. However, given the definition of group that we presented earlier, it would seem that congressional or parliamentary size (300 to 400 members) is somewhere close to this limit. In practice, most work groups, including task forces and committees, usually have between 3 and 20 members.

SIZE AND SATISFACTION The more the merrier? In theory, yes. In fact, however, members of larger groups rather consistently report less satisfaction with group membership than those who find themselves in smaller groups.[8] What accounts for this apparent contradiction?

For one thing, as opportunities for friendship increase, the chance to work on and develop these opportunities might decrease owing to the sheer time and energy required. In addition, in incorporating more members with different viewpoints, larger groups might prompt conflict and dissension, which work against member satisfaction. As group size increases, the time available for verbal participation by each member decreases. Also, many people are inhibited about participating in larger groups.[9] Finally, in larger groups, individual members identify less easily with the success and accomplishments of the group. For example, a particular member of a 4-person cancer research team should be able to identify his or her personal contributions to a research breakthrough more easily than a member of a 20-person team can.

SIZE AND PERFORMANCE Satisfaction aside, do large groups perform tasks better than small groups? This question has great relevance to practical organizational decisions: How many people should a bank assign to evaluate loan applications? How many carpenters should a construction company assign to build a garage? If a school system decides to implement team teaching, how big should the teams be? The answers to these and similar questions depend on the exact task that the group needs to accomplish and on how we define good performance.[10]

Some tasks are **additive tasks**. This means that we can predict potential performance by adding the performances of individual group members together. Building a house is an additive task, and we can estimate potential speed of construction by adding the efforts of individual carpenters. Thus, for additive tasks, the potential performance of the group increases with group size.

 LO 3

Explain how group size and member diversity influence what occurs in groups.

Additive tasks. Tasks in which group performance is dependent on the sum of the performance of individual group members.

Disjunctive tasks.
Tasks in which group performance is dependent on the performance of the best group member.

Process losses. Group performance difficulties stemming from the problems of motivating and coordinating larger groups.

Conjunctive tasks.
Tasks in which group performance is limited by the performance of the poorest group member.

Some tasks are **disjunctive tasks**. This means that the potential performance of the group depends on the performance of its *best member*. For example, suppose that a research team is looking for a single error in a complicated computer program. In this case, the performance of the team might hinge on its containing at least one bright, attentive, logical-minded individual. Obviously, the potential performance of groups doing disjunctive tasks also increases with group size because the probability that the group includes a superior performer is greater.

We use the term "potential performance" consistently in the preceding two paragraphs for the following reason: As groups performing tasks get bigger, they tend to suffer from process losses.[11] **Process losses** are performance difficulties that stem from the problems of motivating and coordinating larger groups. Even with good intentions, problems of communication and decision making increase with size—imagine 50 carpenters trying to build a house. Thus, actual performance = potential performance – process losses.

These points are summarized in Exhibit 3. As you can see in part (a), both potential performance and process losses increase with group size for additive and disjunctive tasks. The net effect is shown in part (b), which demonstrates that actual performance increases with size up to a point and then falls off. Part (c) shows that the *average* performance of group members decreases as size gets bigger. Thus, up to a point, larger groups might perform better as groups, but their individual members tend to be less efficient.

We should note one other kind of task. **Conjunctive tasks** are those in which the performance of the group is limited by its *poorest performer*. For example, an assembly-line operation is limited by its weakest link. Also, if team teaching is the technique used to train employees how to perform a complicated, sequential job, one poor teacher in the sequence will severely damage the effectiveness of the team. Both the potential and actual performance of conjunctive tasks would decrease as group size increases because the probability of including a weak link in the group goes up.

EXHIBIT 3
Relationships among group size, productivity, and process losses.
Source: From Steiner, I.D. (1972). *Group process and productivity*. New York: Academic Press, p. 96. Copyright © 1972.

Explore

Go to MyManagementLab to see an annotated version of this figure.

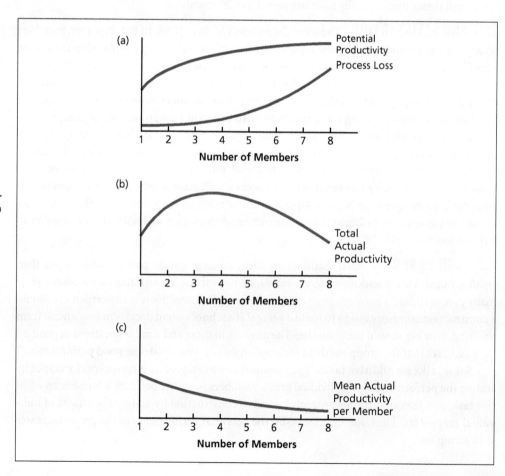

In summary, for additive and disjunctive tasks, larger groups might perform better up to a point but at increasing costs to the efficiency of individual members. By any standard, performance on purely conjunctive tasks should decrease as group size increases.

Diversity of Group Membership

Imagine an eight-member product development task force composed exclusively of 30-something white males of Western European heritage. Then imagine another task force with 50 percent men and 50 percent women from eight different ethnic or racial backgrounds and an age range from 25 to 55. The first group is obviously homogeneous in its membership, while the latter is heterogeneous or diverse. Which task force do you think would develop more quickly as a group? Which would be most creative?

Group diversity has a strong impact on interaction patterns—more diverse groups have a more difficult time communicating effectively and becoming cohesive (we will study cohesiveness in more detail shortly).[12] This means that diverse groups might tend to take longer to do their forming, storming, and norming.[13] Once they do develop, more and less diverse groups can be equally cohesive and productive.[14] However, diverse groups sometimes perform better on certain tasks. For example, diversity in educational background and functional specialty (e.g., marketing versus product design) enhances team creativity and innovation because a wider variety of ideas are considered.[15] In general, any negative effects of "surface diversity" in age, gender, or race are small or wear off over time. For instance, age diversity is unrelated to group performance, while racial and gender diversity have small negative effects.[16] However, "deep diversity" in attitudes toward work or how to accomplish a goal can badly damage cohesiveness.[17]

All this speaks well for the concepts of valuing and managing diversity. When management values and manages diversity, it offsets some of the initial process loss costs of diversity and capitalizes on its benefits for group performance.

Group Norms

Social **norms** are collective expectations that members of social units have regarding the behaviour of each other. As such, they are codes of conduct that specify what individuals ought and ought not to do and standards against which we evaluate the appropriateness of behaviour.

Much normative influence is unconscious, and we are often aware of such influence only in special circumstances, such as when we see children struggling to master adult norms or international visitors sparring with the norms of our culture. We also become conscious of norms when we encounter ones that seem to conflict with each other ("Get ahead" but "Don't step on others") or when we enter new social situations. For instance, the first day on a new job, workers frequently search for cues about what is considered proper office etiquette: Should I call the boss "mister"? Can I personalize my workspace?

NORM DEVELOPMENT *Why* do norms develop? The most important function that norms serve is to provide regularity and predictability to behaviour. This consistency provides important psychological security and permits us to carry out our daily business with minimal disruption.

What do norms develop *about*? Norms develop to regulate behaviours that are considered at least marginally important to their supporters. For example, managers are more likely to adopt norms regarding the performance and attendance of employees than norms concerning how employees personalize and decorate their offices. In general, less deviation is accepted from norms that concern more important behaviours.

How do norms develop? Individuals develop attitudes as a function of a related belief and value. In many cases, their attitudes affect their behaviour. When the members of a group *share* related beliefs and values, we can expect them to share consequent attitudes. These shared attitudes then form the basis for norms.[18] Notice that it really does not make

Review how *norms*, *roles*, and *status* affect social interaction.

Norms. Collective expectations that members of social units have regarding the behaviour of each other.

171

sense to talk about "my personal norm." Norms are *collectively* held expectations, depending on two or more people for their existence.

Why do individuals tend to comply with norms? Much compliance occurs simply because the norm corresponds to privately held attitudes. In addition, even when norms support trivial social niceties (such as when to shake hands or when to look serious), they often save time and prevent social confusion. Most interesting, however, is the case in which individuals comply with norms that *go against* their privately held attitudes and opinions. For example, couples without religious convictions frequently get married in religious services, and people who hate neckties often wear them to work. In short, groups have an extraordinary range of rewards and punishments available to induce conformity to norms.

SOME TYPICAL NORMS There are some classes of norms that seem to crop up in most organizations and affect the behaviour of members. They include the following:

- *Dress norms.* Social norms frequently dictate the kind of clothing people wear to work.[19] Military and quasi-military organizations tend to invoke formal norms that support polished buttons and razor-sharp creases. Even in organizations that have adopted casual dress policies, employees often express considerable concern about what they wear at work. Such is the power of social norms.

- *Reward allocation norms.* There are at least four norms that might dictate how rewards, such as pay, promotions, and informal favours could be allocated in organizations:

  a. Equity—reward according to inputs, such as effort, performance, or seniority.

  b. Equality—reward everyone equally.

  c. Reciprocity—reward people the way they reward you.

  d. Social responsibility—reward those who truly need the reward.[20]

  Most Western organizations tend to stress allocation according to some combination of equity and equality—give employees what they deserve, and no favouritism.

- *Performance norms.* The performance of organizational members might be as much a function of social expectations as it is of inherent ability, personal motivation, or technology.[21] Work groups provide their members with potent cues about what an appropriate level of performance is. New group members are alert for these cues: Is it all right to take a break now? Under what circumstances can I be absent from work without being punished? (See the Research Focus: *Absence Cultures—Norms in Action.*) The official organizational norms that managers send to employees usually favour high performance. However, work groups often establish their own informal performance norms, such as those that restrict productivity under a piece-rate pay system. Groups that set specific, challenging goals will perform at a high level.[22]

Roles

Roles. Positions in a group that have a set of expected behaviours attached to them.

Roles are positions in a group that have a set of expected behaviours attached to them. Thus, roles represent "packages" of norms that apply to particular group members. As we implied in the previous section, many norms apply to all group members to be sure that they engage in *similar* behaviours (such as restricting productivity or dressing a certain way). However, the development of roles is indicative of the fact that group members might also be required to act *differently* from one another.

In organizations, we find two basic kinds of roles. Designated or *assigned roles* are formally prescribed by an organization as a means of dividing labour and responsibility to facilitate task achievement. In general, assigned roles indicate "who does what" and "who can tell others what to do." In a software firm, labels that we might apply to formal roles include president, software engineer, analyst, programmer, and sales manager. In addition to assigned

RESEARCH FOCUS

ABSENCE CULTURES—NORMS IN ACTION

On first thought, you might assume that absenteeism from work is a very individualized behaviour, a product of random sickness or of personal job dissatisfaction. Although these factors contribute to absenteeism, there is growing evidence that group norms also have a strong impact on how much work people miss.

We can see cross-national differences in absenteeism. Traditionally, absence has been rather high in Scandinavia, lower in the United States and Canada, and lower yet in Japan and Switzerland. Clearly, these differences are not due to sickness but rather to differences in cultural values about the legitimacy of taking time off work. These differences get reflected in work group norms.

Within the same country and company we can still see group differences in absenteeism. A company that Gary Johns studied had four plants that made the same products and had identical human resources policies. Despite this, one plant had a 12 percent absence rate while another had an absence rate of 5 percent. Within one plant, some departments had virtually no absence while others approached a rate of 25 percent!

Moving to the small group level, Johns also studied small customer service groups in a utility company. Despite the fact that all employees were doing the same

work in the same firm, there were again striking cross-group differences in absenteeism, ranging from 1 to 13 percent.

These normative differences in absenteeism across groups are called absence cultures. How do they develop? People tend to adjust their own absence behaviour to what they see as typical of their group. Then, other factors come into play. In the utility company study, the groups that monitored each other's behaviour more closely had lower absence. A Canadian study found that air traffic controllers traded off calling in sick so that their colleagues could replace them at double overtime. A U.K. study found that industrial workers actually posted "absence schedules" so that they could take time off without things getting out of hand! All these are examples of norms in action.

The norms underlying absence cultures can dictate presence as well as absence. Recent studies show that "presenteeism," coming to work when feeling unwell, is prevalent in many human services occupations.

Source: Some of the research bearing on absence cultures is described in Johns, G. (2008). Absenteeism and presenteeism: Not at work or not working well. In J. Barling & C.L. Cooper (Eds.), *Sage Handbook of Organizational Behavior* (Vol. 1). London: Sage.

roles, we invariably see the development of *emergent roles*. These are roles that develop naturally to meet the social–emotional needs of group members or to assist in formal job accomplishment. The class clown and the office gossip fulfill emergent social–emotional roles, while an "old pro" might emerge to assist new group members learn their jobs. Other emergent roles might be assumed by informal leaders or by scapegoats who are the targets of group hostility.

ROLE AMBIGUITY **Role ambiguity** exists when the goals of one's job or the methods of performing it are unclear. Ambiguity might be characterized by confusion about how performance is evaluated, how good performance can be achieved, or what the limits of one's authority and responsibility are.

Exhibit 4 shows a model of the process that is involved in assuming an organizational role. As you can see, certain organizational factors lead role senders (such as managers) to

Role ambiguity. Lack of clarity of job goals or methods.

 Explore

Go to MyManagementLab to see an annotated version of this figure.

EXHIBIT 4
A model of the role assumption process.
Source: Adapted from Katz, D. et al. (1966, 1978). *The Social Psychology of Organizations*, 2nd edition, p.196. © 1966, 1978 John Wiley & Sons Inc. New York. Reprinted by permission of John Wiley & Sons, Inc.

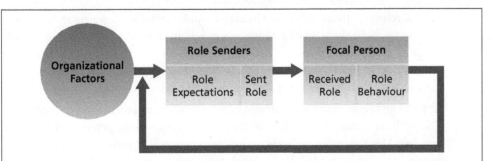

develop role expectations and "send" roles to focal people (such as employees). The focal person "receives" the role and then tries to engage in behaviour to fulfill the role. This model reveals a variety of elements that can lead to ambiguity.

- *Organizational factors.* Some roles seem inherently ambiguous because of their function in the organization. For example, middle management roles might fail to provide the "big picture" that upper management roles do. Also, middle management roles do not require the attention to supervision necessary in lower management roles.

- *The role sender.* Role senders might have unclear expectations of a focal person. Even when the sender has specific role expectations, they might be ineffectively sent to the focal person. A weak orientation session, vague performance reviews, or inconsistent feedback and discipline may send ambiguous role messages to employees.

- *The focal person.* Even role expectations that are clearly developed and sent might not be fully digested by the focal person. This is especially true when he or she is new to the role. Ambiguity tends to decrease as length of time in the job role increases.[23]

What are the practical consequences of role ambiguity? The most frequent outcomes appear to be job stress, dissatisfaction, reduced organizational commitment, lowered performance, and intentions to quit.[24] Managers can do much to reduce unnecessary role ambiguity by providing clear performance expectations and performance feedback, especially for new employees and for those in more intrinsically ambiguous jobs.

ROLE CONFLICT **Role conflict** exists when an individual is faced with incompatible role expectations. Conflict can be distinguished from ambiguity in that role expectations might be crystal clear but incompatible in the sense that they are mutually exclusive, cannot be fulfilled simultaneously, or do not suit the role occupant.

- **Intrasender role conflict** occurs when a single role sender provides incompatible role expectations to the role occupant. For example, a manager might tell an employee to take it easy and not work so hard, while delivering yet another batch of reports that require immediate attention. This form of role conflict seems especially likely to also provoke ambiguity.

- If two or more role senders differ in their expectations for a role occupant, **intersender role conflict** can develop. Employees who straddle the boundary between the organization and its clients or customers are especially likely to encounter this form of conflict. Intersender conflict can also stem exclusively from within the organization. The classic example here is the first-level manager, who serves as the interface between "management" and "the workers." From above, the manager might be pressured to get the work out and keep the troops in line. From below, he or she might be encouraged to behave in a considerate and friendly manner.

- Organizational members necessarily play several roles at one time, especially if we include roles external to the organization. Often, the expectations inherent in these several roles are incompatible, and **interrole conflict** results.[25] One person, for example, might fulfill the roles of a functional expert in marketing, head of the market research group, subordinate to the vice-president of marketing, and member of a product development task force. This is obviously a busy person, and competing demands for her time are a frequent symptom of interrole conflict.

- Even when role demands are clear and otherwise congruent, they might be incompatible with the personality or skills of the role occupant—thus, **person–role conflict** results.[26] Many examples of "whistle-blowing" are signals of person–role conflict. The organization has demanded some role behaviour that the occupant considers unethical.

Role conflict. A condition of being faced with incompatible role expectations.

Intrasender role conflict. A single role sender provides incompatible role expectations to a role occupant.

Intersender role conflict. Two or more role senders provide a role occupant with incompatible expectations.

Interrole conflict. Several roles held by a role occupant involve incompatible expectations.

Person–role conflict. Role demands call for behaviour that is incompatible with the personality or skills of a role occupant.

As with role ambiguity, the most consistent consequences of role conflict are job dissatisfaction, stress reactions, lowered organizational commitment, and turnover intentions.[27] Managers can help prevent employee role conflict by avoiding self-contradictory messages, conferring with other role senders, being sensitive to multiple role demands, and fitting the right person to the right role.

Status

Status is the rank, social position, or prestige accorded to group members. Put another way, it represents the group's *evaluation* of a member. Just *what* is evaluated depends on the status system in question. However, when a status system works smoothly, the group will exhibit clear norms about who should be accorded higher or lower status.

Status. The rank, social position, or prestige accorded to group members.

FORMAL STATUS SYSTEMS All organizations have both formal and informal status systems. Since formal systems are most obvious to observers, let's begin there. The formal status system represents management's attempt to publicly identify those people who have higher status than others. It is so obvious because this identification is implemented by the application of *status symbols* that are tangible indicators of status. Status symbols might include titles, particular working relationships, pay packages, work schedules, and the physical working environment. Just what are the criteria for achieving formal organizational status? One criterion is often seniority in one's work group. Employees who have been with the group longer might acquire the privilege of choosing day shift work or a more favourable office location. Even more important than seniority, however, is one's assigned role in the organization—one's job. Because they perform different jobs, secretaries, labourers, managers, and executives acquire different statuses. Organizations often go to great pains to tie status symbols to assigned roles.

Why do organizations go to all this trouble to differentiate status? For one thing, status and the symbols connected to it serve as powerful magnets to induce members to aspire to higher organizational positions (recall Maslow's need for self-esteem). Second, status differentiation reinforces the authority hierarchy in work groups and in the organization as a whole, since people *pay attention* to high-status individuals.

INFORMAL STATUS SYSTEMS In addition to formal status systems, one can detect informal status systems in organizations. Such systems are not well advertised, and they might lack the conspicuous symbols and systematic support that people usually accord the formal system. Nevertheless, they can operate just as effectively. Sometimes, job performance is a basis for the acquisition of informal status. The "power hitters" on a baseball team or the "cool heads" in a hospital emergency unit might be highly evaluated by co-workers for their ability to assist in task accomplishment. Some managers who perform well early in their careers are identified as "fast trackers" and given special job assignments that correspond to their elevated status. Just as frequently, though, informal status is linked to factors other than job performance, such as gender or race. For example, the man who takes a day off work to care for a sick child may be praised as a model father. The woman who does the same may be questioned about her work commitment.

CONSEQUENCES OF STATUS DIFFERENCES Status differences have a paradoxical effect on communication patterns. Most people like to communicate with others at their own status or higher rather than with people who are below them.[28] The result should be a tendency for communication to move up the status hierarchy. However, if status differences are large, people can be inhibited from communicating upward. These opposing effects mean that much communication gets stalled.

People pay attention to and respect status.[29] Thus, status also affects the amount of various group members' communication and their influence in group affairs. As you might guess, higher-status members do more talking and have more influence.[30] Some of the most convincing evidence comes from studies of jury deliberations, in which jurors with higher social status (such as managers and professionals) participate more and have more effect on the verdict.[31] Unfortunately, there is no guarantee that the highest-status person is the most knowledgeable about the problem at hand!

REDUCING STATUS BARRIERS Although status differences can be powerful motivators, their tendency to inhibit the free flow of communication has led many organizations to downplay status differentiation by doing away with questionable status symbols. The goal is to foster a culture of teamwork and cooperation across the ranks, as seen in the IDEO vignette that opened the chapter. The high-tech culture of Silicon Valley is egalitarian and lacking in conspicuous status symbols, but even old-line industries are getting on the bandwagon, doing away with reserved parking and fancy offices for executives.

Some organizations employ phoney or misguided attempts to bridge the status barrier. Some examples of "casual Friday" policies (which permit the wearing of casual clothes on Fridays) only underline status differences the rest of the week if no other cultural changes are made.

Many observers note that email has levelled status barriers.[32] High-speed transmission, direct access, and the opportunity to avoid live confrontation often encourage lower-status parties to communicate directly with organizational VIPs. This has even been seen in the rank-conscious military.

LO 5

Discuss the causes and consequences of *group cohesiveness.*

Group cohesiveness. The degree to which a group is attractive to its members.

GROUP COHESIVENESS

Group cohesiveness is a critical property of groups. Cohesive groups are those that are especially attractive to their members. Because of this attractiveness, members are especially desirous of staying in the group and tend to describe the group in favourable terms.[33]

The arch-stereotype of a cohesive group is the major league baseball team that begins September looking like a good bet to win its division and make it to the World Series. On the field we see well-oiled, precision teamwork. In the clubhouse, all is sweetness and joviality, and interviewed players tell the world how fine it is to be playing with "a great bunch of guys."

Cohesiveness is a relative, rather than absolute, property of groups. While some groups are more cohesive than others, there is no objective line between cohesive and non-cohesive groups. Thus, we will use the adjective *cohesive* to refer to groups that are more attractive than average for their members.

Factors Influencing Cohesiveness

What makes some groups more cohesive than others? Important factors include threat, competition, success, member diversity, group size, and toughness of initiation.

THREAT AND COMPETITION External threat to the survival of the group increases cohesiveness in a wide variety of situations.[34] As an example, consider the wrangling, uncoordinated corporate board of directors that quickly forms a united front in the face of a takeover bid. Honest competition with another group can also promote cohesiveness.[35] This is the case with the World Series contenders.

Why do groups often become more cohesive in response to threat or competition? They probably feel a need to improve communication and coordination so that they can better cope with the situation at hand. Members now perceive the group as more attractive because it is seen as capable of doing what has to be done to ward off threat or to win. However, under *extreme* threat or very *unbalanced* competition, increased cohesiveness will serve little purpose. For example, the partners in a firm faced with certain financial disaster would be unlikely to exhibit cohesiveness because it would do nothing to combat the severe threat.

SUCCESS It should come as no surprise that a group becomes more attractive to its members when it has successfully accomplished some important goal, such as defending itself

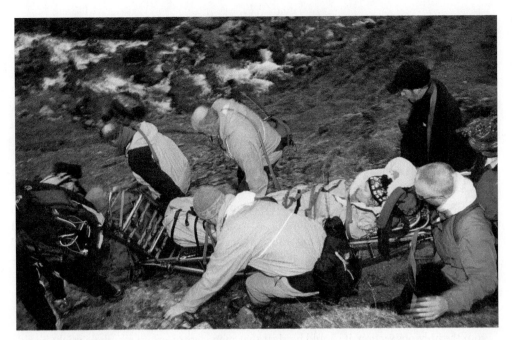

Cohesive groups lead to effective goal accomplishment.

against threat or winning a prize.[36] By the same token, cohesiveness will decrease after failure, although there may be "misery loves company" exceptions. The situation for competition is shown graphically in Exhibit 5. Fit-Rite Jeans owns two small clothing stores (A and B) in a large city. To boost sales, it holds a contest between the two stores, offering $150 worth of merchandise to each employee of the store that achieves the highest sales during the next business quarter. Before the competition begins, the staff of each store is equally cohesive. As we suggested above, when competition begins, both groups become more cohesive. The members become more cooperative with each other, and in each store there is much talk about "us" versus "them." At the end of the quarter, store A wins the prize and becomes yet more cohesive. The group is especially attractive to its members because it has succeeded in the attainment of a desired goal. On the other hand, cohesiveness plummets in the losing store B—the group has become less attractive to its members.

MEMBER DIVERSITY Earlier, we pointed out that groups that are diverse in terms of gender, age, and race can have a harder time becoming cohesive than more homogeneous groups. However, if the group is in agreement about how to accomplish some particular task,

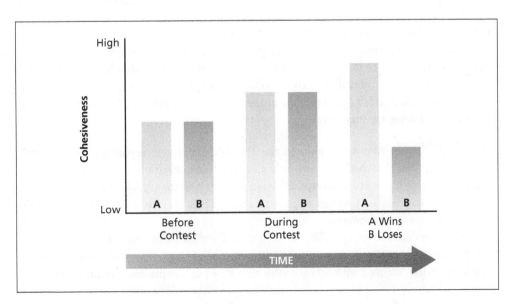

EXHIBIT 5
Competition, success, and cohesiveness.

Explore

Go to MyManagementLab to see an annotated version of this figure.

its success in performing the task will often outweigh surface dissimilarity in determining cohesiveness.[37]

SIZE Other things being equal, bigger groups should have a more difficult time becoming and staying cohesive. In general, such groups should have a more difficult time agreeing on goals and more problems communicating and coordinating efforts to achieve those goals. Earlier, we pointed out that large groups frequently divide into subgroups. Clearly, such subgrouping is contrary to the cohesiveness of the larger group.

TOUGHNESS OF INITIATION Despite its rigorous admissions policies, the Harvard Business School does not lack applicants. Similarly, exclusive yacht and golf clubs might have waiting lists for membership extending several years into the future. All this suggests that groups that are tough to get into should be more attractive than those that are easy to join.[38] This is well known in the armed forces, where rigorous physical training and stressful "survival schools" precede entry into elite units such as the Canadian Special Operations Forces Command or the U.S. Army Rangers.

Consequences of Cohesiveness

From the previous section, it should be clear that managers or group members might be able to influence the level of cohesiveness of work groups by using competition or threat, varying group size or composition, or manipulating membership requirements. The question remains, however, as to whether *more* or *less* cohesiveness is a desirable group property. This, of course, depends on the consequences of group cohesiveness and who is doing the judging.

MORE PARTICIPATION IN GROUP ACTIVITIES Because members wish to remain in the group, voluntary turnover from cohesive groups should be low. Also, members like being with each other; therefore, absence should be lower than in less cohesive groups. In addition, participation should be reflected in a high degree of communication within the group as members strive to cooperate with and assist each other. This communication might well be of a more friendly and supportive nature, depending on the key goals of the group.[39]

MORE CONFORMITY Because they are so attractive and coordinated, cohesive groups are well equipped to supply information, rewards, and punishment to individual members. These factors take on special significance when they are administered by those who hold a special interest for us. Thus, highly cohesive groups are in a superb position to induce conformity to group norms.

Members of cohesive groups are especially motivated to engage in activities that will *keep* the group cohesive. Chief among these activities is applying pressure to deviants to get them to comply with group norms. Cohesive groups react to deviants by increasing the amount of communication directed at these individuals.[40] Such communication contains information to help the deviant "see the light," as well as veiled threats about what might happen if he or she does not. Over time, if such communication is ineffective in inducing conformity, it tends to decrease. This is a signal that the group has isolated the deviant member to maintain cohesiveness among the majority.

MORE SUCCESS Above, we pointed out that successful goal accomplishment contributes to group cohesiveness. However, it is also true that cohesiveness contributes to group success—in general, cohesive groups are good at achieving their goals. Research has found that group cohesiveness is related to performance.[41] Thus, there is a reciprocal relationship between success and cohesiveness.

Why are cohesive groups effective at goal accomplishment? Probably because of the other consequences of cohesiveness we discussed above. A high degree of participation and communication, coupled with active conformity to group norms and commitment, should

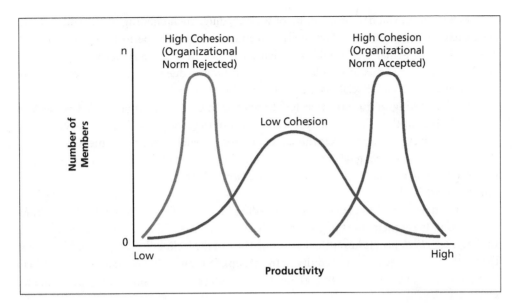

EXHIBIT 6
Hypothetical productivity curves for groups varying in cohesiveness.

✱ Explore

Go to MyManagementLab to see an annotated version of this figure.

ensure a high degree of agreement about the goals the group is pursuing and the methods it is using to achieve those goals. Thus, coordinated effort pays dividends to the group.

Since cohesiveness contributes to goal accomplishment, should managers attempt to increase the cohesiveness of work groups by juggling the factors that influence cohesiveness? To answer this question, we must emphasize that cohesive groups are especially effective at accomplishing *their own* goals. If these goals happen to correspond with those of the organization, increased cohesiveness should have substantial benefits for group performance. If not, organizational effectiveness might be threatened.[42] One large-scale study of work groups reached the following conclusions:

- In highly cohesive groups, the productivity of individual group members tends to be fairly similar to that of other members. In less cohesive groups there is more variation in productivity.

- Highly cohesive groups tend to be *more* or *less* productive than less cohesive groups, depending on a number of variables.[43]

These two facts are shown graphically in Exhibit 6. The lower variability of productivity in more cohesive groups stems from the power of such groups to induce conformity. To the extent that work groups have productivity norms, more cohesive groups should be better able to enforce them. Furthermore, if cohesive groups accept organizational norms regarding productivity, they should be highly productive. If cohesive groups reject such norms, they are especially effective in limiting productivity.

One other factor that influences the impact of cohesiveness on productivity is the extent to which the task really requires interdependence and cooperation among group members (e.g., a football team versus a golf team). Cohesiveness is more likely to pay off when the task requires more interdependence.[44]

In summary, cohesive groups tend to be successful in accomplishing what they wish to accomplish. In a good labour relations climate, group cohesiveness on interdependent tasks should contribute to high productivity. If the climate is marked by tension and disagreement, cohesive groups may pursue goals that result in low productivity.

SOCIAL LOAFING

Have you ever participated in a group project at work or school in which you did not contribute as much as you could have because other people were there to take up the slack? Or have you ever reduced your effort in a group project because you felt that others were not pulling

LO 6

Explain the dynamics of *social loafing*.

Social loafing. The tendency to withhold physical or intellectual effort when performing a group task.

their weight? If so, you have been guilty of social loafing. **Social loafing** is the tendency that people have to withhold physical or intellectual effort when they are performing a group task.[45] The implication is that they would work harder if they were alone rather than part of the group. Earlier we said that process losses in groups could be due to coordination problems or to motivation problems. Social loafing is a motivation problem.

People working in groups often feel trapped in a social dilemma, in that something that might benefit them individually—slacking off in the group—will result in poor group performance if everybody behaves the same way. Social loafers resolve the dilemma in a way that hurts organizational goal accomplishment. Notice that the tendency for social loafing is probably more pronounced in individualistic North America than in more collective and group-oriented cultures.

As the questions above suggest, social loafing has two different forms. In the *free rider effect*, people lower their effort to get a free ride at the expense of their fellow group members. In the *sucker effect*, people lower their effort because of the feeling that others are free riding, that is, they are trying to restore equity in the group. You can probably imagine a scenario in which the free riders start slacking off and then the suckers follow suit. Group performance suffers badly.

What are some ways to counteract social loafing?[46]

- *Make individual performance more visible.* Where appropriate, the simplest way to do this is to keep the group small in size. Then, individual contributions are less likely to be hidden. Posting performance levels and making presentations of one's accomplishments can also facilitate visibility.

- *Make sure that the work is interesting.* If the work is involving, intrinsic motivation should counteract social loafing.

- *Increase feelings of indispensability.* Group members might slack off because they feel that their inputs are unnecessary for group success. This can be counteracted by using training and the status system to provide group members with unique inputs (e.g., having one person master computer graphics programs).

- *Increase performance feedback.* Some social loafing happens because groups or individual members simply are not aware of their performance. Increased feedback, as appropriate, from the boss, peers, and customers (internal or external) should encourage self-correction.

- *Reward group performance.* Members are more likely to monitor and maximize their own performance (and attend to that of their colleagues) when the *group* receives rewards for effectiveness.[47]

Watch

HERMAN MILLER: ORGANIZATIONAL BEHAVIOUR Go to MyManagementLab to watch a video about organizational behaviour.

Simulate

TEAMS Go to MyManagementLab to complete a simulation about teams.

WHAT IS A TEAM?

Some have suggested that a team is something more than a group. They suggest that a group becomes a team when there exists a strong sense of shared commitment and when a synergy develops such that the group's efforts are greater than the sum of its parts.[48] While such differences might be evident in some instances, our definition of a group is sufficient to describe most teams that can be found in organizations. The term *team* is generally used to describe "groups" in organizational settings. Therefore, for our purposes in this chapter, we use the terms interchangeably. Teams have become a major building block of organizations and are now quite common in North America.[49] Research has shown improvements in organizational performance in terms of both efficiency and quality as a result of team-based work arrangements.[50]

Recall that self-efficacy is beliefs individuals have about their ability to successfully perform a task. When it comes to teams, collective efficacy is also important to ensure high performance.[51] **Collective efficacy** consists of *shared* beliefs that a team can successfully

Collective efficacy. Shared beliefs that a team can successfully perform a given task.

perform a given task. Notice that self-efficacy does not necessarily translate into collective efficacy—five skilled musicians do not necessarily result in a good band. In the following sections we cover the factors that contribute to collective efficacy in a team.

DESIGNING EFFECTIVE WORK TEAMS

The double-edged nature of group cohesiveness suggests that a delicate balance of factors dictates whether a work group is effective or ineffective. In turn, this suggests that organizations should pay considerable attention to how work groups are designed and managed.

A good model for thinking about the design of effective work groups is to consider a successful sports team. In most cases, such teams are small groups made up of highly skilled individuals who are able to meld these skills into a cohesive effort. The task they are performing is intrinsically motivating and provides very direct feedback. If there are status differences on the team, the basis for these differences is contribution to the team, not some extraneous factor. The team shows an obsessive concern with obtaining the right personnel, relying on tryouts or player drafts, and the team is coached, not supervised. With this informal model in mind, let's examine the concept of group effectiveness more closely.

J. Richard Hackman of Harvard University (co-developer of the Job Characteristics Model) has written extensively about work group effectiveness.[52] According to Hackman, a work group is effective when (1) its physical or intellectual output is acceptable to management and to the other parts of the organization that use this output, (2) group members' needs are satisfied rather than frustrated by the group, and (3) the group experience enables members to *continue* to work together.

What leads to group effectiveness? In colloquial language, "sweat, smarts, and style." Put more formally, as Hackman notes, group effectiveness occurs when high effort is directed toward the group's task, when great knowledge and skill are directed toward the task, and when the group adopts sensible strategies for accomplishing its goals. And just how does an organization achieve this? There is growing awareness in many organizations that the answer is self-managed work teams.

Self-Managed Work Teams

Self-managed work teams generally provide their members with the opportunity to do challenging work under reduced supervision. Other labels that we often apply to such groups are autonomous, semi-autonomous, and self-directed. The general idea, which is more important than the label, is that the groups regulate much of their own members' behaviour. Much interest in such teams was spurred by the success of teams in Japanese industry. Critical to the success of self-managed teams are the nature of the task, the composition of the group, and the various support mechanisms in place.[53]

TASKS FOR SELF-MANAGED TEAMS Experts agree that tasks assigned to self-managed work teams should be complex and challenging, requiring high interdependence among team members for accomplishment. In general, these tasks should have the qualities of enriched jobs. Thus, teams should see the task as significant, they should perform the task from beginning to end, and they should use a variety of skills. Self-managed teams have to have something useful to self-manage, and it is fairly complex tasks that capitalize on the diverse knowledge and skills of a group. Taking a number of olive stuffers on a food-processing assembly line, putting them in distinctive jumpsuits, calling them the Olive Squad, and telling them to self-manage will be unlikely to yield dividends in terms of effort expended or brainpower employed. The basic task will still be boring, a prime recipe for social loafing!

LO 7

Discuss how to design and support *self-managed teams.*

Self-managed work teams. Work groups that have the opportunity to do challenging work under reduced supervision.

Outside the complexity requirement, the actual range of tasks for which organizations have used self-managed teams is wide, spanning both blue- and white-collar jobs. In the white-collar domain, complex service and design jobs seem especially conducive to self-management. In the blue-collar domain, General Mills and Chaparral Steel of Midlothian, Texas, make extensive use of self-managed work groups. In general, these groups are responsible for dividing labour among various subtasks as they see fit and making a variety of decisions about matters that impinge on the group. When a work site is formed from scratch and lacks an existing culture, the range of these activities can be very broad. Consider the self-managed teams formed in a new U.K. confectionery plant.

> *Production employees worked in groups of 8 to 12 people, all of whom were expected to carry out each of eight types of jobs involved in the production process. Group members were collectively responsible for allocating jobs among themselves, reaching production targets and meeting quality and hygiene standards, solving local production problems, recording production data for information systems, organizing breaks, ordering and collecting raw materials and delivering finished goods to stores, calling for engineering support, and training new recruits. They also participated in selecting new employees. Within each group, individuals had considerable control over the amount of variety they experienced by rotating their tasks, and each production group was responsible for one product line. Group members interacted informally throughout the working day but made the most important decisions—for example, regarding job allocation—at formal weekly group meetings where performance was also discussed.[54]*

If a theme runs through this discussion of tasks for self-managed teams, it is the breakdown of traditional, conventional, specialized *roles* in the group. Group members adopt roles that will make the group effective, not ones that are simply related to a narrow specialty.

COMPOSITION OF SELF-MANAGED TEAMS How should organizations assemble self-managed teams to ensure effectiveness? "Stable, small, and smart" might be a fast answer.[55]

- *Stability.* Self-managed teams require considerable interaction and high cohesiveness among their members. This, in turn, requires understanding and trust. To achieve this, group membership must be fairly stable. Rotating members into and out of the group will cause it to fail to develop a true group identity.[56]

- *Size.* In keeping with the demands of the task, self-managed teams should be as small as is feasible. The goal here is to keep coordination problems and social loafing to a minimum. These negative factors can be a problem for all groups, but they can be especially difficult for self-managed groups. This is because reduced supervision means that there is no boss to coordinate the group's activities and search out social loafers who do not do their share of the work.

- *Expertise.* Group members should have a high level of expertise about the task at hand. Everybody does not have to know everything, but the group as a *whole* should be very knowledgeable about the task. Again, reduced supervision discourages "running to the boss" when problems arise, but the group must have the resources to successfully solve these problems. One set of skills that all members should probably possess to some degree is social skills. Understanding how to talk things out, communicate effectively, and resolve conflict is especially important.

- *Diversity.* Put simply, a team should have members who are similar enough to work well together and diverse enough to bring a variety of perspectives and skills to the task at hand. A product planning group consisting exclusively of new male MBAs might work well together but lack the different perspectives that are necessary for creativity.

One way of maintaining appropriate group composition might be to let the group choose its own members, as occurred at the confectionery plant we described above. A potential problem with this is that the group might use some irrelevant criterion (such as race or gender) to unfairly exclude others. Thus, human resources department oversight is necessary, as are very clear selection criteria (in terms of behaviours, skills, and credentials). The selection stage is critical, since some studies (including the one conducted in the confectionary plant) have shown elevated turnover in self-managed teams.[57] Such turnover can damage team effectiveness because it reduces the capacity for the team to learn and adapt.[58] Thus, "fit" is important, and it is well worth expending the extra effort to find the right people. At Britain's Pret A Manger sandwich and coffee shops, job seekers work in a shop for a day and then the staff votes on whether they can join the team.[59]

The theme running through this discussion of team composition favours *high cohesiveness* and the development of group *norms* that stress group effectiveness.

SUPPORTING SELF-MANAGED TEAMS A number of support factors can assist self-managed teams in becoming and staying effective. Reports of problems with teams can usually be traced back to inadequate support.

- *Training.* In almost every conceivable instance, members of self-managed teams require extensive training. The kind of training depends on the exact job design and on the needs of the workforce. However, some common areas include:
  - *Technical training.* This might include math, computer use, or any tasks that a supervisor formerly handled. Cross-training in the specialties of other teammates is common.
  - *Social skills.* Assertiveness, problem solving, and routine dispute resolution are skills that help the team operate smoothly.
  - *Language skills.* This can be important for ethnically diverse teams. Good communication is critical on self-managed teams.
  - *Business training.* Some firms provide training in the basic elements of finance, accounting, and production so that employees can better grasp how their team's work fits into the larger picture.

- *Rewards.* The general rule here is to mostly tie rewards to team accomplishment rather than to individual accomplishment while still providing team members with some individual performance feedback to counteract social loafing. Microsoft's European product support group went from individual rewards to team-based rewards when it found that the former discouraged engineers from taking on difficult cases.[60] Gain sharing, profit sharing, and skill-based pay are compatible reward systems for a team environment. Skill-based pay is especially attractive because it rewards the acquisition of multiple skills that can support the team.

- *Management.* Self-management will not receive the best support when managers feel threatened and see it as reducing their own power or promotion opportunities. Some schooled in the traditional role of manager may simply not adapt. Those who do can serve important functions by mediating relations *between* teams and by dealing with union concerns, since unions are often worried about the cross-functional job sharing in self-management. One study found that the most effective managers in a self-management environment encouraged groups to observe, evaluate, and reinforce their own task behaviour.[61] This suggests that coaching teams to be independent enhances their effectiveness.[62]

Exhibit 7 summarizes the factors that determine work group effectiveness. Michael Campion and colleagues studied these factors in teams of professional and non-professional workers.[63] Their results provide strong support for many of the relationships shown in the exhibit. Overall, research has shown improvements in team productivity, quality, customer satisfaction, and safety following the implementation of self-managed work teams.[64]

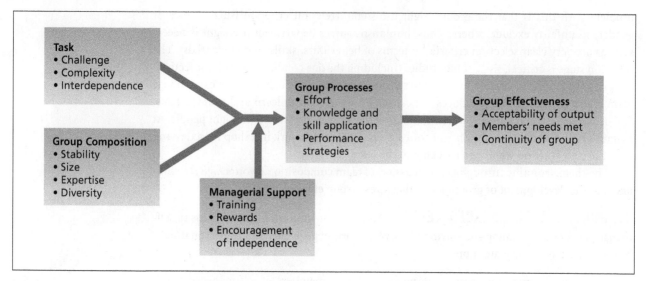

EXHIBIT 7
Factors influencing work group effectiveness.
Source: Based in part on Hackman, J.R. (1987). "The Design of Work Teams" in J.W. Lorsch (Ed.), *Handbook of organizational behaviour*. Englewood Cliffs, NJ: Pearson Education. Used by permission of J.W. Lorsch.

Go to MyManagementLab to see an annotated version of this figure.

Explain the logic behind *cross-functional teams* and describe how they can operate effectively.

Cross-functional teams. Work groups that bring people with different functional specialties together to better invent, design, or deliver a product or service.

Cross-Functional Teams

Let's look at another kind of team that contemporary organizations are using with increasing frequency. **Cross-functional teams** bring people with different functional specialties together to better invent, design, or deliver a product or service. For example, recall that the IDEO Kentucky public housing project brought together experts in architecture, design, anthropology, and psychology.

A cross-functional team might be self-managed and permanent if it is doing a recurrent task that is not too complex. If the task is complex and unique (such as designing a car), cross-functional teams require formal leadership, and their lives will generally be limited to the life of the specific project. In both cases, the "cross-functional" label means that such diverse specialties are necessary that cross-training is not feasible. People have to be experts in their own area but able to cooperate with others.

Cross-functional teams, which have been used in service industries such as banking and hospitals, are probably best known for their successes in product development.[65] Thus, Rubbermaid uses teams to invent and design a remarkable variety of innovative household products. Pharmaceutical development teams at Novartis and Wyeth include toxicologists, biologists, clinicians, chemists, and marketers.

The general goals of using cross-functional teams include some combination of innovation, speed, and quality that comes from early coordination among the various specialties. We can see their value by looking at the traditional way auto manufacturers used to design cars in North America.[66] First, stylists determined what the car would look like and then passed their design on to engineering, which developed mechanical specifications and blueprints. In turn, manufacturing considered how to construct what the stylists and engineers designed. Somewhere down the line, marketing and accounting got their say. This process invariably leads to problems. One link in the chain might have a difficult time understanding what the previous link meant. Worse, one department might resist the ideas of another simply because they "were not invented here." The result of all this is slow, expensive development and early quality problems. In contrast, the cross-functional approach gets all the specialties working together from day one. A complex project, such as a car design, might have over 30 cross-functional teams working at the same time. Global Focus: *A Diverse Global Team Creates the Camaro* describes a small part of the cross-functional teamwork that produced the sporty Chevy, which is built in Oshawa, Ontario.

The speed factor can be dramatic. Manufacturers have reduced the development of a new car model by several years. Boeing used a cross-functional team to reduce certain design analyses from two weeks to only a few minutes.

GLOBAL FOCUS

A Diverse Global Team Creates the Camaro

The handful of designers who gave birth to the reborn Camaro were a diverse group. That theme continued as it was developed all around the globe. When Design Director Tom Peters got a hush-hush assignment from Ed Welburn, VP of Global Design, to come up with a new Camaro to be shown at an upcoming auto show, he was beyond excited. The chance to redefine an American icon is every car designer's dream. Trying to keep his project top secret, he assembled a small team of his most talented young designers. They were SangYup Lee and Steve Kim from Korea and Vlad Kapitonov from Russia. Tom wanted a diverse group who didn't grow up with the Camaro in their backyard—who would bring a fresh perspective to the design. He asked his team to design "the meanest street-fighting dog they've ever seen" and to look at modern aircraft for influence. He did this right before a holiday break.

SangYup took that directive literally, feverishly sketching at the airport on his way to visit family in Korea. Vlad and Steve sketched over the break too, and when everybody regrouped at the design lair known as Studio X, Tom knew he had picked the right guys. Sketches were chosen—SangYup's for the front, and Vlad's for the rear. Designer Micah Jones nailed the interior, fusing high design with high technology. Using these sketches as a guide, the car was fast-tracked to a full-size clay and then fitted with an engine and drivetrain so that it could swagger onto the world's stage at the 2006 North American International Auto Show. And that's where the story really began. Tom and his team now had to build a production car that would lose none of the jaw-dropping style of the concept—a job that would require a flawless blend of engineering and technology.

The team crisscrossed the world in this effort, beginning in Australia. There, the engineering group at Holden were chosen because of their rear-wheel-drive prowess.

Three GM designers who worked on the Camaro: Micah Jones, Rebecca Waldmeir, and SangYup Lee.

Working closely with Tom's team, they created a platform that delivered the pure power any car bearing the name Camaro would need. The Camaro took plenty of other side trips on its journey from concept to production car. It was cold-weather tested in Sweden. Warm-weather tested in Death Valley. And the mighty SS was track tested at Nürburgring, where it clocked a world-class 8:19.

The result of all this combined passion is nothing short of spectacular. You might see a beautifully modern American car when you look at the new Camaro. But Tom Peters sees a car drawn by a Korean, engineered in Australia, tested in Germany, and built in North America. Because he knows firsthand that the only way to build a world-class car is to have the best people in the world build it!

Sources: Excerpted from Chevrolet advertising copy. (2009, May). *Road & Track*, 30. General Motors Corp. Used with permission, GM Media Archives.

PRINCIPLES FOR EFFECTIVENESS A number of factors contribute to the effectiveness of cross-functional teams. We will illustrate several with examples from a past redesign of the Ford Mustang.[67]

- *Composition.* All relevant specialties are necessary, and effective teams are sure not to overlook anyone. Auto companies put labour representatives on car design teams to warn of assembly problems. On the Mustang project, outside suppliers were represented. At IDEO, clients are represented on design teams.

- *Superordinate goals.* **Superordinate goals** are attractive outcomes that can only be achieved by collaboration. They override detailed functional objectives that might be in conflict (e.g., finance versus design). On the Mustang project, the superordinate goal was to keep the legendary name alive in the face of corporate cost cutting.

Superordinate goals. Attractive outcomes that can only be achieved by collaboration.

- *Physical proximity.* Team members have to be located (sometimes relocated) close to each other to facilitate informal contact. Mustang used a former furniture warehouse in Allen Park, Michigan, to house its teams.

- *Autonomy.* Cross-functional teams need some autonomy from the larger organization, and functional specialists need some authority to commit their function to project decisions. This prevents meddling or "micromanaging" by upper-level or functional managers.

- *Rules and procedures.* Although petty rules and procedures are to be avoided, some basic decision procedures must be laid down to prevent anarchy. On the Mustang project, it was agreed that a single manufacturing person would have a veto over radical body changes.

- *Leadership.* Because of the potential for conflict, cross-functional team leaders need especially strong people skills in addition to task expertise. The "tough engineer" who headed the Mustang project succeeded in developing his people skills for that task.

Several of these principles ensure that team members share mental models. **Shared mental models** mean that team members share identical information about how they should interact and what their task is. Shared mental models enhance coordination and contribute greatly to effective team performance, at least when the shared knowledge reflects reality.[68] Although shared mental models are important for all teams, they are a particular challenge to instill in cross-functional teams due to the divergent backgrounds of the team members. Consider this product development team:

> *The team is given the mandate to make a "tough truck." The designer, thinking in terms of styling, conceptualizes "tough" as "powerful looking." The designer then sketches a vehicle with a large grille and large tires, creating a very powerful stance. When seeing this mock-up, an engineer, thinking in terms of functionality and conceptualizing tough as implying durability, is unhappy with the design because it compromises the vehicle's power. Maintaining hauling capacity with large tires implies the need for greater torque output from the engine, adding expense and difficulty to the engineer's part of the problem. When the engineer suggests 16- rather than 20-inch wheels, the designer balks, claiming it makes the vehicle look cartoonish rather than tough.*[69]

Clearly, the designer and the engineer don't share mental models of what "tough" means, and this problem can be greatly magnified with the participation of other functions and disciplines. It can also be magnified in virtual teams, a subject we will now turn to.

Virtual Teams

With the increasing trends toward globalization and the rapid development of high-tech communication tools, a new type of team has emerged that will surely be critical to organizations' success for years to come: virtual teams. **Virtual teams** are work groups that use technology to communicate and collaborate across space, time, and organizational boundaries.[70] Along with their reliance on computer and electronic technology, the primary feature of these teams is the lack of face-to-face contact between team members due to geographic dispersion. This separation often entails linkages across countries and cultures. Furthermore, virtual teams are often cross-functional. Technologies used by virtual teams can be either asynchronous (email, fax, voice mail), allowing team members to reflect before responding, or synchronous (chat, groupware), allowing team members to communicate dynamically in real time. Although not so long ago they were only a dream, virtual teams are now spreading across the business landscape and are used by numerous companies, such as CAE, Sabre, IBM, and Texas Instruments. For an example of a virtual team supported by a blog, see the Applied Focus: *Blog Supports Virtual Change Team.*

Shared mental models.
Team members share identical information about how they should interact and what their task is.

VIRTUAL TEAMS Go to MyManagementLab to complete a simulation about virtual teams.

Understand *virtual teams* and what makes them effective.

Virtual teams. Work groups that use technology to communicate and collaborate across time, space, and organizational boundaries.

APPLIED FOCUS

BLOG SUPPORTS VIRTUAL CHANGE TEAM

An office services firm was implementing major benefits changes for its U.S. employees. Part of the benefits strategy change was a shift away from a paternalistic approach to more employee responsibility. The company knew this represented a major change-management opportunity. It wanted to have its best change-management team lead efforts to announce, engage and manage change efforts but without letting advance word leak out. The change-management team was scattered across the United States, but had to work closely together for several months to effect the desired change results. To work as a virtual team, a secure blog was created for the change-management team members. Only team members had access to ongoing discussions and draft change documents. The blog was a convenient way to provide real-time collaboration as well as a record of discussions and decisions for team members who could not make the live conversations. Team members learned to use the blog as the central repository for all planning and implementation tools. It was the most accessed site on a daily basis, even if no synchronous communication was required between members. The change team's success using the blog for virtual team collaboration was noted as a key element of the change process. The blog tool has since been used by other virtual teams throughout the organization.

Source: Excerpted from Society for Human Resource Management. (2010, First Quarter). Successfully transitioning to a virtual organization: Challenges, impact and technology. *SHRM Research Quarterly*, p. 6.

ADVANTAGES OF VIRTUAL TEAMS Why are these teams becoming so popular? Because linking minds through technology has some definite advantages:

- *Around-the-clock work.* Globally, a virtual team is a 24-hour team that never sleeps. In these "follow the sun" teams, a team member can begin a process in London and pass it on to another team member in New York for more input. From New York, the work can be forwarded to a colleague in San Francisco who, after more work, can send it along to Hong Kong for completion.[71] In today's non-stop economy, the benefits of such continuous workflows are huge.

- *Reduced travel time and cost.* Virtual teaming reduces travel costs associated with face-to-face meetings. In the past, important meetings, key negotiation sessions, and critical junctures in projects required team members to board planes and travel long distances. In the virtual environment, expensive and time-consuming travel can be mostly eliminated. Virtual teams can therefore lead to significant savings of time and money, and concerns over air travel also make virtual teams an attractive alternative.

- *Larger talent pool.* Virtual teams allow companies to expand their potential labour markets and to go after the best people, even if these people have no interest in relocating. The nature of virtual teams can also give employees added flexibility, allowing for a better work–life balance, which is an effective recruiting feature.[72]

CHALLENGES OF VIRTUAL TEAMS While the advantages highlighted above are appealing, virtual teams can also involve some disadvantages.[73] Managers must recognize that these teams present unique challenges and should not be treated as regular teams that just happen to use technology.

- *Trust.* Commentators have noted that trust is difficult to develop between virtual team members. People typically establish trust through physical contact and socialization, which are simply not available to virtual team members. For more on this challenge, see You Be the Manager: *Creating Trust in Virtual Teams at Orange.*

YOU BE THE MANAGER

Creating Trust in Virtual Teams at Orange

Multinational companies have a dual challenge of globalizing operations for purposes of efficiencies and localizing delivery of products and services to support national differences. At Orange, this challenge became all the more obvious when it expanded operations in the late 1990s to become a large, pan-European company. Orange is the mobile operator of France Telecom, providing services to 57 million customers across 17 countries. With presence in Europe, the Middle East, and Africa, Orange realized that to protect and strengthen the Orange brand, product development previously performed within host countries needed to become a global initiative. Although it is tempting to centralize a team that has a global mandate, Orange pursued virtual-team collaboration, which allows firms to increase diversity in their teams and potentially achieve greater productivity and creativity. At Orange, virtual teams were becoming a way of life, as with many high-tech, global corporations, but there were clearly challenges, rooted in the fact that there were less interpersonal similarities (e.g., common backgrounds and experience) among team members.

Within the product development organization at Orange, virtual teams were usually led by a product manager. Members of the team not only had primary responsibilities to the virtual team but also did work for local teams and various functions. As with other virtual teams, those at Orange were required to work across time zones, cultures, and reporting lines. Virtuality meant that team members were unable to interact informally, in face-to-face meetings. Communicating through electronic media (e.g., email, phone, and video conferencing) greatly reduced the ability to interact through non-verbal cues. The lack of informal communication was considered to be a large barrier in team productivity. As one team leader expressed, "Work really only starts after that first face-to-face meeting."

Cultural distance also affected the virtual teams at Orange. In one virtual team, conference calls between the U.K. and Paris offices became particularly strained. The British employees, in an effort to enhance meeting productivity, used humour to encourage participation, but this approach backfired. Without the benefit of seeing facial expressions, paired with the difficulty

At Orange, the creation and leadership of virtual teams is based on the fundamental need to create trust quickly and embed this trust throughout the life of the team.

of relating to the jokes themselves, Parisian employees felt increasingly isolated from their British counterparts and, as with other virtual teams at Orange, had low trust in their colleagues' ability to perform.

Because virtual teams at Orange were vital to the company's overall global strategy, management was keen to find ways to enhance team performance, productivity, and innovation. It was clear that work had to be done to overcome the trust barrier that existed between many of the virtual team members.

Questions

1. Why is trust important in virtual teams, and what influences the degree of trust among team members?

2. How can trust be developed and maintained in virtual teams?

To find out how Orange increased trust between virtual team members, see The Manager's Notebook at the end of this chapter.

Source: Adapted from Lawley, D. (2006, May/June). Creating trust in virtual teams at Orange. *Knowledge Management Review, 9* (2), 12–17.

• *Miscommunication.* The loss of face-to-face communication presents certain risks for virtual teams. Humans use many non-verbal cues to communicate meaning and feeling in a message. Using technology, the richness of face-to-face communication is lost and miscommunication can result. These risks can be particularly high on global virtual teams, as attempts at humour or the use of unfamiliar terms can lead to messages being misconstrued. Some organizations, such as Chevron, encourage global team members to avoid humour or metaphors when communicating online.[74]

- *Isolation.* People have needs for companionship. In self-contained offices, co-workers can meet for lunch, share stories, talk about their kids, and socialize outside of work. Unfortunately, these more casual interactions are not usually possible for virtual teams, a lack that can lead to team members having feelings of isolation and detachment.

- *High costs.* Savings in areas such as travel must be weighed against the costs of cutting-edge technology. Initial set-up costs can be substantial. Budgets must also be devoted to maintenance since, in the virtual environment, the firm's technology must run flawlessly, 24 hours a day, 7 days a week.

- *Management issues.* For managers, virtual teams can create new challenges in terms of dealing with subordinates who are no longer in view. How can you assess individual performance, monitor diligence, and ensure fairness in treatment when your team is dispersed around the globe?

Jessica Mesmer-Magnus and colleagues conducted an informative review of the research on information sharing in virtual teams versus face-to-face teams.[75] They found that virtual teams engaged in a lower volume of information sharing but were in fact more likely to share unique information that was not known by other team members. They suggested that the uniqueness advantage is because virtuality encourages more reflection compared to direct interaction. Paradoxically, however, the performance of virtual teams was especially dependent on them also having a high volume of open communication to complement the unique ideas. This is because openness facilitates the development of cooperation, cohesion, and trust, all of which are challenges for virtuality. The authors also found support for the idea that hybrid teams that combine face-to-face interaction with virtual interaction are especially likely to share information, a point reinforced in the following section.

LESSONS CONCERNING VIRTUAL TEAMS Overall, a number of lessons are beginning to emerge about what managers must do or keep watch for when developing virtual teams.[76]

- *Recruitment.* Choose team members carefully in terms of attitude and personality so that they are excited about these types of teams and can handle the independence and isolation that often define them. Find people with good interpersonal skills, not just technical expertise.

- *Training.* Invest in training for both technical and interpersonal skills. In many cases, virtual teams falter not due to weak technical skills but due to poor communication and cooperation.

- *Personalization.* Encourage team members to get to know one another, either by encouraging informal communication using technology or by arranging face-to-face meetings whenever possible. Reduce feelings of isolation by setting aside time for chit-chat, acknowledging birthdays, and so on.

- *Goals and ground rules.* On the management side, virtual team leaders should define goals clearly, set rules for communication standards and responses, and provide feedback to keep team members informed of progress and the big picture.

The key appears to be recognizing the ways in which these teams are different from those based in a single office environment but not falling into the trap of focusing solely on technology. Many of the general recommendations that apply to any work team also apply to virtual teams. These teams are made up of individuals who have the same feelings and needs as workers in more traditional environments. Virtual teams must be real teams, if not by location, then in mind and spirit.

A WORD OF CAUTION: TEAMS AS A PANACEA

Teams can be a powerful resource for organizations, and this chapter has identified some of the important lessons leading to team success. However, switching from a traditional structure to a team-based configuration is not a cure-all for an organization's problems, even though some managers fall prey to the "romance of teams."[77] It is likely that the research to date on teams has focused almost exclusively on viable, ongoing teams, with little attention being paid to unsuccessful teams. Some observers suggest that the team approach puts unwanted pressure and responsibilities on workers. Others have noted that many organizations have rushed to deploy teams with little planning, often resulting in confusion and contradictory signals to employees. Good planning and continuing support are necessary for the effective use of teams.[78]

THE MANAGER'S NOTEBOOK

Creating Trust in Virtual Teams at Orange

1. Trust is an important ingredient in all teams, regardless of the proximity of members. Trust is considered to enhance overall team performance because it reduces the need for formal checks and balances and increases team members' ability to work through interpersonal challenges. When trust is low, teams require a higher degree of control and leadership, which reduces overall productivity and increases costs. In virtual teams, trust is harder to achieve due to the perceived distances (e.g., geographical and cultural) between team members. To overcome this challenge, members of virtual teams need to be aligned in their thoughts and actions about the work they have been assigned. In virtual teams, trust is built on the perceived ability of team members, benevolence between team members, positive feelings about each other, and the overall integrity of the group. At Orange, experience confirmed that three principles are necessary for building trust in teams: small team size, strong leadership, and a common working framework. At first, Orange attempted to run large, lengthy, cross-functional initiatives through the use of virtual teams. But the company found that the number of relationships and the complexity of the work created significant trust barriers. Over time, Orange moved to smaller virtual teams (under 10 members) to achieve more focused mandates over a shorter period. In addition, Orange recognized that more effective leaders were those who could recognize cultural differences and bridge those differences between members through the use of a common framework. For example, one way to ensure "equality" in a team is to have everyone join a conference call by phone, regardless of the fact that some members are located in the same place and could talk face to face.

2. At Orange, experience indicated that leaders of virtual teams are better off focusing on outputs rather than on team processes. Since it is impossible to know what each team member is doing at any particular time, measuring outputs allows each team member to work when and how he or she chooses, respecting local customs and norms. Orange and their consultants also realized that the start-up of a team is a crucial period when leaders need to develop clear team objectives. To encourage a culture of trust within the team, leaders must therefore be good communicators and coaches, be able to foster an atmosphere of trust, and be independent workers. From the start, the leader must demonstrate trust in team members and encourage trust among team members by identifying their track records and nature of expertise. This effort must be complemented by seeking trust from stakeholders of the project, which, in turn, will generate further trust within the team. At Orange, the creation and leadership of virtual teams is now based on the fundamental need to create trust quickly and to embed this trust throughout the life of the team. Trust has become a planned activity to be achieved through the building of knowledge (understanding objectives and the contribution of others) and team formation.

MyManagementLab | Visit MyManagementLab at **www.mymanagementlab** **.com** for access to online tutorials, interactive exercises, videos, and much more.

LEARNING OBJECTIVES CHECKLIST

1 A *group* consists of two or more people interacting interdependently to achieve a common goal. *Formal work groups* are groups that organizations establish to facilitate the achievement of organizational goals. *Informal groups* are groups that emerge naturally in response to the common interests of organizational members.

2 Some groups go through a series of developmental stages: forming, storming, norming, performing, and adjourning. However, the *punctuated equilibrium* model stresses a first meeting, a period of little apparent progress, a critical midpoint transition, and a phase of goal-directed activity.

3 As groups get bigger, they provide less opportunity for member satisfaction. When tasks are *additive* (performance depends on the addition of individual effort) or *disjunctive* (performance depends on that of the best member), larger groups should perform better than smaller groups if the group can avoid *process losses* due to poor communication and motivation. When tasks are *conjunctive* (performance is limited by the weakest member), performance decreases as the group gets bigger, because the chance of adding a weak member increases. Diverse groups generally develop at a slower pace and be less cohesive than homogeneous groups. While the effects of surface-level demographic diversity can wear off over time, deep diversity differences regarding attitudes are more difficult to overcome.

4 *Norms* are expectations that group members have about one another's behaviour. They provide consistency to behaviour and develop as a function of shared attitudes. In organizations, both formal and informal norms often develop to control dress, reward allocation, and performance. *Roles* are positions in a group that have a set of expected behaviours associated with

them. *Role ambiguity* refers to a lack of clarity of job goals or methods. *Role conflict* exists when an individual is faced with incompatible role expectations, and it can take four forms: *intra-sender, intersender, interrole,* and *person–role.* Both ambiguity and conflict have been shown to provoke job dissatisfaction, stress, and lowered commitment. *Status* is the rank or prestige that a group accords its members. Formal status systems use status symbols to reinforce the authority hierarchy and reward progression. Informal status systems also operate in organizations. Although status differences are motivational, they also lead to communication barriers.

5 *Cohesive groups* are especially attractive to their members. Threat, competition, success, and small size contribute to cohesiveness, as does a tough initiation into the group. The consequences of cohesiveness include increased participation in group affairs, improved communication, and increased conformity. Cohesive groups are especially effective in accomplishing their own goals, which may or may not be those of the organization.

6 *Social loafing* occurs when people withhold effort when performing a group task. This is less likely when individual performance is visible, the task is interesting, there is good performance feedback, and the organization rewards group achievement.

7 Members of *self-managed work teams* do challenging work under reduced supervision. For greatest effectiveness, such teams should be stable, small, well trained, and moderately diverse in membership. Group-oriented rewards are most appropriate. Teams perform best when they have high *collective efficacy*, a shared belief that they can perform a given task. Sharing identical information (*shared mental models*) contributes to such efficacy.

8 *Cross-functional teams* bring people with different functional specialties together to better invent, design, or deliver a product or service. They should have diverse membership, a *superordinate* goal, some basic decision rules, and reasonable autonomy. Members should work in the same physical location, and team leaders require people skills as well as task skills.

9 *Virtual teams* use technology to communicate and collaborate across time, space, and organizational boundaries. These teams offer many advantages, such as reduced travel costs, greater potential talent, and continuous workflows, but pose dangers in terms of miscommunication, trust, and feelings of isolation.

DISCUSSION QUESTIONS

1. Describe the kind of skills that you would look for in members of self-managed teams. Explain your choices. Do the same for virtual teams.

2. Debate: *Effective teamwork is more difficult for individualistic Americans, Canadians, and Australians than for more collectivist Japanese.*

3. When would an organization create self-managed teams? When would it use cross-functional teams? When would it employ virtual teams?

4. Suppose that a group of United Nations representatives from various countries forms to draft a resolution regarding world hunger. Is this an additive, disjunctive, or conjunctive task? What kinds of process losses would such a group be likely to suffer? Can you offer a prediction about the size of this group and its performance?

5. Explain how a cross-functional team could contribute to product or service quality. Explain how a cross-functional team could contribute to speeding up product design.

6. Mark Allen, a representative for an international engineering company, is a very religious person who is active in his church. Mark's direct superior has instructed him to use "any legal means" to sell a large construction project to a foreign government. The vice-president of international operations had informed Mark that he could offer a generous "kickback" to government officials to clinch the deal, although such practices are illegal. Discuss the three kinds of role conflict that Mark is experiencing.

7. Some organizations have made concerted efforts to do away with many of the status symbols associated with differences in organizational rank. All employees now park in the same lot, eat in the same dining room, and have similar offices and privileges. Discuss the pros and cons of such a strategy. How might such a change affect organizational communications?

8. You are an executive in a consumer products corporation. The president assigns you to form a task force to develop new marketing strategies for the organization. You are permitted to choose its members. What things would you do to make this group as cohesive as possible? What are the dangers of group cohesiveness for the group itself and for the organization of which the group is a part?

INTEGRATIVE DISCUSSION QUESTIONS

1. What role do perceptions play in group development? Refer to perceptual processes and biases and discuss the implications for each stage of group development. What are the implications for improving the development of groups?

2. How can groups be motivated? Consider the implications of work motivation theories. What do the theories tell us about how to motivate groups?

ON-THE-JOB CHALLENGE QUESTION

Self-Managed Teams at ISE Communications

ISE Communications was one of the pioneers in using self-managed work teams. The teams were put in place to improve manufacturing flexibility and customer service, both factors being crucial in the highly competitive circuit board industry. Its conversion from an assembly-line style of circuit board manufacturing to teams who identified with "their own" products and customers was deemed a great success by industry observers. One interesting result was that the teams became extremely obsessed with monitoring the promptness and attendance of their members, more so than managers had been before the conversion to teams. They even posted attendance charts and created punishments for slack team members.

Use your understanding of both group dynamics and teams to explain why the employees became so concerned about attendance when they were organized into teams. What had changed?

Source: Barker, J.R. (1993). Tightening the iron cage: Concertive control in self-managing teams. *Administrative Science Quarterly*, 38, 408–437.

EXPERIENTIAL EXERCISE

NASA

The purpose of this exercise is to compare individual and group problem solving and to explore the group dynamics that occur in a problem-solving session. The instructor will begin by forming groups of four to seven members.

The situation described in this problem is based on actual cases in which men and women lived or died, depending on the survival decisions they made. Your "life" or "death" will depend on how well your group can share its present knowledge of a relatively unfamiliar problem, so that the group can make decisions that will lead to your survival.

The Problem

You are a member of a space crew originally scheduled to rendezvous with a mother ship on the lighted surface of the moon. Due to mechanical difficulties, however, your ship was forced to land at a spot some 200 miles from the rendezvous point. During landing, much of the equipment aboard was damaged, and, because survival depends on reaching the mother ship, the most critical items available must be chosen for the 200-mile trip. On the next page are listed the 15 items left intact and undamaged after the landing. Your task is to rank them in terms of their importance to your crew in reaching the rendezvous point. In the first column (step 1) place the number 1 by the first most important, and so on, through number 15, the least important. You have 15 minutes to complete this phase of the exercise.

After the individual rankings are complete, participants should be formed into groups having from four to seven members. Each group should then rank the 15 items as a team. This group ranking should be a general consensus after a discussion of the issues, not just the average of each individual ranking. While it is unlikely that everyone will agree exactly on the group ranking, an effort should be made to reach at least a decision that everyone can live with. It is important to treat differences of opinion as a means of gathering more information and clarifying issues and as an incentive to force the group to seek better alternatives. The group ranking should be listed in the second column (step 2).

The third phase of the exercise consists of the instructor providing the expert's rankings, which should be entered in the third column (step 3). Each participant should compute the difference between the individual ranking (step 1) and the expert's ranking (step 3), and between the group ranking (step 2) and the expert's ranking (step 3). Then add the two "difference" columns—the smaller the score, the closer the ranking is to the view of the experts.

Source: From Ritchie, *Organization and people*, 3rd edition. © 1984 South-Western, a part of Cenage Learning, Inc. Reproduced by permission. www.cengage.com/permissions.

Discussion

The instructor will summarize the results on the board for each group, including (a) the average individual accuracy score, (b) the group accuracy score, (c) the gain or loss between the average individual score and the group score, and (d) the lowest individual score (i.e., the best score) in each group.

The following questions will help guide the discussion:

1. As a group task, is the NASA exercise an additive, disjunctive, or conjunctive task?

2. What would be the impact of group size on performance in this task?

3. Did any norms develop in your group that guided how information was exchanged or how the decision was reached?

4. Did any special roles emerge in your group? These could include a leader, a secretary, an "expert," a critic, or a humourist. How did these roles contribute to or hinder group performance?

5. Consider the factors that contribute to effective self-managed teams. How do they pertain to a group's performance on this exercise?

6. How would group diversity help or hinder performance on the exercise?

NASA tally sheet

Items	Step 1 Your individual ranking	Step 2 The team's ranking	Step 3 Survival expert's ranking	Step 4 Difference between Step 1 & 3	Step 5 Difference between Step 2 & 3
Box of matches					
Food concentrate					
50 feet of nylon rope					
Parachute silk					
Portable heating unit					
Two .45 calibre pistols					
One case dehydrated milk					
Two 100-lb. tanks of oxygen					
Stellar map (of the moon's constellation)					
Life raft					
Magnetic compass					
5 gallons of water					
Signal flares					
First aid kit containing injection needles					
Solar-powered FM receiver-transmitter					

	Total		
(The lower the score the better)		Your score	Team score

CASE INCIDENT

The Group Assignment

Janet, a student, never liked working on group assignments; however, this time she thought it would be different because she knew most of the people in her group. But it was not long before things started going badly. After the first meeting, the group could not agree when to meet again. When they finally did meet, nobody had done anything, and the assignment was due in two weeks. The group then agreed to meet again the next day to figure out what to do. However, two of the group members did not show up. The following week Janet tried in vain to arrange for another meeting, but the other group members said they were too busy and that it would be best to divide the assignment up and have each member work on a section. The night before the assignment was due the group members met to give Janet their work. Finally, Janet thought, we are making progress. However, when she got home and read what the other members had written she was shocked at how bad it was. Janet spent the rest of the night and early morning doing the whole assignment herself. Once the course ended, Janet never spoke to any of the group members again.

1. Refer to the typical stages of group development and explain the development of Janet's group.
2. To what extent was group cohesiveness a problem in Janet's work group? What might have made the group more cohesive?

CASE STUDY

The Creativity Development Committee

Tom was the manager of three research and development laboratories for a large chemical and materials corporation. He supervised general operations, budgeting, personnel, and proposal development for the labs. Each lab had several projects, and each project team was headed by a project director, who was usually a scientist or an engineer. Tom had been project director for 10 years in another of the corporation's labs and had been promoted to lab manager four years ago. Although he had to transfer across the country to take this job, he felt he had earned the respect of his subordinates. He had been regarded as an outsider at first, but he worked hard to be accepted, and the lab's productivity had gone up over the last two years. Tom's major worry was keeping track of everything. His busy schedule kept him from close supervision over projects.

As in most labs, each project generally went its own way. As long as it produced results, a project enjoyed a high degree of autonomy. Morale was usually high among research staff. They knew they were on the leading edge of the corporation's success and they enjoyed it. The visibility and importance of innovative research were shown by the fact that project directors were regularly promoted upward.

It was in this milieu that Tom decided that productivity might be further increased if research creativity were heightened. Research teams often met to discuss ideas and to decide on future directions. In these meetings ideas were often improved upon, but they could also be killed or cut off. Tom had studied research on decision making, which indicated that groups often suppress good ideas without a hearing; the research suggested ways of preventing this suppression and enhancing group creativity. Tom hoped to harness these findings by developing standard procedures through which idea development would be enhanced rather than hindered in these meetings. Tom asked four project directors if they were willing to work with him to review the research and meet regularly over the summer to help formulate appropriate procedures. The four agreed to take on the task and the group began its work enthusiastically.

During the first six weeks of the summer the group met weekly to discuss relevant articles and books and to hear consultants. The group was able to narrow down a set of about 15 procedures and programs to 4 prime possibilities. Eventually, 2 programs emerged as possibilities. However, as the list was narrowed from 4 to 2, there was a clear split in how the group felt.

One procedure was strongly favoured by three of the project directors. The fourth project director liked the procedure better than the other option but was less vocal in showing her support for it. In general, the project directors felt the procedure they favoured was far more consistent with what project teams were currently doing and with the problems faced by the corporation. They believed the second program, which involved a lot of writing and the use of special voting procedures, was too abstract for working research scientists to accept. It would be difficult, they said, to use this procedure because everyone would have to fill out forms and explain ideas in writing before a meeting could be held. Because of already heavy workloads, their people would not go along with the program. Researchers would ridicule the program and be prejudiced against future attempts to stimulate creativity.

Tom argued that the second program was more comprehensive, had a broader conception of problems, and would help develop more creative ideas than the first, which was a fairly conservative "brainstorming" process. Although discussion focused on the substantive nature of each program and its reaction to the objective of creativity, the project directors knew that the program Tom favoured was one he had been trained in at his former lab. Tom was a good friend of the consultant who had developed it. The project directors talked outside meetings about this friendship and questioned whether it was shaping Tom's attitudes. The climate of the group, which had initially been positive and enthusiastic, grew tense as issues connected to the power relations between the manager and project directors surfaced.

Although the project directors knew Tom could choose the program he wanted, how the final choice would be made was never clarified at the beginning of the summer. The time that the project directors spent reading and evaluating the programs created an implicit expectation that they would have an equal say in the final choice. At the same time, the project directors had all worked at the lab for at least four years and had experienced first-hand the relative power of managers and project directors. They heard horror stories of project directors who had got on the manager's "wrong side" and been denied promotion or fired. When push came to shove, they expected the manager to have greater power and to be willing to use it.

At its final meeting the group discussed the two programs for quite some time, but there seemed to be little movement. Somewhat hesitantly, Tom turned to each project director individually and asked, "How upset would you be if I choose the program I prefer?" One project director said he was uncomfortable answering. Two indicated that they felt they would have difficulty using the creativity program as it was currently designed. The fourth said that she thought she could live with it. After these answers were given, Tom told the project directors he would leave a memo in their mailboxes informing them of the final decision.

Two weeks after this discussion, the project directors were told that the second program, the one the manager preferred, would be ordered. The memo also said that the other program would be used, on an experimental basis, by one of the 18 projects. The decision caused considerable resentment. The project directors felt "used." They saw little reason in having spent too much time discussing programs if Tom was just going to choose the program he wanted, regardless of their preferences. When the program began in the fall, one of the project directors told his team that the program would be recommended rather than required, and he explained that it might have to be adapted extensively to fit the unit's style. He made this decision without telling the manager. While the move was in clear violation of Tom's authority, he knew Tom could not visit the teams often and was therefore unlikely to find out about it. Another project director instituted the program but commented afterward that he felt he had not integrated it into his unit well. He questioned how much effort he had actually invested in making the program "work."

The incident had a significant impact on the way Tom was seen by the project directors. Several commented that they had lost their respect for Tom, that they saw Tom as someone who was willing to manipulate people for his own purposes. This opinion filtered to other project directors and scientists through the "grapevine" and caused Tom considerable difficulties in a labour grievance during the following year. In this dispute several researchers banded together and defied the manager because they believed he would eventually back down. In addition, the project director who made the program optional for these workers served as a model for similar defiance by others. Once the directors saw that "optional" use of the program would be go unpunished, they felt free to do it themselves, and Tom's control was further reduced. Tom eventually transferred to another division of the corporation.

Source: FOLGER, JOSEPH P.; POOLE, MARSHALL SCOTT; STUTMAN, RANDALL K., WORKING THROUGH CONFLICT: STRATEGIES FOR RELATIONSHIPS, GROUPS, AND ORGANIZATIONS, 3rd Ed, © 1997, pp. 107–109. Reprinted and Electronically reproduced by permission of Pearson Education, Inc., Upper Saddle River, New Jersey.

QUESTIONS

1. Discuss how the stages of group development and the punctuated equilibrium model apply to the Creativity Development Committee. Did the

group progress through any of the stages of these models? Did the group fail to resolve any issues implied by these models?

2. Is the choice of the best creativity development program an additive, disjunctive, or conjunctive task? Explain your reasoning. Discuss the implications of the task type for what happened on the committee.

3. Did role ambiguity surface in the case? If so, how so?
4. Did role conflict surface in the case? If so, which type or types occurred?
5. How did status issues emerge in the committee?
6. Did the committee share a mental model about its goals and procedures?

REFERENCES

1. www.fastcompany.com/mic/2010/profile/ideo; www.ideo.com/images/uploads/home/IDEO_Fact_Sheet.pdf; Brown, T. (2009). *Change by design: How design thinking transforms organizations and inspires innovation.* New York: HarperCollins; www.businessweek.com/careers/content/jan2001/ca20010111_923.htm (Strong quote); http://pages.towson.edu/aclardy/Working%20Papers/IDEO.pdf; www.ideo.com/work/the-tube/; http://charleslawportfolio.com/charleslaw_assets/charleslaw_creativeessay.pdf; www.ideo.com/images/uploads/hcd_toolkit/IDEO_HCD_ToolKit.pdf.

2. Tuckman, B.W. (1965). Developmental sequence in small groups. *Psychological Bulletin, 63,* 384–399; Tuckman, B.W., & Jensen, M.A.C. (1977). Stages of small-group development revisited. *Group & Organization Studies, 2,* 419–427.

3. Harris, S.G., & Sutton, R.I. (1986). Functions of parting ceremonies in dying organizations. *Academy of Management Journal, 29,* 5–30.

4. Seger, J.A. (1983). No innate phases in group problem solving. *Academy of Management Review, 8,* 683–689. For a study comparing phases with punctuated equilibrium, see Chang, A., Bordia, P., & Duck, J. (2003). Punctuated equilibrium and linear progression: Toward a new understanding of group development. *Academy of Management Journal, 46,* 106–117.

5. Ginnett, R.C. (1990). Airline cockpit crew. In J.R. Hackman (Ed.), *Groups that work (and those that don't).* San Francisco: Jossey-Bass.

6. Gersick, C.J.G. (1989). Marking time: Predictable transitions in task groups. *Academy of Management Journal, 32,* 274–309; Gersick, C.J.G. (1988). Time and transition in work teams: Toward a new model of group development. *Academy of Management Journal, 31,* 9–41.

7. Gersick, 1989, 1988; Hackman, J.R., & Wageman, R. (2005). A theory of team coaching. *Academy of Management Review, 30,* 269–287.

8. Hare, A.P. (1976). *A handbook of small group research.* New York: The Free Press; Shaw, M.E. (1981). *Group dynamics: The psychology of small group behavior* (3rd ed.). New York: McGraw-Hill; Jones, E.E., & Gerard, H.B. (1967). *Foundations of social psychology.* New York: Wiley.

9. Hare, 1976; Shaw, 1981.

10. The following discussion relies upon Steiner, I.D. (1972). *Group process and productivity.* New York: Academic Press.

11. Steiner, 1972; Hill, G.W. (1982). Group versus individual performance: Are n+1 heads better than one? *Psychological Bulletin, 91,* 517–539.

12. Williams, K.Y., & O'Reilly, C.A. III. (1998). Demography and diversity in organizations: A review of 40 years of research. *Research in Organizational Behavior, 20,* 77–140; Jackson, S.E., Stone, V.K., & Alvarez, E.B. (1993). Socialization amidst diversity: The impact of demographics on work team oldtimers and newcomers. *Research in Organizational Behavior, 15,* 45–109.

13. Watson, W.E., Kumar, K., & Michaelson, L.K. (1993). Cultural diversity's impact on interaction process and performance: Comparing homogeneous and diverse task groups. *Academy of Management Journal, 36,* 590–602.

14. Webber, S.S., & Donahue, L.M. (2001). Impact of highly and less job-related diversity on work group cohesion and performance: A meta-analysis. *Journal of Management, 27,* 141–162.

15. Bell, S.T., Villado, A.J., Lukasik, M.A., Belau, L., & Briggs, A.L. (2011). Getting specific about demographic diversity variable and team performance relationships: A meta-analysis. *Journal of Management, 37,* 709–743; see also Joshi, A., & Roh, H. (2009). The role of context in work team diversity research: A meta-analytic review. *Academy of Management Journal, 52,* 599–627.

16. Bell et al., 2011; Joshi & Roh, 2009.

17. Harrison, D.A., Price, K.H., & Bell, M.P. (1998). Beyond relational demography: Time and effects of surface- and deep-level diversity on work group cohesion. *Academy of Management Journal, 41,* 96–107; see also Bell, S.T. (2007). Deep-level composition variables as predictors of team performance: A meta-analysis. *Journal of Applied Psychology, 92,* 595–615.

18. For an example of the social process by which this sharing may be negotiated in a new group, see Bettenhausen, K., & Murnighan, J.K. (1991). The development of an intragroup norm and the effects of interpersonal and structural challenges. *Administrative Science Quarterly, 36,* 20–35.

19. Kanter, R.M. (1977). *Men and women of the corporation.* New York: Basic Books, 37.

20. Leventhal, G.S. (1976). The distribution of rewards and resources in groups and organizations. In L. Berkowitz & E. Walster (Eds.), *Advances in experimental social psychology* (Vol. 9). New York: Academic Press.

21. See Mitchell, T.R., Rothman, M., & Liden, R.C. (1985). Effects of normative information on task performance. *Journal of Applied Psychology, 70,* 48–55.

22. Kleingeld, A., van Mierlo, H., & Arends, L. (2011). The effect of goal setting on group performance: A meta-analysis. *Journal of Applied Psychology, 96,* 1289–1304.

23. Jackson, S.E., & Schuler, R.S. (1985). A meta-analysis and conceptual critique of research on role ambiguity and role conflict in work settings. *Organizational Behavior and Human Decision Processes, 36,* 16–78. For a methodological critique of this domain, see King, L.A., & King, D.W. (1990). Role conflict and role ambiguity: A critical assessment of construct validity. *Psychological Bulletin, 107,* 48–64.

24. Jackson & Schuler, 1985; Tubre, T.C., & Collins, J.M. (2000). Jackson and Shuler (1985) revisited: A meta-analysis of the relationship between role ambiguity, role conflict, and job performance. *Journal of Management, 26,* 155–169.

25. O'Driscoll, M.P., Ilgen, D.R., & Hildreth, K. (1992). Time devoted to job and off-job activities, interrole conflict, and affective experiences. *Journal of Applied Psychology, 77,* 272–279.

26. See Latack, J.C. (1981). Person/role conflict: Holland's model extended to role-stress research, stress management, and career development. *Academy of Management Review, 6,* 89–103.

27. Jackson & Schuler, 1985.

28. Shaw, 1981.

29. Fiske, S.T. (2010). Interpersonal stratification: Status, power, and subordination. In S.T. Fiske, D.T. Gilbert, & G. Lindzey (Eds.), *Handbook of social psychology* (5th ed., Vol. 2). Hoboken, NJ: Wiley.

30. Kiesler, S., & Sproull, L. (1992). Group decision making and communication technology. *Organizational Behavior and Human Decision Processes, 52,* 96–123; Fiske, 2010.

31. Strodbeck, F.L., James, R.M., & Hawkins, C. (1957). Social status in jury deliberations. *American Sociological Review, 22,* 713–719.

32. Kiesler & Sproull, 1992.

33. For other definitions and a discussion of their differences, see Mudrack, P.E. (1989). Defining group cohesiveness: A legacy of confusion? *Small Group Behavior, 20,* 37–49.

34. Stein, A. (1976). Conflict and cohesion: A review of the literature. *Journal of Conflict Resolution, 20,* 143–172. For an interesting example, see Haslam, S.A., & Reicher, S. (2006). Stressing the group: Social identity and the unfolding

dynamics of responses to stress. *Journal of Applied Psychology, 91*, 1037–1052.

35. Cartwright, D. (1968). The nature of group cohesiveness. In D. Cartwright & A. Zander (Eds.), *Group dynamics: Research and theory* (3rd ed., pp. 91–109). New York: Harper & Row.

36. Lott, A., & Lott, B. (1965). Group cohesiveness as interpersonal attraction: A review of relationships with antecedent and consequent variables. *Psychological Bulletin, 64*, 259–309.

37. Anderson, A.B. (1975). Combined effects of interpersonal attraction and goal-path clarity on the cohesiveness of task-oriented groups. *Journal of Personality and Social Psychology, 31*, 68–75; see also Cartwright, 1968.

38. Aronson, E., & Mills, J. (1959). The effects of severity of initiation on liking for a group. *Journal of Abnormal and Social Psychology, 59*, 177–181.

39. Cartwright, 1968; Shaw, 1981.

40. Schacter, S. (1951). Deviation, rejection, and communication. *Journal of Abnormal and Social Psychology, 46*, 190–207; see also Barker, J.R. (1993). Tightening the iron cage: Concertive control in self-managing teams. *Administrative Science Quarterly, 38*, 408–437.

41. Beal, D.J., Cohen, R.R., Burke, M.J., & McLendon, C.L. (2003). Cohesion and performance in groups: A meta-analytic clarification of construct relations. *Journal of Applied Psychology, 88*, 989–1004; Mullen, B., & Copper, C. (1994). The relation between group cohesiveness and performance: An integration. *Psychological Bulletin, 115*, 210–227.

42. Podsakoff, P.M., MacKenzie, S.B., & Ahearne, M. (1997). Moderating effects of goal acceptance on the relationship between group cohesiveness and productivity. *Journal of Applied Psychology, 82*, 974–983.

43. Seashore, S. (1954). *Group cohesiveness in the industrial workgroup*. Ann Arbor, MI: Institute for Social Research; see also Stogdill, R.M. (1972). Group productivity, drive, and cohesiveness. *Organizational Behavior and Human Performance, 8*, 26–43. For a critique, see Mudrack, P.E. (1989). Group cohesiveness and productivity: A closer look. *Human Relations, 42*, 771–785.

44. Gulley, S.M., Devine, D.J., & Whitney, D.J. (1995). A meta-analysis of cohesion and performance: Effects of level of analysis and task interdependence. *Small Group Research, 26*, 497–520.

45. Shepperd, J.A. (1993). Productivity loss in small groups: A motivation analysis. *Psychological Bulletin, 113*, 67–81; Kidwell, R.E., III, & Bennett, N. (1993). Employee propensity to withhold effort: A conceptual model to intersect three

avenues of research. *Academy of Management Review, 18*, 429–456.

46. Shepperd, 1993; Kidwell & Bennett, 1993; George, J.M. (1992). Extrinsic and intrinsic origins of perceived social loafing in organizations. *Academy of Management Journal, 35*, 191–202.

47. Barnes, C.M., Hollenbeck, J.R., Jundt, D.K., DeRue, D.S., & Harmon, S.J. (2011). Mixing individual incentives and group incentives: Best of both worlds or social dilemma? *Journal of Management, 37*, 1611–1635.

48. Guzzo, R.A., & Dickson, M.W. (1996). Teams in organizations: Recent research on performance and effectiveness. *Annual Review of Psychology, 47*, 307–338.

49. Kirkman, B.L., & Shapiro, D.L. (1997). The impact of cultural values on employee resistance to teams: Toward a model of globalized self–managing work team effectiveness. *Academy of Management Review, 22*, 730–757.

50. Guzzo & Dickson, 1996; Kirkman & Shapiro, 1997; Banker, R.D., Field, J.M., Schroeder, R.G., & Sinha, K.K. (1996). Impact of work teams on manufacturing performance: A longitudinal field study. *Academy of Management Journal, 39*, 867–890.

51. Tasa, K., Taggar, S., & Seijts, G.H. (2007). The development of collective efficacy in teams: A multi-level and longitudinal perspective. *Journal of Applied Psychology, 92*, 17–27; Gibson, C.B., & Earley, P.C. (2007). Collective cognition in action: Accumulation, interaction, examination, and accommodation in the development and operation of efficacy beliefs in the workplace. *Academy of Management Review, 32*, 438–458; Tasa, K., Sears, G.J., & Schat, A.C.H. (2011). Personality and teamwork behavior in context: The cross-level moderating role of collective efficacy. *Journal of Organizational Behavior, 32*, 65–85; Stajkovic, A.D., Lee, D., & Nyberg, A.J. (2009). Collective efficacy, group potency, and group performance: Meta-analyses of their relationships, and test of a mediation model. *Journal of Applied Psychology, 94*, 814–828.

52. Hackman, J.R. (1987). The design of work teams. In J.W. Lorsch (Ed.), *Handbook of organizational behavior*. Englewood Cliffs, NJ: Prentice-Hall; see also Hackman, J.R. (2002). *Leading teams: Setting the stage for great performances*. Boston: Harvard Business School Press.

53. Campion, M.A., Medsker, G.J., & Higgs, A.C. (1993). Relations between work group characteristics and effectiveness: Implications for designing effective work groups. *Personnel Psychology, 46*, 823–850.

54. Wall, T.D., Kemp, N.J., Jackson, P.R., & Clegg, C.W. (1986). Outcomes of autonomous workgroups: A field experiment. *Academy of Management Journal, 29*, 280–304.

55. Parts of this section rely on Hackman, 1987.

56. See Ashforth, B.E., & Mael, F. (1989). Social identity theory and the organization. *Academy of Management Review, 14*, 20–39.

57. Wall et al., 1986; Cordery, J.L., Mueller, W.S., & Smith, L.M. (1991). Attitudinal and behavioral effects of autonomous group working: A longitudinal field study. *Academy of Management Journal, 34*, 264–276.

58. van der Vegt, G.S., Bunderson, S., & Kuipers, B. (2010). Why turnover matters in self-managing work teams: Learning, social integration, and task flexibility. *Journal of Management, 36*, 1168–1191.

59. Bainbridge, J. (2009). Inspire and innovate: Personal services. www.guardian.co.uk.

60. Hayward, D. (2003, May 20). Management through measurement. *Financial Post*, BE5.

61. Manz, C.C., & Sims, H.P., Jr. (1987). Leading workers to lead themselves: The external leadership of self-managing work teams. *Administrative Science Quarterly, 32*, 106–128.

62. For reviews of research on self-managed teams, see Chapter 3 of Cummings, T.G., & Molloy, E.S. (1977). *Improving productivity and the quality of working life*. New York: Praeger; Goodman, P.S., Devadas, R., & Hughes, T.L.G. (1988). Groups and productivity: Analyzing the effectiveness of self-managing teams. In J.P. Campbell & R.J. Campbell (Eds.), *Productivity in organizations*. San Francisco: Jossey-Bass; Pearce, J.A., III, & Ravlin, E.C. (1987). The design and activation of self-regulating work groups. *Human Relations, 40*, 751–782.

63. Campion, M.A., Papper, E.M., & Medsker, G.J. (1996). Relations between work team characteristics and effectiveness: A replication and extension. *Personnel Psychology, 49*, 429–452; Campion, Medsker, & Higgs, 1993.

64. Kirkman & Shapiro, 1997; Banker et al., 1996.

65. Farnham, A. (1994, February 7). America's most admired company. *Fortune*, 50–54; Dumaine, B. (1993, December 13). Payoff from the new management. *Fortune*, 103–110.

66. Waterman, R.H., Jr. (1987). *The renewal factor*. New York: Bantam Books; McElroy, J. (1985, April). Ford's new way to build cars. *Road & Track*, 156–158.

67. Pinto, M.B., Pinto, J.K., & Prescott, J.E. (1993). Antecedents and consequences of project team cross-functional cooperation. *Management Science, 39,* 1281–1297; Henke, J.W., Krachenberg, A.R., & Lyons, T.F. (1993). Cross-functional teams: Good concept, poor implementation! *Journal of Product Innovation Management, 10,* 216–229. Mustang examples from White, J.B., & Suris, O. (1993, September 21). How a "skunk works" kept the Mustang alive—on a tight budget. *Wall Street Journal,* A1, A12.

68. Mathieu, J., Maynard, M.T., Rapp, T., & Gilson, L. (2008). Team effectiveness 1997–2007: A review of recent advancements and a glimpse into the future. *Journal of Management, 34,* 410–476; Mesmer-Magnus, J.R., & DeChurch, L.A. (2009). Information sharing and team performance. *Journal of Applied Psychology, 94,* 535–546; Mohammed, S., Ferzandi, L., & Hamilton, K. (2010). Metaphor no more: A 15-year review of the team mental model construct. *Journal of Management, 36,* 876–910; DeChurch, L.A., & Mesmer-Magnus, J.R. (2010). The cognitive underpinnings of effective teamwork: A meta-analysis. *Journal of Applied Psychology, 95,* 32–53.

69. Cronin, M.A., & Weingart, L.R. (2007). Representational gaps, information processing, and conflict in functionally diverse teams. *Academy of Management Review, 32,* 761–773, p. 761.

70. Lipnack, J., & Stamps, J. (2000). *Virtual teams: People working across boundaries with technology.* (2nd ed.). New York: Wiley; Axtell, C.M., Fleck, S.J., & Turner, N. (2004). Virtual Teams: Collaborating across distance. *International Review of Industrial and Organizational Psychology, 19,* 205–248; Staff. (2010, First Quarter). Successfully transitioning to a virtual organization: Challenges, impact and technology. *SHRM Research Quarterly.* Alexandria, VA: Society for Human Resource Management.

71. Willmore, J. (2000, February). Managing virtual teams. *Training Journal,* 18–21.

72. Joinson, C. (2002, June). Managing virtual teams. *HR Magazine,* 68–73.

73. Cascio, W.F. (2000, August). Managing a virtual workplace. *Academy of Management Executive,* 81–90; see also Malhotra, A., Majchrzak, A., & Rosen, B. (2007). Leading virtual teams. *Academy of Management Perspectives,* 60–70; and Gibson, C.B., & Gibbs, J.L. (2006). Unpacking the concept of virtuality: The effects of geographic dispersion, electronic dependence, dynamic structure, and national diversity on team innovation. *Administrative Science Quarterly, 51,* 451–495.

74. Willmore, 2000.

75. Mesmer-Magnus, J.R., DeChurch, L.A., Jimenez-Rodriguez, M., Wildman, J., & Shuffler, M. (2011). A meta-analytic investigation of virtuality and information sharing in teams. *Organizational Behavior and Human Decision Processes, 115,* 214–225.

76. Cascio, 2000; Joinson, 2002; Kirkman, B.L., Rosen, B., Gibson, C.B., Tesluk, P.E., & McPherson, S.O. (2002, August). Five challenges to virtual team success: Lessons from Sabre, Inc. *Academy of Management Executive, 16,* 67–79.

77. Allen, N.J., & Hecht, T.D. (2004). The "romance of teams": Toward an understanding of its psychological underpinnings and implications. *Journal of Occupational and Organizational Psychology, 77,* 439–461.

78. Vallas, S.P. (2003). Why teamwork fails: Obstacles to workplace change in four manufacturing plants. *American Sociological Review, 68,* 223–250; Tudor, T.R., Trumble, R.R., & Diaz, J.J. (1996, Autumn). Work-teams: Why do they often fail? *S.A.M. Advanced Management Journal,* 31–39.

PHOTO CREDITS

CONFLICT AND STRESS

From Chapter 13 of *Organizational Behaviour*, Ninth Edition. Gary Johns and Alan M. Saks. Copyright © 2014 by Pearson Education Canada. All rights reserved.

CONFLICT AND STRESS

THE TORONTO HAIR WAR: GLO VERSUS GLISS

A dispute between two of Yorkville's ritziest hair salons has degenerated into a sniping war involving seized garbage, surprise searches, and a $6.4 million lawsuit. The fight centres on Glo Salon & Spa, a high-end beauty purveyor on [Toronto's] Avenue Road that caters to some of the city's wealthiest women. A Glo cut and colour starts at about $200 and goes up quickly from there.

"(Hairstyling) is a dirty little business, laughed Luis Pacheco, co-owner of nearby Hair on the Avenue, who is watching this scrap from the sidelines. "It's like a cesspool."

Three years ago, hairstylist Perry Neglia and a partner sold Glo to Mary Louise Abrahamse, who was new to the salon business. As part of the $450 000 sale, Neglia agreed to continue working at Glo for a year and not to open a competing business for three years. It's not clear who did what to whom over the next three years, but it's plain that relations between Abrahamse and some of her new staff became strained. On April 1, the day after his non-compete clause expired, Neglia opened a rival salon 100 metres up the street, calling it Gliss. Over the next several weeks, a steady stream of Glo hairstylists and colour technicians followed Neglia the short walk up Avenue Road. More importantly, "a high percentage" of their clients came with them, according to Neglia. He and his new staffers contacted long-time customers to let them know about the switch. "It would be rude not to tell them," Neglia said in an interview. "It would look like we didn't want to take them. They'd feel jilted."

"She thinks she bought the clients," Jarmil Kulik, Neglia's new partner and a former Glo stylist, said of Abrahamse. "And nobody does that," said Neglia. As a result, Glo was left with a denuded staff without well-developed client rosters, according to Abrahamse's lawsuit. One of her lawyers, Bob Klotz, said in an interview that his client's business has been "destroyed." Abrahamse declined comment.

For several weeks, things settled to a low boil. But while Neglia and his staff were building their new business, Abrahamse was working behind the scenes to unsettle them. She hired private investigators to go through Gliss's trash. They sent dummy clients into Gliss to look around. The object of the search was to determine what, if anything, Gliss staff had removed from Glo. Key to that investigation were the so-called "colour cards" that are used to chart the chemical formula for colouring hair. The cards often contain a client's contact info. Abrahamse's legal team asserts that the cards are her property. Neglia counters that cards were the property of individual staffers when he owned Glo, and that the rule was not changed after he sold the business. He claims that his staff copied the information on the cards and left the originals at Glo. "That way (the customers) have a choice about which

Former Glo staff, now at Gliss, embroiled in a $6.4 million suit.

salon they want to go to," said Neglia in an interview. The practice of taking cards and luring away clients often causes ugly breakups in the hairstyling business but is so pervasive that most salon owners grudgingly accept it. "Clients have free will, too. There's no ownership," said Hair on the Avenue owner Pacheco. "Is it fair to take [the cards]? I would say so."

The investigators found enough to persuade a judge to issue an Anton Piller order, an extraordinary legal device that allows a private search without notice so that evidence cannot be destroyed. On the morning of June 4, a team of lawyers and forensic technicians, including a videographer, arrived to search Gliss. "It was like something out of *Law & Order*," said stylist Stephen Jackson, one of those who left Glo to join Neglia. At the same time, another half-dozen people turned up at Neglia's home. Both groups brought police officers to act as peacekeepers. Staffers at Gliss were told to hand over cellphones, the contents of which were then copied. A total of six computers at the business and at Neglia's home were confiscated and cloned. About a thousand colour cards and binders with client information were also taken and have yet to be returned. All of that property is now being held by an independent auditor. Neglia, Kulik, Jackson and five other former Glo staff members then learned they were being sued for a total of $6.4 million. "It's mind-boggling," said Brian Menzies, a colourist and co-defendant.

The fight has caused a flutter around Yorkville, where dozens of high-end salons have clustered in the years since Vidal Sassoon opened his landmark shop in the late '60s. "I think everyone thinks Mary Louise is out of her mind, that she's crazy," said Marianne Marshall, the city's top beauty trade headhunter. She said both Abrahamse and Neglia are her clients. It's also raising questions among hair professionals and their clients about who owns what in the prim world of beauty salons. "What is she (Abrahamse) suing for?" said Marlene Hore, an advertising exec who moved up the street to Gliss to continue getting her hair done by Jackson. "Don't I have a right to go wherever I want to have my hair cut?"

On Monday, Justice Colin Campbell thought better of the Anton Piller order. He intends to set it aside, dealing a blow to Abrahamse's suit. However, Klotz said that his client intends to continue. "Sure, Mary Louise is mad," said headhunter Marshall. "But suing Perry (Neglia) is not going to accomplish anything. This way, everyone gets dragged through the mud. And, in the end, I don't think she's going to win."[1]

GORDON LAW GROUP: CONFLICT AND NEGOTIATION Go to MyManagementLab to watch a video about conflict and negotiation.

Define *interpersonal conflict* and review its causes in organizations.

Interpersonal conflict. The process that occurs when one person, group, or organizational subunit frustrates the goal attainment of another.

In this chapter, we will define *interpersonal conflict*, discuss its causes, and examine various ways of handling conflict, including negotiation. Then we will explore *work stress*, noting its causes and the consequences that it can have for both individuals and organizations. Various strategies for managing stress will be considered.

WHAT IS CONFLICT?

Interpersonal conflict is a process that occurs when one person, group, or organizational subunit frustrates the goal attainment of another. Thus, the curator of a museum might be in conflict with the director over the purchase of a particular work of art. Likewise, the entire curatorial staff might be in conflict with the financial staff over cutbacks in acquisition funds.

In its classic form, conflict often involves antagonistic attitudes and behaviours, as seen in the drama concerning the Toronto hair salons. As for attitudes, the conflicting parties might develop a dislike for each other, see each other as unreasonable, and develop negative stereotypes of their opposites ("Those scientists should get out of the laboratory once in a while"). Antagonistic behaviours might include name calling, sabotage, or even physical aggression. In some organizations, the conflict process is managed in a collaborative way that keeps antagonism at a minimum. In others, conflict is hidden or suppressed and not nearly so obvious (e.g., some gender conflict).[2]

CAUSES OF ORGANIZATIONAL CONFLICT

It is possible to isolate a number of factors that contribute to organizational conflict.[3]

Group Identification and Intergroup Bias

An especially fascinating line of research has shown how identification with a particular group or class of people can set the stage for organizational conflict. In this work, researchers have typically assigned people to groups randomly or on the basis of some trivial characteristic, such as eye colour. Even without interaction or cohesion, people have a tendency to develop a more positive view of their own "in-group" and a less positive view of the "out-group," of which they are not a member.[4] The ease with which this unwarranted intergroup bias develops is disturbing.

Why does intergroup bias occur? Self-esteem is probably a critical factor. Identifying with the successes of one's own group and disassociating oneself from out-group failures boosts self-esteem and provides comforting feelings of social solidarity. Research by one of your authors, for example, found that people felt that their work group's attendance record was superior to that of their occupation in general (and, by extension, other work groups).[5] Attributing positive behaviour to your own work group should contribute to your self-esteem.

In organizations, there are a number of groups or classes with which people might identify. These might be based on personal characteristics (e.g., race or gender), job function (e.g., sales or production), or job level (e.g., manager or non-manager). Furthermore, far from being random or trivial, differences between groups might be accentuated by real differences in power, opportunity, clients serviced, and so on. For instance, the merger between Air Canada and Canadian Airlines made firm identities very salient for employees, and these identities persisted even after the companies merged into a single entity. The best prognosis is that people who identify with some groups will tend to be leery of out-group members. The likelihood of conflict increases as the factors we cover below enter into the relationship between groups.

The increased emphasis on teams in organizations generally places a high premium on getting employees to identify strongly with their team. The prevalence of intergroup bias suggests that organizations will have to pay special attention to managing relationships *between* these teams.

Interdependence

When individuals or subunits are mutually dependent on each other to accomplish *their own* goals, the potential for conflict exists. For example, the sales staff is dependent on the production department for the timely delivery of high-quality products. This is the only way sales can maintain the goodwill of its customers. On the other hand, production depends on the sales staff to provide routine orders with adequate lead times. Custom-tailored emergency orders will wreak havoc with production schedules and make the production department look bad. In contrast, the sales staff and the office maintenance staff are not highly interdependent. Salespeople are on the road a lot and should not make great demands on maintenance. Conversely, a dirty office probably will not lose a sale.

Interdependence can set the stage for conflict for two reasons. First, it necessitates interaction between the parties so that they can coordinate their interests. Conflict will not develop if the parties can "go it alone." Second, interdependence implies that each party has some *power* over the other. It is relatively easy for one side or the other to abuse its power and create antagonism.

Interdependence does not *always* lead to conflict. In fact, it often provides a good basis for collaboration through mutual assistance. Whether interdependence prompts conflict depends on the presence of other conditions, which we will now consider.

Differences in Power, Status, and Culture

Conflict can erupt when parties differ significantly in power, status, or culture.

POWER If dependence is not mutual but one-way, the potential for conflict increases. If party A needs the collaboration of party B to accomplish its goals but B does not need A's assistance, antagonism may develop. B has power over A, and A has nothing with which to bargain. A good example is the quality control system in many factories. Production workers might be highly dependent on inspectors to approve their work, but this dependence is not reciprocated. The inspectors might have a separate boss, their own office, and their own circle of friends (other inspectors). In this case, production workers might begin to treat inspectors with hostility, one of the symptoms of conflict.

STATUS Status differences provide little impetus for conflict when people of lower status are dependent on those of higher status. This is the way organizations often work, and most members are socialized to expect it. However, because of the design of the work, there are occasions when employees who technically have lower status find themselves giving orders to, or controlling the tasks of, higher-status people. The restaurant business provides a good example. In many restaurants, lower-status servers give orders and initiate queries to higher-status chefs. The latter might come to resent this reversal of usual lines of influence.[6] In some organizations, junior staff are more adept with information technology than senior staff. Some executives are defensive about this reversal of roles.

CULTURE When two or more very different cultures develop in an organization, the clash in beliefs and values can result in overt conflict. Hospital administrators who develop a strong culture centred on efficiency and cost-effectiveness might find themselves in conflict with physicians who share a strong culture based on providing excellent patient care at any cost. A telling case of cultural conflict occurred when Apple Computer expanded and hired professionals away from several companies with their own strong cultures.

> *During the first couple of years Apple recruited heavily from Hewlett-Packard, National Semiconductor, and Intel, and the habits and differences in style among these companies were reflected in Cupertino. There was a general friction between the rough and tough ways of the semiconductor men (there were few women) and the people who made computers,*

calculators, and instruments at Hewlett-Packard.... Some of the Hewlett-Packard men began to see themselves as civilizing influences and were horrified at the uncouth rough- and-tumble practices of the brutes from the semiconductor industry.... Many of the men from National Semiconductor and other stern backgrounds harboured a similar contempt for the Hewlett-Packard recruits. They came to look on them as prissy fusspots.[7]

Ambiguity

Ambiguous goals, jurisdictions, or performance criteria can lead to conflict. Under such ambiguity, the formal and informal rules that govern interaction break down. In addition, it might be difficult to accurately assign praise for good outcomes or blame for bad outcomes when it is hard to see who was responsible for what. For example, if sales drop following the introduction of a "new and improved" product, the design group might blame the marketing department for a poor advertising campaign. In response, the marketers might claim that the "improved" product is actually inferior to the old product.

Ambiguous performance criteria are a frequent cause of conflict between managers and employees. The basic scientist who is charged by a chemical company to "discover new knowledge" might react negatively when her boss informs her that her work is inadequate. This rather open-ended assignment is susceptible to a variety of interpretations. Conflict is not uncommon in the film and entertainment industry, in part because a great deal of ambiguity surrounds just what is needed to produce a hit movie or show. In the up-market atmosphere of Yorkville's hair salons, there is apparent ambiguity about who "owns" client information such as colour cards.

Scarce Resources

Differences in power are magnified when resources become scarce. This does not occur without a battle, however, and conflict often surfaces in the process of power jockeying. Limited budget money, secretarial support, or lab space can contribute to conflict. Scarcity has a way of turning latent or disguised conflict into overt conflict. Two scientists who do not get along very well may be able to put up a peaceful front until a reduction in lab space provokes each to protect his or her domain. In the chapter-opening vignette, the battle between Glo and Gliss was most decidedly provoked by scarce resources—wealthy customers willing to pay $200 for a haircut and colour.

LO 2

Explain the *types of conflict* and the process by which conflict occurs.

Relationship conflict. Interpersonal tensions among individuals that have to do with their relationship per se, not the task at hand.

Task conflict. Disagreements about the nature of the work to be done.

Process conflict. Disagreements about how work should be organized and accomplished.

TYPES OF CONFLICT

Is all conflict the same? The answer is no. It is useful to distinguish among relationship, task, and process conflict.[8] **Relationship conflict** concerns interpersonal tensions among individuals that have to do with their relationship per se, not the task at hand. So-called personality clashes are examples of relationship conflicts. **Task conflict** concerns disagreements about the nature of the work to be done. Differences of opinion about goals or technical matters are examples of task conflict. Finally, **process conflict** involves disagreements about how work should be organized and accomplished. Disagreements about responsibility, authority, resource allocation, and who should do what all constitute process conflict.

In the context of work groups and teams, relationship and process conflict tend to be detrimental to member satisfaction and team performance. In essence, such conflict prevents the development of cohesiveness. Occasionally, some degree of task conflict is actually beneficial for team performance, especially when the task is non-routine and requires a variety of perspectives to be considered and when it does not degenerate into relationship conflict.[9] Thus, not all conflict is detrimental, and we shall return to some potential benefits of conflict later in the chapter.

CONFLICT DYNAMICS

A number of events occur when one or more of the causes of conflict we noted above take effect. We will assume here that the conflict in question occurs between groups, such as organizational departments. However, much of this is also relevant to conflict within teams or between individuals. Specifically, when conflict begins, we often see the following events transpire:

- "Winning" the conflict becomes more important than developing a good solution to the problem at hand.
- The parties begin to conceal information from each other or to pass on distorted information.
- Each side becomes more cohesive. Deviants who speak of conciliation are punished, and strict conformity is expected.
- Contact with the opposite party is discouraged except under formalized, restricted conditions.
- While the opposite party is negatively stereotyped, the image of one's own position is boosted.
- On each side, more aggressive people who are skilled at engaging in conflict may emerge as leaders.[10]

You can certainly see the difficulty here. What begins as a problem of identity, interdependence, ambiguity, or scarcity quickly escalates to the point that the conflict process *itself* becomes an additional problem. The elements of this process then work against the achievement of a peaceful solution. The conflict continues to cycle "on its own steam," as illustrated in the "Hair War" vignette.

MODES OF MANAGING CONFLICT

How do you tend to react to conflict situations? Are you aggressive? Do you tend to hide your head in the sand? As conflict expert Kenneth Thomas notes, there are several basic reactions that can be thought of as styles, strategies, or intentions for dealing with conflict. As shown in Exhibit 1, these approaches to managing conflict are a function of both how *assertive* you are in trying to satisfy your own or your group's concerns and how *cooperative* you are in trying to satisfy those of the other party or group.[11] It should be emphasized that none of the five

LO ③

Discuss the various *modes of managing conflict.*

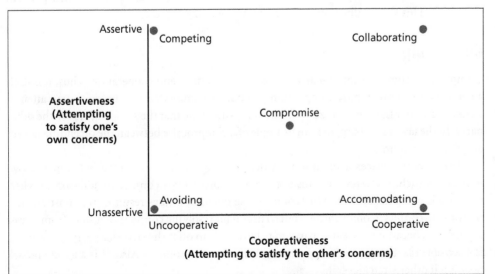

EXHIBIT 1

Approaches to managing organizational conflict.
Source: Thomas, K.W. (1992). Conflict and negotiations in organizations" in M.D. Dunnette, & L.M. Hough, (Eds.) *Handbook of industrial and organizational psychology* (2nd Ed., Vol. 3). Palo Alto, CA: Consulting Psychologists Press. Used by permission of the publisher.

Go to MyManagementLab to see an annotated version of this figure.

styles for dealing with conflict in Exhibit 1 is inherently superior. As we will see, each style might have its place given the situation in which the conflict episode occurs. To diagnose how you manage conflict, try the Experiential Exercise at the end of the chapter.

Avoiding

Avoiding. A conflict management style characterized by low assertiveness of one's own interests and low cooperation with the other party.

The **avoiding** style is characterized by low assertiveness of one's own interests and low cooperation with the other party. This is the "hiding one's head in the sand" response. Although avoidance can provide some short-term stress reduction from the rigours of conflict, it does not really change the situation. Thus, its effectiveness is often limited.

Of course, avoidance does have its place. If the issue is trivial, information is lacking, people need to cool down, or the opponent is very powerful and very hostile, avoidance might be a sensible response.

Accommodating

Accommodating. A conflict management style in which one cooperates with the other party while not asserting one's own interests.

Cooperating with the other party's wishes while not asserting one's own interests is the hallmark of **accommodating**. If people see accommodation as a sign of weakness, it does not bode well for future interactions. However, it can be an effective reaction when you are wrong, the issue is more important to the other party, or you want to build good will.

Competing

Competing. A conflict management style that maximizes assertiveness and minimizes cooperation.

A **competing** style tends to maximize assertiveness for your own position and minimize cooperative responses. In competing, you tend to frame the conflict in strict win–lose terms. Full priority is given to your own goals, facts, or procedures. Bill Gates, the billionaire czar of Microsoft, tends to pursue the competing style:

> *Gates is famously confrontational. If he strongly disagrees with what you're saying, he is in the habit of blurting out, "That's the stupidest…thing I've ever heard!" People tell stories of Gates spraying saliva into the face of some hapless employee as he yells, "This stuff isn't hard! I could do this stuff in a weekend!" What you're supposed to do in a situation like this, as in encounters with grizzly bears, is stand your ground: if you flee, the bear will think you're game and will pursue you, and you can't outrun a bear.[12]*

The competing style holds promise when you have a lot of power, you are sure of your facts, the situation is truly win–lose, or you will not have to interact with the other party in the future. This style is illustrated in the chapter-opening vignette.

Compromise

Compromise. A conflict management style that combines intermediate levels of assertiveness and cooperation.

Compromise combines intermediate levels of assertiveness and cooperation. Thus, it is itself a compromise between pure competition and pure accommodation. In a sense, you attempt to satisfice rather than maximize your outcomes and hope that the same occurs for the other party. In the law, a plea bargain is an example of a compromise between the defending lawyer and the prosecutor.

Compromise places a premium on determining rules of exchange between the two parties. As such, it always contains the seeds for procedural conflict in addition to whatever else is being negotiated. Also, compromise does not always result in the most creative response to conflict. Compromise is not so useful for resolving conflicts that stem from power asymmetry, because the weaker party may have little to offer the stronger party. However, it is a sensible reaction to conflict stemming from scarce resources. Also, it is a good fallback position if other strategies fail.

Collaborating

In the **collaborating** mode, both assertiveness and cooperation are maximized in the hope that an integrative agreement occurs that fully satisfies the interests of both parties. Emphasis is put on a win–win resolution, in which there is no assumption that someone must lose something. Rather, it is assumed that the solution to the conflict can leave both parties in a better condition. Ideally, collaboration occurs as a problem-solving exercise. It probably works best when the conflict is not intense and when each party has information that is useful to the other. Although effective collaboration can take time and practice to develop, it frequently enhances productivity and achievement.[13]

Some of the most remarkable examples of collaboration in contemporary organizations are those between companies and their suppliers. Traditionally, adversarial competition in which buyers try to squeeze the very lowest price out of suppliers, who are frequently played off against each other, has dominated these relationships. This obviously does not provide much incentive for the perpetually insecure suppliers to invest in improvements dedicated toward a particular buyer. Gradually, things have changed, and now it is common for organizations to supply extensive engineering support and technical advice to their suppliers. In a related example, after the 2011 Japanese earthquake and tsunami the country's car manufacturers, usually fierce competitors, collaborated to get the nation's parts suppliers back on line.[14]

Collaboration also helps to manage conflict inside organizations. Cross-functional teams are a good example. Also, research shows that collaboration between organizational departments is particularly important for providing good customer service.[15]

MANAGING CONFLICT WITH NEGOTIATION

The stereotype we have of negotiation is that it is a formal process of bargaining between labour and management or buyer and seller. However, job applicants negotiate for starting salaries, employees negotiate for better job assignments, and people with sick kids negotiate to leave work early. To encompass all these situations, we might define **negotiation** as "a

> **Collaborating.** A conflict management style that maximizes both assertiveness and cooperation.

LO 4

Review a range of *negotiation techniques.*

Negotiation. A decision-making process among interdependent parties who do not share identical preferences.

Collaboration can provide unions and management with win–win solutions.

decision-making process among interdependent parties who do not share identical preferences."[16] Negotiation constitutes conflict management, in that it is an attempt to either prevent conflict or resolve existing conflict.

Negotiation is an attempt to reach a satisfactory exchange among or between the parties. Sometimes, negotiation is very explicit, as in the case of the labour negotiation or the buyer–seller interaction. However, negotiation can also proceed in a very implicit or tacit way.[17] For instance, when an employee is trying to get a more interesting job assignment or to take off from work early, the terms of the exchange are not likely to be spelled out very clearly. Still, this is negotiation.

It has become common to distinguish between distributive and integrative negotiation tactics.[18] **Distributive negotiation** assumes a zero-sum, win–lose situation in which a fixed pie is divided up between the parties. If you re-examine Exhibit 1, you can imagine that distributive negotiation occurs on the axis between competition and accommodation. In theory, the parties will more or less tend toward some compromise. On the other hand, **integrative negotiation** assumes that mutual problem solving can result in a win–win situation in which the pie is actually enlarged before distribution. Integrative negotiation occurs on the axis between avoiding and collaborating, ideally tending toward the latter.

Distributive and integrative negotiations can take place simultaneously. We will discuss them separately for pedagogical purposes.

Distributive Negotiation Tactics

Distributive negotiation is essentially single-issue negotiation. Many potential conflict situations fit this scenario. For example, suppose you find a used car that you really like. Now, things boil down to price. You want to buy the car for the minimum reasonable price, while the seller wants to get the maximum reasonable price.

The essence of the problem is shown in Exhibit 2. Party is a consulting firm who would like to win a contract to do an attitude survey in Other's firm. Party would like to make $90 000 for the job (Party's target) but would settle for $70 000, a figure that provides

Distributive negotiation. Win–lose negotiation in which a fixed amount of assets is divided between parties.

Integrative negotiation. Win–win negotiation that assumes that mutual problem solving can enlarge the assets to be divided between parties.

EXHIBIT 2
A model of distributive negotiation.
Source: Thomas, K.W. (1992). Conflict and negotiations in organizations" in M.D. Dunnette, & L.M. Hough (Eds.) *Handbook of industrial and organizational psychology* (2nd Ed., Vol. 3). Palo Alto, CA: Consulting Psychologists Press. Used by permission of the publisher.

Explore

Go to MyManagementLab to see an annotated version of this figure.

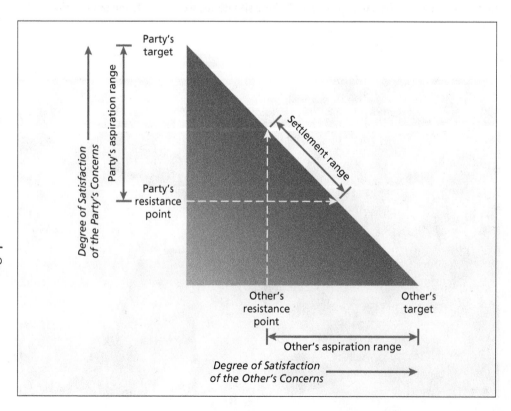

for minimal acceptable profit (Party's resistance point). Other thinks that the survey could be done for as little as $60 000 (Other's target) but would be willing to spend up to $80 000 for a good job (Other's resistance point). Theoretically, an offer in the settlement range between $70 000 and $80 000 should clinch the deal, if the negotiators can get into this range. Notice that every dollar that Party earns is a dollar's worth of cost for Other. How will they reach a settlement?[19]

THREATS AND PROMISES *Threat* consists of implying that you will punish the other party if he or she does not concede to your position. For example, the Other firm might imply that it will terminate its other business with the consulting company if Party does not lower its price on the attitude survey job. *Promises* are pledges that concessions will lead to rewards in the future. For example, Other might promise future consulting contracts if Party agrees to do the survey at a lower price. Of course, the difference between a threat and a promise can be subtle, as when the promise implies a threat should no concession be made.

Threat has some merit as a bargaining tactic if one party has power over the other that corresponds to the nature of the threat, especially if no future negotiations are expected or if the threat can be posed in a civil and subtle way.[20] If power is more balanced and the threat is crude, a counter threat could scuttle the negotiations, despite the fact that both parties could be satisfied in the settlement range. Promises have merit when your side lacks power and anticipates future negotiations with the other side. Both threats and promises work best when they send interpretable signals to the other side about your true position, what really matters to you. Careful timing is critical.

FIRMNESS VERSUS CONCESSIONS How about intransigence—sticking to your target position, offering few concessions, and waiting for the other party to give in? Research shows that such a tactic yields superior economic results, especially in face-to-face negotiations.[21] When some concessions are thought to be appropriate, good negotiators often use face-saving techniques to explain them. For example, the consulting firm might claim that it could reduce the cost of the survey by making it web-based rather than based on paper questionnaires.

PERSUASION Verbal persuasion or debate is common in negotiations. Often, it takes a two-pronged attack. One prong asserts the technical merits of the party's position. For example, the consulting firm might justify its target price by saying "We have the most qualified staff. We do the most reliable surveys." The other prong asserts the fairness of the target position. Here, the negotiator might make a speech about the expenses the company would incur in doing the survey.

Verbal persuasion is an attempt to change the attitudes of the other party toward your target position. Persuaders are most effective when they are perceived as expert, likable, and unbiased. The obvious problem in distributive negotiations is bias—each party knows the other is self-interested. One way to deal with this is to introduce some unbiased parties. For example, the consulting firm might produce testimony from satisfied survey clients. Also, disputants often bring third parties into negotiations on the assumption that they will process argumentation in an unbiased manner.

Salary negotiation is a traditional example of distributive bargaining. A review of studies on gender differences in negotiation outcomes found that although men negotiated significantly better outcomes than women, the overall difference between men and women was small. However, even small differences in salary negotiations would be perpetuated through subsequent salary increases based on percentage of pay. Thus, training programs that enable women to negotiate better starting salaries comparable with men can have short- and long-term benefits.[22] Negotiation is worth doing, as a recent study showed that new hires who negotiated received a $5000 salary premium. Collaborating and competing strategies were superior to compromising and accommodating.[23]

Integrative Negotiation Tactics

As we noted earlier, integrative negotiation rejects a fixed-pie assumption and strives for collaborative problem solving that advances the interests of both parties. At the outset, it is useful but sobering to realize that people have a decided bias for fixed-pie thinking. A good example is seen in the North American manufacturing sector, where such thinking by both unions and management badly damaged the global competitiveness of manufacturing firms.[24]

Why the bias for fixed-pie thinking? First, integrative negotiation requires a degree of creativity. Most people are not especially creative, and the stress of typical negotiation does not provide the best climate for creativity in any event. This means that many of the role models that negotiators have (e.g., following labour negotiations on TV) are more likely to use distributive than integrative tactics. To complicate matters, if you are negotiating for constituents, they are also more likely to be exposed to distributive tactics and likely to pressure you to use them. Nevertheless, attempts at integrative negotiation can be well worth the effort.[25]

COPIOUS INFORMATION EXCHANGE Most of the information exchanged in distributive bargaining is concerned with attacking the other party's position and trying to persuade them of the correctness of yours. Otherwise, mum's the word. A freer flow of information is critical to finding an integrative settlement. The problem, of course, is that we all tend to be a bit paranoid about information being used against us in bargaining situations. This means that trust must be built slowly. One way to proceed is to give away some non-critical information to the other party to get the ball rolling. As we noted earlier, much negotiation behaviour tends to be reciprocated. Also, ask the other party a lot of questions, and *listen* to their responses. This is at odds with the tell-and-sell approach used in most distributive negotiations. If all goes well, both parties will begin to reveal their true interests, not just their current positions.

FRAMING DIFFERENCES AS OPPORTUNITIES Parties in a negotiation often differ in their preferences, for everything from the timing of a deal to the degree of risk that each party wants to assume. Traditionally, such differences are framed as barriers to negotiations. However, such differences can often serve as a basis for integrative agreements because, again, they contain information that can telegraph each party's real interests. For instance, imagine that two co-workers are negotiating for the finishing date of a project that they have to complete by a certain deadline. Due to competing demands, one wants to finish it early, and the other wants to just make the deadline. In the course of the discussion, they realize that they can divide the labour such that one begins the project while the other finishes it, satisfying both parties fully (notice that this is not a compromise).

CUTTING COSTS If you can somehow cut the costs that the other party associates with an agreement, the chance of an integrative settlement increases. For example, suppose that you are negotiating with your boss for a new, more interesting job assignment, but she does not like the idea because she relies on your excellent skills on your current assignment. By asking good questions (see above), you find out that she is ultimately worried about the job being done properly, not about your leaving it. You take the opportunity to inform her that you have groomed a subordinate to do your current job. This reduces the costs of her letting you assume the new assignment.

Integrative solutions are especially attractive when they reduce costs for *all* parties in a dispute. For example, firms in the computer and acoustics industries have joined together to support basic research on technology of interest to all firms. This reduces costly competition to perfect a technology that all parties need anyway.

INCREASING RESOURCES Increasing available resources is a very literal way of getting around the fixed-pie syndrome. This is not as unlikely as it sounds when you realize that two parties, working together, might have access to twice as many resources as one party. One of your authors once saw two academic departments squabbling to get the approval to recruit one new faculty member for whom there was a budget line. Seeing this as a fixed pie leads to one department winning all or to the impossible compromise of half a recruit for each department. The chairs of the two departments used their *combined* political clout to get the dean to promise that they could also have exclusive access to one budget line the following year. The chairs then flipped a coin to see who would recruit immediately and who would wait a year. This minor compromise on time was less critical than the firm guarantee of a budget line.

INTRODUCING SUPERORDINATE GOALS **Superordinate goals** are attractive outcomes that can be achieved only by collaboration.[26] Neither party can attain the goal on its own. Superordinate goals probably represent the best example of creativity in integrative negotiation because they change the entire landscape of the negotiation episode. Many observers have noted how the terrorist attacks on September 11, 2001, created a superordinate goal that prompted collaboration among nations that otherwise might have been mired in conflict over more trivial matters.

Superordinate goals. Attractive outcomes that can be achieved only by collaboration.

Third Party Involvement

Sometimes, third parties come into play to intervene between negotiating parties.[27] Often, this happens when the parties reach an impasse. For example, a manager might have to step in to a conflict between two employees or even between two departments. In other cases, third party involvement exists right from the start of the negotiation. For example, real estate agents serve as an interface between home sellers and buyers.

MEDIATION The process of mediation occurs when a neutral third party helps to facilitate a negotiated agreement. Formal mediation has a long history in labour disputes, international relations, and marital counselling. However, by definition, almost any manager might occasionally be required to play an informal mediating role.

What do mediators do?[28] First, almost anything that aids the *process* or *atmosphere* of negotiation can be helpful. Of course, this depends on the exact situation at hand. If there is tension, the mediator might serve as a lightning rod for anger or try to introduce humour. The mediator might try to help the parties clarify their underlying interests, both to themselves and to each other. Occasionally, imposing a deadline or helping the parties deal with their own constituents might be useful. Introducing a problem-solving orientation to move toward more integrative bargaining might also be appropriate.

The mediator might also intervene in the *content* of the negotiation, highlighting points of agreement, pointing out new options, or encouraging concessions.

Research shows that mediation has a fairly successful track record in dispute resolution. However, mediators cannot turn water into wine, and the process seems to work best when the conflict is not too intense and the parties are resolved to use negotiation to deal with their conflict. If the mediator is not seen as neutral or if there is dissension in the ranks of each negotiating party, mediation does not work so well.[29]

ARBITRATION The process of arbitration occurs when a third party is given the authority to dictate the terms of settlement of a conflict (there is also non-binding arbitration, which we will not consider here). Although disputing parties sometimes agree to arbitration, it can also be mandated formally by law or informally by upper management or parents. The key point is that negotiation has broken down, and the arbitrator has to make a final distributive allocation. This is not the way to integrative solutions.

In *conventional arbitration*, the arbitrator can choose any outcome, such as splitting the difference between the two parties. In *final offer arbitration*, each party makes a final offer, and the arbitrator chooses one of them. This latter invention was devised to motivate the two parties to make sensible offers that have a chance of being upheld. Also, fear of the all-or-nothing aspect of final arbitration seems to motivate more negotiated agreement.[30]

One of the most commonly arbitrated disputes between employers and employees is dismissal for excessive absenteeism. One study found that the arbitrators sided with the company in over half of such cases, especially when the company could show evidence of a fair and consistently applied absentee policy.[31]

IS ALL CONFLICT BAD?

In everyday life, there has traditionally been an emphasis on the negative, dysfunctional aspects of conflict. This is not difficult to understand. Discord between parents and children, severe labour strife, and international disputes are unpleasant experiences. To some degree, this emphasis on the negative aspects of conflict is also characteristic of thinking in organizational behaviour. However, there is growing awareness of some potential *benefits* of organizational conflict.[32] In fact, we suggested this in our previous distinction among task, process, and relationship conflict.

The argument that conflict can be functional rests mainly on the idea that it promotes necessary organizational change:

$$\text{CONFLICT} \rightarrow \text{CHANGE} \rightarrow \text{ADAPTATION} \rightarrow \text{SURVIVAL}^{33}$$

In other words, for organizations to survive, they must adapt to their environments. This requires changes in strategy that may be stimulated through conflict. For example, consider the museum that relies heavily on government funding and consistently mounts exhibits that are appreciated only by "true connoisseurs" of art. Under a severe funding cutback, the museum can survive only if it begins to mount exhibits with more popular appeal. Such a change might occur only after much conflict within the board of directors.

Just how does conflict promote change? For one thing, it might bring into consideration new ideas that would not be offered without conflict. In trying to "one up" the opponent, one of the parties might develop a unique idea that the other cannot fail to appreciate. In a related way, conflict might promote change because each party begins to monitor the other's performance more carefully. This search for weaknesses means that it is more difficult to hide errors and problems from the rest of the organization. Such errors and problems (e.g., a failure to make deliveries on time) might be a signal that changes are necessary. Finally, conflict may promote useful change by signalling that a redistribution of power is necessary. Consider the human resources department that must battle with managers to get diversity programs implemented. This conflict might be a clue that some change is due in power priorities.

All this suggests that there are times when managers might use a strategy of **conflict stimulation** to cause change. But how does a manager know when some conflict might be a good thing? One signal is the existence of a "friendly rut," in which peaceful relationships take precedence over organizational goals. Another signal is seen when parties that should be interacting closely have chosen to withdraw from each other to avoid overt conflict. A third signal occurs when conflict is suppressed or downplayed by denying differences, ignoring controversy, and exaggerating points of agreement.[34]

The causes of conflict, discussed earlier, such as scarcity and ambiguity, can be manipulated by managers to achieve change.[35] For example, when he was appointed vice-chairman of product development at General Motors, Robert Lutz sent out a memo entitled "Strongly Held Beliefs." In it, the product czar said that GM undervalued exciting design, and he panned corporate sacred cows such as the extensive use of consumer focus groups and product planning committees. Lutz stimulated conflict by signalling a shift of resources from marketing to design.[36]

Conflict in organizations, warranted or not, often causes considerable stress. Let's now turn to this topic.

A MODEL OF STRESS IN ORGANIZATIONS

During the last two decades, stress has become a serious concern for individuals and organizations. A U.S. National Institute for Occupational Safety and Health survey found that 40 percent of workers found their jobs extremely or very stressful, and the U.S. Bureau of Labor Statistics determined that stress is a leading cause of worker disability.[37] In fact, in an American Psychological Association survey, work was reported to be a potent source of stress, edging out health and relationships.[38] Stress has been estimated to cost U.S. businesses $300 billion annually and Canadian businesses $16 billion.[39] The model of a stress episode in Exhibit 3 can guide our introduction to this topic.[40]

Stressors

Stressors are environmental events or conditions that have the potential to induce stress. There are some conditions that would prove stressful for just about everyone. These include such things as extreme heat, extreme cold, isolation, or hostile people. More interesting is the fact that the individual personality often determines the extent to which a potential stressor becomes a real stressor and actually induces stress.

Stress

Stress is a psychological reaction to the demands inherent in a stressor that has the potential to make a person feel tense or anxious because the person does not feel capable of coping with these demands.[41] Stress is not intrinsically bad. All people require a certain level of stimulation from their environment, and moderate levels of stress can serve this function. In fact, one would wonder about the perceptual accuracy of a person who *never* experienced tension. On the other hand, stress does become a problem when it leads to especially high levels of anxiety and tension. Obviously, the "Hair War" described in the chapter-opening vignette has provoked much stress.

Stress Reactions

Stress reactions are the behavioural, psychological, and physiological consequences of stress. Some of these reactions are essentially passive responses over which the individual has little direct control, such as elevated blood pressure or a reduced immune function. Other reactions are active attempts to *cope* with some previous aspect of the stress episode. Exhibit 3 indicates that stress reactions that involve coping attempts might be directed toward dealing directly with the stressor or simply reducing the anxiety generated by stress. In general, the former strategy has more potential for effectiveness than the latter because the chances of the stress episode being *terminated* are increased.[42]

LO 6

Distinguish among *stressors*, *stress*, and *stress reactions*.

◉ Watch

EAST HAVEN FIRE DEPARTMENT: MANAGING STRESS Go to MyManagementLab to watch a video about managing stress.

Stressors. Environmental events or conditions that have the potential to induce stress.

Stress. A psychological reaction to the demands inherent in a stressor that has the potential to make a person feel tense or anxious.

Stress reactions. The behavioural, psychological, and physiological consequences of stress.

EXHIBIT 3
Model of a stress episode.

✳ Explore

Go to MyManagementLab to see an annotated version of this figure.

Often, reactions that are useful for the individual in dealing with a stress episode may be very costly to the organization. The individual who is conveniently absent from work on the day of a difficult inventory check might prevent personal stress but leave the organization short-handed (provoking stress in others). Thus, organizations should be concerned about the stress that individual employees experience.

The stress model presented here appears to generalize across cultures. That is, similar factors provoke stress and lead to similar stress reactions around the globe.[43]

LO 7

Discuss the role that personality plays in stress.

Personality and Stress

Personality can have an important influence on the stress experience. As shown in Exhibit 3, it can affect both the extent to which potential stressors are perceived as stressful and the types of stress reactions that occur. Let's look at three key personality traits.

Locus of control. A set of beliefs about whether one's behaviour is controlled mainly by internal or external forces.

LOCUS OF CONTROL

Locus of control concerns people's beliefs about the factors that control their behaviour. Internals believe that they control their own behaviour, while externals believe that their behaviour is controlled by luck, fate, or powerful people. Compared with internals, externals are more likely to feel anxious in the face of potential stressors.[44] Most people like to feel in control of what happens to them, and externals feel less in control. Internals are more likely to confront stressors directly because they assume that this response will make a difference. Externals, on the other hand, are anxious but do not feel that they are masters of their own fate. Thus, they are more prone to simple anxiety-reduction strategies that only work in the short run.

Type A behaviour pattern. A personality pattern that includes aggressiveness, ambitiousness, competitiveness, hostility, impatience, and a sense of time urgency.

TYPE A BEHAVIOUR PATTERN

Interest in the **Type A behaviour pattern** began when physicians noticed that many sufferers of coronary heart disease, especially those who developed the disease relatively young, exhibited a distinctive pattern of behaviours and emotions.[45] Individuals who exhibit the Type A behaviour pattern tend to be aggressive and ambitious. Their hostility is easily aroused, and they feel a great sense of time urgency. They are impatient, competitive, and preoccupied with their work. The Type A individual can be contrasted with the Type B, who does not exhibit these extreme characteristics. Compared with Type B individuals, Type A people report heavier workloads, longer work hours, and more conflicting work demands.[46] We will see later that such factors turn out to be potent stressors. Thus, either Type A people encounter more stressful situations than Type B people do, or they perceive themselves as doing so. In turn, Type A individuals are likely to exhibit adverse physiological reactions in response to stress. These include elevated blood pressure, elevated heart rate, and modified blood chemistry. Frustrating, difficult, or competitive events are especially likely to prompt these adverse reactions. Type A individuals seem to have a strong need to control their work environment. This is doubtless a full-time task that stimulates their feelings of time urgency and leads them to overextend themselves physically.[47]

Research has made it increasingly clear that the major component of Type A behaviour that contributes to adverse physiological reactions is hostility and repressed anger. This may also be accompanied by exaggerated cynicism and distrust of others. When these factors are prominent in a Type A individual's personality, stress is most likely to take its toll.[48]

Negative affectivity. Propensity to view the world, including oneself and other people, in a negative light.

NEGATIVE AFFECTIVITY

Negative affectivity is the propensity to view the world, including oneself and other people, in a negative light. It is a stable personality trait that is a major component of the Big Five personality dimension neuroticism. People high in negative affectivity tend to be pessimistic and downbeat. As a consequence, they tend to report more stressors in the work environment and to feel more subjective stress. They are particularly likely to feel stressed in response to the demands of a heavy workload.[49]

Several factors might be responsible for the susceptibility to stress of those who are high in negative affectivity. These include (a) a predisposition to *perceive* stressors in the workplace, (b) hypersensitivity to existing stressors, (c) a tendency to gravitate to stressful jobs, (d) a tendency to *provoke* stress through their negativity, or (e) the use of passive, indirect coping styles that avoid the real sources of stress.[50]

STRESSORS IN ORGANIZATIONAL LIFE

LO **8**

Review the sources of stress encountered by various organizational role occupants.

A study found that among a sample of employed Canadians, the most common source of stress is *workplace* stressors.[51] In this section, we will examine potential stressors in detail. Some stressors can affect almost everyone in any organization, while others are likely to affect people who perform particular roles.

Executive and Managerial Stressors

Executives and managers make key organizational decisions and direct the work of others. In these capacities, they experience some special forms of stress.

ROLE OVERLOAD **Role overload** occurs when one must perform too many tasks in too short a time period, and it is a common stressor for managers, especially in today's downsized organizations.[52] The open-ended nature of the managerial job is partly responsible for this heavy and protracted workload.[53] Management is an ongoing *process*, and there are few signposts to signify that a task is complete and that rest and relaxation are permitted. Especially when coupled with frequent moves or excessive travel, a heavy workload often provokes conflict between the manager's role as an organizational member and his or her role as a spouse or parent. Thus, role overload may provoke stress, at the same time preventing the manager from enjoying the pleasures of life that can reduce stress.

Role overload. The requirement for too many tasks to be performed in too short a time period.

HEAVY RESPONSIBILITY Not only is the workload of the executive heavy, but it can have extremely important consequences for the organization and its members. A vice-president of

"You've been working awfully hard lately. If you need a little fresh air and sunshine, you can go to www.fresh-air-and-sunshine.com"

labour relations might be in charge of a negotiation strategy that could result in either labour peace or a protracted and bitter strike. To complicate matters, the personal consequences of an incorrect decision can be staggering. For example, the courts have fined and even jailed executives who have engaged in illegal activities on behalf of their organizations. Finally, executives are responsible for people as well as things, and this influence over the future of others has the potential to induce stress. The executive who must terminate the operation of an unprofitable division, putting many out of work, or the manager who must lay off an employee, putting one out of work, may experience guilt and tension.[54]

Operative-Level Stressors

Operatives are individuals who occupy non-professional and non-managerial positions in organizations. In a manufacturing organization, operatives perform the work on the shop floor and range from skilled craftspeople to unskilled labourers. As is the case with other organizational roles, the occupants of operative positions are sometimes exposed to a special set of stressors.

POOR PHYSICAL WORKING CONDITIONS Operative-level employees are more likely than managers and professionals to be exposed to physically unpleasant and even dangerous working conditions. Although social sensibility and union activity have improved working conditions over the years, many employees must still face excessive heat, cold, noise, pollution, and the chance of accidents.

POOR JOB DESIGN Although bad job design can provoke stress at any organizational level (executive role overload is an example), the designs of lower-level blue- and white-collar jobs are particular culprits. It might seem paradoxical that jobs that are too simple or not challenging enough can act as stressors. However, monotony and boredom can prove extremely frustrating to people who feel capable of handling more complex tasks. Thus, research has found that job scope can be a stressor at levels that are either too low or too high.[55]

Boundary Role Stressors, Burnout, and Emotional Labour

Boundary roles. Positions in which organizational members are required to interact with members of other organizations or with the public.

Boundary roles are positions in which organizational members are required to interact with members of other organizations or with the public. For example, a vice-president of public relations is responsible for representing his or her company to the public. At other levels, receptionists, sale reps, and installers often interact with customers or suppliers.

People are especially likely to experience stress as they straddle the imaginary boundary between the organization and its environment. This is yet another form of role conflict in which one's role as an organizational member might be incompatible with the demands made by the public or other organizations. A classic case of boundary role stress involves sales reps. In extreme cases, customers desire fast delivery of a custom-tailored product, such as a new software application. The sales rep might be tempted to "offer the moon" but at the same time is aware that such an order could place a severe strain on his or her organization's software development team. Thus, the sales rep is faced with the dilemma of doing his or her primary job (selling), while protecting another function (software development) from unreasonable demands that could result in a broken delivery contract.

Burnout. A syndrome of emotional exhaustion, cynicism, and reduced self-efficacy.

A particular form of stress (and accompanying stress reactions) experienced by some boundary role occupants is burnout. **Burnout**, as Christina Maslach, Michael Leiter, and Wilmar Schaufeli define it, is a syndrome made up of emotional exhaustion, cynicism, and low self-efficacy.[56] Burnout was originally studied among those working in some capacity with people. Frequently, these people are organizational clients who

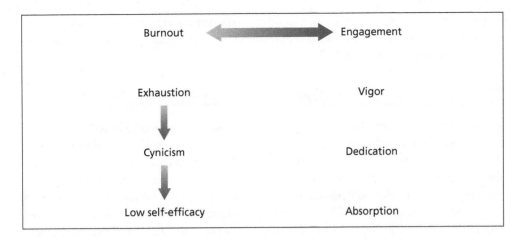

Go to MyManagementLab
to see an annotated
version of this figure.

EXHIBIT 4
**The burnout–
engagement continuum.**

require special attention or who are experiencing severe problems. Thus, teachers, nurses, paramedics, social workers, and police are especially likely candidates for burnout. However, it has now been established that burnout can occur even among non-boundary spanners.

Burnout follows a process that begins with emotional exhaustion (left side of Exhibit 4). The person feels fatigued in the morning, drained by the work, and frustrated by the day's events. One way to deal with this extreme exhaustion is to become cynical and distance oneself from one's clients, the "cause" of the exhaustion. In the extreme, this might involve depersonalizing them, treating them like objects, and lacking concern for what happens to them. The clients might also be seen as blaming the employee for their problems. Finally, the burned-out individual develops feelings of low self-efficacy and low personal accomplishment—"I can't deal with these people, I'm not helping them, I don't understand them." In fact, because of the exhaustion and depersonalization, there might be more than a grain of truth to these feelings. Although the exact details of this progression are open to some question, these three symptoms paint a reliable picture of burnout.[57]

Burnout seems to be most common among people who entered their jobs with especially high ideals. Their expectations of being able to "change the world" are badly frustrated when they encounter the reality shock of troubled clients (who are often perceived as unapprecia-tive) and the inability of the organization to help them. Teachers get fed up with being disci-plinarians, nurses get upset when patients die, and police officers get depressed when they must constantly deal with the "losers" of society. Gender and personality are also related to burnout. Women are more likely to report emotional exhaustion and men are more likely to report depersonalization. In general, those with high self-esteem, high conscientiousness, and internal control report less burnout.[58]

What are the consequences of burnout? Some individuals bravely pursue a new occu-pation, often experiencing guilt about not having been able to cope in the old one. Others stay in the same occupation but seek a new job. For instance, the burned-out nurse may go into nursing education to avoid contact with sick patients. Some people pursue adminis-trative careers in their profession, attempting to "climb above" the source of their difficul-ties. These people often set cynical examples for idealistic subordinates. Finally, some people stay in their jobs and become part of the legion of "deadwood," collecting their paycheques but doing little to contribute to the mission of the organization. Many "good bureaucrats" choose this route.[59]

Much boundary role stress stems from the frequent need for such employees to engage in "emotional labour." Emotional labour involves regulating oneself to suppress negative emotions or to exaggerate positive ones. Thus, police officers are not supposed to express anger at unsafe motorists or drunks, and salon employees are supposed to act friendly and sympathetic to boorish clients. Such suppression and acting takes a toll on cognitive and emotional resources over time.[60]

The Job Demands–Resources Model and Work Engagement

It is obvious that organizations should strive to avoid causing burnout and the extreme detachment from the job that it causes. In fact, organizations should strive to foster exactly the *opposite* of burnout—extreme engagement and enthusiasm for the job. In recent years the subject of engagement has captured the attention of both researchers and managers. In part, this is due to rather low self-reported levels of engagement. Surveys indicate that only 17 percent of Canadians are highly engaged in their work, 66 percent are moderately engaged, and 17 percent are disengaged.[61] **Work engagement** can be defined as "a positive work-related state of mind that is characterized by vigor, dedication, and absorption."[62] (See the right side of Exhibit 4.) Vigour involves high levels of energy and mental resilience at work; dedication means being strongly involved in your work and experiencing a sense of significance, enthusiasm, and challenge; absorption refers to being fully concentrated on and engrossed in your work. In particular, the first two dimensions—vigour and dedication—position engagement as the opposite of burnout.[63]

What determines whether employees tend toward engagement versus burnout? According to the **job demands–resources model** the work environment can be described in terms of demands and resources.[64] Job demands are physical, psychological, social, or organizational features of a job that require sustained physical or psychological effort that in turn can result in physiological or psychological costs. Common demands include work overload, time pressure, role ambiguity, and role conflict. Job resources refer to features of a job that are functional in that they help achieve work goals, reduce job demands, and stimulate personal growth, learning, and development. Job resources can come from the organization (e.g., pay, career opportunities, and job security), interpersonal and social relations (e.g., supervisor and co-worker support, team climate), the organization of work (e.g., role clarity, participation in decision making), and the task itself (e.g., task significance, autonomy, and performance feedback). A central assumption of the model is that high job resources foster work engagement, while high job demands exhaust employees physically and mentally and lead to burnout. Indeed, research has found that job demands are related to burnout, disengagement, and health problems, while job resources lead to work engagement, organizational citizenship behaviour, and organizational commitment. Also, it shows that resources can buffer the negative impact of job demands on well-being.[65]

Exhibit 5 shows the results of a survey of 11 000 U.K. workers in 26 occupations. The occupations are ranked in terms of several outcomes of stress. The low-ranked jobs are "worse," and those in italics are worse than average. These are the jobs that make high demands while supplying limited resources. Later in the chapter we will suggest some ways to reduce stress or improve the ability to cope that involve reducing demands and/or increasing resources.

Some General Stressors

To conclude our discussion of stressors that people encounter in organizational life, we will consider some that are probably experienced equally by occupants of all roles.

INTERPERSONAL CONFLICT Interpersonal conflict can be a potent stressor, especially for those with strong avoidance tendencies. The entire range of conflict, from personality clashes to intergroup strife, is especially likely to cause stress when it leads to real or perceived attacks

Work engagement. A positive work-related state of mind that is characterized by vigour, dedication, and absorption.

Job demands–resources model. A model that specifies how job demands cause burnout and job resources cause engagement.

Rank	Physical Health	Psychological Well–being	Job Satisfaction
1	*Ambulance*	*Social services providing care*	*Prison officer*
2	*Teachers*	*Teachers*	*Ambulance*
3	*Social services providing care*	*Fire brigade*	*Police*
4	*Customer services–call centre*	*Ambulace*	*Customer services–call centre*
5	*Bar staff*	*Vets*	*Social services providing care*
6	*Prison officer*	*Lecturers*	*Teachers*
7	*Mgmt (private sector)*	*Clerical and admin*	*Nursing*
8	*Clerical and admin*	*Mgmt (private sector)*	*Medical/dental*
9	*Police*	*Prison officer*	*Allied health professionals*
10	Teaching assistant	*Research–academic*	Bar staff
11	Head teachers	*Police*	Mgmt (private sector)
12	Secretarial/business support	*Customer services–call centre*	Fire brigade
13	Research–academic	Director (public sector)	Vets
14	Lecturers	Allied health professionals	Clerical and admin
15	Senior police	Bar staff	Mgmt (public sector)
16	Nursing	Nursing	Lecturers
17	Mgmt (public sector)	Medical/dental	Head teachers
18	Allied health professionals	Senior police	Teaching assistant
19	Medical/dental	Secretaria/business support	Secretarial/business support
20	Accountant	Head teachers	Director (public sector)
21	Fire brigade	Mgmt (public sector)	Research–academic
22	Vets	Accountant	Senior police
23	Director (public sector)	Teaching assistant	School lunchtime supervisors
24	Analyst	Analyst	Accountant
25	School lunchtime supervisors	School lunchtime supervisors	Analyst
26	Director/MD (private sector)	Director/MD (private sector)	Director/MD (private sector)

EXHIBIT 5

Occupations ranked on physical health, psychological well-being, and job satisfaction.

Source: Johnson S. (2009). Organizational screening: The ASSET model. In S. Cartwright & C.L. Cooper (Eds.), *The Oxford handbook of organizational well-being.* Oxford: Oxford University Press, p. 145.

Note: The most stressful jobs have the lowest ranks. Jobs worse than average are indicated in italics.

on our self-esteem or integrity. Although conflict can lead to stress in many settings outside of work, we often have the option of terminating the relationship, of "choosing our friends," as it were. This option is often not available at work.

A particular manifestation of interpersonal conflict that has received increased attention is workplace bullying. **Bullying** is repeated negative behaviour directed toward one or more individuals of lower power or status that creates a hostile work environment.[66] Research has clearly demonstrated that it is a potent source of stress and negative well-being.[67]

A number of factors distinguish bullying as a stress-inducing form of conflict.[68] Although bullying can involve physical aggression, it is most commonly a more subtle form of psychological aggression and intimidation. This can take many forms, such as incessant teasing, demeaning criticism, social isolation, or sabotaging others' tools and equipment. An essential feature of bullying is its persistence, and a single harsh incident would not constitute such behaviour. Rather, it is the *repeated* teasing, criticism, or undermining that signals bullying. Another key feature of the bullying process is some degree of power or status imbalance between the bully and the victim. Thus, managers have often been identified as bullies by subordinates, and research has even shown that the behaviour can "trickle down" from managers to supervisors to workers.[69] However, power imbalance can be subtle, and in some

Bullying. Repeated negative behaviour directed toward one or more individuals of lower power or status that creates a hostile work environment.

221

settings even work peers might lack power due to their gender, race, physical stature, low job security, or educational credentials. Also, there is power in numbers, in that subordinates might team up to harass their boss. This is an example of a phenomenon closely associated to bullying called *mobbing*. Mobbing occurs when a number of individuals, usually direct co-workers, "gang up" on a particular employee.[70] Mobbing can be especially intimidating and stressful because it restricts the availability of social support that might be present when there is only a single bully.

The essential point is that victims of bullying and mobbing experience stress because they feel powerless to deal with the perpetrator(s). Most observers note that a combination of factors work together to stimulate this dysfunctional behaviour.

Norway, Sweden, France, and the Canadian provinces of Quebec, Saskatchewan, and Ontario have enacted laws that pertain to bullying in the workplace. Various organizations have also done their part. The U.S. Department of Veterans Affairs and IBM both have active anti-bullying programs. IBM fired several factory workers who mobbed their new supervisor to drive home its seriousness about its policy.[71]

Before continuing, consider You Be the Manager: *Bullying at Veterans Affairs.*

WORK–FAMILY CONFLICT Work–family conflict occurs when either work duties interfere with family life or family life interferes with work responsibilities.[72] A study found that it is costing Canadian companies $6 billion to $10 billion a year in absenteeism, and the Canadian health care system $425 million in increased visits to the doctor.[73]

Two facts of life in contemporary society have increased the stress stemming from the inter-role conflict between being a member of one's family and the member of an organization. First, the increase in the number of households in which both parents work and the increase in the number of single-parent families has led to a number of stressors centred around child care. Finding adequate daycare and disputes between partners about sharing child care responsibilities can prove to be serious stressors. Second, increased life spans have meant that many people in the prime of their careers find themselves providing support for elderly parents, some of whom may be seriously ill. This inherently stressful elder care situation is often compounded by feelings of guilt about the need to tend to matters at work.[74]

Women are particularly victimized by stress due to work–family conflict, although it is a rapidly growing problem for men as well. Much anecdotal evidence suggests that women who take time off work to deal with pressing family matters are more likely than men to be labelled disloyal or undedicated to their work. Also, many managers seem to be insensitive to the demands that these basic demographic shifts are making on their employees, again compounding the potential for stress.[75]

Occupations that require a high degree of teamwork or responsibilities for others tend to provoke the most work–family conflict (e.g., police detectives, firefighters, and family doctors). At the other extreme, tellers, insurance adjusters, and taxi drivers report much lower levels.[76] Also, people who are highly engaged in their work have been shown to have elevated work to family conflict, but more conscientious employees seem to handle this tension between work and family better.[77]

JOB INSECURITY AND CHANGE Secure employment is an important goal for almost everyone, and stress may be encountered when it is threatened. During the last decade, organizations have undergone substantial changes that have left many workers unemployed and threatened the security of those who have been fortunate enough to remain in their jobs. The trend toward mergers and acquisitions, along with reengineering, restructuring, and downsizing, has led to increasingly high levels of stress among employees who either have lost their jobs or must live with the threat of more layoffs, the loss of friends and co-workers,

YOU BE THE MANAGER

Bullying at Veterans Affairs

Jobs in the social service sector regularly entail emotional labour, with workers confronted on a daily basis with high demands from clients concerning social, emotional, and medical problems. While such client–service provider interactions can be emotionally draining, such a work environment can also be a breeding ground for workplace aggression and bullying.

With this in mind, the United States Department of Veterans Affairs (VA), in collaboration with university researchers, launched the Workplace Stress and Aggression Project. The VA provides patient care and federal benefits to veterans and their dependents through central offices, benefits offices, and medical facilities. In the post–September 11 era, the VA had seen an increase in activity with the conflicts in Afghanistan and Iraq. The goal of the project was to assess the prevalence of workplace aggression and bullying within the VA, to understand their impact on employee satisfaction, VA performance, and veteran satisfaction, and to develop intervention strategies.

The research team used archival data, questionnaires, interviews, and discussion groups. Results of the initial surveys clearly indicated that workplace aggression and bullying were issues within the VA. Overall, 36 percent of employees surveyed reported being bullied at work. Bullying was defined as persistent patterns of aggression that workers experienced at least once a week. Of the 36 percent, 29 percent indicated they experienced aggression in the workplace one to five times a week, while 7 percent reported experiencing six or more aggression episodes a week. Another 58 percent of employees reported that they experienced workplace aggression, albeit not on a weekly basis, while only 6 percent of employees indicated that they suffered no workplace aggression. Aggression could be physical or verbal, active (e.g., in a confrontation) or passive (e.g., through exclusion), or direct (e.g., personally targeted) or indirect (e.g., defacing property or spreading rumours). Most incidents were of the verbal, passive, and indirect variety.

Employees indicated that 44 percent of the aggression they experienced emanated from co-workers, 35 percent came from supervisors, and 12 percent came from veterans. In terms of impact on personal well-being, they suffered more stress and lower job satisfaction when a supervisor was the source of the aggression than when co-workers or clients were the

High levels of bullying at various Veterans Affairs facilities worried executives.

source. The research team also found that bullying was linked to lower employee and organizational performance and increases in stress, absenteeism, lateness, turnover, and worker compensation claims. With these data in hand, the project team's focus turned to understanding why aggression occurred and what could be done to reduce it.

Questions

1. What do you think some of the primary causes of workplace aggression and bullying within the VA might be? Do you think the causes would be different across the various VA facilities?

2. Suggest an intervention strategy to reduce the incidence of aggression and bullying in the VA workplace. Who should be involved?

To find out how the VA responded, see The Manager's Notebook at the end of the chapter.

Sources: Scaringi, J., et al. (n.d.). *The VA workplace stress and aggression project—Final report*; Neuman, J.H., and Keashly, L. (2005, August). Reducing aggression and bullying: An intervention project in the U.S. Department of Veterans Affairs. In J. Raver (Chair), *Workplace bullying: International perspectives on moving from research to practice*. Symposium presented at the annual meeting of the Academy of Management, Honolulu, HI; Neuman, J.H. (2004). Injustice, stress, and aggression in organizations. In R.W. Griffin and A.M. O'Leary-Kelly (Eds.), *The dark side of organizational behavior*. San Francisco, CA: Jossey-Bass.

and an increased workload.[78] The fear of job loss has become a way of life for employees at all organizational levels.[79]

At the operative level, unionization has provided a degree of employment security for some, but the vagaries of the economy and the threat of technology and other organizational changes hang heavily over many workers. Among professionals, the very specialization that enables them to obtain satisfactory jobs becomes a millstone whenever social or economic forces change. For example, aerospace scientists and engineers have long been prey to the boom-and-bust nature of their industry. When layoffs occur, these people are often perceived as overqualified or too specialized to easily obtain jobs in related industries. Finally, the executive suite does not escape job insecurity. Recent pressures for corporate performance have made cost-cutting a top priority, and one of the surest ways to cut costs in the short run is to reduce executive positions and thus reduce the total management payroll. Many corporations have greatly thinned their executive ranks in recent years.

ROLE AMBIGUITY We have already noted how role conflict—having to deal with incompatible role expectations—can provoke stress. There is also substantial evidence that role ambiguity can provoke stress.[80] Role ambiguity exists when the goals of one's job or the methods of performing the job are unclear. Such a lack of direction can prove stressful, especially for people who are low in their tolerance for such ambiguity. For example, the president of a firm might be instructed by the board of directors to increase profits and cut costs. While this goal seems clear enough, the means by which it can be achieved might be unclear. This ambiguity can be devastating, especially when the organization is doing poorly and no strategy seems to improve things.

SEXUAL HARASSMENT Sexual harassment is a major workplace stressor, with serious consequences for employees and organizations that are similar to or more negative than those of other types of job stressors.[81] Sexual harassment in the workplace is now considered to be widespread in both the public and private sectors, and most harassment victims are subjected to ongoing harassment and stress.[82] The negative effects of sexual harassment include decreased morale, job satisfaction, organizational commitment, and job performance and increased absenteeism, turnover, and job loss. Sexual harassment has also been found to have serious effects on the psychological and physical well-being

EXHIBIT 6
Sources of stress at various points in the organization.

Go to MyManagementLab to see an annotated version of this figure.

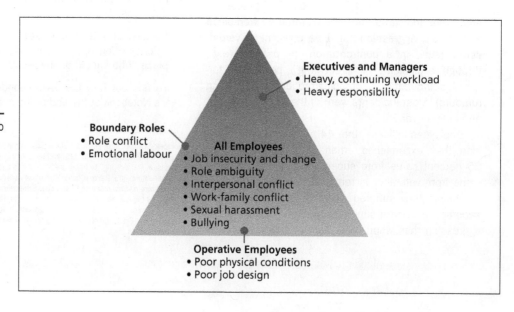

of harassment victims.[83] Victims of sexual harassment experience depression, frustration, nervousness, fatigue, nausea, hypertension, and symptoms of post-traumatic stress disorder.[84] Organizations in which sexual harassment is most likely to be a problem are those that have a climate that is tolerant of sexual harassment and where women are working in traditionally male-dominated jobs and in a male-dominated workplace.[85]

Exhibit 6 summarizes the sources of stress at various points in the organization.

REACTIONS TO ORGANIZATIONAL STRESS

In this section, we examine the reactions that people who experience organizational stress might exhibit. These reactions can be divided into behavioural, psychological, and physiological responses. In general, reactions that result in an addition to one's resources can be seen as good coping with stress. Reactions that increase demands constitute bad coping. Exhibit 7 shows how a sample of more than 31 000 Canadian employees reported coping with stress.

Behavioural Reactions to Stress

Behavioural reactions to stress are overt activities that the stressed individual uses in an attempt to cope with the stress. They include problem solving, seeking social support, modified performance, withdrawal, and the use of addictive substances.

PROBLEM SOLVING In general, problem solving is directed toward terminating the stressor or reducing its potency, not toward simply making the person feel better in the short run. Problem solving is reality-oriented, and while it is not always effective in combating the stressor, it reveals flexibility and realistic use of feedback. Most examples of a problem-solving response to stress are undramatic because problem solving is generally the routine, sensible, obvious approach that an objective observer might suggest. Consider the following examples of problem solving.

- *Delegation.* A busy executive reduces her stress-provoking workload by delegating some of her many tasks to a capable assistant.

Coping Strategies	% of Sample Who Use		
	Rarely	Weekly	Daily
Prioritize	9%	21%	69%
Schedule, organize, and plan my time more carefully	22%	32%	47%
Talk with family or friends	26%	29%	45%
Just work harder (I try to do it all)	31%	26%	43%
Find some other activity to take my mind off it	36%	32%	32%
Talk with colleagues at work	40%	27%	32%
Delegate work to others	49%	24%	27%
Search for help from family or friends	51%	25%	23%
Just try and forget about it	60%	20%	19%
Search for help from colleagues at work	65%	19%	16%
Have an alcoholic drink	65%	23%	12%
Use prescription, over-the-counter, or other drugs	86%	4%	11%
Reduce the quality of the things I do	72%	18%	10%

EXHIBIT 7
How Canadian employees cope with stress.
Source: Higgins, C., Duxbury, L., & Lyons, S. (2006). *Reducing work-life conflict: What works? What doesn't?* Ottawa: Health Canada, p. 131. Reproduced with the permission of the Minister of Public Works and Government Services Canada, 2009.

Explore

Go to MyManagementLab to see an annotated version of this figure.

LO 9

Describe *behavioural, psychological,* and *physiological reactions* to stress and discuss techniques for managing stress.

- *Time management.* A manager who finds the day too short writes a daily schedule, requires his subordinates to make formal appointments to see him, and instructs his secretary to screen phone calls more selectively.

- *Talking it out.* An engineer who is experiencing stress because of poor communication with her non-engineer superior resolves to sit down with the boss and hammer out an agreement concerning the priorities on a project.

- *Asking for help.* A salesperson who is anxious about his company's ability to fill a difficult order asks the production manager to provide a realistic estimate of the probable delivery date.

- *Searching for alternatives.* A machine operator who finds her monotonous job stress-provoking applies for a transfer to a more interesting position for which the pay is identical.

SEEKING SOCIAL SUPPORT Speaking generally, social support simply refers to having close ties with other people. In turn, these close ties can affect stress by bolstering self-esteem, providing useful information, offering comfort and humour, or even providing material resources (such as a loan). Research evidence shows that the benefits of social support are double-barrelled. First, people with stronger social networks exhibit better psychological and physical well-being. Second, when people encounter stressful events, those with good social networks are likely to cope more positively. Thus, the social network acts as a buffer against stress.[86]

Off the job, individuals might find social support in a spouse, family, or friends. On the job, social support might be available from one's superior or co-workers. Research evidence suggests that the buffering aspects of social support are most potent when they are directly connected to the source of stress. This means that co-workers and superiors may be the best sources of support for dealing with work-related stress. But most managers need better training to recognize employee stress symptoms, clarify role requirements, and so on. Unfortunately, some organizational cultures, especially those that are very competitive, do not encourage members to seek support in a direct fashion. In this kind of setting, relationships that people develop in professional associations can sometimes serve as an informed source of social support.

PERFORMANCE CHANGES Stress or stressors frequently cause reduced job performance.[87] However, this statement needs to be qualified slightly. Some stressors are "hindrance" stressors in that they directly damage goal attainment. These include things like role ambiguity and interpersonal conflict. Such stressors damage performance. On the other hand, some stressors are challenging. These include factors such as heavy workload and responsibility. Such stressors can damage performance, but they sometimes stimulate it via added motivation.[88] Because they are discretionary, organizational citizenship behaviours are especially likely to decrease under stressful conditions.[89]

WITHDRAWAL Withdrawal from the stressor is one of the most basic reactions to stress. In organizations, this withdrawal takes the form of absence and turnover. Compared with problem-solving reactions to stress, absenteeism fails to attack the stressor directly. Rather, the absent individual is simply attempting short-term reduction of the anxiety prompted by the stressor. When the person returns to the job, the stress is still there. From this point of view, absence is a dysfunctional reaction to stress for both the individual and the organization. The same can be said about turnover if a person resigns from a stressful job on the spur of the moment merely to escape stress. However, a good case can be made for a well-planned resignation in which the intent is to assume another job that should be less stressful. This is actually a problem-solving reaction that should benefit both the individual and the organization in

RESEARCH FOCUS

PRESENTEEISM IN THE WORKPLACE

Presenteeism refers to going to work when one is ill. Although both managers and work researchers have been interested in absenteeism for years, it is only recently that presenteeism has become a subject of concerted interest. Some of this interest is stimulated by the finding that the aggregate productivity loss that occurs due to working while ill is much greater than that attributed to absence. Presentees are at work, but they are often not working at full capacity. What would cause people to go to work even though they are suffering from asthma, allergies, migraines, or respiratory problems? Many factors appear to be stress-related. This is ironic because it means that some stressors can cause both absenteeism and presenteeism.

High job demands and time pressure have been associated with presenteeism; people feel under pressure to get work done and sense the work piling up if they are absent. This is especially likely if there is a lack of backup, an increasing possibility in today's downsized organizations. Job insecurity may also prompt people to go to work when they are ill. Thus, non-permanent employees exhibit less absenteeism than their permanent counterparts, and this might signal presenteeism on their part. Strict policies against absence and team-oriented work designs have also been implicated in presenteeism. In team settings, people might feel they are letting the team down if they book off sick.

Depression, which is frequently associated with stress, is one of the most common health problems connected to presenteeism. This may be because people do not view it as a legitimate reason to be absent or fear disclosing it as the reason for their absence.

Source: Johns, G. (2010). Presenteeism in the workplace: A review and research agenda. *Journal of Organizational Behavior, 31*, 519–532.

the long run. Absence, turnover, and turnover intentions have often been linked with stress and its causes.[90] For an ironic counter-example, see the Research Focus: *Presenteeism in the Workplace.*

USE OF ADDICTIVE SUBSTANCES Smoking, drinking, and drug use represent the least satisfactory behavioural responses to stress for both the individual and the organization. These activities fail to terminate stress episodes, and they leave employees less physically and mentally prepared to perform their jobs. We have all heard of hard-drinking newspaper reporters and advertising executives, and it is tempting to infer that the stress of their boundary role positions is responsible for their drinking. Indeed, cigarette and alcohol use are associated with work-related stress.[91]

Psychological Reactions to Stress

Psychological reactions to stress primarily involve emotions and thought processes rather than overt behaviour, although these reactions are frequently revealed in the individual's speech and actions. The most common psychological reaction to stress is the use of defence mechanisms.[92]

Defence mechanisms are psychological attempts to reduce the anxiety associated with stress. Notice that, by definition, defence mechanisms concentrate on *anxiety reduction* rather than on actually confronting or dealing with the stressor. Some common defence mechanisms include the following:

Defence mechanisms. Psychological attempts to reduce the anxiety associated with stress.

- *Rationalization* is attributing socially acceptable reasons or motives to one's actions so that they will appear reasonable and sensible, at least to oneself. For example, a male nurse who becomes very angry and abusive when learning that he will not be promoted to supervisor might justify his anger by claiming that the female head nurse discriminates against men.

- *Projection* is attributing one's own undesirable ideas and motives to others so that they seem less negative. For example, a sales executive who is undergoing conflict about offering a bribe to an official of a foreign government might reason that the official is corrupt.

- *Displacement* is directing feelings of anger at a "safe" target rather than expressing them where they may be punished. For example, a construction worker who is severely criticized by the boss for sloppy workmanship might take out his frustrations in an evening hockey league.

- *Reaction formation* is expressing oneself in a manner that is directly opposite to the way one truly feels, rather than risking negative reactions to one's true position. For example, a low-status member of a committee might vote with the majority on a crucial issue rather than stating his true position and opening himself up to attack.

- *Compensation* is applying one's skills in a particular area to make up for failure in another area. For example, a professor who is unable to get his or her research published might resolve to become a superb teacher.

Is the use of defence mechanisms a good or bad reaction to stress? Used occasionally to temporarily reduce anxiety, they appear to be a useful reaction. For example, the construction worker who displaces aggression in an evening hockey league rather than attacking a frustrating boss might calm down, return to work the next day, and "talk it out" with the boss. Thus, the occasional use of defence mechanisms as short-term anxiety reducers probably benefits both the individual and the organization. In fact, people with "weak defences" can be incapacitated by anxiety and resort to dysfunctional withdrawal or addiction.

When the use of defence mechanisms becomes a chronic reaction to stress, however, the picture changes radically. The problem stems from the very character of defence mechanisms—they simply do not change the objective character of the stressor, and the basic conflict or frustration remains in operation. After some short-term relief from anxiety, the basic problem remains unresolved. In fact, the stress might *increase* with the knowledge that the defence has been essentially ineffective.

Physiological Reactions to Stress

Can work-related stress kill you? This is clearly an important question for organizations, and it is even more important for individuals who experience excessive stress at work. Many studies of physiological reactions to stress have concentrated on the cardiovascular system, specifically on the various risk factors that might prompt heart attacks. For example, work stress is associated with electrocardiogram irregularities and elevated levels of blood pressure, cholesterol, and pulse.[93] Stress has also been associated with the onset of diseases such as respiratory and bacterial infections due to its ill effects on the immune system.[94] The accumulation of stress into burnout has been particularly implicated in cardiovascular problems.[95]

ORGANIZATIONAL STRATEGIES FOR MANAGING STRESS

This chapter would be incomplete without a discussion of personal and organizational strategies to manage stress. In general, these strategies either reduce demands on employees or enhance their resources.

Police officers must deal with a unique type of on-the-job stress: workplace violence. There has been an upswing in psychological counselling for officers experiencing stress reactions.

Job Redesign

Organizations can redesign jobs to reduce their stressful characteristics. In theory, it is possible to redesign jobs anywhere in the organization to this end. Thus, an overloaded executive might be given an assistant to reduce the number of tasks he or she must perform. In practice, most formal job redesign efforts have involved enriching operative-level jobs to make them more stimulating and challenging.

Especially for service jobs, there is growing evidence that providing more autonomy in how service is delivered can alleviate stress and burnout.[96] Call centre workers, fast-food employees, some salespeople, and some hospitality workers are highly "scripted" by employers, with the idea that uniformity will be appreciated by customers. This idea is debatable, but what is not debatable is that this lack of personal control goes against the research-supported prescriptions of job enrichment and empowerment, and the job demands–resources model of stress. Boundary role service jobs require a high degree of emotional regulation in any event, and some degree of autonomy allows employees to cope with emotional labour by adjusting their responses to the needs of the moment in line with their own personalities. Guidelines about desired service outcomes can replace rigid scripts, especially for routine (non-emergency) encounters. Also, excessive electronic monitoring should be avoided in call centres.[97]

A special word should be said about the stressful job designs that often emerge from heavy-handed downsizings, restructurings, and mergers. Common symptoms of such jobs are extreme role overload, increased responsibility without corresponding authority to act, and the assignment of tasks for which no training is provided. Executives overseeing such change efforts should obtain professional assistance to ensure proper job designs.

"Family-Friendly" Human Resource Policies

To reduce stress associated with dual careers, child care, and elder care, many organizations are beginning to institute "family-friendly" human resource policies.[98] These policies generally include some combination of formalized social support, material support, and increased flexibility to adapt to employee needs. In the domain of social support, some firms distribute newsletters, such as *Work & Family Life,* that deal with work–family issues. Others have developed company support groups for employees dealing with elder care problems. Some companies have contracted specialized consultants to provide seminars on elder care issues.

A welcome form of material support consists of corporate daycare centres. Flexibility (which provides more *control* over family issues) is also important, and includes flextime, telecommuting, and job sharing, as well as family leave policies that allow time off for caring for infants, sick children, and aged dependents. Although many firms boast of having such flexible policies, a common problem is encouraging managers to *use* them in an era of downsizing and lean staffing. According to a Mediacorp study, some of Canada's most family-friendly employers include Pfizer, Manitoba Hydro, Statistics Canada, and Desjardins.[99] There is growing evidence that such policies contribute to improved health, lower turnover, and higher organizational performance.[100] In general, research shows that perceptions of flexibility, a reasonable workload, supportive supervision, and a supportive culture are associated with less work–family conflict and higher job satisfaction and organizational commitment.[101] For an example of a family-friendly government initiative, see the Applied Focus: *Quebec Certifies Work–Life Balance.*

APPLIED FOCUS

QUEBEC CERTIFIES WORK–LIFE BALANCE

The benefits of work–life balance have been well-touted through surveys, studies, and employee testimonials. But Quebec has decided to take that sentiment a step further in launching a certification standard around work–family balance. Employers of all sizes can now apply to have their work places evaluated by the Bureau de normalisation du Québec (BNQ), with four levels of certification available. The certification requires, at a minimum, employers have a commitment from management around work–family balance (WFB). This should include an internal management policy, demonstrated commitment to WFB, WFB measures for men and women, employee communications, and a designated person responsible for the program. Employers are also required to have a WFB committee that consults with employees; proposes WFB measures and practices; implements, promotes, and evaluates those measures; and presents the results to management and employees every two years.

Frima Studio is a Quebec City-based employer that...[became] the first in the province to attain the standard, according to Stephen Couture, Frima's president. The company started looking at work–life balance in 2008, offering its 275 employees initiatives such as public transportation passes, flexible schedules, longer holidays, fresh fruit, and on-site massages. Frima's program has evolved to include more innovative approaches such as Frima Points. This gives employees points based on their performance, which they can exchange online for different services such as babysitters, plumbers, or gardeners.

"This program was to have our employees spend more time with their families, so (they can) avoid doing extra work when they're home," said Couture. "It's a kind of program for our employees to have a better life outside the hours they spend at work."

As a result, fewer people leave Frima and more people are inclined to stay, he said. And with a competitive video game industry in Quebec and larger companies installing new facilities in the region, there's a lot of pressure on HR and recruitment.

"This kind of program helps to become competitive," he said. "There's a lot of people in the province who have deep pockets for their employees, to attract employees, so we needed to be creative."

Adopting a work–family program is more than just an expense, it's an investment, said Couture.

Source: Excerpted from Dobson, S. (2011, May 23). Quebec certifies work-life balance. *Canadian HR Reporter*, 1,19; see also Dobson, S. (2012, May 7). Quebec certification hits 1-year mark. *Canadian HR Reporter*, 7, 10.

Companies are striving to be much more "family friendly" than in the past. Some organizations offer daycare for children of employees.

Stress Management Programs

Some organizations have experimented with programs designed to help employees "manage" work-related stress. Such programs are also available from independent off-work sources. Some of these programs help physically and mentally healthy employees prevent problems due to stress. Others are therapeutic in nature, aimed at individuals who are already experiencing stress problems. Although the exact content of the programs varies, most involve one or more of the following techniques: meditation, training in muscle-relaxation exercises, biofeedback training to control physiological processes, training in time management, and training to think more positively and realistically about sources of job stress.[102] Evidence suggests that these applications are useful in reducing physiological arousal, sleep disturbances, and self-reported tension and anxiety.[103]

Work–Life Balance, Fitness, and Wellness Programs

Many people have argued that a balanced lifestyle that includes a variety of leisure activities combined with a healthy diet and physical exercise can reduce stress and counteract some of the adverse physiological effects of stress. For some organizations, work–life balance programs and quality-of-life benefits have become a strategic retention tool. Employees are increasingly demanding work–life balance benefits, and employers are realizing that by providing them they can increase commitment and reduce turnover.

At Husky Injection Molding Systems, the cafeteria serves only healthy food. The company's head office in Bolton, Ontario, has a naturopath, a chiropractor, a medical doctor, a nurse, and a massage therapist on staff, and employees are encouraged to use the company's large fitness centre.[104] The DundeeWealth investment firm features weight-loss contests, fitness classes, and consultation on home training programs.[105]

Studies show that fitness training is associated with improved mood, a better self-concept, reduced absenteeism, enhanced job satisfaction, and reports of better performance.[106] Work–life programs are also believed to result in lower health care costs. Some of these improvements probably stem from stress reduction.

THE MANAGER'S NOTEBOOK

Bullying at Veterans Affairs

1. Many of the well-known sources of conflict in the workplace can lead to aggression and bullying. Power and status differences between individuals, rivalries between groups, uncertainty and competition, and a noxious organizational culture can all facilitate bullying and aggression. The VA project team found many of these conditions at the various sites. However, they generally found a distinctive pattern of causes of bullying at each facility. At some sites, a lack of cooperation, respect, and fairness were drivers of aggression and bullying. At other sites, diversity management was the primary issue. Sites that had recently made significant new hires often had clashes between newcomers and old-timers. Sites with poor leadership and a lack of goal alignment were also problems. The results were often communication breakdowns, misinformation, and the growth of rumours. Overall, the project team identified issues in the work climate, although they varied in content from site to site, as the key factor in workplace aggression and bullying.

2. The VA project team realized that, unlike many organizational development prescriptions advocating the establishment of best practices to resolve problems, interventions to quell workplace aggression and bullying would need to be customized at each site to deal with each specific work climate. However, the general process they developed to do this was common to all. In the 11 sites that participated in the more comprehensive version of the project, the research team created action teams of organizational members to guide the project and develop needed interventions. The exercise of bringing people together to learn and discuss issues surrounding bullying and aggression in itself transformed the work climate in a positive way. Interventions often focused on some form of what are known as High Involvement Work Systems, involving information sharing and empowerment. In a follow-up two years after the original data gathering exercise, the research team found that, compared with the 15 sites that did not participate in the intervention, the 11 focal sites reported fewer incidents of aggressive behaviour and fewer injury stress–related behaviours. Work attitudes and performance indicators also improved at the 11 intervention sites compared with the 15 other sites.

MyManagementLab

Visit MyManagementLab at **www.mymanagementlab .com** for access to online tutorials, interactive exercises, videos, and much more.

LEARNING OBJECTIVES CHECKLIST

1. *Interpersonal conflict* is a process that occurs when one person, group, or organizational unit frustrates the goal attainment of another. Such conflict can revolve around facts, procedures, or the goals themselves. Causes of conflict include intergroup bias, high interdependence, ambiguous jurisdictions, and scarce resources. Differences in power, status, and culture are also a factor.

2. *Types of conflict* include *relationship*, *task*, and *process* conflict. Conflict dynamics include the need to win the dispute, withholding information, increased cohesiveness, negative stereotyping of the other party, reduced contact, and emergence of aggressive leaders.

3. Modes of managing conflict include *avoiding*, *accommodating*, *competing*, *compromise*, and *collaborating*.

4 *Negotiation* is a decision-making process among parties that do not have the same preferences. *Distributive negotiation* attempts to divide up a fixed amount of outcomes. Frequent tactics include threats, promises, firmness, concession making, and persuasion. *Integrative negotiation* attempts to enlarge the amount of outcomes available via collaboration or problem solving. Tactics include exchanging copious information, framing differences as opportunities, cutting costs, increasing resources, and introducing *superordinate goals.*

5 When managers perceive that employees are in a rut or avoiding disagreements at the cost of not dealing with important issues, they may want to *stimulate* conflict to reinvigorate the workplace. Although conflict is often considered a negative occurrence, conflict can also be necessary for and beneficial to organizational change initiatives. In the context of change, conflict can generate new ideas, lead to more careful monitoring of the actions of others, and lead to a redistribution of power within the organization.

6 *Stressors* are environmental conditions that have the potential to induce stress. *Stress* is a psychological reaction that can prompt tension or anxiety because an individual feels incapable of coping with the demands made by a stressor. *Stress reactions* are the behavioural, psychological, and physiological consequences of stress.

7 Personality characteristics can cause some individuals to perceive more stressors than others, experience more stress, and react more negatively to this stress. In particular, people with *external locus of control*, high *negative affectivity*, and *Type A behaviour pattern* are prone to such reactions.

8 At the managerial or executive level, common stressors include *role overload* and high responsibility. At the *operative level*, poor physical working conditions and underutilization of potential owing to poor job design are common stressors. *Boundary role occupants* often experience stress in the form of conflict between demands from inside the employing organization and demands from outside. Emotional labour may also provoke stress. *Burnout* may occur when a job produces emotional exhaustion, cynicism, and low self-efficacy. Job insecurity and change, role ambiguity, sexual harassment, interpersonal conflict, and work–family conflicts have the potential to induce stress in all organizational members.

Work engagement is a positive state of mind about work involving dedication, absorption, and vigour. The job demands–resources model explains how demands lead to burnout and resources lead to engagement.

9 *Behavioural reactions* to stress include problem solving, modified performance, withdrawal, and the use of addictive substances. *Problem solving* is the most effective reaction because it confronts the stressor directly and thus has the potential to terminate the stress episode. The most common psychological reaction to stress is the use of *defence mechanisms* to temporarily reduce anxiety. The majority of studies on physiological reactions to stress implicate cardiovascular risk factors. Strategies that can reduce organizational stress include job redesign, family-friendly human resource policies, stress management programs, and work–life balance programs.

DISCUSSION QUESTIONS

1. The manager of a fast-food restaurant sees that conflict among the staff is damaging service. How might she implement a superordinate goal to reduce this conflict?

2. A company hires two finance majors right out of college. Being in a new and unfamiliar environment, they begin their relationship cooperatively. However, over time, they develop a case of deep interpersonal conflict. What factors could account for this?

3. What are some of the factors that make it a real challenge for conflicting parties to develop a collaborative relationship and engage in integrative negotiation?

4. Two social workers just out of college join the same county welfare agency. Both find their case loads very heavy and their roles very ambiguous. One exhibits negative stress reactions, including absence and elevated alcohol use. The other seems to cope very well. Use the stress episode model to explain why this might occur.

5. Imagine that a person who greatly dislikes bureaucracy assumes her first job as an investigator in a very bureaucratic government tax office. Describe the stressors that she might encounter in this situation. Give an example of a problem-solving reaction to this stress. Give an example of a defensive reaction to it.

6. What factors might explain why bullying persists? How do workplace bullies get away with it?

7. Compare and contrast the stressors that might be experienced by an assembly line worker and the president of a company.

8. Discuss the advantages and disadvantages of hiring employees with Type A personality characteristics.

INTEGRATIVE DISCUSSION QUESTIONS

1. Does personality influence the way individuals manage conflict? Consider the relationship among each of the following personality characteristics and the five approaches to managing conflict described in this chapter: the Big Five dimensions of personality, locus of control, self-monitoring, self-esteem, need for power, and Machiavellianism.

2. Can leadership be a source of stress in organizations? Refer to leadership theories (e.g., leadership traits, behaviours, situational theories, participative leadership, strategic leadership, and LMX theory) and explain how leadership can be a source of stress. According to each theory, what can leaders do to reduce stress and help employees cope with it?

ON-THE-JOB CHALLENGE QUESTION

Why Don't People Take Their Vacations?

A Harris/Decima poll determined that almost 25 percent of Canadians fail to use all the vacation days they are entitled to during the year. The unused days ranged from 1.39 in the province of Quebec to 2.81 in Alberta. Although these numbers seem small, they project nationally to 34 million unused days a year. Despite this, 42 percent of those polled reported being tired, stressed, and in need of a vacation. A similar Harris Interactive U.S. poll found that 57 percent of Americans reported unused vacation days.

What do you think explains the reluctance of so many people to forego deserved vacation time? If you were or are a manager, how would you react to staff who don't use all their vacation days? What are the long-term implications of this behaviour?

Sources: Covert, K. (2009, July 9). Vacation phobia spreads. *National Post*, FP11; Censky, A. (2012, May 18). Vacation? No thanks, boss. *CNNMoney*.

EXPERIENTIAL EXERCISE

Strategies for Managing Conflict

Indicate how often you use each of the following by writing the appropriate number in the blank. Choose a number from a scale of 1 to 5, with 1 being "rarely," 3 being "sometimes," and 5 being "always." After you have completed the survey, use the scoring key to tabulate your results.

____ 1. I argue my position tenaciously.

____ 2. I put the needs of others above my own.

____ 3. I arrive at a compromise both parties can accept.

____ 4. I don't get involved in conflicts.

____ 5. I investigate issues thoroughly and jointly.

____ 6. I find fault in other persons' positions.

____ 7. I foster harmony.

____ 8. I negotiate to get a portion of what I propose.

____ 9. I avoid open discussions of controversial subjects.

____ 10. I openly share information with others in resolving disagreements.

____ 11. I enjoy winning an argument.

____ 12. I go along with the suggestions of others.

____ 13. I look for a middle ground to resolve disagreements.

____ 14. I keep my true feelings to myself to avoid hard feelings.

____ 15. I encourage the open sharing of concerns and issues.

____ 16. I am reluctant to admit I am wrong.

____ 17. I try to help others avoid "losing face" in a disagreement.

____ 18. I stress the advantages of "give and take."

____ 19. I encourage others to take the lead in resolving controversy.

____ 20. I state my position as only one point of view.

Scoring Key

Managing Strategy

Total your responses to these questions

Competing 1, 6, 11, 16 _____

Accommodating 2, 7, 12, 17 _____

Compromising 3, 8, 13, 18 _____

Avoiding 4, 9, 14, 19 _____

Collaborating 5, 10, 15, 20 _____

Primary conflict management strategy (highest score): _____

Secondary conflict management strategy (next-highest score): _____

Source: Whetten, D.A., & Cameron, K.S. *Developing management skills* (7th ed.) © 2008. Reproduced by Pearson Education, Inc., Upper Saddle River, NJ. Electronically reproduced by permission of Pearson Education, Inc., Upper Saddle River, NJ.

CASE INCIDENT

Bringing Baby to Work

Ted Swanson liked to think of himself as a progressive, family-friendly kind of guy. Consequently, he couldn't quite believe the words coming out of his mouth, directed at Bryan Papis, his boss and owner of the creative media company ZeusAd. "Bryan, that baby is driving me crazy! The cooing, laughing, and crying are one thing, but some of the creative team and support staff make such a fuss over him that it drives me to distraction. I had a client in here yesterday who didn't know what to make of the whole thing. This just isn't professional."

The four-month-old baby to which Ted was alluding belonged to Glenda Fox, one of the more clever creative types in the company. Although she was eligible for extended maternity leave, she had chosen not to take it. She said she didn't want to "get out of the loop" or let her current project team down. These motives, and Glenda's espoused beliefs in "attachment parenting" had led her to bring her new baby to work on a fairly regular basis, except when her husband could occasionally provide care.

Bryan Papis also prided himself on being a family-friendly employer, but he wondered if ZeusAd needed a formal policy concerning babies at work.

Source: Inspired in part by Boesveld, S. (2012, March 8). When every day is take your kids to work day. *National Post*, A1, A2.

1. A number of news stories have appeared suggesting that babies in the workplace are a source of considerable interpersonal conflict. What are some likely reasons for this?

2. Is bringing a baby to work the ultimate example of work–family integration? Or does it go too far in blurring the distinction between work and family?

3. What considerations should underpin a formal policy concerning babies at work?

CASE STUDY

Tough Guy

A mere half-block away from the office on a pleasing fall day—the kind that caught the attention of most New Yorkers—Jeremy Frazer, an associate at the investment bank Hudson Smith Gordon ("Hudson") thought about Chip Mazey, one of the vice presidents he was working with on a negotiation. Frazer and three other members working on the deal, Jean Fenster, Rich Patten, and Payton Edwards, had finally confided in each other about what it was like to work for the VP.

They found themselves in a difficult situation, one that most of them thought they had no power to change. After all, doing something about Mazey's behavior was tricky business. First was the fear of confronting Mazey. Another concern was the likelihood that Mazey would probably deny his behavior or wouldn't think that a problem existed. Then there was the unease about escalating the discussion to include a conversation with Mazey's boss. Going upstairs might cause a tense situation to become even worse. Not really knowing what to do irked Frazer, though he couldn't exactly say why. He thought about the stories his co-workers had shared.

Bulge, Middle, or Boutique?

The lure of high risk and high reward made investment banking an attractive career for many in the world of finance. Organizations employed investment banks to help work out financial problems. Offering a mix of business activities, investment banks issued securities, helped investors to purchase securities, managed financials assets, traded securities, and provided financial advice. Investment banks came in several sizes. The largest were called "bulge bracket" firms; the "middle market" companies tended to be regionally based; and "boutique" banks were smaller and more specialized. As a "middle market" firm, Hudson was oriented toward financial analysis and program trading.

To support their security sales and trading activities, investment banks hired and maintained large staffs of research analysts. As Frazer described:

> In investment banking, you make deals for companies to raise capital—debt or equity. Research supports that effort. By becoming expert in a particular field, you generate more business. My firm is considered the leading expert on wireless carriers. This reputation translates into wireless communication companies' wanting Hudson to do research on them.

Making the Deal with a Fast-Tracker

Chip Mazey had been with Hudson 10 years and followed the "kiss up, kick down" mantra. His verbal lashings were sharp, unrelenting, and unprovoked. He had developed a nasty reputation among analysts and associates, which was passed to the firm's top management only through their 360° review system. Mazey was very careful not to show his true colors when senior management was within earshot, but as result of the negative comments from below, his initial promotion to vice president was postponed. The decision came as a shock to him, because he believed he had always been submissive to upper management. Despite his poor people skills, Mazey was a solid banker, and he received the promotion as scheduled one year later.

As a vice president, Mazey's swagger and bravado increased exponentially. Mazey always had trouble interacting with his peers, but after his promotion, he was more ruthless to his subordinates than his peers. He often referred to subordinates as "you" or "analyst" and he reminded others of his new title by telling them, "I am superior to you." It was common for him to yell at a subordinate in a rage, only to discover that he had made an error and there was no problem. In such a situation, Mazey would abruptly hang up the phone when he realized his error without a goodbye or apology. The targets of his verbal abuse disliked working with him and tried to spend time working on projects with other bankers.

The first time Frazer worked with Mazey was on a project Mazey was heading up. "I was assigned to this kick-ass multibillion dollar deal," Frazer said. "Even better than that was the fact that the deal team included the vice president, so I was extremely excited about the opportunity." The vice president was in charge of leading the deal and had a reputation of being "dynamic" and on the "fast track." Frazer's enthusiasm faded somewhat when he stepped into Mazey's office. During their initial meeting, Mazey ordered Frazer to stand "right here" and pointed to a spot on the floor in front of his desk. The associate felt uneasy about being spoken to in this manner, but because it was the first time he had worked with Mazey, he decided not to mention anything—it was best to let things go. After all, investment banks had a reputation for being infested with Type A personalities. Some "I-bankers" had told Frazer that the biggest challenge in an investment banking career was to manage upward.

Over the next several weeks, Frazer witnessed Mazey's insulting and derogatory behavior toward other associates and analysts. Tension was part of being around him. "Fortunately, I worked on multiple assignments, reporting to various other managers at the same time," Frazer said. "The dynamics on other assignment were in stark contrast to this particular one. So I realized how much I like the job and how well I fit in—despite being so heavily reprimanded on a continual basis with that VP."

On a Need-to-Know Basis

That Mazey was difficult to deal with was hardly news to most at Hudson. What was worthy of a headline was that Frazer seemed more willing than most to talk about his supervisor's questionable behavior. Others who had been in the organization much longer than Frazer just learned to work around Mazey's behavior—he was a control freak who made a lot of money for the company and that translated into wielding a lot of power. "I became more comfortable with some of my peers and started confiding in a few of them," Frazer said. "I realized my situation was hardly unique since everyone who had at one time worked with that VP had the same story." Things became so ugly, Frazer learned, that some full-time associates within the group bluntly refused to work with him. Jean Fenster, an analyst who also worked with Mazey on a few deals, described her experience:

When I first started, Chip asked me to complete an assignment which would typically take a novice at least three days to finish. I was handed the assignment at 8 p.m. and instructed to have it finished and on his desk to look at first thing the following morning. I sat through the night cracking on the assignment and finally completed what I thought was a pretty comprehensive product. To my good fortune, there were a few experienced staff members at the office during the night who offered to vet my product. They

seemed pretty happy with my work. Slightly before dawn, I laid the finalized assignment on Chip's desk. I thought it would be a great idea to go home, catch up on a couple hours of sleep, and clean up. I arrived back at the office at least 15 minutes before Chip—ready to answer any questions.

As expected Fenster was called over to Mazey's desk the next morning. What followed, however, was unexpected. He questioned every assumption she had made, countered every explanation she offered in a derogatory manner, and nitpicked her work for an entire hour. He then asked her to redo the work based on information he forwarded via e-mail. When Fenster sat down at her desk to rework the material, she was shocked to learn that the VP was privy to that additional information *before he handed her the assignment*, information that would have made it easier to complete the work. She just couldn't fathom why this information was not forwarded to her earlier. Even more discouraging was that although she was asked to complete the work within 24 hours, the e-mail indicated they had two weeks before it was even due. That assignment was a nightmare, and every effort Fenster made toward working on it contributed to the bad dream. "Each session I had with Chip included a series of derogatory and demeaning remarks directed toward me," she said. "From my communication skills, my accent, to the way I dressed, this VP was critical."

Fenster's story sounded eerily familiar to Rich Patten, who described a couple of his experiences with the vice president. During a conference call with a client, Patten was unable to answer a question the client posted. Mazey became enraged and began screaming at both him and the other analyst in the room. Patten said he could have helped Mazey answer the client's questions but Mazey's ranting prevented him from even speaking. "The outburst resembled that of a 2-year-old, and both of us were speechless," Patten said. "Then, still in a rage, Chip grabbed a calculator from his desktop and shattered it against the wall, just above my head!"

Later that day, Mazey apologized for his outburst, and Patter believed his apology was sincere. "I had considered going to speak with the vice president who hired me about the incident," Patten said. "But after the apology I changed my mind," Mazey asked the associate to focus on the task at hand. It was 7 p.m. and there were still at least nine hours of work that had to be completed by an 8 a.m. conference call the next morning, Mazey instructed Patten to come in to work an hour early to prepare for the call.

"I spent the entire night working, arrived home at 4:30 a.m., slept for an hour and a half, and then returned to the office at 7 a.m.," Pattern recalled. "Gulping down my coffee, I went to Chip's office only to find it empty." The 8 a.m. showtime came and went without any word from Mazey, who eventually rolled into the office at 10 a.m. without a word. Patten asked him about the meeting, and Mazey simply said that the meeting was changed. Patten asked another associate who was staffed on the deal about the meeting, and found out that no such meeting was ever planned!

Get to Work—Everyone!

Payton Edwards had another Mazey characteristic to share. "He's very bright and certainly very capable, but he demands complete perfection and treats subordinates as if they were subservient to him and only him," Edwards said. "Occasionally, this man would compliment me for a 'job well done.'" Yet within five minutes, Mazey would come back with some reason why it wasn't "quite right" and force him to redo his work. He was also known for forcing people to do useless, menial tasks. For example, he frequently had his administrative assistant, as well as two analysts, complete the *exact* same task. Mazey said he just want to make absolutely sure that when all was said and done, the task was completed perfectly. Eventually, the analysts and administrative assistant found out that they were all assigned the same task and they were peeved. They felt like he didn't trust them—and he didn't. Edwards said,

Even when it was apparent that Chip had made a mistake, he never openly acknowledged it. One time, he denied that that there were multiple buyers on a particular deal and created a hostile deal environment for many of the concerned parties. He also did not like initiative-taking, much less even consider rewarding it. When I went to him with ideas on topics to research relevant ongoing deals, he shot down my ideas and told me to work on what he wanted me to get done. When it turned out later that my ideas were good, he never gave me credit and pretended that he

had thought of them himself. In fact, he went out of his way to discredit me. For example, when I was still a very novice drinker, Chip would get a kick out of having me order the wine at closing dinners. He wanted to embarrass me in public because of my lack of knowledge about wine.

Chip also made fun of the secretary who came from a poorer part of the city and where everyone seemed to have the same last name. At Christmas parties, the support staff was not allowed to bring spouses while analysts and associates were invited to bring their spouses. Chip told me that he did not feel that it was necessary to "pay to feed the secretary's husband."

Any More Questions?

Life for support staff working for Mazey was a challenge as well. He had an incessant need to know what every person was working on at all times. This was even more pronounced the lower an employee was within the organizational hierarchy. His administrative assistant, Gabriela Salaberrios, found it surprising that the VP needed to know what a secretary was typing at a given moment. Yet Mazey had to know where all employees were at all times. He provided Salaberrios with a cell phone so that he could contact her in the middle of the night to work on last-minute deal items. He was never polite, and refused to take no for an answer. More than a few times, Mazey called in the middle of the night and demanded her presence at the office. Many times he had already sent a car to get Salaberrios before she had said yes. One time, she was vacationing in Tunisia, and he called to demand her immediate return—it seemed that his idea on how a deal should go from beginning to end was to be followed by all.

So What?

Proud of his accomplishment in his career so far, Frazer had sashayed into New York with a youthful certainty that attitude would carry him. He held a job he had thought about for some time in a firm he was convinced would offer even more opportunities. Not once had he expected to get sidetracked over some middle-aged, disgruntled vice president.

Yet that same VP possessed many of the characteristics Frazer had expected and indeed admired on Wall Street. Gathering all this information on Mazey had been almost cathartic. Now what, if anything, should he do with it?

Source: This case was compiled from various student accounts of actual events as a composite case by Gerry Yemen, Senior Case Writer, and James G. Clawson, E. Thayer Bigelow Professor of Business Administration. It was written as a basis for class discussion rather than to illustrate effective or ineffective handling of an administrative situation. Copyright © 2007 by the University of Virginia Darden School Foundation, Charlottesville, VA. All rights reserved. To order copies, send an e-mail to sales@dardenbusinesspublishing.com. No part of this publication may be reproduced, stored in a retrieval system, used in a spreadsheet, or transmitted in any form or by any means—electronic, mechanical, photocopying, recording, or otherwise—without the permission of the Darden School Foundation.

QUESTIONS

1. Earlier in the chapter *conflict* was defined as a process that occurs when one person, group, or organizational subunit frustrates the goal attainment of another. Speculate about how Chip Mazey has frustrated the goal attainment of personnel at Hudson Smith Gordon.

2. Is the conflict observed in the case relationship, task, or process conflict? Please explain your reasoning.

3. The chapter outlined a number of causes of conflict. Which seem to be prevalent in this case? Feel free to cite some other contributors as well.

4. The chapter discusses five modes of managing conflict: avoiding, accommodating, competing, compromise, and collaborating. What mode does Chip Mazey employ? What mode does his staff employ?

5. Chip Mazey's subordinates seem to be suffering from stress, but what is its exact causes? That is, how does his behaviour translate into stress for others?

6. Is Chip a bully? Defend your answer.

7. Despite his obvious reputation, how has Chip managed to retain a position of power?

8. What should Jeremy Fraser do now? What should his goals be?

INTEGRATIVE CASE

Deloitte & Touche: Integrating Arthur Andersen

You have previously answered a number of questions about the Deloitte & Touche Integrative Case that dealt with issues related to learning, perceptions, fairness and job attitudes, motivation, and pay plans. Now you can return to the Integrative Case and enhance your understanding of some of the main issues associated with social behaviour and organizational processes by answering the following questions that deal with groups, socialization and culture, leadership, communication, conflict, and stress.

QUESTIONS

1. Given that employees from the two firms will be working together in groups, what are the implications for group development and group cohesiveness? What advice would you give the integration team for designing effective work teams?

2. Is organizational socialization relevant for the integration of Arthur Andersen employees? What would you tell the integration team about organizational socialization and how it can be helpful for the integration process?

3. What methods of organizational socialization can be used to integrate the Arthur Andersen employees? Explain how you would use each of the methods and indicate what you think would be most effective for the successful integration of Arthur Andersen employees.

4. Review the results of the cultural assessment of the two firms and then compare and contrast

their cultures. How are they similar and different and what are the implications for the successful integration of the two firms?

5. What should the integration team do about the cultural differences between the two firms? Should they integrate the Arthur Andersen employees into the existing Deloitte & Touche culture or should they create a new culture? What do you think the integration team should do and how should they proceed?

6. How important is leadership for the successful integration of the two firms? Consider the implications of the different leadership theories (situational theories, leader–member exchange theory, transformational and transactional leadership, ethical and authentic leadership, and strategic leadership) for the successful integration of

the two firms. What type of leadership do you think is most important and likely to be effective, and why?

7. Identify some challenges or barriers to effective communication in the case. How did Deloitte try to counteract these barriers?

8. Although there is no evidence of open conflict in the case, there is plenty of potential for it. What are some factors that might cause conflict between the Deloitte and Andersen contingents?

9. Consider the potential for stress among the employees of both firms. What stressors are employees most likely to experience and why? What can the integration team do to minimize these stressors and help employees cope with stress?

REFERENCES

1. Excerpted from Kelly, C. (2009, June 17). Rival Yorkville hair salons in ugly battle. www.thestar.com. Reprinted with permission of TorStar Syndication Services.

2. Kolb, D.M., & Bartunek, J.M. (Eds.) (1992). *Hidden conflict in organizations: Uncovering behind-the-scenes disputes.* Newbury Park, CA: Sage.

3. This section relies partly on Walton, R.E., & Dutton, J.M. (1969). The management of interdepartmental conflict: A model and review. *Administrative Science Quarterly, 14,* 73–84; see also De Dreu, C.K.W., & Gelfand, M.J. (2008). Conflict in the workplace: Sources, functions, and dynamics across multiple levels of analysis. In C.K.W. De Dreu & M.J. Gelfand (Eds.), *The psychology of conflict and conflict management in organizations.* New York: Lawrence Erlbaum.

4. Ashforth, B.E., & Mael, F. (1989). Social identity theory and the organization. *Academy of Management Review, 14,* 20–39; Kramer, R.M. (1991). Intergroup relations and organizational dilemmas: The role of categorization processes. *Research in Organizational Behavior, 13,* 191–228; Messick, D.M., & Mackie, D.M. (1989). Intergroup relations. *Annual Review of Psychology, 40,* 45–81.

5. Johns, G. (1994). Absenteeism estimates by employees and managers: Divergent perspectives and self-serving perceptions. *Journal of Applied Psychology, 79,* 229–239.

6. See Whyte, W.F. (1948). *Human relations in the restaurant industry.* New York: McGraw-Hill.

7. Moritz, M. (1984). *The little kingdom: The private story of Apple Computer.* New York: Morrow, 246–247.

8. Jehn, K.A., & Mannix, E.A. (2001). The dynamic nature of conflict: A longitudinal study of intragroup conflict and group performance. *Academy of Management Journal, 44,* 238–251.

9. De Dreu, C.K.W., & Weingart, L.R. (2003). Task versus relationship conflict, team performance, and team member satisfaction: A meta-analysis. *Journal of Applied Psychology, 88,* 741–749; de Wit, F.R.C., Greer, L.L., & Jehn, K.A. (2012). The paradox of intragroup conflict: A meta-analysis. *Journal of Applied Psychology, 97,* 360–390.

10. See Blake, R.R., Shepard, M.A., & Mouton, J.S. (1964). *Managing intergroup conflict in industry.* Houston: Gulf; Sherif, M. (1966). *In common predicament: Social psychology of intergroup conflict and cooperation.* Boston:

Houghton Mifflin; Wilder, D.A. (1986). Social categorization: Implications for creation and reduction of intergroup bias. *Advances in Experimental Social Psychology, 19,* 291–349; Pruitt, D.G. (2008). Conflict escalation in organizations. In De Dreu & Gelfand, 2008.

11. Thomas, K.W. (1992). Conflict and negotiation in organizations. In M.D. Dunnette & L.M. Hough (Eds.), *Handbook of industrial and organizational psychology* (2nd ed., Vol. 3). Palo Alto, CA: Consulting Psychologists Press.

12. Seabrook, J. (1994, January 10). E-mail from Bill. *The New Yorker,* 48–61, 52.

13. Johnson, D.W., Maruyama, G., Johnson, R., Nelson, D., & Skon, L. (1981). Effects of cooperative and individualistic goal structures on achievement: A meta-analysis. *Psychological Bulletin, 89,* 47–62; see also Tjosvold, D. (1991). *The conflict-positive organization.* Reading, MA: Addison-Wesley.

14. Keenan, G. (2011, December 28). Earthquake. Tsunami. Floods. How Japan's car makers are rebuilding after a year of disasters. *Globe and Mail,* B1, B4, B5.

15. Tjosvold, D., Dann, V., & Wong, C. (1992). Managing conflict between departments to serve customers. *Human Relations, 45,* 1035–1054.

16. Neale, M.A., & Bazerman, M.H. (1992, August). Negotiating rationally: The power and impact of the negotiator's frame. *Academy of Management Executive,* 42–51, p. 42; for a recent review, see Thompson, L.L., Wang, J., & Gunia, B.C. (2010). Negotiation. *Annual Review of Psychology, 61,* 491–515.

17. Wall, J.A., Jr. (1985). *Negotiation: Theory and practice.* Glenview, IL: Scott, Foresman.

18. Walton, R.E., & McKerzie, R.B. (1991). *A behavioral theory of labor negotiations* (2nd ed.). Ithaca, NY: ILR Press.

19. What follows draws on Pruitt, D.G. (1981). *Negotiation behavior.* New York: Academic Press.

20. Wall, J.A., Jr., & Blum, M. (1991). Negotiations. *Journal of Management, 17,* 273–303.

21. Hüffmeier, J., Freund, P.A., Zerres, A., Backhaus, K., & Hertel, G. (2011). Being tough or being nice? A meta-analysis on the impact of hard- and softline strategies in distributive negotiations. *Journal of Management,* 0149206311423788.

22. Stuhlmacher, A.F., and Walters, A.E. (1999). Gender differences in negotiation outcome: A meta-analysis. *Personnel Psychology, 52,* 653–677; see also Kulik, C.T., & Olekalns, M. (2012). Negotiating the gender divide: Lessons

from the negotiation and organizational behavior literatures. *Journal of Management, 38,* 1387–1415.

23. Marks, M., & Harold, C. (2011). Who asks and who receives in salary negotiation. *Journal of Organizational Behavior, 32,* 371–394.

24. Bazerman, M.H. (1990). *Judgment in managerial decision making* (2nd ed.). New York: Wiley.

25. The following draws on Bazerman, M.H., & Neale, M.A. (1992). *Negotiating rationally.* New York: The Free Press; see also Bazerman, M.H. (2006). *Judgment in managerial decision making* (6th ed.). Hoboken, NJ: Wiley.

26. Sherif, 1966; Hunger, J.D., & Stern, L.W. (1976). An assessment of the functionality of the superordinate goal in reducing conflict. *Academy of Management Journal, 19,* 591–605.

27. Goldman, B.M., Cropanzano, R., Stein, J., & Benson, L. III. (2008). The role of third parties/mediation in managing conflict in organizations. In De Dreu & Gelfand, 2008.

28. Pruitt, 1981; Kressel, K., & Pruitt, D.G. (1989). *Mediation research.* San Francisco: Jossey-Bass.

29. Kressel & Pruitt, 1989.

30. Pruitt, 1981; Wall & Blum, 1991.

31. Moore, M.L., Nichol, V.W., & McHugh, P.P. (1992). Review of no-fault absenteeism cases taken to arbitration, 1980–1989: A rights and responsibilities analysis. *Employee Rights and Responsibilities Journal, 5,* 29–48; Scott, K.D., & Taylor, G.S. (1983, September). An analysis of absenteeism cases taken to arbitration: 1975–1981. *The Arbitration Journal, 61–70.*

32. For a spirited debate on this, see De Dreu, C.K.W. (2008). The virtue and vice of workplace conflict: Food for (pessimistic) thought. *Journal of Organizational Behavior, 29,* 5–18, and Tjosvold, D. (2008). The conflict-positive organization: It depends on us. *Journal of Organizational Behavior, 29,* 19–28.

33. Robbins, S.P. (1974). *Managing organizational conflict: A nontraditional approach.* Englewood, Cliffs, NJ: Prentice-Hall, 20.

34. Brown, L.D. (1983). *Managing conflict at organizational interfaces.* Reading, MA: Addison-Wesley.

35. Robbins, 1974; see also Brown, 1983.

36. Raynal, W., & Wilson, K.A. (2001, October 15). What about Bob? *Autoweek,* 5.

37. Keita, G.P. (2006, June). The national push for workplace health. *Monitor on Psychology,* 32.

38. American Psychological Association (2012). *Stress in America: Our health at risk*. Washington, DC: APA.

39. Tangri, R. (2007, September). Putting a price on stress. *Canadian Healthcare Manager, 14*, 24–25.

40. This model has much in common with many contemporary models of work stress. For a comprehensive summary, see Kahn, R.L., & Byosiere, P. (1992). Stress in organizations. In M.D. Dunnette & L.M. Hough (Eds.), *Handbook of industrial and organizational psychology* (2nd ed., Vol. 3). Palo Alto, CA: Consulting Psychologists Press.

41. McGrath, J.E. (1970). A conceptual formulation for research on stress. In J.E. McGrath (Ed.), *Social and psychological factors in stress*. New York: Holt, Rinehart, Winston.

42. Roth, S., & Cohen, L.J. (1986). Approach, avoidance, and coping with stress. *American Psychologist, 41*, 813–819.

43. Glazer, S., & Beehr, T.A. (2005). Consistency of implications of three role stressors across four countries. *Journal of Organizational Behavior, 26*, 467–487.

44. Ng, T.W.H., Sorensen, K.L., & Eby, L.T. (2006). Locus of control at work: A meta-analysis. *Journal of Organizational Behavior, 27*, 1057–1087.

45. Friedman, M., & Rosenman, R. (1974). *Type A behavior and your heart*. New York: Knopf.

46. Chesney, M.A., & Rosenman, R. (1980). Type A behavior in the work setting. In C.L. Cooper and R. Payne (Eds.), *Current concerns in occupational stress*. Chichester, England: Wiley. For a typical study, see Jamal, M., & Baba, V.V. (1991). Type A behavior, its prevalence and consequences among women nurses: An empirical examination. *Human Relations, 44*, 1213–1228.

47. Fine, S., & Stinson, M. (2000, February 3). Stress is overwhelming people, study shows. *Globe and Mail*, A1, A7; Matthews, K.A. (1982). Psychological perspectives on the Type A behavior pattern. *Psychological Bulletin, 91*, 293–323.

48. Booth-Kewley, S., & Friedman, H.S. (1987). Psychological predictors of heart disease: A quantitative review. *Psychological Bulletin, 101*, 343–362; Smith, D. (2003, March). Angry thoughts, at-risk hearts. *Monitor on Psychology*, 46–48; Ganster, D.C., Schaubroeck, J., Sime, W.E., & Mayes, B.T. (1991). The nomological validity of the Type A personality among employed adults. *Journal of Applied Psychology, 76*, 143–168.

49. Houkes, I., Janssen, P.P.M., de Jonge, J., & Bakker, A.B. (2003). Personality, work characteristics, and employee well-being: A longitudinal analysis of additive and moderating effects. *Journal of Occupational Health Psychology, 8*, 20–38; Grant, S., & Langan-Fox, J. (2007). Personality and the stressor-strain relationship: The role of the Big Five. *Journal of Occupational Health Psychology, 12*, 20–33; Kammeyer-Mueller, J.D., Judge, T.A., & Scott, B.A. (2009). The role of core self-evaluations in the coping process. *Journal of Applied Psychology, 94*, 177–195.

50. Spector, P.E., Zapf, D., Chen, P.Y., & Frese, M. (2000). Why negative affectivity should not be controlled in stress research: Don't throw out the baby with the bath water. *Journal of Organizational Behavior, 21*, 79–95. For a relevant study, see Barsky, A., Thoresen, C.J., Warren, C.R., & Kaplan, S.A. (2004). Modeling negative affectivity and job stress: A contingency-based approach. *Journal of Organizational Behavior, 25*, 915–936.

51. Fine, S., & Stinson, M. (2000, February 3). Stress is overwhelming people, study shows. *Globe and Mail*, A1, A7.

52. Parasuraman, S., & Alutto, J.A. (1981). An examination of the organizational antecedents of stressors at work. *Academy of Management Journal, 24*, 48–67.

53. Mintzberg, H. (1973). *The nature of managerial work*. New York: Harper & Row.

54. An excellent review of managerial stressors can be found in Marshall, J., & Cooper, C.L. (1979). *Executives under pressure*. New York: Praeger.

55. Xie, J.L., & Johns, G. (1995). Job scope and stress: Can job scope be too high? *Academy of Management Journal, 38*, 1288–1309.

56. Maslach, C., Leiter, M.P., & Schaufeli, W. (2009). Measuring burnout. In S. Cartwright & C.L. Cooper (Eds.), *The Oxford handbook of organizational well-being*. Oxford: Oxford University Press; Maslach, C., & Leiter, M.P. (2008). Early predictors of burnout and engagement. *Journal of Applied Psychology, 93*, 498–512; Maslach, C., & Jackson, S.E. (1984). Burnout in organizational settings. In S. Oskamp (Ed.), *Applied social psychology annual* (Vol. 5). Beverly Hills, CA: Sage.

57. Maslach, C., Schaufeli, W.B., & Leiter, M.P. (2001). Job burnout. *Annual Review of Psychology, 52*, 397–422; Cordes, C.L., & Dougherty, T.W. (1993). A review and integration of research on job burnout. *Academy of Management Review, 18*, 621–656. For a comprehensive study, see Lee, R.T., & Ashforth, B.E. (1993). A longitudinal study of burnout among supervisors and managers: Comparisons of the Leiter and Maslach (1988) and Golembiewski et al. (1986) models. *Organizational Behavior and Human Decision Processes, 54*, 369–398.

58. Purvanova, R.K., & Muros, J.P. (2010). Gender differences in burnout: A meta-analysis. *Journal of Vocational Behavior, 77*, 168–185; Alarcon, G., Eschleman, K.J., & Bowling, N.A. (2009). Relationships between personality variables and burnout: A meta-analysis. *Work & Stress, 23*, 244–263.

59. See Pines, A.M., & Aronson, E. (1981). *Burnout: From tedium to personal growth*. New York: The Free Press.

60. Hülsheger, U.R., & Schewe, A.F. (2011). On the costs and benefits of emotional labor: A meta-analysis of three decades of research. *Journal of Occupational Health Psychology, 16*, 361–389; see also Mesmer-Magnus, J.R., DeChurch, L.A., & Wax, A. (2012). Moving emotional labor beyond surface and deep acting: A discordance–congruence perspective. *Organizational Psychology Review, 2*, 6–53.

61. Galt, V. (2005, November 15). Fewer workers willing to put in 110%. *Globe and Mail*, B8; Carniol, N. (2005, November 15). Fewer workers willing to give 100 percent. *Toronto Star*, D1, D11; Galt, V. (2005, January 26). This just in: Half your employees ready to jump ship. *Globe and Mail*, B1, B9.

62. Schaufeli, W.B., Bakker, A.B., & Van Rhenen, W. (2009). How changes in job demands and resources predict burnout, work engagement, and sickness absenteeism. *Journal of Organizational Behavior, 30*, 893–917; see also Bakker, A.B., & Demerouti, E. (2008). Towards a model of work engagement. *Career Development International, 13*, 209–223.

63. Cole, M.S., Walter, F., Bedeian, A.G., & O'Boyle, E.H. (2012). Job burnout and employee engagement: A meta-analytic examination of construct proliferation. *Journal of Management, 38*, 1550–1581.

64. Bakker, A.B., & Demerouti, E. (2007). The job-demands-resources model: State of the art. *Journal of Managerial Psychology, 22*, 309–328.

65. Bakker & Demerouti, 2007; Schaufeli et al., 2009.

66. Salin, D. (2003). Ways of explaining workplace bullying: A review of enabling, motivating and precipitating structures in the work environment. *Human Relations, 56*, 1213–1232.

67. Bowling, N.A., & Beehr, T.A. (2006). Workplace harassment from the victim's perspective: A theoretical model and meta-analysis. *Journal of Applied Psychology, 91*, 998–1012.

68. Salin, 2003; Rayner, C., & Keashly, L. (2005). Bullying at work: A perspective from Britain and North America. In

S. Fox & P.E. Spector (Eds.), *Counter-productive work behavior: Investigations of actors and targets.* Washington, DC: American Psychological Association.

69. Mawritz, M.B., Mayer, D.M., Hoobler, J.M., Wayne, S.J., & Marinova, S.V. (2012). A trickle-down model of abusive supervision. *Personnel Psychology, 65,* 325–357.

70. This is one interpretation of the distinction between bullying and mobbing. See Zapf, D., & Einarsen, S. (2005). Mobbing at work: Escalated conflicts in organizations. In Fox & Spector, 2005.

71. Dingfelder, S.F. (2006, July–August). Banishing bullying. *Monitor on Psychology,* 76–78.

72. See Ford, M.T., Heinen, B.A., & Lang-kamer, K.L. (2008). Work and family satisfaction and conflict: A meta-analysis of cross-domain relations. *Journal of Applied Psychology, 92,* 57–80.

73. Duxbury, L., & Higgins, C. (2003). *Work–life conflict in Canada in the new millennium: A status report.* Ottawa: Health Canada.

74. For a review of the antecedents of work–family conflict, see Michel, J.S., Kotrba, L.M., Mitchelson, J.K., Clark, M.A., & Baltes, B.B. (2011). Antecedents of work-family conflict: A meta-analytic review. *Journal of Organizational Behavior, 32,* 689–725.

75. Bellavia, G.M., & Frone, M.R. (2005). Work–family conflict. In J. Barling, E.K. Kelloway, & M.R. Frone (Eds.), *Handbook of work stress.* Thousand Oaks, CA: Sage.

76. Dierdorff, E.C., & Ellington, J.K. (2008). It's the nature of the work: Examining behavior-based sources of work–family conflict across occupations. *Journal of Applied Psychology, 93,* 883–892.

77. Halbesleben, J.R.B., Harvey, J., & Bolino, M.C. (2009). Too engaged? A conservation of resources view of the relationship between work engagement and work interference with family. *Journal of Applied Psychology, 94,* 1452–1465.

78. For job loss in particular, see McKee-Ryan, F.M., Song, Z., Wanberg, C.R., & Kinicki, A.J. (2005). Psychological and physical well-being during unemployment: A meta-analytic study. *Journal of Applied Psychology, 90,* 53–76; for mergers and acquisitions, see Cartwright, S. (2005). Mergers and acquisitions: An update and appraisal. *International Review of Industrial and Organizational Psychology, 20,* 1–38.

79. DeFrank, R.S., & Ivancevich, J.M. (1998, August). Stress on the job: An executive update. *Academy of Management Executive,* 55–66.

80. Jackson, S.E., & Schuler, R.S. (1985). Meta-analysis and conceptual critique of research on role ambiguity and conflict in work settings. *Organizational Behavior and Human Decision Processes, 36,* 16–78. For a critique of some of this research, see Fineman, S., & Payne, R. (1981). Role stress—A methodological trap? *Journal of Occupational Behaviour, 2,* 51–64.

81. Fitzgerald, L.F., Drasgow, F., Hulin, C.L., Gelfand, M.J., & Magley, V.J. (1997). Antecedents and consequences of sexual harassment in organizations: A test of an integrated model. *Journal of Applied Psychology, 82,* 578–589; Schneider, K.T., Swan, S., & Fitzgerald, L.F. (1997). Job-related and psychological effects of sexual harassment in the workplace: Empirical evidence from two organizations. *Journal of Applied Psychology, 82,* 401–415.

82. Fitzgerald et al., 1997; Schneider et al., 1997.

83. O'Leary-Kelly, A.M., Bowes-Sperry, L., Bates, C.A., & Lean, E.R. (2009). Sexual harassment at work: A decade (plus) of progress. *Journal of Management, 35,* 503–536; Willness, C.R., Steel, P., & Lee, K. (2007). A meta-analysis of the antecedents and consequences of workplace sexual harassment. *Personnel Psychology, 60,* 127–162.

84. Peirce, E., Smolinski, C.A., & Rosen, B. (1998, August). Why sexual harassment complaints fall on deaf ears. *Academy of Management Executive,* 41–54; Schneider et al., 1997.

85. Fitzgerald et al., 1997; Glomb, T.M., Munson, L.J., Hulin, C.L., Bergman, M.E., & Drasgow, F. (1999). Structural equation models of sexual harassment: Longitudinal explorations and cross-sectional generalizations. *Journal of Applied Psychology, 84,* 14–28.

86. Cohen, S., & Wills, T.A. (1985). Stress, social support, and the buffering hypothesis. *Psychological Bulletin, 98,* 310–357; Kahn & Byosiere, 1992. For recent treatments of social support and relational views of work, see Grant, A.M., & Parker, S.K. (2009). Redesigning work design theories: The rise of relational and proactive perspectives. *Academy of Management Annals, 3,* 317–375, and Baran, B.E., Shanock, L.R., & Miller, L.R. (2012). Advancing organizational support theory into the twenty-first century world of work. *Journal of Business and Psychology, 27,* 123–147.

87. Gilboa, S., Shirom, A., Fried, Y., & Cooper, C. (2008). A meta-analysis of work demand stressors and job performance: Examining main and moderating effects. *Personnel Psychology, 61,* 227–271. For a classic study, see Jamal, M. (1984). Job stress and job performance controversy: An empirical assessment. *Organizational Behavior and Human Performance, 33,* 1–21.

88. LePine, J.A., Podsakoff, N.P., & LePine, M.A. (2005). A meta-analytic test of the challenge stressor-hindrance stressor framework: An explanation for inconsistent relationships among stressors and performance. *Academy of Management Journal, 48,* 764–775.

89. Eatough, E.M., Chang, C.-H., Miloslavic, S.A., & Johnson, R.E. (2011). Relationships of role stressors with organizational citizenship behavior: A meta-analysis. *Journal of Applied Psciyhology, 96,* 619–632.

90. Johns, G. (1997). Contemporary research on absence from work: Correlates, causes and consequences. *International Review of Industrial and Organizational Psychology, 12,* 115–173; Darr, W., & Johns, G. (2008). Work strain, health, and absenteeism from work: A meta-analysis. *Journal of Occupational Health Psychology, 13,* 293–318; Podsakoff, N.P., LePine, J.A., & LePine, M.A. (2007). Differential challenge stressor-hindrance stressor relationships with job attitudes, turnover intentions, turnover, and withdrawal behavior: A meta-analysis. *Journal of Applied Psychology, 92,* 438–454.

91. Beehr, T.A., & Newman, J.E. (1978). Job stress, employee health, and organizational effectiveness: A facet analysis, model, and literature review. *Personnel Psychology, 32,* 665–699; Kahn & Byosiere, 1992; Frone, M.R. (2008). Employee alcohol and illicit drug use: Scope, causes, and organizational consequences. In J. Barling & C.L. Cooper (Eds.), *Sage handbook of organizational behavior* (Vol 1). London: Sage.

92. For reviews, see Cramer, P. (2000). Defense mechanisms in psychology today: Further processes for adaptation. *American Psychologist, 55,* 637–646; Baumeister, R.F., Dale, K., & Sommer, K.L. (1998). Freudian defense mechanisms and empirical findings in modern social psychology: Reaction formation, projection, displacement, undoing, isolation, sublimation, and denial. *Journal of Personality, 66,* 1081–1124.

93. Beehr & Newman, 1978. For a later review and a strong critique of this work, see Fried, Y., Rowland, K.M., & Ferris, G.R. (1984). The physiological measurement of work stress: A critique. *Personnel Psychology, 37,* 583–615. See also Fried, Y. (1989). The future of physiological assessments in work situations. In C.L. Cooper & R. Payne (Eds.), *Causes, coping, and consequences of stress at work.* Chichester, England: Wiley & Sons.

94. Cohen, S., & Herbert, T.B. (1996). Health psychology: Psychological and physical disease from the perspective of human psychoneuroimmunology. *Annual Review of Psychology, 47*, 113–142; Cohen, S., & Williamson, G.M. (1991). Stress and infectious disease in humans. *Psychological Bulletin, 109*, 5–24.

95. Melamed, S., Shirom, A., Toker, S., Berliner, S., & Shapira, I. (2006). Burnout and risk of cardiovascular disease: Evidence, possible causal paths, and promising research directions. *Psychological Bulletin, 132*, 327–353; Kivimaki, M., Virtanen, M., Elovainio, M., Kouvonen, A., Vaananen, A., & Vahtera, J. (2006). Work stress in the etiology of coronary heart disease: A meta-analysis. *Scandinavian Journal of Work, Environment and Health, 32*, 431–442; see also the special issue Stress and the Heart, *Stress and Health*, August 2008.

96. Grandey, A.A., Fisk, G.M., & Steiner, D.D. (2005). Must "service with a smile" be stressful? The moderating role of personal control for American and French employees. *Journal of Applied Psychology, 90*, 893–904; Grandey, A.A., Dickter, D.N., & Sin, H.P. (2004). The customer is not always right: Customer aggression and emotion regulation of service employees. *Journal of Organizational Behavior, 25*, 397–418.

97. See Spriggs, C.A., & Jackson, P.R. (2006). Call centers as lean service environments: Job related strain and the mediating role of work design. *Journal of Occupational Health Psychology, 11*, 197–212.

98. This section relies on a *Wall Street Journal* special section on Work & Family (1993, June 21) and Shellenbarger, S. (1993, June 29). Work & family. *Wall Street Journal,* B1.

99. Canadastop100.com/family/, retrieved May 25, 2012.

100. Ngo, H.-Y., Foley, S., & Loi, R. (2009). Family friendly work practices, organizational climate, and firm performance: A study of multinational corporations in Hong Kong. *Journal of Organizational Behavior, 30*, 665–680; Van Steenbergen, E.F., & Ellemers, N. (2009). Is managing the work–family interface worthwhile? Benefits for employee health and performance. *Journal of Organizational Behavior, 30*, 617–642.

101. Kelly, E.L., Kossek, E.E., Hammer, L.B., Durhman, M., Bray, J., Chermack, K., Murphy, L.A., & Kaskubar, D. (2008). Getting there from here: Research on the effects of work-family initiatives on work-family conflict and business outcomes. *Academy of Management Annals, 2*, 305–309.

102. Richardson, K.M., & Rothstein, H.R. (2008). Effects of occupational stress management intervention programs: A meta-analysis. *Journal of Occupational Health Psychology, 13*, 69–93; Ivancevich, J.M., Matteson, M.T., Freedman, S.M., & Phillips, J.S. (1990). Worksite stress management interventions. *American Psychologist, 45*, 252–261; Cartwright, S., & Cooper, C. (2005). Individually targeted interventions. In Barling et al., 2005.

103. Richardson & Rothstein, 2008; Ivancevich et al., 1990.

104. Lush, T. (1998, October 3). Company with a conscience. *The Gazette* (Montreal), C3.

105. Immen, W., & Brown-Bowers, A. (2008, April 16). Employers get the fitness bug. *Globe and Mail,* C1, C2.

106. Parks, K.M., & Steelman, L.A. (2008). Organizational wellness programs: A meta-analysis. *Journal of Occupational Health Psychology, 13*, 58–63; DeGroot, T., & Kiker, D.S. (2003). A meta-analysis of the non-monetary effects of employee health management programs. *Human Resource Management, 42*, 53–69; Jex, S.M. (1991). The psychological benefits of exercise in work settings: A review, critique, and dispositional model. *Work & Stress, 5*, 133–147.

PHOTO CREDITS

The Strategic Role of Human Resources Management

|||||||||||||||||||||||||||||||||||||||||||||||||||||||||||||||

LEARNING OUTCOMES

AFTER STUDYING THIS CHAPTER, YOU SHOULD BE ABLE TO

DEFINE human resources management and ANALYZE the strategic significance of human resources management.

DESCRIBE the two categories of activities required of HR managers and DISCUSS examples of each.

DISCUSS the internal and external environmental factors affecting human resources management policies and practices and EXPLAIN their impact.

DESCRIBE the three stages in the evolution of HRM.

EXPLAIN how HRM has changed over recent years to include a higher-level advisory role.

|||||||||||||||||||||||||||||||||||||||||||||||||||||||||||||||

REQUIRED PROFESSIONAL CAPABILITIES (RPC)

- Advises on the status of dependent and independent contractors and determinants of employee status

- Contributes to improvements in the organization's structures and work processes

- Gathers, analyzes, and reports relevant business and industry information (including global trends) to influence the development of strategic business HR plans

- Develops business cases for HR activity

- Stays current with professional knowledge

- Fosters and promotes the advancement of the profession

- Keeps current with emerging HR trends

- Guides and facilitates change in organizational culture or values consistent with business strategy

- Provides support and expertise to managers and supervisors with respect to managing people

- Monitors expenditures and timelines

THE STRATEGIC ROLE OF HUMAN RESOURCES MANAGEMENT

human resources management (HRM) The management of people in organizations to drive successful organizational performance and achievement of the organization's strategic goals.

Human resources management (HRM) refers to the management of people in organizations. Human resources professionals are responsible for ensuring that the organization attracts, retains, and engages the diverse talent required to meet operational and performance commitments made to customers and shareholders. Their job is to ensure that the organization finds and hires the best individuals available, develops their talent, creates a productive work environment, and continually builds and monitors these human assets. They have the primary responsibility for managing the workforce that drives organizational performance and achieves the organization's strategic goals.[1]

More specifically, HRM involves formulating and implementing HRM systems (such as recruitment, performance appraisal, and compensation) that are aligned with the organization's strategy to ensure that the workforce has the competencies and behaviours required to achieve the organization's strategic objectives. It is crucial that the HR strategy be aligned with the company's strategic plan (see **Figure 1**).

Just as important as the financial capital that is required for an organization to operate, the knowledge, education, training, skills, and expertise of a firm's workers represent its increasingly valuable **human capital**. More and more organizations are awakening to the importance of human capital as the next competitive advantage.[2]

human capital The knowledge, education, training, skills, and expertise of an organization's workforce.

Research studies over the past two decades have confirmed that effective HR practices are related to better organizational performance.[3] Organizational benefits range from employee empowerment to extensive training that affects the productivity of employees.[4] The resource-based view of the firm suggests that human resource practices contribute to the development of embedded knowledge of a firm's culture, history, processes, and context, which are non-imitable.[5]

RPC

Develops business cases for HR activity.

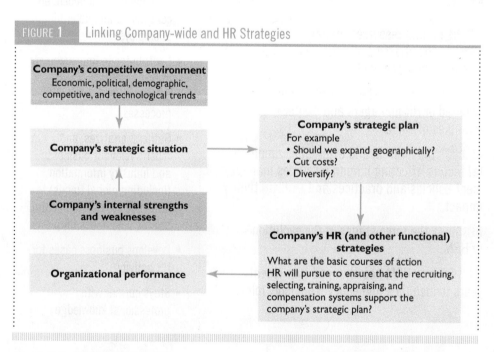

FIGURE 1 Linking Company-wide and HR Strategies

Source: © Gary Dessler, Ph.D., 2007.

More specifically, three HR practices (profit sharing, results-oriented performance appraisal, and employment security) have strong relationships with important accounting measures of performance (return on assets and return on equity).[6] High-performance HR practices (comprehensive employee recruitment and selection procedures, incentive compensation and performance management systems, and extensive employee involvement and training) have a positive relationship with turnover, productivity, and corporate financial performance (gross rate of return on capital).[7]

A BRIEF HISTORY OF HRM

HRM has changed dramatically over time and has assumed an increasingly strategic role. The demands on HR staff and expectations regarding their role have evolved as HRM has changed. HR practices have been shaped by society's prevailing beliefs and attitudes about workers and their rights, which have evolved in three stages.

Scientific Management: Concern for Production

scientific management The process of "scientifically" analyzing manufacturing processes, reducing production costs, and compensating employees based on their performance levels.

Frederick Taylor was the driving force behind **scientific management**, the process of "scientifically" analyzing manufacturing processes, reducing production costs, and compensating employees based on their performance.[8] As a result, management practices in the late 1800s and early 1900s emphasized task simplification and performance-based pay. Such incentives were expected to lead to higher wages for workers, increased profits for the organization, and workplace harmony. Taylor's views were not accepted by all management theorists. For example, Mary Parker Follett, a writer ahead of her time, advocated the use of self-management, cross-functional cooperation, empowerment, and managers as leaders, not dictators.[9]

The Human Resources Movement: Concern for People and Productivity

human resources movement A management philosophy focusing on concern for people and productivity.

HRM is currently based on the theoretical assumptions of the **human resources movement**. Arriving at this joint focus on people and productivity involved four evolutionary phases.[10]

Phase 1

In the early 1900s, HRM—or personnel administration, as it was then called—played a very minor or non-existent role. During this era, personnel administrators assumed responsibility for hiring and firing (a duty formerly looked after by first-line supervisors), ran the payroll department, and administered benefits. Their job consisted largely of ensuring that procedures were followed.

Phase 2

As the *scientific management movement* gained momentum, operational efficiency increased but wage increases did not keep up, causing workers to distrust management. The resulting increase in unionization led to personnel departments serving as the primary contact for union representatives. Following the depression of the 1930s, various pieces of legislation were enacted, including a minimum wage act, an unemployment insurance program, and protection of workers' right to belong to unions. Legal compliance was subsequently added to the responsibilities of personnel managers. During the 1940s and 1950s, personnel managers were also involved in dealing with the impact of the *human relations movement*. Orientation, performance appraisal, and employee relations responsibilities were added to their job.

Phase 3

The third major phase in personnel management was a direct result of government legislation passed during the 1960s, 1970s, and 1980s that affected employees' human rights, wages and benefits, working conditions, health and safety, and established penalties for failure to meet them. The role of personnel departments expanded dramatically. They continued to provide expertise in such areas as compensation, recruitment, and training but in an expanded capacity.

outsourcing The practice of contracting with outside vendors to handle specified business functions on a permanent basis.

Technological advances resulted in outsourcing much of the operational HR activities. **Outsourcing** involves contracting with outside vendors to handle specified business functions on a permanent basis. Although using outside experts to provide employee counselling and payroll services has been common for many years, the outsourcing of other specific HR functions, including pension and benefits administration, recruitment, management development, and training, has become increasingly common.[11]

For example, Air Canada, CIBC, BMO Financial Group, Hewlett-Packard Canada, IBM Canada, Calgary Health, and TELUS have all outsourced part or all of their administrative HR functions. During the latter part of this era, the term "human resources management" emerged. This change represented a shift in emphasis—from maintenance and administration to corporate contribution, proactive management, and initiation of change.[12]

Phase 4

The fourth phase of HRM is the current phase, where the role of HR departments has evolved to that of helping their organization achieve its strategic objectives.[13] HR activities have become ubiquitous, where not only the HR department but also every line manager has responsibilities related to employees as they move through the stages of the human-capital life cycle: selection and assimilation into the organization, development of capabilities while working in the organization, and transition out of the organization. **Figure 2** highlights core job requirements that are found in non-HR roles that were traditionally limited to the HR department, thus providing further evidence for the permeation of HR skills throughout the organization. Thus, all potential managers must be aware of the basics of HR to succeed in their respective roles. HR professionals often serve as subject matter experts or in-house consultants to line managers, offering advice on HR-related matters, formulating HR policies and procedures, and providing a wide range of HR services.

A 2011 national survey of HR professionals identified five critical pieces of knowledge required by HR professionals today. Presented in priority order, they are business acumen, an understanding of employment law and

FIGURE 2 Traditional HR Responsibilities in Non-HR Roles

Senior Managers

- Senior managers may specialize in areas such as finance, marketing, or human resources or in the sale of a particular product or provision of a particular service
- Establish objectives for the company and formulate or approve policies and programs
- Authorize and organize the establishment of major departments and associated senior staff positions

- Allocate material, human, and financial resources to implement organizational policies and programs; establish financial and administrative controls; formulate and approve promotional campaigns; and approve overall personnel planning

- Select middle managers, directors, or other executive staff
- Coordinate the work of regions, divisions, or departments

Financial Auditors and Accountants

- May supervise and train articling students, other accountants, or administrative technicians

Supervisors, General Office and Administrative Support Workers

- Coordinate, assign, and review the work of clerks engaged in word processing, record keeping and filing, operating telephones and switchboards, data entry, desktop publishing, and other activities involving general office and administrative skills
- Establish work schedules and procedures and coordinate activities with other work units or departments

- Resolve work-related problems and prepare and submit progress and other reports
- Train workers in job duties, safety procedures, and company policies
- Ensure smooth operation of office equipment and machinery, and arrange for maintenance and repair work

Industrial and Manufacturing Engineers

- Plan and design plant layouts and facilities
- Study new machinery and facilities and recommend or select efficient combinations

- Develop flexible or integrated manufacturing systems and technological procedures
- Conduct studies and implement programs to determine optimum inventory levels for production and to allow optimum use of machinery, materials, and resources
- Analyze costs of production
- Design, develop, and conduct time studies and work simplification programs

- Determine human resource and skill requirements and develop training programs
- Develop performance standards, evaluation systems, and wage and incentive programs
- Establish programs and conduct studies to enhance industrial health and safety or to identify and correct fire and other hazards
- Supervise technicians, technologists, analysts, administrative staff, and other engineers

Nursing Coordinators and Supervisors

- Supervise registered nurses, licensed practical nurses, and other nursing personnel

- Evaluate patients' needs and ensure that required nursing care is delivered
- Assist in the establishment of unit policies and procedures
- Assist in the selection, evaluation, and professional development of nursing personnel

---

University Professors and Lecturers

- Teach one or more university subjects to undergraduate and graduate students
- Prepare, administer, and grade examinations, laboratory assignments, and reports

- Direct research programs of graduate students and advise on research matters

- Conduct research in field of specialization and publish findings in scholarly journals or books

- May serve on faculty committees dealing with such matters as curriculum planning and degree requirements and perform a variety of administrative duties
- May represent their universities as speakers and guest lecturers
- May provide professional consultative services to government, industry, and private individuals

---

Source: O*NET OnLine, www.onetonline.org, (accessed October 3, 2011).

legislation, talent management, broad HR knowledge, and employee–labour relations knowledge.[14] The results align with an overall trend of increased expectations of HR professionals, suggesting that there are core competencies that those responsible for HR activities (within the HRM department and outside of it) must secure to help deliver value to the organization (see **Figure 3**).

Credible Activist A core HR competency is that of being both credible (respected, listened to, trusted) and active (takes a position, challenges assumptions). Both of these qualities are required to help an organization optimize the value added from its human resources.

The activist role is shared with non-HR positions as well. For example, a recent study conducted by Monster.com found that 73 percent of CEOs spend more than 25 percent of their time on talent-related activities, with three in every five identifying employee satisfaction/engagement as a key goal for their job, and three of every four identifying retention of high-performing employees as one of their goals.[15]

RPC

Guides and facilitates change in organizational culture or values consistent with business strategy

Culture and Change Steward The ability to appreciate, help shape, and articulate an organization's corporate culture includes understanding, guiding, and reacting to both internal and external stakeholder expectations. HR staff has a responsibility to shape and support a culture of change as well as develop programs, strategies, or projects to embed desired change throughout the organization.

employee engagement The emotional and intellectual involvement of employees in their work, such as intensity, focus, and involvement in his or her job and organization.

Intense global competition and the need for more responsiveness to environmental changes put a premium on **employee engagement**, the emotional and intellectual involvement of employees in their work, such as intensity, focus, and involvement in his or her job and organization. Engaged employees drive desired organizational outcomes—they go beyond what is required; understand and share the values and goals of the organization; perceive that there are opportunities for growth, development, and advancement; enjoy collegial relationships with managers and co-workers; trust their leaders; and regard the success of the organization as their success.[16] According to an analysis of a Hewitt Associates database (over 4 million employees from

FIGURE 3   HR Competency Model

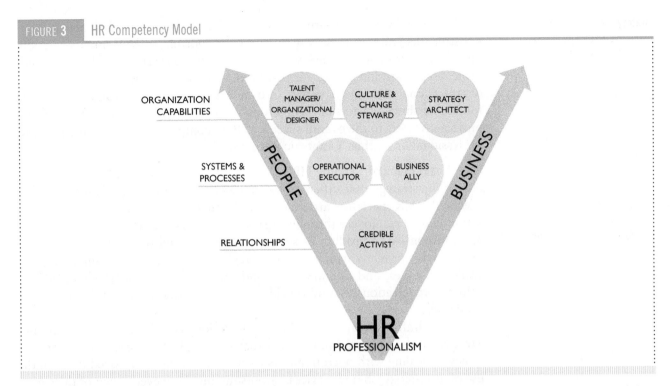

almost 1500 companies), there is a strong positive relationship between engagement and organizational performance (sales growth and total shareholder return).[17]

Talent Manager and Organizational Designer As traditional linear career paths change, the importance of an HR professional's ability to effectively manage human resources has become more critical as employees enter, exit, or move up, down, or across the organization. In this vein, HR specialists must embed theory, research, and practice into the processes, policies, and structures of an organization.

HR professionals and line managers play a pivotal role in *lowering labour costs*, the single largest operating expense in many organizations, particularly in the service sector. Doing so might involve introducing strategies to reduce turnover, absenteeism, and the rate of incidence of occupational illnesses and injuries. It could also mean adopting more effective recruitment, selection, and training programs. At one international tire manufacturing firm, adopting a behaviour-based interview strategy as the basis for selection of entry-level engineers resulted in savings of $500 000 in three years. These savings were due to lower turnover, lower training costs, and improved capabilities of the engineering staff because of a better fit.[18]

Strategy Architect HR professionals significantly contribute to strategy by integrating internal stakeholder and external stakeholder expectations. Through identifying, forecasting, and facilitating organizational responses to an ever-changing internal workforce and often volatile external pressures, HR plays an active role in the establishment and execution of overall strategy.

RPC

Monitors expenditures and timelines

strategy The company's plan for how it will balance its internal strengths and weaknesses with external opportunities and threats to maintain a competitive advantage.

Traditionally, **strategy**—the company's plan for how it will balance its internal strengths and weaknesses with external opportunities and threats to maintain a competitive advantage—was formulated without HR input. But today HR professionals are increasingly involved in both formulating and implementing organizational strategy. A survey of over 1100 corporate managers in Canada found that three-quarters of them strongly believe that the HR function contributes significantly to the overall success of their company and view having an HR professional on staff as a strategic advantage.[19]

Operational Executor Leading HR researcher Brian Becker says, "It isn't the content of the strategy that differentiates the winners and losers, it is the ability to execute."[20] HR specialists are expected to be **change agents** who lead the organization and its employees through organizational change. Making the enterprise more responsive to product or service innovations and technological change is the objective of many management strategies. Flattening the pyramid, empowering employees, and organizing around teams are ways in which HRM can help an organization respond quickly to its customers' needs and competitors' challenges.

change agents Specialists who lead the organization and its employees through organizational change.

Policy drafting, adaption, and implementation, as well as employees' administrative needs, were traditional roles that HR fulfilled. In recent years the efficiency in dealing with operational issues has significantly improved through the use of technology, shared services, or outsourcing. However, much of the expertise in operational aspects of employee-related policies remains largely within the HR professional's realm of responsibility.

Business Ally Organizational goal setting and development of business objectives is highly dependent on external opportunities or threats. HR professionals, together with other organizational managers, play a role in what strategic planners call **environmental scanning**, which involves identifying and analyzing *external* opportunities and threats that may be crucial to the organization's success. These managers can also supply competitive intelligence that may be useful as the company formulates its strategic plans. Details regarding a successful incentive plan being used by a competitor, impending labour shortages, and information about pending legislative changes are examples.

environmental scanning Identifying and analyzing external opportunities and threats that may be crucial to the organization's success.

Resources Consulting
www.cfthr.com/en/index.php

HR Dept
www.hrdept.co.uk

RPC

Provides support and expertise to managers and supervisors with respect to managing people

HR professionals can also add value to the strategy formulation process by supplying information regarding the company's *internal* strengths and weaknesses, particularly as they relate to the organization's workforce. HR professionals not only understand the value and social context of the business, but they are also increasingly relied on to determine how an organization should be structured and how work can be integrated to ensure financial success.

As highlighted in the Strategic HR box, the evolution of HR is far from done. HR's transformation has been underway for several years, but progress has been somewhat inconsistent because of lack of senior management support and the fact that many non-HR managers still view HR as a cost centre. Many HR professionals need to acquire more broad-based business knowledge and skill sets to be considered and respected as equal business partners by other executives in the company.[21] In a few organizations HR remains locked in an operational mode, processing forms and requests, administering compensation and benefits, managing policies and programs, and overseeing hiring and training.[22]

Table 1 illustrates the different focus of operational versus strategic HR activities.

STRATEGIC HR

The HR Role Continues to Evolve

The current shift in human resources management as a department and as a profession will continue to undergo evolution well into the 2020s. There are five major forces driving this change:

1. **Changing Technology.** Technology has helped automate basic HR functions, including managing day-to-day transactions and employee self-service systems. Rather than maintain HR technology experts in-house, nearly half of companies outsource operational functions of HR (payroll, benefits administration, employee education, recruitment processes, and workforce analytics). And rather than commoditizing or marginalizing HR functions, the shift has actually freed up HR professionals from these repetitive tasks to concentrate on more critical functions, such as decreasing turnover, focusing on the quality of talent secured, and developing leaders within the organization.

2. **New Rules.** Corporate accounting scandals that plagued the early 2000s resulted in a more focused alignment of organizational activities with new laws and compliance expectations. The financial crisis that started in 2008 included a series of additional regulations and expectations of organizational accountability. In this highly volatile environment with high accountability expectations, HR's role is increasingly strategic, including helping the organization recover from changes and comply with new regulations.

3. **Succession Planning.** Fifty percent of companies do not have a succession plan in place for their CEO. Tales of disruptive, hastily planned, and overall unsuccessful succession plans highlight the importance of identifying, grooming, and supporting potential successors within an organization. HR's role extends significantly beyond operational tasks to think critically about the complexities, time, and contingencies that must be considered in succession planning. Thus, HR executives are critical to organizational success through development and management of a comprehensive succession planning process.

4. **Identifying Top Talent.** While some companies argue that all employees must be motivated, educated, rewarded, and evaluated, others argue that a better return on investment can be secured by focusing on a smaller portion of workers (for example, the top 3 percent of all employees). HR is continually asked to establish a commitment to talent development that is fair, realistic, aware of limitations, and sustainable. A thoughtful set of criteria for assessing and managing talent goes well beyond administrative activities to include an integrative and strategic approach to HR.

5. **A New Breed of HR Leaders.** The rise of the CHRO (chief HR officer) or CTO (chief talent officer) confirms the seriousness and intent of many boards of directors in elevating and recognizing the role and capabilities of HR in an organization's leadership. Including HR in the C-suite highlights the importance of talent management and HR's perspective on organizational issues. HR's participation at the highest level of organizational decision making marks the transformation of the role of HR from operational expert to strategic expert in a concrete way.

Source: Adapted from D. Kaplan "The End of Human Resources as We Know It." Human Resources Executive Online, www.hreonline.com. (Accessed October 3, 2011). Reprinted from Human Resources Executive, Copyright 2012 all rights reserved.

Measuring the Value of HR: Metrics

metrics Statistics used to measure activities and results.

Today's HR professionals need to be able to measure the value and impact of their organization's human capital and HRM practices. The use of various **metrics**, or statistics to measure the activities and results of HR, is now quite common. Traditional operational measures focused on the amount of activity and the costs of the HR function (such as number of job candidates interviewed per month, cost per hire, and so on), but today's measures need to reflect the quality of people and the effectiveness of HRM initiatives that build workforce capability. These new measures provide critical information that

| TABLE 1 | Operational versus Strategic HR |

Operational	Strategic
Skills	Concepts
Administrative tasks	Planning
Reactive	Proactive
Collecting metrics/measurements	Analyzing metrics/measurements
Working to achieve goals and objectives	Setting the goals and objectives
Following the laws, policies, and procedures	Interpreting, establishing, and revising the laws, policies, and procedures
Employee focus	Organizational focus
Explaining benefits to employees	Designing benefit plans that help the organization achieve its mission and goals
Setting up training sessions for employees	Assessing training needs for the entire organization
Recruiting and selecting employees	Workforce planning and building relationships with external resources
Administering the salary/wage plan	Creating a pay plan that maximizes employees' productivity, morale, and retention
Always doing things the same way	Recognizing that there may be better ways of doing things; recognizing how changes affect the entire organization—not just HR
Works within the organizational culture	Attempts to improve the organizational culture

Source: D.M. Cox and C.H. Cox, "At the Table: Transitioning to Strategic Business Partner," *Workspan* (November 2003), p. 22.

can be linked to organizational outcomes like productivity, product or service quality, sales, market share, and profits. For example, the percentage of first-choice job candidates accepting an offer to hire indicates the strength of the organization's employment brand in the marketplace and directly affects the quality of the workforce.[23]

balanced scorecard A measurement system that translates an organization's strategy into a comprehensive set of performance measures.

Many organizations are using the **balanced scorecard** system that includes measures of the impact of HRM on organizational outcomes. The balanced scorecard approach translates an organization's strategy into a comprehensive set of performance measures. It includes financial measures that tell the results of actions already taken. It complements the financial measures with operational measures of organizational, business unit, or department success that will drive future performance. It balances long-term and short-term actions and measures of success relating to financial results, customers, internal business processes, and human capital management.[24] For example, one measure relating to HRM is the percentage of senior management positions with fully job-ready successors ready to move up.

ENVIRONMENTAL INFLUENCES ON HRM

There are numerous external and internal environmental influences that drive the strategic focus of HRM. To be effective, all managers, including those with responsibility for HR, must monitor the environment on an ongoing basis, assess the impact of any changes, and be proactive in responding to such challenges.

External Environmental Influences

Six major external environmental influences on HRM will be discussed: economic conditions, labour market issues, technology, government, globalization, and environmental concerns.

Economic Conditions

Economic conditions affect supply and demand for products and services, which, in turn, have a dramatic impact on the number and types of employees required as well as on an employer's ability to pay wages and provide benefits. When the economy is healthy, companies often hire more workers as demand for products and services increases. Consequently, unemployment rates fall, there is more competition for qualified employees, and training and retention strategies increase in importance. Conversely, during an economic downturn, some firms reduce pay and benefits to maintain workers' jobs. Other employers are forced to downsize by offering attractive early retirement and early leave programs or by laying off or terminating employees. Unemployment rates rise and employers are often overwhelmed with applicants when vacancies are advertised.

Productivity refers to the ratio of an organization's outputs (goods and services) to its inputs (people, capital, energy, and materials). Canada's relatively low productivity growth rate is of concern because of increasing global competition. To improve productivity, managers must find ways to produce more outputs with current input levels or use fewer resources to maintain current output levels. In most organizations today, productivity improvement is essential for long-term success.

Employment trends in Canada have been experiencing dramatic change. The **primary sector**, which includes agriculture, fishing and trapping, forestry, and mining, now represents only 4 percent of jobs. Employment in the **secondary sector** (manufacturing and construction) has decreased to 19 percent of jobs. The sector that has grown to represent 77 percent of jobs, dominating the Canadian economy, is the **tertiary or service sector**, which includes public administration, personal and business services, finance, trade, public utilities, and transportation/communications.

Since all jobs in the service sector involve the provision of services by employees to individual customers, effectively managing and motivating human resources is critical. Although there are some lesser-skilled jobs (in housekeeping and food services, for example), many service-sector jobs demand highly knowledgeable employees.

Labour Market Issues

Increasing Workforce Diversity Canada's workforce is among the most diverse in the world. Diversity refers to the attributes that humans are likely to use to tell themselves "that person is different from me." These attributes

productivity The ratio of an organization's outputs (goods and services) to its inputs (people, capital, energy, and materials).

primary sector Jobs in agriculture, fishing and trapping, forestry, and mining.

secondary sector Jobs in manufacturing and construction.

tertiary or service sector Jobs in public administration, personal and business services, finance, trade, public utilities, and transportation/communications.

include demographic factors (such as race, gender, and age) as well as values and cultural norms.[25]

The proportion of visible and ethnic minorities entering the Canadian labour market is expected to continue growing at a faster pace than the rest of the population. Today, Canada admits more immigrants per capita than any other country. About two-thirds of visible minorities are immigrants, and approximately 20 percent of the Canadian population could be visible minorities by 2017. Ethnic diversity is also increasing. Currently, more than 200 different ethnic groups are represented among Canadian residents.[26]

As the employment rate for women has continued to converge toward that for men, organizations are accommodating working women and shared parenting responsibilities by offering onsite daycare, emergency childcare support, and flexible work arrangements. Women are now the primary breadwinners for 29 percent of dual-earner couples in Canada.[27]

The Aboriginal population is young and growing at a rate almost twice that of the rest of the Canadian population.[28] Young Aboriginal people represent an untapped source of employees who are still facing considerable difficulty in obtaining jobs and advancing in the workplace.

Canadians with disabilities continue to confront physical barriers to equality every day. Inaccessibility is still the rule, not the exception. Even though studies show that there are no performance differences in terms of productivity, attendance, and average tenure between employees who classify themselves as having a disability and those who do not, persons with disabilities continue, on average, to experience an unemployment rate that is 50 percent higher than that for the able-bodied population and an average income that is 17 percent lower.[29]

Another aspect of diversity is generational differences. There are four generations in the workplace, and nearly half of all Canadians say they have experienced a clash with workers older or younger than themselves. On the other hand, about one-quarter of workers say they don't notice age differences and another one-quarter think this situation provides an excellent learning opportunity.

Traditionalists Individuals born before 1946.

The senior group are the **Traditionalists** (also known as the Silent Generation), born before 1946. They grew up in era of hardship, including a world war and the Great Depression, and they tend to be quiet, loyal, and self-sacrificing. Although many have retired, many remain in the workforce.[30] For example, Walmart employs many seniors, even into their 90s, as greeters in their stores.[31]

Baby Boomers Individuals born between 1946 and 1964.

The **Baby Boomers**, born between 1946 and 1964, are the largest group in the workforce. They grew up in a time of major optimism and change amidst the moon landing and the women's movement. They tend to be career-focused workaholics who experienced a lot of competition in the workplace and are driven to succeed. Boomers are just beginning to retire and as a result the ratio of people not in the labour force (children under the age of 16 and seniors) per hundred people in the working population is expected to increase rapidly, from 44 per hundred in 2005 to 61 per hundred in 2031.[32] There are significantly fewer workers in later generations. This will create a labour shortage because a large, experienced group will be leaving the labour force and there will not be enough workers behind them to take over their jobs.

Generation X Individuals born between 1965 and 1980.

Generation X (individuals born between 1965 and 1980) is a much smaller group than the Boomers and were originally called the Baby Busters. This group grew up as divorce rates skyrocketed, and they were the first technology-literate generation. They tend to be independent and believe that security comes from transferability of skills rather than corporate loyalty. They can provide "out-of-the-box" thinking that can help companies deal with uncertainty. Flexible work–life arrangements and continuous skill development are valued by this generation.[33]

Generation Y Individuals born since 1980.

Generation Y (also known as Millennials and the Net Generation), born since 1980, are the children of the Baby Boomers, who have a reputation for being over-involved parents.[34] Members of this sizable group are beginning to enter the workforce. Although they are techno-savvy, comfortable with diversity, and eager to make a contribution, they tend also to be impatient and action oriented. They expect to change jobs frequently. New approaches to work and career management will be required to keep this group challenged.[35] For example, almost 90 percent of recent graduates in one survey said that they would deliberately seek out an employer with corporate social responsibility behaviour that reflects their own values. Unfortunately, businesses have been slow to catch on.[36] A summary of the attitudes/values/expectations and key characteristics of each generation is shown in **Table 2.**

Half of Canada's population has some postsecondary education (trades, college, or university).[37] Given the higher expectations of the better-educated labour force, managers are expected to ensure that the talents and capabilities of employees are fully utilized and that opportunities are provided for career growth.

RPC

Keeps current with emerging HR trends

TABLE **2**   The Four Generations

	Traditionalists 1922–1945	Baby Boomers 1946–1964	Gen Xers 1965–1980	Gen Ys 1981–2000
Attitudes, Values, and Expectations	• Loyalty • Respect for authority • Dedication • Sacrifice • Conformity • Honour • Privacy • Stability • Economic conservatism	• Optimism • Involvement • Team oriented • Personal growth and gratification • Youthfulness • Equality • Career focused	• Independence • Self-reliance • Pragmatism • Skepticism • Informality • Balance	• Confidence • Diversity • Civic duty • Optimism • Immediate access to information and services
Key Characteristics	• Compliant • Stable • Detail oriented • Hard-working • Dedicated • Fiscally frugal • Trustworthy • Risk averse • Long-term focused	• Driven to succeed • Team player • Relationship focused • Eager to add value • Politically savvy in the workplace • Competitive	• Techno-literate • Flexible and adaptable • Creative • Entrepreneurial • Multitasker • Results driven • Individualistic	• Techno-savvy • Collective action • Expressive and tolerant of differences • Eager to accept challenges • Innovative and creative

Source: Adwoa K. Buahene and Giselle Kovary. Reprinted with permission from *HR Professional* (October/November 2007).

An Ethical | Dilemma

The maintenance department supervisor has just come to you, the HR manager, voicing concern about the safety of two of her reporting employees whom she recently discovered are functionally illiterate. What are your responsibilities to these employees, if any?

On the other hand, a startlingly high proportion (26 percent) have only marginal literacy skills, meaning their ability to understand and use printed and written documents in daily activities to achieve goals and to develop knowledge and potential is limited. A frightening reality is that inadequate reading and writing skills have replaced lack of experience as the major reason for rejecting entry-level candidates.[38] About 15 percent of working-age Canadians are *functionally illiterate*—unable to read, write, calculate, or solve problems at a level required for independent functioning or the performance of routine technical tasks.[39] Functional illiteracy is exacting a toll not only on individual social and economic opportunities, but also on organizations' accident rates and productivity levels.

contingent/non-standard workers
Workers who do not have regular full-time employment status.

Non-Standard or Contingent Workers For the last 30 years or more, the labour market has undergone major structural changes with the growth of **contingent (or "non-standard") workers**, meaning workers that do not fit the traditional definition of permanent, full-time employment with the same employer on an indeterminate basis. The forms of employment involving part-time, fixed-term, temporary, home, and standby workers, those who have more than one job, and the self-employed have become so significant numerically that they now affect about one-third of the workforce. More women fall into this category than men.[40] Non-standard work is often poorly paid, offers little or no job security, and is generally not covered by employment legislation. Some are calling for these laws to be updated so that contingent workers are provided the same legal protection as other workers.[41]

Technology

From Twitter to Facebook to videoconferencing setups that make it seem like everyone is in the same room, there is a wide range of technology available to organizations today. All of this technology can make working in and managing a dispersed workforce easier and can enable people to work anywhere and everywhere. The workplace of today includes "hotels, cafes and conference venues, as well as public areas of lounges and airports."[42] However, it has also brought new concerns as the line between work and family time has become blurred.[43]

Questions concerning data control, accuracy, the right to privacy, and ethics are at the core of a growing controversy brought about by the new information technologies. Sophisticated computerized control systems are used to monitor employee speed, accuracy, and efficiency in some firms. More firms are also monitoring employee email, voice mail, telephone conversations, and computer usage, and some now monitor employee behaviour using video surveillance.[44]

Government

Various laws enacted by governments have had and will continue to have a dramatic impact on the employer–employee relationship in Canada. One of the factors that makes employment law in Canada so challenging is that there are 14 different jurisdictions involved. Each of the ten provinces and three territories has its own human rights, employment standards, labour relations, health and safety, and workers' compensation legislation. In addition, about 10 percent of the workforce (including employees of the federal government and Crown corporations, chartered banks, airlines, national railways, and the Canadian Armed Forces) is covered by federal employment legislation.

Although there is some commonality across jurisdictions, there is also considerable variation. Minimum wage, overtime pay requirements, vacation entitlement, and grounds protected under human rights legislation, for example, vary from one province/territory to another. Furthermore, some jurisdictions have pay equity and employment equity legislation while others do not. This means that companies with employees in more than one jurisdiction have different rules applying to different employees. There are, however, certain laws that apply to all employers and employees across Canada, such as employment insurance and the Canada/Quebec Pension Plan.

Globalization

globalization The emergence of a single global market for most products and services.

The term **globalization** refers to the emergence of a single global market for most products and services. This growing integration of the world economy into a single, huge marketplace is increasing the intensity of competition and leading most organizations to expand their operations around the world.[45] Firms in other parts of the world are also seeing human resources as a source of competitive advantage, as discussed in the Global HRM box.

GLOBAL HRM

Lin Congyin Prizes His Staff

Lin Congyin is the founder and chairperson of Jiumuwang Western-Style Fashional Clothes Co. Ltd. in Quanzhou, the third-largest city in Fujian province in China. His company makes men's trousers and has led the segment's market share for seven consecutive years, beating out more than 110 000 garment enterprises in China. For Lin, the most valuable assets of his undertaking are not capital, products, or brand: "Staff is paramount," he says. In the clothing industry, which has a high employee turnover rate, Jiumuwang's rate always stands at no higher than 1.5 percent, the lowest among his competitors. "Without my staff, we wouldn't have such a renowned brand with a reputation of high quality."

No matter how busy he is, Lin always makes time to sign birthday cards for all his 8000 staff, almost every day. And he has incorporated a monthly birthday party into his routine. "Just imagine a big party for at least 500 people every month," he says with excitement.

Lin has insisted on providing free annual physical examinations for every staff member for the past 10 years.

Moreover, he arranges the same package vacation for all of his staff, including cleaners, every year. "It's my responsibility to take care of all the staff."

"It's quite simple to explain: as a boss, staff is earning your money or helping you to make money," he says. "If being concerned with staff helps you make fortune, then they should be respected," he says. "When I started Jiumuwang, I realized this principle."

Jiumuwang creates a career path tailored to every new staff member when they join the company. "We provide training to help promote staff's abilities. As a result we gain a talent pool," he says. Earlier this year, the All-China Federation of Industry and Commerce and Federation of Trade Unions awarded Lin the National Outstanding Entrepreneur award for staff caring. "If we respect staff and offer them training, their value will be priceless," says Lin.

Source: Adapted from Li Fangfang, "Lin Means Business," *China Business Week* (March 31–April 6, 2008), p. 12.

RPC

Gathers, analyzes, and reports relevant business and industry information (including global trends) to influence the development of strategic business HR plans

There are increasing numbers of multinational corporations—firms that conduct a large part of their business outside the country in which they are headquartered and that locate a significant percentage of their physical facilities and human resources in other countries. For example, Toyota has a large market share in the United States, Europe, and Africa, and is the market leader in Australia. Toyota has factories all over the world, manufacturing or assembling vehicles like the Corolla for local markets. Notably, Toyota has manufacturing or assembly plants in the United States, Japan, Australia, Canada, Indonesia, Poland, South Africa, Turkey, the United Kingdom, France, and Brazil, and has recently added plants in Pakistan, India, Argentina, the Czech Republic, Mexico, Malaysia, Thailand, China, and Venezuela.[46]

Globalization means that HR professionals need to become familiar with employment legislation in other countries and need to manage ethical dilemmas when labour standards are substantially lower than those in Canada. Companies doing business in sub-Saharan Africa, for example, have to deal with a high death rate among employees with AIDS. Some are paying for antiretroviral drugs to keep their employees alive.[47]

Environmental Concerns

Environmental concerns have suddenly (some might say finally) emerged as an issue for people, particularly the younger generations.[48] Sustainability, climate change, global warming, pollution, carbon footprints, extinction of wildlife species, ecosystem fragility, and other related issues are increasingly important to people around the world. There is increasing evidence that interest in environmental issues is motivating the behaviour of employees, and that they are concerned about whether they work for environmentally responsible companies. Companies like Fairmont Hotels have made environmental stewardship a priority for almost 20 years. They have found that developing a reputation as an environmental leader and demonstrating corporate social responsibility have not only helped them to gain market share, but have also been a strong employee retention tool.[49]

Employees are increasingly concerned with social responsibility, including environmental responsibility, on the part of their employer.

Internal Environmental Influences

How a firm deals with the three internal environmental influences of organizational culture, organizational climate, and management practices has a major impact on its ability to meet its objectives.

Organizational Culture

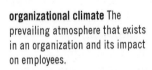

organizational culture The core values, beliefs, and assumptions that are widely shared by members of an organization.

Organizational culture consists of the core values, beliefs, and assumptions that are widely shared by members of an organization. Culture is often conveyed through an organization's mission statement, as well as through stories, myths, symbols, and ceremonies. It serves a variety of purposes:

- communicating what the organization "believes in" and "stands for"
- providing employees with a sense of direction and expected behaviour (norms)
- shaping employees' attitudes about themselves, the organization, and their roles
- creating a sense of identity, orderliness, and consistency
- fostering employee loyalty and commitment

All managers with HR responsibilities play an important role in creating and maintaining the type of organizational culture desired. For example, they may organize recognition ceremonies for high-performing employees and be involved in decisions regarding symbols, such as a logo or the design of new company premises. Having a positive culture has a positive impact on employer branding, recruitment, retention, and productivity.

Organizational Climate

organizational climate The prevailing atmosphere that exists in an organization and its impact on employees.

Organizational climate refers to the prevailing atmosphere, or "internal weather," that exists in an organization and its impact on employees.[50] It can be friendly or unfriendly, open or secretive, rigid or flexible, innovative or stagnant. The major factors influencing the climate are management's leadership style, HR policies and practices, and the amount and style of organizational communication. The type of climate that exists is generally reflected in the level of employee motivation, job satisfaction, performance, and productivity. HR professionals play a key role in helping managers throughout the firm establish and maintain a positive organizational climate.

Employees in fast-food establishments are taught how to provide courteous, efficient customer service.

Management Practices

Management practices have changed considerably over the past decade, with many HRM implications. For example, the traditional bureaucratic structure with many levels of management is being replaced by

261

empowerment Providing workers with the skills and authority to make decisions that would traditionally be made by managers.

flatter organizational forms using cross-functional teams and improved communication. Since managers have more people reporting to them in flat structures, they cannot supervise their employees as closely and employee **empowerment** has greatly increased.

GROWING PROFESSIONALISM IN HRM

RPC

Stays current with professional knowledge

Fosters and promotes advancement of the profession

Today, HR practitioners must be professionals in terms of both performance and qualifications.[51] Every profession has several characteristics: (1) a common body of knowledge; (2) benchmarked performance standards; (3) a representative professional association; (4) an external perception as a profession; (5) a code of ethics; (6) required training credentials for entry and career mobility; (7) an ongoing need for skill development; and (8) a need to ensure professional competence is maintained and put to socially responsible uses. Every province has an association of HR practitioners (Prince Edward Island is included in Nova Scotia's) that currently assumes dual roles: first, as a professional association serving the interests of its members, and second, as a regulatory body serving the public. These two roles sometimes conflict, such as when the disciplinary role of a regulator conflicts with the professional interests of a member.[52]

Canadian Council of Human Resources Associations **www.cchra.ca/en/**

World Federation of People Management Associations **www.wfpma.com**

The Canadian Council of Human Resources Associations (CCHRA) is the 40 000-member national body through which all provincial HR associations are affiliated. The CCHRA is in turn a member of the World Federation of People Management Associations (WFPMA). The International Personnel Management Association (IPMA)–Canada is the national association for public-sector and quasi-public-sector HR professionals.

Other important associations for HR specialists include the Canadian Industrial Relations Association; WorldatWork for compensation and rewards issues; health and safety associations, such as the Industrial Accident Prevention Association, the Construction Safety Association, and Safe Communities Canada; and the Canadian Society for Training and Development.

certification Recognition for having met certain professional standards.

The Certified Human Resources Professional (CHRP) designation is a nationally recognized **certification** for Canadian HR professionals (there are approximately 21 000 of them at present).[53] Managed by the CCHRA and administered through provincial HR associations, the CHRP is similar to other professional designations, such as Chartered Accountant (CA) and Professional Engineer (P.Eng.); it recognizes members' qualifications and experience based on established levels of 187 required professional capabilities in seven functional dimensions: (1) professional practice; (2) organizational effectiveness; (3) staffing; (4) employee and labour relations; (5) total compensation; (6) organizational learning, training, and development; and (7) occupational health, safety, and wellness. The national certification requirements are shown in **Figure 4**. A recently launched SHRP designation (Senior Human Resources Professional) is aimed at professionals who possess other internationally recognized designations (for example, the US Society for Human Resource Management), or a work history demonstrating leadership, advisory capabilities, strategic orientation, a breadth of general business knowledge (not just limited to HR), and significant impact of their organization and profession.

In addition to the international- and national-level broad HR designations, a series of more specialized or specific professional designations in Canada allows those who may be interested in specialized areas to gain recognition for a deeper level of subject matter expertise. **Table 3** highlights a series of additional HR designations.[54]

FIGURE **4**   National CHRP Certification Requirements

Please note that throughout the certification and recertification process, provincial variations may apply. Always contact the provincial HR association of which you are a member to ensure you have the most updated information that applies to you (www.hranb.org/cchra-member-association.php).

A. Initial Certification

To fulfill the academic requirements for the CHRP designation, a candidate must:

1. Become a member of a provincial human resources professionals association; and

2. Pass

(1) The National Knowledge Exam® (assesses knowledge of major human resources functions), and

(2) National Professional Practice Assessment® (measures human resources "experience"); must be written within 5 years of passing the National Knowledge Exam®. (Please note that the NPPA is not mandatory in Quebec and Ontario.)

As of January 1, 2011, CHRP Candidates—those who have passed the National Knowledge Exam® (NKE) – will require a minimum of a bachelor's degree from an accredited college or university in order to register for the National Professional Practice Assessment® and qualify for the CHRP designation. In some provinces, the degree requirement varies, or additional requirements may be applicable. Please contact your provincial HR association for more details.

B. Sign the National Code of Ethics (or your provincial association's equivalent)

C. Recertification

Every three years, all CHRPs will be required to recertify based on a set of professional development criteria, including seminars, conferences, volunteer work, or continuing education. Provincial variations may apply.

Source: Adapted from Canadian Council of Human Resources Associations, *What Is the CHRP Designation?* www.cchra.ca (July 29, 2009). Reproduced with permission of the Canadian Council of Human Resources Associations.

TABLE 3 Professional HR Designations in Canada (as of 2006)

Designation	Designation Holders in Canada
Certified Human Resources Professional (CHRP)	18 000
Group Benefits Associate (GBA)	1430
Registered Professional Recruiter (RPR)	1200
Canadian Payroll Manager (CPM)	1200
Certified Employee Benefits Specialist (CEBS)	896
Payroll Compliance Practitioner (PCP)	850
Certified Compensation Professional (CCP)	734
Retirement Plans Associate (RPA)	652
Canadian Management Professional (CMP)	550
International Personnel Management Association (IPMA) – Certified Practitioner	266
Registered Assessment Specialist (RAS)	250
Certified Training and Development Professional (CTDP)	250
Registered Professional Trainer (RPT)	200
Compensation Management Specialist (CMS)	174
Global Remuneration Professional (GPR)	37
Senior Professional in HR (SPHR)	37

Source: Adapted from S. Klie, "Senior HR Designations Unveiled," *Canadian HR Reporter*, July 7, 2009. Reprinted by permission of Canadian HR Reporter. © Copyright Thomson Reuters Canada Ltd., (2012) Toronto, Ontario, 1-800-387-5164. Web: www.hrreporter.com

Chapter SUMMARY

1. Human resources management (HRM) refers to the management of people in organizations. Strategic HRM involves linking HRM with strategic goals and objectives to improve business performance. In more and more firms, HR professionals are becoming strategic partners in strategy formulation and execution.

2. The two major stages in the evolution of management thinking about workers were (1) scientific management, which focused on production, and (2) the human resources movement, in which it was recognized that organizational success is linked to operational and strategic management of labour.

3. Core roles HR professionals must fulfill today include the roles of talent manager, culture/change steward, strategic architect, operational executor, business ally, and credible activist. These roles are shared with managers and executives in the organization, with HR professionals often assuming roles of advisers or subject matter experts.

4. Activities of employee management, empowerment, training, and guidance are often shared between managers in the organization (executive and line managers) and HR professionals. Therefore, managers, executives,

and HR personnel are all influential in effective human resources management.

5. Human resources activities are now being seen as falling into two categories. The first is the traditional operational (administrative) category, where HR hires and maintains employees and then manages employee separations. The second is the more recent strategic category, where HR is focused on ensuring that the organization is staffed with the most effective human capital to achieve its strategic goals.

6. A number of external factors have an impact on HRM, including economic factors, labour market issues, technology, government, globalization, and environmental concerns.

7. There are numerous professional designations that will boost a career trajectory in human resources. The most basic of these is the Canadian Human Resources Professional (CHRP). However, additional designations exist that are important and may be influential in building expertise and careers in management or human resources management.

MyManagementLab

Visit MyManagementLab to access a personalized Study Plan and additional study tools for this chapter.

Key TERMS

Baby Boomers
balanced scorecard
certification
change agents
contingent/non-standard workers
employee engagement
empowerment
environmental scanning
Generation X
Generation Y
globalization
human capital
human resources management (HRM)

human resources movement
metrics
organizational climate
organizational culture
outsourcing
primary sector
productivity
scientific management
secondary sector
strategy
tertiary or service sector
Traditionalists

Review and Discussion QUESTIONS

1. Describe the transformation that HR underwent over the years. Discuss how changes in internal and external factors contributed to the evolution in HR.

2. Describe the role of HR in strategy formulation and strategy implementation.

3. Describe how the external environment influences HR.

4. Differentiate between organizational culture and organizational climate.

5. Describe the multiple jurisdictions related to employment legislation affecting HRM in Canada.

6. Discuss the six core competencies required of HR professionals. Identify how these competencies are also embedded in the roles of line managers, senior managers, and C-level executives in an organization.

7. Explain how HR has become professionalized and describe the value of this professionalization.

Critical Thinking QUESTIONS

1. Explain how demographics and workforce diversity have had an impact on the organization in which you are working or one in which you have worked. What policies or practices did managers or HR in the organization have in place to help assist with the management of a diverse internal labour force?

2. Explain how changing economic and competitive pressures have had an impact on the organization in which you are working or one in which you have worked. How has your business responded to these pressures?

3. A firm has requested your assistance in ensuring that its multigenerational workforce functions effectively as a team. What strategies or programs would you recommend? Why?

4. Choose a non-HR role you have had in your previous jobs. Identify how you used the core competencies of HR professionals in that role and how it affected your job performance.

Experiential EXERCISES

1. Working alone or with a small group of classmates, interview an HR manager and prepare a short essay regarding his or her role in strategy formulation and implementation.

2. Review job ads for five senior HR roles on job posting websites or corporate websites. Identify common competencies required for those roles as per the ads. Contrast these required competencies (both implied and explicit) with the core HR professional competencies highlighted in this chapter. Discuss the most consistently required competency and the impact of that competency on organizational success.

3. Review job ads for five executive roles (such as CEO, vice-president, or president) on job posting websites or corporate websites. Identify common competencies required for those roles as per the ads. Contrast these required competencies (both implied and explicit) with the core HR professional competencies highlighted in this chapter. Discuss the most consistently required competency and how it is important in non-HR roles.

4. According to a 2011 study of the world's most attractive firms (released by Universum), the top 10 employers for career seekers with a business background were (in priority order): Google, KPMG, PricewaterhouseCoopers, Ernst & Young, Deloitte, Microsoft, Procter & Gamble, J.P. Morgan, Apple, and Goldman Sachs. In groups, review the company websites of these organizations to determine the corporate strategy, objectives, and markets that these organizations target. As a team, discuss the similarities and differences among the strategies, objectives, and markets of these 10 employers. Explain how these factors might affect Generation Y perceiving these companies as desirable employers.

5. Using the sample balanced scorecard template provided by your professor, in pairs develop a balanced scorecard measure for a hypothetical company in the retail urban clothing sector. This company has many stores in large and small cities in Ontario and Quebec. Be sure to take into consideration current economic conditions as you develop your measures.

   Exchange your completed set of measures with another pair. Compare and contrast your measures. Is one set "better" than the other? Why or why not? Debrief as instructed.

Running CASE

Introduction

HRM—activities like recruiting, selecting, training, and rewarding employees—is not just the job of a central HR group, but rather one in which every manager must engage. Perhaps nowhere is this more apparent than in the typical small service business, where the owner–manager usually has no HR staff to rely on. However, the success of such an enterprise often depends largely on the effectiveness with which workers are recruited, hired, trained, evaluated, and rewarded. To help illustrate and emphasize the front-line manager's HR role, we will use a case based on an actual small business in Ottawa's high-tech region. Owner–managers Jennifer Lau and Pierre LeBlanc confront and solve HRM problems each day by applying the concepts and techniques presented in this text.

LearnInMotion.com: A Profile

Jennifer and Pierre graduated from university as business majors in June 2008 and got the idea for LearnInMotion.com as a result of a project they worked on together their last semester in their entrepreneurship class. The professor had divided the students into two- or three-person teams and asked them to "create a business plan for a high-tech company." The idea the two came up with was LearnInMotion.com. The basic idea of the website was to list a vast array of web-based, CD-ROM–based, or textbook-based continuing education-type business courses for working people who wanted to take a course from the comfort of their own homes. Users could come to the website to find and then take a course in one of several ways. Some courses could be completed interactively on the web via the site; others were in a form that was downloadable directly to the user's computer; others (which were either textbook or CD-ROM–based) could be ordered and delivered (in several major metropolitan areas) by independent contractor delivery people. Their business mission was "to provide work-related learning when, where, and how you need it."

Based on their research, they knew the market for work-related learning was booming. At the same time, professional development activities like these were increasingly Internet-based. Tens of thousands of on- and offline training firms, universities, associations, and other content providers were trying to reach their target customers via the Internet. Jennifer and Pierre understandably thought they were in the right place at the right time.

Jennifer's father had some unused loft space in Kanata, Ontario, so with about $45 000 of accumulated savings, Jennifer and Pierre incorporated and were in business. They retained the services of an independent programmer and hired two people—a web designer to create the graphics for the site (which would then be programmed by the programmer) and a content manager whose job was to enter information onto the site as it came in from content providers. By the end of 2008, they also completed upgrading their business plan into a form they could show to prospective venture capitalists. They sent the first version to three Canadian venture capitalists. Then they waited.

And then they waited some more. They never heard back from the first three venture capitalists, so they sent their plan to five more. They still got no response. But Pierre and Jennifer pressed on. By day they called customers to get people to place ads on their site, to get content providers to list their available courses, and to get someone—anyone—to deliver textbook- and CD-ROM–based courses, as needed, across Canada. By May 2009 they had about 30 content providers offering courses and content through LearnInMotion.com. In the summer, they got their first serious nibble from a venture capital firm. They negotiated with this company through much of the summer, came to terms in the early fall, and closed the deal—getting just over $1 million in venture funding—in November 2009.

After a stunning total of $75 000 in legal fees (they had to pay both their firm's and the venture capital firm's lawyers to navigate the voluminous disclosure documents and agreements), they had just over $900 000 to spend. The funding, according to the business plan, was to go toward accomplishing five main goals: redesigning and expanding the website; hiring about seven more employees; moving to a larger office; designing and implementing a personal information manager (PIM)/calendar (users and content providers could use the calendar to interactively keep track of their personal and business schedules); and last but not least, driving up sales. LearnInMotion was off and running.

1 What is human resources management and does it have a role to play in this organization? If so, in what ways specifically?

2 What environmental influences will affect the role that human resources management could play within this organization?

Case INCIDENT

Jack Nelson's Problem

As a new member of the board of directors for a local bank, Jack Nelson was being introduced to all the employees in the home office. When he was introduced to Ruth Johnson he was curious about her work and asked her what the machine she was using did. Johnson replied that she really did not know what the machine was called or what it did. She explained that she had only been working there for two months. She did, however, know precisely how to operate the machine. According to her supervisor, she was an excellent employee.

At one of the branch offices, the supervisor in charge spoke to Nelson confidentially, telling him that "something was wrong," but she didn't know what. For one thing, she explained, employee turnover was too high, and no sooner had one employee been put on the job than another one resigned. With customers to see and loans to be made, she continued, she had little time to work with the new employees as they came and went.

All branch supervisors hired their own employees without communication with the home office or other branches. When an opening developed, the supervisor tried to find a suitable employee to replace the worker who had quit.

After touring the 22 branches and finding similar problems in many of them, Nelson wondered what the home office should do or what action he should take. The banking firm was generally regarded as a well-run institution that had grown from 27 to 191 employees in the past eight years. The more he thought about the matter, the more puzzled Nelson became. He couldn't quite put his finger on the problem, and he didn't know whether to report his findings to the president.

QUESTIONS

1 What do you think is causing some of the problems in the bank's branches?

2 Do you think setting up an HR unit in the main office would help?

3 What specific functions should an HR unit carry out? What HR functions would then be carried out by supervisors and other line managers? What role should the Internet play in the new HR organization?

Source: Claude S. George, *Supervision in Action: Art Managing Others,* 4th Ed., ©1985. Reprinted and Electronically reproduced by permission of Pearson Education, Inc., Upper Saddle River, New Jersey.

MyManagementLab

Visit MyManagementLab to access a personalized Study Plan and additional study tools for this chapter.

CBC ⬤ To view the CBC videos, read a summary, and answer discussion questions, go to MyManagementLab

NOTES

1. O. Parker, *The Strategic Value of People: Human Resource Trends and Metrics* (Ottawa, ON: The Conference Board of Canada, July 2006); E. Andrew, "Most Canadian Companies Are Still Not Treating Human Resources as a Serious Strategic Issue," *Workspan Focus Canada* (February 2006), pp. 14–16; S. Prashad, "All Aligned: How to Get HR on Board with Business," *HR Professional* (February/March 2005), pp. 19–29.

2. O. Parker, *It's the Journey That Matters: 2005 Strategic HR Transformation Study Tour.* (Ottawa, ON: The Conference Board of Canada, March 2006).

3. N. Bontis, "Made to Measure: Linking Human Capital Metrics with Organizational Performance," *HR Professional* (August/September 2007), pp. 16–20; B. Becker, M. Huselid, P.S. Pickus, and M.F. Spratt, "HR as a Source of Shareholder Value: Research and Recommendations," *Human Resource Management* 36, no. 1 (Spring 1997), pp. 39–47; B. Becker and B. Gerhart, "The Impact of Human Resource Management on Organizational Performance: Progress and Prospects," *Academy of Management Journal*, 39, no. 4 (August 1996), pp. 779–801; M. Huselid, "The Impact of Human Resources Management Practices on Turnover, Productivity, and Corporate Performance," *Academy of Management Journal*, 38 (1995), pp. 635–672; P. Wright, G. McMahan, B. McCormick, and S. Sherman, "Strategy, Core Competence, and HR Involvement as Determinants of HR Effectiveness and Refinery," *Human Resource Management*, 37, no. 37 (1998), pp. 17–31.

4. C. Clegg, M. Patterson, A. Robinson, C. Stride, T.D. Wall, and S.J. Wood, "The Impact of Human Resource and Operational Management Practices on Company Productivity: A Longitudinal Study," *Personnel Psychology*, 61 (Autumn 2008), pp. 467–501.

5. A. Lado and M.C. Wilson, "Human Resource Systems and Sustained Competitive Advantage: A Competency-Based Perspective," *Academy of Management Review*, 19 (1994), pp. 699–727.

6. J.E. Delery and D.H. Doty, "Modes of Theorizing in Strategic Human Resource Management: Tests of Universalistic, Contingency, and Configurational Performance Predictions," *Academy of Management Journal*, 39, no. 4 (1996), pp. 802–835.

7. M. Huselid, "The Impact of Human Resources Management Practices on Turnover, Productivity, and Corporate Performance," *Academy of Management Journal*, 38 (1995), pp. 635–672.

8. F.W. Taylor, "The Principles of Scientific Management," in J.M. Sharfritz and J.S. Ott (eds.), *Classics of Organization Theory*, 2nd ed. (Chicago, IL: The Dorsey Press, 1987), pp. 66–81.

9. D.G. Nickels, J.M. McHugh, S.M. McHugh, and P.D Berman, *Understanding Canadian Business*, 2nd ed. (Toronto, ON: Irwin, 1997), p. 220.

10. This discussion is based on E.E. Lawler III, "Human Resources Management," *Personnel* (January 1988), pp. 24–25.

11. J. Miller, "HR Outsourcing and the Bottom Line," *Workspan* (October 2008), pp. 76–81; J. Berkow, "People Skills Required," *National Post* (October 19, 2005).

12. R.J. Cattaneo and A.J. Templer, "Determining the Effectiveness of Human Resources Management," in T.H. Stone (ed.), *ASAC: Personnel and Human Resources Division Proceedings* (Halifax, NS: St. Mary's University, June 1988), p. 73.

13. T. Belford, "HR Focusing on How It Can Add Value," *Globe and Mail* (March 25, 2002), p. B11.

14. S. Dobson, "Business Acumen Critical for HR: Survey," *Canadian HR Reporter* (May 9, 2011).

15. S. Modi, "Is the CEO the New Chief Talent Officer in Global Recruitment and HR?" Monster Thinking, (July 6, 2011), www.monsterthinking.com/2011/07/06/is-the-ceo-the-new-chief-talent-officer-in-global-recruitment-and-hr/ (accessed September 26, 2011).

16. R. Wright, *Measuring Human Resources Effectiveness Toolkit* (Ottawa, ON: The Conference Board of Canada, 2004); U. Vu, "The HR Leader's Contribution in an Engaged Organization," *Canadian HR Reporter* (May 22, 2006); D. Brown, "Measuring Human Capital Crucial, ROI Isn't, Says New Think-Tank Paper," *Canadian HR Reporter* (October 25, 2004), pp. 1, 4; J. Douglas and T. Emond, "Time to Pop the Question: Are Your Employees Engaged?" *WorldatWork Canadian News* (Third Quarter, 2003), pp. 12–14.

17. R. Baumruk, "The Missing Link: The Role of Employee Engagement in Business Success," *Workspan* (November 2004), pp. 48–52; N. Winter, "Tuned In and Turned On," *Workspan* (April 2003), pp. 48–52.

18. D.S. Cohen, "Behaviour-Based Interviewing," *Human Resources Professional* (April/May 1997), p. 29.

19. *CCHRA Awareness Study* (Toronto, ON: CCHRA and Ekos Research Associates, 2008).

20. B.E. Becker, M.A. Huselid, and D. Ulrich, *The HR Scorecard: Linking People, Strategy and Performance* (Boston, MA: Harvard Business School Press, 2001); D. Brown, "Measuring the Value of HR," *Canadian HR Reporter* (September 24, 2001), pp. 1, 5. See also E. Beaudan, "The Failure of Strategy: It's All in the Execution, *Ivey Business Journal* (January/February 2001).

21. A. Aijala, B. Walsh, and J. Schwartz, *Aligned at the Top: How Business and HR Executives View Today's Most Significant People Challenges—And What They're Doing About It.* Deloitte Development LLC, 2007.

22. *Canada's Demographic Revolution: Adjusting to an Aging Population* (Ottawa, ON: The Conference Board of Canada, March 2006).

23. O. Parker, *The Strategic Value of People: Human Resource Trends and Metrics* (Ottawa, ON: The Conference Board of Canada, July 2006).

24. R. Kaplan and D. Norton, *The Strategy-Focused Organization: How Balanced Scorecard Companies Thrive in the New Business Environment* (Boston, MA: Harvard Business School Press, 1996); S. Mooraj, D. Oyon, and D. Hostettler, "The Balanced Scorecard: A Necessary Good or an Unnecessary Evil?" *European Management Journal* 17, no. 5 (October 1999), pp. 481–491; B. Becker, M. Huselid, and D. Ulrich, *The HR Scorecard: Linking People, Strategy and Performance* (Boston, MA: Harvard Business School Press, 2001); M. Huselid, B. Becker, and R. Beatty, *The Workforce Scorecard: Managing Human Capital to Execute Strategy* (Boston, MA: Harvard Business School Press, 2006).

25. G. Ferris, D. Frink, and M.C. Galang, "Diversity in the Workplace: The Human Resources Management Challenge," *Human Resource Planning* 16, no. 1 (1993), p. 42.

26. "Study: Canada's Visible Minority Population in 2017," *The Daily*, Statistics Canada (March 2005); *Canada's Ethnocultural Portrait: The Changing Mosaic*, Statistics Canada, Catalogue No. 96 F0030 XIE 2001 0082004.

27. Statistics Canada, "Wives as Primary Breadwinners," *Perspectives* (August 2006), p. 3, Catalogue # 75-001-XIE; Statistics Canada, "Labour Force Characteristics by Age and Sex," CANSIM Table 282-0087, www.statcan,gc,ca/subjects-sujets/labour-travail/lfs-epa/t090710al-eng.htm (accessed July 31, 2009).

28. M. Hutchinson, "Aboriginal Workforce Poised to Replace Retiring Baby Boomers," http://www.aboriginalhr.ca/en/programs/MAI/Business_case (August 17, 2006).

29. C. Williams, "Disability in the Workplace," *Perspectives on Labour and Income* 18, no. 1 (February 2006), pp. 16–24.

30. S.P. Eisner, "Managing Generation Y," *S.A.M. Advanced Management Journal*, 70, no. 4 (2005), pp. 4–15; "Canadians Plan to Work Past Traditional Retirement Age, Survey Finds," www.worldatwork.org/waw/adimComment?id=3085&printable (March 11, 2009); "More Than Half of Canadians Plan to Work in Retirement," *Canadian HR Reporter* (January 8, 2007).

31. S. Dobson, "Age-Free Culture Goal of Top Employers," *Canadian HR Reporter* (January 12, 2009).

32. A. Belanger, L. Martel, and E. Caron-Malenfant, *Population Projections for Canada, Provinces and Territories: 2005–2031*, Statistics Canada, Catalogue No. 91-520-XIE (December 2005), pp. 16–17; *Canada's*

Demographic Revolution: Adjusting to an Aging Population (Ottawa, ON: The Conference Board of Canada, March 2006).

33. Based on material cited in "News and Views: Flex Appeal," compiled by M. Griffin, *HR Professional* (February/March 1999), p. 10; research reported by P.L. Nyhof in "Managing Generation X: The Millennial Challenge," *Canadian HR Reporter* (May 22, 2000), pp. 7–8; R. Berry, "Observations on Generational Diversity," *Profiles in Diversity Journal* 4, no. 3 (2002).

34. A. Glass, "Understanding Generational Differences for Competitive Success," *Industrial and Commercial Training*, 39, no. 2 (2007), pp. 98–103.

35. Jean-Philippe Naud, "Generation Y at Work," *WorldatWork Canadian News* (Second Quarter, 2005), pp. 6–8; D. Piktialis, "The Generational Divide in Talent Management," *Workspan* (March 2006), pp. 10–12; G. Kovary and A. Buahene, "Recruiting the Four Generations," *Canadian HR Reporter* (May 23, 2005), p. R6.

36. *Managing Tomorrow's People: The Future of Work to 2020*. (London UK: PricewaterhouseCoopers, 2007).

37. Statistics Canada, *Labour Force Historical Review*, Catalogue No.71F0004XCB, 2007.

38. A. Campbell and N. Gagnon, *Literacy, Life and Employment: An Analysis of Canadian International Adult Literacy Survey (IALS) Microdata* (Ottawa, ON: Conference Board of Canada, January 2006).

39. P. Bleyer, "Let's Make Productivity Work for Canadians," Canadian Council on Social Development, 2005, www.ccsd.ca/pr/2005/ccsd_prebudget.htm (accessed January 6, 2007).

40. J. Bernier, *The Scope of Federal Labour Standards and Nontraditional Work Situations* (Submission to the Federal Labour Standards Review, October 2005), pp. 5–13.

41. M. Townson, *Women in Non-Standard Jobs: The Public Policy Challenge* (Ottawa, ON: Status of Women Canada, 2003); M. Townson, "The Impact of Precarious Employment," in L.O. Stone (ed.), *New Frontiers of Research on Retirement*, Statistics Canada, Catalogue No. 75-511-XIE, 2006, pp. 355–382; R.P. Chaykowski, *Non-standard Work and Economic Vulnerability*, Canadian Policy Research Network, Vulnerable Workers Series, No. 3 (March 2005); G. Valeé, *Towards Enhancing the Employment Conditions of Vulnerable Workers: A Public Policy Perspective*, Canadian Policy Research Network, Vulnerable Workers Series, No. 2 (March 2005).

42. M. Vartiainen, M. Hakonen, S. Koivisto, P. Mannonen, M. P. Nieminen, V. Ruohomaki, and A. Vartola, *Distributed and Mobile: Places, People and Technology* (Helsinki Finland: Oy Yliopistokustannus University Press, 2007), p. 75.

43. C. Clark, "The World Is Flat: Work-Life Trends to Watch," *Workspan* (January 2009), pp. 17–19.

44. K. Williams, "Privacy in a Climate of Electronic Surveillance," *Workplace News* (April 2005), p. 10.

45. P. Benimadhu, "Startling Business Shifts Causing a Rethink of Work," *InsideEdge* (Summer 2008), p. 10.

46. "Multinational Corporation," http://en.wikipedia.org/wiki/Multinational_corporation (accessed August 17, 2006).

47. S. Nolen, "Step 1: Keep Workers Alive," *Globe and Mail* (August 5, 2006), pp. B4–B5.

48. U. Vu, "Climate Change Sparks Attitude Shift," *Canadian HR Reporter* (March 26, 2007), p. 11.

49. S. Dobson, "Fairmont Finds It's Easy Being Green," *Canadian HR Reporter* (March 26, 2007).

50. R. Stringer, *Leadership and Organizational Climate* (Upper Saddle River, NJ: Prentice-Hall, 2002).

51. This section is based on www.cchra.ca.

52. C. Balthazard, "The Difference between a Professional Association and a Regulatory Body," *Canadian HR Reporter* (August 11, 2008); C. Balthazard, "Regulatory Agenda at HRPA," *Canadian HR Reporter* (November 3, 2008).

53. This section is based on www.cchra.ca.

54. S. Klie, "Senior HR Designation Unveiled," *Canadian HR Reporter* (July 7, 2009).

PHOTO CREDITS

Recruitment

THE STRATEGIC IMPORTANCE OF RECRUITMENT

recruitment The process of searching out and attracting qualified job applicants, which begins with the identification of a position that requires staffing and is completed when résumés or completed application forms are received from an adequate number of applicants.

recruiter A specialist in recruitment whose job is to find and attract capable candidates.

Recruiters Café
www.recruiterscafe.com
Great Place to Work Institute Canada
www.greatplacetowork.ca

employer branding The image or impression of an organization as an employer based on the benefits of being employed by the organization.

Human talent is beginning to be referred to as the world's most sought-after commodity.[1] The quality of an organization's human resources begins with a strategic perspective in the management of recruitment. **Recruitment** is the process of searching out and attracting qualified job applicants. It begins with the identification of a position that requires staffing and is completed when résumés or completed application forms are received from an adequate number of applicants. A Watson Wyatt study found that organizations with superior recruiting practices financially outperform those with less effective programs and that successful recruiting is a strong indicator of higher shareholder value.[2]

Authority for recruitment is generally delegated to HR staff members, except in small businesses where line managers usually recruit their own staff. In large organizations where recruiting is done on a continual basis, the HR team typically includes specialists, known as **recruiters**, whose job is to find and attract qualified applicants. Recruiters are becoming increasingly critical to achieving an organization's strategic objectives as competition for the employees necessary for strategy implementation increases due to the growing talent shortage.

Organizations are increasingly seeking the high profile given to an "employer of choice," such as those included in lists such as Mediacorp's "Top 100 Employers," the Hewitt Associates "50 Best Employers," and the *Financial Post*'s "Ten Best Companies to Work for." Employers such as Scotiabank, Purolator, Tim Hortons, and many others are also applying the marketing concept of branding to strengthen their recruitment activities.[3]

Employer Branding

Gabriel Bouchard, founder of the Monster Canada online job board, says, "In an increasingly tight job market, employers must remain permanently visible to potential employees, establishing and maintaining relationships with potential candidates before they even begin pursuing a new job. This is particularly crucial when it comes to hard-to-fill or mission-critical positions."[4] Proactive employers are trying to obtain a competitive advantage in recruitment by establishing themselves as employers of choice through employer branding. The purpose of an employer brand is to attract people to apply to work at the organization and to earn the loyalty of current employees.

Employer branding is the image or impression of an organization as an employer based on the perceived benefits of being employed by the organization. It is the experience of an employee when working for a company, based on feelings, emotions, senses, realities, and benefits (functional benefits such as personal development, economic benefits such as monetary rewards, and psychological benefits such as feelings of purpose, belonging, and recognition). It is essentially a promise made to employees and their perception of how well that promise is delivered.[5]

Employer branding is particularly important during the recruitment process, not just for applicants who are eventually hired but also for those not hired who are out in the marketplace communicating their experience as an applicant to other job seekers.[6] Inconsiderate recruiting practices can be brand suicide for companies. Branding includes the experiences a candidate goes through while interacting with a company throughout the recruitment process, including[7]

- what candidates experience when they go to the company's website,
- whether HR sends an acknowledgement letter or email thanking each candidate who sends in a résumé,
- how candidates are greeted by the receptionist when they make initial contact by phone or in person, and
- whether the HR person who interviews candidates is a good spokesperson who can articulate the organization's values and culture.

Employer branding involves three steps.[8] Step 1 is to define the target audience, where to find them, and what they want from an employer. The target group may be one of the four generations in today's workforce, the underemployed, or the four employment equity groups. McDonald's may target potential Generation Y employees who are seeking career development. At Southland Transportation, a school bus service provider in Alberta, the target audience is retired police officers, recent retirees, and parents with young children.[9]

Step 2 is to develop the employee value proposition—the specific reasons why the organization is a unique place to work and a more attractive employer for the target audience compared to other organizations. The use of concrete facts, programs, policies, survey results, and information will clearly portray the organization as an employer of choice. It is also important to ensure that current managers are prepared to deliver the value proposition by guiding and mentoring employees.[10] Loblaw and Fairmont Hotels offer potential employees the opportunity to participate in "green" environmental initiatives.[11] At PCL Construction of Alberta, 80 percent of employees own stock in the company.[12]

Step 3 is to communicate the brand by incorporating the value proposition into all recruitment efforts. The communication should reinforce and remind current and potential employees of promises in the employee value proposition and of the organization's ability to deliver it through their managers. An integrated marketing approach to internal and external communication should use various channels, such as television, radio, print, websites, social media, and so on.[13]

McDonald's Recruiting
www.worksforme.ca/mcd

McDonald's used focus groups to identify the interests of one of their target markets for recruitment (young people). The results of the focus groups suggest that this target market is interested in balancing their own freedom and goals with making money. As a result, McDonald's offered flexible hours, uniform choices, scholarships, and discount cards to support its value proposition slogan "We take care of our employees." This value proposition was also communicated through television ads and a recruiting website. Following the introduction of this branding initiative, McDonald's saw a surge in the number of young people who recognized McDonald's as a great place to work.[14] With the right branding strategy, job seekers line up to apply for jobs. A successful brand results in job seekers saying "I'd like to work there."[15]

THE RECRUITMENT PROCESS

As illustrated in **Figure 1**, the recruitment process has a number of steps:

1. Job openings are identified through HR planning (based on the organization's strategic plan) or manager request. HR plans play a vital role in the identification process, because they indicate present and future openings and specify which should be filled internally and which externally. Openings do arise unexpectedly, though, when managers request that a new employee be hired.

2. The job requirements are determined. This step involves reviewing the job description and the job specifications and updating them, if necessary. Job analysis describes how to collect and interpret job descriptions and specifications.

3. Appropriate recruiting source(s) and method(s) are chosen. The major decision here is whether to start with internal or external recruiting. There is no single, best recruiting technique, and the most appropriate for any given position depends on a number of factors, which will be discussed in the next section.

4. A pool of qualified recruits is generated. The requirements of employment equity legislation (if any) and the organization's diversity goals should be reflected in the applicant pool.

A recruiter must be aware of constraints affecting the recruitment process to be successful in his or her job. Constraints arise from organizational policies, such as promote-from-within policies, which mean that a recruiter cannot start recruiting externally for a specified period, even if he or she is aware that there are no suitable internal candidates. Constraints also arise from compensation policies, since they influence the attractiveness of the job to potential applicants. If there is an employment equity plan, it will specify goals for increasing recruitment from the designated groups. Monetary and non-monetary inducements offered by competitors impose a constraint, since recruiters must try to meet the prevailing standards of the company or use alternative inducements.

Perhaps the biggest constraint on recruiting activity at this time is the current labour shortage, which makes recruiting more difficult. One survey by Hewitt Associates found that recruitment practices will have to undergo "enormous change" over the next several years.[16] Some initiatives are already underway to attract foreign recruits, as explained in the Global HRM box.

FIGURE 1   An Overview of the Recruitment Process

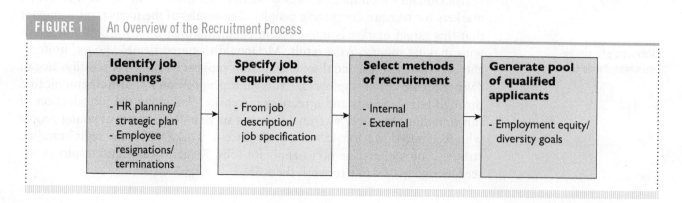

274

GLOBAL HRM

Recruiting European Candidates

An often overlooked option for managing the talent shortage is to recruit more candidates from Europe. Canada has strong ties to the European Union, and Europeans have a lot to offer the Canadian marketplace, including global business perspectives.

"An important value-added Europeans can bring to the Canadian market is their ability to interact and negotiate within a multicultural environment and context. This aptitude strengthens Canadian companies' ability to function better in Canada's increasingly multicultural environment," says David Delfini, head of business development at Volareweb/Alitalia.

For Europeans, Canada offers an opportunity for advancement they might not get at home. In Italy, for example, it is almost impossible to move up the ranks if you haven't dedicated at least 20 years to the company. A 2007 study by BlueSteps.com polled over 933 senior executives worldwide and revealed that traditional values about job tenure and loyalty remain well-ingrained with executives. The research also highlighted that 76 percent of European executives cited a lack of career advancement opportunities as the number one motivator to leave a company.

The borders have changed with the crisis of retiring Baby Boomers and impending talent shortages.

Countries are opening their doors. The world is building broader intellectual capacity and perspectives and better preparation for the global market. Europeans can offer Canadian organizations needed experience and a global perspective in a tightening labour market.

One company pursuing this strategy is EBA Engineering Consultants of Edmonton. They have successfully recruited people in the UK to relocate to western Canada by using a high-tech/high-touch promotional tool that communicates EBA's employment brand in a powerful way. A leather-bound album features stunning photographs of western Canada, testimonials from EBA employees who had been previously recruited from overseas, and a USB key that links candidates to a comprehensive website. At the back of the album, a leather luggage tag is mounted as a call to action, inviting candidates to pack their bags and join the EBA family in Canada.

Source: Adapted from A. Mirza, "Recruiting International Candidates," *HR Professional* (December 2008/January 2009), p. 27; and from K. Peters, "Public Image Ltd.," *HR Professional* (December 2007/January 2008), pp. 24–30. Reprinted with permission of *HR Professional*.

DEVELOPING AND USING APPLICATION FORMS

For most employers, completion of an application form is the last step in the recruitment process. An application form provides an efficient means of collecting verifiable historical data from each candidate in a standardized format; it usually includes information about education, prior work history, and other job-related skills.

A completed application form can provide the recruiter with information on the applicant's education and experience, a brief overview of the applicant's career progress and growth, and information that can be used to predict whether or not the candidate will succeed on the job. Even when detailed résumés have been submitted, most firms also request that a standardized company application form be completed. There are many reasons for this practice:

- Candidate comparison is facilitated because information is collected in a uniform manner.

- The information that the company requires is specifically requested, rather than just what the candidate wants to reveal.

- Candidates are typically asked to complete an application form while on the company premises, and thus it is a sample of the candidate's own work (obtaining assistance with résumés is common, given that many job boards offer online résumé building options).

- Application forms typically ask the candidate to provide written authorization for reference checking.

- Candidates are asked to acknowledge that the information provided is true and accurate, which protects the company from applicants who falsify their credentials.

- Many application forms today have an optional section regarding designated group member status. An example is provided in **Figure 2**. The data collected are used for employment equity tracking purposes.

biographical information blank (BIB) A detailed job application form requesting biographical data found to be predictive of success on the job, pertaining to background, experiences, and preferences. Responses are scored.

One type of application form that can be used to predict performance is a **biographical information blank (BIB)**, also known as a biodata form. Essentially, it is a more detailed version of an application form, focusing on biographical data found to be predictive of job success. Questions relating to age, gender, race, or other grounds prohibited under human rights legislation cannot be used. Candidates respond to a series of questions about their background, experiences, and preferences, including willingness to travel and leisure activities. Because biographical questions rarely have right or wrong answers, BIBs are difficult to fake. The development of a BIB requires that the items that are valid predictors of job success be identified and that scores be established for different responses to these items. By totalling the scores for each item, it is possible to obtain a composite score for each applicant.

There has been a shift in the format of the forms from the traditional pen and paper methods to online applications given the exposure to the World Wide Web and the advances in human resource information systems. **Figure 3** provides an example of an online application used by Canadian Tire to collect the same information that was traditionally collected in pen and paper format. Online applications significantly reduce the risk of lost applications, increase the exposure level of the job ad (global reach), and can reduce the likelihood of biases associated with other forms of face-to-face recruitment.

However, online application forms can result in a large number of applicants (for example, Google receives over 3000 applications per day[18]), therefore putting pressure on staff to manage the high volume of applicants. HRIS can be extremely useful here in automatically coding and storing applications, allowing HR professionals to search through the applications using specified search functions. The HRIS can also pre-screen applicants against predetermined criteria, providing an automated shortlist of qualified candidates. This significantly reduces the need for HR staff to screen résumés, but increases the importance of the content of the résumés and the validity of the pre-screening criteria. Due to the convenience and ubiquity of web browsers, application forms are increasingly being used online to allow applicants to build a profile and submit information directly or indirectly to potential employers. This offers around-the-clock convenience since applicants can create and submit applications or résumés on an ongoing and continuous real-time basis.

FIGURE 2   Self-Identification for Employment Equity Purposes

Employee Self-Identification Form

(Confidential when completed)

- This form is designed to collect information on the composition of the Public Service workforce to comply with legislation on employment equity and to facilitate the planning and implementation of employment equity activities. Your response is **voluntary** and you may identify in more than one designated group.

- The information you provide will be used in compiling statistics on employment equity in the federal Public Service. With your consent (see Box E), it may also be used by the employment equity coordinator of your department for human resource management purposes. This includes referral for training and developmental assignments and, in the case of persons with disabilities, facilitating appropriate accommodation in the workplace.

- Employment equity information will be retained in the Employment Equity Data Bank (EEDB) of the Treasury Board Secretariat and its confidentiality is protected under the *Privacy Act*. You have the right to review and correct information about yourself and can be assured that it will not be used for unauthorized purposes.

Step 1:   Complete boxes A to E. In boxes B, C and D, refer to the definitions provided.

Step 2:   Sign and date the form and return it to your department's EE coordinator.

*** Thank you for your cooperation.***

TBS/PPB 300-02432
TBS/SCT 330-78 (Rev. 1999–02)

A.

[   ]   [   ]

Family Name   Given Name and Initial

[   ]

Department or Agency/Branch

[(   )   ]   [   ]

Telephone # (office)   Personal Record Identifier (PRI)

○ Female   ○ Male

B. A person with a disability . . . (i) . . . has a long-term or recurring physical, mental, sensory, psychiatric, or learning impairment and

1. considers himself/herself to be disadvantaged in employment by reason of that impairement, or,

2. believes that an employer or potential employer is likely to consider him/her to be disadvantaged in employment by reason of that impairment,
   and includes persons whose functional limitations owing to their impairment have been accommodated in their current job or workplace.

ARE YOU A PERSON WITH A DISABILITY?

○ No

○ Yes, check all that apply

11 ○ **Co-ordination or dexterity** *(difficulty using hands or arms, for example, grasping or handling a stapler or using a keyboard)*

12 ○ **Mobility** *(difficulty moving around, for example, from one office to another or up and down stairs)*

16 ○ **Blind or visual impairment** *(unable to see or difficulty seeing)*

19 ○ **Deaf or hard of hearing** *(unable to hear or difficulty hearing)*

13 ○ **Speech impairment** *(unable to speak or difficulty speaking and being understood)*

continued

FIGURE 2 *(Continued)*

23 ○ **Other disability** *(including learning disabilities, developmental disabilities and all other types of disabilities)*

(Please specify) _____

C. An Aboriginal person . . .

. . . is a North American Indian or a member of a First Nation or who is Métis or Inuit. North American Indians or members of a First Nation include status, treaty or registered Indians, as well as non-status and non-registered Indians.

ARE YOU AN ABORIGINAL PERSON

○ No

○ Yes, check the appropriate circle

03 ○ North American Indian/First Nation

02 ○ Métis

01 ○ Inuit

D. A person in a visible minority . . .

. . . in Canada is someone (other than an Aboriginal person as defined in C above) who is non-white in colour/race, regardless of place of birth.

ARE YOU IN A VISIBLE MINORITY GROUP

○ No

○ Yes, check the circle which best describes your visible minority group or origin

41 ○ Black

45 ○ Chinese

51 ○ Filipino

47 ○ Japanese

48 ○ Korean

56 ○ South Asian/East Indian *(including Indian from India; Bangladeshi; Pakistani; East Indian from Guyana; Trinidad; East Africa; etc.)*

58 ○ Southeast Asian *(including Burmese; Cambodian; Laotian; Thai; Vietnamese; etc.)*

57 ○ Non-White West Asian, North African and Arab *(including Egyptian; Libyan; Lebanese; Iranian; etc.)*

42 ○ Non-White Latin American *(including indigenous persons from Central and South America, etc.)*

44 ○ Persons of Mixed Origin *(with one parent in one of the visible minority groups listed above)*

59 ○ Other Visible Minority Group

(Please specify) _____

E. 99○ The information in this form may be used for human resources management

_____   _____

Signature   Date (DD/MM/YY)

Source: Employee Self-Identification Form, www.tbs-sct.gc.ca/gui/iden2-eng.asp, Treasury Board of Canada Secretariat, 2002. Reproduced with the permission of the Minister of Public Works and Government Services Canada, 2012.

FIGURE 3 Sample Online Application Form—Canadian Tire

Source: Reproduced with permission of Canadian Tire.

RECRUITING FROM WITHIN THE ORGANIZATION

Although recruiting often brings job boards and employment agencies to mind, current employees are generally the largest source of recruits. Filling open positions with inside candidates has several advantages. According to human capital theory, the accumulation of firm-specific knowledge and experience involves a joint investment by both the employee and employer, therefore, both parties benefit from maintaining a long-term relationship. Employees see that competence is rewarded, thus enhancing their commitment, morale, and performance. Having already been with the firm for some time, insiders may be more committed to the company's goals and less likely to leave. Managers (as agents of the organization) are provided with a longer-term perspective when making business decisions. It is generally safer to promote from within, because the firm is likely to have a more accurate assessment of the person's skills and performance level than would otherwise be the case. In addition, inside candidates require less orientation than outsiders do.

Recruiting from within also has a number of drawbacks. Employees who apply for jobs and don't get them may become discontented (informing unsuccessful applicants as to why they were rejected and what remedial action they might take to be more successful in the future is thus essential).[19] Managers may be required to post all job openings and interview all inside candidates, even when they already know whom they want to hire, thus wasting considerable time and creating false hope on the part of those employees not genuinely being considered. Employees may be less satisfied with and accepting of a boss appointed from within their own ranks than they would be with a newcomer; it is sometimes difficult for a newly chosen leader to adjust to no longer being "one of the gang."[20] There is also a possibility of "inbreeding." When an entire management team has been brought up through the ranks, they may have a tendency to make decisions "by the book" and to maintain the status quo when a new and innovative direction is needed.

Internal Recruitment Methods

Recruiting from within can be accomplished by using job posting, human resources records, and skills inventories.

Job Posting

job posting The process of notifying current employees about vacant positions.

Job posting is a process of notifying current employees about vacant positions. Most companies now use computerized job-posting systems, where information about job vacancies can be found on the company's intranet. This involves a notice outlining the job title, duties (as listed in the job description), qualifications (taken from the job specification), hours of work, pay range, posting date, and closing date, as shown in **Figure 4**. Not all firms use intranets. Some post jobs on bulletin boards or in employee publications. As illustrated in **Figure 5**, there are advantages and disadvantages to using job postings to facilitate the transfer and promotion of qualified internal candidates.

An Ethical Dilemma

Suppose a manager has already made up his or her mind about who will be selected for an internal position. But an internal job posting and subsequent interviews have shown another equally qualified candidate. Who should be offered the position?

Human Resources Records

Human resources records are often consulted to ensure that qualified individuals are notified, in person, of vacant positions. An examination of employee files, including résumés and application forms, may uncover employees who are working in jobs below their education or skill levels, people who already have the requisite KSAs, or individuals with the potential to move into the vacant position if given some additional training.

Skills Inventories

Skills inventories are an even better recruitment tool. Although such inventories may be used instead of job postings, they are more often used as a supplement. Whether computerized or manual, referring to such inventories ensures that qualified internal candidates are identified and considered for transfer or promotion when opportunities arise.

Limitations of Recruiting from Within

It is rarely possible to fill all non-entry-level jobs with current employees. Middle- and upper-level jobs may be vacated unexpectedly, with no internal replacements yet qualified or ready for transfer or promotion; or the jobs may require such specialized training and experience that there are no potential internal replacements. Even in firms with a policy of promoting from within, potential external candidates are increasingly being considered to meet strategic objectives. Hiring someone from outside may be preferable in order to acquire the latest knowledge and expertise or to gain new ideas and revitalize the department or organization.[21]

FIGURE 4   Sample Job Posting: University of Alberta

Faculty of Physical Education and Recreation—Academic Programs

Competition No.: A103814421   Closing Date: June 3, 2011

The Academic Programs area of the Faculty of Physical Education and Recreation oversees and manages the academic programs of approximately 920 undergraduates in four undergraduate degree programs and 135 graduate students at the master's and doctoral level. The goal of this unit is to provide an optimal learning experience for our students. It is also responsible for the appointment and management of Sessional Instructors for the Fall and Winter courses and a combination of Graduate Teaching Assistants (GTAs) and Sessional staff for the Spring and Summer courses.

In order to aid in the overall strategic direction and planning of this unit, as well as undertaking necessary day-to-day service functions, this unit is seeking an Academic Programs Administrative Professional Officer (APO) who will lead important administrative aspects in a collegial working environment. Out of the 11 continuing staff members who work in the Academic Programs Unit, this position is one of two that reports directly to the Vice Dean. The APO is accountable for establishing/coordinating an efficient and effective administrative support system for the teaching and service functions of the Academic Programs Unit.

Responsibilities:

- Identifies, recruits, conducts preliminary interviews and makes final decision on appointments regarding the hiring of Sessional Academic Staff (Contract Academic Staff: Teaching (CAST)); prepares all data for the production of the CAST contracts for Fall and Winter terms and advises the Vice Dean on these appointments
- Manages and supervises the Faculty's Sessional teaching instructors including preparing and monitoring the Faculty's CAST budget
- Responsible for all human resource functions for seven full-time support staff including supervision and performance evaluations
- Responsible for the administrative support of the Faculty Evaluation Committee (FEC) process within the Faculty; for this activity the position is responsible to the Dean, as Chair of FEC within the Faculty
- Responsible for the preparation of the annual Academic Programs operating budget
- Advises the Academic Planning Committee on the relevant Faculty and University policies in all areas of operation
- Contributes to the development of policies and procedures for the Academic Unit and represents the best interests of the unit through membership on Faculty ad hoc task forces, committees, etc.
- Responsible for the Faculty of Physical Education and Recreation's section of the UofA calendar
- Schedules academic courses, final exams, course restrictions, and Management & Balancing Lab/Seminar sections
- Maintains and upgrades the functionality of the Faculty's Teaching Assignment database

Qualifications

- Bachelor's degree in Physical Education, Recreation, Kinesiology, or a related allied health field preferred; undergraduate degrees in other disciplines may be considered
- Excellent interpersonal, communication and written skills
- Ability to work effectively both in a team environment and independently
- Ability to work under tight timelines and make decisions involving the recruitment and appointment of CAST instructional staff
- Excellent PeopleSoft skills with both Campus Solutions and Human Capital Management
- Superior information systems skills including: MS Office Suite, WWW, etc.
- Superior analytical, problem-solving and critical-thinking skills
- Demonstrated ability to provide precise and concise information/advice to all areas in the unit
- Demonstrated strong leadership capabilities and organizational skills
- Strong financial analysis/reporting skills and attention to detail; ability to develop and monitor operating budgets in the Academic Programs Unit
- Well-developed planning and organization skills
- Extensive knowledge of University and Faculty Policies & Procedures

In accordance with the Administrative Professional Officer agreement, this full-time continuing position offers a comprehensive benefits package and annual salary range of $55,388–$92,316 (subject to current negotiations).

How to Apply

Apply Online

Note: Online applications are accepted until midnight Mountain Standard Time of the closing date.

Mail

Dr. Dan Syrotuik, Vice Dean
Academic Programs Office
Faculty of Physical Education and Recreation
University of Alberta
E407 Van Vliet Centre
EDMONTON, Alberta, T6G 2H9

Email
Dan.Syrotuik@ualberta.ca

Fax
(780) 492-6583

The University of Alberta hires on the basis of merit. We are committed to the principle of equity in employment. We welcome diversity and encourage applications from all qualified women and men, including persons with disabilities, members of visible minorities and Aboriginal persons.)

Source: Reprinted by permission of Recruitment Services, Human Resources, University of Alberta.

FIGURE 5 Advantages and Disadvantages of Job Posting

Advantages

- Provides every qualified employee with a chance for a transfer or promotion.
- Reduces the likelihood of special deals and favouritism.
- Demonstrates the organization's commitment to career growth and development.
- Communicates to employees the organization's policies and guidelines regarding promotions and transfers.
- Provides equal opportunity to all qualified employees.

Disadvantages

- Unsuccessful job candidates may become demotivated, demoralized, discontented, and unhappy if feedback is not communicated in a timely and sensitive manner.
- Tensions may rise if it appears that a qualified internal candidate was passed over for an equally qualified or less qualified external candidate.
- The decision about which candidate to select may be more difficult if there are two or more equally qualified candidates.

RECRUITING FROM OUTSIDE THE ORGANIZATION

RPC

Identifies the potential sources of internal and external qualified candidates

Unless there is a workforce reduction, even in firms with a promote from within policy, a replacement from outside must eventually be found to fill the job left vacant once all eligible employees have been given the opportunity for transfer or promotion. In addition, most entry-level positions must be filled by external candidates. The advantages of external recruitment include the following:

- the generation of a larger pool of qualified candidates, which may have a positive impact on the quality of the selection decision
- the availability of a more diverse applicant pool, which can assist in meeting employment equity goals and timetables
- the acquisition of skills or knowledge not currently available within the organization or the introduction of new ideas and creative problem-solving techniques
- the elimination of rivalry and competition caused by employees jockeying for transfers and promotions, which can hinder interpersonal and interdepartmental cooperation
- the potential cost savings resulting from hiring individuals who already have the required skills, rather than providing extensive training

Planning External Recruitment

When choosing the external recruitment method(s), several factors should be considered in addition to the constraints mentioned earlier. The type of job to be filled has a major impact on the recruitment method selected. For example, most firms normally rely on professional search firms for recruiting executive-level employees. In contrast, Internet advertising is commonly used for recruiting other salaried employees.

Yield ratios help to indicate which recruitment methods are the most effective at producing qualified job candidates. A **yield ratio** is the percentage of applicants that proceed to the next stage of the selection process. A recruiting yield pyramid, such as that shown in **Figure 6**, can be devised for each method by calculating the yield ratio for each step in the selection process.

The hypothetical firm in Figure 6 typically hires 50 entry-level accountants each year. As the figure illustrates, this company knows that if they recruit 1 200 potential new hires only 200 will be invited for interviews (a 6:1 ratio of leads generation to candidates interviewed). In other words, of six leads generated through college/university recruiting efforts, one applicant is invited to attend an interview. Of those, only 150 will actually make it to the interview process with a mere 100 being offered a position, and of those only 50 will accept and eventually be hired. The firm calculates that this method leads to a ratio of offers made to actual new hires of two to one (about half of the candidates to whom offers are made accept). The firm also knows that the ratio of candidates interviewed to offers made is three to two, while the ratio of candidates invited for interviews to candidates actually interviewed is generally four to three. Finally, the firm knows that the ratio between leads generated and candidates selected for interviews is six to one. Given these ratios, the firm knows that using this particular recruitment method, 1 200 leads must be generated to hire 50 new accountants. While this example identifies how yields are calculated and used, each organization typically determines their own desired yields based on industry, position, size, and resources of the organization to determine their own internal yield targets.

The average number of days from when the company initiates a recruitment method to when the successful candidate begins to work is called *time-lapse data*. Assume that the accounting company in the above example found the following scenario: Six days elapsed between submission of application forms and résumés to invitation for an interview; five days then passed from invitation to actual interview; five days from interview to job offer; six days from job offer to acceptance; and 23 days from acceptance of job offer to commencement of work. These data indicate that, using on-campus recruiting, the firm must initiate recruitment efforts at least 45 days before the anticipated job opening date. Calculating time-lapse data for each recruitment method means that the amount

yield ratio The percentage of applicants that proceed to the next stage of the selection process.

RPC

Evaluates recruiting effectiveness

| FIGURE 6 | Recruiting Yield Pyramid |

50 — New hires
100 — Offers made (100:50 = 2:1)
150 — Candidates interviewed (150:100 = 3:2)
200 — Candidates invited (200:150 = 4:3)
1200 — Leads generated (1200:200 = 6:1)

of lead time available can be taken into account when deciding which strategy or strategies would be most appropriate.

External Recruitment Methods

Many methods of recruiting from the external labour market are in use. A 2010 study by Right Management of 5 858 job seekers found that the most successful way to find a job was through traditional networking, followed by online job boards. The results of the study are highlighted in **Figure 7**. Traditional networking includes employee referrals, former employees who have remained in contact with the organization, concentrated job fairs based on relationships formed with educational institutes, professional and trade associations, labour organizations, and military personnel. Online job boards include traditional online job boards, corporate websites, and government-initiated job boards.

Employee Referrals

Some organizations encourage applications from friends and relatives of current employees by mounting an employee referral campaign. Openings are announced in the company's intranet or newsletter along with a request for referrals. Cash awards or prizes may be offered for referrals that culminate in a new hire. Because no advertising or agency fees are involved, paying bonuses still represents a low recruiting cost.

nepotism A preference for hiring relatives of current employees.

The disadvantages associated with employee referrals include the potential for inbreeding and **nepotism** to cause morale problems and dissatisfaction among employees whose referrals are not hired. Perhaps the biggest drawback, however, is that this method may result in systemic discrimination.

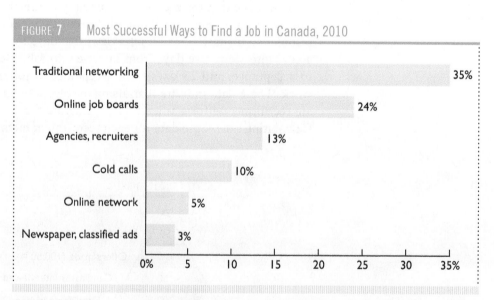

FIGURE 7   Most Successful Ways to Find a Job in Canada, 2010

Note: Often candidates rely on more than one method (for example, networking leads to an awareness about a job posted online in a colleague's company). The above survey forced respondents to identify only one tool that they used to find their most recent job.

Source: Survey by Right Management, published in "Networking Gets the Job Done," *Canadian HR Reporter* (August 15, 2011), p. 4.

Former Employees

In these times of talent shortage and diminishing employee loyalty, some organizations are making efforts to keep in touch with former employees who may be interested in rejoining the organization in future. Organizations such as Microsoft, Ernst & Young, and Procter & Gamble are establishing alumni networks that offer benefits such as healthcare, job boards, and alumni parties. About 25 percent of hires at the manager level and above at Microsoft are returning employees, known as "boomerangs."[22]

Educational Institutions

Recruiting at educational institutions is extremely effective when candidates require formal training but need relatively little full-time work experience. High schools can provide recruits for clerical and some blue-collar jobs. For example, Encana, an oil and gas company headquartered in Calgary, is facing an ongoing shortage of skilled workers. It has started a program called "Oil and Gas Production Field Operator Career Pathway," which offers high school students an opportunity to earn credits while learning about field production work. Beginning in Grade 10, students in participating high schools can sign up for a distance-learning course supplied by Calgary-based Southern Alberta Institute of Technology (SAIT). Students who progress through the course in all three years will graduate with a production field operation certificate from SAIT. Students will have a chance of getting one of at least six paid 8-week summer internship positions with Encana following each year.[23]

Many companies take recruitment campaigns into high schools to sell careers to a younger generation. This type of recruitment helps a variety of industries meet future recruitment demands. Here, students learn how to work on a car.

Most high schools, colleges, and universities have counselling centres that provide job-search assistance to students through such activities as skills assessment testing and workshops on résumé preparation and interview strategies. Sometimes they arrange for onsite job fairs, at which employers set up displays outlining the types of job opportunities available. The Halifax Career Fair, a partnership among Nova Scotia's universities and colleges, is the foremost recruiting event in Atlantic Canada. Every year the event attracts about 100 companies from across the country and 1 200 students.[24]

Cooperative (co-op) education and field placement programs have become increasingly popular in Canada. These programs require students to spend a specified amount of time working in organizations as an integral part of the academic program, thereby gaining some hands-on skills in an actual work setting. Co-op programs are offered in some high schools, as well as in colleges and universities.

Career Edge
www.careeredge.ca
Job Postings (Student Job Magazine)
www.jobpostings.ca
Halifax Career Fair
www.halifaxcareerfair.com

Summer internship programs hire college or university students to complete summer projects between their second-last and final year of study. Their performance is assessed, and those who are judged to be superior are offered permanent positions following graduation. Other firms offer internship opportunities to graduates, thereby enabling them to acquire hands-on skills to supplement their education. As with student internships, outstanding performers are often offered full-time employment at the end of the program. It is now possible for firms to recruit graduate interns online through Career Edge, an organization committed to helping university, college, and high school graduates gain essential career-related experience through internships. Career Edge uses the Internet as its sole means of bringing companies and youth together. More than 8 000 young Canadians have started their careers through the program in more than 1 000 organizations. Within a few months of completing their internship, nearly 80 percent of interns have found permanent employment with competitive salaries, and nearly 60 percent of the interns are hired by host organizations on a full-time basis.[25]

Internship, co-op, and field placement programs can produce a win–win result. The employer is provided with an inexpensive opportunity to assess potential employees while benefiting from the current knowledge and enthusiasm of bright, talented individuals. Because co-op students and interns have been exposed to the organization, they are less likely to leave shortly after permanent hire than recruits with no previous exposure to the firm.[26] Recognizing these benefits has made such programs a major recruitment method in many organizations.

Open Houses and Job Fairs

Another popular recruitment method involves holding an open house. Common in retail firms looking to staff a new store from the ground up, open houses have also been the choice of corporations trying to draw out scarce talent in an ultra-tight job market. A similar recruitment method involves holding a job fair onsite. At such events, recruiters share information about the organization and job opportunities with those attending in an informal, relaxed setting. Some organizations are now holding job fairs online (known as virtual job fairs) to connect with a wider geographical audience. Top prospects are invited to visit the firm or to return at a later date for a more in-depth assessment.

Professional and Trade Associations

CA Source
www.casource.com

Hire Authority
www.hireauthoritycanada.com

Professional and trade associations can be extremely helpful when recruiters are seeking individuals with specialized skills in such fields as IT, engineering, HR, and accounting, particularly if experience is a job requirement. Many such associations conduct ongoing placement activities on behalf of their members, and most regularly send their members newsletters or magazines in which organizations can place job advertisements. Such advertising may attract individuals who hadn't previously thought about changing jobs, as well as those actively seeking employment. For example, the Human Resources Professionals Association (HRPA) in Ontario has an employment service called the Hire Authority. For a nominal fee, employers can post HR-related employment opportunities on the HRPA website, where they can be viewed by HRPA members. Additionally, employers can pay for access to an online database of member résumés and can search, sort, and pre-screen qualified candidates for vacant positions.[27]

Labour Organizations

Some firms, particularly in the construction industry, obtain recruits through union hiring halls. The union maintains a roster of members (typically skilled trades people, such as carpenters, pipe fitters, welders, plumbers, and electricians), whom it sends out on assignment as requests from employers are received. Once the union members have completed their contracted work at one firm, they notify the union of their availability for another assignment.

Military Personnel

Military reservists are also potential recruits. The Canadian Forces Liaison Council (CFLC) is responsible for promoting the hiring of reservists by civilian employers. The CFLC also encourages civilian employers to give reservists time off for military training. Reserve force training develops skills and attributes sought after in the civilian workforce, such as leadership, planning, coordination, and teamwork.[28] Many organizations—such as Home Depot Canada and Énergie New Brunswick Power—have recognized the value of such leave and have joined the 4 700 organizations in Canada that have signed a statement of support for the reserve forces with the CFLC.[29] The CFLC's Reserve Employment Assistance Program (REAP) allows employers to place job postings for skilled personnel at more than 300 military units across the country at no charge.[30]

Online Recruiting

The majority of companies now use *online recruitment*, and a majority of Canadian workers use the Internet to research prospective employers, review job postings, complete online applications, and post their résumés. The Internet provides recruiters with a large audience for job postings and a vast talent pool. Online recruiting can involve accessing one or more Internet job boards, using a corporate website, or using social networking sites.

Internet Job Boards Online job boards are fast, easy, and convenient and allow recruiters to search for candidates for positions in two ways. First, companies can post a job opening online (often for a fee) and customize it by using corporate logos and adding details about the company benefits and culture. Job seekers can search through the job postings, often by job type, region, or other criterion, and apply for the position online through the job board. The popularity of Internet job boards among job seekers is high because of the number of job postings available on one site.

Second, job seekers can post their résumés on job boards, and firms can search the database. Canada has hundreds of job boards, ranging from the two largest, Workopolis and Monster, to many smaller job boards serving specific fields from tourism to medicine.[31] Job board meta-crawlers such as simplyhired. ca enable job seekers to search multiple job boards with one query.

The advantages of job boards include candidate assistance with self-assessment and résumé writing, and pre-screening assistance for recruiters. One problem with Internet job boards is their vulnerability to privacy breaches. Fake job postings can lead to identity theft from submitted résumés, and résumés are sometimes copied onto competing job boards or other sites.[32] As a result, job boards are now providing tips for job seekers on maintaining privacy and confidentiality.[33]

Corporate Websites With the overabundance of applicants found on most online job boards, employers are now using their own corporate websites to recruit.

Career pages provide a single platform for recruitment that promotes the employer brand, educates the applicant about the company, captures data about the applicant, and provides an important link to job boards where a company's positions may be advertised.[34] Virtual workplace tours using video can be provided to attract top talent aligned with the employer brand.[35] Corporate websites also help the company create a pool of candidates who have already expressed interest in the organization.[36]

Using pre-screening strategies is essential, however. The volume of résumés definitely does not diminish when the firm accepts them online. At Hewlett-Packard, for example, more than 1 million online applications are received each year.[37] One way of coping with this volume is to generate automatic replies acknowledging receipt of applications.[38] Applicant tracking software is available to help recruiters track individual candidates through the recruitment and selection processes and to enable candidates to keep their profiles up to date.

Active job seekers are not the only potential future employees who visit corporate websites. Customers, investors, and competitors also visit them.[39] Many of those visiting career websites are "happily employed" individuals (known as "passive" job seekers) who are likely to arrive at the career site after browsing the company's main pages for other reasons, such as research into products or services. Therefore, it is important that a firm have a prominently positioned link on the homepage leading directly to the careers section to make it easy for passive job seekers to pursue job opportunities within the company.[40]

Tips FOR THE FRONT LINE

Best practices for career websites include the following:

- Include candid information about company culture, career paths, and business prospects.

- Include third-party sources of information on your company, such as articles, rankings, and awards.

- Design separate sections for different types of job seekers, such as students and part-timers.

- Have a direct link from the homepage to the career page.

- Have a job search tool that allows applicants to search open job positions by location and job category.

- Have a standardized application or résumé builder to allow for easy applicant screening.

- Use "email to a friend" options for visitor referrals.[41]

Human Resources and Skills Development Canada (HRSDC)

Job Bank
www.jobbank.gc.ca

Training and Careers
www.jobsetc.gc.ca

Through various programs, including those for youth, Aboriginals, and persons with disabilities, HRSDC helps unemployed individuals find suitable jobs and helps employers locate qualified candidates to meet their needs—at no cost to either party. The Job Bank is the largest web-based network of job postings available to Canadian employers free of charge, and it provides access to 700 000 new jobs each year, with more than 40 000 jobs at any given time and up to 2 000 new jobs posted every day. HRSDC also operates Job Match, a web-based recruitment tool that can match employers' skill requirements with individuals' skill sets. Job seekers receive a list of employers with a matching job vacancy and employers receive a list of qualified candidates.[42]

Executive Search Firms

Employers use executive search firms to fill critical positions in a firm, usually middle- to senior-level professional and managerial positions. Such firms often specialize in a particular type of talent, such as executives, sales, scientific, or middle-management employees. They typically know and understand the marketplace, have many contacts, and are especially adept at contacting qualified candidates who are employed and not actively looking to change jobs (which is why they have been given the nickname "headhunters"). Generally, one-third of the fee is payable as a retainer at the outset. Compared with the value of the time savings realized by the client firm's executive team, however, such a fee often turns out to be insignificant.

Using this recruitment method has some potential pitfalls.[43] Executive search firms cannot do an effective job if they are given inaccurate or incomplete information about the job or the firm. It is therefore essential for employers to explain in detail the type of candidate required—and why. A few headhunters are more salespeople than professionals, and they are more interested in persuading the employer to hire a candidate rather than in finding one who really meets the job specifications. Some firms have also been known to present an unpromising candidate to a client simply to make their one or two other prospects look that much better. The Association of Canadian Search, Employment, and Staffing Services (ACSESS) sponsors the Certified Personnel Consultant (CPC) designation, which signifies that recruiters have met specific educational and testing requirements and confirms an individual's commitment to best industry practices.[44]

Private Employment Agencies

Private employment agencies are often called on to provide assistance to employers seeking clerical staff, functional specialists, and technical employees. The "staffing" business has grown into a $6 billion industry that places hundreds of thousands of job seekers each year.[45] Generally, it is the employer who pays the agency fee. It is not uncommon for employers to be charged a fee equal to 15 to 30 percent of the first year's salary of the individual hired through agency referral. This percentage may vary depending on the volume of business provided by the client and the type of employee sought.

These agencies take an employer's request for recruits and then solicit job seekers, relying primarily on Internet job boards, advertising, and walk-ins/write-ins. Employment agencies serve two basic functions: (1) expanding the applicant pool and (2) performing preliminary interviewing and screening. Specific situations in which an employment agency might be used for recruiting include the following:

- The organization does not have an HR department or does not have anyone with the requisite time and/or expertise.

- The firm has experienced difficulty in generating a pool of qualified candidates for the position or a similar type of position in the past.

Association of Canadian Search, Employment, and Staffing Services (ACSESS)
www.acsess.org

- A particular opening must be filled quickly.

- There is a desire to recruit a greater number of designated group members than the firm has been able to attract on its own.

- The recruitment effort is aimed at reaching individuals who are currently employed and might therefore feel more comfortable answering ads placed by and dealing with an employment agency.

Tips FOR THE FRONT LINE

It should be noted, however, that the amount of service provided varies widely, as does the level of professionalism and the calibre of staff. Although most agencies carefully screen applicants, some simply provide a stream of applicants and let the client's HR department staff do the screening. Agency staff is usually paid on a commission basis, and their desire to earn a commission may occasionally compromise their professionalism (for example, encouraging job seekers to accept jobs for which they are neither qualified nor suited).

Cold Calls: Walk-Ins and Write-Ins

Individuals who go to organizations in person to apply for jobs without referral or invitation are called walk-ins. People who submit unsolicited résumés to organizations are known as write-ins. Walk-ins and write-ins are an inexpensive recruitment method. Their résumés are generally screened by the HR department and if an applicant is considered suitable, his or her résumé is retained on file for three to six months or passed on to the relevant department manager if there is an immediate or upcoming opening for which the applicant is qualified. Some organizations, such as RBC Financial Group, are using computer databases to store the information found on the résumés and application forms of walk-in and write-in candidates. Whether the original document is paper based or submitted online, it can be scanned and stored in databases for fast, easy access using a few key words.[46]

Online Networking Sites

Many organizations are turning to social networking sites like Facebook to find young, tech-savvy recruits. Some create virtual recruitment booths and others create a company profile where they can post jobs and publicize their employer brand. Other users seeking jobs can become "friends" of potential employers and upload their profiles, which contain more information than résumés. Ernst & Young is one firm that has used this approach—it has even established its own company social networking site for employees and alumni.[47]

An Ethical Dilemma

Is it ethical to use personal information on social networking sites to assess job candidates?

The advantage of using social networking for recruitment purposes is the opportunity to connect with millions of other users at little or no cost. One disadvantage is the possibility of unhappy employees or customers posting negative comments on the site.[48]

Print Advertising

Despite the advent of online recruiting, traditional advertising in newspapers and other print media is still a very common method of recruiting.[49] For advertising to bring the desired results, two issues must be addressed: the media to be used and the construction of the ad.[50] The selection of the best medium—whether it is the local newspaper, a national newspaper, a technical journal, or even a billboard—depends on the types of positions for which the organization is recruiting. Reaching individuals who are already employed and not actively seeking alternative employment requires a different medium than is appropriate to attract those who are unemployed.

To achieve optimum results from an advertisement, the following four-point guide, called AIDA, should be kept in mind as the ad is being constructed:

1. The ad should *attract attention*. The ads that stand out have borders, a company logo or picture, and effective use of empty white space. To attract attention, key positions should be advertised in display ads, rather than classified ads.

2. The ad should develop *interest* in the job. Interest can be created by the nature of the job itself, by pointing out the range of duties or the amount of challenge or responsibility involved. Sometimes other aspects of the job, such as its location or working conditions, are useful in attracting interest. To ensure that the individuals attracted are qualified, the job specifications should always be included.

3. The ad should create a *desire* for the job. This may be done by capitalizing on the interesting aspects of the job itself or by pointing out any unique benefits or opportunities associated with it, such as the opportunity for career development or travel. Desire may also be created by stressing the employer's commitment to employment equity. The target audience should be kept in mind as the ad is being created.

4. The ad should instigate *action*. To prompt action, ads often include a closing date and a statement such as "Call today," "Send your résumé today," "Check out our website for more information," or "Go to the site of our next job fair."

When properly constructed, advertisements can be an effective instrument for recruiting, as well as for communicating the organization's corporate image to the general public.

There are two general types of newspaper advertisements: want ads and blind ads. **Want ads** describe the job and its specifications, the compensation package, and the hiring employer. Although the content pertaining to the job, specifications, and compensation is identical in **blind ads**, such ads omit the identity and address of the hiring employer. Although many job seekers do not like responding to blind ads because there is always the danger of unknowingly sending a résumé to the firm at which they are currently employed, such ads do result in the opening remaining confidential (which may be necessary if the position is still staffed).

Many factors make advertising a useful recruiting method. Employers can use advertisements to reach and attract potential job applicants from a diverse labour market in as wide or narrow a geographical area as desired. To meet employment equity goals and timetables, ads can be placed in publications read by designated group members, such as a minority-language newspaper or the newsletter of a not-for-profit agency assisting individuals who have a particular mental or physical disability.

Recruiting Non-Permanent Staff

In recent years, many companies have increased their use of contingent workers to attain labour flexibility and acquire employees with special skills on an as needed basis. In these firms, recruiters are spending more time seeking temporary

want ad A recruitment ad describing the job and its specifications, the compensation package, and the hiring employer. The address to which applications or résumés should be submitted is also provided.

blind ad A recruitment ad in which the identity and address of the employer are omitted.

(term, seasonal, casual) and contract workers and less time recruiting permanent staff.[51] Two common sources of non-permanent staff are temporary help agencies and contract workers.

Temporary Help Agencies

Temporary help agencies, such as Kelly Services and Office Overload, exist in major cities in Canada. They specialize in providing temporary workers to cover for employees who are ill, on vacation, or on a leave of absence. Firms also use temporary employees to handle seasonal work, peak workloads, and special projects for which no current employees have the time or expertise. Temporary workers (temps) are agency employees and are reassigned to another employer when their services are no longer required.

Temps provide employers with three major benefits:

1. They cost much less than permanent employees, as they generally receive less compensation than permanent staff. There are also savings related to the hiring and training costs associated with permanent employees. In fact, training has become the central investment in the business strategy of many temporary employment agencies. For example, Accountemps invests in the skills and training of employees after they have worked for a specified amount of time. This training includes online tutoring in software they may use on the job and tuition reimbursement for skills training.[52]

2. If a temp performs unsatisfactorily, a substitute can be requested immediately. Generally, a suitable replacement is sent to the firm within one business day.

3. Individuals working as temps who are seeking full-time employment are often highly motivated, knowing that many firms choose full-time employees from the ranks of their top-performing temps.

The number of temporary and freelance workers is increasing all over the world. Freelancing allows employers to match their job needs to independent workers who complete tasks on an as needed basis.

Contract Workers

contract workers Employees who develop work relationships directly with the employer for a specific type of work or period of time.

Contract workers are employees who develop work relationships directly with the employer for a specific type of work or period of time.[53] For example, Parc Aviation is a major supplier of contract workers to the airline industry. Airline organizations benefit from the services of contract engineers by having them cover seasonal or unplanned peaks in business, carry out special tasks or projects, and reduce the necessity for airlines to downsize permanent staff during cyclical downturns.[54]

Many professionals with specialized skills become contract workers, including project managers, accountants, and lawyers. Some have consciously made a decision to work for themselves; others have been unable to obtain full-time employment in their field of expertise or have found themselves out of a full-time job because of

An Ethical : Dilemma

Is it ethical to keep extending the contracts of contract workers rather than hiring them as permanent employees to avoid the cost of employee benefits?

cutbacks. Thus, some want to remain self-employed; others work a contract while hoping to obtain a full-time position eventually. Some firms hire former employees (such as retirees) on a contract basis.

RECRUITING A MORE DIVERSE WORKFORCE

Recruiting a diverse workforce is not just socially responsible—it's a necessity. As noted previously, the composition of Canada's workforce is changing dramatically. Trends of particular significance include the increasing necessity of hiring older employees, a decrease in the availability of young workers, and an increase in the number of women, visible minorities, Aboriginal people, and persons with disabilities in the workforce.

Attracting Older Workers

Prime50
www.prime50.com

Many employers, recognizing the fact that the workforce is aging, are encouraging retirement-age employees to stay with the company or are actively recruiting employees who are at or beyond retirement age. For example, 20 percent of Home Depot Canada's workforce is over the age of 50.[55] Hiring and retaining older employees has significant benefits. These workers typically have high job satisfaction, a strong sense of loyalty and organizational commitment, a strong work ethic, good people skills, and a willingness to work in a variety of roles, including part time.[56]

To make a company attractive to older workers, it is important to deal with stereotypical attitudes toward older workers through education, ensure that HR policies do not discourage recruitment of older workers, develop flexible work arrangements, and redesign jobs to accommodate decreased dexterity and strength. Canadian employers have been encouraged to take action to retain and recruit older workers as they represent a large, underutilized, skilled labour pool, but so far little effort has been made to attract these people.[57] A 2008 Conference Board of Canada study found that the most common recruitment strategy for older workers was rehiring former employees and retirees. Less than 20 percent were using recruitment campaigns directed specifically at mature workers.[58]

Attracting Younger Employees

Many firms are recognizing the benefits of a multigenerational workforce and are not only trying to attract older workers, but are also taking steps to address the pending shortage of younger employees. Although older employees have comparatively wider experience and wisdom, the young bring energy, enthusiasm, and physical strength to their positions.

Successful organizations balance these different kinds of experience. McDonald's Restaurants of Canada (one of the largest employers of youth in the country and an active recruiter of seniors) feels that it is critical for organizations in the service industry to have employees who mirror their customer base. Its experience is that each member of the multi-age teams brings a particular strength, which leads to synergy, respect, and team building.[59]

Younger members of the workforce are part of the Generation X and Generation Y cohorts. To appeal to Generation Xers, it is important to stress that they will be able to work independently and that work–life balance is supported. Potential employees from Generation Y will want to know that they will be working with experts from across the organization and that the will have a variety of experiences, as described in the Strategic HR box. They will be attracted by organizations that value social responsibility, diversity, and creativity.[60] Accounting firm Meyers Norris Penny built an award-winning student recruiting campaign around the question "What do you want?" which resulted in continuously improving the quality of the students hired.[61]

STRATEGIC HR

Attracting the Younger Generation

The authors of the book *Bridging the Generation Gap* asked 500 Gen Ys this question: "What's important to you on the job?" The top three responses were quality of friendships, feeling they can make a contribution on the job, and a feeling of safety. These young workers want an organization where they can create friendships, much as they did in school. In other words, the organization must have a social flair to catch their eye. Some examples include a company sports league and company social events like movie nights or meeting after work for a drink. But these quality relationships must go along with a feeling that what they do adds value to the organization.

The Gen Ys said that the top three ways an organization can entice their generation to want employment with the organization are offering a competitive salary, a casual work environment, and growth/development opportunities such as mentoring and training. Other benefits that organizations can offer to entice younger workers include state-of-the-art technology, opportunities to volunteer in the community (on company time), regular feedback, tuition reimbursement programs, strong reward and recognition programs, and a connection to the mission and vision of the organization.

The younger generation aims to take advantage of every form of technology to make their job search successful and easier. Organizations need to advertise jobs on multiple online job boards, including local, national, and trade related. Organizations should also create a job board on the company's website that should be regularly updated and provide an easy and responsive way for candidates to apply online. The posting should include an email address for the HR department or an online application process. For the process to succeed, organizations must regularly check the applications and follow-up with candidates.

The actual copy of the ads is critical. Certain key words attract these individuals to an organization's ads when they do online searches. The younger generation likes short, snappy copy that gets right to the point of what they will be doing. But of equal or more importance, the ad needs to advertise the culture of the organization as it relates to the values of this generation. The ads should include statements such as "fast-paced environment," "individual contribution," "work–life balance," "do it your way," "opportunity to grow," "no rules," and "state-of-the-art technology." Of course, organizations should only list these kinds of features in the ads if they truly offer them. Otherwise, the organization will see just how fast these workers will leave a company that doesn't fulfill its promises.

Source: Adapted from R. Throckmorton and L. Gravett, "Attracting the Younger Generation," *Canadian HR Reporter* (April 23, 2007).

Recruiting Designated Group Members

Most of the recruitment methods already discussed can be used to attract members of designated groups (Aboriginal people, women, visible minorities, and persons with disabilities), provided that the employer's commitment to

After struggling to restart his career in Canada, Sibaway Issah found the assistance he needed with Career Edge, a not-for-profit agency that links qualified immigrants with possible employers.

Aboriginal Human Resource Council
http://aboriginalhr.ca

Canadian Council on Rehabilitation and Work
www.ccrw.org

WORKink
www.workink.com

HireImmigrants.ca
www.hireimmigrants.ca

equality and diversity is made clear to all involved in the recruitment process—whether it is employees who are asked for referrals or private employment agencies. This can also be stressed in all recruitment advertising. Alternative publications targeted at designated group members should be considered for advertising, and linkages can be formed with organizations and agencies specializing in assisting designated group members. Specific examples follow.

The Aboriginal Human Resource Council, headquartered in Saskatoon, Saskatchewan, sponsors the Aboriginal Inclusion Network, which offers a job board, résumé database, and other tools to hire, retain, and promote Aboriginal talent. The Inclusion Network is linked to 350 Aboriginal employment centres across Canada, and the number of job seekers on the network increased 70 percent from 2009 to 2011.[62]

The Society for Canadian Women in Science and Technology (SCWIST) is a not-for-profit, volunteer organization aimed at improving attitudes and stereotypes about and assisting women in scientific, technological, and engineering careers. Employers can access valuable resources such as websites, employment agencies, and publications to attract professional women for employment opportunities in industries where they generally have a low representation.[63]

WORKink is Canada's most powerful online career development and employment portal for Canadians with disabilities. The WORKink site offers a full complement of employment and recruitment resources and services for job seekers with disabilities and for employers looking to create an inclusive workplace. WORKink is sponsored by the Canadian Council on Rehabilitation and Work. Employers can post job openings free of charge, browse résumés of people with disabilities, or access information on how to adapt the work environment to accommodate people with disabilities in their region.[64]

The Ontario Ministry of Community and Social Services sponsors a program called Paths to Equal Opportunity intended to provide links to information on removing and preventing barriers so that people with disabilities can work, learn, and play to their fullest potential. In conjunction with the Canadian Abilities Foundation, the program publishes a resource booklet called *Abilities @ Work*, which provides specific information to employers who want to find out about recruiting, interviewing, hiring, and working with people with disabilities. It also provides information to employees and job seekers with disabilities who want information on looking for work, accommodation in the workplace, and maintaining employment.

Another useful tool is the guidebook *Tapping the Talents of People with Disabilities: A Guidebook for Employers*, which is available through the Conference Board of Canada. More information on hiring people with disabilities is provided in the Workforce Diversity box.

WORKFORCE DIVERSITY

The Disconnect in Recruiting People with Disabilities

The good news is that employers want to hire people with disabilities, and qualified candidates are available. But putting employers and job seekers together needs improved coordination to create more success stories. Employers have bottom-line reasons for building workforce diversity. Inclusiveness is a competitive advantage that lets an organization better connect with a diverse community and customer base. Inclusiveness provides access to a larger pool of strong job candidates in a time of skills shortages and enhances an organization's reputation as an employer of choice.

So why aren't more employers tapping into the wealth of human potential in people with disabilities? After all, as a group they make up roughly 13 percent of the working-age population. That is precisely what the Canadian Abilities Foundation set out to determine in its recently completed Neglected or Hidden study, the findings of which may surprise employers.

Likely the most revealing finding that illustrates the need for a new employment strategy for people with disabilities is the disconnect that exists among employers, people with disabilities, and the service providers who help these individuals enter the workforce.

With few exceptions, these stakeholders just don't seem to know how to communicate with one another,

if they are fortunate enough to find one another in the first place. The commitment and passion of workers with disabilities and those assisting them is sound. Meanwhile, hundreds of disability-related organizations across Canada provide some level of employment support to their clients. The Neglected or Hidden study suggests that the number of Canadian employers willing to hire people with disabilities should be more than adequate to meet the availability of disabled job seekers.

The good news is that a small number of disability organizations have made significant inroads in their regions by using employer partnerships. One example is the Dartmouth Work Activity Society in Nova Scotia, which started its new approach with just a single employer "partner" who was highly satisfied with the services provided. EmployAbilities, a full-time service agency serving Edmonton and northern Alberta for more than 35 years, has also launched a partnership-building strategy. A unique feature of the agency's approach is its partnership with the local chamber of commerce through which it offers advice on disability issues to employers.

Source: Adapted from A. Prost, "Successful Recruiting from an Untapped Source," *Canadian HR Reporter* (January 16, 2006), pp. 11–12.

Chapter SUMMARY

1. Recruitment is the process of searching out and attracting qualified job applicants. It begins with the identification of a position that requires staffing and is completed when résumés or completed application forms are received. In order to manage the increasing talent shortage, proactive employers are trying to obtain a competitive advantage in recruitment by establishing themselves as employers of choice through employer branding.

2. The recruitment process has four steps. First, job openings are identified through HR planning or manager request. Second, the job description and job specifications are reviewed to determine the job requirements. Third, appropriate recruiting source(s) and method(s) are chosen. Fourth, using these strategies, a pool of qualified candidates is generated.

3. Application forms have been largely replaced by online applications, where candidates provide information on education and experience, a brief overview of past career progress, and other information that can be used to predict whether an applicant will succeed on the job.

4. Job posting is the process of notifying existing employees about vacant positions. Human resources records may indicate appropriate applicants for vacant positions. Skills inventories may provide even better information.

5. External recruitment methods include traditional networking, online job boards, agencies, recruiters, cold calls, online networks, and print ads.

6. Two strategies for obtaining non-permanent staff include using temporary help agencies and hiring contract workers.

7. Recruiting a diverse workforce is a necessity, given the shrinking labour force. In particular, recruiters are trying to attract older workers, younger workers, women, visible minorities, Aboriginal people, and people with disabilities.

MyManagementLab

Visit MyManagementLab to access a personalized Study Plan and additional study tools for this chapter.

Key TERMS

biographical information blank (BIB)
blind ad
contract workers
employer branding
job posting

nepotism
recruiter
recruitment
want ad
yield ratio

Review and Discussion QUESTIONS

1. Discuss the advantages and disadvantages of recruiting from within the organization. Identify and describe the three tools that are used in this process.

2. Brainstorm the advantages of external recruitment. Discuss the risks associated with external recruiting.

3. Explain the difference between an Internet job board and a corporate career website.

4. Under what circumstances should a private employment agency be used?

5. Describe the advantages of using online application forms or résumé repositories as part of the recruitment process.

Critical Thinking QUESTIONS

1. What potential problems may result if the employer branding value proposition presented during the recruitment process is not reinforced once the new recruit is working for the organization? What could organizations do to avoid this situation?

2. What potential problems could be created by offering referral bonuses to existing employees?

3. Compare and contrast the advantages and disadvantages of traditional and virtual career fairs.

4. As the labour supply gets tighter and tighter, would you be in favour of loosening requirements for foreign-trained professionals (for example, doctors, professors, accountants, engineers) to become immediately qualified in Canada? Why or why not? Identify the underlying assumptions in the position you took.

5. What are some of the specific reservations that a 30-year-old candidate might have about applying for a job that requires managing a workforce that is on average 10 years older than he or she is?

6. Assume you are the HR manager in a highly homogenous company that now wants to better reflect the diversity of the target client group in its employee population. What must you consider as you think about implementing your new recruitment strategy?

Experiential EXERCISES

1. Go to your university's or college's career centre and gather information on all the services they provide. How many companies come to recruit students through the centre each year? What services does the centre provide to employers seeking to hire graduating students? Employers seeking to hire summer students? Employers seeking to hire students for internships?

2. Given the importance of networking to recruitment success, organize the class around core jobs that students would like to have. In each group, brainstorm sources of networking. Poll the group to determine how many people in the group are taking advantage of each available network. Highlight reasons for low involvement and brainstorm ideas about how these challenges can be overcome.

3. Considering the current economic situation and using the following list of jobs, identify all of the sources that could be used to recruit qualified applicants:

- Registered nurses to work in the critical care unit of a new regional hospital

- Carpenters to work on a new home building project

- Chief financial officer for an international engineering firm with a head office located in Vancouver

- Retail sales associates to work in an urban clothing chain

- Customer service representatives to work in a bank branch

- Bilingual administrative assistants for a Canadian financial services company operating internationally

Running CASE

Getting Better Applicants

If Jennifer and Pierre were asked what the main problem was in running their business, their answer would be quick and short: hiring good people. They were simply astonished at how hard it was to attract and hire good candidates. After much debate, they decided to post openings for seven positions: two salespeople, one web designer, two content management people, one office manager, and one web surfer.

Their first approach was to design and place a large display ad in two local newspapers. The display ad listed all the positions available. Jennifer and Pierre assumed that by placing a large ad with the name of the company prominently displayed and a bold border around the ad, it would draw attention and therefore generate applicants. For two consecutive weekends, the ad cost the fledgling company close to $1000, but it produced only a handful of applicants. After speaking with them by phone, Jennifer and Pierre rejected three outright, two said they weren't interested, and two scheduled interviews but never showed up.

The owners therefore decided to change their approach. They used different recruiting methods for each position. In the paper, they placed ads for the salespeople under "Sales" and for the office manager under "Administrative."

They advertised for a web designer by placing an ad on Monster.ca. And for the content managers and web surfer they placed neatly typed help wanted ads in the career placement offices of a technical college and a community college about 10 minutes away from their office. They also used this job posting approach to find independent contractors they could use to physically deliver courses to users' homes or offices.

The results were disappointing. Over a typical weekend, literally dozens of want ads for experienced salespeople appear, as well as almost as many for office managers. The ad for salespeople generated three calls, one of whom Jennifer and Pierre felt might be a viable candidate, although the person wanted a much higher salary than they had planned to pay. One possible candidate emerged for the office manager position.

They decided to change the positioning of the sales ad in the newspaper from "Salespersons Wanted" to "Phone Sales," which is a separate category (since the job involved entirely inside phone sales). Many of the calls they got (not all of them, but many) were from salespeople who were used to working in what some people called "boiler-room" operations. In other words, they sit at the phone all day making cold calls from lists provided by their employers, selling anything from burglar alarms to investments, all under very high-pressure conditions. They weren't interested in LearnInMotion, nor was LearnInMotion interested in them.

They fared a little better with the web designer ad, which produced four possible applicants. They got no phone calls from the local college job postings; when they called to ask the placement offices why, they were told that their posted salary of $8 per hour was "much too low." They went back and replaced the job postings with $10 hourly rates.

"I just don't understand it," Jennifer finally said. Especially for the sales job, Jennifer and Pierre felt that they were offering perfectly acceptable compensation packages, so the lack of applicants surprised them. "Maybe a lot of people just don't want to work for dot-coms anymore," said Pierre, thinking out loud. "When the bottom fell out of the dot-com market, a lot of good people were hurt by working for a series of two or three failed dot-coms. Maybe they've just had enough of the wired world."

QUESTIONS

1. Describe how the recruitment process (including all of the steps) outlined in Figure 1 will be of assistance to Jennifer and Pierre to solve their recruitment problems.

2. Draft a new job posting for each of the seven positions discussed in the case. Then discuss how you put the job postings together and why, using Figure 2 and Figure 3 as examples.

Case INCIDENT

Solving a Potential Recruitment Dilemma

Rachel Lucas is the human resources manager of a prestigious accounting firm. Rachel recently attended a local human resources professionals' association meeting where recruitment was the topic up for discussion. At this meeting all aspects of the recruitment process, including recruitment methods and how to increase diversity through the use of application forms, were to be discussed. Rachel couldn't wait to apply what she learned at this meeting to her job.

While listening to the scheduled speaker for the evening, Rachel started to think about the current recruitment initiatives she was dealing with at work. The firm was entering its traditional busy season where many clients would need tax returns completed. This time every year she needed to source and hire quality, qualified candidates to fill 50 tax preparer positions. The partners were relying heavily on her this year to get higher quality candidates because of the complex returns that would have to be completed, and to have them in place within three weeks.

As the speaker was finishing his presentation, Rachel wondered what recruitment process and techniques she should use. What would be the best decisions for the firm?

QUESTIONS

1 Should Rachel use internal or external recruitment techniques to staff these 50 positions?

2 Rachel is hoping to recruit qualified candidates from a variety of diverse demographics. Will she have to use different recruitment techniques to do this? If so, what ones are the most effective to attract these candidates (older workers, designated group members, and so on)?

3 Rachel plans on hiring recruiters to assist her in staffing these 50 positions. Knowing the company will require the recruiters to adhere to the concept of employer branding, describe what steps Rachel should take to orient the new recruiters to the branding process.

MyManagementLab

Visit MyManagementLab to access a personalized Study Plan and additional study tools for this chapter.

 To view the CBC videos, read a summary, and answer discussion questions, go to MyManagementLab

NOTES

1. G. Bouchard, "Strong Employer Brand Can Tap Scarce Resource: Talent," *Canadian HR Reporter* (November 19, 2007), p. 10.

2. "Effective Recruiting Tied to Stronger Financial Performance," *WorldatWork Canadian News* (Fourth Quarter, 2005), pp. 18–19.

3. K. Peters, "Public Image Ltd," *HR Professional* (December 2007/January 2008), pp. 24–30; S. Klie, "Getting Employees to Come to You," *Canadian HR Reporter* (November 19, 2007), pp. 9–10; S. Klie, "Tuning into TV's Recruitment Reach," *Canadian HR Reporter* (September 25, 2006).

4. G. Bouchard, "Strong Employer Brand Can Tap Scarce Resource: Talent," *Canadian HR Reporter* (November 19, 2007), p. 10.

5. K. Peters, "Public Image Ltd," *HR Professional* (December 2007/January 2008), pp. 24–30; G. Bouchard, "Strong Employer Brand Can Tap Scarce Resource: Talent," *Canadian HR Reporter* (November 19, 2007), p. 10; M. Morra, "Best in Show," *Workplace News* (September/October 2006), pp. 17–21; M. Shuster, "Employment Branding: The Law of Attraction!" *Workplace* (January/February 2008), pp. 14–15.

6. M. Morra, "Best in Show," *Workplace News* (September/October 2006), pp. 17–21.

7. G. Bouchard, "Strong Employer Brand Can Tap Scarce Resource: Talent," *Canadian HR Reporter* (November 19, 2007), p. 10.

8. S. Klie, "Getting Employees to Come to You," *Canadian HR Reporter* (November 19, 2007), pp. 9–10; M. Shuster, "Employment Branding: The Law of Attraction!" *Workplace* (January/February 2008), pp. 14–15.

9. K. Peters, "Public Image Ltd," *HR Professional* (December 2007/January 2008), pp. 24–30; S. Dobson, "The Little School Bus Company That Could," *Canadian HR Reporter* (April 23, 2007).

10. M. Shuster, "Employment Branding: The Law of Attraction!" *Workplace* (January/February 2008), pp. 14–15.

11. A. Watanabe, "From Brown to Green, What Colour Is Your Employment Brand?" *HR Professional* (February/March 2008), pp. 47–49.

12. M. Morra, "Best in Show," *Workplace News* (September/October 2006), pp. 17–21.

13. R. Milgram, "Getting the Most Out of Online Job Ads," *Canadian HR Reporter* (January 28, 2008).

14. K. Peters, "Public Image Ltd," *HR Professional* (December 2007/January 2008), pp. 24–30; S. Klie, "Getting Employees to Come to You," *Canadian HR Reporter* (November 19, 2007), pp. 9–10.

15. S. Klie, "Getting Employees to Come to You," *Canadian HR Reporter* (November 19, 2007), pp. 9–10; M. Shuster, "Employment Branding: The Law of Attraction!" *Workplace* (January/February 2008), pp. 14–15.

16. "Recruitment Tops HR Areas Expecting 'Enormous Change,'" *Canadian HR Reporter* (December 6, 2004), p. G3; *Hewitt Associates Timely Topic Survey* (February 2004).

17. H.N. Chait, S.M. Carraher, and M.R. Buckley, "Measuring Service Orientation with Biodata," *Journal of Management Issues* (Spring 2000), pp. 109–120; V.M. Catano, S.F. Cronshaw, R.D. Hackett, L.L. Methot, and W.H. Weisner, *Recruitment and Selection in Canada*, 2nd ed. (Scarborough, ON: Nelson Thomson Learning, 2001), p. 307; J.E. Harvey-Cook and R.J. Taffler, "Biodata in Professional Entry-Level Selection: Statistical Scoring of Common-Format Applications," *Journal of Occupational and Organizational Psychology* (March 1, 2000), pp. 103–118; Y.Y. Chung, "The Validity of Biographical Inventories for the Selection of Salespeople," *International Journal of Management* (September 2001).

18. L. Petrecca, "With 3000 Job Applications a Day, Google Can Be Picky," *USA Today* (May 18, 2010), (accessed September 9, 2012). http://www.usatoday.com/money/workplace/2010-05-19-jobs19_VA_N.htm

19. D. Dahl and P. Pinto, "Job Posting, an Industry Survey," *Personnel Journal* (January 1977), pp. 40–41.

20. J. Daum, "Internal Promotion—Psychological Asset or Debit? A Study of the Effects of Leader Origin," *Organizational Behavior and Human Performance*, 13 (1975), pp. 404–413.

21. See, for example, A. Harris, "Hiring Middle Management: External Recruitment or Internal Promotion?" *Canadian HR Reporter* (April 10, 2000), pp. 8–10.

22. M. Sharma, "Welcome Back!" *HR Professional* (February/March 2006), pp. 38–40; E. Simon, "You're Leaving the Company? Well, Don't Be a Stranger," *Globe and Mail* (December 22, 2006), p. B16.

23. U. Vu, "Encana Builds Talent Pipeline into High School Classrooms," *Canadian HR Reporter* (April 11, 2005), p. 3.

24. Halifax Career Fair, www.halifaxcareerfairs.com (accessed May 31, 2009).

25. Career Edge, www.careeredge.ca (accessed May 31, 2009).

26. N. Laurie and M. Laurie, "No Holds Barred in Fight for Students to Fill Internship Programs," *Canadian HR Reporter* (January 17, 2000), pp. 15–16.

27. Human Resources Professionals Association of Ontario, www.hrpao.org (accessed June 25, 2003).

28. D. Hurl, "Letting the Armed Forces Train Your Managers," *Canadian HR Reporter* (December 3, 2001), pp. 8–9.

29. L. MacGillivray, "Cashing in on the Canadian Forces," *Workplace Today* (October 2001), pp. 40–41.

30. L. Blake, "Ready-Trained, Untapped Source of Skilled Talent—Courtesy Canadian Forces," *Workplace*, www.workplace-mag.com (accessed December 2, 2008).

31. U. Vu, "Security Failures Expose Résumés," *Canadian HR Reporter* (May 24, 2003); P. Lima, "Talent Shortage? That Was Yesterday. Online Recruiters Can Deliver More Candidates for Your Job Openings and Help You Find Keepers," *Profit: The Magazine for Canadian Entrepreneurs* (February/March 2002), pp. 65–66; "Online Job Boards," *Canadian HR Reporter* (February 11, 2002), pp. G11–G15.

32. U. Vu, "Security Failures Expose Résumés," *Canadian HR Reporter* (May 24, 2003).

33. S. Bury, "Face-Based Recruiting," *Workplace* (September/October 2008), pp. 19–21.

34. G. Stanton, "Recruiting Portals Take Centre Stage in Play for Talent," *Canadian HR Reporter* (September 25, 2000), pp. G1–G2.

35. A. da Luz, "Video Enhances Online Job Ads," *Canadian HR Reporter* (February 11, 2008).

36. D. Brown, "Canadian Government Job Boards Lag on Best Practices," *Canadian HR Reporter* (January 13, 2003), p. 2.

37. T. Martell, "Résumé Volumes Push Firms to Web," *ComputerWorld Canada* (April 7, 2000), p. 45.

38. A. Altass, "E-Cruiting: A Gen X Trend or Wave of the Future?" *HR Professional* (June–July 2000), p. 33.

39. "Corporate Spending Millions on Ineffective Web Recruiting Strategies," *Canadian HR Reporter* (September 25, 2000), p. G5.

40. A. Snell, "Best Practices for Web Site Recruiting," *Canadian HR Reporter* (February 26, 2001), pp. G7, G10.

41. D. Brown, "Who's Looking Online? Most Firms Don't Know," *Canadian HR Reporter* (August 13, 2001), pp. 2, 12; "Corporate Spending Millions on Ineffective Web Recruiting Strategies," *Canadian HR Reporter* (September 25, 2000), p. G5; A. Snell, "Best Practices for Web Site Recruiting," *Canadian HR Reporter* (February 26, 2001), pp. G7, G10.

42. Service Canada, Job Bank, http://jb-ge.hrdc-drhc.gc.ca (accessed May 31, 2009).

43. J.A. Parr, "7 Reasons Why Executive Searches Fail," *Canadian HR Reporter* (March 12, 2001), pp. 20, 23.

44. Association of Canadian Search, Employment and Staffing Services (ACSESS), www.acsess.org (accessed August 8, 2006).

45. Statistics Canada, *The Daily* (April 8, 2005); Association of Canadian Search, Employment and Staffing Services (ACSESS), "Media Kit: Media Fact Sheet," www.acsess.org/NEWS/factsheet.asp (accessed May 31, 2009).

46. A. Doran, "Technology Brings HR to Those Who Need It," *Canadian HR Reporter* (October 6, 1997), p. 8.

47. S. Bury, "Face-Based Recruiting," *Workplace* (September/October 2008), pp. 19–21.

48. D. Harder, "Recruiting in Age of Social Networking," *Canadian HR Reporter* (April 21, 2008).

49. L. Barrington and J. Shelp, "Looking for Employees in All the Right Places," *The Conference Board Executive Action Series* (December 2005).

50. A. Pell, *Recruiting and Selecting Personnel* (New York, NY: Regents, 1969), pp. 16–34.

51. T. Lende, "Workplaces Looking to Hire Part-Timers," *Canadian HR Reporter* (April 22, 2002), pp. 9, 11.

52. K. LeMessurier, "Temp Staffing Leaves a Permanent Mark," *Canadian HR Reporter* (February 10, 2003), pp. 3, 8.

53. A. Ryckman, "The 5 Keys to Getting Top Value from Contractors," *Canadian HR Reporter* (December 2, 2002), p. 25; S. Purba, "Contracting Works for Job Hunters," *Globe and Mail* (April 24, 2002).

54. "Flexible Staffing in the Aerospace Industry," *Airfinance Journal I Aircraft Economic Yearbook* (2001), pp. 14–17.

55. M. Potter, "A Golden Opportunity for Older Workers to Energize Firms," *Canadian HR Reporter* (April 25, 2005), p. 13.

56. L. Cassiani, "Looming Retirement Surge Takes on New Urgency," *Canadian HR Reporter* (May 21, 2001), pp. 1, 10.

57. O. Parker, *Too Few People, Too Little Time: The Employer Challenge of an Aging Workforce* (Ottawa, ON: The Conference Board of Canada Executive Action, July 2006).

58. K. Thorpe, *Harnessing the Power: Recruiting, Engaging, and Retaining Mature Workers.* (Ottawa, ON: Conference Board of Canada, 2008).

59. S.B. Hood, "Generational Diversity in the Workplace," *HR Professional* (June/July 2000), p. 20.

60. G. Kovary and A. Buahene, "Recruiting the Four Generations," *Canadian HR Reporter* (May 23, 2005), p. R6.

61. S. Klie, "Firm Asks Students: What Do You Want?" *Canadian HR Reporter* (May 5, 2008).

62. Inclusion Network, www.inclusionnetwork.ca (accessed May 31, 2009); Aboriginal Human Resource Council, http://aboriginalhr.ca (accessed May 31, 2009).

63. Society for Canadian Women in Science and Technology, www.harbour.sfu.ca/scwist/index_files/Page1897.htm (accessed May 31, 2009); C. Emerson, H. Matsui, and L. Michael, "Progress Slow for Women in Trades, Tech, Science," *Canadian HR Reporter* (February 14, 2005), p. 11.

64. WORKInk, www.workink.com (accessed May 31, 2009).

PHOTO CREDITS

Selection

THE STRATEGIC IMPORTANCE OF EMPLOYEE SELECTION

selection The process of choosing among individuals who have been recruited to fill existing or projected job openings.

Selection is the process of choosing among individuals who have been recruited to fill existing or projected job openings. Whether considering current employees for a transfer or promotion or outside candidates for a first-time position with the firm, information about the applicants must be collected and evaluated. Selection begins when a pool of applicants has submitted their résumés or completed application forms as a result of the recruiting process.

The selection process has important strategic significance. More and more managers have realized that the quality of the company's human resources is often the single most important factor in determining whether the firm is going to survive and be successful in reaching the objectives specified in its strategic plan. Those individuals selected will be implementing strategic decisions and, in some cases, creating strategic plans. Thus, successful candidates must fit with the strategic direction of the organization. For example, if the organization is planning to expand internationally, language skills and international experience will become important selection criteria.

When a poor selection decision is made and the individual selected for the job is not capable of acceptable performance in the job, strategic objectives will not be met. In addition, when an unsuccessful employee must be terminated, the recruitment and selection process must begin all over again, and the successor must be properly oriented and trained. The "hidden" costs are frequently even higher, including internal disorganization and disruption and customer alienation. For example, the City of Waterloo was forced to fire its new chief administrative officer after three weeks on the job when it was found that he had provided inaccurate and misleading information to city council in a previous job.[1]

There are also legal implications associated with ineffective selection. Human rights legislation in every Canadian jurisdiction prohibits discrimination in all aspects, terms, and conditions of employment on such grounds as race, religion or creed, colour, marital status, gender, age, and disability. Firms must ensure that all their selection procedures are free of both intentional and systemic discrimination (see **Appendix 1**, which provides the Canadian Human Rights Commission's *Guide to Screening and Selection in Employment*). Organizations required by law to implement an employment equity plan must ensure that all their employment systems, including selection, are bias-free and do not have an adverse impact on members of the four designated groups—women, visible minorities, Aboriginal people, and persons with disabilities.

An Ethical : Dilemma

As the company recruiter, how would you handle a request from the CEO that you hire her son for a summer job, knowing that, given current hiring constraints, the sons and daughters of other employees will not be able to obtain such positions?

Another legal implication is employer liability for negligent or wrongful hiring. Courts are increasingly finding employers liable when employees with unsuitable backgrounds are hired and subsequently engage in criminal activities falling within the scope of their employment. British Columbia has a law that requires schools, hospitals, and employers of childcare workers to conduct criminal record checks for all new employees.[2]

Suggested guidelines for avoiding negative legal consequences, such as human rights complaints, liability for negligent hiring, and wrongful dismissal suits, include the following:

1. Ensure that all selection criteria and strategies are based on the job description and the job specifications.
2. Adequately assess the applicant's ability to meet performance standards or expectations.
3. Carefully scrutinize all information supplied on application forms and résumés.
4. Obtain written authorization for reference checking from prospective employees, and check references carefully.
5. Save all records and information obtained about the applicant during each stage of the selection process.
6. Reject applicants who make false statements on their application forms or résumés.

Supply Challenges

Although it is desirable to have a large, qualified pool of recruits from which to select applicants, this is not always possible. Certain vacant positions may be subject to a labour shortage (based on job requirements, location, work environment, and so on), while other simultaneous vacant positions may be subject to a labour surplus (due to external environment factors, training and education levels, immigration patterns, and so on). A **selection ratio** is the ratio of the number of applicants hired to the total number of applicants available, as follows:

selection ratio The ratio of the number of applicants hired to the total number of applicants.

Number of Applicants Hired ÷ Total Number of Applicants = Selection Ratio

A small selection ratio, such as 1:2, may be indicative of a limited number of applicants from which to select, and it may also mean low-quality recruits. If this is the case, it is generally better to start the recruitment process over again, even if it means a hiring delay, rather than taking the risk of hiring an employee who will be a marginal performer at best.

A large selection ratio, such as 1:400, may be indicative that the job ad is too vague, that the organization's HR team may need to automate the screening process, or that there is a need for more resources to find the right job candidate amongst the high number of applicants.

The Selection Process

multiple-hurdle strategy An approach to selection involving a series of successive steps or hurdles. Only candidates clearing the hurdle are permitted to move on to the next step.

Most firms use a sequential selection system involving a series of successive steps— a **multiple-hurdle strategy**. Only candidates clearing a "hurdle" (selection techniques including pre-screening, testing, interviewing, and background/reference checking) are permitted to move on to the next step. Clearing the hurdle requires meeting or exceeding the minimum requirements established for that hurdle. Thus, only candidates who have cleared all of the previous hurdles remain in contention for the position at the time that the hiring decision is being made.

To assess each applicant's potential for success on the job, organizations typically rely on a number of sources of information. The number of steps in the selection process and their sequence vary with the organization. An abbreviated selection process for entrepreneurs and small business owners is provided in the Entrepreneurs and HR box. The types of selection instruments

ENTREPRENEURS and HR

Employment Testing and Interviewing

For the small business, one or two hiring mistakes could be disastrous, so a formal testing program is advisable. Some tests are so easy to use that they are particularly good for smaller firms. Several examples follow.

- The Wonderlic Personnel Test measures general mental ability. It takes less than 15 minutes to administer the four-page booklet. The tester reads the instructions and then keeps time as the candidate works through the 50 problems on the two inside sheets. The tester scores the test by adding up the number of correct answers. Comparing the candidate's score with the minimum scores recommended for various occupations shows whether the candidate achieved the minimally acceptable score for the type of job in question.

- The Predictive Index measures work-related personality traits, drives, and behaviours—in particular, dominance, extroversion, patience, and blame avoidance—on a two-sided sheet. A template makes scoring simple. The Predictive Index program includes 15 standard personality patterns. For example, there is the "social interest" pattern for a person who is generally unselfish, congenial, persuasive, patient, and unassuming. This person would be good with people and a good personnel interviewer, for instance.

- Computerized testing programs are especially useful for small employers. For example, many employers rely on informal typing tests when hiring office help. A better approach is to use a program like the Minnesota Clerical Assessment Battery published by Assessment Systems Corporation. It runs on a PC and includes a typing test, proofreading test, filing test, business vocabulary test, business math test, and clerical knowledge test.

Interviewing

A practical, streamlined employment interview process would proceed as follows:

- Preparing for the interview: Even a busy entrepreneur or small business manager can quickly specify the kind of person who would be best for the job. One way to do so is to focus on four basic required factors—knowledge and experience, motivation, intellectual capacity, and personality—and to ask the following questions:

  - Knowledge and experience: What must the candidate know to perform the job? What experience is absolutely necessary to perform the job?

  - Motivation: What should the person like doing to enjoy this job? Is there anything the person should not dislike? Are there any essential goals or aspirations the person should have? Are there any unusual energy demands on the job?

  - Intellectual capacity: Are there any specific intellectual aptitudes required (mathematical, mechanical, and so on)? How complex are the problems the person must solve? What must a person be able to demonstrate he or she can do intellectually? How should the person solve problems (cautiously, deductively, and so on)?

  - Personality: What are the critical personality qualities needed for success on the job (ability to withstand boredom, decisiveness, stability, and so on)? How must the job incumbent handle stress, pressure, and criticism? What kind of interpersonal behaviour is required in the job up the line, at peer level, down the line, and outside the firm with customers?

- Specific factors to probe in the interview: A combination of situational questions and open-ended questions like those in **Figure 6** should be asked to probe the candidate's suitability for the job. For example:

  - Knowledge and experience factor: Situational questions such as "How would you organize such a sales effort?" or "How would you design that kind of website?" can probe for information on this factor.

  - Intellectual factor: Here, such things as complexity of tasks the person has performed, grades in school, test results (including scholastic aptitude tests and so on), and how the person organizes his or her thoughts and communicates are assessed.

  - Motivation factor: The person's likes and dislikes (for each task, what he or she liked or disliked about it), aspirations (including the validity of each goal in terms of the person's reasoning about why he or she chose it), and energy level should be probed, perhaps by asking what he or she does on, say, a "typical Tuesday."

  - Personality factor: Questions probing for selfdefeating behaviours (aggressiveness, compulsive fidgeting, and so on) and exploring the person's past interpersonal relationships should be asked. Additional questions about the person's

continued

past interactions (working in a group at school, working with fraternity brothers or sorority sisters, leading the work team on the last job, and so on) should also be asked. A judgment about the person's behaviour in the interview itself can also be made—is the candidate personable? Shy? Outgoing?

- Conducting the interview. Devise and use a plan to guide the interview. According to interviewing expert John Drake, significant areas to cover include the candidate's
  - college or university experiences
  - work experiences—summer, part time
  - work experience—full time
  - goals and ambitions
  - reactions to the job you are interviewing for
  - self-assessments (by the candidate of his or her strengths and weaknesses)
  - military experiences
  - present outside activities
- Follow the plan: Begin with an open-ended question for each topic, such as, "Could you tell me about what you did when you were in high school?"

Keep in mind that information must be elicited regarding four main traits—intelligence, motivation, personality, and knowledge and experience. The information in each of these four areas can then be accumulated as the person answers. Follow-up questions on particular areas such as "Could you elaborate on that, please?" can then be used.

- Match the candidate to the job: After following the interview plan and probing for the four factors, conclusions can be drawn about the person's intellectual capacity, knowledge and experience, motivation, and personality, and the candidate's general strengths and limitations can be summarized using an interview evaluation form (for instance, see **Figure 7**). The conclusions can then be compared to both the job description and the list of behavioural requirements developed when preparing for the interview. This should provide a rational basis for matching the candidate to the job based on an analysis of the traits and aptitudes the job actually requires.

Source: Based on John Drake, *Interviewing for Managers: A Complete Guide to Employment Interviewing* (New York, NY: AMCOM, 1982). Reprinted with permission.

and screening devices used are also not standardized across organizations. Even within a firm, the number and sequence of steps often vary with the type and level of the job, as well as the source and method of recruitment. **Figure 1** illustrates the steps commonly involved.

At each step in the selection process, carefully chosen selection criteria must be used to determine which applicants will move on to the next step. It is through job analysis that the duties, responsibilities, and human requirements for each job are identified. By basing selection criteria on these requirements, firms can create a legally defensible hiring system.[3] Individuals hired after thorough screening against these carefully developed selection criteria (based directly on the job description and job specifications) learn their jobs readily, are productive, and generally adjust to their jobs with a minimum of difficulty.

Designing an effective selection process involves composing a series of job-related questions to be asked of all applicants for a particular job. There are also a few job-related, candidate-specific questions. Doing so involves the following five steps, the first two of which should occur before recruitment:[4]

1. Decide who will be involved in the selection process and *develop selection criteria*. Specifying selection criteria involves clarifying and weighting the information in the job description and job specifications and holding discussions among the interview-team members, especially those most familiar with the job and co-workers.

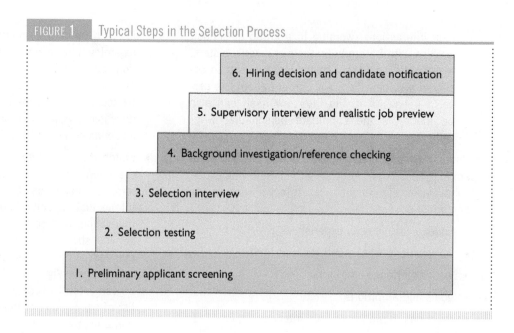

FIGURE 1 Typical Steps in the Selection Process

6. Hiring decision and candidate notification

5. Supervisory interview and realistic job preview

4. Background investigation/reference checking

3. Selection interview

2. Selection testing

I. Preliminary applicant screening

must criteria Requirements that are absolutely essential for the job, include a measurable standard of acceptability, or are absolute and can be screened initially on paper.

want criteria Those criteria that represent qualifications that cannot be screened on paper or are not readily measurable, as well as those that are highly desirable but not critical.

RPC

Supports managers in the selection of candidates

2. *Specify* musts *and* wants *and weight the* wants. Once agreed on, the selection criteria should be divided into the two categories: musts and wants.[5] **Must criteria** are those that are absolutely essential for the job, include a measurable standard of acceptability, or are absolute. There are often only two musts: a specific level of education (or equivalent combination of education and work experience) and a minimum amount of prior work experience. These criteria can be initially screened, based on the applicants' résumés or applications. The **want criteria** include skills and abilities that cannot be screened on paper (such as verbal skills) or are not readily measurable (such as leadership ability, teamwork skills, and enthusiasm), as well as qualifications that are desirable but not critical.

3. Determine assessment strategies and *develop an evaluation form*. Once the must and want criteria have been identified, appropriate strategies for learning about each should be specified. For some qualifications, especially those that are critically important, the team may decide to use several assessment strategies. For example, leadership skills might be assessed through behavioural questions, situational questions, a written test, and an assessment centre. Once all want criteria have been agreed on and weighted, it becomes the basis for candidate comparison and evaluation, as illustrated in **Figure 2**.

4. *Develop interview questions* to be asked of all candidates. Questions should be developed for each KSA to be assessed during the interview. *Job-knowledge questions* and *worker-requirements questions* to gauge the applicants' motivation and willingness to perform under prevailing working conditions, such as shift work or travel, should also be included.

5. *Develop candidate-specific questions*. A few open-ended, job-related questions that are candidate specific should be planned, based on each candidate's résumé and application form.

FIGURE 2 Worksheet—Comparison of Candidates for an Administrative Assistant Position

Criteria

Alternatives						
	A Smith		**B** Brown		**C** Yuill	
Must	Info	Go/No	Info	Go/No	Info	Go/No
Education — Office Admin. diploma or equivalent experience (3 years' clerical/secretarial experience)	Office admin. diploma	Go	Office admin. diploma	Go	No diploma, 1 year related experience	No Go
Experience — At least 2 years' secretarial/clerical experience	3 years' experience	Go	2 years' experience	Go		Go

		A Smith			**B** Brown			**C** Yuill		
Wants	Wt.	Info	Sc.	Wt. Sc.	Info	Sc.	Wt. Sc.	Info	Sc.	Wt. Sc.
Keyboarding/word processing	10	Word processing test	9	90	Word processing test	10	100			
Good oral communication	9	Interview assessment	9	81	Interview assessment	9	81			
Good spelling/grammar	9	Test results	8	72	Test results	9	81			
Organizational ability	9	Interview questions/simulation/reference checking	8	72	Interview questions/simulation/reference checking	9	81			
Initiative	8	Interview questions/simulation/reference checking	7	56	Interview questions/simulation/reference checking	8	64			
High ethical standards	7	Interview questions/simulation/reference checking	7	49	Interview questions/simulation/reference checking	7	49			
Shorthand skills (or speed writing)	4	Interview question and test results	4	16	Interview question and test results	0	0			
Designated group member, other than white female	2	Application form	2	4	Application form	0	0			
				440			456			

TOP CANDIDATE

Acquiring Employees and the Law

The entire recruitment and selection procedure must comply with human rights legislation. All information collected from the time an ad is posted to the time that the selection decision is made must be free from questions that would directly or indirectly classify candidates on the basis of any of the prohibited grounds under human rights legislation; potential employers cannot ask for a photograph, information about illnesses, disabilities or workers' compensation claims, or information that could lead to direct, intentional discrimination, such as age, gender, sexual orientation, marital status, maiden name, date of birth, place of origin, number of dependents, and so on.

If the process collects any information that is considered a prohibited ground for discrimination, an unsuccessful candidate may challenge the legality of the entire recruitment and selection processes. In such cases, the burden of proof is on the employer. Thus, taking human rights legislation requirements into consideration when designing effective recruitment and selection procedures is imperative. *A Guide to Screening and Selection in Employment* in **Appendix 1** provides helpful hints. Specific guidelines regarding questions that can and cannot be asked on application forms are available through the human rights commissions in each jurisdiction.

Managing the process in a legally defensible way involves keeping the following guidelines in mind:

1. Selection personnel cannot ask questions that would violate human rights legislation, either directly or indirectly. Questions cannot be asked about candidates' marital status, childcare arrangements, ethnic background, or workers' compensation history, for example.

2. All candidates must be treated in the same manner. Any agent of the organization cannot ask only female factory position applicants to demonstrate their lifting abilities, for example, or question female sales applicants about their willingness to travel but not ask male candidates. However, accommodation must be provided to applicants with disabilities (see the Workforce Diversity box).

3. Cutting short an interview based on preconceived notions about the gender or race of the "ideal" candidate must also be avoided, because this is another example of illegal differential treatment.

4. A helpful phrase to keep in mind when designing selection criteria is "This job requires . . ." Organization representatives who focus on the job description and job specifications can gather all the information required to assess applicants without infringing on the candidates' legal rights.

STEP 1: PRELIMINARY APPLICANT SCREENING

Initial applicant screening is generally performed by members of the HR department. Application forms and résumés are reviewed, and those candidates not meeting the essential selection criteria are eliminated first. Then, the remaining applications are examined and those candidates who most closely match the remaining job specifications are identified and given further consideration.

The use of technology is becoming increasingly popular to help HR professionals improve the initial screening process. Almost all large firms or firms with high turnover use technological applications to help screen large numbers of candidates and generate short lists of individuals who will move on to the next step in the selection process.

WORKFORCE DIVERSITY

Principles for Assessment Accommodations

There are four principles those responsible for assessment should be guided by in determining accommodations when assessing persons with disabilities.

Principle 1: Provide all applicants with an equal opportunity to fully demonstrate their qualifications.

A disability may hinder a person from fully demonstrating his or her qualifications using a particular assessment instrument. Therefore, adjustments need to be made to the administration procedures or to the assessment instrument itself so that the person is in a position to fully demonstrate his or her qualifications.

Principle 2: Determine assessment accommodations on a case-by-case basis.

Three key elements must be considered when determining appropriate accommodations:

- The nature and the extent of the individual's functional limitation

- The type of assessment instrument being used

- The nature and level of the qualification being assessed

Principle 3: Do not alter the nature or level of the qualification being assessed.

For example, although providing additional time to complete a test could be appropriate when the qualification "knowledge of the organization's mandate and its business" is assessed, providing additional time could be inappropriate for a test assessing the qualification "verify information rapidly and accurately." In the latter case, the obtained result may not be representative of the applicant's true ability to do the task rapidly, considering the additional time given.

Principle 4: Base assessment accommodations on complete information.

To make appropriate decisions when determining assessment accommodations, there is a need to rely on complete information on the three elements mentioned earlier, justifying the case-by-case approach:

1. The nature and the extent of the individual's functional limitations: For example, the appropriate accommodation for one person who is partially sighted may require a large print format of a test; while for another person who is also partially sighted, the appropriate accommodation may require special lighting. These differences arise because the nature and extent of the functional limitations vary from one individual to another.

2. Type of assessment instrument: For example, someone who has functional limitations that affect his or her manual writing speed may need some additional time to write an essay-style exam, while the same person may not need additional time for a multiple-choice exam that does not require written responses beyond filling in circles on a response sheet.

3. Nature of the qualification being assessed: For example, allowing the use of a calculator for a test assessing "ability to perform financial calculations" could be appropriate. However, allowing the use of a calculator when the "ability to do mental calculations" is assessed would be inappropriate. In the latter case, the provision of the calculator would invalidate the result, as it would not be representative of the applicant's ability to do the task mentally.

Source: Guide for Assessing Persons with Disabilities, http://www.psc-cfp.gc.ca/plcy-pltq/guides/assessment-evaluation/apwd-eph/pdf/apwd-eph-eng.pdf (pp. 10–12), Public Service Commission of Canada, Policy Development Directorate, July 2007. Reproduced with the permission of the Minister of Public Works and Government Services Canada, 2012.

STEP 2: SELECTION TESTING

Selection testing is a common screening device used by approximately two-thirds of Canadian organizations to assess specific job-related skills as well as general intelligence, personality characteristics, mental abilities, interests, and preferences.[6] Testing techniques provide efficient, standardized procedures for screening large numbers of applicants. Several thousand psychological and personality tests are on the market.[7]

The Importance of Reliability and Validity

Tests and other selection techniques are only useful if they provide reliable and valid measures.[8] All reputable tests will provide information to users about the reliability and validity of the test.

Reliability

reliability The degree to which interviews, tests, and other selection procedures yield comparable data over time; in other words, the degree of dependability, consistency, or stability of the measures used.

The degree to which interviews, tests, and other selection procedures yield comparable data over time is known as **reliability**. Reliability is the degree of dependability, consistency, or stability of the measures used. For example, a test that results in widely variable scores (for example, if the same candidate completes the test three times and secures scores of 60 percent, 82 percent, and 71 percent) when it is administered on different occasions to the same individual is unreliable. Reliability also refers to the extent to which two or more methods yield the same results or are consistent. For example, applicants with high scores on personality tests for impulsivity or lack of self-control are correlated with the likelihood of failing background checks due to criminal behaviour.[9] Reliability also means the extent to which there is agreement between two or more raters (inter-rater reliability).

When dealing with tests, another measure of reliability that is taken into account is internal consistency. For example, suppose a vocational interest test has 10 items, all of which were supposed to measure, in one way or another, the person's interest in working outdoors. To assess internal reliability, the degree to which responses to those 10 items vary together would be statistically analyzed (which is one reason that tests often include questions that appear rather repetitive). Reliability can be diminished when questions are answered randomly, when the test setting is noisy or uncomfortable, and when the applicant is tired or unwell.

Validity

validity The accuracy with which a predictor measures what it is intended to measure.

Validity, in the context of selection, is an indicator of the extent to which data from a selection technique, such as a test or interview, are related to or predictive of subsequent performance on the job. For example, high impulsivity is correlated with low productivity.[10] Separate validation studies of selection techniques should be conducted for different subgroups, such as visible minorities and women, to assess **differential validity**. In some cases, the technique may be a valid predictor of job success for one group (such as white males) but not for other applicants, thereby leading to systemic discrimination.

differential validity Confirmation that the selection tool accurately predicts the performance of all possible employee subgroups, including white males, women, visible minorities, persons with disabilities, and Aboriginal people.

Three types of validity are particularly relevant to selection: criterion-related, content, and construct validity.

criterion-related validity The extent to which a selection tool predicts or significantly correlates with important elements of work behaviour.

Criterion-Related Validity The extent to which a selection tool predicts or significantly correlates with important elements of work behaviour is known as **criterion-related validity**. Demonstrating criterion-related validity requires proving that those who exhibit strong sales ability on a test or in an interview, for example, also have high sales on the job, and that those individuals who do poorly on the test or in the interview have poor sales results.

content validity The extent to which a selection instrument, such as a test, adequately samples the knowledge and skills needed to perform the job.

Content Validity When a selection instrument, such as a test, adequately samples the knowledge and skills needed to perform the job, **content validity** is assumed to exist. The closer the content of the selection instrument is to actual samples of work or work behaviour, the greater the content validity. For example, asking a candidate for a secretarial position to demonstrate word processing skills, as required on the job, has high content validity.

Construct Validity The extent to which a selection tool measures a theoretical construct or trait deemed necessary to perform the job successfully is known as **construct validity**. Intelligence, verbal skills, analytical ability, and leadership skills are all examples of constructs. Measuring construct validity requires demonstrating that the psychological trait or attribute is related to satisfactory job performance, as well as showing that the test or other selection tool used accurately measures the psychological trait or attribute. As an example of poor construct validity, an accounting firm was selecting applicants for auditor positions based on a test for high extroversion, when the job in fact required working alone with data. A test to select applicants with high introversion would have had higher construct validity and would have helped to avoid the high turnover rate the firm was experiencing.[11]

Professional standards for psychologists require that tests be used as supplements to other techniques, such as interviews and background checks; that tests be validated in the organization where they will be used; that a certified psychologist be used to choose, validate, administer, and interpret tests; and that private, quiet, well-lit, and well-ventilated settings be provided to all applicants taking the tests.[12]

Tests of Cognitive Abilities

Ensuring validity of selection tools when assessing candidates with disabilities may require accommodation of the disability. Some guidelines are provided in the Workforce Diversity box. Included in the category of tests of cognitive abilities are tests of general reasoning ability (intelligence), tests of emotional intelligence, and tests of specific cognitive abilities, like memory and inductive reasoning.

Intelligence Tests

Intelligence (IQ) tests are tests of general intellectual abilities (also referred to as general mental abilities) and have been used since the end of World War I.[13] They measure not a single "intelligence" trait, but rather a number of abilities, including memory, vocabulary, verbal fluency, and numerical ability. An IQ score is actually a *derived* score, reflecting the extent to which the person is above or below the "average" adult's intelligence score. Empirical research suggests that general mental ability is the strongest general predictor of job performance at one's chosen occupation.[14] Intelligence is often measured with individually administered tests, such as the Stanford-Binet test or the Wechsler test. Other IQ tests, such as the Wonderlic Personnel Test, can be administered to groups of people. These are relatively quick pen and paper or online tests that can be accessed for a nominal fee.

Emotional Intelligence Tests

Emotional intelligence (EI) tests measure a person's ability to monitor his or her own emotions and the emotions of others and to use that knowledge to guide thoughts and actions. Someone with a high emotional quotient (EQ) is self-aware, can control his or her impulses, is self-motivated, and demonstrates empathy and social awareness. Many people believe that EQ, which can be modified through conscious effort and practice, is actually a more important determinant of success

---

construct validity The extent to which a selection tool measures a theoretical construct or trait deemed necessary to perform the job successfully.

RPC

Evaluates the effectiveness of selection processes, tools, and outcomes

RPC

Determines the appropriate selection tools and develops new tools as required

intelligence (IQ) tests Tests that measure general intellectual abilities, such as verbal comprehension, inductive reasoning, memory, numerical ability, speed of perception, spatial visualization, and word fluency.

emotional intelligence (EI) tests Tests that measure a person's ability to monitor his or her own emotions and the emotions of others and to use that knowledge to guide thoughts and actions.

than a high IQ. However, there is extremely limited and somewhat highly controversial empirical evidence to support the importance of EI in the workplace.[15] Self-assessment EI tests include the Emotional Quotient Inventory (EQ-i), the EQ Map, the Mayer-Salovey-Caruso Emotional Intelligence Test (MSCEIT), and the Emotional Intelligence Questionnaire (EIQ). The Emotional Competence Inventory (ECI) is a 360-degree assessment in which several individuals evaluate one person to get a more complete picture of the individual's emotional competencies.[16]

**Emotional Intelligence Consortium
www.eiconsortium.org**

Specific Cognitive Abilities

There are also measures of specific thinking skills, such as inductive and deductive reasoning, verbal comprehension, memory, and numerical ability. Tests in this category are often called **aptitude tests**, since they purport to measure the applicant's aptitude for the job in question, that is, the applicant's potential to perform the job once given proper training. An example is the test of mechanical comprehension illustrated in **Figure 3**. It tests the applicant's understanding of basic mechanical principles. It may therefore reflect a person's aptitude for

aptitude tests Tests that measure an individual's aptitude or potential to perform a job, provided he or she is given proper training.

FIGURE 3   Two Problems from the Test of Mechanical Comprehension

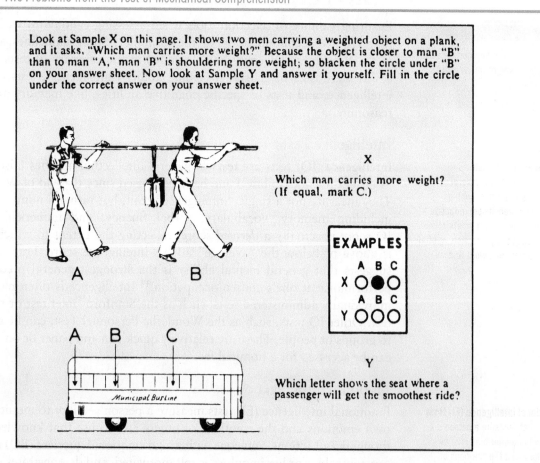

jobs—like that of machinist or engineer—that require mechanical comprehension. Multidimensional aptitude tests commonly used in applicant selection include the General Aptitude Test Battery (GATB).

Tests of Motor and Physical Abilities

There are many *motor abilities* that a firm might want to measure. These include finger dexterity, manual dexterity, speed of arm movement, and reaction time. The Crawford Small Parts Dexterity Test, as illustrated in **Figure 4**, is an example. It measures the speed and accuracy of simple judgment, as well as the speed of finger, hand, and arm movements. Other tests include the Stromberg Dexterity Test, the Minnesota Rate of Manipulation Test, and the Purdue Pegboard.

Tests of physical abilities may also be required.[17] For example, some firms are now using functional abilities evaluations (FAE) to assist with placement decisions. An FAE, which measures a whole series of physical abilities—ranging from lifting, to pulling and pushing, sitting, squatting, climbing, and carrying—is particularly useful for positions with a multitude of physical demands, such as a firefighter or police officer.[18] Ensuring that physical abilities tests do not violate human rights legislation requires basing such tests on job duties identified through job analysis and a physical demands analysis, ensuring that the tests duplicate the actual physical requirements of the job, developing and imposing such tests honestly and in good faith, ensuring that those administering the tests are properly trained and administer the tests in a consistent manner, and ensuring that testing standards are objectively related to job performance.[19]

FIGURE 4	Crawford Small Parts Dexterity Test

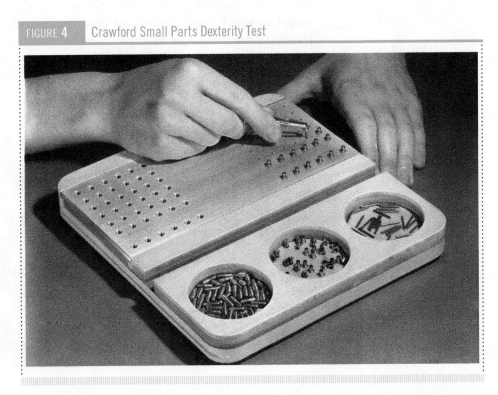

Source: Photo of the Crawford Small Parts Dexterity Test. Copyright 1946, 1956, 1981 by NCS Pearson, Inc. Reproduced with permission. All rights reserved.

Measuring Personality and Interests

A person's mental and physical abilities are seldom sufficient to explain his or her job performance. Other factors, such as the person's motivation and interpersonal skills, are important too. Personality and interest inventories are sometimes used as predictors of such intangibles.

Personality tests can measure basic aspects of an applicant's personality, such as introversion, stability, and motivation. The use of such tests for selection assumes that it is possible to find a relationship between a measurable personality trait (such as conscientiousness) and success on the job.[20] Many of these tests are *projective*. In the Thematic Apperception Test, an ambiguous stimulus (like an inkblot or clouded picture) is presented to the test taker, and he or she is asked to interpret or react to it. Because the pictures are ambiguous, the person's interpretation must come from within—the viewer supposedly *projects* into the picture his or her own emotional attitudes about life. Thus, a security-oriented person might have a very different description of what he or she sees compared to someone who is not.

The Myers-Briggs Type Indicator instrument, which has been in use for more than 50 years, is believed to be the most widely used personality inventory in the world. More than 2 million assessments are administered annually in the United States alone.[21] Another example of a common personality test is the Minnesota Multiphasic Personality Inventory (MMPI), which measures traits like hypochondria and paranoia.

Research studies confirm that personality tests can help companies hire more effective workers. For example, industrial psychologists often talk in terms of the "Big Five" personality dimensions as they apply to employment testing: *extroversion, emotional stability, agreeableness, conscientiousness,* and *openness to experience.*[22] These dimensions can be measured using the NEO Five-Factor Inventory (NEO-FFI) and similar tests. One study focused on the extent to which these dimensions predicted performance (in terms of job and training proficiency, for example) for professionals, police officers, managers, sales workers, and skilled/semi-skilled workers. Conscientiousness showed a consistent relationship with all performance criteria for every occupation.

personality tests Instruments used to measure basic aspects of personality, such as introversion, stability, motivation, neurotic tendency, self-confidence, self-sufficiency, and sociability.

Psychometric Assessments
www.psychometrics.com

Research INSIGHT

FIGURE 5 Sample Picture from Thematic Apperception Test: How Do You Interpret It?

Extroversion was a valid predictor of performance for managers and sales employees—the two occupations involving the most social interaction. Both openness to experience and extroversion predicted training proficiency for all occupations.[23]

There has been an ongoing debate in the research world on whether personality can be faked. In a test of 77 experienced assessors, over 70 percent agreed that "faking is a serious threat to the validity of personality inventory in the assessment process."[24] Evidence supports two specific trends in personality tests and faking: (1) people can fake personality inventories when they are motivated to do so, and (2) individual differences exist in the ability to fake.[25]

Interest inventories compare a candidate's interests with those of people in various occupations. Thus, a person taking the Strong-Campbell Interest Inventory would receive a report comparing his or her interests with those of people already in occupations such as accountant, engineer, manager, or medical technologist. Interest inventories have many uses. One is career planning, since people generally do better in jobs involving activities in which they have an interest. Another is selection. If the firm can select people whose interests are roughly the same as those of high-performing incumbents in the jobs for which it is hiring, the new employees are more likely to be successful.[26]

Achievement Tests

An **achievement test** is basically a measure of what a person has learned. Most of the tests taken in school are achievement tests. They measure knowledge or proficiency in such areas as economics, marketing, or HRM. Achievement tests are also widely used in selection. For example, the Purdue Test for Machinists and Machine Operators tests the job knowledge of experienced machinists with such questions as "What is meant by 'tolerance'?" Other tests are available for electricians, welders, carpenters, and so forth. In addition to job knowledge, achievement tests measure the applicant's abilities; a keyboarding test is one example.

Work Sampling

Work samples focus on measuring job performance directly and thus are among the best predictors of job performance. In developing a work-sampling test, experts first list all the possible tasks that jobholders would be required to perform. Then, by listing the frequency of performance and relative importance of each task, key tasks are identified. Each applicant then performs the key tasks, and his or her work is monitored by the test administrator, who records the approach taken. Finally, the work-sampling test is validated by determining the relationship between the applicants' scores on the work samples and their actual performance on the job. Once it is shown that the work sample is a valid predictor of job success, the employer can begin using it for selection.[27]

Management Assessment Centres

In a two- to three-day **management assessment centre**, the management potential of 10 or 12 candidates is assessed by expert appraisers who observe them performing realistic management tasks. The centre may be a plain conference room, but it is often a special room with a one-way mirror to facilitate unobtrusive

Research Psychologists Press
www.rpp.on.ca

interest inventories Tests that compare a candidate's interests with those of people in various occupations.

achievement tests Tests used to measure knowledge or proficiency acquired through education, training, or experience.

management assessment centre A comprehensive, systematic procedure used to assess candidates' management potential that uses a combination of realistic exercises, management games, objective testing, presentations, and interviews.

A management game or simulation is a typical component in a management assessment centre.

observations. Examples of the types of activities and exercises involved include the following:

1. *An in-basket exercise.* Each candidate is faced with an accumulation of reports, memos, messages from incoming phone calls, letters, and other materials collected in the in-basket of the simulated job that he or she is to take over and is required to take appropriate action. For example, he or she must write letters, return phone calls, and prepare meeting agendas. The trained evaluators then review the results.

2. *A leaderless group discussion.* A leaderless group is given a discussion question and told to arrive at a group decision. The raters evaluate each candidate's interpersonal skills, acceptance by the group, leadership ability, and individual influence.

3. *Management games.* Participants engage in realistic problem solving, usually as members of two or more simulated companies that are competing in the marketplace. Decisions might have to be made about issues such as how to advertise and manufacture and how much inventory to keep in stock.

4. *Individual presentations.* During oral presentations on an assigned topic, each participant's communication skills and persuasiveness are evaluated.

5. *Objective tests.* Candidates may be asked to complete paper and pencil or computer-based personality, aptitude, interest, or achievement tests.

6. *An interview.* Most centres also require an interview between at least one of the expert assessors and each participant to evaluate interests, background, past performance, and motivation.

Situational Testing

situational tests Tests in which candidates are presented with hypothetical situations representative of the job for which they are applying and are evaluated on their responses.

In **situational tests,** candidates are presented with hypothetical situations representative of the job for which they are applying (often on video) and are evaluated on their responses.[28] Several of the assessment centre exercises described above are examples of situational tests. In a typical test, a number of realistic scenarios are presented and each is followed by a multiple-choice question with several possible courses of action, from which candidates are asked to select the "best" response, in their opinion.[29] The level of each candidate's skills is then evaluated, and an assessment report can be easily generated, making the simulation easier and less expensive to administer than other screening tools. Simulations also provide a realistic job preview by exposing candidates to the types of activities they will encounter on the job.

Research INSIGHT

A research study of situational testing on 160 civil service employees demonstrated the validity of the situational test in predicting overall job performance as well as three performance dimensions: core technical proficiency, job dedication, and interpersonal facilitation. The situational test provided valid predictive information over and above cognitive ability tests, personality tests, and job experience.[30]

Micro-Assessments

micro-assessment A series of verbal, paper-based, or computer-based questions and exercises that a candidate is required to complete, covering the range of activities required on the job for which he or she is applying.

An entirely performance-based testing strategy that focuses on individual performance is a **micro-assessment**. In a micro-assessment, each applicant completes a series of verbal, paper-based, or computer-based questions and exercises that cover the range of activities required on the job for which he or she is applying. In addition to technical exercises, participants are required to solve a set of work-related problems that demonstrate their ability to perform well within the confines of a certain department or corporate culture. Exercises are simple to develop because they are taken directly from the job.

Physical Examination, Substance Abuse Testing, and Polygraph Tests

The use of medical examinations in selection has decreased, in part because of the loss of physically demanding manufacturing and natural resource jobs. Before 1980, 25 percent of new hires underwent a medical exam, but by 2001, only 11 percent were required to do so.[31] Three main reasons that firms may include a medical examination as a step in the selection process are (1) to determine that the applicant *qualifies for the physical requirements* of the position and, if not, to document any *accommodation requirements*; (2) to establish a *record and baseline* of the applicant's health for the purpose of future insurance or compensation claims; and (3) to *reduce absenteeism and accidents* by identifying any health issues or concerns that need to be addressed, including communicable diseases of which the applicant may have been unaware. Medical exams are only permitted after a written offer of employment has been extended (except in the case of bona fide occupational requirements, as for food handlers).

The purpose of pre-employment substance abuse testing is to avoid hiring employees who would pose unnecessary risks to themselves and others or perform below expectations. However, in Canada, employers are not permitted to screen candidates for substance abuse. Alcohol and drug addiction is considered to be a disability under human rights codes, and an employee cannot be discriminated against during the selection process based on a disability.[32]

A polygraph test (also referred to as a lie detector test) involves using a series of controlled questions while simultaneously assessing physiological conditions of individuals such as blood pressure, pulse, respiration, and skin conductivity, with the assumption that deceptive responses produce different physiological responses than truthful responses. Such tests have been widely rejected by the scientific community since they have failed to produce valid or reliable results. In Ontario, the Employment Standards Act specifically prohibits use of polygraphs in pre-employment selection. Validated tests of honesty or integrity are more useful and reliable in the selection process.

Interactive employment tests administered on the computer are becoming popular as screening devices at many firms.

STEP 3: THE SELECTION INTERVIEW

selection interview A procedure designed to predict future job performance on the basis of applicants' oral responses to oral inquiries.

The interview is used by virtually all organizations for selecting job applicants. The **selection interview**, which involves a process of two-way communication between the interviewee and the interviewer, can be defined as "a procedure designed to predict future job performance on the basis of applicants' oral responses to oral inquiries."[33]

Interviews are considered to be one of the most important aspects of the selection process and generally have a major impact on both applicants and interviewers. Interviews significantly influence applicants' views about the job and organization, enable employers to fill in any gaps in the information provided on application forms and résumés, and supplement the results of any tests administered. They may also reveal entirely new types of information.

RPC

Administers a variety of selection tools, including tests, interviews, reference checks, and so on

A major reason for the popularity of selection interviews is that they meet a number of the objectives of both the interviewer and interviewee. Interviewer objectives include assessing applicants' qualifications and observing relevant aspects of applicants' behaviour, such as verbal communication skills, degree of self-confidence, and interpersonal skills; providing candidates with information about the job and expected duties and responsibilities; promoting the organization and highlighting its attractiveness; and determining how well the applicants would fit into the organization. Typical objectives of job applicants include presenting a positive image of themselves, selling their skills and marketing their positive attributes to the interviewer(s), and gathering information about the job and the organization so that they can make an informed decision about the job, career opportunities in the firm, and the work environment.[34]

Types of Interviews

Selection interviews can be classified according to the degree of structure, their content, and the way in which the interview is administered.

The Structure of the Interview

unstructured interview An unstructured, conversational-style interview. The interviewer pursues points of interest as they come up in response to questions.

First, interviews can be classified according to the degree to which they are structured. In an **unstructured interview**, questions are asked as they come to mind. Thus, interviewees for the same job may or may not be asked the same or similar questions, and the interview's unstructured nature allows the interviewer to ask questions based on the candidate's last statements and to pursue points of interest as they develop. Unstructured interviews generally have low reliability and validity.[35]

structured interview An interview following a set sequence of questions.

The interview can also be structured. In the classical **structured interview**, the questions and acceptable responses are specified in advance and the responses are rated for appropriateness of content.[36] In practice, however, most structured interviews do not involve specifying and rating responses in advance. Instead, each candidate is asked a series of predetermined, job-related questions based on the job description and specifications. Such interviews are generally high in validity and reliability. However, a totally structured interview does not provide the flexibility to pursue points of interest as they develop, which may result in an interview that seems quite mechanical to all concerned.

mixed (semi-structured) interview An interview format that combines the structured and unstructured techniques.

Between these two extremes is the **mixed (semi-structured) interview**, which involves a combination of pre-set, structured questions based on the job description and specification, and a series of candidate-specific, job-related questions based on information provided on the application form or résumé. The questions asked of all candidates facilitate candidate comparison, while the job-related, candidate-specific questions make the interview more conversational. A realistic approach that yields comparable answers and indepth insights, the mixed interview format is extremely popular.

A study of 92 real employment interviews found that the interviewers using high levels of structure in the interview process evaluated applicants less favourably than those who used semi-structured or unstructured interviews, and those applicants who were evaluated using a semi-structured interview were rated slightly higher than those evaluated by unstructured interviews. Additionally, the study found that significant differences occur in the way that female and male interviewers evaluate their applicants. Although male interviewers' ratings were unaffected by the interview structure, female interviewers' ratings were substantially higher in unstructured and semi-structured interviews than in highly structured interviews.[37]

The Content of the Interview

Interviews can also be classified according to the content of their questions. A **situational interview** is one in which the questions focus on the individual's ability to project what his or her *future* behaviour would be in a given situation.[38] The underlying premise is that intentions predict behaviour. For example, a candidate for a supervisory position might be asked how he or she would respond to an employee coming to work late three days in a row. The interview can be both *structured* and *situational*, with predetermined questions requiring the candidate to project what his or her behaviour would be. In a structured situational interview, the applicant could be evaluated, say, on whether he or she would try to determine if the employee was experiencing some difficulty in getting to work on time or would simply issue a verbal or written warning to the employee.

The **behavioural interview**, also known as a **behaviour description interview (BDI)**, involves describing various situations and asking interviewees how they behaved *in the past* in such situations.[39] The underlying assumption is that the best predictor of future performance is past performance in similar circumstances.

Administering the Interview

Interviews can also be classified based on how they are administered:

- One-on-one or by a panel of interviewers
- Sequentially or all at once
- Face-to-face or technology aided (such as videoconferencing or by phone)

The majority of interviews are sequential, face-to-face, and one-on-one. In a *sequential* interview the applicant is interviewed by several persons in sequence before a selection decision is made. In an *unstructured sequential* interview each interviewer may look at the applicant from his or her own point of view, ask different questions, and form an independent opinion of the candidate. Conversely, in a *structured sequential* (or serialized) interview, each interviewer rates the candidate on a standard evaluation form, and the ratings are compared before the hiring decision is made.[40]

Research INSIGHT

situational interview A series of job-related questions that focus on how the candidate would behave in a given situation.

behavioural interview or behaviour description interview (BDI) A series of job-related questions that focus on relevant past job-related behaviours.

panel interview An interview in which a group of interviewers questions the applicant.

A **panel interview** involves the candidate being interviewed simultaneously by a group (or panel) of interviewers, including an HR representative, the hiring manager, and potential co-workers, superiors, or reporting employees. The key advantages associated with this technique are the increased likelihood that the information provided will be heard and recorded accurately; varied questions pertaining to each interviewer's area of expertise; minimized time and travel/accommodation expenses as each interviewee only attends one interview; reduced likelihood of human rights/employment equity violations since an HR representative is present; and less likelihood of interviewer error, because of advanced planning and preparation.

A more stressful variant of the panel interview is the *mass interview*, which involves a panel simultaneously interviewing several candidates. The panel poses a problem to be solved and then sits back and watches which candidate takes the lead in formulating an answer.

A panel interview is an efficient and cost-effective way of permitting a number of qualified persons to assess a candidate's KSAs.

Common Interviewing Mistakes

Several common interviewing errors that can undermine the usefulness of interviews are discussed in the following section. These interviewer errors can be reduced by properly planning and training interviewers on the process, as well as educating interviewers about these risks.

Poor Planning

Many selection interviews are simply not carefully planned and may be conducted without having prepared written questions in advance. Lack of planning often leads to a relatively unstructured interview, in which whatever comes up is discussed. The end result may be little or no cross-candidate job-related information. The less structured the interview is, the less reliable and valid the evaluation of each candidate will be.[41]

Snap Judgments

One of the most consistent literature findings is that interviewers tend to jump to conclusions—make snap judgments—during the first few minutes of the interview or even before the interview begins based on the candidates' test scores or résumé data. Thus, candidates feel pressure to start off on the right foot with the interviewer. However, snap judgments are not accurate or reliable in the selection process and should be avoided.

Negative Emphasis

Many interviewers seem to have a consistent negative bias. They are generally more influenced by unfavourable than favourable information about the candidate. Also, their impressions are much more likely to change from favourable to unfavourable than vice versa. Providing information about the value or weight of criteria in the selection process can ensure that the interviewer assesses the criteria accordingly.

Halo Effect

It is also possible for a positive initial impression to distort an interviewer's rating of a candidate, because subsequent information is judged with a positive bias. This is known as the **halo effect**. Having gained a positive impression of the candidate on one or more factors, the interviewer may not seek contradictory information when listening to the candidate's answers to the questions posed or may interpret/frame all responses positively.

Poor Knowledge of the Job

Interviewers who do not know precisely what the job entails and what sort of candidate is best suited for it usually make their decisions based on incorrect stereotypes about what a good applicant is. Interviewers who have a clear understanding of what the job entails conduct more effective interviews.

Contrast (Candidate-Order) Error

Contrast or candidate-order error means that the order in which applicants are seen can affect how they are rated. In one study, managers were asked to evaluate a candidate who was "just average" after first evaluating several "unfavourable" candidates. The average candidate was evaluated more favourably than he or she might otherwise have been because, in contrast to the unfavourable candidates, the average one looked better than he or she actually was.

Influence of Nonverbal Behaviour

Interviewers are also influenced by the applicant's nonverbal behaviour, and the more eye contact, head moving, smiling, and other similar nonverbal behaviours, the higher the ratings. These nonverbal behaviours often account for more than 80 percent of the applicant's rating. This finding is of particular concern since nonverbal behaviour is tied to ethnicity and cultural background. An applicant's attractiveness and gender also play a role. Research has shown that those rated as being more physically attractive are also rated as more suitable for employment, well ahead of those rated average looking and those regarded as physically unattractive. Although this bias is considered to be unconscious, it may have serious implications for aging employees.[42]

Leading

Some interviewers are so anxious to fill a job that they help the applicants to respond correctly to their questions by asking leading questions or guiding the candidate to the expected answer. An obvious example might be a question like: "This job calls for handling a lot of stress. You can do that, right?" The leading is not always so obvious. Subtle cues regarding the preferred response, such as a smile or nod, are also forms of leading.[43]

Too Much/Too Little Talking

If the applicant is permitted to dominate the interview, the interviewer may not have a chance to ask his or her prepared questions and often learns very little about the candidate's job-related skills. At the other extreme, some interviewers talk so much that the interviewee is not given enough time to answer questions. One expert suggests using the 30/70 rule: During a selection interview, encourage the candidate to speak 70 percent of the time, and restrict the interviewer speaking to just 30 percent of the time.[44]

Similar-to-Me Bias

Interviewers tend to provide more favourable ratings to candidates who possess demographic, personality, and attitudinal characteristics similar to their own, regardless of the value of those characteristics to the job.[45] The result can be a lack of diversity in the organization and a poor fit with the job if secured.

Designing an Effective Interview

Problems like those just described can be avoided by designing and conducting an effective interview. Combining several of the interview formats previously discussed enables interviewers to capitalize on the advantages of each.[46] To allow for probing and to prevent the interview from becoming too mechanical in nature, a semi-structured format is recommended. Given their higher validity in predicting job performance, the focus should be on situational and behavioural questions.

Conducting an Effective Interview

Although the following discussion focuses on a semi-structured panel interview, the steps described apply to all selection interviews.[47]

Planning the Interview

Before the first interview, agreement should be reached on the procedure that will be followed. Sometimes all members of the team ask a question in turn; in other situations, only one member of the team asks questions and the others serve as observers. Sitting around a large table in a conference room is much more appropriate and far less stressful than having all panel members seated across from the candidate behind a table or desk, which forms both a physical and a psychological barrier. As noted earlier, special planning is required when assessing candidates with disabilities.

The rapport established with a job applicant not only puts the person at ease but also reflects the company's attitude toward its public.

Establishing Rapport

The main purpose of an interview is to find out as much as possible about the candidate's fit with the job specifications, something that is difficult to do if the individual is tense and nervous. The candidate should be greeted in a friendly manner and put at ease.

Asking Questions

The questions written in advance should then be asked in order. Interviewers should listen carefully, encourage the candidate to express his or her thoughts and ideas fully, and record the candidate's answers briefly but thoroughly. Taking notes increases the validity of the interview process, since doing so (1) reduces the likelihood of forgetting job-relevant information and subsequently reconstructing forgotten information in accordance with biases and stereotypes; (2) reduces the likelihood of making a snap judgment and helps to prevent the halo effect, negative emphasis, and candidate-order errors; and (3) helps to ensure that all candidates are assessed on the same criteria.[48] Some examples of appropriate interview questions are shown in **Figure 6**.

Closing the Interview

Toward the end of the interview, time should be allocated to answer any questions that the candidate may have and, if appropriate, to advocate for the firm and position. It is useful to also inform the candidate about the next steps and timelines that the organization will follow at this point.

Evaluating the Candidate

Immediately following each interview, the applicant's interview performance should be rated by each panel member independently, based on a review of his or her notes or an observation form like the one shown in **Figure 7**. Since interviews are only one step in the process, and since a final decision cannot be reached until all assessments (including reference checking) have been completed, these evaluations should not be shared at this time.

FIGURE 6   Suggested Supplementary Questions for Interviewing Applicants

1. How did you choose this profession?
2. What did you enjoy most about your previous job?
3. What did you like least about your previous job?
4. Why did you leave your last job? What were the circumstances?
5. What has been your greatest frustration on your current job? Why?
6. Why should we be hiring you?
7. What do you expect from us?
8. What are three things you will not do in your next job?
9. What would your last employer say your three weaknesses are?
10. What would your last employer say your three major strengths are?
11. How can your manager best help you obtain your goals?
12. How did your manager rate your job performance?
13. Would you change your last supervisor? How?
14. What are your career goals during the next 1–3 years? 5–10 years?
15. How will working for this company help you reach those goals?
16. What did you do the last time you received instructions with which you disagreed?
17. What are some of the disagreements between you and your manager? What did you do?
18. Which do you prefer, working alone or working with teams?
19. What motivated you to do better at your last job?
20. Do you consider your progress on that job representative of your ability? Why?
21. Do you have any questions about the duties of the job for which you have applied?
22. How do you think you can perform the essential functions of the job for which you have applied?

Source: Based on www.HR.BLR.com

FIGURE 7	Interview Evaluation Form

Name of candidate:

Date interviewed:

Position:

Completed by:

Date:

Instructions: Circle one number for each criterion, then add them together for a total.

KNOWLEDGE OF SPECIFIC JOB AND JOB-RELATED TOPICS

0. No knowledge evident.
1. Less than we would prefer.
2. Meets requirements for hiring.
3. Exceeds our expectations of average candidates.
4. Thoroughly versed in job and very strong in associated areas.

EXPERIENCE

0. None for this job; no related experience either.
1. Would prefer more for this job. Adequate for job applied for.
2. More than sufficient for job.
3. Totally experienced in job.
4. Strong experience in all related areas.

COMMUNICATION

0. Could not communicate. Will be severely impaired in most jobs.
1. Some difficulties. Will detract from job performance.
2. Sufficient for adequate job performance.
3. More than sufficient for job.
4. Outstanding ability to communicate.

INTEREST IN POSITION AND ORGANIZATION

0. Showed no interest.
1. Some lack of interest.
2. Appeared genuinely interested.
3. Very interested. Seems to prefer type of work applied for.
4. Totally absorbed with job content. Conveys feeling only this job will do.

OVERALL MOTIVATION TO SUCCEED

0. None exhibited.
1. Showed little interest in advancement.
2. Average interest in advancement.
3. Highly motivated. Strong desire to advance.
4. Extremely motivated. Very strong desire to succeed and advance.

POISE AND CONFIDENCE

0. Extremely distracted and confused. Displayed uneven temper.
1. Sufficient display of confusion or loss of temper to interfere with job performance.
2. Sufficient poise and confidence to perform job.
3. No loss of poise during interview. Confidence in ability to handle pressure.
4. Displayed impressive poise under stress. Appears unusually confident and secure.

COMPREHENSION

0. Did not understand many points and concepts.
1. Missed some ideas or concepts.
2. Understood most new ideas and skills discussed.
3. Grasped all new points and concepts quickly.
4. Extremely sharp. Understood subtle points and underlying motives.

_____ **TOTAL POINTS**

ADDITIONAL REMARKS:

Source: Reprinted with permission of the publisher, Business & Legal Reports, Inc. Copyright Business & Legal Reports, Inc., 2011. www.HR.BLR.com

STEP 4: BACKGROUND INVESTIGATION/ REFERENCE CHECKING

Background investigation and reference checking are used to verify the accuracy of the information provided by candidates on their application forms and résumés. In an ideal world, every applicant's story would be completely accurate, but in real life this is often not the case, as illustrated in **Figure 8**. At least one-third of applicants lie—overstating qualifications or achievements, attempting to hide negative information, or being deliberately evasive or untruthful.[49]

Unfortunately, some employers do not check references, which can have grave consequences. Background checks are thus necessary to avoid negligent hiring lawsuits when others are placed in situations of unnecessary and avoidable risk.[50] Cases in Canada have included a nurse who practised in a Toronto hospital for almost two years without a registered nurse qualification, a manufacturing plant payroll officer who embezzled almost $2 million, and a teacher arrested for possessing child pornography.[51] Other problems can also be addressed through background checks. Loblaw recently took action to reduce its $1 billion disappearing goods problem by making criminal record checks mandatory for all prospective employees. As a result, 7.5 percent of prospective hires have been eliminated because of criminal records.[52]

Surveys indicate that at least 90 percent of Canadian organizations conduct background checks.[53] Many firms use reference-checking services or hire a consultant to perform this task. Obtaining such assistance may be a small price to pay to avoid the time and legal costs associated with the consequences of failing to do a thorough background check.

Whether requesting reference information in writing or asking for such information over the telephone, questions should be written down in advance. If enough time is taken and the proper questions are asked, such checking is an inexpensive and straightforward way of verifying factual information about the applicant. This may include current and previous job titles, salary, dates of employment, and reasons for leaving, as well as information about the applicant's fit with the prospective job and organizational culture.

CKR Global
www.ckrglobal.com

BackCheck
www.backcheck.ca

Investigative Research Group
www.irgcanada.com

FIGURE **8**	Top Seven Résumé Lies

1 Dates of employment

2 Job title (inflated rank)

3 Salary level

4 Criminal records

5 Education (bogus degrees, diploma mills)

6 Professional licence (MD, RN, etc.)

7 "Ghost" company (self-owned business)

Source: AccuScreen Inc., www.accuscreen.com/TOP7 (accessed May 24, 2009). Used with permission.

Information to Be Verified

A basic background check includes a criminal record check, independent verification of educational qualifications, and verification of at least five years' employment, together with checks of three performance-related references from past supervisors. For financially sensitive positions, a credit check may also be included.

Obtaining Written Permission

As a legal protection for all concerned, applicants should be asked to indicate, in writing, their willingness for the firm to check with current or former employers and other references. There is generally a section on the application form for this purpose. Many employers will not give out any reference information until they have received a copy of such written authorization. Because background checks may provide information on age or other prohibited grounds for discrimination, some employers do not conduct background checks until a conditional offer of employment has been extended.[54]

However, other employers do not hesitate to seek out information in the public domain at any time, without permission. A recent survey found that almost one-quarter of employers are using social networking sites like Facebook to gather information on job applicants. A third of those employers find enough negative information (such as the items listed in **Figure 9**) to eliminate a candidate from further consideration, and one-quarter of them find favourable content that supports the candidate's application.[55]

Providing References

In providing reference information, the concept of *qualified privilege* is important. Generally speaking, if comments are made in confidence for a public purpose, without malice, and are honestly believed, the defence of qualified privilege exists.

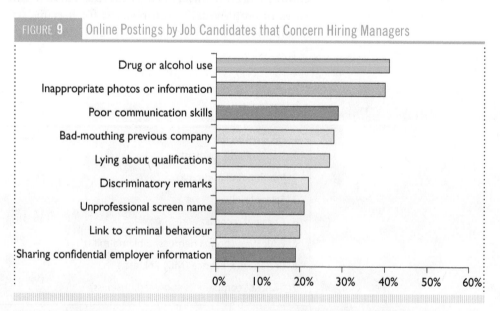

FIGURE 9 Online Postings by Job Candidates that Concern Hiring Managers

Source: Data from R. Zupek, "Is Your Future Boss Researching You Online?" CareerBuilder.ca, www.careerbuilder.ca/blog/2008/10/09/cb-is-your-future-boss-researching-you-online (accessed May 24, 2009). Copyright Sept. 10, 2008 Career Builder, LLC. - Reprinted with permission.

Thus, if honest, fair, and candid references are given by an individual who is asked to provide confidential information about the performance of a job applicant, then the doctrine of qualified privilege generally protects the reference giver, even if negative information is imparted about the candidate.[56] An overly positive reference, however, describing an employee dismissed for theft as "trustworthy," for example, can be considered *negligent misrepresentation* if the former employee steals from a new employer.[57] Due to concerns about the possibility of civil litigation, some Canadian companies have adopted a "no reference" policy regarding previous employees or are only willing to confirm the position held and dates of employment—especially in the case of discharged employees.[58]

STEP 5: SUPERVISORY INTERVIEW AND REALISTIC JOB PREVIEW

The two or three top candidates typically return for an interview with the immediate supervisor, who usually makes the final selection decision. The supervisory interview is important because the supervisor knows the technical aspects of the job, is most qualified to assess the applicants' job knowledge and skills, and is best equipped to answer any job-specific questions from the candidate. Also, the immediate supervisor generally has to work closely with the selected individual and must feel comfortable with that person. The selected individual must fit with the current members of the hiring department, something that the supervisor is often best able to assess. When a supervisor makes a hiring recommendation, he or she is usually committed to the new employee's success and will try to provide assistance and guidance. If the new hire is not successful, the supervisor is more likely to accept some of the responsibility.

realistic job preview (RJP)
A strategy used to provide applicants with realistic information—both positive and negative—about the job demands, the organization's expectations, and the work environment.

A **realistic job preview (RJP)** should be provided at the time of the supervisory interview. The purpose of an RJP is to create appropriate expectations about the job by presenting realistic information about the job demands, the organization's expectations, and the work environment.[59] Studies have reported that RJPs lead to improved employee job satisfaction, reduced voluntary turnover, and enhanced communication.[60] Although some candidates may choose not to accept employment with the firm after an RJP, those individuals probably would not have remained with the firm long had they accepted the job offer.[61]

STEP 6: HIRING DECISION AND CANDIDATE NOTIFICATION

RPC

Establishes appointment procedures for candidates selected through the recruitment process, ensuring that conditions of employment are documented and consistent with established policies

To make the hiring decision, information from the multiple selection techniques used must be combined, and the applicant who is the best fit with the selection criteria must be identified. HR department staff members generally play a major role in compiling all the data. It is the immediate supervisor who is usually responsible for making the final hiring decision, though. Firms generally make a subjective evaluation of all the information gleaned about each candidate and arrive at an overall judgment. The validity and reliability of these judgments can be improved by using tests that are objectively scored and by devising a candidate-rating sheet based on the weighted want criteria.

Another approach involves combining all the pieces of information according to a formula and giving the job to the candidate with the highest score. Research studies have indicated that this approach, called a **statistical strategy**, is generally more reliable and valid than is a subjective evaluation.[62]

statistical strategy A more objective technique used to determine whom the job should be offered to; involves identifying the most valid predictors and weighting them through statistical methods, such as multiple regression.

Regardless of collection methodology, all information used in making the selection decision should be kept in a file, including interview notes, test results, reference-checking information, and so on. In the event of a human rights challenge, negligent hiring charge, or union grievance about the selection decision, such data are critical.

Once the selection decision has been made, a job offer is extended to the successful candidate. Often, the initial offer is made by telephone, but it should be followed up with a written employment offer that clearly specifies important terms and conditions of employment, such as starting date, starting salary, probation period, and so on.

RPC

Supports managers in the negotiation of terms and conditions of employment

Candidates should be given a reasonable length of time in which to think about the offer and not be pressured into making an immediate decision. If there are two candidates who are both excellent and the first-choice candidate declines the offer, the runner-up can then be offered the job.

An Ethical Dilemma

As the HR manager, how much feedback should you provide to those individuals not selected for a position?

Chapter SUMMARY

1. Selection is the process of choosing among individuals who have been recruited to fill existing or projected job openings. The purpose of selection is to find the "best" candidate. Because the quality of the company's human resources is often a competitive advantage in achieving the company's strategic objectives, selection of employees has considerable strategic importance. Those individuals selected will be implementing strategic decisions and, in some cases, creating strategic plans. Thus, the successful candidates must fit with the strategic direction of the organization.

2. Reliability (the degree to which selection techniques are dependable, consistent, and stable) and validity (which relates to accuracy) of selection tests and interviews are critically important for effective selection of the best candidate and to satisfy legal requirements.

3. The different types of tests used for selection include intelligence tests, emotional intelligence tests, aptitude tests, tests of motor and physical

abilities, personality tests, interest inventories, achievement tests, the work-sampling technique, management assessment centres, situational testing, micro-assessments, and medical examinations. Pre-employment substance abuse testing is not permitted under human rights legislation in Canada.

4. Selection interviewing can be unstructured, structured, or semi-structured. The content varies between situational interviews (focus on future behaviour) and behavioural interviews (focus on past behaviour). Interviews can be administered on a one-on-one basis, sequentially, or by using a panel.

5. Reference checking is an important source of information about job candidates. Failure to check references can lead to negligent or wrongful-hiring lawsuits. When providing references, the legal concept of qualified privilege means that if honest, fair, and candid references are given, the reference-giver is protected from litigation, even if negative information is

imparted about the candidate. Providing falsely positive references can lead to charges of negligent misrepresentation by subsequent employers. Fear of civil litigation has led some Canadian companies to adopt a policy of "no references" or to only confirm a former employee's position and dates of employment.

MyManagementLab

Visit MyManagementLab to access a personalized Study Plan and additional study tools for this chapter.

Key TERMS

achievement tests
aptitude tests
behavioural interview or behaviour description interview (BDI)
construct validity
content validity
contrast or candidate-order error
criterion-related validity
differential validity
emotional intelligence (EI) tests
halo effect
intelligence (IQ) tests
interest inventories
management assessment centre
micro-assessment
mixed (semi-structured) interview

multiple-hurdle strategy
must criteria
panel interview
personality tests
realistic job preview (RJP)
reliability
selection
selection interview
selection ratio
situational interview
situational tests
statistical strategy
structured interview
unstructured interview
validity
want criteria

Review and Discussion QUESTIONS

1. Explain the differences among criterion-related validity, content validity, and construct validity.

2. Describe five different types of testing that may be used in the selection process and give an example of each.

3. Describe any four activities involved in a management assessment centre.

4. Name and describe the pros and cons of the three different types of interview structures.

5. Explain the difference between situational and behavioural interviews. Give examples of situational and behavioural interview questions.

6. Briefly discuss any five common interviewing mistakes and explain how such errors can be avoided.

7. Why is the supervisory interview so important in the selection process?

Critical Thinking QUESTIONS

1. If you were asked to design an effective selection process for retail sales representatives working on a 100 percent commission basis, which of the steps described in this chapter would you include and why? Justify the omission of any steps and explain why the quality of the selection decision will not be compromised by their elimination.

2. Assume that you have just been hired as the employment manager in a small manufacturing firm that has never done any selection testing. Write a memorandum to the CEO describing the types of tests that you would recommend the firm consider using in the future. Also list some of the legal and ethical concerns pertaining to such testing and how such concerns can be overcome, and the benefits to the firm for using the recommended testing.

3. Describe strategies that you could use to (a) establish rapport with an extremely nervous candidate, (b) get an interviewee who is rambling "back on track," (c) clarify a statement made by an applicant during an interview, and (d) obtain detailed reference information from an individual who seems reluctant to say much.

4. Alberta oil and gas companies are using pre-employment substance abuse testing even though it is prohibited. Their argument is that, because they have multibillion-dollar projects underway with a lot of potential for accidents, environmental damage, and so on, they want to be sure that they are not hiring employees who have substance abuse problems. They know that their young, transient, and relatively wealthy oil sands workforce commonly abuses drugs and alcohol. How could this situation be resolved in the spirit of the law on accommodating disabilities?

Experiential EXERCISES

1. Design a semi-structured interview questionnaire for a position with which you are extremely familiar, basing the candidate-specific questions on your own résumé. Ensure that behavioural, situational, job-knowledge, and worker-requirements questions are included. Once you have done so, select a partner. Role-play two selection interviews—one based on your questionnaire and the other based on your partner's questionnaire. The individual who wrote the questions is to play the role of interviewee, with his or her partner serving as the interviewer. Do not forget to build rapport, ask the questions in order, take effective notes, and bring the interview to a close. Once you have completed the two role-plays, critically evaluate each interview questionnaire.

2. Create an offer of employment for a successful customer service representative at a call centre, outlining the terms and conditions of employment. Keep in mind that a copy of the letter should be signed and returned by the new hire and that a signed letter of offer becomes an employment contract.

3. Develop two situational and two behavioural interview questions for either a college or university professor along with an outline of a "good" answer for each that you expect from the interviewees. Share and critique both questions and answers. Discuss how taking the time to complete this activity can help in candidate selection.

Running CASE

The Better Interview

Like virtually all the other HR-related activities at LearnInMotion.com, the company has no organized approach to interviewing job candidates. Three people, Jennifer, Pierre, and Greg (from the board of directors), interview each candidate, and the three then get together for a discussion. Unfortunately, they usually reach strikingly different conclusions. For example, Greg thought a particular candidate was "stellar" and would not only be able to sell but also eventually assume various administrative responsibilities to take the load off Jennifer and Pierre. Pierre thought this particular candidate was hopeless: "I've been selling for eight years and have hired many salespeople, and there's no way this person's going to be a closer," he said. Jennifer, noting that a friend of her mother had recommended this particular candidate, was willing to take a wait-and-see attitude: "Let's hire her and see how she does," she said. Pierre replied that this was no way to hire a salesperson, and, in any case, hiring another administrator was pretty far down their priority list. "I wish Greg would stick to the problem at hand, namely hiring a 100-percent salesperson."

Jennifer was sure that inadequate formal interviewing practices, procedures, and training accounted for at least some of the problems they were having in hiring and keeping good salespeople. They did hire one salesperson whom they thought was going to be terrific, based on the praise provided by her references and on what they understood her previous sales experience had been; she stayed for a month and a half, sold hardly anything, cost the company almost $10 000 of its precious cash, and then left for another job.

The problem wasn't just with the salespeople. They also hired a programmer largely based on his assertion that he was expert in various web-related programming languages, including HTML, XML, and JavaScript. They followed up with one of his references, who was neutral regarding the candidate's programming abilities. But, being desperate, Jennifer and Pierre hired him anyway—only to have him leave three weeks later, more or less by mutual consent.

"This is a total disaster," said Jennifer, and Pierre could only agree. It was obvious that in some respects their interviews were worse than not interviewing at all. For example, if they didn't have interviews, perhaps they would have used more caution in following up with the candidates' references. In any case, they now want you, their management consultant, to tell them what to do.

QUESTIONS

1. How would you restructure LearnInMotion's selection process?

2. Should Pierre and Jennifer use the multiple-hurdle strategy? Why or why not?

3. What are some of the legal implications of a new selection process that Jennifer and Pierre need to be aware of?

Case INCIDENT

The Case of What Should Have Been Known

Sunrise Academy, a privately run technical college, has been operating now for four successful years. Executive Director Ron Phillips is responsible for overseeing the college. He has just been reviewing the latest enrollment figures and is pleasantly surprised again by the projected number for the upcoming school year. This will mean that a new professor will be needed in the business administration program. Ron picks up the phone and calls the director of human resources to start the process for drafting a job posting to advertise the position both internally and externally.

A week goes by and HR calls Ron to indicate that they have many applications available to be reviewed for potential interviews. Ron reviews the applicants and a short list is developed and called for interviews. After a round of four "okay, but not spectacular" interviews, Ron was beginning to think they would never find a good candidate. However, the last interviewee, Rita Miller, turned out to be the successful choice and was subsequently offered the position. HR checked two references prior to offering Rita the position in writing. HR also asked Rita to bring an original copy of her Masters of Business Administration degree once it was received, as this degree was a requirement in the professor posting.

Rita brought a copy of her degree to HR within a week of being offered the position. HR's policy is also to call the issuing institution to verify degrees. Things became busy in the department so it was nearly two months later when someone finally checked Rita's degree. The results indicated Rita's degree was forged. HR called Ron with the news, and Ron has asked you to come in to help him decide what to do next.

QUESTIONS

1 Are there any legal implications to be aware of as a result of this selection decision?

2 What should have been done differently in the selection process?

3 How should the background-checking process be improved at Sunrise Academy?

MyManagementLab

Visit MyManagementLab to access a personalized Study Plan and additional study tools for this chapter.

 To view the CBC videos, read a summary, and answer discussion questions, go to MyManagementLab

Subject	Avoid Asking	Preferred	Comment
Name	about name change: whether it was changed by court order, marriage, or other reason maiden name		ask after selection if needed to check on previously held jobs or educational credentials
Address	for addresses outside Canada	ask place and duration of current or recent address	
Age	for birth certificates, baptismal records, or about age in general	ask applicants whether they are eligible to work under Canadian laws regarding age restrictions	if precise age is required for benefits plans or other legitimate purposes, it can be determined after selection
Sex	males or females to fill in different applications about pregnancy, childbearing plans, or childcare arrangements	ask applicant if the attendance requirements can be met	during the interview or after selection, the applicant, for purposes of courtesy, may be asked which of Dr., Mr., Mrs., Miss, or Ms. is preferred
Marital Status	whether the applicant is single, married, divorced, engaged, separated, widowed, or living common law whether an applicant's spouse may be transferred about spouse's employment	if transfer or travel is part of the job, the applicant can be asked if he or she can meet these requirements ask whether there are any circumstances that might prevent completion of a minimum service commitment	information on dependants can be determined after selection if necessary
Family Status	number of children or dependants about childcare arrangements	if the applicant would be able to work the required hours and, where applicable, overtime	contacts for emergencies and/or details on dependants can be determined after selection
National or Ethnic Origin	about birthplace, nationality of ancestors, spouse, or other relatives whether born in Canada for proof of citizenship	since those who are entitled to work in Canada must be citizens, permanent residents, or holders of valid work permits, applicants can be asked if they are legally entitled to work in Canada	documentation of eligibility to work (papers, visas, etc.) can be requested after selection
Military Service	about military service in other countries	inquire about Canadian military service where employment preference is given to veterans by law	
Language	mother tongue where language skills obtained	ask whether applicant understands, reads, writes, or speaks languages required for the job	testing or scoring applicants for language proficiency is not permitted unless it is job related
Race or Colour	about race or colour, including colour of eyes, skin, or hair		*continued*

Subject	Avoid Asking	Preferred	Comment
Photographs	for photo to be attached to applications or sent to interviewer before interview		photos for security passes or company files can be taken after selection
Religion	whether applicant will work a specific religious holiday about religious affiliation, church membership, frequency of church attendance for references from clergy or religious leader	explain the required work shift, asking whether such a schedule poses problems for the applicant	reasonable accommodation of an employee's religious beliefs is the employer's duty
Height and Weight			no inquiry unless there is evidence that they are genuine occupational requirements
Disability	for list of all disabilities, limitations, or health problems whether applicant drinks or uses drugs whether applicant has ever received psychiatric care or been hospitalized for emotional problems whether applicant has received workers' compensation		the employer should: – disclose any information on medically related requirements or standards early in the application process – then ask whether the applicant has any condition that could affect his or her ability to do the job, preferably during a pre-employment medical examination a disability is only relevant to job ability if it: – threatens the safety or property of others – prevents the applicant from safe and adequate job performance even when reasonable efforts are made to accommodate the disability
Medical Information	whether currently under a physician's care name of family doctor whether receiving counselling or therapy		medical exams should be conducted after selection and only if an employee's condition is related to job duties offers of employment can be made conditional on successful completion of a medical exam
Pardoned Conviction	whether applicant has ever been convicted whether applicant has ever been arrested whether applicant has a criminal record	if bonding is a job requirement, ask whether the applicant is eligible	inquiries about criminal records or convictions are discouraged unless related to job duties

continued

Subject	Avoid Asking	Preferred	Comment
Sexual Orientation	about the applicant's sexual orientation		contacts for emergencies and/or details on dependants can be determined after selection
References			the same restrictions that apply to questions asked of applicants apply when asking for employment references

Source: A Guide to Screening and Selection in Employment, Canadian Human Rights Commission. www.chrc-ccdp.ca/publications/screening_employment-en.asp. Reprinted with permission of the Minister of Public Works and Government Services Canada, 2009.

NOTES

1. D. Brown, "Waterloo Forced to Fire Top Bureaucrat Weeks After Hiring," *Canadian HR Reporter* (October 11, 2004), p. 3.

2. British Columbia Criminal Records Review Act, www.pssg.gov.bc.ca/criminal-records-review/index.htm (accessed May 31, 2009).

3. C. Kapel, "Giant Steps," *Human Resources Professional* (April 1993), pp. 13–16.

4. P. Lowry, "The Structured Interview: An Alternative to the Assessment Center?" *Public Personnel Management,* 23, no. 2 (Summer 1994), pp. 201–215.

5. Steps two and three are based on the Kepner-Tregoe Decision-Making Model.

6. S.A. Way and J.W. Thacker, "Selection Practices: Where Are Canadian Organizations?" *HR Professional* (October/November 1999), p. 34.

7. L.J. Katunich, "How to Avoid the Pitfalls of Psych Tests," *Workplace News Online* (July 2005), p. 5; *Testing and Assessment—FAQ/Finding Information About Psychological Tests,* APA Online, www.apa.org/science/faq-findtests.html (accessed August 1, 2006).

8. M. McDaniel et al., "The Validity of Employment Interviews: A Comprehensive Review and Meta-analysis," *Journal of Applied Psychology,* 79, no. 4 (1994).

9. "Hiring: Psychology and Employee Potential," *HR Professional* (August/September 2008), p. 16.

10. Ibid.

11. S. Bakker, "Psychometric Selection Assessments," *HR Professional* (April/May 2009), p. 21.

12. Canadian Psychological Association, *Guidelines for Educational and Psychological Testing,* www.cpa.ca/documents/PsyTest.html (accessed May 31, 2009).

13. R.M. Yerkes, "Psychological Examining in the U.S. Army: Memoirs of the National Academy of Sciences," Washington DC: U.S. Government Printing Office, Vol. 15 (1921).

14. F.L. Schmidt and J. Hunter, "General Mental Ability in the World of Work: Occupational Attainment and Job Performance," *Journal of Personality and Social Psychology,* 86, no. 1 (2004), 162–173.

15. M. Zeidner, I. G. Matthews, and R.D. Roberts, "Emotional Intelligence in the Workplace: A Critical Review" *Applied Psychology: An International Review,* 53, no.3 (2004), pp. 371–399

16. "Emotional Intelligence Testing," *HR Focus* (October 2001), pp. 8–9.

17. Results of meta-analyses in one recent study indicated that isometric strength tests were valid predictors of both supervisory ratings of physical performance and performance on work simulations. See B.R. Blakley, M. Quinones, M.S. Crawford, and I.A. Jago, "The Validity of Isometric Strength Tests," *Personnel Psychology,* 47 (1994), pp. 247–274.

18. C. Colacci, "Testing Helps You Decrease Disability Costs," *Canadian HR Reporter* (June 14, 1999), p. G4.

19. K. Gillin, "Reduce Employee Exposure to Injury with Pre-Employment Screening Tests," *Canadian HR Reporter* (February 28, 2000), p. 10.

20. This approach calls for construct validation, which, as was pointed out, is extremely difficult to demonstrate.

21. Myers-Briggs Type Indicator (MBTI) Assessment, www.cpp.com/products/mbti/index.asp (accessed May 31, 2009).

22. See, for example, D. Cellar et al., "Comparison of Factor Structures and Criterion Related Validity Coefficients for Two Measures of Personality Based on the Five-Factor Model," *Journal of Applied Psychology,* 81, no. 6 (1996), pp. 694–704; J. Salgado, "The Five Factor Model of Personality and Job Performance in the European Community," *Journal of Applied Psychology,* 82, no. 1 (1997), pp. 30–43.

23. M.R. Barrick and M.K. Mount, "The Big Five Personality Dimensions and Job Performance: A Meta-Analysis," *Personnel Psychology,* 44 (Spring 1991), pp. 1–26.

24. C. Robie, K. Tuzinski, and P. Bly, "A Survey of Assessor Beliefs and Practices Related to Faking," *Journal of Managerial Psychology* (October 2006), pp. 669–681.

25. C. Robie, "Effects of Perceived Selection Ratio on Personality Test Faking," *Social Behavior and Personality,* 34, no. 10 (2006), 1233–1244.

26. E. Silver and C. Bennett, "Modification of the Minnesota Clerical Test to Predict Performance on Video Display Terminals," *Journal of Applied Psychology,* 72, no. 1 (February 1987), pp. 153–155.

27. L. Siegel and I. Lane, *Personnel and Organizational Psychology* (Homewood, IL: Irwin, 1982), pp. 182–183.

28. J. Weekley and C. Jones, "Video-Based Situational Testing," *Personnel Psychology,* 50 (1997), p. 25.

29. Ibid, pp. 26–30.

30. D. Chan and N. Schmitt, "Situational Judgment and Job Performance," *Human Performance,* 15, no. 3 (2002), pp. 233–254.

31. S. Klie, "Screening Gets More Secure," *Canadian HR Reporter* (June 19, 2006).

32. Canadian Human Rights Commission, *Canadian Human Rights Commission Policy on Alcohol and Drug Testing* (June 2002).

33. M. McDaniel et al., "The Validity of Employment Interviews: A Comprehensive Review and Meta-Analysis," *Journal of Applied Psychology,* 79, no. 4 (1994), p. 599.

34. J.G. Goodale, *The Fine Art of Interviewing* (Englewood Cliffs, NJ: Prentice Hall Inc., 1982), p. 22; see also R.L. Decker, "The Employment Interview," *Personnel Administrator,* 26 (November 1981), pp. 71–73.

35. M. Campion, E. Pursell, and B. Brown, "Structured Interviewing: Raising the Psychometric Properties of the Employment Interview," *Personnel Psychology,* 41 (1988), pp. 25–42.

36. M. McDaniel et al., "The Validity of Employment Interviews: A Comprehensive Review and Meta-Analysis," *Journal of Applied Psychology,* 79, no. 4 (1994).

37. D.S. Chapman and P.M. Rowe, "The Impact of Video Conferencing Technology, Interview Structure, and Interviewer Gender on Interviewer Evaluations in the Employment Interview: A Field Experiment," *Journal of Occupational and Organizational Psychology,* 74 (September 2001), pp. 279–298.

38. M. McDaniel et al., "The Validity of Employment Interviews: A Comprehensive Review and Meta-Analysis," *Journal of Applied Psychology,* 79, no. 4 (1994), p. 601.

39. Ibid.

40. "Lights, Camera...Can I Have a Job?" *Globe and Mail* (March 2, 2007), p. C1; A. Pell, *Recruiting and Selecting Personnel* (New York, NY: Regents, 1969), p. 119.

41. J.G. Goodale, *The Fine Art of Interviewing* (Englewood Cliffs, NJ: Prentice Hall Inc., 1982), p. 26.

42. See R.D. Arvey and J.E. Campion, "The Employment Interview: A Summary and Review of Recent Research," *Personnel Psychology,* 35 (1982), pp. 281–322; M. Heilmann and L. Saruwatari, "When Beauty Is Beastly: The Effects of Appearance and Sex on Evaluation of Job Applicants for Managerial and Nonmanagerial Jobs," *Organizational Behavior and Human Performance,* 23 (June 1979), pp. 360–722; C. Marlowe, S. Schneider, and C. Nelson, "Gender and Attractiveness Biases in Hiring Decisions: Are More Experienced Managers Less Biased?" *Journal of Applied Psychology,* 81, no. 1 (1996), pp. 11–21; V. Galt, "Beauty Found Not Beastly in the Job Interview," *Globe and Mail* (April 15, 2002).

43. A. Pell, "Nine Interviewing Pitfalls," *Managers* (January 1994), p. 29; T. Dougherty, D. Turban, and J. Callender, "Confirming First Impressions in the Employment Interview: A Field Study of Interviewer Behavior," *Journal of Applied Psychology,* 79, no. 5 (1994), p. 663.

44. See A. Pell, "Nine Interviewing Pitfalls," *Managers* (January 1994), p. 29; P. Sarathi, "Making Selection Interviews Effective," *Management and Labor*

Studies, 18, no. 1 (1993), pp. 5–7; J. Shetcliffe, "Who, and How, to Employ," *Insurance Brokers' Monthly* (December 2002), pp. 14–16.

45. G.J. Sears and P.M. Rowe, "A Personality-Based Similar-to-Me Effect in the Employment Interview: Conscientious, Affect-versus-Competence Mediated Interpretations, and the Role of Job Relevance," *Canadian Journal of Behavioural Sciences,* 35 (January 2003), p. 13.

46. This section is based on E.D. Pursell, M.A. Campion, and S.R. Gaylord, "Structured Interviewing: Avoiding Selection Problems," *Personnel Journal,* 59 (1980), pp. 907–912; G.P. Latham, L.M. Saari, E.D. Pursell, and M.A. Campion, "The Situational Interview," *Journal of Applied Psychology,* 65 (1980), pp. 422–427; see also M. Campion, E. Pursell, and B. Brown, "Structured Interviewing: Raising the Psychometric Properties of the Employment Interview," *Personnel Psychology,* 41 (1988), pp. 25–42; J.A. Weekley and J.A. Gier, "Reliability and Validity of the Situational Interview for a Sales Position," *Journal of Applied Psychology,* 72 (1987), pp. 484–487.

47. A. Pell, *Recruiting and Selecting Personnel* (New York, NY: Regents, 1969), pp. 103–115.

48. W.H. Wiesner and R.J. Oppenheimer, "Note-Taking in the Selection Interview: Its Effect upon Predictive Validity and Information Recall," *Proceedings of the Annual Conference Meeting. Administrative Sciences Association of Canada* (Personnel and Human Resources Division, 1991), pp. 97–106.

49. V. Tsang, "No More Excuses," *Canadian HR Reporter* (May 23, 2005); L.T. Cullen, "Getting Wise to Lies," *TIME* (May 1, 2006), p. 27.

50. Ibid.

51. L. Fischer, "Gatekeeper," *Workplace News* (August 2005), pp. 10–11.

52. "Background Checks," *HR Professional* (June/July 2008), p. 16.

53. T. Humber, "Recruitment Isn't Getting Any Easier," *Canadian HR Reporter* (May 23, 2005).

54. C. Hall and A. Miedema, "But I Thought You Checked?" *Canadian HR Reporter* (May 21, 2007).

55. R. Zupek, "Is Your Future Boss Researching You Online?" CareerBuilder.ca, www.careerbuilder.ca/blog/2008/10/09/cb-is-your-future-boss-researching-you-online (accessed May 24, 2009).

56. J.R. Smith, "Damaging Reference Survives Alberta Privacy Challenge," *Canadian HR Reporter* (January 28, 2008).

57. A.C. Elmslie, "Writing a Reference Letter—Right or Wrong?" *Ultimate HR Manual,* 44 (January 2009), pp. 1–3.

58. A. Moffat, "The Danger of Digging too Deep," *Canadian HR Reporter* (August 11, 2008); see also P. Israel, "Providing References to Employees: Should You or Shouldn't You?" *Canadian HR Reporter* (March 24, 2003), pp. 5–6; T. Humber, "Name, Rank and Serial Number," *Canadian HR Reporter* (May 19, 2003), pp. G1, G7.

59. J.A. Breaugh, "Realistic Job Previews: A Critical Appraisal and Future Research Directions," *Academy of Management Review,* 8, no. 4 (1983), pp. 612–619.

60. P. Buhler, "Managing in the '90s: Hiring the Right Person for the Job," *Supervision* (July 1992), pp. 21–23; S. Jackson, "Realistic Job Previews Help Screen Applicants and Reduce Turnover," *Canadian HR Reporter* (August 9, 1999), p. 10.

61. S. Jackson, "Realistic Job Previews Help Screen Applicants and Reduce Turnover," *Canadian HR Reporter* (August 9, 1999), p. 10.

62. B. Kleinmutz, "Why We Still Use Our Heads Instead of Formulas: Toward an Integrative Approach," *Psychological Bulletin,* 107 (1990), pp. 296–310.

PHOTO CREDITS

Orientation and Training

From Chapter 8 of *Human Resources Management in Canada*, Twelfth Edition. Gary Dessler, Nita Chhinzer, and Nina D. Cole.

Orientation and Training

The terms "orientation" and "training" are associated, but actually represent slightly different variations of employee assimilation efforts. Orientation refers to a long-term, continuous socialization process in which employee and employer expectations or obligations are considered. With a focus on organization-specific topics, orientation attempts to transfer learning into behaviour using disciplined, consistent efforts.[1] In comparison, training refers to short-term, discrete efforts in which organizations impart information and instructions in an effort to help the recipient gain the required skills or knowledge to perform the job at adequate levels. Given that training often occurs after the orientation process, this chapter first reviews the process of orienting employees, followed by a review of the training process.

ORIENTING EMPLOYEES

Once employees have been recruited and selected, the next step is orienting them to their new company and their new job. A strategic approach to recruitment and retention of employees includes a well-integrated orientation program, both before and after hiring.[2] New employees need a clear understanding of company policies, expectations regarding their performance, and operating procedures. In the long term, a comprehensive orientation (also called onboarding) program can lead to reductions in turnover, increased morale, fewer instances of corrective discipline, and fewer employee grievances. It can also reduce the number of workplace injuries, particularly for young workers.[3] The bottom-line implications of successful orientation can be dramatic, as described in the Strategic HR box.

Purpose of Orientation Programs

employee orientation (onboarding)
A procedure for providing new employees with basic background information about the firm and the job.

Employee orientation (**onboarding**) provides new employees with basic background information about the employer and specific information that they need to perform their jobs satisfactorily. At the Law Society of Upper Canada, any time a new employee walks through the door the organization acts quickly to help the person get started on the right foot. The Law Society views orientation as an investment in the retention of talent. The essence of the orientation program is to introduce people to the culture, give them a common bond, teach the importance of teamwork in the workplace, and provide the tools and information to be successful at the Law Society.[4]

socialization The ongoing process of instilling in all employees the prevailing attitudes, standards, values, and patterns of behaviour that are expected by the organization.

Orientation is actually one component of the employer's new-employee socialization process. **Socialization** is the ongoing process of instilling in all employees the prevailing attitudes, standards, values, and patterns of behaviour that are expected by the organization.[5] During the time required for socialization to occur, a new employee is less than fully productive. A strong onboarding program can speed up the socialization process and result in the new employee achieving full productivity as quickly as possible.

reality shock (cognitive dissonance)
The state that results from the discrepancy between what the new employee expected from his or her new job and the realities of it.

Orientation helps the employee to perform better by providing necessary information about company rules and practices. It helps to clarify the organization's expectations of an employee regarding his or her job, thus helping to reduce the new employee's first-day jitters and **reality shock** (also referred to as **cognitive dissonance**)—the discrepancy between what the new employee expected from his or her new job and its realities.

STRATEGIC HR

Onboarding: The First Step in Motivation and Retention

Professor Jerry Newman is one of the authors of a best-selling book on compensation. He worked undercover as a crew member in seven fast-food restaurants during a 14-month period to research total rewards. One of his findings was that the onboarding (also known as employee orientation) process played a significant role in long-term perceptions of management's leadership abilities and the quality of non-monetary rewards.

In the best restaurant he worked for, he walked in and asked a counter worker for an application. She handed it to him, suggested that he fill out the application in the lobby, and in one simple gesture, created a positive first impression by asking "Would you like a soda?" Although it may seem trivial, it was one of the few times anyone went to any lengths, however minor, to satisfy the needs of a future employee.

The first days and weeks of employment are crucial in the turnover reduction process as reality begins to converge or diverge with an employee's needs and aspirations. Making good first impressions goes a long way toward shaping a future view of non-monetary rewards.

In recent years, the fast-food industry has made concerted efforts to reduce turnover. Many chains have cut turnover in half during the past five years. Why? Because when they start to analyze costs, the results of successful onboarding are dramatic.

Assume a typical store does $1 million in sales and profits are 10 percent ($100 000). A typical turnover, according to most brands, costs between $1 500 and $2 000. If turnover is 150 percent and the typical store has 40 employees, then 60 employees turn over during the course of the year. Taking the midpoint of the replacement cost, 60 employees at $1750 each equals $105 000. With profits at $100 000, the turnover costs eat up a store's profitability. This is why fast food has made reducing turnover a high priority. And the cost of turnover in, say, high-tech industries is much higher than $1 500 or $2 000. It quickly becomes apparent that reducing turnover, partially accomplished through a positive and successful onboarding experience, can have very positive payoffs.

An important part of any effective orientation program is sitting down and deciding on work-related goals with the new employee. These goals provide the basis for early feedback and establish a foundation for ongoing performance management.[6] Orientation is the first step in helping the new employee manage the learning curve; it helps new employees become productive more quickly than they might otherwise.

Some organizations commence orientation activity before the first day of employment. At Ernst & Young, the firm keeps in touch with people who have been hired but have not yet started work by sending them internal newsletters, inviting them to drop by for chats, and hosting dinners for them.[7] Others use orientation as an ongoing "new-hire development process" and extend it in stages throughout the first year of employment to improve retention levels and reduce the overall costs of recruitment.[8]

Online onboarding systems that can be provided to new employees as soon as they accept the job offer are increasingly being used to engage employees more quickly and accelerate employee performance.[9] Online onboarding provides strategic benefits starting with building the brand as an employer of choice. This approach engages new hires in a personalized way and accelerates their time-to-productivity by completing benefits decisions, payroll forms, new-hire data, introduction of policies and procedures, and preliminary socialization using videos and graphics before the first day on the job, leading to a productive day one.[10]

Content of Orientation Programs

Orientation programs range from brief, informal introductions to lengthy, formal programs. In the latter, the new employee is usually given (over an extended period of time) the following:

- Internal publications, including employee handbooks that cover matters such as company history, current mission, activities, products, and people
- Facility tour and staff introductions
- Job-related documents, including an explanation of job procedures, duties and responsibilities, working hours, and attendance expectations; vacations and holidays; payroll, employee benefits, and pensions; and work regulations and policies such as personal use of company technology
- Expected training to be received (when and why)
- Performance appraisal criteria, including the estimated time to achieve full productivity.

Hints **TO ENSURE LEGAL COMPLIANCE**

Note that some courts have found employee handbook contents to represent a contract with the employee. Therefore, disclaimers should be included that make it clear that statements of company policies, benefits, and regulations do not constitute the terms and conditions of an employment contract, either express or implied. Firms should think twice before including such statements in the handbook as "No employee will be terminated without just cause," or statements that imply or state that employees have tenure; these could be viewed as legal and binding commitments.

In an orientation, the supervisor explains the exact nature of the job, introduces new colleagues, and familiarizes new employees with the workplace.

Responsibility for Orientation

The first day of the orientation usually starts with the HR specialist, who explains such matters as working hours and vacation. The employee is then introduced to his or her new supervisor, who continues the orientation by explaining the exact nature of the job, introducing the person to his or her new colleagues, and familiarizing the new employee with the workplace. Sometimes, another employee at a peer level will be assigned as a "buddy" or mentor for the newly hired employee for the first few weeks or months of employment.[11] It is a good idea for the HR department to follow up with each new employee about three months after the initial orientation to address any remaining questions.

Special Orientation Situations

Diverse Workforce

In an organization that has not had a diverse workforce in the past, orienting new employees from different backgrounds poses a special challenge. The values of the organization may be new to the new employees if these values were not part of their past experience. New employees should be advised to expect a variety of reactions from current employees to someone from a different background and be given some tips on how to deal with these reactions. In particular, they need to know which reactions are prohibited under human rights legislation and how to report these, should they occur. In addition, as diversity of the internal workforce increases, existing employees can be oriented toward a broader range of employee perceptions and effective communication techniques.

Mergers and Acquisitions

Employees of a newly merged company need to receive information about the details of the merger or acquisition as part of the information on company history. They also need to be made aware of any ongoing, as-yet-unresolved difficulties regarding day-to-day operational issues related to their work. A further orientation issue arises with respect to the existing employees at the time of the merger or acquisition: A new company culture will evolve in the merged organization, and everyone will experience a resocialization process. This presents an opportunity for the merged organization to emphasize the new organizational values and beliefs, thereby reinforcing corporate culture and furthering the new organization's business objectives.[12]

Union versus Non-Union Employees

New employees in unionized positions need to be provided with a copy of the collective bargaining agreement and be told which information relates specifically to their particular job. They also need to be introduced to their union steward, have payroll deduction of union dues explained, and be informed of the names of union executive members. New employees, both unionized and non-unionized, need to be made aware of which jobs are unionized and which ones are not.

Multi-Location Organizations

New employees in a multi-location company need to be made aware of where the other locations are and what business functions are performed in each location. The Ontario Ministry of Education is one such organization, and it uses a web-based, online orientation to deliver corporate-level information.[13] All employees have equal access regardless of their location, and the same message is delivered to each one. Updates can be made instantaneously, and employees can view the information at their own pace.

IBM has been piloting two virtual onboarding programs for interns in China and India. In the Chinese pilot, US-based HR staff and Chinese interns create individual avatars to build relationships, learn about their functions, and hold meetings within Second Life (an online artificial 3-D world). In India, IBM is using another virtual tool called Plane Shift to allow virtual teams to simulate project work.[14]

Problems with Orientation Programs

A number of potential problems can arise with orientation programs. Often, *too much information* is provided in a short time (usually one day) and the new employee is overwhelmed. New employees commonly find themselves inundated with forms to fill out for payroll, benefits, pensions, and so on. Another problem is that *little or no orientation* is provided, which means that new employees must personally seek answers to each question that arises and work without a good understanding of what is expected of them. This is a common problem for part-time and contract workers. Finally, the orientation information provided by the HR department can be *too broad* to be meaningful to a new employee, especially on the first day; whereas the orientation information provided by the immediate supervisor may be *too detailed* to realistically be remembered by the new employee.

Evaluation of Orientation Programs

Orientation programs should be evaluated to assess whether they are providing timely, useful information to new employees in a timely and cost-effective manner. Three approaches to evaluating orientation programs are as follows:

1. *Employee reaction.* Interview or survey new employees for their opinion on the usefulness of the orientation program. Also, evaluate job performance within specified time periods to assess transference of learning and behaviours where possible.

2. *Socialization effects.* Review new employees at regular intervals to assess progress toward understanding and acceptance of the beliefs, values, and norms of the organization.

3. *Cost/benefit analysis.* Compare (1) orientation costs, such as printing handbooks and time spent orienting new employees by HR staff and immediate supervisors, with (2) benefits of orientation, including reduction in errors, rate of productivity, efficiency levels, and so on.

Executive Integration

The orientation process is a continuous, long-term process aimed at moulding desired behaviours and aligning values of the employee and the organization. As such, there is a formal component of orientation that often occurs when a new employee first joins the organization. There is also an ongoing informal orientation process, with the aim to build a strong employee bond with organizational values, history, and tradition. This can include staff involvement such as mentoring, management guidance (by using high level staff, firms communicate the importance of messages and experiences in a more meaningful way), and through employee empowerment (indoctrination of values and information to guide workplace behaviour).

Additionally, newly hired or promoted executives typically do not participate in formal orientation activities, and there is little planning regarding how they will be integrated into their new position and company. The common assumption is that the new executive is a professional and will know what to do, but full executive integration can take up to 18 months. [15] To make things even more difficult, executives are often brought in as change agents, in which case they can expect to face considerable resistance. Thus, a lack of attention to executive integration can result in serious problems with assimilation and work effectiveness. It is common to perceive executive integration as an orientation issue, but integration at senior levels in the

An Ethical Dilemma

Is it ethical to withhold information from an incoming executive about critical problems that he or she will face?

organization requires an ongoing process that can continue for months as the new executive learns about the unspoken dynamics of the organization that are not covered in orientation programs, such as how decisions are really made and who holds what type of power.[16]

Executive integration is of critical importance to a productive relationship between a new executive and his or her organization, and it is important to review previous successes and failures at executive integration on an ongoing basis. Key aspects of the integration process include the following:

- Identifying position specifications (particularly the ability to deal with and overcome jealousy)
- Providing realistic information to job candidates and providing support regarding reality shock
- Assessing each candidate's previous record at making organizational transitions
- Announcing the hiring with enthusiasm
- Stressing the importance of listening as well as demonstrating competency, and promoting more time spent talking with the boss
- Assisting new executives who are balancing their work to change cultural norms while they themselves are part of the culture itself.[17]

THE TRAINING PROCESS

training The process of teaching employees the basic skills/competencies that they need to perform their jobs.

Training employees involves a learning process in which workers are provided with the information and skills that they need to successfully perform their jobs. Training might mean showing a production worker how to operate a new machine, a new salesperson how to sell the firm's product, or a new supervisor how to interview and appraise employees. Whereas *training* focuses on skills and competencies needed to perform employees' current jobs, *development* is training of a long-term nature. Its aim is to prepare current employees for future jobs within the organization.

Canadian Society for Training and Development (CSTD)
www.cstd.ca

It is important to ensure that business and training goals are aligned and that training is part of an organization's strategic plan.[18] A training professional in today's business world has to understand the organization's business, speak its language, and demonstrate the business value of training investment.[19] Purolator, one of Canada's largest courier services, has 12 500 employees in Canada, and Stephen Gould, senior vice-president of HR, says it's critical to the success of the business that the company's trainers understand the business strategy.[20]

In today's service-based economy, highly knowledgeable workers can be the company's most important assets. Thus, it is important to treat training as a strategic investment in human capital.[21] For example, Vancouver's Sierra Systems, an information technology consulting company, offers ongoing in-house training and more than 2 000 online courses for its employees. Their senior HR manager explains: "Training and development is critical to our business. We're a professional services firm and our people are how we deliver our business."[22] Unfortunately, formal training levels have been reducing over the last few years, as discussed in the Strategic HR box.

STRATEGIC HR

The Role of Training and Orientation in a Tough Economy

In 2008, Canadian organizations dedicated roughly 1.5 percent of their payroll to training and orientation activities, resulting in more than 11 million working Canadians experiencing some form of workplace-related training. A Conference Board of Canada survey of Canadian organizations provides detailed information about the status of training and orientation in recent years.

Canada's lagging productivity is partially attributed to the skills shortage in Canada, as well as the inability to create new products and successfully commercialize them. In addition, the pressures of an increasingly diverse and aging workforce, demand for more knowledge-based activities in the workplace, and economic globalization present challenges that an organization can only meet by renewing, developing, and upgrading workers' skills.

Yet, organizations have been rapidly reducing investments in training and development. According to a 2009 Learning and Development Outlook survey, the amount of training each employee received annually was the equivalent of 20 hours, compared to 28.5 hours just four years earlier. Also, the real term expenditure on training and orientation activities averaged $787 per employee, representing a 40 percent decrease from levels 15 years ago.

There are a number of possible explanations for this, including the move to more informal training (which increased 56 percent over four years); the use of more cost-effective, immediate, and relevant training; and a lack of monitoring of training and orientation activities of the organization.

In addition, it may be possible that the responsibility for training and development shifted from the organization to the employee as the economy contracted. In a tight labour market, unemployed persons and those who are looking to change jobs are pressured to make themselves more enticing to potential employers. As a result, individuals often engage in initiatives such as licensing, education, training, and professional certifications outside of the workplace environment, which can have a depressionary effect on workplace training metrics (including cost and time).

Source: Learning and Development Outlook 2009: Learning in Tough Times, by P. Derek Hughes and Alison Campbell. Used with permission from the Conference Board of Canada.

A federal government report concluded that:

> To remain competitive and keep up with the accelerating pace of technological change, Canada must continuously renew and upgrade the skills of its workforce. We can no longer assume that the skills acquired in youth will carry workers through their active lives. Rather, the working life of most adults must be a period of continuous learning.[23]

Already, a skills crisis has arisen in the manufacturing sector, where lack of qualified personnel is a major problem. Skills in greatest need of improvement are problem solving, communications, and teamwork.[24] Training is therefore moving to centre stage as a necessity for improving employers' competitiveness. The federal government has called for businesses to increase spending on training, and business has asked the government to expand programs for professional immigrants to get Canadian qualifications in their fields. In response, the Canadian Council on Learning was created by the federal government to promote best practices in workplace learning. The Quebec government has legislated that all firms with a payroll of more than $250 000 must spend 1 percent of payroll on employee training (or else pay a tax in the same amount).[25]

Another benefit of increased training is the fact that training can strengthen employee commitment. It implies faith in the future of the company and of the individual employee. Few things can better illustrate a firm's commitment to its employees than continuing developmental opportunities to improve themselves, and such commitment is usually reciprocated.[26] This loyalty is one reason that a high-commitment firm like the Bank of Montreal provides seven days of training per year for all employees at a cost of $1 800 per employee—more than double the national average.[27] Today's young employees view learning and growth as the pathway to a successful and secure future and are attracted to organizations that have a commitment to keeping and growing their talent.[28]

Training and Learning

Training is essentially a learning process. To train employees, therefore, it is useful to know something about how people learn. For example, people have three main learning styles: *auditory*, learning through talking and listening; *visual*, learning through pictures and print; and *kinesthetic*, tactile learning through a whole-body experience. Training effectiveness can be enhanced by identifying learning styles and personalizing the training accordingly.[29]

First, it is easier for trainees to understand and remember material that is meaningful. At the start of training, provide the trainees with an overall picture of the material to be presented. When presenting material, use as many visual aids as possible and a variety of familiar examples. Organize the material so that it is presented in a logical manner and in meaningful units. Try to use terms and concepts that are already familiar to trainees.

Second, make sure that it is easy to transfer new skills and behaviours from the training site to the job site. Maximize the similarity between the training situation and the work situation and provide adequate training practice. Give trainees the chance to use their new skills immediately on their return to work. Train managers first and employees second to send a message about the importance of the training, and control contingencies by planning rewards for trainees who successfully complete and integrate the new training.[30]

Third, motivate the trainee. Motivation affects training outcomes independently of any increase in cognitive ability. Training motivation is affected by individual characteristics like conscientiousness and by the training climate.[31] Therefore, it is important to try to provide as much realistic practice as possible. Trainees learn best at their own pace and when correct responses are immediately reinforced, perhaps with a quick "Well done." For many younger employees, the use of technology can motivate learning. Simulations, games, virtual worlds, and online networking are revolutionizing how people learn and how learning experiences are designed and delivered. Learners who are immersed in deep experiential learning in highly visual and interactive environments become intellectually engaged in the experience.[32]

Fourth, effectively prepare the trainee. Research evidence shows that the trainee's pre-training preparation is a crucial step in the training process. It is important to create a perceived need for training in the minds of

Research INSIGHT

participants.[33] Also, provide preparatory information that will help to set the trainees' expectations about the events and consequences of actions that are likely to occur in the training environment (and, eventually, on the job). For example, trainees learning to become first-line supervisors might face stressful conditions, high workload, and difficult employees. Studies suggest that the negative impact of such events can be reduced by letting trainees know ahead of time what might occur.[34]

Legal Aspects of Training

negligent training Occurs when an employer fails to adequately train an employee who subsequently harms a third party.

International Personnel Assessment Council **www.ipacweb.org**

Under human rights and employment equity legislation, several aspects of employee training programs must be assessed with an eye toward the program's impact on designated group members.[35] For example, if relatively few women or visible minorities are selected for the training program, there may be a requirement to show that the admissions procedures are valid—that they predict performance on the job for which the person is being trained. It could turn out that the reading level of the training manuals is too advanced for many trainees for whom English is not their first language, which results in their doing poorly in the program, quite aside from their aptitude for the jobs for which they are being trained. The training program might then be found to be unfairly discriminatory. On the other hand, employees who refuse a lawful and reasonable order to attend a training program may be considered to have abandoned their position.[36]

Negligent training is another potential problem. **Negligent training** occurs when an employer fails to train adequately, and an employee subsequently harms a third party. Also, employees who are dismissed for poor performance or disciplined for safety infractions may claim that the employer was negligent in that the employee's training was inadequate.

The Five-Step Training Process

A typical training program consists of five steps, as summarized in **Figure 1**. The purpose of the *needs analysis* step is to identify the specific job performance skills needed, to analyze the skills and needs of the prospective trainees, and to develop specific, measurable knowledge and performance objectives. Managers must make sure that the performance deficiency is amenable to training rather than caused by, say, poor morale because of low salaries. In the second step, *instructional design*, the actual content of the training program is compiled and produced, including workbooks, exercises, and activities. The third step is *validation*, in which the bugs are worked out of the training program by presenting it to a small, representative audience. Fourth, the training program is *implemented*, using techniques like those discussed in this chapter (such as on-the-job training and programmed learning). Fifth, there should be an *evaluation* and follow-up step in which the program's successes or failures are assessed.

FIGURE 1 The Five Steps in the Training and Development Process

1. NEEDS ANALYSIS

- Identify specific job performance skills needed to improve performance and productivity.
- Analyze the audience to ensure that the program will be suited to their specific levels of education, experience, and skills, as well as their attitudes and personal motivations.
- Use research to develop specific measurable knowledge and performance objectives.

2. INSTRUCTIONAL DESIGN

- Gather instructional objectives, methods, media, description of and sequence of content, examples, exercises, and activities. Organize them into a curriculum that supports adult learning theory and provides a blueprint for program development.
- Make sure all materials (such as video scripts, leaders' guides, and participants' workbooks) complement each other, are written clearly, and blend into unified training geared directly to the stated learning objectives.
- Carefully and professionally handle all program elements—whether reproduced on paper, film, or tape—to guarantee quality and effectiveness.

3. VALIDATION

- Introduce and validate the training before a representative audience. Base final revisions on pilot results to ensure program effectiveness.

4. IMPLEMENTATION

- When applicable, boost success with a train-the-trainer workshop that focuses on presentation knowledge and skills in addition to training content.

5. EVALUATION AND FOLLOW-UP

- Assess program success according to

  REACTION—Document the learners' immediate reactions to the training.

  LEARNING—Use feedback devices or pre- and post-tests to measure what learners have actually learned.

  BEHAVIOUR—Note supervisors' reactions to learners' performance following completion of the training. This is one way to measure the degree to which learners apply new skills and knowledge to their jobs.

  RESULTS—Determine the level of improvement in job performance and assess needed maintenance.

Source: This article was originally published in IOMA's monthly newsletter *HRFocus®* and is republished here with the express written permission of IOMA. © 2009. Further use of, electronic distribution, or reproduction of this material requires the permission of IOMA. www.ioma.com

STEP 1: TRAINING NEEDS ANALYSIS

RPC

Conducts training needs assessments

The first step in training is to determine what training is required, if any. The main task in assessing the training needs of new employees is to determine what the job entails and to break it down into subtasks, each of which is then taught to the new employee. Assessing the training needs of current employees can be more complex, because it involves the added task of deciding whether or not training is the solution. For example, performance may be down not because of lack of training but because the standards are not clear or because the person is not motivated.

task analysis A detailed study of a job to identify the skills and competencies it requires so that an appropriate training program can be instituted.

Task analysis and performance analysis are the two main techniques for identifying training needs. **Task analysis**—an analysis of the job's requirements—is especially appropriate for determining the training needs of employees who are *new* to their jobs. **Performance analysis** appraises the performance of *current* employees to determine whether training could reduce performance problems (such as excess scrap or low output). Other techniques used to identify training needs include supervisors' reports, HR records, management requests, observations, tests of job knowledge, and questionnaire surveys.[37]

performance analysis Verifying that there is a performance deficiency and determining whether that deficiency should be rectified through training or through some other means (such as transferring the employee).

Whichever technique is used—task analysis, performance analysis, or some other—employee input is essential. It is often true that no one knows as much about the job as the people actually doing it, so soliciting employee input is usually wise.[38]

Task Analysis: Assessing the Training Needs of New Employees

Task analysis—identifying the broad competencies and specific skills required to perform job-related tasks—is used for determining the training needs of employees who are new to their jobs. Particularly with entry-level workers, it is common to hire inexperienced people and train them.[39] Thus, the aim is to develop the skills and knowledge required for effective performance—like soldering (in the case of an assembly worker) or interviewing (in the case of a supervisor).

The job description and job specifications are helpful here. These list the specific duties and skills required on the job and become the basic reference point in determining the training required to perform the job.

Task Analysis Record Form

Some employers supplement the current job description and specification with a task analysis record form. This consolidates information regarding the job's required tasks and skills in a form that is especially helpful for determining training requirements. As illustrated in **Table 1**, a task analysis record form contains six types of information:

1. *Column 1, Task List.* Here, the job's main tasks and subtasks are listed.
2. *Column 2, When and How Often Performed.* Here, the frequency with which the tasks and subtasks are performed is indicated.
3. *Column 3, Quantity and Quality of Performance.* Here, the standards of performance for each task and subtask are described in measurable terms, like "tolerance of 0.007 inches," or "within two days of receiving the order," for instance.

TABLE 1 Task Analysis Record Form

Task List	When and How Often Performed	Quantity and Quality of Performance	Conditions Under Which Performed	Competencies and Specific Knowledge Required	Where Best Learned
1. Operate paper cutter	4 times per day		Noisy press room:		
1.1 Start motor			distractions		
1.2 Set cutting distance		± tolerance of 0.007 in.		Read gauge	On the job
1.3 Place paper on cutting table		Must be completely even to prevent uneven cut		Lift paper correctly	On the job
1.4 Push paper up to cutter				Must be even	On the job
1.5 Grasp safety release with left hand	100% of time, for safety			Essential for safety	On the job but practise first with no distractions
1.6 Grasp cutter release with right hand				Must keep both hands on releases	On the job but practise first with no distractions
1.7 Simultaneously pull safety release with left hand and cutter release with right hand					
1.8 Wait for cutter to retract	100% of time, for safety			Must keep both hands on releases	On the job but practise first with no distractions
1.9 Retract paper				Wait till cutter retracts	On the job but practise first with no distractions
1.10 Shut off	100% of time, for safety				On the job but practise first with no distractions
2. Operate printing press					
2.1 Start motor					
.					
.					
.					

Note: Task analysis record form showing some of the tasks and subtasks performed by a right-handed printing press operator.

4. *Column 4, Conditions Under Which Performed.* This column indicates the conditions under which the tasks and subtasks are to be performed.

5. *Column 5, Competencies and Specific Knowledge Required.* This is the heart of the task analysis form. Here, the competencies and specific skills or knowledge required for each task and subtask are listed, specifying exactly what knowledge or skills must be taught. Thus, for the subtask "Set cutting distance," the trainee must be taught how to read the gauge.

6. *Column 6, Where Best Learned.* The decision as to whether the task is learned best on or off the job is based on several considerations. Safety is one: For example, prospective jet pilots must learn something about the plane off the job in a simulator before actually getting behind the controls.

Once the essential skills involved in doing the job are determined, new employees' proficiency in these skills can be assessed and training needs identified for each individual.

Performance Analysis: Determining the Training Needs of Current Employees

Performance analysis means verifying whether there is a significant performance deficiency and, if so, determining whether that deficiency should be rectified through training or some other means (such as transferring the employee). The first step is to appraise the employee's performance because, to improve it, the firm must first compare the person's current performance with what it should be. Examples of specific performance deficiencies follow:

> "Salespeople are expected to make ten new contacts per week, but John averages only six."

> "Other plants our size average no more than two serious accidents per month; we are averaging five."

Distinguishing between *can't do* and *won't do* problems is at the heart of performance analysis. First, the firm must determine whether it is a *can't do* problem and, if so, its specific causes. For example, the employees do not know what to do or what the standards are; there are obstacles in the system (such as a lack of tools or supplies); job aids are needed; poor selection has resulted in hiring people who do not have the skills to do the job; or training is inadequate. Conversely, it might be a *won't do* problem. In this case, employees *could* do a good job if they wanted to. If so, the reward system might have to be changed, perhaps by implementing an incentive program.

Training Objectives

Once training needs have been identified, training objectives can be established, which should be concrete and measurable. Objectives specify what the trainee should be able to accomplish after successfully completing the training program. They thus provide a focus for the efforts of both the trainee and the trainer and provide a benchmark for evaluating the success of the training program. A training program can then be developed and implemented with the intent to achieve these objectives. These objectives must be accomplished within the organization's training budget.

STEP 2: INSTRUCTIONAL DESIGN

After the employees' training needs have been determined and training objectives have been set, the training program can be designed. Descriptions of the most popular traditional training techniques and more recent e-learning techniques follow.

Traditional Training Techniques

On-the-Job Training

On-the-job training (OJT) involves having a person learn a job by actually performing it. Virtually every employee—from mailroom clerk to company president—gets some on-the-job training when he or she joins a firm. In many companies, OJT is the only type of training available. It usually involves assigning new employees to experienced workers or supervisors who then do the actual training.[40]

OJT has several advantages: it is relatively inexpensive, trainees learn while producing, and there is no need for expensive off-job facilities, like classrooms or manuals. The method also facilitates learning, since trainees learn by actually doing the job and get quick feedback about the quality of their performance.

Apprenticeship Training

More employers are going "back to the future" by implementing apprenticeship training programs, an approach that began in the Middle Ages. Apprenticeship training basically involves having the learner/apprentice study under the tutelage of a master craftsperson.

Apprentices become skilled workers through a combination of classroom instruction and on-the-job training. Apprenticeships are widely used to train individuals for many occupations, including those of electrician and plumber. In Canada, close to 170 established trades have recognized apprenticeship programs.[41]

Apprenticeship training is critical today as more than half of skilled trades workers are expecting to retire by 2020. Federal, provincial, and territorial governments are increasing their funding of apprenticeship training programs to meet this growing need for more trades people.[42]

On-the-job training is structured and concrete. Here, a supervisor teaches an employee to use a drum-forming machine.

Informal Learning

About two-thirds of industrial training is not "formal" at all but rather results from day-to-day unplanned interactions between the new worker and his or her colleagues. Informal learning may be defined as "any learning that occurs in which the learning process is not determined or designed by the organization."[43]

Job Instruction Training

job instruction training (JIT) The listing of each job's basic tasks along with key points to provide step-by-step training for employees.

Many jobs consist of a logical sequence of steps and are best taught step by step. This step-by-step process is called **job instruction training (JIT)**. To begin, all necessary steps in the job are listed, each in its proper sequence. Alongside each step, a corresponding "key point" (if any) should be noted. The steps show *what* is to be done, while the key points show *how* it is to be done and *why*. Here is an example of a job instruction training sheet for teaching a right-handed trainee how to operate a large, motorized paper cutter:

Steps	Key Points
1. Start motor	None
2. Set cutting distance	Carefully read scale to prevent wrong-sized cut
3. Place paper on cutting table	Make sure paper is even to prevent uneven cut
4. Push paper up to cutter	Make sure paper is tight to prevent uneven cut
5. Grasp safety release with left hand	Do not release left hand to prevent hand from being caught in cutter
6. Grasp cutter release with right hand	Do not release right hand to prevent hand from being caught in cutter
7. Simultaneously pull cutter and safety releases	Keep both hands on corresponding releases to avoid hands being on cutting table
8. Wait for cutter to retract	Keep both hands on releases to avoid having hands on cutting table
9. Retract paper	Make sure cutter is retracted; keep both hands away from releases
10. Shut off motor	None

In today's service economy, job instruction training for step-by-step manual work is being superseded by behaviour modelling for service workers.

Classroom Training

Classroom training continues to be the primary method of providing corporate training in Canada, and lectures are a widely used method of classroom training delivery. Lecturing has several advantages. It is a quick and simple way of providing knowledge to large groups of trainees, as when the sales force must be taught the special features of a new product.

Classroom learning has evolved to maintain its relevance in the technological age. For Generation Y employees familiar with Web 2.0 features such as wikis, blogs, and podcasts, learning opportunities must reflect their new abilities and needs. Blended learning, using a combination of instructor-led training and online e-learning, has been found to provide better learning results and higher learner engagement and enthusiasm than expected. In blended learning, the in-class training becomes tightly integrated with the online experience, and the relevance to the learner is vastly improved. Thus the classroom has evolved to include interactions with remote colleagues and instructors, e-learning in many forms, coaching, assessment, and feedback.[44]

Audiovisual Techniques

Audiovisual techniques (CDs or DVDs) can be very effective and are widely used. Audiovisuals can be more expensive than conventional lectures to develop, but offer some advantages. Trainers should consider using them in the following situations:

1. *When there is a need to illustrate how a certain sequence should be followed over time*, such as when teaching wire soldering or telephone repair. The stop-action, instant-replay, or fast- or slow-motion capabilities of audiovisuals can be useful.

2. *When there is a need to expose trainees to events not easily demonstrable in live lectures*, such as a visual tour of a factory or open-heart surgery.

3. *When the training is going to be used organization-wide* and it is too costly to move the trainers from place to place.

There are three options when it comes to audiovisual material: buying an existing product, making one, or using a production company. Dozens of businesses issue catalogues that list audiovisual programs on topics ranging from applicant interviewing to zoo management.

Videoconferencing, in which an instructor is televised live to multiple locations, is now a common method for training employees. It has been defined as "a means of joining two or more distant groups using a combination of audio and visual equipment."[45] Videoconferencing allows people in one location to communicate live with people in another city or country or with groups in several places at once. It is particularly important to prepare a training guide ahead of time, as most or all of the learners will not be in the same location as the trainer. It is also important for the trainer to arrive early and test all equipment that will be used.

videoconferencing Connecting two or more distant groups by using audiovisual equipment.

Programmed Learning

Whether the programmed instruction device is a textbook or a computer, **programmed learning** consists of three functions:

1. Presenting questions, facts, or problems to the learner
2. Allowing the person to respond
3. Providing feedback on the accuracy of his or her answers

programmed learning A systematic method for teaching job skills that involves presenting questions or facts, allowing the person to respond, and giving the learner immediate feedback on the accuracy of his or her answers.

The main advantage of programmed learning is that it reduces training time by about one-third.[46] Programmed instruction can also facilitate learning because it lets trainees learn at their own pace, provides immediate feedback, and (from the learner's point of view) reduces the risk of error. However, trainees do not learn much more from programmed learning than they would from a traditional textbook. Therefore, the cost of developing the manuals or software for programmed instruction has to be weighed against the accelerated but not improved learning that should occur.

Vestibule or Simulated Training

vestibule or simulated training Training employees on special off-the-job equipment, as in airplane pilot training, whereby training costs and hazards can be reduced.

Vestibule or simulated training is a technique by which trainees learn on the actual or simulated equipment that they will use on the job, but they are trained off the job. Therefore, it aims to obtain the advantages of on-the-job training without

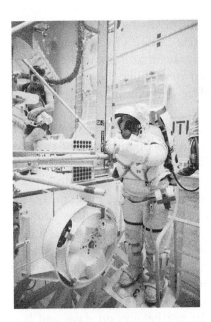

Vestibule training simulates flight conditions at NASA headquarters.

e-learning Delivery and administration of learning opportunities and support via computer, networked, and web-based technology to enhance employee performance and development.

actually putting the trainee on the job. Vestibule training is virtually a necessity when it is too costly or dangerous to train employees on the job. Putting new assembly-line workers right to work could slow production, for instance, and when safety is a concern—as with pilots—vestibule training may be the only practical alternative.

Vestibule training may just place a trainee in a separate room with the equipment that he or she will actually be using on the job; however, it often involves the use of equipment simulators. In pilot training, for instance, the main advantages of flight simulators are safety, learning efficiency, and cost savings (on maintenance costs, pilot cost, fuel cost, and the cost of not having the aircraft in regular service).[47]

E-Learning

Electronic training techniques have been developed that allow trainers to provide learning in a more flexible, personalized, and cost-effective manner. **E-learning** is the delivery and administration of learning opportunities and support via computer, networked, and web-based technology to enhance employee performance and development. Canadian employers are using e-learning to become more productive and innovative and to make self-directed, lifelong learners of their employees.[48]

Effective e-learning requires good instructional design. It is critical to motivate learners by describing the benefits they will gain from the training, providing content designed to the learner's specific needs, and offering interactivity, such as application of the material to common problems in the context of the learner's workplace and intrinsic feedback.[49]

The Canadian Society for Training and Development has found that e-learning is generally as effective as other forms of learning, but at a reduced cost. The primary users of e-learning in Canada are professional and technical employees; clerical, service, and support employees; and managers. Interestingly, learners are more satisfied when web-based learning involves high levels of human interaction.[50] Mobile technologies are growing in influence in training and development. Short videos, instant messages, podcasts, and email are examples of smartphone features that can be used for training.[51]

There are three major types of e-learning: computer-based training, online training, and electronic performance support systems (EPSS).

Computer-Based Training

In computer-based training (CBT), the trainee uses a computer-based system to interactively increase his or her knowledge or skills. Computer-based training almost always involves presenting trainees with integrated computerized simulations and using multimedia (including video, audio, text, and graphics) to help the trainee learn how to do the job.[52] Cisco Systems developed a binary math game intended to improve the effectiveness of network engineers and made it available for free on its website and for use on mobile devices. This simple game solved a key training problem and also turned out to be an effective corporate marketing tool.[53]

A new generation of simulations has been developed to simulate role-play situations designed to teach behavioural skills and emotional intelligence. Body language, facial expressions, and subtle nuances are programmed in. These new simulations offer authentic and relevant scenarios involving pressure situations that tap users' emotions and force them to act.[54] At L'Oréal Canada, new product managers participate in a training program that combines e-learning and a virtual simulation where they apply their new skills. Teams of trainees compete as virtual companies in the marketplace and continue to learn when they see their results compared to the others.[55]

A higher percentage of Canadian firms use CBT compared with American firms, primarily because of Canada's geography. CBT is often more cost-effective than traditional training methods, which require instructors or trainees to travel long distances to training sites.[56] Alberta Pacific Forest Industries (Al-Pac) had such good results from using CBT as a staple of its training program that it launched a new component to enable employees to learn the skills of another trade. Employees benefit from having training that is accessible 24 hours a day, which addresses shift work and different learning styles. This training program also helps to keep non-union staff members satisfied, as the multi-skilling resulting from CBT enables many employees to rotate jobs.[57]

CBT programs can be very beneficial. Advantages include instructional consistency (computers, unlike human trainers, do not have good days and bad days), mastery of learning (if the trainee does not learn it, he or she generally cannot move on to the next step in the CBT), flexibility for the trainee, and increased trainee motivation (resulting from the responsive feedback of the CBT program).

Online Training

Web-based training is now commonly used by Canadian organizations. It is generally estimated that online training costs about 50 percent less than traditional classroom-based training. Also, online learning is ideal for adults, who learn what they want, when they want, and where they want. Online training is often the best solution for highly specialized business professionals who have little time available for ongoing education. Students (the workers of tomorrow) thrive in online learning environments. They do not find it to be an isolated or lonely experience, and they find that they have more time to reflect on the learning material, which leads to livelier interaction.[58] Further, online training is ideal for global organizations that want consistent training for all employees worldwide. Alcan Inc. is using this approach to standardize its training programs for 72 000 employees in 55 countries.[59]

However, critics point out that content management, sound educational strategy, learner support, and system administration should receive more attention, as they are often the critical determining factors in successful training outcomes. In the last few years, "learner content management systems" have been developed to deliver personalized content in small "chunks" or "nuggets" of learning. These systems complement "learning management systems" that are focused on the logistics of managing learning. Together, they form a powerful combination for an e-learning platform. This development is considered part of the "second wave" of e-learning, involving greater standardization and the emergence of norms. Another problem is that the freedom of online learning means that unless learners are highly motivated, they may not complete the training. It is estimated that learners don't complete 50 to 90 percent of online courses. In general, it is important to seek "blended learning," including both personal interaction and online training tools.[60]

Electronic Performance Support Systems (EPSS)

electronic performance support systems (EPSS) Computer-based job aids, or sets of computerized tools and displays, that automate training, documentation, and phone support.

Electronic performance support systems (EPSS) are computer-based job aids, or sets of computerized tools and displays, that automate training, documentation, and phone support. EPSS provides support that is faster, cheaper, and more effective than traditional paper-based job aids, such as manuals. When a customer calls a Dell Computer service representative about a problem with a new computer, for example, the representative is probably asking questions prompted by an EPSS, which takes the service representative and the customer through an analytical sequence, step by step. Without the EPSS, Dell would have to train its service representatives to memorize an unrealistically large number of solutions. Learners say that an EPSS provides significant value in maximizing the impact of training. If a skill is taught but the trainees don't need to use it until several weeks or months later, the learning material is always available through the EPSS.[61]

STEPS 3 AND 4: VALIDATION AND IMPLEMENTATION

RPC

Ensures arrangements are made for training schedules, facilities, trainers, participants, equipment, and course materials

Validation of the training program that has been designed is an often-overlooked step in the training process. In order to ensure that the program will accomplish its objectives, it is necessary to conduct a pilot study, or "run through," with a representative group of trainees. The results of the pilot study are used to assess the effectiveness of the training.

Revisions to the program can be made to address any problems encountered by the pilot group of trainees in using the training material and experiences provided to them. Testing at the end of the pilot study can measure whether or not the program is producing the desired improvement in skill level. If the results fall below the level of the training objectives, then more work must be undertaken to strengthen the instructional design.

Once the program has been validated, it is ready to be implemented by professional trainers. In some cases, a train-the-trainer workshop may be required to familiarize trainers with unfamiliar content or with unique and innovative new methods for presenting the training content.

STEP 5: EVALUATION OF TRAINING

transfer of training Application of the skills acquired during the training program into the work environment and the maintenance of these skills over time.

It is important to assess the return on investment in human capital made through training by determining whether the training actually achieved the objectives. **Transfer of training** is the application of the skills acquired during the training program into the work environment and the maintenance of these skills over time. A number of actions can be taken before, during, and after a training program to enhance transfer of training.[62]

Before training, potential trainees can be assessed on their level of ability, aptitude, and motivation regarding the skill to be taught, and those with higher levels can be selected for the training program. Trainees can be involved in designing the training, and management should provide active support at this stage.

During the training, it is important to provide frequent feedback, opportunities for practice, and positive reinforcement. After the training program, trainees can use goal-setting and relapse-prevention techniques to increase the likelihood of applying what they have learned. Management can enhance transfer of training by providing opportunities to apply new skills and by continuing to provide positive reinforcement of the new skills while being tolerant of errors.

After trainees complete their training (or at planned intervals during the training), the program should be evaluated to see how well its objectives have been met and the extent to which transfer of training has occurred. Thus, if assemblers should be able to solder a junction in 30 seconds, or a photocopier technician repair a machine in 30 minutes, then the program's effectiveness should be measured based on whether these objectives are attained. For example, are trainees learning as *much* as they can? Are they learning as *fast* as they can? Is there a *better method* for training them? These are some of the questions that are answered by properly evaluating training efforts.

Overall, there is little doubt that training and development can be effective. Formal studies of training programs substantiate the potential positive impact of such programs. Profitable companies spend the most on training, and those rated as being among the 100 best companies to work for in Canada spend the most per employee on training.[63]

There are two basic issues to address when evaluating a training program. The first is the design of the evaluation study and, in particular, whether controlled experimentation will be used. The second is the training effect to be measured.

Controlled experimentation is the best method to use in evaluating a training program. A controlled experiment uses both a training group and a control group (that receives no training). Data (for example, on quantity of production or quality of soldered junctions) should be obtained both before and after the training effort in the training group, and before and after a corresponding work period in the control group. In this way, it is possible to determine the extent to which any change in performance in the training group resulted from the training itself, rather than from some organization-wide change like a raise in pay, which would likely have affected employees in both groups equally.

Training Effects to Measure

Four basic categories of training outcomes can be measured:[64]

1. *Reaction.* First, evaluate trainees' reactions to the program. Did they like the program? Did they think it worthwhile? One expert suggests using an evaluation form like the one shown in **Figure 2** to evaluate employee reaction to the training program.[65]
2. *Learning.* Second, test the trainees to determine whether they learned the principles, skills, and facts that they were supposed to learn.
3. *Behaviour.* Next, ask whether the trainees' behaviour on the job changed because of the training program. For example, are employees in the store's complaint department more courteous toward disgruntled customers than they were previously? These measures determine the degree of transfer of training.

RPC
Facilitates post-training support activities to ensure transfer of learning to the workplace

controlled experimentation Formal methods for testing the effectiveness of a training program, preferably with a control group and with tests before and after training.

FIGURE 2 | Sample Training Evaluation Form

PROGRAM NAME: _____ DATE: _____

YOUR NAME (Optional): _____ FACILITATOR(S): _____

OVERALL PROGRAM RATING	Poor		Fair		Good		Excellent
	1	2	3	4	5	6	7

What did you like **best** about the program?	What did you like **least** about the program?	What would you like to have spent **more** time on?

Please complete this form to help us assess how well this program met your needs and our objectives. Your feedback is important to us and will be used in our continuous efforts to improve the quality and usefulness of this program. Circle the number that best expresses your reaction to each item.

	Strongly Disagree		Disagree		Agree		Strongly Agree
1. The program was well-organized	1	2	3	4	5	6	7
2. The sequence of material presented was logical	1	2	3	4	5	6	7
3. The content of the program was understandable	1	2	3	4	5	6	7
4. The program activities were effective in helping me learn the concepts and skills presented	1	2	3	4	5	6	7
5. The objectives of the program were clear	1	2	3	4	5	6	7
6. The program met its stated objectives	1	2	3	4	5	6	7
7. The facilitator(s) grasped the material and activities they presented	1	2	3	4	5	6	7
8. The knowledge and skills learned in this program will help me do my job better	1	2	3	4	5	6	7

9. The length of the program   was appropriate   should be shorter   should be longer

Thank you for your participation and feedback!

Source: Reproduced, with permission, from the *Ultimate HR Manual*, published by and copyright CCH Canadian Limited, Toronto, Ontario.

4. *Results.* Last, but probably most important, ask questions such as these: "Did the number of customer complaints about employees drop?" "Did the rejection rate improve?" "Was turnover reduced?" "Are production quotas now being met?" and so on. Improvements in these "metrics"—specific measures of workplace results—are especially important. The training program may succeed in terms of the reactions from trainees, increased learning, and even changes in behaviour, but if the results are not achieved, then in the final analysis the training has not achieved its goals. If so, the

problem may be related to inappropriate use of a training program. For example, training is ineffective when environmental factors are the cause of poor performance.

Although the four basic categories are understandable and widely used, there are several things to keep in mind when using them to measure training effects. First, there are usually only modest correlations among the four types of training criteria (that is, scoring "high" on learning does not necessarily mean that behaviour or results will also score "high," and the converse is true as well). Similarly, studies show that "reaction" measures (for example, asking trainees "How well did you like the program?") may provide some insight into how trainees felt about the program, but probably will not provide much insight into what they learned or how they will behave once they are back on the job.

TRAINING FOR SPECIAL PURPOSES

Training increasingly does more than just prepare employees to perform their jobs effectively. Training for special purposes—increasing literacy and adjusting to diversity, for instance—is required too. The following is a sampling of such special-purpose training programs.

Literacy and Essential Skills Training

National Adult Literacy Database
www.nald.ca

Functional illiteracy is a serious problem for many employers. As the Canadian economy shifts from goods to services, there is a corresponding need for workers who are more skilled, more literate, and better able to perform at least basic arithmetic. Not only does enhanced literacy give employees a better chance for success in their careers, but it also improves bottom-line performance of the employer—through time savings, lower costs, and improved quality of work.[66]

In 2008, the Canadian Council on Learning reported that almost half of Canadian adults are below the internationally accepted literacy standard for coping in a modern society.[67] A 2010 update of this research suggests that Canada's largest cities (like Toronto, Vancouver, and Ottawa) will see a substantial increase in the illiteracy rate of the workforce, largely due to the spike in the number of seniors and the growing number of immigrants.[68] Research by University of Ottawa economists for Statistics Canada has shown that investments in essential skills training to improve literacy and numeracy pay off. For every increase of 1 percent in national literacy scores relative to the international average, a country will realize a 2.5 percent gain in productivity and a 1.5 percent increase in per capita GDP over the long term.[69]

Employers are responding to this issue in two main ways. Organizations such as diamond mining company BHP Billiton, steel giant Dofasco, the Construction Sector Council, and the Canadian Trucking Human Resources Council have implemented a training strategy with the objective of raising the essential skills of their workforce. Essential skills of workers can be measured with the Test of Workplace Essential Skills (TOWES), developed by Bow Valley College in Calgary. In 2005, the federal government made funding available for

RPC

Identifies and accesses external sources of training funding available to employees training professionals to develop enhanced language training (ELT) to provide job-specific English instruction to help immigrants gain employment in their area of expertise.[70]

Training for Global Business and Diverse Workforces

With increasingly diverse workforces and customers, there is a strong business case for implementing global business and diversity training programs. Research by Healthy Companies International has found that success in the global marketplace is predicted by developing leaders at all levels of business and by placing a high value on multicultural experience and competencies. The research identified four global literacies, or critical competencies, required to succeed in the global economy:

- personal literacy—understanding and valuing oneself
- social literacy—engaging and challenging other people
- business literacy—focusing and mobilizing the business
- cultural literacy—understanding and leveraging cultural differences[71]

Diversity training enhances cross-cultural sensitivity among supervisors and non-supervisors, with the aim of creating more harmonious working relationships among a firm's employees. It also enhances the abilities of salespeople to provide effective customer service.[72]

Two broad approaches to diversity training are cross-cultural communication training and cultural sensitivity training. *Cross-cultural communication training* focuses on workplace cultural etiquette and interpersonal skills. *Cultural sensitivity training* focuses on sensitizing employees to the views of different cultural groups toward work so that employees from diverse backgrounds can work together more effectively. All employees should be involved in managing diversity, and diversity initiatives should be planned and supported as any other business opportunity would be.[73]

Diversity Training
www.diversityatwork.org
www.diversitytraining.com

Customer Service Training

More and more retailers are finding it necessary to compete based on the quality of their service, and many are therefore implementing customer service training programs. The basic aim is to train all employees to (1) have excellent product knowledge and (2) treat the company's customers in a courteous and hospitable manner. The saying "The customer is always right" is emphasized by countless service companies today. However, putting the customer first requires employee customer service training.

The Canadian retail industry has struggled in the past with poorly trained workers who were not equipped to provide quality customer service. Retailers now understand that they need to make a serious investment in their employees.[74] The Retail Council of Canada offers a national customer service certification program for retail sales associates and retail first-level managers, based on national occupational standards and essential skills profiles for each group. Certification requires the completion of a workbook, a multiple-choice exam, an in-store evaluation-of-performance interview, and experience (600 hours for sales associates, one year for first-level managers). The certification program for sales associates includes the topics of professionalism, customer service and sales, inventory, store appearance, security and safety, and communication. Topics for first-level managers include professionalism, communication, leadership, human resources, operations, marketing, sales, customer service, administration, and planning.[75]

Training for Teamwork

An increasing number of firms today use work teams to improve their effectiveness. However, many firms find that teamwork does not just happen and that employees must be trained to be good team members.

Some firms use outdoor training—such as Outward Bound programs—to build teamwork. Outdoor training usually involves taking a group of employees out into rugged terrain, where, by overcoming physical obstacles, they learn team spirit, cooperation, and the need to trust and rely on each other.[76]

An example of one activity is the "trust fall." Here, an employee has to slowly lean back and fall backward from a height of, say, three metres into the waiting arms of five or ten team members. The idea is to build trust in one's colleagues.

Not all employees are eager to participate in such activities. Firms like Outward Bound have prospective participants fill out extensive medical evaluations to make sure that participants can safely engage in risky outdoor activities. Others feel that the outdoor activities are too contrived to be applicable back at work. However, they do illustrate the lengths to which employers will go to build teamwork.

An Ethical Dilemma

Is it ethical to require employees to participate in weekend and evening training programs if they do not want to because it is going to take time that they would otherwise be spending on personal and family responsibilities?

Training for First-Time Supervisors/Managers

As Baby Boomers head into retirement, young employees are rising to positions of authority quickly and in large numbers. They are assuming supervisory and managerial roles at much younger ages than their counterparts were only 10 to 15 years ago, with some university graduates being hired into management training programs right after graduation. Along with the steep learning curve that all first-time supervisors/managers face, the latest group faces the challenges of managing employees from previous generations who are still present in the workforce.

New supervisors/managers are often chosen for their technical ability, and their interpersonal and communication skills get overlooked. But it is precisely these skills that will determine success as a manager, which requires networking and the ability to get work done through other people. New managers also need to learn to define their personal management style, how to give and receive feedback, how to motivate others, and how to manage conflict.[77]

The transition demands crucial training because first-time supervisors/managers need to learn a new set of skills. Formal training is required, and higher-level managers need to coach, mentor, and provide performance feedback to new young supervisors.[78] This type of training can be provided by external organizations like the Canadian Management Centre.

Canadian Management Centre
www.cmctraining.org

Chapter SUMMARY

1. A strategic approach to recruitment and retention of employees includes a well-integrated orientation (onboarding) program both before and after hiring. New employees need a clear understanding of company policies, expectations regarding their performance, and operating procedures. Orientation is part of the socialization process that instills in new employees the prevailing attitudes, standards, values, and patterns of behaviour that are expected by the organization. Onboarding helps to reduce reality shock—the discrepancy between what the new employee expected from his or her job and its realities.

2. The basic training process consists of five steps: needs analysis, instructional design, validation, implementation, and evaluation.

3. Two techniques for assessing training needs are (1) task analysis to determine the training needs of employees who are new to their jobs, and (2) performance analysis to appraise the performance of current employees to determine whether training could reduce performance problems.

4. Traditional training techniques include on-the-job-training, apprenticeship training, informal learning, job instruction training, classroom training, audiovisual techniques, programmed learning, and vestibule or simulated training.

5. Three types of e-learning are computer-based training, online training, and electronic performance support systems.

6. In evaluating the effectiveness of a training program, four categories of outcomes can be measured: reaction, learning, behaviour, and results.

7. Today's organizations often provide training for special purposes, including literacy training, diversity training, customer service training, training for teamwork, and training for first-time supervisors/managers.

MyManagementLab

Visit MyManagementLab to access a personalized Study Plan and additional study tools for this chapter.

Key TERMS

controlled experimentation
electronic performance support systems (EPSS)
e-learning
employee orientation (onboarding)
job instruction training (JIT)
negligent training
performance analysis
programmed learning

reality shock (cognitive dissonance)
socialization
task analysis
training
transfer of training
vestibule or simulated training
videoconferencing

Review and Discussion QUESTIONS

1. Prepare an orientation program checklist for your current or most recent job.

2. Identify and describe three special orientation situations that may be encountered.

3. Choose a task you are familiar with—such as mowing the lawn or using a chat room—and develop a job instruction training sheet for it.

4. Ali Khan is an undergraduate business student majoring in accounting. He has just failed the first accounting course, Accounting 101, and is understandably upset. Explain how you would use performance analysis to identify what, if any, are Ali's training needs.

5. Describe how you would go about determining the best way to train a group of newly hired managers on how to conduct selection interviews.

6. Think about a job you have had in the past. For this job, identify which training technique was used and reflect on reasons why you think that system was used. Next, select a different training technique from the chapter that you think would have been good to use, providing a justification as to why this would be a suitable technique.

Critical Thinking QUESTIONS

1. "A well-thought-out onboarding program is especially important for employees (like many recent graduates) who have had little or no work experience." Explain why you agree or disagree with this statement.

2. What do you think are some of the main drawbacks of relying on informal on-the-job training for teaching new employees their jobs?

3. This chapter points out that one reason for implementing special global training programs is to avoid business loss because of cultural insensitivity. What sort of cultural insensitivity do you think is meant, and how might that translate into lost business? What sort of training programs would you recommend to avoid such cultural insensitivity?

4. Most training programs are not formally evaluated beyond a reaction measure. Why do you think employers do not measure the impact of training on learning, behaviour, and results more often?

5. Assume that your company president wants to develop a more customer-focused organization. For the past 10 years, the company has focused on cost containment while growing the business. Write a memo to your company president that supports the investment in customer service training as part of the strategic plan.

Experiential EXERCISES

1. Obtain a copy of an employee handbook from your employer or from some other organization. Review it and make recommendations for improvement.

2. Working individually or in groups, follow the steps in **Figure 1** and prepare a training program for a job that you currently hold or have had in the past.

3. In small groups of four to six students, complete the following exercise:

   WestJet has asked you to quickly develop the outline of a training program for its new reservation clerks. Airline reservation clerks obviously need numerous skills to perform their jobs. (You may want to start by listing the job's main duties, using the information provided below.)

Produce the requested training outline, making sure to be very specific about what you want to teach the new clerks and what methods and aids you suggest using to train them.

Duties of Airline Reservation Clerks:

Customers contact airline reservation clerks to obtain flight schedules, prices, and itineraries. The reservation clerks look up the requested information on the airline's flight schedule systems, which are updated continuously. The reservation clerk must deal courteously and expeditiously with the customer and be able to quickly find alternative flight arrangements to provide the customer with the itinerary that fits his or her needs. Alternative flights and prices must be found quickly so that the customer is not kept waiting and so that the reservation operations group maintains its efficiency standards. It is often necessary to look under various routings, since there may be a dozen or more alternative routes between the customer's starting point and destination.

4. Working in groups of four to six students, complete the following exercise:

Determine who in your group knows how to make paper objects such as cranes, boxes, balloons, ninja darts, fortunes, boats, and so on. Select one person who is willing to be a subject matter expert (SME) to assist your group in developing an on-the-job training program to make one product.

Using the expertise of your SME, develop, document (refer to the sample job instruction template earlier in the chapter), and validate a training plan to make the chosen product. Modify the documented plan as required after your pilot. Ensure that everyone in your group has a copy of the plan and can reliably make the product to standards. Once this is accomplished, each group member will pair up with a member of another group that made a different product. Each person in the resulting pairs will train his or her partner on how to make the products using the training plan and sample he or she created.

Debrief the exercise as instructed.

Running CASE

Running Case: LearnInMotion.com

The New Training Program

"I just don't understand it," said Pierre. "No one here seems to follow instructions, and no matter how many times I've told them how to do things, they seem to do them their own way." At present, LearnInMotion.com has no formal onboarding or training policies or procedures. Jennifer believes this is one reason why employees generally ignore the standards that she and Pierre would like them to adopt.

Several examples illustrate this problem. One job of the web designer (her name is Maureen) is to take customer copy for banner ads and adapt it for placement on LearnInMotion.com. She has been told several times not to tinker in any way with a customer's logo: Most companies put considerable thought and resources into logo design, and as Pierre has said, "Whether or not Maureen thinks the logo is perfect, it's the customer's logo, and she's to leave it as it is." Yet just a week ago, they almost lost a big customer when Maureen, to "clarify" the customer's logo, modified its design before posting it on LearnInMotion.com.

That's just the tip of the iceberg. As far as Jennifer and Pierre are concerned, it is the sales effort that is completely out of control. For one thing, even after several months on the job, it still seems as if the salespeople don't know what they're talking about. For example, LearnInMotion has several co-brand arrangements with websites like Yahoo! This setup allows users on other sites to easily click through to LearnInMotion.com if they are interested in ordering educational courses or CDs. Jennifer has noticed that, during conversations with customers, the two salespeople have no idea which sites co-brand with LearnInMotion, or how to get to the LearnInMotion site from the partner website. The salespeople also need to know a lot more about the products themselves. For example, one salesperson was trying to sell someone who produces programs on managing call centres on the idea of listing its products under LearnInMotion's "communications" community. In fact, the "communications" community is for courses on topics like interpersonal communications and how to be a better listener; it has nothing to do with managing the sorts of call centres that, for instance, airlines use for handling customer inquiries.

As another example, the web surfer is supposed to get a specific email address with a specific person's name for the salespeople to use; instead he often just comes back with an "information" email address from a website. The list goes on and on.

Jennifer feels the company has had other problems because of the lack of adequate employee training and orientation. For example, a question came up recently when employees found out they weren't paid for the Canada Day holiday. They assumed they would be paid, but they were not. Similarly, when a salesperson left after barely a month on the job, there was considerable debate about whether the person should receive severance pay and accumulated vacation pay. Other matters to cover during an orientation, says

Jennifer, include company policy regarding lateness and absences; health and hospitalization benefits (there are none, other than workers' compensation); and matters like maintaining a safe and healthy workplace, personal appearance and cleanliness, personal telephone calls and email, substance abuse, and eating on the job.

Jennifer believes that implementing orientation and training programs would help ensure that employees know how to do their jobs. She and Pierre further believe that it is only when employees understand the right way to do their jobs that there is any hope those jobs will in fact be carried out in the way the owners want them to be. Now they want you, their management consultant, to help them.

QUESTIONS

1 How would you change LearnInMotion's orientation program? Should this company rename this process to an onboarding program instead?

2 Should Pierre and Jennifer be involved in the onboarding program to emphasize the importance of this process to their staff?

3 Should management of each department assist in the development and subsequent enforcement of the new onboarding program? Why or why not?

Case INCIDENT

A Case of Too Little Training Too Late!

It's late Friday afternoon in Thunder Bay, Ontario, and Jeff Hartley, a returning summer student, is looking forward to the end of the workday so that he can join his team from the paint department at the baseball game tonight. At the same time, in the office area adjacent to the plant, Julie Adler is working on the finishing touches to a new training program she will be requiring all new employees to take prior to being hired at Simplas Inc. Julie just completed hiring back all of the summer students who were on staff last year and is anxious to have them attend this required training/onboarding program scheduled for Monday morning.

The company has never had a formal onboarding program before, including no Workplace Hazardous Materials Information System (WHMIS) training regarding chemicals and their affects in the workplace. Julie has been noticing some unsafe behaviours lately and wants to take this opportunity to put appropriate training in place. Another part of Julie's plan for this training is to emphasize the supervisor's role in each department with regard to promoting safe behaviours, especially in the area of proper handling of chemicals in the workplace.

An hour later Julie has put the finishing touches on her new orientation/training program, has confirmed the trainer scheduled to certify everyone in WHMIS on Monday, and has received top management support for her program when she hears screams coming from the paint department. Running down the stairs to the paint department, she sees Jeff Hartley unconscious on the floor. The sound of the arrival of the ambulance erupts into the air. After Jeff is taken to the hospital, Julie is desperate to investigate what happened. She turns to his supervisor and demands to know all the details. Apparently, in his hurry to be done for the day, Jeff did not wear his face mask while he was painting a final part and must have passed out from the paint fumes collecting in the area. Julie sighs and realizes just how much more training will be needed at this company; onboarding is just a start. Please assist Julie by answering the following questions.

QUESTIONS

1 What legal aspects regarding the obvious lack of training in this case will Julie, as HR manager, and the company have to deal with?

2 How can the five-step training process assist in this scenario?

3 Should Julie put together specific training for all summer students?

MyManagementLab

Visit MyManagementLab to access a personalized Study Plan and additional study tools for this chapter.

CBC To view the CBC videos, read a summary, and answer discussion questions, go to MyManagementLab

NOTES

1. M. Akdere and S. Schmidt, "Measuring the Effects of Employee Orientation Training on Employee Perception," *The Business Review* (Summer 2007), pp. 322–327.

2. B.W. Pascal, "The Orientation Wars," *Workplace Today* (October 2001), p. 4.

3. B. Pomfret, "Sound Employee Orientation Program Boosts Productivity and Safety," *Canadian HR Reporter* (January 25, 1999), pp. 17–19.

4. L. Shelat, "First Impressions Matter—A Lot," *Canadian HR Reporter* (May 3, 2004), pp. 11, 13.

5. For a recent discussion of socialization, see, for example, G. Chao et al., "Organizational Socialization: Its Content and Consequences," *Journal of Applied Psychology*, 79, no. 5 (1994), pp. 730–743.

6. S. Jackson, "After All That Work in Hiring, Don't Let New Employees Dangle," *Canadian HR Reporter* (May 19, 1997), p. 13.

7. A. Macaulay, "The Long and Winding Road," *Canadian HR Reporter* (November 16, 1998), pp. G1–G10.

8. R. Biswas, "Employee Orientation: Your Best Weapon in the Fight for Skilled Talent," *Human Resources Professional* (August/September 1998), pp. 41–42.

9. "Employee Onboarding Guides New Hires," *Workspan* (January 2009), p. 119.

10. D. Chhabra, "What Web-Based Onboarding Can Do for Your Company," *Workspan* (May 2008), pp. 111–114.

11. R. Harrison, "Onboarding: The First Step in Motivation and Retention," *Workspan* (September 2007), pp. 43–45.

12. D. Barnes, "Learning Is Key to Post-Merger Success," *Canadian HR Reporter* (July 12, 1999), pp. 16–17.

13. C. Gibson, "Online Orientation: Extending a Welcoming Hand to New Employees," *Canadian HR Reporter* (November 30, 1998), pp. 22–23.

14. "Onboarding: Virtual Orientation at IBM," *HR Professional* (August/September 2008), p. 12.

15. D. Brown, "Execs Need Help Learning the Ropes Too," *Canadian HR Reporter* (April 22, 2002), p. 2.

16. Ibid.

17. "The Critical Importance of Executive Integration," *Drake Business Review* (December 2002), pp. 6–8.

18. S. Mingail, "Employers Need a Lesson in Training," *Canadian HR Reporter* (February 11, 2002), pp. 22–23.

19. U. Vu, "Trainers Mature into Business Partners," *Canadian HR Reporter* (July 12, 2004), pp. 1–2.

20. S. Klie, "Training Isn't Always the Answer," *Canadian HR Reporter* (December 5, 2005), pp. 13–14.

21. V. Galt, "Training Falls Short: Study," *Globe and Mail* (July 9, 2001), p. M1.

22. D. Harder, "Sierra Systems Earns Top Marks for Training," *Canadian HR Reporter* (February 2, 2009).

23. *Knowledge Matters: Skills and Learning for Canadians* (Government of Canada, 2002), p. 3, www11.sdc.gc.ca/sl-ca/doc/summary.shtml (accessed June 7, 2006).

24. A. Tomlinson, "More Training Critical in Manufacturing," *Canadian HR Reporter* (November 4, 2002), p. 2.

25. D. Brown, "PM Calls for Business to Spend More on Training," *Canadian HR Reporter* (December 16, 2002), pp. 1, 11; D. Brown, "Budget Should Include More for Training: Critics," *Canadian HR Reporter* (March 10, 2003), pp. 1–2; D. Brown, "Legislated Training, Questionable Results," *Canadian HR Reporter* (May 6, 2002), pp. 1, 12.

26. N.L. Trainor, "Employee Development the Key to Talent Attraction and Retention," *Canadian HR Reporter* (November 1, 1999), p. 8.

27. Bank of Montreal, www.bmo.com (accessed May 31, 2009).

28. L. Johnston, "Employees Put High Price on Learning, Development," *Canadian HR Reporter* (November 3, 2008); S. Klie, "Higher Education Leads to Higher Productivity," *Canadian HR Reporter* (December 3, 2007).

29. D. LaMarche-Bisson, "There's More than One Way to Learn," *Canadian HR Reporter* (November 18, 2003), p. 7.

30. M. Belcourt, P.C. Wright, and A.M. Saks, *Managing Performance through Training and Development*, 2nd ed. (Toronto, ON: Nelson Thomson Learning, 2000); see also A.M. Saks and R.R. Haccoun, "Easing the Transfer of Training," *Human Resources Professional* (July–August 1996), pp. 8–11.

31. J.A. Colquitt, J.A. LePine, and R.A. Noe, "Toward an Integrative Theory of Training Motivation: A Meta-Analytic Path Analysis of 20 Years of Research," *Journal of Applied Psychology*, 85 (2000), pp. 678–707.

32. M. Georghiou, "Games, Simulations Open World of Learning," *Canadian HR Reporter* (May 5, 2008).

33. K.A. Smith-Jentsch et al., "Can Pre-Training Experiences Explain Individual Differences in Learning?" *Journal of Applied Psychology*, 81, no. 1 (1986), pp. 100–116.

34. J.A. Cannon-Bowers et al., "A Framework for Understanding Pre-Practice Conditions and Their Impact on Learning," *Personnel Psychology*, 51 (1988), pp. 291–320.

35. Based on K. Wexley and G. Latham, *Developing and Training Human Resources in Organizations* (Glenview, IL: Scott, Foresman, 1981), pp. 22–27.

36. G. Na, "An Employer's Right to Train," *Canadian HR Reporter* (October 6, 2008).

37. B.M. Bass and J.A. Vaughan, "Assessing Training Needs," in C. Schneier and R. Beatty, *Personnel Administration Today* (Reading, MA: Addison-Wesley, 1978), p. 311; see also R. Ash and E. Leving, "Job Applicant Training and Work Experience Evaluation: An Empirical Comparison of Four Methods," *Journal of Applied Psychology*, 70, no. 3 (1985), pp. 572–576; J. Lawrie, "Break the Training Ritual," *Personnel Journal*, 67, no. 4 (April 1988), pp. 95–77; T. Lewis and D. Bjorkquist, "Needs Assessment—A Critical Reappraisal," *Performance Improvement Quarterly*, 5, no. 4 (1992), pp. 33–54.

38. See, for example, G. Freeman, "Human Resources Planning—Training Needs Analysis," *Human Resources Planning*, 39, no. 3 (Fall 1993), pp. 32–34.

39. J.C. Georges, "The Hard Realities of Soft Skills Training," *Personnel Journal*, 68, no. 4 (April 1989), pp. 40–45; R.H. Buckham, "Applying Role Analysis in the Workplace," *Personnel*, 64, no. 2 (February 1987), pp. 63–65; J.K. Ford and R. Noe, "Self-Assessed Training Needs: The Effects of Attitudes towards Training, Management Level, and Function," *Personnel Psychology*, 40, no. 1 (Spring 1987), pp. 39–54.

40. K. Wexley and G. Latham, *Developing and Training Human Resources in Organizations* (Glenview, IL: Scott, Foresman, 1981), p. 107.

41. "German Training Model Imported," *BNA Bulletin to Management* (December 19, 1996), p. 408; L. Burton, "Apprenticeship: The Learn While You Earn Option," *Human Resources Professional* (February/March 1998), p. 25; H. Frazis, D.E. Herz, and M.W. Harrigan, "Employer-Provided Training: Results from a New Survey," *Monthly Labor Review*, 118 (1995), pp. 3–17.

42. "Apprenticeship Grant Gets Going," *Canadian HR Reporter* (January 25, 2007); "New Funding for Apprenticeships," *Canadian HR Reporter* (May 3, 2004), p. 2; "Ontario Boosts Apprenticeship Program with $37 Million Investment," *Canadian HR Reporter* (April 7, 2000); ThinkTrades (Alberta Aboriginal Apprenticeship Project), www.thinktrades.com/candidates.htm (accessed June 13, 2006).

43. N. Day, "Informal Learning Gets Results," *Workforce* (June 1998), p. 31.

44. S. Williams, "'Classroom' Training Alive and Changing," *Canadian HR Reporter* (October 6, 2008).

45. M. Emery and M. Schubert, "A Trainer's Guide to Videoconferencing," *Training* (June 1993), p. 60.

46. G.N. Nash, J.P. Muczyk, and F.L. Vettori, "The Role and Practical Effectiveness of Programmed Instruction," *Personnel Psychology*, 24 (1971), pp. 397–418.

47. K. Wexley and G. Latham, *Developing and Training Human Resources in Organizations* (Glenview, IL: Scott, Foresman, 1981), p. 141; see also

R. Wlozkowski, "Simulation," *Training and Development Journal,* 39, no. 6 (June 1985), pp. 38–43.

48. "Pros and Cons of E-learning," *Canadian HR Reporter* (July 16, 2001), pp. 11, 15; D. Murray, *E-learning for the Workplace* (Ottawa, ON: Conference Board of Canada, 2001); see also M. Rueda, "How to Make E-Learning Work for Your Company," *Workspan* (December 2002), pp. 50–53; U. Vu, "Technology-Based Learning Comes of Age," *Canadian HR Reporter* (April 21, 2003), pp. 3, 17.

49. S. Mingail, "Good E-Learning Built on Good Instructional Design," *Canadian HR Reporter* (March 22, 2004), p. 12.

50. S. Carliner, M. Ally, N. Zhao, L. Bairstow, S. Khoury, and L. Johnston, *A Review of the State of the Field of Workplace Learning: What We Need to Know About Competencies, Diversity, E-Learning, and Human Performance Impact* (Canadian Society for Training and Development, 2006).

51. G. Siemens, "5 Things to Watch in E-learning," *Canadian HR Reporter* (October 6, 2008).

52. See, for example, T. Falconer, "No More Pencils, No More Books!" *Canadian Banker* (March/April 1994), pp. 21–25.

53. M. Georghiou, "Games, Simulations Open World of Learning," *Canadian HR Reporter* (May 5, 2008).

54. W. Powell, "Like Life?" *Training & Development* (February 2002), pp. 32–38; see also A. Macaulay, "Reality-Based Computer Simulations Allow Staff to Grow through Failure," *Canadian HR Reporter* (October 23, 2000), pp. 11–12.

55. S. Klie, "L'Oreal Plays Games with Training," *Canadian HR Reporter* (October 6, 2008).

56. A. Czarnecki, "Interactive Learning Makes Big Dent in Time, Money Requirements for T&D," *Canadian HR Reporter* (November 18, 1996), pp. L30–L31.

57. L. Young, "Self-Directed Computer-Based Training That Works," *Canadian HR Reporter* (April 24, 2000), pp. 7–8.

58. F. Manning, "The Misuse of Technology in Workplace Learning," *Canadian HR Reporter* (April 24, 2000), p. 7, 10; T. Purcell, "Training Anytime, Anywhere," *Canadian HR Reporter* (July 16, 2001), pp. 11, 15; L. Cassini, "Student Participation Thrives in Online Learning Environments," *Canadian HR Reporter* (May 2, 2001), p. 2.

59. O. Diss, "Deploying a New E-Learning Program?" *HR Professional* (October–November 2005), p. 16.

60. P. Weaver, "Preventing E-Learning Failure," *Training & Development* (August 2002), pp. 45–50; K. Oakes, "E-Learning," *Training & Development* (March 2002), pp. 73–75; see also P. Harris, "E-Learning: A Consolidation Update," *Training & Development* (April 2002), pp. 27–33; C.R. Taylor, "The Second Wave," *Training & Development* (October 2002), pp. 24–31; E. Wareham, "The Educated Buyer," *Computing Canada* (February 18, 2000), p. 33; A. Tomlinson, "E-Learning Won't Solve All Problems," *Canadian HR Reporter* (April 8, 2002), pp. 1, 6.

61. P. Weaver, "Preventing E-Learning Failure," *Training & Development* (August 2002), pp. 45–50.

62. M. Belcourt, P.C. Wright, and A.M. Saks, *Managing Performance through Training and Development,* 2nd ed. (Toronto, ON: Nelson Thomson Learning, 2002), pp. 188–202.

63. Ibid, p. 9.

64. D. Kirkpatrick, "Effective Supervisory Training and Development," Part 3,

"Outside Programs," *Personnel,* 62, no. 2 (February 1985), pp. 39–42. Among the reasons training might not pay off on the job are a mismatching of courses and trainees' needs, supervisory slip-ups (with supervisors signing up trainees and then forgetting to have them attend the sessions when the training session is actually given), and lack of help in applying skills on the job.

65. N.L. Trainor, "Evaluating Training's Four Levels," *Canadian HR Reporter* (January 13, 1997), p. 10.

66. C. Knight, "Awards for Literacy Announced," *Canadian HR Reporter* (December 29, 1997), p. 10.

67. *Reading the Future: Planning to Meet Canada's Future Literacy Needs* (Ottawa, ON: Canadian Council on Learning, 2008).

68. "New Report Reveals the Future of Literacy in Canada's Largest Cities," Canadian Council on Learning, www.ccl-cca.ca/CCL/Newsroom/Releases/20100908literacy2031.html (accessed July 7, 2011).

69. S. Coulombe, J-F. Tremblay, and S. Marchand, *International Adult Literacy Study: Literacy Scores, Human Capital and Growth Across 14 OECD Countries,* Statistics Canada, Catalogue No. 89-552-MIE, 2004; S. Mingal, "Tackling Workplace Literacy a No-Brainer," *Canadian HR Reporter* (November 22, 2004), pp. G3, G10; D. Brown, "Poor Reading, Math Skills a Drag on Productivity, Performance," *Canadian HR Reporter* (February 28, 2005), pp. 1, 10.

70. U. Vu, "Workplace Language Training Gets Cash Boost," *Canadian HR Reporter* (May 19, 2008); K. Wolfe, "Language Training for the Workplace," *Canadian HR Reporter* (June 6, 2005), pp. 1, 13.

71. R. Rosen and P. Digh, "Developing Globally Literate Leaders," *Training & Development* (May 2001), pp. 70–81.

72. B. Siu, "Cross-Cultural Training and Customer Relations: What Every Manager Should Know," *Canadian HR Reporter* (November 15, 1999), pp. G3, G15.

73. D. Roberts and B. Tsang, "Diversity Management Training Helps Firms Hone Competitive Edge," *Canadian HR Reporter* (June 19, 1995), pp. 17–18.

74. L. Young, "Retail Sector Seeks to Upgrade Education, Training to Solve Human Resource Woes," *Canadian HR Reporter* (February 8, 1999), p. 11; see also B. Nagle, "Superior Retail Training Blends Customer Service, Product Knowledge," *Canadian HR Reporter* (July 15, 2002), pp. 7–8; D. Brown, "Is Retail Ready to Buy Training?" *Canadian HR Reporter* (July 15, 2002), pp. 7–8.

75. Canadian Retail Institute, www.retaileducation.ca/cms/sitem.cfm/certification_&_training (accessed May 31, 2009).

76. Based on J. Laabs, "Team Training Goes Outdoors," *Personnel Journal* (June 1991), pp. 56–63; see also S. Caudron, "Teamwork Takes Work," *Personnel Journal,* 73, no. 2 (February 1994), pp. 41–49.

77. B. Donais, "Training Managers in Handling Conflict," *Canadian HR Reporter* (March 12, 2007); A. Tomlinson, "A Dose of Training for Ailing First-Time Managers," *Canadian HR Reporter* (December 3, 2001), pp. 7, 10.

78. L.C. McDermott, "Developing the New Young Managers," *Training & Development* (October 2001), pp. 42–48; A. Tomlinson, "A Dose of Training for Ailing First-Time Managers," *Canadian HR Reporter* (December 3, 2001), pp. 7, 10.

PHOTO CREDITS

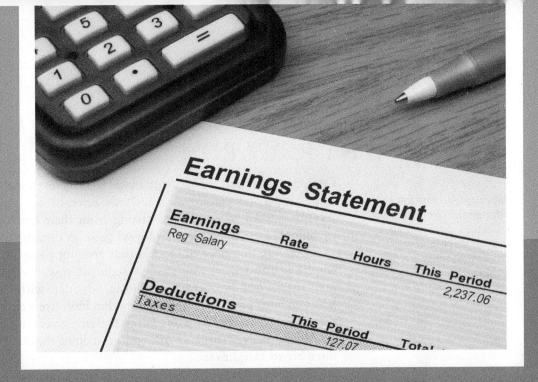

Strategic Pay Plans

AFTER STUDYING THIS CHAPTER, YOU SHOULD BE ABLE TO

EXPLAIN the strategic importance of total rewards.

EXPLAIN in detail each of the three stages in establishing pay rates.

DISCUSS competency-based pay.

DESCRIBE the five basic elements of compensation for managers.

DEFINE pay equity and EXPLAIN its importance today.

- Monitors the competitiveness of the total compensation strategy on an ongoing basis

- Monitors the competitiveness of the compensation program relative to comparable organizations

- Provides for delivery of payroll services in compliance with applicable legislation and company policy and advises the organization on related matters

- Ensures compliance with legally required programs

- Ensures accurate and timely delivery of pay

- Ensures pay records are accurate and complete

- Recommends job price and pay ranges based on relevant internal and external factors

THE STRATEGIC IMPORTANCE OF TOTAL EMPLOYMENT REWARDS

total employment rewards An integrated package of all rewards (monetary and non-monetary, extrinsic and intrinsic) gained by employees arising from their employment.

Compensation and rewards management is extremely important to every employee. **Total employment rewards** refer to an integrated package of all rewards gained by employees arising from their employment. These rewards encompass everything that employees value in the employment relationship.

There are a variety of models that attempt to define the elements of total employee rewards. Some models segment rewards based on the monetary (extrinsic), non monetary (intrinsic) divide, with further differentiation between bash payments and benefits that have are a cash expense for the organization, but are not paid as cash to the employees, as illustrated in **Figure 1**.[1]

Alternatively, WorldatWork conceptualized the total rewards model within three broad categories:

Compensation (extrinsic), benefits (extrinsic), and *non-monetary rewards (intrinsic)*. Recently, the work experience category was further refined by splitting it into three parts—work–life programs, performance and recognition, and development and career opportunities—resulting in five categories of total rewards, as shown in **Figure 2**.

The total rewards approach, as opposed to the previous approach of managing different elements of compensation in isolation, has arisen from the changing business environment of the last several decades. The economies of developed nations like Canada have evolved from a largely industrialized base to become far more virtual, knowledge-based, and service-based, where employees are increasingly regarded as drivers of productivity. A total rewards approach considers individual reward components as part of an integrated whole to determine the best mix of rewards that are aligned with

RPC

Monitors the competitiveness of the total compensation strategy on an ongoing basis

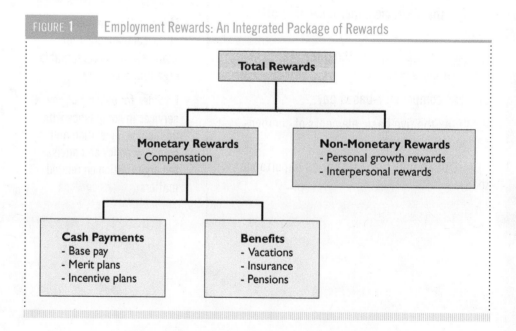

FIGURE 1 Employment Rewards: An Integrated Package of Rewards

FIGURE 2   The Total Rewards Model

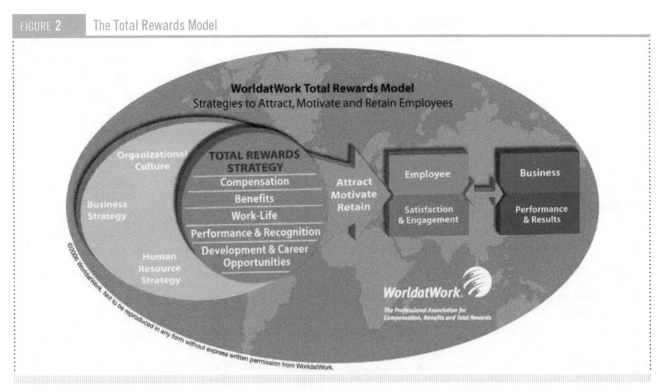

Source: Total Rewards: WorldatWork Introduces a New View 2006. Reprinted with permission of WorldatWork, Scottsdale, AZ. www.worldatwork.org.

business strategy and that provide employee value, all within the cost constraints of the organization. Alignment is the extent to which rewards support outcomes that are important to achieving the organization's strategic objectives. For example, when competitive advantage relies on relentless customer service, this behaviour should be reinforced. Employee value is created when rewards are meaningful to employees and influence their affiliation with the organization.[2]

The Five Components of Total Rewards

1. *Compensation.* This category includes direct financial payments in the form of wages, salaries, incentives, commissions, and bonuses. Wages and salaries are discussed in this chapter.

2. *Benefits.* This category includes indirect payments in the form of financial benefits, like employer-paid insurance and vacations. It also includes employee services.

3. *Work–life programs.* This category of rewards relates to programs that help employees do their jobs effectively, such as flexible scheduling, telecommuting, childcare, and so on.

4. *Performance and recognition.* This category includes pay-for-performance and recognition programs.

5. *Development and career opportunities.* This category of rewards focuses on planning for the advancement or change in responsibilities to best suit individual skills, talents, and desires. Tuition assistance, professional development, sabbaticals, coaching and mentoring opportunities, succession planning, and apprenticeships are all examples of career-enhancing programs.

The world's most admired companies excel at taking a total rewards approach, as discussed in the Strategic HR box.

STRATEGIC HR

Rewards Program Effectiveness at the World's Most Admired Companies

Every year, the world's most admired companies (MACs) are featured in *Fortune* magazine. In 2009, these companies excelled in six key areas related to reward program effectiveness:

1. focusing on excellence in the execution of rewards programs

2. ensuring their rewards programs are aligned with organizational goals, strategy, and culture

3. promoting a total rewards view across the organization and effectively leveraging intangible rewards

4. having stronger programs for developing talent from within, resulting in lower base salaries than that of their peers

5. better leveraging their managers' skills in rewards program implementation

6. reinforcing HR's role in helping managers succeed at putting reward programs into action

One key reason MACs are more successful at aligning their rewards programs with their organizational goals is that they tend to take a more global, centralized approach to managing rewards strategy, compensation structures, and performance management programs. They also excel at communicating their business strategies to managers and employees. The emphasis on communication also extends to the rewards arena.

MACs understand that employees are motivated by much more than money. They are more likely to take a total rewards approach, covering not just tangible rewards like base salary, incentives, and other monetary benefits, but also intangible rewards such as career-growth opportunities, quality of work, recognition, and work climate.

MACs generally pay lower base salaries than their peers. On average, MACs pay approximately 5 percent less in base pay for management and professional roles than other organizations. This is most likely the result of the emphasis that MACs place on intangible rewards like career development. They have a stronger pool of homegrown talent to choose from when job vacancies arise, so they are less reliant on hiring expensive external talent.

Organizations tend to fuss and fret about the design of their rewards programs, but these companies exemplify what research has indicated: Impressive design is not why rewards programs generally work well. It is the way they are put into action and then sustained by the organization that drives their effectiveness.

Source: Adapted from T. McMullen, M. Royal, and M. Stark, "Rewards-Program Effectiveness: What Makes the World's Most Admired Companies Great?" *WorldatWork Journal*, 18, no. 1, pp. 65–74. Contents © 2009. Reprinted with permission from WorldatWork. Content is licensed for use by purchaser only. No part of this article may be reproduced, excerpted, or redistributed in any form without express written permission from WorldatWork.

Impact of Rewards

Towers Perrin (now known as Towers Watson)
www.towerswatson.com

The purposes of rewards are to attract, retain, motivate, and engage employees. *Engagement* refers to a positive emotional connection to the employer and a clear understanding of the strategic significance of the job, which results in discretionary effort on the part of the employee. The *2007–2008 Global*

Workforce Study by Towers Perrin (now known as Towers Watson) consultants found that, for Canadians, competitive base pay was the number one factor in attracting employees to an organization, having excellent career opportunities was the most important factor in retaining employees, and senior management's interest in employee well-being was the top factor influencing employee engagement.[3] Similarly, a study of 446 organizations across Canada by Western Compensation and Benefits Consultants found that the most effective attraction strategy was offering competitive base salaries, and the top reason for turnover among employees was dissatisfaction with cash compensation. Opportunities for advancement, work–life balance programs, and competitive benefits programs are also used by over 70 percent of Canadian companies to attract talent.[4]

BASIC CONSIDERATIONS IN DETERMINING PAY RATES

Four basic considerations influence the formulation of any pay plan: legal requirements, union issues, compensation policy, and equity.

Legal Considerations in Compensation

Hints TO ENSURE LEGAL COMPLIANCE

All of the 14 jurisdictions regulating employment in Canada (ten provinces, three territories, and the federal jurisdiction) have laws regulating compensation. Thus, HR managers must pay careful attention to which legislation affects their employees. Further, these laws are constantly changing and require continual monitoring to ensure compliance. Legislation affecting compensation administration is discussed below.

Employment/Labour Standards Acts (Canada Labour Code)

Employment/labour laws set minimum standards regarding pay, including minimum wage, maximum hours of work, overtime pay, paid vacation, paid statutory holidays, termination pay, record keeping of pay information, and more. There are variations in some of the minimum standards for students, trainees, domestics, nannies, seasonal agricultural workers, and others. Executive, administrative, and professional employees are generally exempt from the overtime pay requirements.

Pay Equity Acts

Pay equity laws were enacted to address the historical undervaluation of "women's work" by providing equal pay for work of equal (or comparable) value performed by men and women. Employers are required to identify male- and female-dominated jobs, and then use a gender-neutral job evaluation system based on specific compensable factors (such as skill, effort, responsibility, and working conditions) to evaluate the jobs. Pay for female-dominated jobs that are equivalent in value to male-dominated jobs must be increased to the pay level of the comparable male-dominated job. Not all Canadian jurisdictions have pay equity laws, as will be discussed later in this chapter.

Human Rights Acts

All jurisdictions have enacted human rights laws to protect Canadians from discrimination on a number of grounds in employment and other areas. These grounds differ somewhat among jurisdictions, but most prohibit discrimination in employment (such as in compensation and promotion) on the basis of age, sex, colour, race/ancestry/place of origin, religion/creed, marital/family status, and physical or mental disability.

Canada/Quebec Pension Plan

All employees and their employers must contribute to the Canada/Quebec Pension Plan throughout the employee's working life. Pension benefits based on the employee's average earnings are paid during retirement.

Other Legislation Affecting Compensation

Association of Workers' Compensation Boards of Canada **www.awcbc.org**

Each province and territory, as well as the federal government, has its own *workers' compensation laws*. The objective of these laws is to provide a prompt, sure, and reasonable income to victims of work-related accidents and illnesses. The Employment Insurance Act is aimed at protecting Canadian workers from total economic destitution in the event of employment termination that is beyond their control. Employers and employees both contribute to the benefits provided by this act. This act also provides up to 45 weeks of compensation for workers unemployed through no fault of their own (depending on the unemployment rate in the claimant's region and other factors). Maternity leave, parental leave, and compassionate care leave benefits are also provided under the Employment Insurance Act.[5]

Union Influences on Compensation Decisions

Work stoppages may reflect employee dissatisfaction with pay plans and other forms of compensation, such as pensions.

Unions and labour relations laws also influence how pay plans are designed. Historically, wage rates have been the main issue in collective bargaining. However, other issues—including time off with pay, income security (for those in industries with periodic layoffs), cost-of-living adjustments, and pensions—are also important.[6]

The Canada Industrial Relations Board and similar bodies in each province and territory oversee employer practices and ensure that employees are treated in accordance with their legal rights. Their decisions underscore the need to involve union officials in developing the compensation package.

Union Attitudes toward Compensation Decisions

Several classic studies shed light on union attitudes toward compensation plans and on commonly held union fears.[7] Many union leaders fear that any system used to evaluate the worth of a job can become a tool for management malpractice. They tend to believe that no one can judge the relative value of jobs better than the workers themselves. In addition, they believe that management's

Research INSIGHT

usual method of using several compensable factors (like "degree of responsibility") to evaluate and rank the worth of jobs can be a manipulative device for restricting or lowering the pay of workers. One implication is that the best way in which to gain the cooperation of union members in evaluating the worth of jobs is to get their active involvement in this process and in assigning fair rates of pay to these jobs. However, management has to ensure that its prerogatives—such as the right to use the appropriate job evaluation technique to assess the relative worth of jobs—are not surrendered.

Compensation Policies

RPC

Provides for delivery of payroll services in compliance with applicable legislation and company policy and advises the organization on related matters

An employer's compensation policies provide important guidelines regarding the wages and benefits that it pays. A number of factors are taken into account when developing a compensation policy, including whether the organization wants to be a leader or a follower regarding pay, business strategy, and the cost of different types of compensation. Important policies include the basis for salary increases, promotion and demotion policies, overtime pay policy, and policies regarding probationary pay and leaves for military service, jury duty, and holidays. Compensation policies are usually written by the HR or compensation manager in conjunction with senior management.[8]

Equity and Its Impact on Pay Rates

external equity Employees perceives his or her pay as fair given the pay rates in other organizations.

internal equity Employees perceives his or her pay as fair given the pay rates of others in the organization.

A crucial factor in determining pay rates is the need for equity, specifically **external equity** and **internal equity**. Research has indicated that employee perceptions of fairness are one of the two key conditions for effective reward programs.[9] Externally, pay must compare favourably with rates in other organizations or an employer will find it hard to attract and retain qualified employees. Pay rates must also be equitable internally: Each employee should view his or her pay as equitable given other pay rates in the organization.

ESTABLISHING PAY RATES

RPC

Ensures accurate and timely delivery of pay

In practice, the process of establishing pay rates that are both externally and internally equitable requires three stages:

1. Determine the worth of jobs within the organization through job evaluation (to ensure internal equity), and group jobs with similar worth into pay grades.
2. Conduct a wage/salary survey of what other employers are paying for comparable jobs (to ensure external equity).
3. Combine the job evaluation (internal) and salary survey (external) information to determine pay rates for the jobs in the organization.

Each of these stages will be explained in turn.

Stage 1: Job Evaluation

job evaluation A systematic comparison to determine the relative worth of jobs within a firm.

Job evaluation is aimed at determining a job's relative worth. It is a formal and systematic comparison of jobs within a firm to determine the worth of one job relative to another, and it eventually results in a job hierarchy.

The basic procedure is to compare the content of jobs in relation to one another, for example, in terms of their effort, responsibility, skills, and working conditions. Job evaluation usually focuses on **benchmark jobs** that are critical to the firm's operations or that are commonly found in other organizations. Rohm and Haas, a multinational chemical company, ensures that its benchmark jobs represent all the various business units and departments in the organization, are drawn from all levels of the organization, have large numbers of incumbents, are clear and well known in the industry, are stable and easily understood in terms of purpose and work content, and are visible and well understood by all employees.[10] The resulting evaluations of benchmark jobs are used as reference points around which other jobs are arranged in order of relative worth.

Compensable Factors

Jobs can be compared intuitively by deciding that one job is "more important" or "of greater value or worth" than another without digging any deeper into why in terms of specific job-related factors. This approach, called the *ranking method*, is hard to defend to employees or others who may not agree with the resulting job hierarchy. As an alternative, jobs can be compared by focusing on certain basic factors that they have in common. In compensation management, these basic factors are called **compensable factors**. They are the factors that determine the definition of job content, establish how the jobs compare with one another, and set the compensation paid for each job.

Some employers develop their own compensable factors. However, most use factors that have been popularized by packaged job evaluation systems or by legislation. For example, most of the pay equity acts in Canada focus on four compensable factors: *skill, effort, responsibility*, and *working conditions*. As another example, the job evaluation method popularized by the Hay Group consulting firm focuses on four compensable factors: *know-how, problem solving, accountability*, and *working conditions*. Often, different job evaluation systems are used for different departments, employee groups, or business units.

Identifying compensable factors plays a pivotal role in job evaluation. All jobs in each employee group, department, or business unit are evaluated *using the same compensable factors*. An employer thus evaluates the same elemental components for each job within the work group and is then better able to compare jobs—for example, in terms of the degree of skill, effort, responsibility, and working conditions present in each.[11]

Job Evaluation Committee

Job evaluation is largely a judgmental process and one that demands close cooperation among supervisors, compensation specialists, and the employees and their union representatives. The main steps involved include identifying the need for the program, getting cooperation, and choosing an evaluation committee; the committee then carries out the actual job evaluation.[12]

A **job evaluation committee** is established to ensure the representation of the points of view of various people who are familiar with the jobs in question, each of whom may have a different perspective regarding the nature of the jobs. The committee may include employees, HR staff, managers, and union representatives.

benchmark job A job that is critical to the firm's operations or that is commonly found in other organizations.

compensable factor A fundamental, compensable element of a job, such as skill, effort, responsibility, and working conditions.

job evaluation committee A diverse group (including employees, HR staff, managers, and union representatives) established to ensure the fair and comprehensive representation of the nature and requirements of the jobs in question.

The job evaluation committee typically includes several employees and has the important task of evaluating the worth of each job using compensable factors.

Tips : FOR THE FRONT LINE

classification/grading method A method for categorizing jobs into groups.

classes Groups of jobs based on a set of rules for each class, such as amount of independent judgment, skill, physical effort, and so forth. Classes usually contain similar jobs—such as all secretaries.

grades Groups of jobs based on a set of rules for each grade, where jobs are similar in difficulty but otherwise different. Grades often contain dissimilar jobs, such as secretaries, mechanics, and firefighters.

grade/group description A written description of the level of compensable factors required by jobs in each grade; sed to combine similar jobs into grades or classes.

point method A job evaluation method in which a number of compensable factors are identified, the degree to which each of these factors is present in the job is determined, and an overall point value is calculated.

The evaluation committee first identifies 10 or 15 key benchmark jobs. These will be the first jobs to be evaluated and will serve as the anchors or benchmarks against which the relative importance or value of all other jobs can be compared. Then the committee turns to its most important function—actually evaluating the worth of each job. For this, the committee will probably use either the job classification method or the point method.

Classification Method

The **classification/grading method** involves categorizing jobs into groups. The groups are called **classes** if they contain similar jobs or **grades** if they contain jobs that are similar in difficulty but otherwise different.

This method is widely used in the public sector. The federal government's UT (University Teaching) job group is an example of a job class because it contains similar jobs involving teaching, research, and consulting. Conversely, the AV (Audit, Commerce, and Purchasing) job group is an example of a job grade because it contains dissimilar jobs, involving auditing, economic development consulting, and purchasing.

There are several ways in which to categorize jobs. One is to draw up class descriptions (similar to job descriptions) and place jobs into classes based on their correspondence to these descriptions. Another is to draw up a set of classifying rules for each class (for instance, the amount of independent judgment, skill, physical effort, and so on that the class of jobs requires). Then the jobs are categorized according to these rules.

The usual procedure is to choose compensable factors and then develop class or grade descriptions that describe each class in terms of the amount or level of compensable factor(s) in jobs. The federal government's classification system, for example, employs different compensable factors for various job groups. Based on these compensable factors, a **grade/group description** (like that in **Figure 3**) is written. Then, the evaluation committee reviews all job descriptions and slots each job into its appropriate class or grade.

The job classification method has several advantages. The main one is that most employers usually end up classifying jobs anyway, regardless of the job evaluation method that they use. They do this to avoid having to work with and develop pay rates for an unmanageable number of jobs; with the job classification method, all jobs are already grouped into several classes. The disadvantages are that it is difficult to write the class or grade descriptions and that considerable judgment is required in applying them. Yet many employers use this method with success.

Point Method

The **point method** is widely used in the private sector and requires identifying several compensable factors. The extent or degree to which each factor is present in the job is evaluated, a corresponding number of points is assigned for each factor, and the number of points for each factor is summed to arrive at an overall point value for the job.

FIGURE 3   Example of a Group Definition in the Federal Government

Correctional Services (CX) Group Definition

The Correctional Services Group comprises positions that are primarily involved in the custody, control and correctional influence of inmates in the institutions of Correctional Service Canada and the training of staff engaged in custodial and correctional work at a Staff College of Correctional Service Canada.

Inclusions

Notwithstanding the generality of the foregoing, for greater certainty, it includes positions that have as their primary purpose, responsibility for one or more of the following activities:

1. the custody and control of inmates and the security of the institution;

2. the custody and control of detainees being held under Immigration and Refugee Protection Act (IRPA) Security Certificates;

3. the correctional influence of inmates with the continuing responsibility to relate actively and effectively to inmates;

4. the admission and discharge of inmates, and the control of inmate visits and correspondence;

5. the organization and implementation of recreational activities, the surveillance and control of inmates engaged in these activities and the custody and issue of recreational equipment;

6. the training of staff in custodial and correctional procedures and techniques; and

7. the leadership of any of the above activities.

Exclusions

Positions excluded from the Correctional Services Group are those whose primary purpose is included in the definition of any other group or those in which one or more of the following activities is of primary importance:

1. the operation of heating plant, sewage facilities and water supplies and the provision of maintenance services;

2. the provision of patient care that requires the application of a comprehensive knowledge of or specialized expertise in physical and mental health care;

3. the provision of services and supplies to inmates; and

4. the instruction of inmates in workshops, crafts and training programs.

Source: Correctional Services (CX) Classification Standard. www.tbs-sct.gc.ca/cla/def/cx-eng.asp, Treasury Board of Canada Secretariat, 2004. Reproduced with the permission of the Minister of Public Works and Government Services Canada, 2012.

1. *Preliminary steps.* To use the point method, it is necessary to have current job descriptions and job specifications based on a thorough job analysis. The foundation of the job evaluation plan is a number of compensable factors that must be agreed upon. In Canada, four compensable factors are commonly used: skill, effort, responsibility, and working conditions. These factors are general and can mean different things in different workplaces. Therefore sub-factors of each one may also be determined to clarify the specific meaning of each factor, as shown below.

Factor	Sub-Factors
Skill	Education and Experience Interpersonal Skill
Effort	Physical Effort Mental Effort
Responsibility	Supervision of Others Planning
Working Conditions	Physical Environment Travel

Each sub-factor must be carefully defined to ensure that the evaluation committee members will apply them consistently. An example of a sub-factor definition is presented in **Figure 4**.

FIGURE 4	Sub-Factor Definition

Responsibility for Others

This sub-factor is used to measure the responsibility that the incumbent of the position assumes for the direction and/or supervision of volunteers, external suppliers/contractors and staff. The following characteristics of the work are to be considered in selecting a level: the nature of supervision given, based either on accountability for results or functional guidance (how-to), and the number of employees or others directed/supervised. Occasional supervision, such as that performed during the absence of the supervisor on vacation or sick leaves, is not to be considered. **This sub-factor does NOT include the academic supervision of students or the activities of others outside of an employee-type relationship.**

Source: Based on McMaster University CAW Local 555 Job Evaluation Plan, www.workingatmcmaster.ca/jjesc (accessed March 23, 2009).

2. *Determine factor weights and degrees.* The next step is to decide on the maximum number of points (called "weight") to assign to each factor. Assigning factor weights is generally done by the evaluation committee. The committee members carefully study each factor and determine the relative value of the factors. For example:

Skill	30 percent
Effort	30 percent
Responsibility	30 percent
Working conditions	10 percent
	100 percent

Then definitions of varying amounts (called "degrees" or "levels") of each sub-factor (or overall factor if no sub-factors are used) are prepared so that raters can judge the degree of a sub-factor/factor existing in a job. Thus, sub-factor "physical environment" for the factor "working conditions" might have three degrees—occasional, frequent, continuous—defined as follows:

Degree 1: Occasional—less than 30 percent of the time on an annual basis. Typically occurs once in a while, but not every day, or every day for less than 30 percent of the day.

Degree 2: Frequent—30 percent to 60 percent of the time on an annual basis. A regular feature of the job that occurs during any given day, week, or season.

Degree 3: Continuous—More than 60 percent of the time on an annual basis. Typically occurs for most of the regular work day, all year round (on average).

The number of degrees usually does not exceed five or six, and the actual number depends mostly on judgment. It is not necessary to have the same number of degrees for each factor, and degrees should be limited to the number necessary to distinguish among jobs.

3. *Assign points for each degree of each sub-factor.* Points are then assigned to each factor, as in **Table 1**. For example, suppose that it is decided to use a total number of 1 000 points in the point plan. Then, since the factor "skill" had a weight of 30 percent, it would be assigned a total of 30 percent of

		Degrees					Maximum Weight	
Factor	Sub-Factors	1	2	3	4		Points	
Skill	Education and Experience	50	100	150	200	200		
	Interpersonal Skill	25	50	75	100	100		
							300	30%
Effort	Physical Effort	25	50	75	100	100		
	Mental Effort	50	100	150	200	200		
							300	30%
Responsibility	Supervision of Others	50	100	150		150		
	Planning	50	100	150		150		
							300	30%
Working Conditions	Physical Environment	20	40	60		60		
	Travel	10	20	30	40	40		
							100	10%
							1000	100%

TABLE 1 — Point Method Job Evaluation Plan

1 000 = 300 points. This automatically means that the highest degree for each sub-factor of the skill factor would be 300 points. Points are then assigned to the other degrees for this factor, in equal amounts from the lowest to the highest degree. This step is repeated for each factor and its sub-factors, resulting in the final job evaluation plan, as shown in Table 1. All these decisions are recorded in a job evaluation manual to be used by the job evaluation committee.

4. *Evaluate the jobs.* Once the manual is complete, the actual evaluations can begin. Each job is evaluated factor by factor to determine the number of points that should be assigned to it. First, committee members determine the degree (first degree, second degree, and so on) to which each factor is present in the job. Then they note the corresponding points (see Table 1) that were assigned to each of these degrees. Finally, they add up the points for all factors, arriving at a total point value for the job. Raters generally start by rating benchmark jobs and obtaining consensus on these, and then they rate the rest of the jobs.

Point systems involve a quantitative technique that is easily explained to and used by employees. However, it can be difficult and time-consuming to develop a point plan and to effectively train the job evaluation user group. This is one reason why many organizations adopt a point plan developed and marketed by a consulting firm. In fact, the availability of a number of ready-made plans probably accounts in part for the wide use of point plans in job evaluation.

If the committee assigned pay rates to each individual job, it would be difficult to administer since there might be different pay rates for hundreds or even thousands of jobs. Even in smaller organizations there is a tendency to try to simplify wage and salary structures as much as possible. Therefore, the committee will probably want to group similar jobs (in terms of their number of points, for instance) into grades for pay purposes. Then, instead of having to deal with pay rates for hundreds of jobs, it might only have to focus on pay rates for 10 or 12 groupings of jobs.

A **pay grade** comprises jobs of approximately equal value or importance, as determined by job evaluation. If the point method was used, the pay grade consists of jobs falling within a range of points. If the classification system was used, then the jobs are already categorized into classes or grades. The next stage is to obtain information on market pay rates by conducting a wage/salary survey.

Stage 2: Conduct a Wage/Salary Survey

Compensation or **wage/salary surveys** play a central role in determining pay rates for jobs.[13] An employer may use wage/salary surveys in three ways. First, survey data are used to determine pay rates for benchmark jobs that serve as reference points or anchors for the employer's pay scale, meaning that other jobs are then paid based on their relative worth compared to the benchmark jobs. Second, an increasing number of positions are paid solely based on the marketplace (rather than relative to the firm's benchmark jobs).[14]

As a result of the current shift away from long-term employment, compensation is increasingly shaped by market wages and less by how it fits into the hierarchy of jobs in one organization. Finally, surveys also collect data on employee benefits, work–life programs, pay-for-performance plans, recognition plans, and so on to provide a basis on which to make decisions regarding other types of rewards.

Formal and Informal Surveys by the Employer

Most employers rely heavily on formal or informal surveys of what other employers are paying.[15] Informal telephone surveys are good for collecting data on a relatively small number of easily identified and quickly recognized jobs, such as when a bank's HR director wants to determine the salary at which a newly opened customer service representative's job should be advertised. Informal discussions among human resources specialists at regular professional association meetings are other occasions for informal salary surveys. Some employers use formal questionnaire surveys to collect compensation information from other employers, including things like number of employees, overtime policies, starting salaries, and paid vacations.

Commercial, Professional, and Government Salary Surveys

Many employers also rely on surveys published by various commercial firms, professional associations, or government agencies. For example, Statistics Canada provides monthly data on earnings by geographic area, by industry, and by occupation. **Table 2** provides an example of earnings data by industry and occupation.

The Toronto Board of Trade conducts five compensation surveys annually, covering executive; management; professional, supervisory, and sales; information technology; and administrative and support positions. The surveys include information from small, medium, and large employers in the Greater Toronto Area. A separate survey of employee benefits and employment practices is also conducted.

---

pay grade Comprises jobs of approximately equal value.

wage/salary survey A survey aimed at determining prevailing wage rates. A good salary survey provides specific wage rates for comparable jobs. Formal written questionnaire surveys are the most comprehensive.

TABLE 2 Average Weekly Earnings by Industry 2004–2009

Geography=Canada
Type of employees=All employees
Overtime=Including overtime

North American Industry Classification System (NAICS)	2004	2005	2006	2007	2008	2009
Industrial aggregate excluding unclassified businesses	709.41	737.29	755.48	788.06	810.52	823.53
Mining, quarrying, and oil and gas extraction	1,278.11	1,296.35	1,325.73	1,437.44	1,527.90	1,594.04
Utilities	1,261.08	1,298.32	1,350.66	1,421.49	1,424.73	1,500.79
Construction	846.38	877.34	900.32	961.16	1,014.51	1,048.42
Manufacturing	862.60	896.35	904.69	940.67	949.54	917.73
Wholesale trade	826.89	865.92	905.24	937.14	956.59	988.89
Retail trade	425.65	441.18	449.86	458.80	475.17	486.70
Transportation and warehousing	807.78	828.07	834.40	864.51	883.28	874.69
Information and cultural industries	916.99	952.30	955.52	1,003.44	1,003.54	1,077.16
Finance and insurance	887.00	921.01	951.17	998.93	1,002.03	1,036.81
Real estate and rental and leasing	654.56	698.06	710.73	756.11	772.87	771.83
Professional, scientific and technical services	937.42	989.94	1,016.41	1,060.36	1,093.67	1,129.10
Management of companies and enterprises	1,012.41	1,005.19	1,050.28	1,086.16	1,087.91	1,144.86
Admistrative and support, waste management and remediation services	546.15	583.67	600.98	648.97	673.97	671.44

Source: Statistics Canada, CANSIM database, Table 281-0027, 2011. Available for free at www.statcan.gc.ca/pub/72-002-x/72-002-x2011002-eng.pdf.

Monster.ca Salary & Benefits Centre
http://career-advice.monster.ca/
Salary-Benefits/careers.aspx

Private consulting or executive recruiting companies, such as Towers Watson, Mercer, and Hewitt Associates, annually publish data covering the compensation of senior and middle managers and members of boards of directors. Professional organizations, such as the Certified General Accountants and Professional Engineers Ontario, conduct surveys of compensation practices among members of their associations.

For some jobs, salaries are determined directly based on formal or informal salary surveys like those available from Monster.ca. In most cases, though, surveys are used to price benchmark jobs around which other jobs are then slotted based on their relative worth as determined through job evaluation.

Salary Survey Interpretation and Use

RPC

Monitors the competitiveness of the compensation program relative to comparable organizations

Data from the Hay Group consulting firm indicate that large organizations participate in an average of 11 compensation surveys and use information from seven of them to administer their own compensation practices.[16]

Upward bias can be a problem regardless of the type of compensation survey used. At least one compensation expert argues that the way in which most surveys are constructed, interpreted, and used leads almost invariably to a situation in which firms set higher wages than they otherwise might. For example, "companies like to compare themselves against well-regarded, high-paying, and high-performing companies," so baseline salaries tend to be biased upward.

Similarly, "companies that sponsor surveys often do so with an implicit (albeit unstated) objective: to show the company [is] paying either competitively or somewhat below the market, so as to justify positive corrective action." For these and similar reasons, it is probably wise to review survey results with a skeptical eye and to acknowledge that upward bias may exist and should perhaps be considered when making decisions.[17]

Whatever the source of the survey, the data must be carefully assessed for accuracy before they are used to make compensation decisions. Problems can arise when the organization's job descriptions only partially match the descriptions contained in the survey, the survey data were collected several months before the time of use, the participants in the survey do not represent the appropriate labour market for the jobs being matched, and so on.[18]

Now all the information necessary to move to the next stage—determining pay for jobs—has been obtained.

Stage 3: Combine the Job Evaluation and Salary Survey Information to Determine Pay for Jobs

The final stage is to assign pay rates to each pay grade. (Of course, if jobs were not grouped into pay grades, individual pay rates would have to be assigned to each job.) Assigning pay rates to each pay grade (or to each job) is usually accomplished with a **wage curve**.

The wage curve graphically depicts the market pay rates currently being paid for jobs in each pay grade, relative to the job evaluation points for each job or grade. An example of a wage curve is presented in **Figure 5**. Note that pay rates are shown on the vertical axis, while the points for pay grades are shown along the horizontal axis. The purpose of the wage curve is to show the relationship between the value of the job as determined by one of the job evaluation methods and the current average pay rates for each job or grade.

RPC

Recommends job price and pay ranges based on relevant internal and external factors

wage curve A graphic description of the relationship between the value of the job and the average wage paid for this job.

| FIGURE **5** | Plotting a Wage Curve |

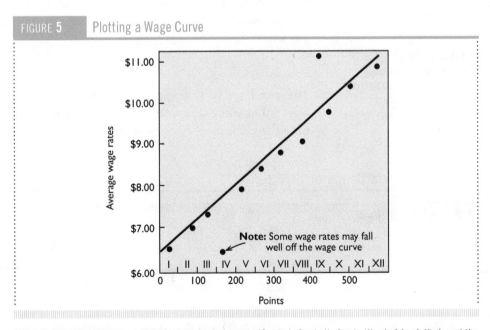

Note: The average market pay rate for jobs in each grade (Grade I, Grade II, Grade III, etc.) is plotted, and the wage curve is fitted to the resulting points.

An Ethical : Dilemma

What should employers do when there is a shortage of a certain type of skill and they cannot attract any workers unless they pay a market rate above the maximum of their salary range for that job? How should other jobs (without a skills shortage) in the same company in the same salary range be paid?

There are several steps in determining pay for pay grades using a wage curve. First, find the average pay for each pay grade, since each of the pay grades consists of several jobs. Next, plot the pay rates for each pay grade, as was done in **Figure 5**. Then fit a line (called a "wage line") through the points just plotted. This can be done either freehand or by using a statistical method known as regression analysis. Finally, determine pay for jobs. Wages along the wage line are the target wages or salary rates for the jobs in each pay grade.

Developing Rate Ranges

pay ranges A series of steps or levels within a pay grade, usually based on years of service.

Most employers do not just pay one rate for all jobs in a particular pay grade. Instead, they develop **pay ranges** for each grade so that there might, for instance, be 10 levels or "steps" and 10 corresponding pay rates within each pay grade. This approach is illustrated in **Table 3**, which shows the pay rates and levels for some of the federal government pay grades. As of the time of this pay schedule, for instance, employees in positions that were classified in grade CX-1 could be paid annual salaries between $52 604 and $66 413, depending on the level at which they were hired into the grade, the amount of time they were in the grade, and their merit increases (if any). Another way to depict the rate ranges for each grade is with a wage structure, as in **Figure 6**. The wage structure graphically depicts the range of pay rates (in this case, per hour) to be paid for each grade.

The use of pay ranges for each pay grade has several benefits. First, the employer can take a more flexible stance with respect to the labour market; for example, some flexibility makes it easier to attract experienced, higher-paid employees into a pay grade where the starting salary for the lowest step may be too low to attract such experienced people. Pay ranges also allow employers to provide for performance differences between employees within the same grade or between those with differing seniority. As in **Figure 6**, most employers structure their pay ranges to overlap a bit so that an employee with greater experience or seniority may earn more than an entry-level person in the next higher pay grade.

broadbanding Reducing the number of salary grades and ranges into just a few wide levels or "bands," each of which then contains a relatively wide range of jobs and salary levels.

Broadbanding

The trend today is for employers to reduce their salary grades and ranges from 10 or more down to three to five, a process that is called **broadbanding**. Broadbanding means combining salary grades and ranges into just a few wide

TABLE 3 Federal Government Pay Schedules CX-1 and CX-2

| Rate Levels within Grade | | | | | |
Grade	1	2	3	4	5
CX-1	$52 604	55 761	59 107	62 652	66 413
CX-2	$55 826	59 176	62 726	66 489	70 477

Source: CX - Correctional Services Group Annual Rates of Pay, www.tbs-sct.gc.ca/pubs_pol/hrpubs/coll_agre/cx/cx08-eng.asp, Treasury Board of Canada Secretariat, 2006. Reproduced with the permission of the Minister of Public Works and Government Services Canada, 2012.

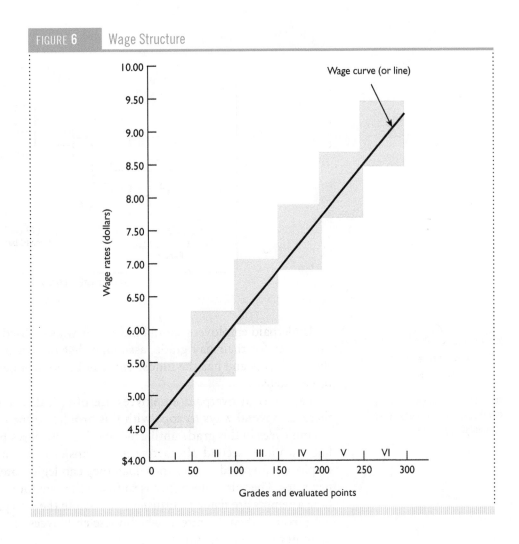

FIGURE 6 Wage Structure

Wage curve (or line)

Wage rates (dollars)

Grades and evaluated points

levels or "bands," each of which then contains a relatively wide range of jobs and salary levels (see **Figure 7**).

Broadbanding a pay system involves several steps. First, the number of bands is decided on and each is assigned a salary range. The bands usually have wide salary ranges and also overlap substantially. As a result, there is much more flexibility to move employees from job to job within bands and less need to "promote" them to new grades just to give them higher salaries.

Broadbanding's basic advantage is that it injects greater flexibility into employee compensation.[19] The new, broad salary bands can include both supervisors and those reporting to them. Broadbanding also facilitates less specialized, boundaryless jobs and organizations. Less specialization and more participation in cross-departmental processes generally mean enlarged duties or capabilities and more possibilities for alternative career tracks.

Correcting Out-of-Line Rates

The actual wage rate for a job may fall well off the wage line or well outside the rate range for its grade. This means that the average pay for that job is currently too high or too low relative to other jobs in the firm. If a point falls well below the line, a pay raise for the job may be required. If the plot falls well above the wage line, pay cuts or a pay freeze may be required.

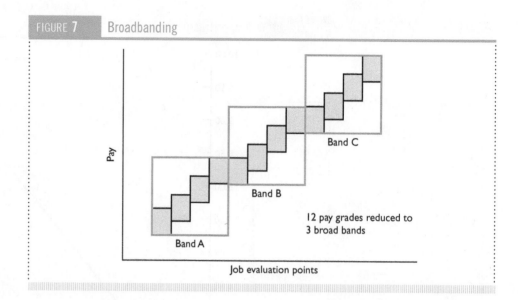

FIGURE 7 Broadbanding

12 pay grades reduced to 3 broad bands

Band A

Band B

Band C

Pay

Job evaluation points

red circle pay rate A rate of pay that is above the pay range maximum.

Underpaid employees should have their wages raised to the minimum of the rate range for their pay grade, assuming that the organization wants to retain the employees and has the funds. This can be done either immediately or in one or two steps.

Pay rates of overpaid employees are often called **red circle pay rates**, and there are several ways to cope with this problem. One is to freeze the rate paid to employees in this grade until general salary increases bring the other jobs into line with it. A second alternative is to transfer or promote some or all of the employees involved to jobs for which they can legitimately be paid their current pay rates. The third alternative is to freeze the rate for six months, during which time attempts are made to transfer or promote the overpaid employees. If this is not possible, then the rate at which these employees are paid is cut to the maximum in the pay range for their grade.

PAY FOR KNOWLEDGE

Pay-for-knowledge systems are known as *competency-based pay* (for management and professional employees) and *skill-based pay* (for manufacturing employees). These plans pay employees for the range, depth, and types of knowledge that they are capable of using, rather than for the job that they currently hold. Competencies are individual knowledge, skills, and behaviours that are critical to successful individual or corporate performance based on their relation to the organization's visions, values, and business strategy.[20]

Core competencies describe knowledge and behaviours that employees throughout the organization must exhibit for the organization to succeed, such as "customer service orientation" for all hotel employees. *Functional competencies* are associated with a particular organizational function, such as "negotiation skills" for salespeople, or "safety orientation" for pilots. *Behavioural competencies* are expected behaviours, such as "always walking a customer to the product they are looking for rather than pointing."[21] A pay-for-knowledge program should include the following:

Tips **FOR THE FRONT LINE**

- Competencies and skills—directly important to job performance—that can be defined in measurable and objective terms. Skills tend to be easier to define and measure than competencies.

- New and different competencies that replace obsolete competencies or competencies that are no longer important to job performance. If additional competencies are needed, the obsolete competency should be removed from the program.
- On-the-job training, not "in the classroom" training. Those who possess the competencies or skills should teach them. Also include on-the-job assessment, which can be supplemented by paper-and-pencil exams administered on the job.[22]

As an example, in a manufacturing plant setting, workers would be paid based on their attained skill levels. In a three-level plan:

1. Level 1 would indicate limited ability, such as knowledge of basic facts and ability to perform simple tasks without direction.
2. Level 2 would mean that the employee has attained partial proficiency and could, for instance, apply technical principles on the job.
3. Level 3 would mean that the employee is fully competent in the area and could, for example, analyze and solve production problems.

Construction workers today are often compensated for their work through the method of skill-based pay.

Increased workforce flexibility is one of the most significant advantages of pay for knowledge. Employees rotate between different jobs or production areas to encourage the learning of new competencies and skills. This process fosters flexibility by encouraging workers to learn multiple competencies and skills and to willingly switch tasks.[23]

Experience has shown that competency-based pay is more efficient in the first years of its existence. The greatest challenge is measurement of competencies. As time goes on, employees often become dissatisfied if these measurements are not valid or if the people responsible for assessing competencies are considered incompetent or biased.[24]

Another major employee concern is that pay be linked sufficiently to performance as well as competencies. Some compensation consultants suggest that firms should not pay for competencies at the exclusion of rewards for high performance results. For example, competencies could be linked to the determination of base salary combined with bonuses that are based on performance.[25] One final issue for many Canadian companies is that pay-for-knowledge systems do not meet pay equity requirements.[26]

Although only about 15 to 20 percent of workplaces use pay for knowledge at present, experts predict that the viewpoint that people, rather than jobs, provide advantages to organizations will continue to grow in popularity. They foresee the emergence of new pay systems combining competencies and market values.[27]

PAY FOR EXECUTIVE, MANAGERIAL, AND PROFESSIONAL JOBS

Developing a compensation plan to pay executive, managerial, and professional employees is similar in many respects to developing a plan for other employees.[28] The basic aims of the plan are the same in that the goal is to attract good employees and maintain their commitment. Yet for executive, managerial, and professional jobs, job evaluation provides only a partial answer to the question of how to pay these employees. Executives, managers, and professionals are almost always paid based on their performance as well as on the basis of static job demands, like working conditions.

Compensating Executives and Managers

There are five elements in an executive/managerial compensation package: salary, benefits, short-term incentives, long-term incentives, and perquisites.[29] The amount of salary paid usually depends on the value of the person's work to the organization and how well the person is honouring his or her responsibilities. Salary is the cornerstone of executive compensation, because it is the element on which the others are layered, with benefits, incentives, and perquisites often awarded in some proportion to base pay.

An Ethical Dilemma

Is it right that CEOs earn enormous amounts of money when most employees are getting small increases each year (sometimes even less than inflation)?

Research INSIGHT

Executive compensation tends to emphasize performance incentives more than other employee pay plans do, since organizational results are likely to reflect the contributions of executives more directly than those of other employees. The heavy incentive component of executive compensation can be illustrated by using some of Canada's best-paid executives as an example.[30] The highest paid executive in Canada in 2010 was Hank Swartout, CEO of Precision Drilling Corporation, who earned a total compensation of $74 824 331, of which $840 000 was base salary. Hunter Harrison, CEO of Canadian National Railway, received total compensation of $56 219 494, which included his base salary of $1 665 950. A study on CEO pay determined that firm size accounts for 40 percent of the variance of total CEO pay, while firm performance accounts for less than 5 percent of the variance.[31]

There has been considerable debate regarding whether top executives are worth what they are paid. Some argue that the job of an executive is increasingly difficult. The stakes are high, and job tenure is often short. Expectations are getting higher, the questions from shareholders are more direct, and the challenge of navigating an organization through difficult economic times has never been so great. However, shareholder activism regarding executive pay has attempted to tighten the restrictions on what firms pay their top executives.

Some believe that pay for performance is taking hold, with companies now making stronger links between company performance and CEO total compensation. Others believe that linking pay to performance is still inadequate in the majority of companies. Most agree that better disclosure of executive pay is required, and groups such as the Canadian Securities Administrators and the Canadian Coalition for Good Governance are pressing for dramatic changes in executive compensation disclosure.[32]

Compensating Professional Employees

Compensating non-supervisory professional employees, like engineers and scientists, presents unique problems. Analytical jobs require creativity and problem solving, compensable factors not easily compared or measured. Furthermore, the professional's economic impact on the firm is often related only indirectly to the person's actual efforts; for example, the success of an engineer's invention depends on many factors, like how well it is produced and marketed.

In theory, the job evaluation methods explained previously can be used for evaluating professional jobs.[33] The compensable factors here tend to focus on problem solving, creativity, job scope, and technical knowledge and expertise. The job classification method is commonly used—a series of grade descriptions are written, and each position is slotted into the grade having the most appropriate definition.

In practice, traditional methods of job evaluation are rarely used for professional jobs since it is so difficult to identify compensable factors and degrees of factors that meaningfully capture the value of professional work. "Knowledge and the skill of applying it," as one expert notes, "are extremely difficult to quantify and measure."[34]

As a result, most employers use a *market-pricing approach* in evaluating professional jobs. They price professional jobs in the marketplace to the best of their ability to establish the values for benchmark jobs. These benchmark jobs and the employer's other professional jobs are then slotted into a salary structure. Specifically, each professional discipline (like mechanical engineering or electrical engineering) usually ends up having four to six grade levels, each of which requires a fairly broad salary range. This approach helps ensure that the employer remains competitive when bidding for professionals whose attainments vary widely and whose potential employers are found literally worldwide.[35]

PAY EQUITY

Historically, the average pay for Canadian women has been considerably lower than that for men. In 1967, women's average wages were 46.1 percent of men's average wages. **Table 4** shows the most recent wage gap statistics. Some of this gap is due to the fact that women do more part-time work than men, but even when full-year, full-time workers are compared, the gap has stalled at approximately 30 percent since 1998 (see Workforce Diversity box). The wage gap is narrower for single women over those who are married, and for younger women when compared to those who are older.[36]

Moreover, the gap persists even when women have the same qualifications and do the same type of work as men. A 2004 study showed that, two years after graduation, female university graduates in the Maritime provinces working full time earned 78 percent of the weekly wage of males, even after accounting for differences in field of study, occupation, location, and hours worked.[37]

Although such factors as differences in hours worked, experience levels, education levels, and level of unionization contribute to the wage gap, systemic discrimination is also present.[38] The purpose of pay equity legislation is to redress systemic gender discrimination in compensation for work performed by employees in female-dominated job classes. **Pay equity** requires that equal wages be paid for jobs of equal value or "worth" to the employer, as determined by gender-neutral (i.e., free of any bias based on gender) job evaluation techniques.

pay equity Providing equal pay to male-dominated job classes and female-dominated job classes of equal value to the employer.

The legal process involved can be lengthy. A final decision is still pending in a pay equity complaint filed against Canada Post in 1983 claiming that 6 000 clerical workers had been subjected to systemic discrimination.[39] In 2006,

TABLE 4 Male–Female Average Earnings Ratio* for Full-Year, Full-Time Workers, 1998–2008

Geography=Canada

Work activity=Full-year full-time workers

Earnings	Average earnings, females (dollars)	Average earnings, males (dollars)	Female-to-male average earnings ratio (percent)
1998	40,500	56,300	71.9
1999	38,900	56,900	68.4
2000	40,200	56,900	70.6
2001	40,600	58,100	69.9
2002	40,800	58,200	70.2
2003	40,700	57,900	70.2
2004	42,000	59,900	70.1
2005	41,800	59,400	70.5
2006	43,200	60,000	71.9
2007	44,100	61,700	71.4
2008	44,700	62,600	71.3

*Earnings stated in constant year 2006 dollars.

Source: Statistics Canada, CANSIM Table 202-0102, http://estat.statcan.gc.ca/cgi-win/CNSMCGI.EXE (accessed August 20, 2011).

WORKFORCE DIVERSITY

Women Work for Free as of September 17

For women in Ontario, the middle of September means more than the end of summer. It is a stark reminder of the gender pay gap that persists in the province. As of September 17, the year is 71 percent of the way through, and with women in Ontario earning an average of 71 cents for every dollar men earn, it also marks the day women start working for free, according to the Equal Pay Coalition.

With an overall 29 percent gender pay gap, women are effectively denied their fair pay from September 17 until the end of the year while men get their full pay, states the coalition. Ontario's Pay Equity Act, which turned 20 years old in 2008, was supposed to end this devaluation by requiring employers to pay women's and men's jobs the same when they were of comparable value. The pay gap has decreased from 38 percent in 1988 to 29 percent today, but that is still too high, according to the coalition.

Canada ranks seventeenth among 22 Organisation for Economic Co-operation and Development countries and is behind the United States, which has a 23 percent wage gap. The World Economic Forum's *2007 Global Gender Gap Report* highlighted the key role gender "remuneration gaps" play in preventing economies from realizing their full potential. Businesses, communities, and governments all benefit from pay equity enforcement.

Discriminatory pay affects women throughout their lives, beginning with their first jobs and continuing into retirement. Young women graduating from high school earn 27 percent less than male high school graduates; young women graduating from university earn 16 percent less than male graduates. But this pay gap widens as their careers progress. The median income of retired women is almost half that of retired men. Over a lifetime these pay gaps add up to enormous financial losses for working women, estimating the total for each woman to be between US$700 000 and US$2 million, depending on education level.

Source: Adapted from "Women Work for Free as of Sept. 17," *Canadian HR Reporter* (September 18, 2008); and M. Cornish, "Much Work to Be Done on Pay Equity," *Canadian HR Reporter* (February 28, 2008). Reprinted by permission of Canadian HR Reporter. © Copyright Thomson Reuters Canada Ltd., (2012) Toronto, Ontario, 1-800-387-5164. Web: www.hrreporter.com

Saskatchewan workers demonstrate for pay equity.

the Supreme Court of Canada ruled against a Canadian Human Rights Tribunal decision that female Air Canada flight attendants' jobs could not be compared with those of mainly male mechanics and pilots and sent the case back to the tribunal. The court condemned Air Canada's use of legal technicalities to delay the case, which began in 1991.[40]

Six provinces (Ontario, Quebec, Manitoba, Nova Scotia, New Brunswick, and Prince Edward Island) have created separate proactive legislation that specifically requires that pay equity be achieved. Ontario and Quebec require pay equity in both the public and the private sectors, whereas the legislation in the other four provinces applies only to the public sector. In the federal jurisdiction and the Yukon (public sector only), human rights legislation requires equal pay for work of equal value.

The wage gap has narrowed since the introduction of pay equity legislation, but there is still no explanation other than systemic discrimination for much of the 30 percent gap that still persists.[41] In the long term, the best way to remove the portion of the wage gap resulting from systemic discrimination is to eliminate male- and female-dominated jobs by ensuring that women have equal access to and are equally represented in all jobs.

Chapter SUMMARY

1. A total rewards approach considers individual reward components as part of an integrated whole to determine the best mix of rewards that are aligned with business strategy and provide employee value, all within the cost constraints of the organization. Alignment is the extent to which rewards support outcomes that are important to achieving the organization's strategic objectives. For example, when competitive advantage relies on relentless customer service, this behaviour should be reinforced. Employee value is created when rewards are meaningful to employees and influence their affiliation with the organization.

2. Establishing pay rates involves three stages: job evaluation (to ensure internal equity), conducting wage/salary surveys (to ensure external equity), and combining job evaluation and salary survey results to determine pay rates. Job evaluation is aimed at determining the relative worth of jobs within a firm. It compares jobs with one another based on their content, which is usually defined in terms of compensable factors, such as skill, effort, responsibility, and working conditions. Jobs of approximately equal value are combined into pay grades for pay purposes. Salary surveys collect data from other employers in the marketplace who are competing for employees in similar kinds of positions. The wage curve shows the average market wage for each pay grade (or job). It illustrates what the average wage for each grade should be and whether any present wages or salaries are out of line.

3. Competency-based pay plans provide employee compensation based on the skills and knowledge that they are capable of using, rather than the job that they currently hold.

4. The five basic elements of compensation for managers are salary, benefits, short-term incentives, long-term incentives, and perquisites.

5. Pay equity is intended to redress systemic gender discrimination as measured by the wage gap, which indicates that full-time working women in Canada make about 71 cents for every dollar made by full-time working men. Pay equity requires equal pay for female-dominated jobs of equal value to male-dominated jobs (where value is determined through job evaluation).

MyManagementLab

Visit MyManagementLab to access a personalized Study Plan and additional study tools for this chapter.

Key TERMS

benchmark job
broadbanding
classes
classification/grading method
compensable factor
external equity
grade/group description
grades
internal equity
job evaluation

job evaluation committee
pay equity
pay grade
pay ranges
point method
red circle pay rate
total employment rewards
wage curve
wage/salary survey

Review and Discussion QUESTIONS

1. What are the five components of total rewards?

2. Describe what is meant by the term "benchmark job."

3. Identify and briefly describe the three stages in establishing pay rates.

4. What are the pros and cons of the following methods of job evaluation: ranking, classification, factor comparison, point method?

5. Explain the term "competencies" and explain the differences among core, functional, and behavioural competencies.

6. Explain what is meant by the market-pricing approach in evaluating professional jobs.

7. Explain what pay equity legislation is intended to accomplish, what action is required by the legislation to accomplish it, and how effective the legislation has been in accomplishing its objectives.

Critical Thinking QUESTIONS

1. Do you think that transactional or relational rewards have more impact on overall organizational performance?

2. Why do companies pay for compensation surveys where job matching may be difficult rather than conducting their own surveys?

3. It was recently reported in the news that the base pay for Canadian bank CEOs range in the millions of dollars, and the pay for the governor of the Bank of Canada is less than half of that of the lowest paid bank CEO. How do you account for this difference? Should anything be done about this? Why or why not?

4. Do you agree with paying people for competencies and skills that they are rarely required to use on the job?

5. What are some of the potential reasons that gender-based pay discrimination is so hard to eradicate?

6. Why do you think there is such a discrepancy between the pay rates of executives and employees? Is this fair? Why or why not?

Experiential EXERCISES

1. Working individually or in groups, conduct salary surveys for the positions of entry-level accountant and entry-level chemical engineer. What sources did you use, and what conclusions did you reach? If you were the HR manager for a local engineering firm, what would you recommend that each job be paid?

2. Obtain information on the pay grades and rate ranges for each pay grade at your college or university. Do they appear to be broadbands? If not, propose specific broadbands that could be implemented.

3. You have been asked by the owner of your medium-sized import and export company (200+ people) to develop a way to standardize pay ranges for different jobs in the company. He says he is tired of employees complaining about the pay they get compared to others and is concerned that if he does nothing someone will complain about inequitable pay practices. Outline the steps you will follow to do this. Make sure to give a rationale for the type of job evaluation system you propose as well as for the method you suggest to obtain comparable salary data. The jobs he is most concerned about are

   - sales representative
   - shipping and receiving manager
   - multilingual contract negotiator
   - accounts receivable clerk
   - shipping clerk.

4. You are the HR manager at a large construction firm headquartered in Edmonton. Most of the company's administrative staff are also in Edmonton. You have regional and local site offices across the country. Draft a memo to employees about your company's new pay-for-knowledge and skills policy. Make sure to document at least one fully complete section on how this policy will be administered. Your professor may give you some ideas on what might be considered or you may create your own circumstances under which pay for knowledge and skills will be applied.

Running CASE

The New Pay Plan

LearnInMotion.com does not have a formal wage structure, nor does it have rate ranges or use compensable factors. Jennifer and Pierre base wage rates almost exclusively on those prevailing in the surrounding community, and they temper these by trying to maintain some semblance of equity among what workers with different responsibilities are paid. As Jennifer says, "Deciding what to pay dot-com employees is an adventure: Wages for jobs like web designer and online salesperson are always climbing dramatically, and there's not an awful lot of loyalty involved when someone else offers you 30 percent or 40 percent more than you're currently making." Jennifer and Pierre are therefore continually scanning various sources to see what others are paying for positions like theirs. They peruse the want ads almost every day and conduct informal surveys among their friends at other dot-coms. Once or twice a week, they also check compensation websites like Monster.ca.

Although the company has taken a somewhat unstructured, informal approach to establishing its compensation plan, the firm's actual salary schedule is guided by several basic pay policies. For one thing, the difficulty they had recruiting and hiring employees caused them to pay salaries 10 to 20 percent above what the market would seem to indicate. Jennifer and Pierre write this off to the need to get and keep good employees. As Jennifer says,

"If you've got 10 web designers working for you, you can afford to go a few extra weeks without hiring another one, but when you need one designer and you have none, you've got to do whatever you can to get that one designer hired." Their somewhat informal approach has also led to some potential inequities. For example, the two salespeople—one a man, the other a woman—are earning different salaries, and the man is making about 30 percent more. If everything was going fine—for instance, if sales were up and the calendar was functional—perhaps they wouldn't be worried. However, the fact is that the two owners are wondering if a more structured pay plan would be a good idea. Now they want you, their management consultant, to help them decide what to do.

QUESTIONS

1 Describe the total rewards model and its five components and whether it would benefit LearnInMotion.

2 What are some basic considerations in determining pay rates that LearnInMotion must be aware of?

3 Using the three stages of establishing pay rates, provide recommendations to LearnInMotion in regard to job evaluation, wage/salary surveys, and how to combine the first two steps to determine pay rates for LearnInMotion's jobs.

Case INCIDENT

Salary Inequities at Acme Manufacturing

Joe Blackenship was trying to figure out what to do about a problem salary situation that he had in his plant. Blackenship recently took over as president of Acme Manufacturing. The founder, Bill George, had been president for 35 years. The company is family-owned and located in a small eastern Manitoba town. It has approximately 250 employees and is the largest employer in the community. Blackenship is a member of the family that owns Acme, but he had never worked for the company prior to becoming president. He has an MBA and a law degree, plus 15 years of management experience with a large manufacturing organization where he was senior vice-president of human resources when he made his move to Acme.

A short time after joining Acme, Blackenship started to notice that there was considerable inequity in the pay structure for salaried employees. A discussion with the HR director led him to believe that salaried employees' pay was very much a matter of individual bargaining with the past president. Hourly paid factory workers were not part of the problem because they were unionized and their wages were set by collective bargaining. An examination of the salaried payroll showed that there were 25 employees, whose pay ranged from that of the president to that of the receptionist. A closer examination showed that 14 of the salaried employees were female. Three of these were front-line factory supervisors, and one was the HR director. The rest were non-management employees.

This examination also showed that the HR director appeared to be underpaid and that the three female supervisors were paid somewhat less than any of the male supervisors. However, there were no similar supervisory jobs in which there were both male and female incumbents. When asked, the HR director said that she thought the female supervisors may have been paid at a lower rate mainly because they were women, and perhaps George did not think that women needed as much money because they had working husbands. However, she added the thought that they might be paid less because they supervised lesser-skilled employees than did male supervisors. Blackenship was not sure that this was true.

The company from which Blackenship had moved had a good job evaluation system. Although he was thoroughly familiar and capable with this compensation tool, Blackenship did not have time to create a job evaluation study at Acme. Therefore, he decided to hire a compensation consultant from a nearby university to help him. Together, they decided that all 25 salaried jobs should be in the same job evaluation cluster, that a modified ranking system of job evaluation should be used, and that the job descriptions recently completed by the HR director were current, accurate, and usable in the study.

The job evaluation showed that there was no evidence of serious inequities or discrimination in the non-management jobs, but that the HR director and the three female supervisors were being underpaid relative to comparable male salaried employees.

Blackenship was not sure what to do. He knew that if the underpaid supervisors took their case to the local pay equity commission, the company could be found guilty of sex discrimination and then have to pay considerable back wages. He was afraid that if he gave these women an immediate salary increase large enough to bring them up to where they should be, the male supervisors would be upset and the female supervisors might comprehend the total situation and want back pay. The HR director told Blackenship that the female supervisors had never complained about pay differences, and they probably did not know the law to any extent.

The HR director agreed to take a sizable salary increase with no back pay, so this part of the problem was solved. Blackenship believed that he had four choices relative to the female supervisors:

- Do nothing.
- Increase the female supervisors' salaries gradually.
- Increase their salaries immediately.
- Call the three supervisors into his office, discuss the situation with them, and jointly decide what to do.

QUESTIONS

1 What would you do if you were Blackenship?
2 How do you think the company got into a situation like this in the first place?

3 Why would you suggest that Blackenship pursue your suggested alternative?

Source: Based on a case prepared by Professor James C. Hodgetts of the Fogelman College of Business and Economics at the University of Memphis. All names are disguised. Used with permission.

MyManagementLab

Visit MyManagementLab to access a personalized Study Plan and additional study tools for this chapter.

To view the CBC videos, read a summary, and answer discussion questions, go to MyManagementLab

NOTES

1. S. O'Neal, "Total Rewards and the Future of Work," *Workspan* (January 2005), pp. 18–26; S. Watson, "Total Rewards: Building a Better Employment Deal," *Workspan* (December 2003), pp. 48–51.

2. S. O'Neal, "Total Rewards and the Future of Work," *Workspan* (January 2005), pp. 18–26; L. Wright, "Total Rewards Can Mean More HR Work than You Think," *Canadian HR Reporter* (October 6, 2003), pp. 9, 12; K.D. Scott, D. Morajda, and J.W. Bishop, "Increase Company Competitiveness: 'Tune Up' Your Pay System," *WorldatWork Journal* (First Quarter, 2002), pp. 35–42.

3. *Towers Perrin 2007–2008 Global Workforce Study* (Stamford CT: Towers Perrin, 2008), www.towersperrin.com/tp/getwebcachedoc?webc=HRS/USA/2008/200802/GWS_handout_web.pdf (accessed September 26, 2011).

4. "Employee Attraction and Retention," Western Compensation and Benefits Consultants, www.wcbc.ca/news/attractionretention (accessed September 26, 2011).

5. J. Dawe, "Compassionate Care Benefit: A New Alternative for Family Caregivers," *Workplace Gazette* (Summer 2004); S. Klie, "Feds Expand Eligibility for Compassionate Care," *Canadian HR Reporter* (July 17, 2006).

6. "GM, Daimler-Chrysler Workers Ratify Agreements," *Workplace Today* (December 1999), p. 11.

7. Harold Jones, "Union Views on Job Evaluations: 1971 vs. 1978," *Personnel Journal,* 58 (February 1979), pp. 80–85.

8. R. Sahl, "Job Content Salary Surveys: Survey Design and Selection Features," *Compensation and Benefits Review* (May–June 1991), pp. 14–21.

9. M.A. Thompson, "Rewards, Performance Two Biggest Words in HR Future," *WorldatWork Canadian News,* 10 (2002), pp. 1, 2, 11.

10. E. Sibray and J.B. Cavallaro, "Case Study: Market Data and Job Evaluation Equals the Best of Both Worlds," *Workspan,* (July 2007), pp. 27–30.

11. Job analysis can be a useful source of information on compensable factors, as well as on job descriptions and job specifications. For example, a quantitative job analysis technique like the position analysis questionnaire generates quantitative information on the degree to which the following five basic factors are present in each job: having decision making/communication/social responsibilities, performing skilled activities, being physically active, operating vehicles or equipment, and processing information. As a result, a job analysis technique like the PAQ is actually also appropriate as a job evaluation technique (or, some say, more appropriate), in that jobs can be quantitatively compared with one another on those five dimensions, and their relative worth thus ascertained.

12. H. Risher, "Job Evaluation: Validity and Reliability," *Compensation and Benefits Review,* 21 (January–February 1989), pp. 22–36.

13. S. Werner, R. Konopaske, and C. Touhey, "Ten Questions to Ask Yourself about Compensation Surveys," *Compensation and Benefits Review,* 31 (May/June 1999), pp. 54–59.

14. P. Cappelli, *The New Deal at Work: Managing the Market-Driven Workforce* (Boston, MA: Harvard Business School Press, 1999).

15. S. Werner, R. Konopaske, and C. Touhey, "Ten Questions to Ask Yourself about Compensation Surveys," *Compensation and Benefits Review,* 31 (May/June 1999), pp. 54–59.

16. "Compensation Surveys on the Internet," *Canadian HR Reporter* (February 10, 1997), p. 6.

17. F.W. Cook, "Compensation Surveys Are Biased," *Compensation and Benefits Review* (September–October 1994), pp. 19–22.

18. K.R. Cardinal, "The Art and Science of the Match, or Why Job Matching Keeps Me Up at Night," *Workspan* (February 2004), pp. 53–56; S. Werner, R. Konopaske, and C. Touhey, "Ten Questions to Ask Yourself about Compensation Surveys," *Compensation and Benefits Review,* 31 (May/June 1999), pp. 1–6; see also U. Vu, "Know-How Pays in Comp Surveys," *Canadian HR Reporter* (April 7, 2003), p. 13.

19. D. Hofrichter, "Broadbanding: A 'Second Generation' Approach," *Compensation and Benefits Review* (September–October 1993), pp. 53–58; see also G. Bergel, "Choosing the Right Pay Delivery System to Fit Banding," *Compensation and Benefits Review,* 26 (July–August 1994), pp. 34–38.

20. C. Bacca and G. Starzmann, "Clarifying Competencies: Powerful Tools for Driving Business Success," *Workspan* (March 2006), pp. 44–46.

21. Ibid.

22. P.K. Zingheim and J.R. Schuster, "Reassessing the Value of Skill-Based Pay," *WorldatWork Journal* (Third Quarter, 2002).

23. R. Long, "Paying for Knowledge: Does It Pay?" *Canadian HR Reporter* (March 28, 2005), pp. 12–13.

24. S. St.-Onge, "Competency-Based Pay Plans Revisited," *Human Resources Professional* (August/September 1998), pp. 29–34; J. Kochanski and P. Leblanc, "Should Firms Pay for Competencies: Competencies Have to Help the Bottom Line," *Canadian HR Reporter* (February 22, 1999), p. 10.

25. F. Giancola, "Skill-Based Pay—Issues for Consideration," *Benefits & Compensation Digest,* 44, no. 5 (May 2007), pp. 10–15.

26. D. Tyson, *Canadian Compensation Handbook* (Toronto, ON: Aurora Professional Press, 2002).

27. P.K. Zingheim, J.R. Schuster, and M.G. Dertien, "Measuring the Value of Work: The 'People-Based' Pay Solution," *WorldatWork Journal* (Third Quarter, 2005), pp. 42–49.

28. D. Yoder, *Personnel Management and Industrial Relations* (Englewood Cliffs, NJ: Prentice Hall, 1970), pp. 643–645.

29. B.R. Ellig, "Executive Pay: A Primer," *Compensation & Benefits Review* (January–February 2003), pp. 44–50.

30. "The Top 1000: Top 50 Highest Paid Executives, 2007," www.reportonbusiness.com/v5/content/tp1000-2007/index.php?view-top_50_execs (accessed November 26, 2008).

31. H.L. Tosi, S. Werner, J.P. Katz, and L.R. Gomez-Mejia, "How Much Does Performance Matter? A Meta-Analysis of CEO Pay Studies," *Journal of Management,* 26 (2000), pp. 301–339.

32. M.A. Thompson, "Investors Call for Better Disclosure of Executive Compensation in Canada," *Workspan Focus Canada* (2006), pp. 5–6.

33. P. Moran, "Equitable Salary Administration in High-Tech Companies," *Compensation and Benefits Review,* 18 (September–October 1986), pp. 31–40.

34. R. Sibson, *Compensation* (New York, NY: AMACOM, 1981), p. 194.

35. B. Bridges, "The Role of Rewards in Motivating Scientific and Technical Personnel: Experience at Elgin AFB," *National Productivity Review* (Summer 1993), pp. 337–348.

36. M. Drolet, "The Male–Female Wage Gap," *Perspectives,* Statistics Canada (Spring 2002), pp. 29–37; E. Carey, "Gender Gap in Earnings Staying Stubbornly High," *Toronto Star* (March 12, 2003), p. A9.

37. "Female Grads Make Less than Males," *Canadian HR Reporter* (April 19, 2004), p. 2.

38. D. Brown, "StatsCan Unable to Explain Gender Wage Gap," *Canadian HR Reporter* (January 31, 2000), p. 3.

39. "PSAC Prepares for Federal Court of Appeal Hearing on Pay Equity Complaint at Canada Post," (July 10, 2008), www.psac.com/news/2008/what/2080710-e.shtml (accessed March 23, 2009).

40. "Air Canada Loses Pay Equity Decision, For Now," *Canadian HR Reporter* (February 13, 2006), p. 2.

41. D. Brown, "StatsCan Unable to Explain Gender Wage Gap," *Canadian HR Reporter* (January 31, 2000), p. 3.

PHOTO CREDITS

Photo Credits are listed in order of appearance.
Solidsdman/Dreamstime.com/GetStock
The Canadian Press(Frank Gunn)
Yuri Arcurs/Shutterstock
Jupiter/Comstock
Regina Leader-Post/Patrick Pettit

Performance Management

LEARNING OUTCOMES

AFTER STUDYING THIS CHAPTER, YOU SHOULD BE ABLE TO

EXPLAIN the five steps in the performance management process.

DESCRIBE five performance appraisal methods and the pros and cons of each.

DISCUSS the major problems inhibiting effective performance appraisals.

DISCUSS 360-degree appraisal from multiple sources.

DESCRIBE the three types of appraisal interviews.

DISCUSS the future of performance management.

REQUIRED PROFESSIONAL CAPABILITIES (RPC)

- Provides development information, support activities, and procedures for learners, supervisors, and managers to assist in achieving performance improvement

- Assists and coaches supervisors to help employees achieve required performance levels

From Chapter 10 of *Human Resources Management in Canada*, Twelfth Edition. Gary Dessler, Nita Chhinzer, and Nina D. Cole.

THE STRATEGIC IMPORTANCE OF PERFORMANCE MANAGEMENT

performance management The process encompassing all activities related to improving employee performance, productivity, and effectiveness.

In any organization, achieving strategic objectives requires employee productivity above all else as organizations strive to create a high-performance culture by using a minimum number of employees. Thus, it has been suggested that better performance management represents a largely untapped opportunity to improve company profitability.[1] Many companies are still dealing with the reality that their performance management systems are ineffective—for example, they need to downsize poor performers, but performance appraisal records indicate that all employees are performing adequately.

Performance management is a process encompassing all activities related to improving employee performance, productivity, and effectiveness. It includes *goal setting, pay for performance, training and development, career management,* and *disciplinary action.* The performance management system must provide an integrated network of procedures across the organization that will influence all work behaviour.[2] There are three major purposes of performance management: it aligns employee actions with strategic goals, it is a vehicle for culture change, and it provides input into other HR systems such as development and remuneration.[3]

THE PERFORMANCE MANAGEMENT PROCESS

Performance management is of considerable strategic importance to today's organizations because the most effective way for firms to differentiate themselves in a highly competitive, service-oriented, global marketplace is through the quality of its employees.[4] The performance management process contains five steps:[5]

1. Defining performance expectations and goals
2. Providing ongoing feedback and coaching
3. Conducting performance appraisal and evaluation discussions
4. Determining performance rewards/consequences
5. Conducting development and career opportunities discussions

Robert Thorndike researched performance management processes and suggests that employment decisions (such as a performance appraisal system) must be valid, practical, reliable, and free from bias.[6] Failure to measure and use appraisal results effectively in human resource decision making and career development negates the primary purpose of performance evaluations. Effective performance management thus begins with defining the job and its performance standards, which will now be discussed.

STEP 1: DEFINING PERFORMANCE EXPECTATIONS

Defining performance expectations and goals is a critical step in employees' understanding of how their work makes a contribution to achieving business results. Over the last 30 years there has been more recognition that job

task performance An individual's direct contribution to their job related processes.

performance is a multidimensional construct which can be split into what has become widely acknowledged as *task* versus *contextual* performance.[7]

Task performance reflects an individual's direct contribution to their job-related processes. Focusing on tasks means that performance expectations are grounded in realistic job demands and align with the organization's strategic objectives and implementation plans. They may also be partially based on previous performance evaluations.

However, as part of the movement toward more corporate social responsibility, expectations are beginning to extend beyond job skills and skills required for promotion to addressing the concept of whole person development (aligned with the direction, attitudes, motivation, and advancement opportunities of the employee). In addition to task performance, contextual performance is often evaluated as a second factor contributing to an employee's overall work-related performance. **Contextual performance** reflects an individual's indirect contribution to the organization by improving the organizational, social, and psychological behaviours that contribute to organizational effectiveness beyond those specified for the job. This includes extra-role behaviours and contextual factors like "demonstrates a positive attitude" and "pitches in to help others when needed," which have surfaced as contextual performance expectations.[8] These goals may be informally known, but not formally defined, which can become problematic in performance management. Employees also need to be aware of which behaviours are expected and which are discretionary to maintain the legitimacy of the performance management system.

contextual performance An individual's indirect contribution to the organization by improving the organizational, social, and psychological behaviours that contribute to organizational effectiveness beyond those specified for the job.

Research finds that most employees require much more clarification of their performance expectations and how these contribute to the organization's overall results.[9] For example, the sales associate job description may list such duties as "supervise support staff" and "be responsible for all customer liaisons." However, one particular sales associate may be expected to personally sell at least $600 000 worth of products per year by handling the division's two largest accounts, to keep the sales assistants happy, and to keep customers away from company executives.[10]

Ultimately, the performance management process cannot be separated from performance measurement. Performance expectations need to be developed in a legally defensible (correlated with job activities), clear, and measurable way. In addition, they must be communicated and supported as such by the organization. Aligned with the sales associate example, a "personal selling" activity can be measured in terms of how many dollars of sales the associate is to generate personally. "Keeping customers away from executives" can be measured with a standard of no more than 10 customer complaints per year being the sales associate's target. In general, employees should always know ahead of time how and on what basis they will be appraised. It is important to note that expectations cannot discriminate directly or indirectly against anyone on protected grounds (gender, age, disability, and so on).

Hints TO ENSURE LEGAL COMPLIANCE

In global companies, performance appraisal criteria may need to be modified to be consistent with cultural norms and values. An interesting study found that some criteria are acceptable in many cultures, as discussed in the Global HRM box.

GLOBAL HRM

Performance Appraisal Criteria in China

Performance appraisal gradually has become more widely used in Chinese enterprises since 1978, when Deng Xiaoping's "open-door" policy began. The appraisal criteria used then were "good moral practice" (*de*), which refers to virtue or moral integrity; "adequate competence" (*neng*), which relates to one's educational background, physical condition, and ability to lead and manage; "positive working attitude" (*qing*), which covers diligence, attendance, and sense of responsibility; and "strong performance record" (*jie*), which refers mainly to work effectiveness, including work quality and quantity.

In the west, where individuals have an inalienable right to choose their own lifestyles and moralities, performance criteria cannot be based on personal character, but instead need to focus on more objective criteria, such as job competence, abilities, and achievements. In China, however, the attitudes and moral character of a person have been regarded as highly relevant to performance. The Confucian view stresses that the most important aspect of an individual is the moral base of his or her character. Chinese culture tends to ascribe achievement more to effort (that is, diligence, which reflects one's morality) than to ability (which, conceived as an inborn trait, requires no moral effort). For the Chinese, hard work reflects admirably on one's character, and achievement is thought to be closely related to moral character. These deeply rooted Confucian values in China thus lead to an emphasis on appraisals that are based upon personal attitudes and moral characteristics (a practice that is clearly antithetical to the appraisal practices in western societies) that appear to reflect traditional Chinese values, such as working hard and being loyal and respectful toward senior staff. Some specific examples are accepting overtime work; being punctual, careful, helpful, loyal, and respectful toward senior staff; as well as being persistent, adaptable, dedicated, and hard working.

Researchers Robert Taormina and Jennifer Gao from the University of Macau gave Chinese workers a list of appraisal items from both western and Chinese sources and asked which ones would be acceptable. They found three performance appraisal factors that were very acceptable to Chinese employees: work dedication, work efficiency, and teamwork. Work dedication behaviours, such as punctuality, loyalty, working hard, and dedication toward one's work, exist in both eastern and western cultures. Employee efficiency has long been considered important to good job performance, as it is considered to be a means to achieve organizational goals. Chinese employees appear to recognize this managerial objective since they were willing to be evaluated on criteria that assess the efficiency of their work. Teamwork is a behavioural manifestation of the group orientation in eastern cultures.

These findings indicate that relevant and carefully selected appraisal criteria can be applicable across cultures.

Source: Robert J. Taormina and Jennifer H. Gao (2009). Identifying Acceptable Performance Appraisal Criteria: An International Perspective. *Asia Pacific Journal of Human Resources* 47(1), pp. 102–125. Copyright © 2009, Australian Human Resources Institute. Used with permission from John Wiley and Sons.

STEP 2: PROVIDING ONGOING COACHING AND FEEDBACK

Throughout the performance management process, managers and their reports should continue to discuss progress. **Figure 1** provides an example of a performance improvement plan (often referred to as a PIP) that can be used to focus such discussions and facilitate ongoing performance improvement. It is important to have open two-way communication, and both the employee and the manager need to check in frequently throughout the performance management process to talk about progression toward goals.

In some organizations, strategies and objectives change quickly. In such cases, managers and employees may need to change their goals to be consistent. Employees are responsible for monitoring their own performance and asking for help. This promotes employee ownership and control over the process.

FIGURE 1   Example of a Performance Improvement Plan

Sample Performance Improvement Plan

TO: [Employee's Name]

FROM: [   ]

SUBJECT: [30/60/90] Day Performance Improvement Plan

DATE: [   ]

This memorandum is written as a [30/60/90] Day Performance Improvement Plan designed to focus your attention on substantially improving your performance in several key areas.

[As was discussed in your most recent performance review dated _____ , you received several "1's" in key areas and an overall rating of "1" meaning you did not meet expectations.]

[Since your performance review on _____, your performance has been unsatisfactory in several respects. For example, _____ .]

This being the case, I have outlined the following Performance Improvement Plan which sets forth objectives that you must accomplish in order to bring your performance up to minimal acceptable standards. The plan is as follows:

1.

2.

3. [list fair objectives – they can be both objective and subjective – in clear terms that could reasonably be accomplished within the required time frame]

4.

5.

You have [30/60/90] days from today to meet these objectives. I will meet with you twice over the next [30/60/90] days to discuss your progress. Our first meeting will be on _____ at _____ and the second meeting will be on _____ at _____ . Both meetings will be in my office.

It is your responsibility to contact me at anytime during this time period regarding your performance and to seek assistance in removing roadblock(s) you may come up against which may impede your progress.

MILW_513764.1

Source: Docstoc, Documents & Resources for Small Businesses & Professionals, www.docstoc.com/docs/4960973/ Sample-Performance-Improvement-Plan-TO-FROM-SUBJECT-DATE-Employee.

STEP 3: PERFORMANCE APPRAISAL AND EVALUATION DISCUSSION

The appraisal itself is generally conducted with the aid of a predetermined and formal method, like one or more of those described in this section.

Formal Appraisal Methods

Graphic Rating Scale

graphic rating scale A scale that lists a number of traits and a range of performance for each. The employee is then rated by identifying the score that best describes his or her level of performance for each trait.

The **graphic rating scale** is the simplest and most popular technique for appraising performance. **Figure 2** shows a typical rating scale. It lists traits (such as reliability) and a range of performance values (from unsatisfactory to outstanding) for each one. The supervisor rates each employee by circling or checking the score that best describes his or her performance for each trait. The assigned values are then totalled.

Instead of appraising generic traits or factors, many firms specify the duties to be appraised. For a payroll coordinator, these might include being the liaison with accounting and benefits staff, continually updating knowledge regarding relevant legislation, maintenance of payroll records, data entry and payroll calculations, and ongoing responses to employee inquiries regarding payroll issues.

Alternation Ranking Method

alternation ranking method Ranking employees from best to worst on a particular trait.

Ranking employees from best to worst on a trait or traits is another method for evaluating employees. Because it is usually easier to distinguish between the worst and best employees than to rank them, an **alternation ranking method** is popular. First, list all employees to be rated, and then cross out the names of any not known well enough to rank. Then, on a form such as that shown in **Figure 3**, indicate the employee who is the highest on the characteristic being measured and also the one who is the lowest. Then choose the next highest and the next lowest, alternating between highest and lowest until all the employees to be rated have been ranked.

Paired Comparison Method

paired comparison method Ranking employees by making a chart of all possible pairs of employees for each trait and indicating the better employee of the pair.

The **paired comparison method** helps to make the ranking method more precise. For every trait (quantity of work, quality of work, and so on), every employee is paired with and compared with every other employee.

Suppose that five employees are to be rated. In the paired comparison method, a chart is prepared, as in **Figure 4**, of all possible pairs of employees for each trait. Then, for each trait, indicate (with a + or −) who is the better employee of the pair. Next, the number of times that an employee is rated as better is added up. In Figure 4, employee Maria was ranked highest (she has the most + marks) for quality of work, while Art was ranked highest for creativity.

Forced Distribution Method

forced distribution method Predetermined percentages of ratees are placed in various performance categories.

Jack Welch, retired chief executive officer of General Electric (GE), is most often associated with the **forced distribution method**, which places predetermined percentages of ratees in performance categories. At GE, the bell curve was used to identify the top 10–20% of the workforce (which are then identified as those exceeding

FIGURE 2   Sample Graphic Rating Scale Form

Sample Performance Rating Form

Employee's Name _____   Level: Entry-level employee

Manager's Name _____

Key Work Responsibilities   Results/Goals to be Achieved
1. _____   1. _____
2. _____   2. _____
3. _____   3. _____
4. _____   4. _____

Communication

	1	2	3	4	5

Below Expectations	Meets Expectations	Role Model
Even with guidance, fails to prepare straight-forward communications, including forms, paperwork, and records, in a timely and accurate manner; products require extensive corrections. Even with guidance, fails to adapt style and materials to communicate straightforward information.	With guidance, prepares straightforward communications, including forms, paperwork, and records, in a timely and accurate manner; products require minimal corrections. With guidance, adapts style and materials to communicate straightforward information.	Independently prepares communications, such as forms, paperwork, and records, in a timely, clear, and accurate manner; products require few, if any, corrections. Independently adapts style and materials to communicate information.

Organizational Know-How

	1	2	3	4	5

Below Expectations	Meets Expectations	Role Model
<performance standards appear here>	<performance standards appear here>	<performance standards appear here>

Personal Effectiveness

	1	2	3	4	5

Below Expectations	Meets Expectations	Role Model
<performance standards appear here>	<performance standards appear here>	<performance standards appear here>

Teamwork

	1	2	3	4	5

Below Expectations	Meets Expectations	Role Model
<performance standards appear here>	<performance standards appear here>	<performance standards appear here>

Achieving Business Results

	1	2	3	4	5

Below Expectations	Meets Expectations	Role Model
<performance standards appear here>	<performance standards appear here>	<performance standards appear here>

continued

Results Assessment

Accomplishment 1: _____

1	2	3	4	5
Low Impact		**Moderate Impact**		**High Impact**
The efficiency or effectiveness of operations remained the same or improved only minimally. The quality of products remained the same or improved only minimally.		The efficiency or effectiveness of operations improved quite a lot. The quality of products improved quite a lot.		The efficiency or effectiveness of operations improved tremendously. The quality of products improved tremendously.

Accomplishment 2: _____

1	2	3	4	5
Low Impact		**Moderate Impact**		**High Impact**
The efficiency or effectiveness of operations remained the same or improved only minimally. The quality of products remained the same or improved only minimally.		The efficiency or effectiveness of operations improved quite a lot. The quality of products improved quite a lot.		The efficiency or effectiveness of operations improved tremendously. The quality of products improved tremendously.

Narrative

_____

_____

_____

_____

_____

Areas to Be Developed	Actions	Completion Date

Manager's Signature _____ Date _____

Employee's Signature _____ Date _____

The above employee signature indicates receipt of, but not necessarily concurrence with, the evaluation herein.

Source: Adapted from Elaine Pulakos, *Performance Management* (SHRM Foundation, 2004) pp. 16–17. Reprinted by permission of Society for Human Resource Management Foundation.

FIGURE 3 Alternation Ranking Scale

ALTERNATION RANKING SCALE

For the Trait: _____

For the trait you are measuring, list all the employees you want to rank. Put the highest-ranking employee's name on line 1. Put the lowest-ranking employee's name on line 20. Then list the next highest ranking on line 2, the next lowest ranking on line 19, and so on. Continue until all names are on the scale.

Highest-ranking employee

1. _____	11. _____
2. _____	12. _____
3. _____	13. _____
4. _____	14. _____
5. _____	15. _____
6. _____	16. _____
7. _____	17. _____
8. _____	18. _____
9. _____	19. _____
10. _____	20. _____

Lowest-ranking employee

FIGURE 4 Ranking Employees by the Paired Comparison Method

FOR THE TRAIT "QUALITY OF WORK"

Employee Rated:

As Compared with:	A Art	B Maria	C Chuck	D Diane	E José
A Art		+	+	−	−
B Maria	−		−	−	−
C Chuck	−	+		+	−
D Diane	+	+	−		+
E José	+	+	+	−	

Maria Ranks Highest Here

FOR THE TRAIT "CREATIVITY"

Employee Rated:

As Compared with:	A Art	B Maria	C Chuck	D Diane	E José
A Art		−	−	−	−
B Maria	+		−	+	+
C Chuck	+	+		−	+
D Diane	+	−	+		−
E José	+	−	−	+	

Art Ranks Highest Here

Note: "+" means "better than" and "−" means "worse than." For each chart, add up the number of + signs in each column to get the highest-ranked employee.

expectations, with a focus on receiving the highest compensation increases and advancement opportunities), the bottom 10% (which are identified as those not meeting expectations, with a focus on coaching for improvement or possible termination). The remaining employees, by default, are considered the backbone of the workforce and receive moderate compensation increases and development opportunities. While the method allows for a concentration of effort and resources on those deemed to be top performers, this method has been criticized as being demotivating since the majority of the workforce are classified as at or below average.[11]

Critical Incident Method

critical incident method Keeping a record of uncommonly good or undesirable examples of an employee's work-related behaviour and reviewing the list with the employee at predetermined times.

With the **critical incident method,** the supervisor keeps a log of desirable or undesirable examples or incidents of each employee's work-related behaviour. Then, every six months or so, the supervisor and employee meet to discuss the latter's performance by using the specific incidents as examples.

This method has several advantages. It provides specific hard facts for explaining the appraisal. It also ensures that a manager thinks about the employee's appraisal throughout the year, because the incidents must be accumulated; therefore, the rating does not just reflect the employee's most recent performance. Keeping a running list of critical incidents should also provide concrete examples of what an employee can do to eliminate any performance deficiencies.

The critical incident method can be adapted to the specific job expectations laid out for the employee at the beginning of the year. Thus, in the example presented in **Table 1**, one of the assistant plant manager's continuing duties is to supervise procurement and to minimize inventory costs. The critical incident shows that the assistant plant manager let inventory storage costs rise 15 percent; this provides a specific example of what performance must be improved in the future.

The critical incident method is often used to supplement another appraisal technique, like a ranking system. It is useful for identifying specific examples of good and poor performance and for planning how deficiencies can be corrected. It is not as useful by itself for comparing employees nor, therefore, for making salary decisions.

Narrative Forms

Some employers use narrative forms to evaluate employees. For example, the form in Figure 1 presented a suggested format for identifying a performance issue and presenting a *performance improvement plan* (PIP). The performance problem is described in specific detail, and its organizational impact is specified. The improvement plan identifies measurable improvement goals, provides directions regarding training and any other suggested activities to address the performance issue, and encourages the employee to add ideas about steps to be taken to improve performance. Therefore, a PIP essentially facilitates a constructive discussion between an employee and his or her manager, and provides

TABLE 1   Examples of Critical Incidents for an Assistant Plant Manager

Continuing Duties	Targets	Critical Incidents
Schedule production for plant	Full utilization of employees and machinery in plant; orders delivered on time	Instituted new production scheduling system; decreased late orders by 10 percent last month; increased machine utilization in plant by 20 percent last month
Supervise procurement of raw materials and inventory control	Minimize inventory costs while keeping adequate supplies on hand	Let inventory storage costs rise 15 percent last month; overordered parts "A" and "B" by 20 percent; underordered part "C" by 30 percent
Supervise machinery maintenance	No shutdowns because of faulty machinery	Instituted new preventative maintenance system for plant; prevented a machine breakdown by discovering faulty part

clarity as to how to improve work performance. Finally, the outcomes and consequences, both positive and negative, are explicitly stated. A summary performance appraisal discussion then focuses on problem solving.[12]

Behaviourally Anchored Rating Scales

behaviourally anchored rating scale (BARS) An appraisal method that aims to combine the benefits of narratives, critical incidents, and quantified ratings by anchoring a quantified scale with specific narrative examples of good and poor performance.

A **behaviourally anchored rating scale (BARS)** combines the benefits of narratives, critical incidents, and quantified ratings by anchoring a series of quantified scales, one for each performance dimension, with specific behavioural examples of good or poor performance. The guiding principle to BARS is that by elaboration of the dimension and rating scale, it gives raters a uniform interpretation as to the types of behaviour being measured.[13] BARS usually involves a scale of nine anchors, although seven and five anchors have also been used.[14]

The midpoint scales are more difficult to develop in a standardized format than the scale extremes. Recent efforts have focused on addressing midpoint scale development to influence inter-rater reliability and inter-rater agreement.[15] The research suggests that all levels of the scale be anchored with statements reflecting how users are to interpret them to increase uniform use of the scale. As well, developers of the scales should be involved in the training of users to increase the consistency in how the scale is used, which increases the effectiveness and legal defensibility of the performance appraisal. **Figure 5** provides an example of a BARS for one performance dimension: "sales skills."

FIGURE 5 Behaviourally Anchored Rating Scale

SALES SKILLS

Skilfully persuading customers to purchase products; using product benefits and opportunities effectively; closing skills; adapting sales techniques appropriately to different customers; effectively overcoming objections to purchasing products.

5 — If a customer insists on a particular brand name, the salesperson perseveres. Although products with this particular brand name are not available, the salesperson does not give up; instead, the salesperson persuades the customer that his or her needs could be better met with another product.

4 — The salesperson treats objections to purchasing the product seriously; works hard to counter the objections with relevant positive arguments regarding the benefits of the product.

3 — When a customer is deciding on which product to purchase, the salesperson tries to sell the product with the highest profit magin.

2 — The salesperson insists on describing more features of the product even though the customer wants to purchase it right now.

1 — When a customer states an objection to purchasing a product, the salesperson ends the conversation, assuming that the prospect must not be interested.

Developing a BARS can be more time-consuming than developing other appraisal tools, like graphic rating scales. But BARS may also have important advantages:[16]

1. *A more accurate measure.* People who know the job and its requirements better than anyone else does develop BARS. The result should therefore be a good measure of performance on that job.

2. *Clearer standards.* The critical incidents along the scale help to clarify what is meant by extremely good performance, average performance, and so forth.

3. *Feedback.* The critical incidents may be more useful in providing feedback to appraisees than simply informing them of their performance rating without providing specific behavioural examples.

4. *Independent dimensions.* Systematically clustering the critical incidents into five or six performance dimensions (such as "knowledge and judgment") should help to make the dimensions more independent of one another. For example, a rater should be less likely to rate an employee high on all dimensions simply because he or she was rated high in "conscientiousness."

5. *Consistency.* BARS evaluations also seem to be relatively consistent and reliable in that different raters' appraisals of the same person tend to be similar.[17]

Management by Objectives (MBO)

management by objectives (MBO)
Involves setting specific measurable goals with each employee and then periodically reviewing the progress made.

Stripped to its essentials, **management by objectives (MBO)** requires the manager and employee to jointly set specific measurable goals and periodically discuss progress toward these goals, aligned with a comprehensive, *organization-wide goal-setting and appraisal program.* When managers and employees set goals collaboratively, employees become more engaged and committed to the goal, leading to a higher rate of success.[18] While there is a notion that difficult goals (also referred to as "stretch goals") can increase personal growth and professional development, and improve organizational effectiveness,[19] it is important to set objectives that match the job description and the person's abilities. Goals that push an employee too far beyond his or her abilities may lead to burnout.[20] To motivate performance, the objectives must be fair and attainable.

1. *Set the organization's goals.* Establish an organization-wide plan for the next year and set goals.

2. *Set departmental goals.* Department heads and their superiors jointly set goals for their departments.

3. *Discuss departmental goals.* Department heads discuss the department's goals with all employees in the department (often at a department-wide meeting) and ask them to develop their own individual goals; in other words, how can each employee contribute to the department's attainment of its goals?

4. *Define expected results* (set individual goals). Here, department heads and employees set short-term performance targets.

5. *Performance reviews: Measure the results.* Department heads compare the actual performance of each employee with the expected results.

6. *Provide feedback.* Department heads hold periodic performance review meetings with employees to discuss and evaluate progress in achieving expected results.

Problems to Avoid Using MBO has three potential problems. *Setting unclear, unmeasurable objectives* is the main one. Such an objective as "will do a better job of training" is useless. Conversely, "will have four employees promoted during the year" is a measurable objective. Second, MBO is *time-consuming*. Taking the time to set objectives, measure progress, and provide feedback can take several hours per employee per year, over and above the time already spent doing each person's appraisal. Third, setting objectives with an employee sometimes turns into a *tug of war*; managers push for higher goals and employees push for lower ones. It is thus important to know the job and the person's ability. To motivate performance, the objectives must be fair and attainable.

Mixing the Methods

Most firms combine several appraisal techniques. The form shown in Figure 2 is a graphic rating scale with behavioural incidents included to define values for the traits being measured. The quantifiable ranking method permits comparisons of employees and is therefore useful for making salary, transfer, and promotion decisions. The critical incidents provide specific examples of performance relative to expectations and can be used to develop the high and low anchors for the BARS technique.[21] Ultimately, no one single solution is best for all performance management systems. Instead, resource constraints (time, money, people) and organizational factors (budget, turnover, strategy) will help determine which of the options is best for each organization.

The Use of Technology in Performance Appraisals

Over the past few years, web-based performance management has moved from being a leading-edge approach adopted by only large companies to a mainstream practice that is quickly becoming an industry standard among medium and small organizations.[22] It enables managers to keep computerized notes on employees, combine these with ratings on several performance traits, and then generate written text to support each part of the appraisal.

But the true value in web-based performance management goes beyond simply automating time-consuming, tedious tasks like tracking down paper-based appraisal forms. They ultimately improve the overall performance management process, starting with higher completion rates, which can dramatically increase the value of performance management within organizations of all sizes. Performance management systems provide employees with a clear development path and a better understanding of how their goals are aligned with those of the organization, which in turn increases their support of the process. Managers have the information they need to ensure development plans are relevant and executed. Executives have a clear picture of the organization's talent strategy and how it ties into the bottom line.

Most web-based performance management systems provide advanced reporting capabilities, which allow managers to track the status of performance management initiatives easily. Goal management functions enable organizations to link individual goals to strategic corporate goals, meaning that executives have insight into the progress being made on corporate objectives. Succession planning tools provide executives with a clear plan to build a talent pool to meet the organization's business needs and address potential attrition.

In a relatively short time, employee performance management has undergone a rapid evolution with the development of powerful, web-based tools. HR professionals are no longer mired in paperwork and other mundane administrative tasks. They have more time to focus on meeting strategic objectives, better tools to implement best practices programs, and access to critical workforce metrics they can share with their executive team.

electronic performance monitoring (EPM) Having supervisors electronically monitor the amount of computerized data an employee is processing per day and thereby his or her performance.

Electronic performance monitoring (EPM) is in some respects the ultimate in computerized appraising. Electronic performance monitoring means having supervisors electronically observe the employee's output or whereabouts. This typically involves using computer networks and wireless audio or video links to monitor and record employees' work activities. It includes, for instance, monitoring a data clerk's hourly keystrokes, tracking via GPS the whereabouts of delivery drivers, and monitoring the calls of customer service clerks.

This food service supervisor is conducting a feedback session about an employee's performance during a major banquet to keep communications open and build employee commitment.

Research INSIGHT

Performance Appraisal Problems and Solutions

Few of the things a manager does are fraught with more peril than appraising employees' performance. Employees in general tend to be overly optimistic about what their ratings will be, and they also know that their raises, career progress, and peace of mind may well hinge on how they are rated. Thus, an honest appraisal inevitably involves an emotional component, which is particularly difficult when managers are not trained on formal appraisal discussion skills. The result is often dishonest appraisals or avoidance of appraisals.[23]

Even more problematic, however, are the numerous structural problems that can cast serious doubt on just how fair the whole process is. Fortunately, research shows that action by management to implement a more acceptable performance appraisal system can increase employee trust in management.[24] According to several studies, the majority of organizations view their performance management systems as ineffective. More focus on the execution of performance appraisal is required instead of searching for new techniques and methods.[25] Some of the main appraisal problems and how to solve them, as well as several other pertinent appraisal issues, will now be reviewed.

Validity and Reliability

Appraisal systems must be based on performance criteria that are valid for the position being rated and must be reliable, in that their application must produce consistent ratings for the same performance. Employee concerns about appraisal fairness are influenced by these characteristics of the performance appraisal system.

Criteria used in performance appraisal must be accurate, or valid, to produce useful results. Criteria must be (1) relevant to the job being appraised, (2) broad enough to cover all aspects of the job requirements, and (3) specific. For example, including a broad criterion, such as "leadership," may not be relevant to non-management jobs and may be so vague that it can be interpreted in many different ways.

Effective appraisal criteria are precise enough to result in consistent measures of performance when applied across many employees by many different raters. This is difficult to achieve without quantifiable and measurable criteria.

Rating Scale Problems

Seven main problems can undermine appraisal tools like graphic rating scales: unclear standards, the halo effect, central tendency, leniency or strictness, appraisal bias, the recency effect, and the similar-to-me bias.

The problem of **unclear performance standards** is illustrated in **Table 2**. Although the graphic rating scale seems objective, it would probably result in unfair appraisals because the traits and degrees of merit are open to interpretation. For example, different supervisors would probably differently define "good" performance, "fair" performance, and so on. The same is true of traits, such as "quality of work" or "creativity." There are several ways in which to rectify this problem. The best way is to develop and include descriptive phrases that define each trait, as in Figure 2. There, the form specified what was meant by "outstanding," "very good," and "good" quality of work. This specificity results in appraisals that are more consistent and more easily explained.

The **halo effect** means that the rating of an employee on one trait (such as "gets along with others") biases the way that person is rated on other traits (such as "reliability"). This problem often occurs with employees who are especially friendly (or unfriendly) toward the supervisor. For example, an unfriendly employee will often be rated unsatisfactory for all traits rather than just for the trait "gets along well with others." Being aware of this problem is a major step toward avoiding it. Supervisory training can also alleviate the problem.[26]

Many supervisors have a **central tendency** when filling in rating scales. For example, if the rating scale ranges from one to seven, they tend to avoid the highs (six and seven) and lows (one and two) and rate most of their employees between three and five. If a graphic rating scale is used, this central tendency could mean that all employees are simply rated "average." Such a restriction can distort the evaluations, making them less useful for promotion, salary, or counselling purposes. Ranking employees instead of using a graphic rating scale can avoid this central tendency problem, because all employees must be ranked and thus cannot all be rated average.

Some supervisors tend to rate all of their employees consistently high (or low), just as some instructors are notoriously high graders and others are not. Fear of interpersonal conflict is often the reason for leniency.[27] Conversely, evaluators

unclear performance standards An appraisal scale that is too open to interpretation of traits and standards.

halo effect In performance appraisal, the problem that occurs when a supervisor's rating of an employee on one trait biases the rating of that person on other traits.

central tendency A tendency to rate all employees in the middle of the scale.

TABLE 2 A Graphic Rating Scale with Unclear Standards

	Excellent	Good	Fair	Poor
Quality of work				
Quantity of work				
Creativity				
Integrity				

Note: For example, what exactly is meant by "good," "quantity of work," and so forth?

strictness/leniency The problem that occurs when a supervisor has a tendency to rate all employees either low or high.

tend to give more weight to negative attributes than to positive ones.[28] This **strictness/leniency** problem is especially serious with graphic rating scales, since supervisors are not necessarily required to avoid giving all of their employees low (or high) ratings. However, when ranking employees, a manager is forced to distinguish between high and low performers. Thus, strictness/leniency is not a problem with the ranking or forced distribution approaches.

Individual differences among ratees in terms of a wide variety of characteristics, such as age, race, and sex, can affect their ratings, often quite apart from their actual performance.[29] In fact, research shows that less than half of performance evaluation ratings are actually related to employee performance and that most of the rating is based on idiosyncratic factors.[30] This is known as **appraisal bias.** Not only does this bias result in inaccurate feedback, but it is also illegal under human rights legislation. Although age-related bias is typically thought of as affecting older workers, one study found a negative relationship between age and performance evaluation for entry-level jobs in public accounting firms.[31] A related issue is described in the Workforce Diversity box.

appraisal bias The tendency to allow individual differences, such as age, race, and sex, to affect the appraisal ratings that these employees receive.

Canadian Human Rights Commission **www.chrc-ccdp.ca**

Interestingly, the friendliness and likeability of an employee have been found to have little effect on that person's performance ratings.[32] However, an employee's previous performance can affect the evaluation of his or her current performance.[33] The actual error can take several forms. Sometimes the rater may systematically overestimate improvement by a poor worker or decline by a good worker, for instance. In some situations—especially when the change in behaviour is more gradual—the rater may simply be insensitive to improvement or decline. In any case, it is important to rate performance objectively. Such factors as previous performance, age, or race should not be allowed to influence results.

WORKFORCE DIVERSITY

Watch for Cultural Biases in Assessing Employees

Canadian organizations are increasingly turning to immigrants as the supply of workers dries up in Canada. This demographic shift poses some unique challenges for organizations in integrating these new Canadians into the workplace, particularly when it comes to performance management.

Values, beliefs, and perspectives vary by culture. Typical group and individual behaviours in Canada may not be the norm for people from other cultures. The performance appraisal, with its goal-setting procedures and inherent feedback process, is a western concept that can be a cultural disconnect for employees with different cultural roots. In eastern cultures, appraisals are as likely to deal with attributes such as cooperation and sociability as they are with achievement of results. And because status is so important in eastern cultures (it is crucial to an individual's sense of worth and contribution), it is important to ensure that the employee does not become insulted or lose face.

In some cultures, managers provide explicit directions and employees are more deferential to their superiors. Technical expertise is the proven path to promotion rather than taking initiative and seeking new responsibilities. Also, performance is more often assessed on a group basis, with recognition and rewards being assigned for strong group performance; the individual is expected to work for the good of the group. Typical performance criteria used in Canada are more individual-focused and may not value group-oriented performance.

Cultural diversity in the workplace provides an opportunity to maximize sales and profits while creating a work atmosphere appropriate for all cultures. Managers and executives in an economy becoming more dependent on the successful integration of highly skilled internationally trained professionals owe it to their organizations—and their futures as business leaders—to successfully manage the entire diverse workforce.

Source: Adapted from R. Singer, "Watch for Cultural Biases in Assessing Employees," *Canadian HR Reporter* (June 19, 2006). Reprinted by permission of Canadian HR Reporter. © Copyright Thomson Reuters Canada Ltd., (2012) Toronto, Ontario, 1-800-387-5164. Web: www.hrreporter.com

recency effect The rating error that occurs when ratings are based on the employee's most recent performance rather than on performance throughout the appraisal period.

similar-to-me bias The tendency to give higher performance ratings to employees who are perceived to be similar to the rater in some way.

RPC

Provides development information, support activities, and procedures for learners, supervisors, and managers to assist in achieving performance improvement

The **recency effect** occurs when ratings are based on the employee's most recent performance, whether good or bad. To the extent that this recent performance does not exemplify the employee's average performance over the appraisal period, the appraisal is biased.

If a supervisor tends to give higher ratings to employees with whom he or she has something in common, the **similar-to-me bias** is occurring. This bias can be discriminatory if it is based on similarity in race, gender, or other prohibited grounds.

How to Avoid Appraisal Problems

There are at least four ways in which managers can minimize the impact of appraisal problems, such as bias and central tendency. First, raters must be familiar with the problems just discussed. Understanding the problem can help to prevent it.

Second, training supervisors on how to eliminate rating errors, such as the halo effect, leniency, and central tendency, can help them avoid these problems.[34] In a typical training program, raters are shown videos of jobs being performed and are asked to rate the worker. Ratings made by each participant are then placed on a flip chart and the various errors (such as leniency and halo) are explained. For example, if a trainee rated all criteria (such as quality, quantity, and so on) about the same, the trainer might explain that a halo error had occurred. Typically, the trainer gives the correct rating and then illustrates the rating errors made by the participants.[35] According to one study, computer-assisted appraisal training improved managers' ability to conduct performance appraisal discussions with their employees.[36]

Rater training will not eliminate all rating errors or ensure absolute accuracy. In practice, several factors—including the extent to which pay is tied to performance ratings, union pressure, employee turnover, time constraints, and the need to justify ratings—may be more important than training. This means that improving appraisal accuracy calls not only for training but also for reducing outside factors, such as union pressure and time constraints.[37] It has also been found that employee reaction to current performance reviews is affected by past appraisal feedback, which is beyond the control of the current manager.[38]

Third, raters must choose the right appraisal tool. Each tool, such as the graphic rating scale or critical incident method, has its own advantages and disadvantages. For example, the ranking method avoids central tendency but can cause ill feelings when employees' performances are, in fact, all "high" (see **Table 3**).

Fourth, errors in performance appraisals can be reduced by using multiple raters in the evaluation. Multiple raters increase the validity and accuracy of the rating by controlling for individual biases or idiosyncrasies. Also, responsibility for poor appraisals is diffused; therefore, raters are more comfortable giving a poor rating. When raters are accountable for their rating, reliability also increases.[39] As an additional benefit, multiple ratings may be more legally defensible.

Who Should Do the Appraising?

Who should actually rate an employee's performance? Several options exist as to who can be involved in the performance management appraisal process.

TABLE 3 Important Advantages and Disadvantages of Appraisal Tools

	Advantages	Disadvantages
Graphic rating scale	Simple to use; provides a quantitative rating for each employee.	Standards may be unclear; halo effect, central tendency, leniency, and bias can also be problems.
Alternation ranking	Simple to use (but not as simple as graphic rating scale); avoids central tendency and other problems of rating scales.	Can cause disagreements among employees and may be unfair if all employees are, in fact, excellent.
Paired comparison method	A more precise ranking method that involves multiple traits.	Difficult to use as employee numbers increase; differences may not be noticeable enough to rank.
Forced distribution method	End up with a predetermined number of people in each group.	Appraisal results depend on the adequacy of the original choice of cutoff points.
Critical incident method	Helps specify what is "right" and "wrong" about the employee's performance; forces the supervisor to evaluate employees on an ongoing basis.	Difficult to rate or rank employees relative to one another; cannot be used to defend salary decisions.
Narrative form	Explicitly states improvement goals and associated outcomes or consequences.	Employees may take these too personally.
Behaviourally anchored rating scale (BARS)	Provides behavioural "anchors"; very accurate; high inter-rater reliability.	Difficult to develop.
Management by objectives	Tied to jointly agreed-upon performance objectives.	Risk of unclear performance measures, time-consuming, and inflated/deflated goals due to tug of war.

The best performance appraisal systems are those in which the supervisor or manager makes an ongoing effort to coach and monitor employees instead of leaving evaluation to the last minute.

Supervisors

Supervisors' ratings are still the heart of most appraisal systems. Getting a supervisor's appraisal is relatively easy and also makes a great deal of sense. The supervisor should be—and usually is—in the best position to observe and evaluate the performance of employees reporting to him or her and is responsible for their performance.

Self

Employees' self-ratings of performance are sometimes used, generally in conjunction with supervisors' ratings. Employees value the opportunity to participate in performance appraisal more for the opportunity to be heard than for the opportunity to influence the end result.[40] Nevertheless, the basic problem with self-ratings is that employees usually rate themselves higher than they are rated by supervisors or peers.[41] In one study, for example, it was found that when asked to rate their own job performance, 40 percent of the employees in jobs of all types placed themselves in the top 10 percent ("one of the best"), while virtually all remaining employees rated themselves either in the top 25 percent ("well above average") or at least in the top 50 percent ("above average"). Usually no more than 1 percent or 2 percent will place themselves in a below-average category, and then almost invariably in the top below-average category. However, self-ratings have been found to correlate more highly with performance measures if employees know that this comparison will be made and if they are instructed to compare themselves with others.[42]

Supervisors requesting self-appraisals should know that their appraisals and their employees' self-appraisals may accentuate appraiser–appraisee differences, and rigidify positions.[43] Furthermore, even if self-appraisals are not formally requested, each employee will enter the performance review meeting with his or her own self-appraisal in mind, and this will usually be higher than the supervisor's rating.

Peers

The appraisal of an employee by his or her peers can be effective in predicting future management success. Peers may have more opportunity to observe ratees and to observe them at more revealing times than supervisors do. One potential problem is *logrolling*; here, all the peers simply get together to rate each other highly.

With more firms using self-managing teams, peer or team appraisals are becoming more popular. One study found that peer ratings had an immediate positive impact on perceptions of open communication, motivation, group cohesion, and satisfaction, and these were not dependent on the ratio of positive to negative feedback.[44] Thus, peer appraisals would appear to have great potential for work teams.

Committees

Many employers use rating committees to evaluate employees. These committees usually comprise the employee's immediate supervisor and three or four other supervisors. Using multiple raters can be advantageous. Although there may be a discrepancy in the ratings made by individual supervisors, the composite ratings tend to be more reliable, fair, and valid.[45] Using several raters can help cancel out problems like bias and the halo effect on the part of individual raters. Furthermore, when there are variations in raters' ratings, they usually stem from the fact that raters often observe different facets of an employee's performance and the appraisal ought to reflect these differences.[46] Even when a committee is not used, it is common to have the appraisal reviewed by the manager immediately above the one who makes the appraisal.

Subordinates

Traditionally, supervisors feared that being appraised by their employees would undermine their management authority. However, with today's flatter organizations and empowered workers, much managerial authority is a thing of the past, and employees are in a good position to observe managerial performance.[47] Thus, more firms today are letting employees anonymously evaluate their supervisors' performance, a process many call *upward feedback*.[48] When conducted throughout the firm, the process helps top managers diagnose management styles, identify potential "people" problems, and take corrective action with individual managers as required. Such employee ratings are especially valuable when used for developmental rather than evaluative purposes.[49] Managers who receive feedback from employees who identify themselves view the upward appraisal process more positively than do managers who receive anonymous feedback; however, employees (not surprisingly) are more comfortable giving anonymous responses, and those who have to identify themselves tend to provide inflated ratings.[50] Research comparing employee and peer ratings of managers found them to be comparable. [51]

Upward feedback from reporting employees is quite effective in terms of improving the supervisor's behaviour, according to the research evidence. One study examined data for 92 managers who were rated by one or more reporting employees in each of four administrations of an upward feedback survey over two and a half years. The reporting employees were asked to rate themselves and their managers in surveys that consisted of 33 behavioural statements. The feedback to the managers also contained results from previous administrations of the survey so that they could track their performance over time.

According to the researchers, managers whose initial performance level was lower than the average employee performance level improved performance by the next performance assessment and sustained this improvement two years later. Interestingly, the results also suggest that it is not necessarily the specific feedback that caused the performance improvement, because low-performing managers seemed to improve over time even if they did not receive any feedback. Instead, learning what the critical supervisory behaviours were (as a result of themselves filling out the appraisal surveys) and knowing that they might be appraised may have been enough to result in the improved supervisory behaviours. In a sense, therefore, it is the existence of the formal upward feedback program rather than the actual feedback itself that may signal and motivate supervisors to get their behaviours in line with what they should be.[52]

360-Degree Appraisal

360-degree appraisal A performance appraisal technique that uses multiple raters including peers, employees reporting to the appraisee, supervisors, and customers.

Many Canadian firms are now using what is called **360-degree appraisal**, or "multisource feedback." Here, as shown in **Figure 6**, performance information is collected "all around" an employee—from his or her supervisors, subordinates, peers, and internal or external customers.[53] This feedback was originally used only for training and development purposes, but it has rapidly

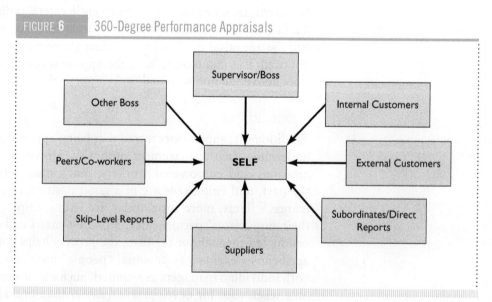

FIGURE 6 360-Degree Performance Appraisals

Source: Alma M. McCarthy, Thomas N. Garavan, "360° Feedback Process: Performance, Improvement and Employee Career Development," *Journal of European Industrial Training*, 25, no. 1 (2001), pp. 5–32. © Emerald Group Publishing Limited all rights reserved.

spread to the management of performance and pay.[54] The 360-degree approach supports the activities of performance feedback, coaching, leadership development, succession planning, and rewards and recognition.[55]

There are a number of reasons for the rapid growth of 360-degree appraisal, despite the significant investment of time required for it to function successfully. Today's flatter organizations employ a more open communicative climate conducive to such an approach, and 360-degree appraisal fits closely with the goals of organizations committed to continuous learning. A multiple-rater system is also more meaningful in today's reality of complex jobs, with matrix and team reporting relationships. A 360-degree appraisal can be perceived as a jury of peers, rather than the supervisor as a single judge, which enhances perceptions of fairness.[56]

Most 360-degree appraisal systems contain several common features (including Internet-based 360-degree feedback systems. They are usually applied in a confidential and anonymous manner. Appropriate parties—peers, superiors, employees, and customers, for instance—complete survey questionnaires about an individual. The questionnaires must be custom-designed and linked to the organization's strategic direction, vision, and values.[57] All this information is then compiled into individualized reports. When the information is being used for self-development purposes only, the report is presented to the person being rated, who then meets with his or her own supervisor and information pertinent for the purpose of developing a self-improvement plan is shared. When the information is being used for management of performance or pay, the information is also provided to the ratee's supervisor, and a supportive and facilitative process to follow up is required to ensure that the behavioural change required for performance improvement is made.[58]

Research INSIGHT

There is a limited amount of research data on the effectiveness of 360-degree feedback. Some organizations have abandoned it for appraisal purposes because of negative attitudes from employees and inflated ratings.[59] Some studies have found that the different raters often disagree on performance ratings.[60] A recent study by researchers at Concordia University in Montreal found that 360-degree feedback is popular among Canadian employers, despite such problems as the amount of time and effort involved, lack of trust in the system by employees, and lack of fit with strategic goals and other HR practices. The results showed that organizations that successfully implemented 360-degree feedback were those that had the most clarity on what their initial objectives were. Organizations that rely exclusively on external consultants to establish 360-degree appraisal have less success than organizations that are more sensitive to contextual factors, such as the readiness of employees and the culture of the organization.[61]

An Ethical Dilemma

Is it fair to factor in employee self-ratings in 360-degree performance appraisal, when we know that these appraisals tend to be inflated?

Some experts suggest that 360-degree feedback be used for developmental purposes only.[62] In general, it is advisable to use 360-degree feedback for developmental/career-planning purposes initially, and then to determine whether the organization is ready to use it for evaluative appraisal purposes. A pilot test in one department is often recommended. Once a decision to use 360-degree appraisal has been made, organizations should consider the following advice:[63]

Tips FOR THE FRONT LINE

- Have the performance criteria developed by a representative group that is familiar with each job.

- Be clear about who will have access to reports.
- Provide training for all supervisors, raters, and ratees.
- Assure all raters that their comments will be kept anonymous.
- Plan to evaluate the 360-degree feedback system for fine-tuning.

Formal Appraisal Discussions

formal appraisal discussion An interview in which the supervisor and employee review the appraisal and make plans to remedy deficiencies and reinforce strengths.

The essence of a performance appraisal is the feedback provided in a one-on-one conversation called the **formal appraisal discussion.** This is an interview in which the supervisor and employee review the appraisal and make plans to remedy deficiencies and reinforce strengths. Unfortunately, surveys show that less than half of companies describe their performance appraisal systems as effective or very effective because of weak execution due to managers abdicating their responsibility for screening out poor performers.[64] This discussion is often avoided by supervisors and managers who have not been trained to provide constructive feedback and to deal with defensive employees. Ultimately, feedback should be ongoing, making the formal appraisal discussion one of many performance discussions.

Types of Interviews

There are three basic types of formal appraisal discussions, each with its own objectives:[65]

Formal Appraisal Discussion Type	Formal Appraisal Discussion Objective
(1) Satisfactory performance—Promotable employee	(1) Make development plans
(2) Satisfactory performance—Nonpromotable employee	(2) Maintain performance
(3) Unsatisfactory performance—Correctable	(3) Plan correction

If the employee's performance is unsatisfactory and the situation uncorrectable, there is usually no need for any formal appraisal discussion because the person's performance is not correctable anyway. Either the person's poor performance is tolerated for now, or he or she is dismissed.

Satisfactory—Promotable

Here, the person's performance is satisfactory and there is a promotion ahead. This is the easiest of the three formal appraisal discussions. The objective is to discuss the person's career plans and to develop a specific action plan for the educational and professional development that the person needs to move to the next job.

Satisfactory—Not Promotable

This interview is for employees whose performance is satisfactory but for whom promotion is not possible. Perhaps there is no more room in the company; some employees are happy where they are and do not want a promotion.[66] The objective here is not to improve or develop the person but to maintain satisfactory performance.

This situation is not easy. The best option is usually to find incentives that are important to the person and are enough to maintain satisfactory performance. These might include extra time off, a small bonus, additional authority to handle a slightly enlarged job, and verbal reinforcement in the form of "Well done!"

Unsatisfactory—Correctable

When the person's performance is unsatisfactory but correctable, the interview objective is to lay out an *action plan* (as explained later) for correcting the unsatisfactory performance.

Preparing for the Formal Appraisal Discussion

An important component of the performance management process is the effective use of feedback. This often happens in a formal appraisal discussion after the performance has been evaluated. There are three things to do in preparation for the interview.[67] First, assemble the data. Study the person's job description, compare the employee's performance to the standards, and review the files of the employee's previous appraisals. Next, prepare the employee. Give the employee at least a week's notice to review his or her own work, read over his or her job description, analyze problems he or she may be dealing with, and gather questions and comments for the interview. Finally, find a mutually agreeable time and place and allow plenty of time for the interview. Interviews with non-supervisory staff should take no more than an hour. Appraising management employees often takes two or three hours. Be sure that the interview is conducted in a private place where there will be no interruptions. It is important to keep in mind what is said and how it is said. The Strategic HR box provides an example of how management teams in a global company were guided on managing the formal appraisal discussion.

How to Conduct the Interview

Constructive feedback is considered a positive and motivating experience.[68] There are four things to keep in mind when conducting a formal appraisal discussion to ensure the feedback is constructive.[69]

1. *Be direct and specific.* Talk in terms of objective work data. Use examples, such as absences, tardiness, quality records, inspection reports, scrap or waste, orders processed, productivity records, material used or consumed, timeliness of tasks or projects, control or reduction of costs, numbers of errors, costs compared with budgets, customers' comments, product returns, order processing time, inventory level and accuracy, accident reports, and so on.

2. *Do not get personal.* Do not say, "You are too slow in producing those reports." Instead, try to compare the person's performance with a standard ("These reports should normally be done within 10 days"). Similarly, do not compare the person's performance with that of other people ("He is quicker than you are").

3. *Encourage the person to talk.* Stop and listen to what the person is saying; ask open-ended questions, such as, "What do you think we can do to improve the situation?" Use phrases such as, "Go on," or "Tell me more." Restate the person's last point as a question, such as, "You do not think that you can get the job done?"

RPC

Assists and coaches supervisors to help employees achieve required performance levels

Tips | **FOR THE FRONT LINE**

STRATEGIC HR

Jaguar Land Rover Formal Appraisal Discussion Training

In 2008, an Indian conglomerate (Tata) took over the Jaguar Land Rover carmaker. This triggered a new set of management behaviours, including the redesign of the performance management process. The contract to develop a companywide performance management system for the 1500 managers (from line level to board level) went to learning and development specialist Ashorne Hill.

As part of this process, management was educated on a standardized approach to performance evaluation. Management was coached on techniques for managing behaviour during the formal appraisal discussion, including the following suggestions:

- Say what you see—acknowledging signposting by reflecting behaviour back to the individual in words
- Empathy—demonstrating genuine understanding and concern, even when challenging specific behaviours or questioning performance standards
- Broken record—interrupting without creating confrontation

- Active listening—focusing on what is being said and responding directly
- Questioning—using open, closed, and probing questions, as required, to elicit information
- Reassurance—being supportive of the other person's point of view, where appropriate
- Nonverbal communication—adopting body language that encourages communication
- Calm, even tone and pace—bringing the conversation back to a considered, mutual exchange of views whenever emotion threatens to disrupt the discussion or lead it into a dead end.

The training program is viewed as a success by management and participants alike. Jaguar Land Rover believes that managers are now equipped with the skills to implement the performance management system successfully.

Source: J. Hicks, "Jaguar Land Rover Bosses Get to Grips with Performance Management: Program Teaches Practical Skills for the Workplace," *Human Resource Management International Digest* (2011), volume 19, issue 4, pp. 10–12. © Emerald Group Publishing Limited all rights reserved.

4. *Develop an action plan.* Do not get personal, but do make sure that by the end of the interview you have (a) provided specific examples of performance that does and does not need attention or improvement, (b) made sure the person understands how he or she should improve his or her performance, (c) obtained an agreement from the person that he or she understands the reasons for the appraisal, and (d) developed an action plan that shows steps to achieving specified goals and the results expected. Be sure that a timeline is included in the plan.

How to Handle Criticism and Defensive Employees

When criticism is required, it should be done in a manner that lets the person maintain his or her dignity and sense of worth. Specifically, criticism should be provided constructively, in private, and immediately following poor performance. Provide examples of critical incidents and specific suggestions of what could be done and why. Finally, ensure that criticism is objective and free of any personal biases.

When poor performance by an employee is described, the first reaction will often be denial. By denying the fault, the person avoids having to question his or her own competence. Others react to criticism with anger and aggression. This helps them let off steam and postpones confronting the immediate problem until they are able to cope with it. Still others react to criticism by retreating into a shell.

Understanding and dealing with defensiveness is an important appraisal skill that requires the following:[70]

1. Recognize that defensive behaviour is normal.

2. Never attack a person's defences. Do not try to "explain someone" to himself or herself by saying things like, "You know the real reason you are using that excuse is that you cannot bear to be blamed for anything." Instead, try to concentrate on the act itself ("sales are down") rather than on the person ("you are not selling enough").

3. Postpone action. Sometimes it is best to do nothing at all. People frequently react to sudden threats by instinctively hiding behind their "masks." Given sufficient time, however, a more rational reaction usually takes over.

4. Recognize human limitations. Do not expect to be able to solve every problem that comes up, especially the human ones. More importantly, remember that a supervisor should not try to be a psychologist. Offering employees understanding is one thing; trying to deal with deep psychological problems is another matter entirely.

Ensuring That the Formal Appraisal Discussion Leads to Improved Performance

It is important to clear up performance problems by setting goals and a schedule for achieving them. However, even if you have obtained agreement from your employees about the areas for performance improvement, they may or may not be satisfied with their appraisal. In one study, researchers found that whether or not employees expressed satisfaction with their formal appraisal discussion depended mostly on three factors: (1) not feeling threatened during the interview, (2) having an opportunity to present their ideas and feelings and to influence the course of the interview, and (3) having a helpful and constructive supervisor conduct the interview.[71]

Ultimately, the main objective of performance apprasials is to improve employee performance, keeping performance expectations clear and targeted on activities that build value for the organization. In dealing with employee performance issues, legal experts suggest that management follow seven steps to ensure that performance appraisals have the desired effect and are legally defensible:

1. Let the employee know that his or her performance is unacceptable and explain your minimum expectations.

2. Ensure that your expectations are reasonable.

3. Let employees know that warnings play a significant role in the process of establishing just cause; employees must be warned and told that discharge will result if they continue to fail to meet minimum standards.

4. Ensure that you take prompt corrective measures when required; failure to do so could lead to a finding that you condoned your employee's conduct.

5. Avoid sending mixed messages, such as a warning letter together with a "satisfactory" performance review.

6. Provide the employee with a reasonable amount of time to improve performance.

7. Be prepared to provide your employees with the necessary support to facilitate improvement.[72]

How to Handle a Formal Written Warning

There will be times when an employee's performance is so poor that a formal written warning is required. Such written warnings serve two purposes: (1) They may serve to shake the employee out of his or her bad habits, and (2) they can help the manager defend his or her rating of the employee, both to his or her boss and (if needed) to a court or human rights commission.

Written warnings should identify the standards under which the employee is judged, make it clear that the employee was aware of the standard, specify any violation of the standard, indicate that the employee has had an opportunity to correct his or her behaviour, and specify what the employee must now do to correct his or her behaviour.

STEP 4: DETERMINE PERFORMANCE REWARDS/CONSEQUENCES

Some time after the performance review has taken place, the manager should use the salary planning guidelines to determine the appropriate rewards or consequences, comparing actual performance against the defined levels. Performance rewards are given through merit pay or extra payment such as a cash bonus. The two most important aspects used to determine the appropriate reward/consequence are achievement of goals and how the employee meets the defined standards.

STEP 5: CAREER DEVELOPMENT DISCUSSION

During this discussion, the manager and employee discuss opportunities for development to strengthen or improve the employee's knowledge, skills, and abilities. Business needs must be balanced with the employee's preferences. These opportunities may focus on actions to boost performance in the area of current goals or to develop new knowledge aimed at a future career plan.

LEGAL AND ETHICAL ISSUES IN PERFORMANCE MANAGEMENT

Ethics should be the bedrock of performance management. Accurate, well-documented performance records and performance appraisal feedback are necessary to avoid legal penalties and to defend against charges of bias based on grounds prohibited under human rights legislation, such as age, sex, and so on. As one commentator puts it,

> The overall objective of high-ethics performance reviews should be to provide an honest assessment of performance and to mutually develop a plan to improve the individual's effectiveness. That requires that we tell people where they stand and that we be straight with them.[73]

Ashland Canada Ltd., an automotive products marketing company in British Columbia, was fined $20 000 for dismissing a sales employee based on an "unacceptable" performance rating even though the employee had exceeded his sales goals. The British Columbia Supreme Court found that the performance rating was unwarranted and undeserved, and criticized Ashland's human resources department for a "reprehensible and substantial departure" from good faith dealings with the employee.[74] In another case, a worker in a government mental health facility was terminated for unsatisfactory performance after 10 years of work with no performance evaluations and no disciplinary record. An adjudicator determined that the employer had failed to establish that the worker's job performance was unsatisfactory, that she had not been given a chance to improve, and that the employer did not have just cause for termination. The employer was required to pay compensation in lieu of reinstatement.[75]

Guidelines for developing an effective appraisal process include the following:[76]

1. Conduct a job analysis to ascertain characteristics (such as "timely project completion") required for successful job performance. Use this information to create job performance standards.

2. Incorporate these characteristics into a rating instrument. (The professional literature recommends rating instruments that are tied to specific job behaviours, that is, BARS.)

3. Make sure that definitive performance standards are provided to all raters and ratees.

4. Use clearly defined individual dimensions of job performance (like "quantity" or "quality") rather than undefined, global measures of job performance (like "overall performance").

5. When using a graphic rating scale, avoid abstract trait names (such as "loyalty," "honesty") unless they can be defined in terms of observable behaviours.

6. Employ subjective supervisory ratings (essays, for instance) as only one component of the overall appraisal process.

7. Train supervisors to use the rating instrument properly. Give instructions on how to apply performance appraisal standards ("outstanding," "satisfactory," and so on) when making judgments. Ensure that subjective standards are not subject to bias.

8. Allow appraisers regular contact with the employee being evaluated.

9. Whenever possible, have more than one appraiser conduct the appraisal, and conduct all such appraisals independently. This process can help to cancel out individual errors and biases.

10. Use formal appeal mechanisms and a review of ratings by upper-level managers.

11. Document evaluations and reasons for any termination decision.

12. Where appropriate, provide corrective guidance to assist poor performers in improving their performance.

THE FUTURE OF PERFORMANCE MANAGEMENT

Effective appraisals are the basis for successful performance management. Although performance appraisal is a difficult interpersonal task for managers, it cannot be eliminated.

Managers need some way to review employees' work-related behaviour, and no one has offered any concrete alternative. Despite the difficulties involved, performance management is still the basis for fostering and managing employee skills and talents, and it can be a key component of improved organizational effectiveness. Performance management techniques in high- and low-performing organizations are essentially the same, but managers in high-performing organizations tend to conduct and implement appraisals and manage performance on a daily basis more effectively.[77]

Recent research indicates that effective performance management involves

- linking individual goals and business strategy,
- showing leadership and accountability at all levels of the organization,
- ensuring close ties among appraisal results, rewards, and recognition outcomes,
- investing in employee development planning, and
- having an administratively efficient system with sufficient communication support. [78]

The key success factor for effective performance appraisal that will lead to optimum employee performance is the quality of the performance appraisal dialogue between a manager and an employee.[79] Managers need to engage in training on an ongoing basis to ensure that they are in a position to engage in high-quality formal appraisal discussions.

Overall, the solution is to create more effective appraisals, as described in this chapter. Effective appraisals are essential to managing the performance required of an organization's employees to achieve that organization's strategic objectives.

Chapter SUMMARY

1. The five steps in the performance management process are (1) defining performance expectations and goals, (2) providing ongoing feedback and coaching, (3) conducting performance appraisal and evaluation discussions, (4) determining performance rewards/consequences, and (5) conducting development and career opportunities discussions.

2. There are a number of performance appraisal methods. Graphic rating scales are simple to use

and facilitate comparison of employees, but the performance standards are often unclear and bias can be a problem. Alternation ranking is a simple method that avoids central tendency, but it can be unfair if most employees are doing well. Paired comparison ensures that all employees are compared with each other, but it can also be unfair if most employees are performing similarly. Narrative forms provide concrete information to the employee but are time-consuming and can be subjective. The forced distribution method ensures differentiation of performance ratings but can be demotivating for employees classified as less than average. The critical incident method is very specific about the employee's strengths and weaknesses and forces the supervisor to evaluate employees on an ongoing basis, but it makes it difficult to compare employees. BARS is very accurate, but is difficult and time-consuming to develop. MBO ties performance ratings to jointly agreed-upon performance objectives, but it is time-consuming to administer.

3. Appraisal problems to be aware of include unclear standards, the halo effect, central tendency, leniency or strictness, appraisal bias, the recency effect, and the similar-to-me bias.

4. The use of 360-degree feedback has grown rapidly. Performance information is collected from the individual being appraised, his or her supervisor, other employees reporting to the person being appraised, and customers. This approach supports the activities of performance appraisal, coaching, leadership development, succession planning, and employee rewards and recognition.

5. There are three types of formal appraisal discussion. When performance is unsatisfactory but correctable, the objective of the interview is to set out an action plan for correcting performance. For employees whose performance is satisfactory but for whom promotion is not possible, the objective of the interview is to maintain satisfactory performance. Finally, the satisfactory-and-promotable interview has the main objective of discussing the person's career plans and developing a specific action plan for the educational and professional development that the person needs to move on to the next job.

6. Although appraisals can be a difficult interpersonal task for managers, they cannot be eliminated. There is no alternative method for assessing employee performance, which is essential for talent management and improved organizational effectiveness. The key success factor is the quality of the performance appraisal dialogue between managers and employees. More training on how to effectively conduct these discussions is required.

MyManagementLab

Visit MyManagementLab to access a personalized Study Plan and additional study tools for this chapter.

Key TERMS

360-degree appraisal
alternation ranking method
appraisal bias
behaviourally anchored rating scale (BARS)
central tendency
contextual performance
critical incident method
electronic performance monitoring (EPM)
forced distribution method
formal appraisal discussion

graphic rating scale
halo effect
management by objectives (MBO)
paired comparison method
performance management
recency effect
similar-to-me bias
strictness/leniency
task performance
unclear performance standards

Review and Discussion QUESTIONS

1. Describe the five steps in the performance appraisal process.
2. Explain how to ensure that the performance appraisal process is carried out ethically and without violating human rights laws.
3. Discuss the pros and cons of using different potential raters to appraise a person's performance.
4. What are the four key actions in conducting a formal appraisal discussion?
5. Explain how to handle a defensive employee in a formal appraisal discussion.

Critical Thinking QUESTIONS

1. Assume you are presenting to an upper-year group of business students and one student asks the question, "Which performance appraisal system is the best?" How would you respond to that question?
2. How can the problem of inconsistency between managers who are rating workers be solved or at least diminished? Make two or more suggestions.
3. Given the difficulty with providing traditional performance standards for jobs that are quite flexible, what sort of "standards" could be developed for these flexible jobs?
4. Some HR professionals avoid using BARS given that it is so time-consuming to develop. How could the development steps be streamlined?
5. Do you agree with the use of forced distribution methods to rate employees? Why or why not?
6. How might a supervisor handle a situation in which negative appraisals in the past have caused an employee to undervalue his or her performance?
7. Discuss how employees might respond to the proposed implementation of electronic performance management systems, such as call monitoring, and so on. How might an organization deal with employees' reactions?
8. How might a supervisor deal with an extremely defensive yet productive member of his or her team in the event of having to deliver the "improvement portion" of the employee's performance appraisal? What techniques would the supervisor need to use to maximize the efficacy of the appraisal and reduce the defensibility of the employee?

Experiential EXERCISES

1. Working individually or in groups, develop a graphic rating scale for a retail sales associate and a fast-food restaurant manager.

2. Working individually or in groups, develop, over a week, a set of critical incidents covering the classroom performance of one of your instructors. Categorize the critical incidents to identify themes within activities that are viewed positively and negatively. Expand on this identification by assessing how the one-week period may be affecting the results and what differences you would have expected had you selected a different week within the year to conduct the assessment.

3. Working in groups, using the NOC job description for cafeteria staff at a local university or college and the example of a performance rating form in Figure 2, develop a graphic rating scale with behavioural incidents for a job of a chef within the cafeteria. You may also want to consider your own experience when constructing your form.

Once you have drafted your form, exchange forms with another student or group. Critique and suggest possible improvements to the forms. Then with your revised form in hand, develop statements of behavioural incidents for two of your rating scale items to address the following circumstances:

- The employee has achieved outstanding results.
- The employee meets acceptable standards.
- The employee has performed very poorly in this aspect of the job.

Be prepared to share and critique statements developed by other students. Debrief the exercise as directed.

Running CASE

The Performance Appraisal

Jennifer and Pierre disagree over the importance of having performance appraisals. Pierre says it's quite clear whether any particular LearnInMotion.com employee is doing his or her job. It's obvious, for instance, if the salespeople are selling, if the web designer is designing, if the web surfer is surfing, and if the content management people are managing to get the customers' content up on the website in a timely fashion. Pierre's position, like that of many small-business managers, is that "we have 1000 higher-priority things to attend to," such as boosting sales and creating the calendar. And in any case, he says, the employees already get plenty of day-to-day feedback from him or Jennifer regarding what they're doing right and what they're doing wrong.

This informal feedback notwithstanding, Jennifer believes that a more formal appraisal approach is required. For one thing, they're approaching the end of the 90-day "introductory" period for many of these employees, and the owners need to make decisions about whether they should go or stay. And from a practical point of view, Jennifer simply believes that sitting down and providing formal, written feedback is more likely to reinforce what employees are doing right and get them to modify things they may be doing wrong. "Maybe this is one reason we're not getting enough sales," she says. They've been debating this for about an hour. Now, they want you, their management consultant, to advise them on what to do.

QUESTIONS

1 What performance appraisal problems will LearnInMotion encounter if they continue on the course of not using formalized performance appraisals?

2 What guidelines would you recommend to Pierre and Jennifer for developing an effective appraisal system?

Case INCIDENT

A Performance Dilemma

Brenda Jackson, a newly hired human resources manager, has been on the job for approximately six months and is in the process of trying to create a new performance appraisal system for her employer, Starbrite Manufacturing Systems. Brenda has reviewed the company's current employee files and has noted that no formal performance appraisals exist in the files. This situation is of great concern to Brenda.

In response, Brenda schedules a meeting with the CEO to discuss her concerns and to gain his support to ultimately recommend the designing of a new performance appraisal system. After the meeting, Brenda is happy at gaining the CEO's approval but starts to feel overwhelmed at the large task she has in pulling the new performance management system together. This is where you come in to help Brenda by answering the following questions.

1 Discuss the performance management process highlighted in the chapter and how it will aid Brenda in creating this new performance appraisal system for her employer.

2 Discuss and suggest the type of appraisal methods that Brenda should recommend the company use.

3 Discuss the rating errors that Brenda must be aware of and how these can be avoided.

MyManagementLab

Visit MyManagementLab to access a personalized Study Plan and additional study tools for this chapter.

CBC 🍁   To view the CBC videos, read a summary, and answer discussion questions, go to MyManagementLab

NOTES

1. J.T. Rich, "The Solutions for Employee Performance Management," *Workspan* (February 2002), pp. 32–37.

2. J.A. Rubino, "Aligning Performance Management and Compensation Rewards Successfully," *WorldatWork Canadian News* (Fourth Quarter, 2004), pp. 12–16.

3. P. Nel, O. Van Dyk, G. Haasbroek, H. Schultz, T. Sono, and A. Werner, *Human Resource Management,* (Cape Town, South Africa: Oxford University Press, 2004).

4. D. Brown, "HR Improving at Performance Management," *Canadian HR Reporter* (December 2, 2002), pp. 1, 14.

5. "The Performance-Management Process," *Workspan* (October 2006), p. 96.

6. R. Thorndike, "Concepts of Culture-Fairness," *Journal of Educational Measurement* (Summer, 1971), pp. 63–70.

7. S. Motowidlo and J. Van Scotter, "Evidence That Task Performance Should Be Distinguished from Contextual Performance," *Journal of Applied Psychology* (November 1993), pp. 475–480.

8. R. Tett, K. Fox, and P. Palmer, "Task and Contextual Performance as Formal and Expected Work Behaviors," Paper presented at the 18th annual Society of Industrial Organizational Psychologists conference (Orlando, FL, April, 2002).

9. A. Sung and E. Todd, "Line of Sight: Moving Beyond the Catchphrase," *Workspan* (October 2004), pp. 65–69.

10. For further discussion, see G. English, "Tuning Up for Performance Management," *Training and Development Journal* (April 1991), pp. 56–60.

11. C.L. Hughes, "The Bell-Shaped Curve That Inspires Guerrilla Warfare," *Personnel Administrator* (May 1987), pp. 40–41.

12. R. Girard, "Are Performance Appraisals Passé?" *Personnel Journal,* 67, no. 8 (August 1988), pp. 89–90.

13. D. Bernardin and P. Smith, "A Clarification of Some Issues Regarding the Development and Use of Behaviorally Anchored Ratings Scales (BARS)," *Journal of Applied Psychology* (August 1981), pp. 458–463.

14. D. Bownas and H. Bernardin, "Critical Incident Technique," in S. Gael (Ed.), *The Job Analysis Handbook for Business, Industry, and Government* (New York, NY: Wiley, 1988), pp. 1120–1137.

15. N. Hauenstein, R. Brown, and A. Sinclair, "BARS and Those Mysterious, Missing Middle Anchors," *Journal of Business and Psychology* (May 2010), pp. 663–672.

16. J. Goodale and R. Burke, "Behaviorally Based Rating Scales Need Not Be Job Specific," *Journal of Applied Psychology,* 60 (June 1975).

17. K.R. Murphy and J. Constans, "Behavioral Anchors as a Source of Bias in Rating," *Journal of Applied Psychology,* 72, no. 4 (November 1987), pp. 573–577.

18. E. Mone and M. London, *Employee Engagement through Effective Performance Management: A Manager's Guide* (New York, NY: Routledge, 2009).

19. S. Kerr and S. Landouer, "Using Stretch Goals to Promote Organizational Effectiveness and Personal Growth: General Electric and Goldman Sachs," *Academy of Management Executive* (November 2004), pp. 134–138.

20. C. Maslach and M. Leiter, "Early Predictors of Job Burnout and Engagement," *Journal of Applied Psychology* (May 2008), pp. 498–512.

21. M. Levy, "Almost-Perfect Performance Appraisals," *Personnel Journal,* 68, no. 4 (April 1989), pp. 76–83.

22. P. Loucks, "Plugging into Performance Management," *Canadian HR Reporter* (February 26, 2007).

23. C. Howard, "Appraise This!" *Canadian Business* (May 23, 1998), p. 96.

24. E. Farndale, V. Hope-Hailey, and C. Kelliher, "High Commitment Performance Management: The Roles of Justice and Trust," *Personnel Review* (2011), pp. 5–23.

25. E. Mone, C. Eisinger, K. Guggenheim, B. Price, and C. Stine, "Performance Management at the Wheel: Driving Employee Engagement in Organizations," *Journal of Business and Psychology* (May 2011), pp. 205–212.

26. K.S. Teel, "Performance Appraisal: Current Trends, Persistent Progress," *Personnel Journal,* 59, no. 4 (April 1980), pp. 296–316.

27. D. Brown, "Performance Management Systems Need Fixing: Survey," *Canadian HR Reporter* (April 11, 2005), pp. 1, 10; M. Waung and S. Highhouse, "Fear of Conflict and Empathic Buffering: Two Explanations for the Inflation of Performance Feedback," *Organizational Behavior and Human Decision Processes,* 71 (1997), pp. 37–54.

28. Y. Ganzach, "Negativity (and Positivity) in Performance Evaluation: Three Field Studies," *Journal of Applied Psychology,* 80 (1995), pp. 491–499.

29. T.J. Maurer and M.A. Taylor, "Is Sex by Itself Enough? An Exploration of Gender Bias Issues in Performance Appraisal," *Organizational Behavior and Human Decision Processes,* 60 (1994), pp. 231–251; see also C.E. Lance, "Test for Latent Structure of Performance Ratings Derived from Wherry's (1952) *Theory of Ratings,*" *Journal of Management,* 20 (1994), pp. 757–771.

30. S.E. Scullen, M.K. Mount, and M. Goff, "Understanding the Latent Structure of Job Performance Ratings," *Journal of Applied Psychology,* 85 (2001), pp. 956–970.

31. A.M. Saks and D.A. Waldman, "The Relationship between Age and Job Performance Evaluations for Entry-Level Professionals," *Journal of Organizational Behavior,* 19 (1998), pp. 409–419.

32. W.C. Borman, L.A. White, and D.W. Dorsey, "Effects of Ratee Task Performance and Interpersonal Factors in Supervisor and Peer Performance Ratings," *Journal of Applied Psychology,* 80 (1995), pp. 168–177.

33. K. Murphy, W. Balzer, M. Lockhart, and E. Eisenman, "Effects of Previous Performance on Evaluations of Present Performance," *Journal of Applied Psychology,* 70, no. 1 (1985), pp. 72–84; see also K. Williams, A. DeNisi, B. Meglino, and T. Cafferty, "Initial Decisions and Subsequent Performance Ratings," *Journal of Applied Psychology,* 71, no. 2 (May 1986), pp. 189–195.

34. S. Appelbaum, M. Roy, and T. Gillilan, "Globalization of Performance Appraisals: Theory and Applications," *Management Decision* (2011), pp. 570–585.

35. J. Hedge and M. Cavanagh, "Improving the Accuracy of Performance Evaluations: Comparison of Three Methods of Performance Appraiser Training," *Journal of Applied Psychology,* 73, no. 1 (February 1988), pp. 68–73.

36. B. Davis and M. Mount, "Effectiveness of Performance Appraisal Training Using Computer Assistance Instruction and Behavior Modeling," *Personnel Psychology,* 37 (Fall 1984), pp. 439–452.

37. T. Athey and R. McIntyre, "Effect of Rater Training on Rater Accuracy: Levels of Processing Theory and Social Facilitation Theory Perspectives," *Journal of Applied Psychology,* 72, no. 4 (November 1987), pp. 567–572.

38. M.M. Greller, "Participation in the Performance Appraisal Review: Inflexible Manager Behavior and Variable Worker Needs," *Human Relations,* 51 (1998), pp. 1061–1083.

39. R. Arvey, and J. Campion, (1982). "The Employment Interview: A Summary and Review of Recent Research," *Personnel Psychology* (June 1982), pp. 281–322; W. Wiesner and S. Cronshaw, "A Meta-Analytic Investigation of the Impact of Interview Format and Degree of Structure on the Validity of the Employment Interview," *Journal of Occupational Psychology* (1988), pp. 275–290; K. Murphy, and J. Cleveland, *Understanding Performance Appraisal: Social, Organizational, and Goal-Based Perspectives* (Thousand Oaks, CA: Sage, 1995).

40. B.D. Cawley, L.M. Keeping, and P.E Levy, "Participation in the Performance Appraisal Process and Employee Reactions: A Meta-Analytic Review of Field Investigations," *Journal of Applied Psychology,* 83 (1998), pp. 615–633.

41. J.W. Lawrie, "Your Performance: Appraise It Yourself!" *Personnel,* 66, no. 1 (January 1989), pp. 21–33; includes a good explanation of how self-appraisals can be used at work; see also A. Furnham and P. Stringfield, "Congruence in Job-Performance Ratings: A Study of 360° Feedback Exam-

ining Self, Manager, Peers, and Consultant Ratings," *Human Relations,* 51 (1998), pp. 517–530.

42. P.A. Mabe III and S.G. West, "Validity of Self-Evaluation of Ability: A Review and Meta-Analysis," *Journal of Applied Psychology,* 67, no. 3 (1982), pp. 280–296.

43. J. Russell and D. Goode, "An Analysis of Managers' Reactions to Their Own Performance Appraisal Feedback," *Journal of Applied Psychology,* 73, no. 1 (February 1988), pp. 63–67; M.M. Harris and J. Schaubroeck, "A Meta-Analysis of Self–Supervisor, Self–Peer, and Peer–Supervisor Ratings," *Personnel Psychology,* 41 (1988), pp. 43–62.

44. V.V. Druskat and S.B. Wolff, "Effects and Timing of Developmental Peer Appraisals in Self-Managing Work Groups," *Journal of Applied Psychology,* 84 (1999), pp. 58–74.

45. M.M. Harris and J. Schaubroeck, "A Meta-Analysis of Self–Supervisor, Self–Peer, and Peer–Supervisor Ratings," *Personnel Psychology,* 41 (1988), pp. 43–62.

46. W.C. Borman, "The Rating of Individuals in Organizations: An Alternate Approach," *Organizational Behavior and Human Performance,* 12 (1974), pp. 105–124.

47. H.J. Bernardin and R.W. Beatty, "Can Subordinate Appraisals Enhance Managerial Productivity?" *Sloan Management Review* (Summer 1987), pp. 63–73.

48. M. London and A. Wohlers, "Agreement between Subordinate and Self-Ratings in Upward Feedback," *Personnel Psychology,* 44 (1991), pp. 375–390.

49. Ibid, p. 376.

50. D. Antonioni, "The Effects of Feedback Accountability on Upward Appraisal Ratings," *Personnel Psychology,* 47 (1994), pp. 349–355.

51. T.J. Maurer, N.S. Raju, and W.C. Collins, "Peer and Subordinate Performance Appraisal Measurement Equivalence," *Journal of Applied Psychology,* 83 (1998), pp. 693–702.

52. R. Reilly, J. Smither, and N. Vasilopoulos, "A Longitudinal Study of Upward Feedback," *Personnel Psychology,* 49 (1996), pp. 599–612.

53. K. Nowack, "360-Degree Feedback: The Whole Story," *Training and Development* (January 1993), p. 69; for a description of some of the problems involved in implementing 360-degree feedback, see M. Budman, "The Rating Game," *Across the Board,* 31, no. 2 (February 1994), pp. 35–38.

54. C. Romano, "Fear of Feedback," *Management Review* (December 1993), p. 39; see also M.R. Edwards and A.J. Ewen, "How to Manage Performance and Pay with 360-Degree Feedback," *Compensation and Benefits Review,* 28, no. 3 (May/June 1996), pp. 41–46.

55. G.P. Latham, J. Almost, S. Mann, and C. Moore, "New Developments in Performance Management," *Organizational Dynamics,* 34, no. 1 (2005), pp. 77–87; R. Brillinger, "The Many Faces of 360-Degree Feedback," *Canadian HR Reporter* (December 16, 1996), p. 21.

56. J.F. Milliman, R.A. Zawacki, C. Norman, L. Powell, and J. Kirksey, "Companies Evaluate Employees from All Perspectives," *Personnel Journal,* 73, no. 11 (November 1994), pp. 99–103.

57. R. Brillinger, "The Many Faces of 360-Degree Feedback," *Canadian HR Reporter* (December 16, 1996), p. 20.

58. Ibid.

59. D.A. Waldman, L.A. Atwater, and D. Antonioni, "Has 360-Degree Feedback Gone Amok?" *Academy of Management Executive,* 12 (1998), pp. 86–94.

60. P.E. Levy, B.D. Cawley, and R.J. Foti, "Reactions to Appraisal Discrepancies: Performance Ratings and Attributions," *Journal of Business and Psychology,* 12 (1998), pp. 437–455.

61. M. Derayeh and S. Brutus, "Learning from Others' 360-Degree Experiences," *Canadian HR Reporter* (February 10, 2003), pp. 18, 23.

62. A.S. DeNisi and A.N. Kluger, "Feedback Effectiveness: Can 360-Degree Appraisal Be Improved?" *Academy of Management Executive,* 14 (2000), pp. 129–139.

63. T. Bentley, "Internet Addresses 360-Degree Feedback Concerns," *Canadian HR Reporter* (May 8, 2000), pp. G3, G15.

64. D. Brown, "Performance Management Systems Need Fixing: Survey," *Canadian HR Reporter* (April 1, 2005), pp. 1, 10.

65. See also J. Greenberg, "Using Explanations to Manage Impressions of Performance Appraisal Fairness," *Employee Responsibilities and Rights Journal,* 4, no. 1 (March 1991), pp. 51–60.

66. R.G. Johnson, *The Appraisal Interview Guide,* Chapter 9 (New York, NY: AMACOM, 1979).

67. J. Block, *Performance Appraisal on the Job: Making It Work* (New York, NY: Executive Enterprises Publications, 1981), pp. 58–62; see also T. Lowe, "Eight Ways to Ruin a Performance Review," *Personnel Journal,* 65, no. 1 (January 1986).

68. J.W. Smither and M. London, "Best Practices in Performance Management," in J.W. Smither & M. London (Eds.), *Performance Management: Putting Research into Action* (San Francisco, CA: Jossey-Bass, 2009).

69. J. Block, *Performance Appraisal on the Job: Making It Work* (New York, NY: Executive Enterprises Publications, 1981), pp. 58–62.

70. M. Feinberg, *Effective Psychology for Managers* (New York, NY: Simon & Schuster, 1976).

71. J. Pearce and L. Porter, "Employee Response to Formal Performance Appraisal Feedback," *Journal of Applied Psychology,* 71, no. 2 (May 1986), pp. 211–218.

72. D.B. Jarvis and R.E. McGilvery, "Poor Performers," *HR Professional* (June/July 2005), p. 32.

73. L. Axline, "Ethical Considerations of Performance Appraisals," *Management Review* (March 1994), p. 62.

74. M. McDougall and L. Cassiani, "HR Cited in Unfair Performance Review," *Canadian HR Reporter* (September 10, 2001), pp. 1, 6.

75. "Health Worker's Performance Review Unfair," *Workplace Today* (June 2001), p. 23.

76. G. Barrett and M. Kernan, "Performance Appraisal and Terminations: A Review of Court Decisions Since Brito v. Zia with Implications for Personnel Practices," *Personnel Psychology,* 40, no. 3 (Autumn 1987), pp. 489–504.

77. J. Kochnarski and A. Sorenson, "Managing Performance Management," *Workspan* (September 2005), pp. 20–37.

78. E.E. Lawler and M. McDermott, "Current Performance Management Practices," *WorldatWork Journal,* 12, no. 2, pp. 49–60.

79. D. Bell, J. Blanchet, and N. Gore, "Performance Management: Making It Work Is Worth the Effort," *WorldatWork Canadian News,* 12, no. 11 (Fourth Quarter, 2004), pp. 1, 27–28.

PHOTO CREDITS

Index